The Social Construction of Race and Ethnicity in the United States

The Social Construction of Race and Ethnicity in the United States

Joan Ferrante
Prince Brown, Jr.

Northern Kentucky University

 LONGMAN

An imprint of Addison Wesley Longman, Inc.

New York • Reading, Massachusetts • Menlo Park, California • Harlow, England
Don Mills, Ontario • Sydney • Mexico City • Madrid • Amsterdam

Editor-in-Chief	Priscilla McGeehon
Executive Editor	Alan McClare
Marketing Manager	Suzanne Daghlian
Project Coordination and Text Design	York Production Services
Cover Design:	Sandra Watanabe
Cover Illustration/Photo	©1997 PhotoDisc, Inc.
Photo Researcher	Julie Tesser
Full Service Production Manager	Valerie Zaborski
Manufacturing Manager	Hilda Koparanian
Electronic Page Makeup	York Production Services
Printer and Binder	The Maple-Vail Book Manufacturing Group
Cover Printer	Coral Graphic Services, Inc.

For permission to use copyrighted material, grateful acknowledgment is made to the copyright holders on pp. 525–529, which are hereby made part of this copyright page.

Library of Congress Cataloging-in-Publication Data
The social construction of race and ethnicity in the United States/[edited by] Joan Ferrante, Prince Brown, Jr.
    p. cm.
    Includes bibliographical references and index.
    ISBN 0-321-01133-3
    1. United States—Race relations. 2. United States—Ethnic relations. 3. Race—Classification.
  4. Ethnicity—United States—Classification. 5. United States—Race relations—Government policy.
  6. United States—Ethnic relations—Government policy.
I. Ferrante-Wallace, Joan, 1955- II. Brown, Prince.
E184.A1S667   1997
305.8'00973—dc21

                                                    97-17604
                                                     CIP

ISBN 0-321-011 33-3

 2 3 4 5 6 7 8 9 10—MA—0 0 9 9 9 8

To:

Elizabeth, Eric, and Christopher Brown
Robert K. Wallace

CONTENTS

PART 3
Ethnic Classification   187

PART 4
The Persistence, Functions, and
Consequences of Social Classification   269

PART 5
Toward a New Paradigm: Transcending Categories   **377**

PREFACE

The Social Construction of Race and Ethnicity in the United States is a five-part book that challenges conventional views of race and ethnicity by describing and critiquing the foundation of those views: the U.S. system of racial and ethnic classification. Readings in this textbook call attention to (1) the personal and systematic consequences of classifying people, (2) the U.S. government's obsession with "nonwhite peoples" reflected in its ongoing attempts to create racial categories and construct rules governing classification, (3) the scientific research disputing the logic of classifying people into race and ethnic categories; (4) the reasons classification persists in the face of overwhelming evidence disputing that logic, and (5) a new paradigm for thinking about "race/ethnicity" and "race-ethnic" relations.

The Social Construction of Race and Ethnicity in the United States is not just a book of readings. Each of the five parts leads off with an in-depth essay or overview that grounds the set of readings in sociological theory. Readings were selected for their potential to stimulate critical thinking and self-examination. In addition, each reading begins with one or more study questions to help readers clarify/identify key concepts and issues.

The idea for this book grew out of our frustration with the misleading way in which the idea of "race" is treated in most textbooks that address this concept. The authors, for example, accurately point out that race is not a meaningful biological concept but then proceed to define race in a way that highlights biological traits and to show photographs suggesting that race is a definitive, clear-cut attribute.

This book also developed out of a shared commitment to improve the quality of our teaching and to gain a fuller understanding of the impact the idea of race has on a society that is consumed by it. The logic, organization, articles, and ideas evolved in conversation with each other and from students responses to class material. As one example of how student input helped to shape this book, we asked students to respond in writing to the idea that "race" is a myth and is based on the false assumption that people can be divided into distinct racial categories. While there are always a few students not surprised by this idea, the majority cannot see how this is possible—as these sample comments show:

- *I don't understand how this is possible but I am open-minded about it.*
- *If there is no such thing as race, why can I look around at the people in the class and know their race?*
- *If race is a myth, why is race such a big deal in this country?*

Such responses motivated us to ask and answer several difficult questions that are central to this book: (1) How is it that racial categories are treated as mutually exclusive when we can identify many cases in which people have complex biological histories? (2) If classification schemes in fact are based on a false assumption, why do they seem so clear-cut? (3) Why have government officials spent so much physical and mental energy devising rules for classifying people according to race? (4) "Why do we so easily recognize races when walking down the street if race is a myth?" (Haney López 1994:19). (5) If race is a myth, should we dismantle classification schemes?

In writing and selecting the readings, we struggled with how to refer to "race." Should we always put the word *race* in quotation marks? Should we always qualify references to a person's race with the words *people classified as* black, white, and so on? In the end, we concluded that the idea of race is real if only because its consequences are real. However, we believe that people must shift their understanding of the meaning of race away from a term referring to clear biological divisions of humanity, to a term referring to "a way in which one group designates itself as 'insider' and other groups as 'outsiders' to reinforce or enforce its wishes and/or ideas in social, economic, and political realms" (Rorhl 1996:96). *The Social Construction of Race and Ethnicity in the United States* was created with the goal of helping readers make this conceptual transition.

Acknowledgments

The ideas in this book are not new. For example, *Race: A Study in Modern Superstition* by Jacques Barzun was published in 1937 and reissued in 1965. In the preface to the 1965 edition, Barzun states "This book is coming back into print because the idea of race it treats of, although repeatedly killed, is nevertheless undying" (pp. ix).

Recall also that W. E. B. Du Bois was preoccupied with the "strange meaning of being black here in the dawning of the Twentieth Century." His preoccupation was no doubt affected by the fact that his father, born in Haiti, was of French and African descent and his mother, born in the United States, was of Dutch and African descent. In *The Philadelphia Negro: A Social Study,* Du Bois (1899) wrote about popular ideas of race and compared them to reality. Du Bois documented that blacks and whites married and paired off despite laws prohibiting marriage and that they did have children (who, by definition cannot fit into one racial category).

We mention Du Bois and Barzun as a way of acknowledging those who came before but whose ideas were not received in the same way as those who write about race as a social construction today. The dates on which many of the readings included in *The Social Construction of Race and Eth-*

nicity in the United States were originally published also point to the many contributors and the long process behind the development of new paradigms.

To our knowledge, this is the first reader written and compiled with the exclusive goal of explaining race as a social construction. For this opportunity, we thank Alan McClare, who signed the book in November 1995. On signing, the book was in rough draft form. Margaret Loftus, former Associate Editor at Addison Wesley Longman, saw the project through to its completion almost 18 months later. We thank Margaret for the encouragement she offered, her insights about how to improve the book, and her excellent ability to synthesize in writing and in conversation the many reviews she secured for this project. In this regard, we are grateful to:

Professor Richard E. Bradfield, *Western New Mexico University*

Professor Michael Collins, *University of Wisconsin*

Professor Lillian Daughada, *Murray State University*

Professor Jan Fiola, *Moorhead State University*

Professor Cecilia Garza, *Texas A&M International University*

Professor Donald Hayes, *Sam Houston University*

Professor Beverly M. John, *Hampton University*

Professor Joane Nagel, *University of Kansas*

Professor Ron Stewart, *State University of New York College at Buffalo*

We would like to thank our research assistant, Angela Vaughn, Class of 1998 at Northern Kentucky University, who helped us track down books, articles, internet documents, and other materials we needed to write and edit this book. She also served as a student reviewer, offering valuable comments and suggestions about how to make this book more effective for student readers. Thanks also goes to Bobby Hussey, an NKU student who drew the artwork titled, "In the U.S. the Offspring of a Multiracial Union is a Single Race."

Special thanks goes to Annalee Taylor Ferrante, for handling the correspondence connected with securing permissions for the readings we reprinted. She also checked all references and quotes for accuracy, and maintained the files. We know of no person who could do this detailed work with the same level of care and accuracy as Annalee.

We dedicate this book to Robert K. Wallace and to Elizabeth, Eric, and Christopher Brown and thank them for their tireless support. We also dedicate this book to the thousands of people who jeopardized their lives, education, and careers in the on-going struggle to alleviate the impact of racial classification in the United States.

The Social Construction
of Race and Ethnicity
in the United States

INTRODUCTION

Every ten years since 1790 (the year of the first census), the United States government has attempted to count the number of people living under its jurisdiction and classify them according to race. On the surface, this seems like a relatively simple task: Obviously we think determining race can be done by simple observation, and we assume that everyone knows his or her race. The Census Bureau data in Table 1 suggests that everyone in the United States belongs to one of five broad racial categories: (1) White; (2) Black; (3) American Indian, Eskimo, Aleut; (4) Asian or Pacific Islander; or (5) Other race. Note there is no mixed-race category nor is there a "don't know" category.

Recently we asked students in a Race and Gender class and in an Introduction to Sociology course if they knew of someone who might find it difficult to answer the race question used by the U.S. Bureau of the Census—that is, did they know of someone who could check more than one of the racial categories provided? (See Table 2.) If so, we asked them to please take a few minutes and write about that person. Of the 70 students in the Race and Gender class, 19 (27 percent) responded in the affirmative. Of the 80 students in the Introduction to Sociology course, 70 (88 percent) knew of someone. Here are some examples.

- *I am of mixed ancestry but because I have to choose one category I usually fill in the white category. I am Japanese-American, and I know many other Japanese-Americans. Many of us never know what circle to fill in. Just the other day I took my brother to the doctor's office, and he asked me which one he should circle, and I told him white. Then he asked me which do I usually fill in and circle, because he was confused too. I told him I usually circle white.*
- *Carolyn, a tall white lady in her 30s, lives with her black husband in a small, predominantly white county. They have one daughter who is five years old and looks a great deal like her father. She is beautiful*

Table I   1990 Population in the United States by Race

RACE (UNIVERSE: PERSONS)	
White	199,827,064
Black	29,930,524
American Indian, Eskimo, or Aleut	2,015,143
Asian or Pacific Islander	7,226,986
Other race	9,710,156

Source: U.S. Bureau of the Census (1996).

Table 2   Race Question for the 1990 Census

---

4. Race

Fill ONE circle for the race that the person considers himself/herself to be.

If Indian (Amer.), print the name of the enrolled or principal tribe.→

○ White
○ Black or Negro
○ Indian (Amer.) (Print the name of the enrolled or principal tribe.)

[ ]

○ Eskimo
○ Aleut

       Asian or Pacific Islander (API)

○ Chinese   ○ Japanese
○ Filipino   ○ Asian Indian
○ Hawaiian   ○ Samoan

If Other Asian or Pacific Islander (API), print one group, for example: Hmong, Fijian, Laotian, Thai, Tongan, Pakistani, Cambodian, and so on. →

○ Korean   ○ Guamanian
○ Vietnamese   ○ Other API ↓

[ ]

If Other race, print race.→

○ Other race (Print race.) ↑

Instructions for Question 4

Fill ONE circle for the race each person considers himself/herself to be.

If you fill the "Indian (Amer.)" circle, print the name of the tribe or tribes in which the person is enrolled. If the person is not enrolled in a tribe, print the name of the principal tribe(s).

If you fill the "Other API" circle [under Asian or Pacific Islander (API)], only print the name of the group to which the person belongs. For example, the "Other API" category includes persons who identify as Burmese, Fijia Hmong, Indonesian, Laatian, Bangladeshi, Pakistani, Tongan, Thai, Cambodian, Sri Lankan, and so on.

If you fill the "Other race" circle, be sure to print the name of the race.

If the person considers himself/herself to be "White," "Black or Negro," "Eskimo," or "Aleut," fill one circle only. Do not print the race in the box.

The "Black or Negro" category also includes persons who identify as African-American, Afro-American, Haitian, Jamaican, West Indian, Nigerian, and so on.

All persons, regardless of citizenship status, should answer this question.

Source: del Pinal and Lapham (1993: 448–49).

---

with long curly black hair, brown skin, and bright brown eyes. They are also awaiting the birth of a second child. Carolyn is already anticipating what the baby will look like.

- *One of my friends has a dark complexion and long hair (male). Recently he was pulled over by a police officer and cited for speeding. The officer marked his race as Native American/Eskimo on the citation. Actually, my friend considers himself white with some Indian ancestry.*

- *I am Filipino, but my birth certificate says I am white. Also I was born in Virginia. My parents are both Filipino, however. Not too many people can figure out, without asking, that I am Filipino; they assume I am Asian.*
- *A friend of mine's mother is Vietnamese and her dad is white. She looks Vietnamese, and most people see her as just that. People who don't know have asked if she can speak English. She just looks at them, almost annoyed at the question because she speaks it plain as day. She was born in the U.S. and has lived here all her life.*
- *Kristen was born to a Native-American mother and an African-American father in 1974. Kristin's grandmother forced her daughter, who was only 16 years old, to give Kristen up for adoption. A white couple eventually adopted her. Kristen makes it a point to inform herself about Native American peoples. She belongs to the local chapter of the NAACP and is the black affairs editor of a college campus newspaper.*
- *I decided to write about myself. I came to the United States from Brazil two years ago. The most intriguing thing about the United States is its ideas about race. It is appalling how Americans insist on placing me in a racial category. When someone in this class asked me "what race do I declare myself in situations in which I must list my race?" and I said "black," one of my "white" friends said in complete disbelief, "You are not black!" While a "black" friend said: "I am very glad, I consider you a sister."*

Apparently these student-generated examples are not unusual.[1] According to the results of the *1990 Census of Population and Housing Content Reinterview Survey* (1993), approximately one in 20 people reported a race on the Content Reinterview Survey that was different from the race they reported on the 1990 Census form (see Table 3).

These survey results, along with student-generated examples, raise an important question: How is it that racial categories are treated as mutually exclusive when we can identify many cases in which people have complex biological histories? Maybe race is not a biological factor, or an inherited trait like eye color or hair color. Perhaps *race* refers to that which is produced through racial classification (Webster 1993). In other words, the fact that everyone seems to fit into a single racial category is the result of the system of racial classification used in the United States. It is not the objective placement of individual human beings in "natural" biological categories.

Perhaps the best example of how the U.S. system of racial classification determines race is the criteria used to specify classification of mixed-race persons. As late as 1980, any person of mixed parentage was "classified according to the race of the nonwhite parent, and mixtures of nonwhite races

Table 3 Race Reported on U.S. Bureau of the Census Form versus Race Reported on Reinterview Form

Reinterview Classification	Total Reported	Census Classification					
		1	2	3	4	5	6
Total Reported	24,539	20,919	2375	118	454	81	592
Item Responses							
1. White	21,034	20,564	30	43	12	36	349
2. Black or Negro	2406	59	2306	2	2	3	34
3. Indian/Eskimo/Aleut	116	37	5	69	0	0	54
4. Asian or Pacific Islander	449	24	0	0	410	410	9
5. Other API	80	6	7	0	21	21	32
6. Other Race	454	229	27	4	9	9	163

24,539 people who answered the race question on the 1990 U.S. Bureau of the Census form were asked to name their race on the 1990 Census of Population and Housing Content Reinterview Survey. Of these 24,539 people, 20,919 said their race was "White" on the 1990 census form, while only 20,564 reported their race as "White" on the Reinterview form. This difference means that 355 people who said they were "White" on the census identified themselves as another race on the reinterview survey. Of those 355, 59 said they were "Black," 37 said they were "Indian/Eskimo/Aleut," 24 said they were "Asian or Pacific Islander," six said they were "Other Asian Pacific Islander," and 229 identified themselves as "Other Race."

Source: U.S. Bureau of the Census (1993: 21).

are classified according to the race of the father, with the special exceptions noted above" (U.S. Bureau of the Census 1993:21). An example of a special exception applies to persons of mixed Negro and Indian descent. In such cases no matter what the father's race, the person is classified as Negro "unless the Indian ancestry very definitely predominates or unless the individual is regarded as an Indian in the community" (p. 21).

As another example, consider the diagram taken from the U.S. Bureau of the Census (1994) interviewing manual (see Fig. 1). The diagram is a flowchart of decisions interviewers must make about *problem cases,* respondents who say they are more than one race or who name a race not listed as a response. Notice how the flowchart directs interviewers to classify the so-called problem respondent as belonging to one race.

The flaws of the racial classification scheme used in the United States are especially evident when we come across people who do not fit into a single racial category, who are forced into a single category, or who must choose between categories. Such cases tell us that race is not an easily de-

Figure 1   Diagram of Procedures for Recording Problem Race Cases

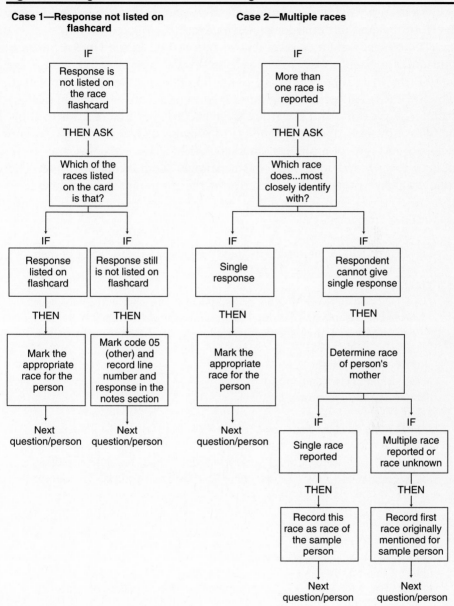

Source: U.S. Bureau of the Census (1994:C3–17).

finable characteristic immediately evident on the basis of physical clues, but is a category defined and maintained by people through a complex array of formal and informal social mechanisms.

The official system of racial classification used in the United States is not unlike a classification scheme devised by a third-grade class in Riceville, Iowa. In 1970, teacher Jane Elliot conducted a classic experiment in which she divided her students into two groups according to a physical attribute—eye color—and rewarded them accordingly. She did this to show her class how easy it is for people (1) to assign social worth, (2) to explain behavior in terms of a physical characteristic such as eye color, and (3) to build a reward system around this seemingly insignificant attribute. The following excerpt from the transcript of the program "A Class Divided" (*Frontline* 1985) shows how Elliot established the ground rules for the classroom experiment.

ELLIOT: It might be interesting to judge people today by the color of their eyes . . . would you like to try this?

CHILDREN: Yeah!

ELLIOT: Sounds like fun doesn't it? Since I'm the teacher and I have blue eyes, I think maybe the blue-eyed people should be on top the first day. . . . I mean the blue-eyed people are the better people in this room. . . . Oh yes they are the—blue-eyed people are smarter than brown-eyed people. . . .

BRIAN: My dad isn't that stupid.

ELLIOT: Is your dad brown-eyed?

BRIAN: Yeah.

ELLIOT: One day you came to school and you told us that he kicked you.

BRIAN: He did.

ELLIOT: Do you think a blue-eyed father would kick his son? My dad's blue-eyed, he's never kicked me. Ray's dad is blue-eyed, he's never kicked him. Rex's dad is blue-eyed, he's never kicked him. This is a fact. Blue-eyed people are better than brown-eyed people. Are you brown-eyed or blue-eyed?

BRIAN: Blue.

ELLIOT: Why are you shaking your head?

BRIAN: I don't know.

ELLIOT: Are you sure that you're right? Why? What makes you sure that you're right?

BRIAN: I don't know.

ELLIOT: The blue-eyed people get five extra minutes of recess, while the brown-eyed people have to stay in. . . . The brown-eyed people do not get to use the drinking fountain. You'll have to use the paper cups. You brown-eyed people are not to play with the blue-eyed people on the playground, because you are not as good as blue-eyed people. The brown-eyed people in this room today are going to wear collars. So that we can tell from a distance what color your eyes are. [Now], on page 127—one hundred twenty-seven. Is everyone ready? Everyone but Laurie. Ready, Laurie?

CHILD: She's a brown-eye.

ELLIOT: She's a brown-eye. You'll begin to notice today that we spend a great deal of time waiting for brown-eyed people (*Frontline* transcript 1985:3–5).

As soon as Elliot set the rules, the blue-eyed children accepted and enforced them eagerly. During recess, the children took to calling each other by their eye colors. Some brown-eyed children got into fights with blue-eyed children who called them "brown-eye." The teacher observed that these "marvelous, cooperative, wonderful, thoughtful children" turn into nasty, vicious, discriminating little third-graders in a space of fifteen minutes" (p. 7).

On the first reading, you might dismiss this demonstration as interesting but as something that could never happen in real life. Eye color as a means of classifying and ranking people—how absurd! In addition to the obvious fact that eye color is an attribute over which people have no control, even the most simple-minded person could readily identify the flaw in this scheme: eye colors fall into more than two categories. Thus a two-category classification scheme could not accommodate people with green, hazel, gray, or mixed-color eyes (one blue eye and one brown eye). We might even laugh at the fact that the teacher and the children agreed to use collars as a way to clearly distinguish the brown-eyed people from the blue-eyed people. All of us can see that dividing people in this manner makes no sense.

Such a strategy is similar to racial classification in the United States in that people are classified according to criteria over which they have no control, either formally by the government or other institutions, or informally as part of everyday interaction. Ernest Evans Kilker (1993) points out that state definitions of who is black have ranged from Georgia's "any known ancestry" to Ohio's "preponderance of blood." Other methods of determining race include "'exhibiting' a child of questionable race to a jury (e.g., Nebraska, California, North Carolina, Kentucky); showing photographs or even crayon portraits (notice the kinky hair) of family members of the individual in question; general reputation; and 'classification by association'—assigning 'color' based on the color of those the individual has normally associated with" (p. 252).

As in the third-grade experiment, a major shortcoming of the U.S. system of racial classification is that not all people fit neatly into the categories the U.S. government designates as important. Even so, as we will learn in this book, people use many conscious and unconscious strategies to make others fit into categories. Likewise, many people employ a number of strategies to make sure they themselves fit into some designated category.

In "Interpreting Census Classifications of Race," sociologist Sharon M. Lee (1993) points out that although the racial classification scheme in the United States has changed in significant ways over time, four dominant themes prevailed: (1) a preoccupation with skin color as the defining indicator of race, (2) a belief in racial purity or in the idea that people can be classified as belonging to one race, (3) a pattern of transforming many ethnic groups into one panethnic racial group, and (4) no sharp distinction between race, ethnicity, and national origin.

The preoccupation with skin color (item 1) suggests that the biological facts do not matter. As one of my students wrote:

> I can't be anything but what my skin color tells people I am. I am black because I look black. It does not matter that my family has a complicated biological heritage. One of my great-great-grandmothers looked white but she was of French and African-American descent. Another great-great-grandmother looked Indian but she was three-fourths Cherokee and one-quarter black. My great-grandfather looked white but his sister was so black she looked purple. My coloring is a middle shade of brown, but I have picked up a lot of red tones in my hair from my Indian heritage. My family is a good example of how classifying people according to skin color is ridiculous.

The features of General Colin Powell are a more famous example of why skin color cannot be regarded as a reliable indicator of biological ancestry. Powell is referred to as a retired black/African-American general but in reality he is the son of Jamaican immigrants with "African, English, Irish, Scottish, Jewish, and probable Arawak Indian ancestry" (Gates 1995:65). Similarly Eldrick "Tiger" Woods, who classifies himself as Asian, is known as a "black" golf prodigy. "His mother, from Thailand, is half Thai, a quarter Chinese, and a quarter white. His father is half black, a quarter Chinese, and a quarter American Indian" (Page 1996:285).

With regard to items 2 and 3, notice in Table 4 that there are four official or major racial categories. Notice also that each racial category encompasses a range of national origin and ethnic groups. The Asian or Pacific Islander category includes ethnic or national origin groups such as Chinese, Asian Indian, Hawaiian, and Guamanian. Note in the instructions to the race question (see Table 2), the "Black" or "Negro" category includes

Table 4   U.S. Population by Race and Selected Subcategories within Each Race

RACE (UNIVERSE: PERSONS)	
White	199,827,064
Black	29,930,524
American Indian, Eskimo, or Aleut:	
American Indian	1,937,391
Eskimo	55,674
Aleut	22,078
Asian or Pacific Islander:	
Asian:	
Chinese	1,648,696
Filipino	1,419,711
Japanese	866,160
Asian Indian	786,694
Korean	797,304
Vietnamese	593,213
Cambodian	149,047
Hmong	94,439
Laotian	147,375
Thai	91,360
Other Asian	282,395
Pacific Islander:	
Polynesian:	
Hawaiian	205,501
Samoan	57,679
Tongan	16,707
Other Polynesian	3,998
Micronesian:	
Guamanian	47,754
Other Micronesian	7,216
Melanesian	7,218
Pacific Islander, not specified	4,519
Other Race	9,710,156

Notice that while the U.S. Bureau of the Census counts the number of people in each of the four official racial categories, it also counts specific subcategories within each racial category. The Census Bureau makes no clear distinction as to whether respondents are to think of the subcategory as a national origin, an ethnicity, or a race. For example, should a person born in the Philippines check "Filipino" if he or she is of Spanish ancestry? (Recall that the Philippines is a former colony of Spain.) Should a person of Italian ancestry who has lived in Hawaii check "Hawaiian," a subcategory under Pacific Islander, or "White"?

Source: U.S. Bureau of the Census (1996).

persons who identify as "African-Americans, Afro-American, Haitian, Jamaican, West Indian, Nigerian, and so on." Keep in mind that people who identify as Haitian, Jamaican, West Indian, or Nigerian can be of any race just as people who identify as American can be of any race. The point is that in the process of transforming many groups into one, the U.S. government makes no sharp distinction among race, ethnicity, and nationality (item 4).

In this book, we begin by considering the various ways in which racial classification schemes affect people's lives. Part 1 includes a number of case studies; each points to the fact that classification schemes are important to people's lives whether individuals fit clearly into a racial category or resist classification. We examine several cases, each representing one or more of the following situations:

1. People who cannot be easily classified and the discomfort and crisis of meaning others feel when they cannot easily place those people into an alleged racial category
2. People classified as belonging to one racial category but raised by parents of another category
3. People who do not fit others' conceptions of the racial category to which they claim to belong
4. People for whom the racial categories to which they belong change in importance from moderate to extreme
5. People whose work (i.e., writing, music, art) is classified as representing that of a particular racial category
6. People who find that racial categories to which they have been assigned dominate interpretations of what is taking place and the course of interaction.

Once we understand the tremendous significance of racial categories, we can identify the shortcomings of racial classification schemes. In Part 2, we present evidence showing that such schemes are based on at least two false assumptions: (1) that people can be divided into clear-cut categories so that everyone fits into one category only, and (2) that each category tells us something meaningful about the persons assigned to it that differentiates them from people assigned to the other categories. If the assumptions supporting classification are problematic, then by extension, so are any generalizations we make about the people in each category. For example, the ongoing and seemingly endless debate as to whether attributes such as intelligence (as measured by IQ tests) or behaviors such as criminal activity (as measured by arrest rates) can be traced to racial or ethnic differences can be laid to rest. If it is clear that race is not a biologically meaningful category, then claiming that race explains differences in behavior proves simply to be a waste of time (Fish 1995).

In Part 3, we critique the U.S. system of ethnic classification. We do this for several reasons. First, as mentioned earlier, the U.S. government has followed a pattern of transforming many ethnic groups into one panethnic racial group. In addition the U.S. government makes no distinction between race, ethnicity, and national origin. Second, according to official policy, the only ethnic categories which federal agencies must use when they collect and present data about the United States population are (1) Hispanic/Spanish origin and (2) not Hispanic/Spanish origin. Although federal agencies may use other categories, all categories must ultimately fall under these two official categories. Finally, we critique ethnic classification because many people believe that classifying people according to ethnicity is a more meaningful criterion than race.

Our goal in critiquing classification schemes is *not* to create "better" categories with clearer dividing lines, but to show the futility of trying to classify people in this manner at all. In other words, the goal is to explore how people come to define arbitrary categories as clear-cut and the mechanisms by which they maintain the illusion of independent or pure categories. This goal is not to be confused with a desire to show that since there is no such thing as race, "race" no longer matters. The important point is that people construct classification schemes that carry real consequences. Classification schemes are problematic because they are used to assign social significance and status value to categories over which people most effected by being categorized have little or no control. When that occurs, persons who possess one variety of a characteristic (white skin versus brown, blond hair versus dark hair) are regarded as more valuable and more worthy of reward than persons who possess other varieties. In other words, categories affect *life chances,* a critical set of potential social advantages including "everything from the chance to stay alive during the first year after birth to the chance to view fine art, the chance to remain healthy and grow tall, and if sick to get well again quickly, the chance to avoid becoming a juvenile delinquent—and very crucially, the chance to complete an intermediary or higher educational grade" (Gerth and Mills 1954:313).

In Part 4, we ask "If classification schemes in fact are arbitrary, why do they seem so clear-cut?" The answer to this question is not simple. We identify at least eight factors that make classification schemes seem clear-cut and appear to be a natural way to divide people: ignorance of history, legal mechanisms, informal mechanisms, adhering to unexamined norms, ideology, social vulnerability, selective inattention, and the scientific method.

Finally, in Part 5, we examine the complex issue of challenging and modifying classification schemes. We consider the real consequences of current schemes and the advantages and disadvantages of modifying them. We recognize that classification, however arbitrary, is connected to discrimination. Although the first impulse may be to call for the elimination of all classification schemes, we must recognize that on some level we need these schemes to monitor discrimination and to appraise efforts to combat discrimination. Given this dilemma—classification as a mechanism supporting discrimination versus classification as a means of monitoring inequality and discrimination—we need a new paradigm to help us consider what categories mean, a vocabulary to help us think about our position in relation to others, and a framework to help us to discuss differences among people and across constructed categories. The readings in Part 5 are a first step in this direction.

In light of the fact that racial categories are social constructions, we struggled with the question of how to refer to "race". Should we always put the word race in quotation marks? Should we always qualify references to a person's race with the words people *classified as* or *who identify as* black, white, and so on? In the end we concluded that the idea of race is real if only because its consequences are real. However we believe that people must shift their understanding of the meaning of race away from a term referring to clear biological divisions of humanity, to a term referring to "a way in which one group designates itself as 'insider' and other groups as 'outsiders' to reinforce or enforce its wishes and/or ideas in social, economic, and political realms" (Rorhl 1996:96). Therefore, we continue to see race as an important concept for thinking about the structure of social relationships but we ask that readers work to make this important conceptual shift.

Notes

[1] Some additional examples from students in these two classes make this point even more clear.

- *I worked with a man with one set of grandparents who were mixed (1 white, 1 black). His parents were also mixed. He looks black. This man is now married to a "white" woman, and their kids* look *black.*

   I don't know how we even came to talk of this one day. I always just thought he was black when he's very mixed up. We kind of just made jokes with him about it because he always said how when filling out applications he just checked "other."

- *I went to high school with a boy who grew up in America Somoa. His mother is from the U.S. and has Cherokee and Irish blood. His father is considered black but has African and Asian blood. My classmates and I never really talked about it, but we all knew he was different from the rest of us.*

- *An alum of my sorority is Cherokee Indian and white. Now she has married a Puerto Rican Hispanic, and they have a daughter who is classified as Hispanic on her birth certificate because her dad is.*

- *My sister's friend could not fit into any of the categories. Her mother is white and her father is black. I never asked her what she considered herself. I do remember when I was in high school and she was in junior high, a couple of the Senior guys nicknamed her "mix." I know it hurt her feelings, but I don't know how she replied to the comment.*

- *I have a white friend from Nigeria who has a black boyfriend. They have a little girl who is light-skinned. The U.S. Census Bureau would probably have a hard time figuring out which racial group to put her in.*

- *When I was in high school I played high school football with a multiracial person. His mother was white and his father was black. He associated with both white and black students inside and outside of school. He lived in the black part of a segregated neighborhood. I think that if he had to choose a category he would circle the black category.*

These photos are Gregory Howard Williams and his family. Williams is author of *Life on the Color Line: The True Story of a White Boy Who Discovered He Was Black.* These photos show that relying on physical features to determine a person's "race" simplifies ancestry.

Photo A: Gregory Howard Williams' grandmother (Sallie Williams), his father (James "Buster" Williams) and his great aunt (Bessie Pharris), circa 1917.

Photo B: Gregory Howard Williams' grandmother with his father, cira 1920.

Photo C: Gregory Howard Williams, 4th grade class picture from Garfield Elementary School, Muncie, 1954

Photo D: Gregory Howard Williams and family, 1992. Left to right: Zach, Anthony, Natalia Dora, Carlos, Sara, and Gregory Howard Williams.

The people shown in the three photographs below self-identify as Native Americans. Yet they do not possess the physical characteristics commonly associated with that label.

GROUP OF SEMINOLE BRAVES.

◆ Photo of newly freed slaves. Based on their physical characteristics many in this photograph would not be labeled "black." Yet because of their mixed biological ancestry and the classification rules of the time they all suffered slave status.

◆ Tiger Woods is socially assigned the status "black" in the United States despite his known Asian and Native American ancestries.

◆ This boy possesses physical features (i.e., blue eyes and dark skin) which are associated with two "distinct" racial categories. However, the current system of classification in the United States requires that he self-identify with one category only. If not the Census Bureau will assign him to a single category.

◆ This boy of mixed Negro-Filipino parentage with his white step-mother appears to possess no specific physical marker to call attention to his Filipino ancestry. Depending on the uninformed observer's point of view this child is likely to be labeled as "black" only.

◆ Erika Ngambi ul Kuo with her husband. At first glance Erika looks as if she might be a different "race" than her husband. However, Erika is considered Afro-German as her father was a "black" Cameroon who worked for a German freight and cruise ship and who eventually settled in Hamburg. Erika's mother was a German Jew. ◆ Photo B shows the couple's daughter with Erika.

The photos below show people who are popularly known as "Amerasians." They are offspring of U.S. servicemen stationed in Asia and local women. ◆

PART · I

The Personal Experience of Classification Schemes

Wherever you look—mind, self, family, state, and society— racial categories represent legal and social fictions, pseudo-scientific genetic nonsense, and contradictory claims which can only leave a reasonable person drowning in a sea of confusion. Whether in the area of racial designation at birth, census classification, affirmative action categorization, or state and federal legal definition for purposes of immigration and naturalization, the chaos of categories and casuistries[1] employed to underpin the concept of race only serve to underline its own ultimate intellectual groundlessness. However, to paraphrase W. I. Thomas: "If a phenomena is perceived to be real, it is real in its consequences"—for all those, who voluntarily or not, benefit or suffer from its social construction.

Ernest Evans Kilker
BLACK AND WHITE IN AMERICA (1993:253)

In this section, we explore the personal experience of racial and ethnic classification schemes. Obviously, personal experience is best understood on the level of *social interaction,* everyday events in which at least two or more people communicate and respond through language and other symbolic gestures in order to affect one another's behavior and thinking. When we encounter another, we make many assumptions about what that person ought to be. Judging from an array of clues, we anticipate his or her identity (or category) and the qualities that we believe to be ordinary and normal for a member of that category. We say "here is someone with a characteristic that places him or her in a certain category. Let me see how he or she fits my conception of what I believe a person in that category should be like." We do not say "here is a person, let me find out what he or she is like without making reference to that category" (Montagu 1964).

We will also consider several interaction situations: situations in which people claiming membership in a particular category do not fit others' conceptions of what someone in the category is like, situations in which people possess characteristics which others use to assign them to a particular category, and situations in which people possess ambiguous characteristics which do not allow others to easily place them into a category. We begin with the case of the Mashpee Indians, a group that does not fit others' conceptions of what Indians are supposed to be like.

The Mashpee Indians

Imagine that you have been selected as a jury member for a case in which you and fellow jurors are asked to decide whether a group of people who call themselves the Mashpee constitutes a tribe and whether the Mashpee people have managed to keep alive a core Indian identity over the past 350 years. This question is important for the Mashpee Wampanoag Council because the tribe is suing, in Federal District Court, a large land development company and other property owners to regain 16,000 acres of community land that they had lost in the mid-nineteenth century. Before the Mashpee can bring the suit to court, however, they must prove that they are the biological and cultural descendants of the Mashpee who inhabited the area when it was settled by colonists and who subsequently lost their land in 1850. If the jury decides in favor of the Mashpee on the question of identity, they will not immediately win their claim to the disputed land. A favorable decision only gives the Mashpee the right to a second trial, which will address the land question. In theory, the identity trial is separate from the land trial.

The lawyers representing the Mashpee argue that in spite of enormous odds, the Mashpee have managed to keep alive a core Indian identity since 1850. The defense, on the other hand, argues that a Mashpee tribe never existed because the federal government never recognized them as a sovereign people. In fact, the town of Mashpee possesses no characteristics to distinguish it from any other small rural community in the United States (Brodeur 1978). At best, says the defense, the Mashpee can be described as a small, mixed community fighting for equality and citizenship while abandoning most of its heritage by choice and coercion (Clifford 1988).

For 41 days, you listen to testimony from both sides, which centers around whether the Mashpee have lost their culture or distinct way of life. You listen to testimony from Mashpee who speak with New England accents; few of them look "Indian." In fact, some could pass as black; others, as white.

You learn that the Mashpee language has not been spoken commonly since 1800. One witness, in her seventies, recalls that some of her older relatives knew the language but that English was always spoken at home. She heard the old tongue spoken once when her grandfather's mother was sick and her grandfather held a long conversation with her. After that, the witness recalled her mother saying "Dad, why didn't you tell me you could speak Indian?" When he did not answer, the witness followed up by asking "Grandpa, why didn't you tell us you could speak Indian? Why didn't you teach us?" He replied, "I just want my children to learn the English language and learn it as well as they can" (Clifford 1988:285–86).

During the testimony you learn that over the past three years, Mashpee Indians have intermarried with members of other Indian groups, with whites, with slaves, with Cape Verde Islanders,[2] with Hessian mercenaries employed to fight for England during the American Revolution (who later deserted from the British Army), and with black servicemen stationed nearby at Camp Edwards during World War II (Brodeur 1978).[3] Outsiders sometimes identify the Mashpee as "colored." The witnesses embody this mixed racial and ethnic heritage. One teenage witness, the daughter of a Portuguese father and a Mashpee mother states that she considers herself Mashpee. When asked under cross-examination "How do you know you're an Indian?" she answers, "My mother told me" (Clifford 1988:301).

You learn from witnesses, who identify themselves as Mashpee, that Mashpee routinely move into and out of the community to go to college, to serve in the military, to look for work. Sometimes the moves are temporary; at other times, permanent. For example, one witness lived away from Mashpee for 18 years while he was stationed in Korea and Japan. After leaving the military, he held jobs in Philadelphia and Boston.

Finally, you hear the following kinds of exchanges between lawyers and Mashpee witnesses:

Q: *You don't eat much Indian food, do you?*
A: *Only sometimes.*
Q: *You use regular doctors, don't you?*
A: *Yes, and herbs, as well.*
Q: *How do you know your ancestry?*
A: *My mother, grandparents, word of mouth.*
Q: *What about being a devout Baptist and Indian?*
A: *Grandmother moon and the earth and all those things. . . . They are very dear to me, and I respect them. But I also respect God through my Christian belief. And to me God and the Great Spirit are the same* (Clifford 1988:287).

———————

Q: *I notice you have a headband and some regalia?*
A: *Yes.*
Q: *How long have you been wearing such clothing?*
A: *Oh, I have been wearing a headband as long as needed, when my hair was long enough.*
Q: *How long has that been?*
JUDGE: *That which you have on there, is that an Indian headband?*
A: *It is a headband.*

JUDGE: *It has some resemblance to an ordinary red bandanna?*
A: *Right, that's what the material is, yes.*
JUDGE: *A bandanna you buy in the store and fold up in that manner?*
A: *Yes* (Clifford 1988:346).

After all the testimony, you are expected to decide whether the 1976 Mashpee are biological and cultural descendants of the 1850 Mashpee. What is your verdict? The jury in this case decides "no." Anthropologist James Clifford (1988), who covered the case, argues that the Mashpee never really had a chance of winning the case in the first place because of the narrow way in which most people think about race and ethnicity. For most people these entities have clear boundaries and when someone steps outside them he or she becomes contaminated causing that person's claims to membership to become suspect. Because the Mashpee have intermarried with other Indian groups, with whites, with blacks, with Cape Verde Islanders who can be of any race, and others, the jury cannot see the Mashpee as a separate people.

Likewise, the idea of a Mashpee culture carries associations of a distinct way of life, "of roots, of a stable, territorialized existence" (p. 338). Many people believe that a culture dies if historical continuity is broken. Few regard cultures as phenomena in flux, which adapt to or are transformed by changing circumstances. Because the Mashpee Indians could not point to a physical or cultural characteristic that set them apart or that had remained unchanged, the jury could not see how the Mashpee people could manage to keep alive a core Indian identity over the past 350 years. In addition, the members of the jury brought with them preconceived conceptions about what it means to be Indian that they may have "gleaned from old John Wayne movies and TV reruns of *The Lone Ranger*" (Riley 1992:136). For example, in this case a Masphee could only be "Mashpee Indian" if they started fires with pieces of flint rather than using matches, if they hunted with bow and arrow rather than rifles, or if they wore deerskin rather than cotton clothing. The reading "Adventures of an Indian Princess" by Patricia Riley (1992) alerts us to some of the ways people pick up such preconceptions about Native Americans.

From the jury's viewpoint, no Mashpee who took the witness stand was an authentic Indian; all had become contaminated (voluntarily or involuntarily) by outside events. The Mashpee could not be authentic because, according to the impossible standards of authenticity, they would have had to remain "pristine" or untouched by the events going on around them over the past 350 years. It seems that the standards of authenticity become less rigid when the dominant groups in society benefit from more flexible standards. The reading "Expelled in 1877, Indian Tribe is Now

Wanted as a Resource" by Timothy Egan (1996) offers an interesting contrast to the Mashpee situation in that some residents of Joseph, Oregon, believe the Nez Percé Indians can return to Wallowa Valley after 120 years and reestablish their identity.

Authenticity

Sociologist Richard Handler argues that the idea of authenticity is a "cultural construct of the modern Western world" (1986:2). He argues that "[o]ur search for authentic cultural experience—for the unspoiled, pristine, genuine, untouched and traditional—says more about us than about others" (p. 2). Handler hypothesizes that questions about authenticity become most relevant when ethnic or racial groups find themselves in a struggle for recognition, whether that recognition be for national sovereignty, for a separate category in the responses to the race question on the census, for the right to speak a language different from the dominant group, or for civil rights (i.e., the right to vote, free speech, equal opportunity). Although the Mashpee land claim was, in theory, not part of the identity trial, one might speculate that the jury could not free themselves of this fact and considered only the question of identity in reaching a verdict.

The case of the Mashpee reminds us that ideas of authenticity are deeply embedded in judgments about whether people are members of the categories to which they claim to belong (Handler 1986). Thus every person, but especially those in categories outside the dominant group, are subjected to conscious or unconscious authenticity tests by those within and outside of the category to which they claim to belong. In the reading "Black Man with a Nose Job" by Lawrence Otis Graham (1995), we learn how Graham struggled with issues of authenticity when he decided to undergo rhinoplasty. He describes friends' and acquaintances' reactions to his changed bridge, nostrils, and profile—to his "longer, thinner nostrils." While white friends and classmates who had undergone the surgical procedure could justify their rhinoplasty with "I just want to look better," Graham cannot escape the question of whether he had launched an assault on his history, identity, culture, and people.

In a similar vein, writers who are not considered members of the dominant group are subjected to authenticity tests. In "Culture Wars in Asian America" by Garrett Hongo (1995), we learn that many reviewers and critics see it as their job to classify non-white authors as authentic or inauthentic and to question the ability of "white" authors to write about "non-white experiences." Many people assume that writers classified as Asian-Americans write (or should write) "Asian-American literature." Classifying writers according to their race or ethnicity sets up a false distinction between so-called mainstream American literature and multicultural literature with all its subspecialities—African, Asian, Native American. Such a false distinction flattens differences, denies variation, represses independence among writers, and denies them "the legitimacy of their own interpretation of events" (Hongo 1995:27). Assuming an automatic correspondence between an author's race or ethnicity and his or her topic and writing style reveals an inability to see Asian-Americans and other groups as highly heterogeneous with regard to experience, national origin, and length of residence in the United States (Hongo 1994). Related to this false dichotomy between mainstream and multicultural literature is a pressure on authors labeled as outside the mainstream to be authentic.

The readings by Graham and Hongo suggest that questioning someone's authenticity pressures him or her into taking action to prove they are "genuine." In addition, such pressure can make the challenged person feel as if he or she is under a microscope or is on stage performing before an audience. Here the dramaturgic model of social interaction offers some insights.

Erving Goffman (1959), the sociologist associated with this model, views social interaction as though it were a theater and people as though they were actors giving performances to audiences. People in social interaction resemble actors in that they must be convincing to others and must demonstrate who they are and what they are about through verbal and nonverbal clues. In social interaction, as on a stage, people manage the setting, their dress, their appearance, their words, and their gestures to correspond to the impressions they are trying to make or to the image they are trying to project to their audience. This process is called *impression management.*

On the surface, the process of impression management may strike us as manipulative and deceitful. Most of the time, however, people are not even aware that they are engaged in impression management because they are simply behaving in ways they regard as natural. But when people are aware that an audience is skeptical about who they are, impression management can become a self-conscious, even deliberate, process. When this occurs, impression management presents people with a dilemma. If they do not conceal thoughts and behavior deemed inappropriate for or not expected of someone in their category, they risk offending or losing their audience. Yet, if they conceal their "true" feelings, wishes, or reactions, they may feel they are being deceitful, insincere, or dishonest, or that they are selling out. According to Goffman, the people involved weigh the costs of losing their audiences against the costs of losing their integrity. If keeping the audience is important, concealment is necessary; if showing our true reactions is important we may risk losing the audience (see "Thyra Johnson, 91, Symbol of Racial Distinctions, Dies").

To this point we have discussed situations in which people's racial and ethnic authenticity is questioned—that is they do not display the distinctive popularly held and imposed characteristic which places them solidly in the category of a Mashpee Indian, a black man, or an Asian writer. But what happens when people display that distinctive characteristic which places them solidly in a social category? Here we can turn to Erving Goffman's theory of stigma for some insights.

Stigma

A *stigma* is an attribute that is deeply discrediting. When someone possesses a stigma, he or she is reduced in the eyes of others from a multifaceted person to a person with one tainted status.[4] The attribute dominates the course of interaction and also the way others think about the person with the discrediting attribute. Consider the situation of Mitzi Uehara-Carter (1996) as she describes it in "On Being Blackanese." Uehara-Carter is both Japanese and Black, and people can't see her as mixed or even as Japanese. Her black heritage dominates the view others have of her to the point that they can only see her as Black. As another example of how a stigma reduces a person in the eyes of others from a multifaceted person to a one dimensional being, consider the situation of noted historian John Hope Franklin (1990) where the element of race affects the ways in which people describe and evaluate his accomplishments:

> It's often assumed that I'm a scholar of Afro-American history, but the fact is that I haven't taught a course in Afro-American history in 30-some—odd years. They say I'm the author of 12 books on black history, when several of those books focus mainly on whites. I'm called a leading black historian, never minding the fact that I've served as president of the American Historical Association, the Organization of American Historians, the Southern Historical Association, Phi Beta Kappa, and on and on. The tragedy . . . is that black scholars so often have their specialties forced on them. My specialty is the history of the South, and that means I teach the history of blacks and whites. (1990:13)

Goffman was particularly interested in social encounters known as "mixed-contacts" or interactions between stigmatized persons and normals. Goffman did not use the term *normal* in the literal sense of the "well-adjusted" or "healthy." Instead, he used it to refer to those people who are

Thyra Johnston, 91, Symbol of Racial Distinctions, Dies

ROBERT McG. THOMAS JR.

Thyra Johnston, a blue-eyed fair-skinned New Hampshire homemaker who became a symbol of the silliness of racial distinctions when she and her husband announced that they were black, died on Nov. 22 at her home in Honolulu. She was 91.

She was the real-life heroine of "Lost Boundaries," a movie that stunned the nation in 1949.

It is doubtful that Norman Rockwell could have dreamed up a family that better epitomized the small-town Depression-era American ideal than Albert and Thyra Johnston and their four children.

Dr. Johnston, who was born in Chicago, graduated with honors from the University of Chicago Medical School and studied radiology at Harvard. He was such a respected figure that in the 10 years that he practiced in Gorham, N.H., he headed the school board, was a selectman, was president of the county medical society and became chairman of the local Republican Party.

Mrs. Johnston, who was born in New Orleans, grew up in Boston and married her husband when he was a medical student, and was at once a model homemaker and mother and a civic and social leader whose well-appointed home in exclusive Prospect Hill was the scene of the annual Christmas social of the Congregational Church.

But Mrs. Johnston, described by her son Albert Jr. as looking as Irish as any of her neighbors, had a secret. In a society of such perverse attitudes that black "blood" was simultaneously scorned and regarded as so powerful that the tiniest trace was considered the defining racial characteristic, she was born one-eighth black, enough to qualify her as "Negro" on her birth certificate.

Although he was listed on his birth certificate as white, according to his son, Dr. Johnston was also part black, as well as part Indian. He was black enough to be one of two "black" students admitted to his medical class under a racial quota. But after graduation he could not find a job at one of the few hospitals that accepted black interns.

When Maine General Hospital in Portland accepted his application without inquiring about his race, a deception of sorts began. "We never once intended to pass over as white," Mrs. Johnston said years later. "It just happened accidentally."

So, too, did the denouement.

It began in 1940, when the Navy recruited Dr. Johnston and then withdrew his commission after the Naval intelligence authorities had questioned him about reports that he had "colored blood." Stung by the rejection, Dr. Johnston, who moved his family to Keene in southern New Hampshire in 1939, told his children about their background.

A few years later Albert Jr. told the story to Louis De Rochemont, the movie producer, who immediately grasped its implications. As a result, the family's story was told, first in a widely

Continued

Thyra Johnston *(Continued)*

read article in the *Reader's Digest* in 1947 by William L. White, then in a book and, lastly, in "Lost Boundaries," which starred Mel Ferrer and Beatrice Pearson.

The movie, which won a series of major awards, was so powerful that when the lights came up after the world premiere in New York, the audience sat in stunned silence.

No wonder. The movie undermined the very foundation of social attitudes that link race and personal characteristics. Its message to white America was unmistakable. Because if you did not know that a person is black, he would be the very one you would want to examine your X-rays and run your school system, and she would be the one you would want to play bridge with and work with on civic projects, what possible difference could it make if you did know?

In Keene the answer was essentially none. The Johnstons' friends seemed to realize that the family had not been passing as white, but as Americans.

Their children, who had, after all, grown up in a society that regarded race as defining, had to make some psychological adjustments. But there was virtually no social backlash, and Dr. Johnston's practice actually grew, until he accepted a lucrative offer to move to Hawaii in 1966.

In 1989, a year after her husband's death, when she attended a movie reunion in Keene, Mrs. Johnston offered her own prism for looking at her palette of grandchildren and great-grandchildren. "I just call them flowers in a garden," she said.

In addition to Albert Jr. of Honolulu, surviving are two other sons, Donald, of Thornton, Colo., and Paul, of Buzzards Bay, Mass.; a daughter, Anne Breen of North Granby, Conn.; a sister, Antoinette Reed of Tuskegee, Ala.; six grandchildren, and eight great-grandchildren.

in the majority or who possess no discrediting attributes in the context of a particular setting. Goffman's choice of this word is unfortunate because some readers forget how Goffman intended it to be used.

In keeping with this focus, Goffman wrote about *mixed contacts,* "the moments when stigmatized and normals are in the same 'social situation,' that is, in one another's immediate physical presence, whether in a conversation-like encounter or in the mere co-presence of an unfocused gathering" (Goffman 1963:12). According to Goffman, when normals and stigmatized interact, the stigma comes to dominate the course of interaction. In the reading "A Rescue Without Cheers," Peter Kramer (1995) describes how one characteristic—skin color—can dominate the course of social interaction: specifically, how the parties involved define, interpret, and attach meaning to an encounter. The encounter—the rescue and subsequent resuscitation of a drowning African-American youth by a white lifeguard, nurse, and psychiatrist—is set at a public beach known informally as a "white beach" and is staffed by black employees. On the day of the incident, however, it was the site of a company picnic attended by black employees. No conversation or encounter can escape the facts of the setting. The author concludes that the incident at the beach reflects two irreconcilable perspectives. From his perspective, the incident reflects one of life's hopeful moments; to the African-American bystanders, the incident only causes further cynicism and despair. The point is that even if the victim's race had no bearing on the action taken by the whites to save him, the rescue could not be separated from the larger context—a public beach defined informally as belonging to whites but populated that day by "outsiders."

A stigma comes to dominate the course of interaction in many ways. First, the very anticipation of contact can cause "normals" and stigmatized individuals to avoid one another. One reason is that interaction threatens their sense of racial, ethnic, or cultural "purity" or loyalty. In the reading "The Burden of Race" (pp. 126–31), an excerpt taken from *Days of Grace: A Memoir* by Arthur Ashe (1993), Ashe explains that being black, not having AIDS, is the heaviest burden that he has had to bear in life. One reason that race was a "burden" for Ashe was that he could never relax, especially in integrated settings because he had to constantly anticipate how others within and outside of the black community might react to his (or his family's) actions and words and then alter his and his family's behavior accordingly. Ashe recalls a time in 1992 when he and his family sat with Stan Smith and his family at a fund raising event for the defeat of AIDS prior to the U.S. Open. Stan Smith's seven-year-old daughter came with twin dolls—one for Ashe's daughter Camera and one for herself. As the event started, Ashe looked over and noticed that Camera was playing with a blond doll in "full view of the attentive network television cameras" (p. 129). Ashe anticipates the reaction many people might have to this scene and decides that he must do something "to get Camera to put that doll down" (p. 129).

Another reason the stigmatized and the normals choose to avoid each other is to escape the other's scrutiny. Persons of the same race and ethnicity may prefer to interact with each other so as to avoid the discomfort, rejections, and suspicions they encounter from people of another racial or ethnic group and even from their own. ("I have a safe space. I don't have to defend myself or hide anything, and I am not judged on my physical appearance" (Atkins 1991:B8). Goffman (1963) suggests that the stigmatized individual has good reason to feel anxious about mixed social interaction and that "we normals will find these situations shaky too" (p. 18). Normals feel "that the stigmatized individual is either too aggressive or too shame-faced, and in either case too ready to read unintended meanings into our actions." Normals may feel that if they show direct sympathetic concern they are calling attention to differences when they should be "color-blind." Yet, if normals forget about the stigma, they may put the stigmatized person in an impossible situation (such as the one Arthur Ashe faced in "The Burden of Race") or unthinkingly make remarks about people who have been stigmatized. Each potential source of discomfort for the stigmatized "can become something we sense he is aware of, aware that we are aware of, and even aware of our state of awareness about his awareness" (Goffman 1963:18).

A second way in which a stigma comes to dominate the course of mixed-contact interaction is that normals often define accomplishments by the stigmatized, even minor accomplishments "as signs of remarkable and noteworthy capacities" (Goffman 1963:14) or as evidence that they have met someone from that category who is an exception to the rule (i.e., he or she is just "like us"). As well as defining the accomplishments of the stigmatized as something unusual, normals also tend to behave according to a third pattern and interpret the stigmatized failings, major and even minor, as related to the stigma.

When normals observe a failing in a stigmatized person, they attribute the cause of the failure to the stigma and ignore other contributing factors that would cause anyone difficulty. A fourth way in which a stigma comes to dominate mixed-contact interaction is that the stigmatized are likely to experience invasion of privacy, whether the invasion be experienced through stares, intrusive questions, or added scrutiny. If the stigmatized show their displeasure at such treatment, normals often treat such complaints as exaggerated, unreasonable, or much to do about nothing. Their argument is that everyone suffers discrimination in some way and that the stigmatized do not have the monopoly on oppression. They announce that they are tired of the complaining and that perhaps the stigmatized are not doing enough to help themselves. This is how one woman from Nigeria reacted to the situation of American blacks. In an excerpt from "What Will My Mother Say," Dympna Ugwu-Oju (1995) recounts the level of ignorance Americans have about Africa and the insensitive and downright humiliating questions they ask. In spite of these experiences, Ugwu-Oju, who did not see herself as a black person, dismissed American blacks' reactions to discrimination as "groundless whining" until she learned that, in the United States, she *was* black and that her skin color was the most prominent characteristic by which she was judged.

This discussion should not lead you to believe that the stigmatized are passive victims who are at the mercy of those in the dominant categories. Goffman describes at least five ways in which the stigmatized respond to people who fail to accord them respect or who treat them as members of a category. One way is to attempt to correct that which is defined as the failing, as when people change the visible characteristics that they believe represent barriers to status and belonging. The stigmatized may undergo cosmetic surgery, straighten their hair, bleach their skin, enroll in a school to change an accent, change friends, or dress in a different manner.

The stigmatized may respond in a second way. Instead of taking direct action and changing the visible attributes that normals define as failings, they may attempt an indirect response. That is, they may devote a great deal to trying to overcome the stereotypes or to appear as if they are in full control of everything around them. They may try to be perfect—to always be in a good mood, to outperform everyone else, or to master an activity ordinarily thought to be beyond the reach of or closed to people in that category. The stigmatized may press harder to prove their uniqueness and their difference from others assigned to their category. Japanese-American David Mura recounts how he wanted "to star in football and basketball, wanted to make it in the glamour sports, not in fencing or golf, where the few Asian American athletes played" (1996:83).

Another strategy the stigmatized take to show their uniqueness from those in their category is to take issue with the way normals respond to them as does Geeta Kothari, an American-born daughter of parents from India, when people she does not know ask her "Where are you from?" Here Kothari comments about a bartender who asked her this question.

> The only context for this question is my skin color and his need to classify me. I am sure he doesn't expect me to say New York. I look different, therefore it's assumed that I must be from somewhere, somewhere that isn't here, America. It would never occur to him to ask my boyfriend, who is white—and Canadian—where he's from.
>
> For years I practiced saying "New York," in answer to that question. When I was younger, I complained to my parents about people asking where I was "really" from. My dad insisted on an answer something like "I am an American citizen, born and raised," which sounds like the words of an immigrant. . . . (1995:153)

Another way for the stigmatized to show their uniqueness is to take special actions to distance themselves from others in their category as in the following situation described by Alexandria Neville, a student in an Introduction to Sociology class, involving her Chinese roommate, Elizabeth.

Elizabeth's parents, who met each other more than 25 years ago while attending college in the U.S., speak Chinese at home and follow traditional Chinese practices. This is often a point of embarrassment to Elizabeth who often refers to them as being "straight off the boat." Elizabeth dates only blond-haired, blue-eyed U.S.-born boys. Recently Elizabeth's parents came to town for her graduation. Elizabeth acted embarrassed to be seen with them. When she introduced them she would say "Aren't they the cutest little Chinese couple?" Her parents never said a word, but one time her mother looked at me and rolled her eyes. The entire day Elizabeth talked to her parents as if they were dumb. At one point, her father ordered filet mignon and Elizabeth said, "No, he will have the New York strip, medium well." Her mother interrupted her and said, "Your father knows what he wants for dinner; he doesn't need your help deciding." Elizabeth thinks that because her parents have thick accents they need help being understood. Actually no one had trouble understanding them.

Sometimes the stigmatized respond in a third way: they use their subordinate status for secondary gains, including personal profit, or "as an excuse for ill success that has come [their] way for other reasons" (Goffman 1963:10).

A fourth response is to view discrimination as a blessing in disguise, especially for its ability to build character or for what it teaches a person about life and humanity. Finally, the stigmatized can condemn all of the normals and view them negatively.

To this point, we have examined two situations: (1) situations in which people claiming membership in a particular category do not fit others' conceptions of what someone in the category is like and (2) situations in which people possess characteristics which allow others to *easily* place them in a particular social category. Now we turn to a third: (3) situations in which people possess ambiguous characteristics which do *not* allow others to easily place them into a category.

The writing of sociologist Robert E. Park (1967) on the *marginal man* provides some insights about people in this kind of situation. The *marginal man* is a person facing a social dilemma. He or she belongs to two groups that society treats as separate entities which have no overlap. Given this larger social context, the marginal man is a cultural hybrid, a person living and sharing intimately in the lives of two seemingly distinct peoples. Yet, at the same time, the marginal man lives on the margin of two groups. Thus the marginal man is simultaneously an insider and outsider. As an outsider, the marginal man takes on the perspective of a stranger: He or she "is not radically committed to the unique ingredients and peculiar tendencies" of either group and "therefore approaches them with the specific attitude of 'objectivity.' But objectivity does not simply involve passivity and detachment; it is a particular structure composed of distance and nearness, indifference and involvement" (Simmel 1950:404). As a result of this position in relationship to each group, the stranger tends to survey "conditions with less prejudice; his [her] criteria for them are more general and more objective ideals" (Simmel 1950:405).

We look at five cases in which people are simultaneously insiders and outsiders. In the reading "Choosing Up Sides," author Judy Scales-Trent (1995) must come to terms with the dilemma of her self-identification as a "black" person and her features which sometimes lead others to describe her as "white" in a society which does not handle anomalies very well. Although she is living proof that categories which are treated as clear-cut do not exist, most of the people she encounters struggle to find a way to place her in a single category: "I am perceived by some as white, by some as black, by yet others as a black person but 'really white.'" Scales-Trent finds that in order to survive as a person, she must question the very existence of categories and the absurdity of a classification system which asks people to "choose up sides" (p. 63).

In the reading "Identity Matters," an excerpt from Marilyn Halter's *Between Race and Ethnicity* (1993), an interesting parallel to Scales-Trent's situation is represented. We are introduced to two Cape Verdean Americans, Joaquim A. "Jack" Custodio and Lucille Ramos. Both faced the dilemma of being identified by the larger society as "black" while self-identifying as white.

Sarah Van't Hul, in "How It Was for Me" (1995), describes the subtle prejudice she experiences from white people and the overt hostility she encounters from black people when they learn that she is a black person who has been adopted by a white family. Like Custodio and Ramos, Van't Hul comes to terms with her marginal status by questioning the constructed nature and meaning of racial categories.

In "Mojado Like Me" we encounter the case of Joseph Tovares (1995), a free lance documentary film producer who poses as a Latino farm worker with two colleagues as part of an undercover story for ABC's "PrimeTime Live." Although it had been 25 years since Tovares had worked in the fields, he thought "there had developed a great distance between who I had been and who I had become." He learns that only a change of clothes and a 1979 Ford truck allowed him to become a "Mexican farm worker" and lose his status as a professional.

Finally we consider the marginal status of Yuri Koehiyama, a young Japanese woman, who was one of the estimated 120,000 people of Japanese descent (80 percent of whom were U.S. citizens) living on the

"Just your style," the sister echoed and resumed picking the gum off her face.

Arletta looked around her, assessed the situation, and decided she was outnumbered. She knew they wouldn't hear her even if she voiced her objections. They never listened when she talked. When she had arrived at their home, they had seemed to be full of curiosity about what it was like to be Indian. But all the questions they fired at her, they eventually answered themselves, armed as they were with a sophisticated knowledge of Indian people gleaned from old John Wayne movies and TV reruns of *The Lone Ranger.*

Arletta imagined she could survive this experience. She had survived a great many things these last two years. Her father's death. Her mother's illness. An endless series of foster homes. She was getting tired of being shuffled around like a worn-out deck of cards. All she wanted right now was to be able to stay in one place long enough for her mother to track her down and take her home. She knew her mother must be well by now and probably getting the run-around from the welfare office as to her daughter's whereabouts. For the time being, staying with the Rapiers' was the only game in town, and she felt compelled to play along. She arranged what she hoped would pass for a smile on her face and said nothing. Behind the silent mask, she ground her teeth together.

The midsummer sun blazed off the shiny chrome hubcaps someone had nailed above the trading post door and reflected sharply into their eyes, making the transition from air-conditioned car to parking lot momentarily unbearable. Mr. Rapier was the first to brave the thick, heated air. He wiped a yellowed handkerchief across his balding head, which had begun to sweat almost immediately upon leaving the car. He adjusted the strap that held his camera around his neck and waited while his wife and daughters quickly climbed out of the car and made their way with swift steps to a battered red Coke machine that stood beside the trading post's open door.

Arletta hung back, squinting her eyes against the brightness. She had no interest in the trading post and was determined to stay outside. Off to the left of the Coke machine, she saw a tall, dark man suddenly walk around the side of the building leading a fleabitten pinto pony with a blanket draped awkwardly across its back. Arletta had to laugh at the way he looked because a Cherokee, or any other kind of respectable Indian, wouldn't dress like that on his worst day. Before her mother's illness, Arletta had traveled with her throughout the United States, dancing at one powwow or another all summer long. She knew how the people dressed, and she learned to recognize other tribes by the things they wore as well. This man had his tribes all mixed up. He wore a fringed buckskin outfit, with Plains-style geometric beaded designs, a Maidu abalone shell choker, and moccasins with Chippewa floral designs beaded on the toes. On his head was a huge, drooping feather headdress, almost identical to the one pictured in the sign beside the road. Arletta noticed that there was something else not quite right about the way he looked. His skin looked funny, all dark and light, almost striped in places. As he came closer, she could see that the dark color of his skin had been painted on with makeup and that the stripes had been made by the sweat running down his skin and spoiling the paint job. Arletta had never in all her life known an Indian who looked the way this man did.

After buying everything they wanted, the Rapier family came spilling out of the trading post just in time to be impressed by the cut-and-paste "Indian."

"Oh, Arletta," Mrs. Rapier said. "Look what you found. A real live Indian! Go on over there like a good girl, and I'll have Jackson take a nice picture of the two of you together. It's so seldom you ever see one of your own people."

Arletta froze. She couldn't believe Mrs. Rapier was serious, but then she knew she was. Mrs. Rapier and her entire family actually believed that the man they saw before them was a bonafide Cherokee chief. What is wrong with these people? she thought. Can't they see this guy's a fake?

Mr. Rapier walked behind Arletta and put his sweaty hands on both her shoulders. For a moment, she thought he was going to give her a reprieve, to tell her that she didn't have to do this, that it was all just a joke. Instead, he pushed her forward, propelling her toward the man with the rapidly melting face. She knew then that they were giving her no choice.

Mr. Rapier arranged the girl and the costumed man in what he thought was a suitable pose and stepped back for a look through his camera. Dissatisfied with what he saw, he turned and walked back into the trading post to return minutes later with an enormous rubber tomahawk, a bedraggled turkey feather war bonnet, a smaller version of the one worn by the costumed man, and a shabbily worked beaded medallion necklace with a purple and yellow thunderbird design. He thrust the tomahawk into Arletta's hand, plunked the headdress on her head sideways, and arranged the necklace around her neck with the quickness of a ferret. Surveying his creation, he smiled and returned to his previous position to adjust his camera lens.

"Smile real big for me, honey," he said. "And say the magic word. Say Cherokee!"

Mr. Rapier grinned, his pale beady eyes twinkled at his clever remark. Arletta felt her mouth go sour and a strange contortion of pain began to move around in the bottom of her belly.

The costumed man took her hand and squeezed it. "Come on now, honey. Smile fer the pitcher," he said. His breath was stale rye whiskey and chewing tobacco. Standing next to him, Arletta could smell the pungent sweat that rolled off of him in waves, making his paint job look even worse than it had when she first saw him. Her stomach felt as if she'd swallowed an electric mixer, and she bit her lips to keep the burning in the back of her eyes from sliding down her face. Through her humiliation, Arletta glared defiantly at the man behind the camera and stubbornly refused to utter Mr. Rapier's magic word, no matter how much he coaxed and cajoled. Finally the camera whirred once like a demented bumblebee and it was done.

Mrs. Rapier dabbed at the perspiration that puddled in her cleavage with a crumpled tissue and praised her husband's photographic genius. "That was perfect, Jackson," she said. "You got her real good. Why, she looks just like an Indian princess."

Appeased by his wife's esteem, Mr. Rapier bought everyone a round of cold drinks and then shepherded Arletta and his rapidly wilting family back into the dilapidated station wagon for the long ride home. The superheated air inside the closed-up car was stifling. Arletta suddenly felt as if she were being walled up alive in some kind of tomb. The syrupy soda that had been so cold when she drank it boiled now as it pitched and rolled inside her stomach. She took off the hideous turkey feather headdress and dropped it, along with the phony rubber tomahawk, onto the floor of the car. Slowly, deliberately, Arletta removed the cheap beaded medallion with its crude rendering of a thunderbird from around her neck. Her fingers trembled as she ran them across the tops of the large, ugly, and uneven beads. Turning the medallion over, she read the tiny words printed faintly on the shiny vinyl backing while the painful turbulence inside her stomach increased.

"Mr. Rapier, could you stop the car?" she said. "Mr. Rapier, I don't feel so good."

Mr. Rapier adjusted the knob on the air conditioner's control panel to high and drove on without acknowledging that Arletta had ever spoken. He was already envisioning how her picture would look in the photo album where he and his wife kept the captured images of all of the foster children they had cared for over the years. He hoped she hadn't spoiled the shot with that stubborn expression of hers. He wanted to put it next to the one of the little black girl they had last year. She sure had looked cute all dressed up in those African clothes standing next to that papier-mâché lion at Jungle World.

Mrs. Rapier pulled down the sun visor and began to pull at her perspiration-soaked hair with jerky, irritated movements. She looked at Arletta in the visor's mirror and frowned.

"Arletta," she said, "you need to hush. You've just worn yourself out from the heat and playing Indian. You'll be just fine as soon as the car cools off."

For an instant, Arletta pleaded with her eyes. Then she threw up all over the genuine Indian goods: "Made in Japan."

"Arletta!" Mrs. Rapier screamed. "Look what you've done! You've ruined all those lovely things we bought. Aren't you ashamed of yourself?"

Arletta flashed a genuine smile for the first time that day. "No, ma'am," she said. "No, ma'am, I'm not."

······················

EXPELLED IN 1877, INDIAN TRIBE IS NOW WANTED AS A RESOURCE

Timothy Egan

Study Questions

1. Based on the background information presented in this reading, is there evidence to suggest that the 1996 "Nez Percé Indians" are more "Indian" than the Mashpee?
2. What factors are behind Wallowa County's recognition that the Nez Percé are a distinct Indian culture?

Joseph, Ore.—They saved Lewis and Clark from starvation, helped many an Oregon Trail straggler find the way west, and outfoxed the United States Army in battles that are studied by military historians to this day.

Yet for all their standing in the history books, the Nez Percé Indians have never been able to regain a foothold in the land they were forced from in 1877—an exile that led to one of the last major Indian wars in North America.

But now, in a turn of history and uncommon fate, the people who live in the mountain valley that was taken from the Nez Percé want the Indians to return and are even assembling the financing to buy a large patch of real estate for them. They regard the return of the Nez Percé as a way to help replace the dying logging and ranching economy that was created as a justification for removing the Indians in the first place.

"They're opening the door for the trail home—I never thought I'd see the day," said Earl (Taz) Conner, one of about 4,000 Nez Percé in North America. Mr. Conner is a direct descendant of Old Chief Joseph, for whom this town is named and whose burial site is a prime tourist attraction here in the Wallowa Valley, in northeastern Oregon. "It is really ironic, asking us Indians to return after booting us out of there in 1877."

These days, the people in the valley see the tribe as a potent economic resource. They hope to set aside land for an interpretive center they believe will be a tourist magnet, as well as a year-round cultural and camping site for the Nez Percé.

A remote, mountainous area, four hours of hard driving from the nearest city of any size, Wallowa County has suffered economically in the last decade as timber mills have shut down and cattle prices have plunged. The Nez Percé have long since disappeared, leaving behind only a little cemetery at the foot of Wallowa Lake. Also known as the Sahaptin, they were given the name Nez Percé (meaning pierced nose) by the French because some of the Indians wore nose pendants.

Tourists from all over the world come to see it and the heart-stopping scenery. In Germany, where the fascination with American Indians knows few bounds, the Wallowa Valley may be as well known as Cooperstown is to American baseball fans.

Until now, among the ranchers and cowboys here, there has been ambivalence about the Indians who were driven out.

"I wouldn't call it guilt, but now that some of the old-timers here have fallen on hard times, they can appreciate a little better what happened to the Nez Percé," said Paul Henderson, the National Park Service coordinator for the Oregon end of the 1,100-mile Nez Percé National Historic Trail, which commemorates the 1877 war.

What has happened here has happened in other Western counties where Indian cultural events have become a big attraction. About 10 years ago, some Nez Percé Indians started to return for the annual rodeo here, setting up a powwow on nearby grounds. Before long, the powwows were attracting more people than the rodeo, which was named Chief Joseph Days.

In all the sorry history of American Indians, the Nez Percé story stands as a singular tale. This year, in Stephen E. Ambrose's best-selling book about Lewis and Clark—"Undaunted Courage: Meriwether Lewis, Thomas Jefferson, and the Opening of the American West" (Simon & Schuster)—a new generation of Americans is learning about the tribe that saved the expedition known as the Corps of Discovery from starvation in 1805 and 1806.

For months, the explorers lived among the Nez Percé, marveling at their elaborate economy, their horse-breeding skills, their athleticism, their ability to prosper in the vast reaches of the Columbia River Plateau.

In part because of their longstanding good relations with the Federal Government dating to that expedition, in 1855 the Nez Percé were given official recognition of the land they lived on, about 13 million acres covering parts of what are now Oregon, Washington and Idaho. Included in that original treaty was the Wallowa Valley, where the Joseph band of the tribe had lived for centuries.

But trespassers inevitably came, as part of the gold rushes in the 1860s and 1870s; the treaty was broken; and by the 1870's, the Army ordered the Nez Percé out of the Wallowa region and onto a much smaller reservation in Idaho. Rather than be rounded up, the Wallowa band fled, led by Young Chief Joseph—son of the older chief.

Their 1600-mile march, with the military in pursuit, over several months was page-one news around the world—with the Indians winning most of the battles.

"On our part, the war was in its origin and motive nothing short of a gigantic blunder and a crime," the *New York Times* wrote in 1877.

Finally, just short of the Canadian border in what is now Montana, where the tribe had hoped to be taken in by other Indians, the starving, freezing band of Nez Percé surrendered.

Some 250 Nez Percé warriors, joined by 500 women, children and old people, had fought with about 2,000 Army soldiers in 20 battles and skirmishes. Later, the Army estimated that a total of 151 Indians had been killed. It was, said Gen. William Tecumseh Sherman, "the most extraordinary of Indian wars."

Afterward, the Government scattered the Nez Percé all across the continent, from Canada to Oklahoma, but never allowed them to return to this valley. Young Joseph was buried in 1904 in the chalky volcanic soil of eastern Washington. He died, it was said, of a broken heart.

Though the Nez Percé made numerous appeals to the Government, and through the courts, to get their Wallowa Valley land back, they were rebuffed. The Government pointed to a revised treaty—signed by some Nez Percé leaders in Idaho, but never signed by Joseph or his band—as the legal basis for keeping the tribe out of Oregon.

Mr. Conner, whose great-grandfather Ollokot fought in the war, noticed a change in attitude a few years ago, as the Wallowa economy went into tailspin.

"I was working for the Forest Service, the only Indian walking around there, and I was approached by this economic development guy from the city of Wallowa," Mr. Conner recalled. "He said he thought the Indians could save this county. I had to laugh at that."

These days, tourists by the busload cannot get enough of the vanquished Joseph band, said Mr. Henderson, the Park Service coordinator.

"Joseph has become one of those transcendent figures in American history," he said. "There is just this huge interest. They come here, to the end of the road, and they see what Joseph was fighting for."

Down the road from Joseph, in the town of Wallowa, community leaders say the aura of the Nez Percé may be the No. 1 draw. Their visitor brochures now proclaim Wallowa as "Gateway to the Land of Chief Joseph," and the Nez Percé Powwow—which is separate from the gathering in Joseph—is now in its sixth year.

Seeing a chance for economic revitalization, the valley's community leaders have joined with the Indians to develop a big Nez Percé cultural and interpretive center. They obtained a $250,000 grant from an Oregon historical group, and plan to use the money to buy 160 acres atop a bluff not far from the river where the Nez Percé used to fish for salmon, just outside the town of Wallowa. They intend to begin a major fund-raising effort for the rest of the money, an amount yet to be determined, to build the center.

The Nez Percé, it turns out, have been something of a lost gem in this valley. "We're just a bunch of white folks—we didn't have a clue at first," said Terry Crenshaw, one of the leaders behind the effort to build a cultural and interpretive center.

But the recent developments have a different meaning for Nez Percé like Soy Redthunder, a descendant of Joseph who lives on the Colville Indian Reservation in Washington State, where Young Joseph is buried.

"The whites may look at it as an economic plus, but we look at it as homecoming," Mr. Redthunder said.

He said the tribe would have to be very careful, given that anti-Indian sentiment still lingers in the valley. "I don't think we want to rush in there and take over the county," he said. "But I see a serious effort to return the Nez Percé people to the Wallowa Valley."

Until a few years ago, Mr. Redthunder said, he had always felt shunned here. "At their cowboy festival, they were highly indifferent to native people—they considered us drunken Indians," he said.

Up in another part of this county, the Nez Percé are about to take possession of 10,000 acres along a creek where Young Joseph was born. This land is being purchased by the Bonneville Power Administration, which markets electricity from the string of Federal dams along the Columbia and Snake Rivers. Having destroyed the salmon runs on which the Indians used to depend, the dam operators are required by law to offer something in return.

In this case, they are buying Wallowa County land and turning it over to the Indians for management. No Indians will live there, but they will get hunting, fishing and management rights. It would be controlled by the band of Nez Percé living on the reservation in Idaho—a group that has been separate from the Joseph band since 1860.

Standing near the Wallowa River, where generations of Nez Percé have long fished for the big chinook salmon and steelhead trout that make their way into the Oregon interior, Mr. Conner could scarcely believe the changes that are under way.

A Navy veteran, he has always felt that people in other parts of the world appreciated the Nez Percé more than people in his home in the Pacific Northwest.

"I was in Spain once," Mr. Conner recalled, "and this guy said to me, 'You're Indian, right? What are you, Sioux?' I told him I was Nez Percé, and his face lit up. He said, 'Nez Percé! Chief Joseph.'"

The return of the Nez Percé here, "would be a tremendous happening for our people," Mr. Conner said, adding, "We're pretty close to being home."

BLACK MAN WITH A NOSE JOB

LAWRENCE OTIS GRAHAM

Study Questions

1. How will Lawrence Otis Graham know if his operation is a success?
2. Where does Graham get his images of "ideal" noses to show the plastic surgeon?
3. When Graham was growing up, with whom did he compare his physical features?
4. What are the "racial" issues bound up with Graham's decision to have rhinoplasty?
5. Do you think Graham can ever know if his decision to undergo rhinoplasty represents a wish to simply "look better" or a wish to look "less black"?

"**D**ad, slow down some."

The relentless spring breeze finally calmed as my father let up from the accelerator and swerved us into a right-hand lane.

This man, who was normally quite solicitous of his youngest son and who almost never drove above fifty miles per hour, was suddenly sighing indignantly over my interference with his driving speed.

"What's wrong?" I asked.

He stared straight ahead, occasionally glancing at the stream of cars that were now passing us by. "Nothing," he answered.

As we reached the Henry Hudson tollbooths that would take us out of Manhattan, three young black faces peered into the side window.

"What the hell happened to *you?*"

"Somebody fucked his shit up—look at that shit!"

Three black guys in their early twenties looked down from their Jeep into my open window and shook their heads with perverse amusement.

Determined to get a response, the driver finally asked, "You get shot?"

Dad moved us up another car length as I put the ice pack beneath my eyes and moved into a reclining position.

"Extra token and a receipt."

"My goodness—is everything all right in there?" the blue-jacketed toll woman asked as she stared into the backseat at my head: an oversized bowling ball of white gauze, plaster, and hospital tape. Unbeknownst to me, melting ice was quietly transforming the gauze-covered bloodstains, making them a more prominent red color and giving them a surreal, almost tie-dye-like quality underneath the white material.

I think I nodded faintly.

"Just a nose job," my father answered while retrieving his change.

"Really?" She seemed surprised by my father's air of nonchalance.

Or was it an air of contempt?

As I lay reclined, with my head practically in the backseat of the little maroon BMW, I wondered what my father thought of me now. A man of a different generation—born and raised in the segregated South—educated and trained in an almost exclusively black world where the concept of an oxymoron readily included such things as a black man with a nose job.

For my entire life, until yesterday, I had displayed his same nostrils, bridge, and profile. Tomorrow I wouldn't. Tomorrow I'd look like someone else. Staring up at the back of my father's head, I realized that the success of my operation would be measured in direct proportion to how much differently my nose looked from his. It was a shameful contrast to make with someone I loved so much, but when looking at my sketches, it was an accurate one nevertheless.

"This is the one I want," I had said while handing the opened magazine to Dr. Wilson.

"Which?" he asked.

I scanned the well-lit Upper East Side office, then crossed my legs with an air of affected nonchalance. "I actually don't care. Any of those would do."

This black plastic surgeon—one who had been practicing on the Upper East Side for longer than my time on this earth—had no doubt met my kind before: that overly anxious patient who displays reckless confidence in the miracles of modern medicine. Walking the streets with desperation in our eyes and portfolios under our arms, we young, well-to-do seekers of cosmetic enhancement bear a strange resemblance to professional models, except that inside *our* portfolios is a lifetime supply of dog-eared photos and print ads depicting *other people's* faces, features, and body parts that we wish *we* had been born with and that we hope can still be affixed—Mr. Potato-head-like—onto the various appendages and extremities of our bodies.

Having torn more than fifty or sixty shots of sharp-nosed, square-jawed, model-handsome, near-black-looking or practically black-looking men from some of the best store catalogs and hippest fashion magazines in New York, I felt I'd done more than my share of the legwork. I was now ready to pay whatever it cost and submit myself to whatever tests, X rays, computer imaging, or painful surgical procedures were necessary.

Dr. Wilson flipped ahead with a ruffled brow. "What magazine are these pictures from?"

I leaned over his desk and looked at the pages. "That's the Brooks Brothers catalog. But I've got lots of other noses and faces mixed in from other catalogs and magazines."

The good doctor—I'd been told one of the best in New York—had no idea of how long I'd agonized over this project. I'd been saving noses and profiles for the prior three years, tearing out pages from magazines, catalogs—even stealing a poster from a Boston red-line subway car one Sunday afternoon—all in the search for the right features. I stuck all this into a bulging April 1987 issue of *Ebony.*

"Mr. Graham," the sensitive doctor began as he reached for my chin and turned my head to either side. "There is only a certain amount of alteration that is possible, or even desirable, for any one nose."

"I know what you're going to say," I interrupted. "That you can't make me look like those guys because they have white noses. But if you notice, those are all *black* men on these pages I've given you. They're all *black.*"

"Hmm."

The least black-looking collection of black men either one of us had ever seen compiled.

"Even if I *could* do this—and it would be unlikely—such a long thin prominent nose wouldn't work on your face."

"Okay, then what about this one?" I showed him a page from a nine-month-old *Sports Illustrated.*

The good doctor shook his head.

"But he's black too." Yeah, black and something else.

"Umm."

"What about this one?" I showed him several shots of a brown-skinned model in a *GQ* layout. Probably a black Cuban.

He waved me on.

I pulled out a recent issue of *Essence* and turned to the first of the paper-clipped pages, which featured models who were suddenly displaying darker skin and wider, flatter noses. "How about that?" I pointed to the *Essence* man who stood holding an elegant glass of whiskey.

"Why don't I sketch out what I think we can consider."

But I wasn't giving up yet. "Wait—let me just show you this last one. I got this tourism ad out of *Ebony.* You must at least be able to do *that.*"

He looked down at the brownest of all my men. "Mr. Graham, that nose would never be in harmony with your lips and chin. They would never work together."

"My lips and chin?" I asked. I had to pause a few seconds and consider the significance of his remark. "Then change them," I finally howled. "Change them. I'll pay whatever it costs. Change them. Just change them!"

Sometimes it takes very little to send some of us down the slippery slope toward black self-hatred.

Eventually I entered a hospital on Manhattan's Upper West Side to undergo that common surgical procedure we all call rhinoplasty. While this procedure is performed nearly a hundred thousand times each year, I had the feeling that my case was different. It was shortly after being wheeled into the large, brightly lit recovery room that I became certain that I had just launched an assault on my identity and my people. But now it was too late to go back. I was, forever, a black man who had gotten a nose job.

Although I'd grown up in a white neighborhood where male and female adolescents got their noses narrowed, chins and cheeks enhanced, and skin chemically peeled as a coming-of-age ritual during junior high and high school vacations, I had never seriously considered plastic surgery for myself. Yes, I wanted to be thought of as more handsome, but no one in my family had ever undergone cosmetic surgery. For these white friends and classmates who had undergone surgical changes, their explanations focused simply on cosmetics: They wanted to look "better." Not surprisingly, no one ever seemed to impute any other motive or to psychoanalyze the real meaning of "better." For me and my family, physical appearance and its alteration were issues of ethnicity and heritage. Black people had wide nostrils, thick lips, protruding mouths, and dark skin—and any desire to change those features was, by definition, a negative commentary on our people and our own racial identity.

For the most part, I never even compared my looks to those of the white kids or white adults around me. During my adolescence, I did, however, draw contrasts with the young blacks in my own world of black professionals and their families who socialized in our black social clubs and vacation places. There were numerous occasions as a child, and later as an adult, when hosting summer cookouts in Sag Harbor, Long Island, or Oak Bluffs, Martha's Vineyard; attending our Jack & Jill family gatherings; or partying at the Sisters of Ethos all-black dances at Wellesley College, when I'd run into dozens of well-to-do, light-skinned, straight-haired, thin-featured black childhood friends. After returning to the security of my own bedroom mirror, I would critique my features against those other blacks in my life who had "sharper," "nicer," "finer" (all words that meant more attractive and less Negroid) physical characteristics.

I would flatten my thick lips against my teeth, protrude my chin, and try but fail to attach a wooden clothespin on the wide fleshy tip of my nose. The pain of this primitive procedure was outweighed by the satisfaction I got from capturing a glimpse of longer, thinner nostrils.

Except for those occasions when I flipped through men's magazines or passed by some daytime or nighttime TV soap opera, it was rare that I ever compared my features to whites around me. Unlike young girls, I was fortunate that as little boys, my brother and I weren't saddled with trying to find our image and, hence, our self-worth, in the similarities we shared with the face and features of a white Barbie and Ken doll. In spite of the ambivalence that I once had about my looks, I've always felt that black boys are far luckier than the black girls who get ambushed by white girls in school and summer camp who tell them, "You'd be really pretty if it wasn't for that black nappy hair of yours."

My color ambivalence manifested itself in many different ways during my adolescence. I'm reminded of the Hasbro G.I. Joe army and astronaut set I used to play with. One afternoon I put brown shoe polish all over my 1967 G.I. Joe astronaut's entire pink body and later melted his tiny nose away with the heat from my Mattel "Creepy Crawlers" cooking iron. I don't know if I can ascribe my actions to black pride or a desire to punish Joe, but I never took him out in public after that.

Finally, after considering hundreds of magazine and catalog layouts and doctor's sketches, after writing a check for $4,000 to a black surgeon, and after having the operation, I still sometimes feel like I've upset the standard of blackness that I'd been raised to accept and appreciate.

When I told a former black classmate about my operation, she accused me of trying to pass out of the black race. It was hardly the sympathetic response I had expected from an intelligent woman who had been one of my first friends in law school. In fact, her contempt was so great and questions so numerous, I really began to wonder if she was right about my motives.

Did I have this operation in order to become less black—to have features that were more white? Had I bought into the white definition of beauty—the sharp nose, the thin lips, the straight hair? Did I think that my less Negroid-looking black friends were more attractive than me?

My wife says my decision is personal and that I shouldn't feel compelled to defend it or explain it to anyone else. I'd like to think she is right. Maybe she's right about not needing to justify my acts to white coworkers or white neighbors. But what about my black relatives, my black friends, my black coworkers, my black secretary? Don't I owe them an explanation? Don't I have to let them know I wasn't saying that I wanted to be white when I pared down my wider, rounder Negroid nose?

Of course, I could take the easy way out and tell onlookers that one's racial identity is not embodied in one's nose. It certainly should be obvious in my case. After all, my dark brown skin and curly black hair are still intact. A different nose won't make me look white. But that's really not the point I need to address, is it?

For two years prior to my operation, I agonized over the ethnic ramifications of cosmetic surgery. According to the American Society of Plastic and Reconstructive Surgeons, 640,000 cosmetic procedures were performed in the United States in 1994. Since the preponderance of those patients were white, I am fairly certain that many of them felt no obligation to justify their surgery to members of their ethnic group.

All of this leads me to conclude that my defenses are a wasted effort. While my white friends have guiltlessly selected profiles and implants with their surgeons, I was making a futile attempt to validate my ethnic loyalty by developing arguments to prove that a nose job would not make me less black.

I shouldn't have to defend my surgery any more than those 640,000 patients who pass under the scalpel each year—or for any person who makes any type of cosmetic changes in his or her natural appearance. After all, an Italian person rarely feels guilty for turning his brown hair blond. Few Jewish people apologize for having their noses shaved down. Not many Asian people have to justify putting waves into their straight hair. Many people, in fact, are surprised to learn that in both Japan and Korea, as well as in the United States, it is quite common for male and female Japanese and Korean people of all ages to have their eyes done (for less than $1,500, a surgeon creates a more westernized eye by creating a fold in the eyelid that makes it appear rounder) and their noses enhanced (for about $2,500, a surgeon creates a more Caucasian nose by raising the bridge and tip by inserting a plastic or cartilage implant). With so many other groups undergoing the same procedures, it is ludicrous for black cosmetic surgery to be taken as a form of heresy against the race.

I am discovering that many whites as well as blacks perceive a black person's cosmetic surgery as a sign of self-hatred or the desire to be less black—an accusation often aimed at singer Michael Jackson, who in spite of his claims about rare skin diseases and naturally changing bone structure, pinched his nose, bleached his skin, tattooed his eyes, enhanced his chin, and straightened his hair. Even black talk-show host Montel Williams felt compelled to explain his nose job to his viewers. His claim: He'd done it because he'd had difficulty breathing. Whether we believe his explanation or not, none of us have the right to challenge such a decision.

An equally presumptuous attitude prevailed a while back with regard to colored contact lenses. No one objected when white actors, models, and consumers wore the cosmetic lenses, but when black talk-show host Oprah Winfrey wore them on TV, there was an immediate avalanche of attacks from both whites and blacks who could not understand why a black person would wear green contacts. White people seemed to be threatened by the notion that black people could actually avail themselves of cosmetic advances and appropriate the beauty characteristics that white people had theretofore defined as exclusively their own. Black audiences, too, looked at rich, powerful, and famous Oprah and feared that she was somehow about to "buy" herself out of the black race and leave us bereft of one more black heroine and role model. In the end, when the host held her ground on her black identity, black and white viewers wised up and realized that the ever dedicated and down-to-earth Winfrey wasn't going anywhere she didn't belong. Colored contacts weren't going to change her.

Black plastic-surgery patients or lens-wearers should not have to address the issue of ethnicity any more than white people who go to a tanning salon or get a collagen shot to thicken their lips—as so many white actors, models, and fashion-conscious citizens are doing today. Black people who get their hair straightened each month should be able to do so just because they want to sample a noncurly style.

Because I've narrowed my nose, some of my black friends say I have sought to deny my ethnicity, and oddly enough, some of my white friends—even those who have had nose jobs themselves—say I'm representative of the young black professional who wants to assimilate into the white culture. Perhaps it is true that the media images and the white kids who surrounded me as a child sometimes caused me to judge my own attractiveness on some other group's standard of beauty, but I dismiss the suggestion that any black who seeks to alter his natural physical characteristics has turned on his people and attempted to "pass" as a member of some other race.

Once the bandages were finally taken off (a few years ago), friends discovered that I am no less black than I was before the operation. I still had the same black friendships, still supported the same black causes, and still maintained the same black consciousness. As my father, the stoic black southerner, was able to do, my friends continue to allow me to take pleasure in my new appearance. For them to view this as anything more than a cosmetic procedure would be to suggest that the culture, feelings, and history of black people are awfully superficial.

CULTURE WARS IN ASIAN AMERICA

GARRETT HONGO

Study Questions
1. Describe the criticism Cynthia Kadohata received for her novel *The Floating World?*
2. What issue did Robert Butler have to confront about his work?
3. What does Hongo's account of his exchange with a *Newsday* reporter tell us about how the media covers issues related to "race"?

During the summer of 1989, on a book tour after the publication of her novel *The Floating World,* writer Cynthia Kadohata, a Japanese American, was making a routine appearance at Cody's Books in Berkeley. The crowd was unusually large for a first-time novelist, packed with interested Asian American students and some UC faculty too. Her book had been receiving good notices in the mainstream press, and a chapter of it had run in *The New Yorker* prior to publication. She read quietly but clearly, with a fine delicacy of voice and a minimum of physical movement. The audience seemed charmed. But in the question and answer session that followed, she was chastised for not writing about the concentration camp experience. Her novel, partially set during the time of World War II, tells the story of an itinerant family of Japanese Americans wandering through the West and South in search of work, doing without community except for each other. It never once mentions the federally ordered evacuation of citizens of Japanese ancestry from the West Coast. But there was a powerful faction among Japanese American intellectuals who felt it was illegitimate of Kadohata to have refrained from any overt references to the internment camp experience.

"You mean to tell me that you have this family of Japanese Americans running around through Arizona, Colorado, and Utah, and you *never* say anything about the camps!" a scholar shouted from the audience. "You should be ashamed of yourself for falsifying our history!" he yelled.

More shouting ensued as a few other Asian Americans joined this public castigation. Kadohata responded by saying that she didn't *intend* to write about the camps, that her novel wasn't *about* the camps, that she was writing about a family of loners and misfits, writing from *her* experience, and that was that. She was then criticized for abdicating her responsibilities as a Japanese American writer, denounced for not fulfilling expectation, for not writing from the public truth of the time.

She told me later that the whole incident puzzled and upset her. It hurt that people, especially other Asian Americans, felt compelled to attack her for what she *didn't* write even more than for what she *did* write. Kadohata was wondering why there was so much vehemence, so much anger, and so much "attitude" among Asian Americans *against* Asian American writers. She hadn't defended herself then, but the episode made a deep and lasting impression. She told me that the next time she was out there, she'd be ready. She wasn't going to get beaten up again without a fight.

I once remarked that Asian America is so immature as a culture and so unused to seeing cultural representations of itself that, whenever representation does occur, many respond with anger because of the pain released. It is as if they recognize *their* story in the outlines of the story one of the writers is telling, but feel even more alienated rather than absolved because that story isn't theirs *exactly*, or doesn't present the precise tone and tenor of their inner feeling regarding an experience they feel the writer, as an Asian American, should understand. It's like a bunch of family members at a holiday dinner sitting around, trying to tell a story about a maiden aunt, a matriarch, or a black sheep. One starts it up, and, before you know it, six others chime in, saying the first didn't get it right, that their version is the one that is true and has all the facts. It has to do with issues of primacy, proprietorship, a claim of proper descent and legitimacy, and a claim to specialized knowledge. It is complex. And charged with passion. Whenever someone singles out a certain storyline, an interpretive angle, there are always those who would dispute its legitimacy, even to the point of trying to erode the confidence of the storyteller. . . .

A couple of years ago, I got a phone call at my home in Oregon from a reporter at *Newsday,* the daily paper for Long Island. Just the day before, Robert Olen Butler had been awarded the Pulitzer Prize in Fiction for his collection of short stories called *A Good Scent from a Strange Mountain.* The narrator of each story is Vietnamese, each a different survivor of the war in Vietnam, most of them living in this country. The reporter wanted to know what I, as an Asian American writer, thought about the prize being awarded to a white male who wrote stories in the personae of male and female Vietnamese refugees.

I told him I was personally delighted that Butler had won the Pulitzer, that I was glad that the prize had finally gone to someone who was known as a dedicated laborer in the fields of creative writing, who wrote for long years in obscurity, who wrote well and without recognition except from his peers in the business, who taught a heavy teaching load at a regional branch of a state university, who was a single parent who gave to his community and to the community of Vietnamese immigrants. I stalled, wanting a little time to think.

"Yes," the reporter said, "but what is your opinion about his being white and writing in the voices of Asians? Of him *adopting* the identity of Vietnamese individuals in order to write his fiction?"

I had suspected there was something hot behind his questioning. On matters of race, American culture has the chronic habit of organizing itself in terms of opposition first, even with regard to a book that, to me, was a sincere attempt to create commonality.

On the one hand, there was the history of stereotyping and ventriloquizing Asians in this country. There was certainly a history of abuse there. And it was a history that was vague in the minds of most Americans who were not Asians—an "invisible" history, one that did not penetrate daily consciousness unless one were oneself Asian American. Butler's collection of stories, in the act of taking on the voices of Vietnamese people, could be interpreted by some as perpetuating that tradition.

On the other hand, there was my own feeling that Butler's book was kind of a breakthrough for American books on the Vietnam experience. Until Butler published his stories, most every piece of writing from Americans had to do with the tragedy of the American experience in Vietnam. Tim O'Brien and Larry Heinemann had written powerful fiction from the point of view of American soldiers. Michael Herr had published nonfiction from a similar perspective, while Yusef Komunyakaa had written a stunning book of poems—it, too, based on his GI experience. Very little had been published from the Vietnamese point of view, and almost nothing about the Vietnamese experience in America. Butler's book had created characters and described an ethos much unknown to mainstream America—that of the Viet Kieu, Vietnamese survivors of the war who had emigrated to the U.S. and were struggling over their losses, their identity, and the difficulties of acculturation. Sympathetic without being sentimental, Butler's treatment gave the outlines of their lives great human dimension and humor without ignoring the multiple tragedies of their having lost homelands, loved ones, and a certain continuity of cultural identity. *A Good Scent from a Strange Mountain,* though written by someone who was white and not Vietnamese, could not easily be seen as yet another piece of "minstrelsy" by the white culture ventriloquizing the ethnic experience and colonizing the mind of the Other for the purpose of reinforcing cultural dominance. It is a work which seemed to me at once more complex than that, and yet I could not say so within the simplistic framework in which the reporter was asking his question.

I told the reporter that I couldn't give him a short answer and gave him the long one instead. I begged off making any kind of *ultimate* political judgment. Since I am not from the Vietnamese American community, I couldn't presume to speak to the issue of whether or not his characterizations and tales infringed upon some "right" of theirs to define themselves in our culture. I felt uncomfortable being asked to speak "as an Asian American," knowing that we are an extremely diverse group in terms of generations, cultures of origin, and economics. I urged him to ask a Vietnamese American. I told him that, by asking me for my opinion, I knew he was operating as if Asians in America were one vast, homogenous category, and making the false assumption that any one of us, no matter that our ethnicities were different, could speak "on behalf" of the entire race.

He tried to press me, but gave up after a few more exchanges. He couldn't pin me down because I didn't want to be. Frustrated, the reporter thanked me and hung up. It was obvious I hadn't helped his story angle. He wanted a fight between Butler and Asians, and he wanted me either to defend Butler or to attack him. He wanted my answers to be *simple* and unqualified. On one side or the other. I guess, on that issue, I was sitting on a fence. The reporter's coming to me was itself another act of racism, and I worried about participating in that.

But I continued to feel uncomfortable about the incident. Why couldn't I have given the reporter something more definitive? Why hadn't I been more ready to give a strong opinion on the matter? What was it that made me speak on both sides of the issue? Was I, in fact, in being so equivocal, acting as an apologist for white colonization of ethnic cultural space? Was I—of *all* things—acting like a goddamn Uncle Tom? What are the issues here and how could I rethink myself through them? I questioned myself but hesitated to bring it up among my friends, whether Asian or not. I feared policing and I feared judgment. I wanted some space to think. I decided to look for other writers who could help me to do this kind of thinking.

There was indeed a political dimension to this issue, but it is not one regarding a given writer's "right" to represent a culture. There is a profound difference between the idea that any group has an exclusive right to engage in authorized acts of cultural representation and the idea that cultural representations are not open to criticism, whether by a group or an individual critic. Although our system of prestige can itself be seen as a kind of rule of unwritten laws, I myself believe that we cannot, finally, create legislation regarding cultural properties in the verbal arts—i.e., provide cultural laws empowering and licensing only certain individuals to do what we will prohibit others from doing with regard to language and the arts. At the same time, I do not think that anyone can be above being criticized for what they choose to do with this kind of liberty. I think we can applaud [David] Mura for raising a political objection to a work of art, but we can also critique—though not silence—Butler on political grounds for the work of art he has produced. I think we can critique Mura as well, and we can praise Butler too—for his humanistic politics as well as for his powerful artistry. The confusions, then, have less to do with the practices of the individual artists and much more to do with the way general thought in our culture (as enacted by media and the ephemeral communal mind) tends to oversimplify complex social and artistic issues, with the habitual comminglings and false oppositions of matters of art with matters of social justice. The problem, ultimately, has to do with confusing and, finally, conflating the two realms.

ON BEING BLACKANESE

MITZI UEHARA-CARTER

Study Questions

1. What societal forces "push" Mitzi Uehara-Carter into the category "black"?
2. In spite of these societal pressures, how does she come to maintain a sense of "Japaneseness"?
3. What identity does she prefer?

"**U**mm . . . excuse me. Where are you from?"

"I'm from Houston, Texas."

"Oh . . . but your parents, where are they from?"

(Hmm. Should I continue to play stupid or just tell them.) "My dad is from Houston, and my mom is from Okinawa, Japan."

"And your dad is black then?"

"Yup."

"So do you speak Japanese?"

"Some."

"Wow. Say something."

This is not a rare conversation. I cannot count the number of times I've pulled this script out to rehearse with random people who have accosted me in the past. "That's so exotic, so cool that you're mixed." It's not that these questions or comments bother me or that I am offended by their bluntness. I think it's more of the attitudes of bewilderment and the exoticism of my being and even the slight bossiness to do something "exotic" that annoy me. I think I am also annoyed because I am still exploring what it means to be both Japanese and Black and still have difficulty trying to express what that means to others.

In many ways and for many years I have grappled with the idea of being a product of two cultures brought together by an unwanted colonization of American military bases on my mother's homeland of Okinawa. Author of "In the Realm of a Dying Emperor," Norma Field expressed these sentiments more clearly than I ever could. "Many years into my growing up, I thought I had understood the awkward piquancy of biracial children with the formulation, they are nothing if not the embodiment of sex itself; now, I modify it to, the biracial offspring of war are at once more offensive and intriguing because they bear the imprint of sex as domination." Of course this is not how I feel about myself all the time, but rather it is the invisible bug that itches under my skin every now and then. It itches when I read about Okinawan girls being raped by U.S. Servicemen, when I see mail order bride ads, when I notice the high divorce or separation rate among Asian women and GI's who were married a few years after WWII, when I see the half-way hidden looks of disgust at my mother by other Japanese women when I walk by her side as a daughter. Our bodies, our presence, our reality is a nuisance to some because we defy a definite and demarcated set of boundaries. We confuse those who are trying to organize ethnic groups by highlighting these boundaries because they don't know how to include us or exclude us. We are blackanese, hapas, eurasians, multiracial. . . .

My mother has been the center of jokes and derogatory comments since my older sister was born. She was the one who took my sister by the hand and led her through the streets of Bangkok and Okinawa as eyes stared and people gathered to talk about the sambo baby. She was the one who took all my siblings to the grocery stores, the malls, the park, school, Burger King, hospitals, church. In each of these public arenas we were stared at either in fascination because we were a new "sight" or stared at with a look of disgust or both. Nigga-chink, Black-Jap, Black-Japanese mutt. The neighborhood kids, friends, and adults labeled my siblings and me with these terms especially after they recognized that my mother was completely intent on making us learn about Okinawan culture. On New Year's Day, we had black eyed peas and mochi. We cleaned the house to start the year fresh and clean. "Don't laugh with your mouth too wide and show yo teeth too much," my mom would always tell us. "Be like a woman." I had not realized that I covered my mouth each time I laughed until someone pointed it out in my freshman year in college. When we disobeyed my mother's rule or screamed, we were being too "American." If I ever left the house with rollers in my hair, my mom would say I shouldn't do American things. "Agijibiyo . . . Where you learn this from? You are Okinawan too. Dame desuyo. Don't talk so much like Americans; listen first." There were several other cultural traits and values that I had inevitably inherited (and cherish) being raised by a Japanese mother.

Growing up in an all Black neighborhood and attending predominately Black and Latino schools until college influenced my identity also. I was definitely not accepted in the Japanese circles as Japanese for several reasons, but that introduces another subject on acceptance into Japanese communities. Now this is not to say that the Black community I associated with embraced me as Blackanese, even though I think it is more accepting of multiracial people than probably any other group (because of the one-drop rule, etc.). There is still an exclusion for those who wish to encompass all parts of their heritage with equal weight, and there is also a subtle push to identify more with one's black heritage than the other part because "society won't see you as mixed or Japanese but BLACK." I can't count the number of times I have heard this argument. What I do know is that no society can tell me that I am more of one culture than another because of the way someone else defines me. I am Blackanese—a mixture of the two in ways that cannot be divided. My body and mentality is not split down the middle where half is black and the other half is Japanese. I have taken the aspects of both worlds to create my own worldview and identity. Like Anna Vale said in Itabari Njeri's article "Sushi and Grits," my mother raised me the best way she knew how, "to be a good Japanese daughter."

My father on the otherhand never constantly sat down to "teach" us about being Black. We were surrounded by Blackness and lived it. He was always tired when he came home from work. He'd sit back in his sofa and blast his jazz. My mom would be in the kitchen with her little tape player listening to her Japanese and Okinawan tapes my aunt sent every other month from California. My siblings and I would stay at my grandmother's house once in a while (she cooked the best collard greens), and when my mom came to pick us up she'd teach her how to cook a southern meal for my father. Our meals were somewhat of an indicator of how much my mom held onto her traditions. My father would make his requests for chicken, steak or okra and my mom had learned to cook these things, but we always had Japanese rice on the side with nori and tofu and fishcake with these really noisome beans that are supposed to be good for you (according to my mom. I swear she knows what every Japanese magazine has to say about food and health). It was my mother who told us that we would be discriminated against because of our color, and it was my Japanese mother to whom we ran when we were called niggers at the public swimming pool in Houston. To say to this woman, "Mom, we are just Black" would be a disrespectful slap in the face. The woman who raised us and cried for years from her family's coldness and rejection because of her decision to marry interracially, cried when my father's sister wouldn't let her be a part of the family picture because she was a "Jap." This woman who happens to be my mother will never hear "Mom, I'm just Black" from my mouth because I'm not and no person—society or government—will force me to do that and deny my reality and my being, no matter how offensive I am to their country or how much of a nuisance I am to their cause. I am Blackanese.

A Rescue Without Cheers

Peter Kramer

Study Questions

1. What factors does the author present as possible explanations for why "blacks" might feel as they did about the rescue?
2. Does the author present evidence (with accounts of precise behavior or quotes) to support the attitudes he attributes to "blacks" about the rescue?
3. Try to recall a situation when you were in a similar emergency situation, as presented in the reading. How did the persons closest to the victim react as they waited for help to arrive?

Last summer, I was granted a privilege rarely vouchsafed a psychiatrist: I felt a human being return to life under my hands. The moment—haunting, humbling—immediately turned bittersweet.

The setting was a New England pond, one my family has visited over many years. Though open to the public, the pond's beach tends to attract locals, largely middle-class whites, drivers of station wagons and jeeps. On that summer's day, the parking lot overflowed with campers and Cadillacs with out-of-state tags. I asked the kid who checks stickers what was up. "Company picnic."

"I hope they're not all in the water," I said, and he gave me a funny look. I soon understood why. The employees were all black; the kid thought I was making a racist remark.

The park felt crowded. Boom boxes were at full blast, and the pond, which we had chosen for its innocuousness—we were hoping to make our youngest more comfortable in the water—was roiled by splashing limbs. Suddenly the lifeguard raced into the pond.

"This is for real," I told my wife, and I headed to the water's edge. From only five yards out, the guard dragged the limp body of a boy. As soon as the victim hit the beach, a competent-looking woman checked for respiration and blew two breaths into his mouth. She announced herself as a cardiac nurse, and I felt immense relief. It's been some time since I've had my hands on a lifeless body. I felt for a pulse—there was none—and began pumping the chest. The lifeguard helped to steady the man's neck. Someone ran to a car phone.

The crowd was agitated around us, but I saw only the body. A short teen-age boy, skin purplish brown with a sickly, pale cast. Counting, thrusting, listening to the nurse. And then a pulse, not the subtle kind you search for in the arteries, but a big thump-thumping right under my hand.

Not until the heartbeat returned did I give a thought to race. But as the young man began to groan and sputter, I felt self-conscious about my white hands on this dusty maroon chest, and the whiteness of the nurse and lifeguard, and the angry energy—for they did, I now realized, sound hostile—of the crowd. It was as if I were doing something of dubious worth in an alien culture, rather than something of unquestioned worth in my own.

We had been through six cycles of breathing and pumping, under a minute. It had seemed interminable. The flood of impressions was as you might imagine: the youth of the boy, the vibes from the crowd, the steadiness of the nurse—I was immensely grateful to her—and the vulnerability of the lifeguard, who was huge and sturdy and terribly shaken over this having happened on his watch.

The police arrived with oxygen. The young man tried to vomit but could not. Then came the rescue squad. How long was he under, they wanted to know? Three minutes, the crowd said. Having just endured an interminable 60 seconds, I knew this estimate might be wrong. It was then that I understood how we looked.

The crowd believed that the lifeguard had acted too slowly because he was inattentive to black voices, because black lives do not matter, because no one wants black swimmers in the white man's water. The estimate of his delay began to rise. Five minutes, a woman said. I showed you where he was in the water, and I called five minutes before you came.

What with the noisy waterfront, might someone have shouted unheard for five minutes? For three? Unlikely—the strand is 20 yards wide. What was clear is what is too often clear, the incompatibility of divergent perspectives.

The aftermath was telling. No one thanked us. How stunning to save a life in the sight of dozens of a boy's friends and receive not a word of thanks. The crowd dispersed angrily, regathered at a barbecue pit.

Anger with the lifeguard was perhaps understandable. And when there is so much emotion—death, life—people do vent by arguing and accusing. But what about the nurse, fortuitously tending her children at this spot? In the age of drug-resistant tuberculosis and heaven knows what else, she pressed her mouth to a stranger's and gave him breath.

White bystanders praised the guard belligerently. Splendid rescue. The lifeguard, the nurse and I were a group apart, comrades trusting only one another. He looked shattered. I said that in emergencies you rarely do things just the way you wish. Now and then you do well enough. At any other time in history, before the dissemination of CPR techniques, before car phones, before police departments with oxygen, this young man would have been dead. Now he was alive. This was one of the good stories.

I would say, upon reflection, that it is an American story, one tainted, as American stories are, by racial division. How did the many African-American observers see the rescue? Filtered, surely, through awareness that a large black presence is unusual on most New England beaches, through concern that a youth was at risk for unknown reasons (because he had not been taught to swim? because past medical care had failed him?), through resentment that the rescuers were to a person white. And the lifeguard, why had he not interrupted the bathers' horseplay, quieted the radios, since they made his job impossible? At the crucial moment, did he assume that just any level of shouting is normal for blacks?

I have thought of that day repeatedly in the past year. The murder of abortionists brings back that scene, and the grousing of dismissed O.J. jurors, and the intensity of the Michigan militia. We are a nation plagued by irreconcilable perspectives. Our capacity for resentment and mistrust seems limitless.

America's forte is allowing difference to flourish, through tolerance. Today we are in civic imbalance and lack the tolerance needed to contain our diversity. The road back, if any can be found, is via attention to perspective. But it is hard to be sanguine when our starting points are so distant, when what to me is one of life's most hopeful moments is to you, and quite legitimately from your vantage, only further cause for cynicism and despair.

THE BURDEN OF RACE

ARTHUR ASHE

Study Questions

1. Explain the meaning of "burden of race."
2. What historical research findings influence Ashe's need to respond in the way he did?
3. Should Stan Smith and his wife have anticipated the problems Ashe and his family might have faced with the gift of a white doll to Ashe's daughter Camera in a highly visible public setting?

I had spent more than an hour talking in my office at home with a reporter for *People* magazine. Her editor had sent her to do a story about me and how I was coping with AIDS. The reporter's questions had been probing and yet respectful of my right to privacy. Now, our interview over, I was escorting her to the door. As she slipped on her coat, she fell silent. I could see that she was groping for the right words to express her sympathy for me before she left.

"Mr. Ashe, I guess this must be the heaviest burden you have ever had to bear, isn't it?" she asked finally.

I thought for a moment, but only a moment. "No, it isn't. It's a burden, all right. But AIDS isn't the heaviest burden I have had to bear."

"Is there something worse? Your heart attack?"

I didn't want to detain her, but I let the door close with both of us still inside. "You're not going to believe this," I said to her, "but being black is the greatest burden I've had to bear."

"You can't mean that."

"No question about it. Race has always been my biggest burden. Having to live as a minority in America. Even now it continues to feel like an extra weight tied around me."

I can still recall the surprise and perhaps even the hurt on her face. I may even have surprised myself, because I simply had never thought of comparing the two conditions before. However, I stand by my remark. Race is for me a more onerous burden than AIDS. My disease is the result of biological factors over which we, thus far, have had no control. Racism, however, is entirely made by people, and therefore it hurts and inconveniences infinitely more.

Since our interview (skillfully presented as a first-person account by me) appeared in *People* in June 1992, many people have commented on my remark. A radio station in Chicago aimed primarily at blacks conducted a lively debate on its merits on the air. Most African Americans have little trouble understanding and accepting my statement, but other people have been baffled by it. Even Donald Dell, my close friend of more than thirty years, was puzzled. In fact, he was so troubled that he telephoned me in the middle of the night from Hamburg, Germany, to ask if I had been misquoted. No, I told him, I had been quoted correctly. Some people have asked me flatly, what could *you,* Arthur Ashe, possibly have to complain about? Do you want more money or fame than you already have? Isn't AIDS inevitably fatal? What can be worse than death?

The novelist Henry James suggested somewhere that it is a complex fate being an American. I think it is a far more complex fate being an African American. I also sometimes think that this indeed may be one of those fates that are worse than death.

I do not want to be misunderstood. I do not mean to appear fatalistic, self-pitying, cynical, or maudlin. Proud to be an American, I am also proud to be an African American. I delight in the accomplishments of fellow citizens of my color. When one considers the odds against which we have labored, we have achieved much. I believe in life and hope and love, and I turn my back on death until I must face my end in all its finality. I am an optimist, not a pessimist. Still, a pall of sadness hangs over my life and the lives of almost all African Americans because of what we as a people have experienced historically in America, and what we as individuals experience each and every day. Whether one is a welfare recipient trapped in some blighted "housing project" in the inner city or a former Wimbledon champion who is easily recognized on the streets and whose home is a luxurious apartment in one of the wealthiest districts of Manhattan, the sadness is still there.

In some respects, I am a prisoner of the past. A long time ago, I made peace with the state of Virginia and the South. While I, like other blacks, was once barred from free association with whites, I returned time and time again, under the new rule of desegregation, to work with whites in my hometown and across the South. But segregation had achieved by that time what it was intended to achieve: It left me a marked man, forever aware of a shadow of contempt that lays across my identity and my sense of self-esteem. Subtly the shadow falls on my reputation, the way I know I am perceived; the mere memory of it darkens my most sunny days. I believe that the same is true for almost every African American of the slightest sensitivity and intelligence. Again, I don't want to overstate the case. I think of myself, and others think of me, as supremely self-confident. I know objectively that it is almost impossible for someone to be as successful as I have been as an athlete and to lack self-assurance. Still, I also know that the shadow is always there; only death will free me, and blacks like me, from its pall.

The shadow fell across me recently on one of the brightest days, literally and metaphorically, of my life. On August 30, 1992, the day before the U.S. Open, the USTA and I together hosted an afternoon of tennis at the National Tennis Center in Flushing Meadows, New York. The event was a benefit for the Arthur Ashe Foundation for the Defeat of AIDS. Before the start, I was nervous. Would the invited stars (McEnroe, Graf, Navratilova, et al.) show up? Would they cooperate with us, or be difficult to manage? And, on the eve of a Grand Slam tournament, would fans pay to see light-hearted tennis? The answers were all a resounding yes (just over ten thousand fans turned out). With CBS televising the event live and Aetna having provided the air time, a profit was assured. The sun shone brightly, the humidity was mild, and the temperature hovered in the low 80s.

What could mar such a day? The shadow of race, and my sensitivity, or perhaps hypersensitivity, to its nuances. Sharing the main stadium box with Jeanne, Camera, and me, at my invitation, were Stan Smith, his wife Marjory, and their daughter Austin. The two little girls were happy to see one another. During Wimbledon in June, they had renewed their friendship when we all stayed near each other in London. Now Austin, seven years old, had brought Camera a present. She had come with twin dolls, one for herself, one for Camera. A thoughtful gesture on Austin's part, and on her parents' part, no doubt. The Smiths are fine, religious people. Then I noticed that Camera was playing with her doll above the railing of the box, in full view of the attentive network television cameras. The doll was the problem; or rather, the fact that the doll was conspicuously a blond. Camera owns dolls of all colors, nationalities, and ethnic varieties. But she was now on national television playing with a blond doll. Suddenly I heard voices in my head, the voices of irate listeners to a call-in show on some "black format" radio station. I imagined insistent, clamorous callers attacking Camera, Jeanne, and me:

"Can you believe the doll Arthur Ashe's daughter was holding up at the AIDS benefit? Wasn't that a shame?"

"Is that brother sick or what? Somebody ought to teach that poor child about her true black self!"

"What kind of role model is Arthur Ashe if he allows his daughter to be brainwashed in that way?"

"Doesn't the brother understand *that he is corrupting his child's mind with notions about the superiority of the white woman? I tell you, I thought we were long past that!"*

The voices became louder in my head. Despite the low humidity, I began to squirm in my seat. What should I do? Should I say, To hell with what some people might think? I know that Camera likes her blond dolls, black dolls, brown dolls, Asian dolls, Indian dolls just about equally; I know that for a fact, because I have watched her closely. I have searched for signs of racial partiality in her, indications that she may be dissatisfied with herself, with her own color. I have seen none. But I cannot dismiss the voices. I try always to live practically, and I do not wish to hear such comments on the radio. On the other hand, I do not want Austin's gift to be sullied by an ungracious response. Finally, I act.

"Jeanne," I whisper, "we have to do something."

"About what?" she whispers back.

"That doll. We have to get Camera to put that doll down."

Jeanne takes one look at Camera and the doll and she understands immediately. Quietly, cleverly, she makes the dolls disappear. Neither Camera nor Austin is aware of anything unusual happening. Smoothly, Jeanne has moved them on to some other distraction.

I am unaware if Margie Smith has noticed us, but I believe I owe her an explanation. I get up and go around to her seat. Softly I tell her why the dolls have disappeared. Margie is startled, dumbfounded.

"Gosh, Arthur, I never thought about that. I never *ever* thought about anything like that!"

"*You* don't have to think about it," I explain. "But it happens to us, in similar situations, all the time."

"All the time?" She is pensive now.

"All the time. It's perfectly understandable. And it certainly is not your fault. You were doing what comes naturally. But for us, the dolls make for a bit of a problem. All for the wrong reasons. It shouldn't be this way, but it is."

I return to my seat, but not to the elation I had felt before I saw that blond doll in Camera's hand. I feel myself becoming more and more angry. I am angry at the force that made me act, the force of racism in all its complexity, as it spreads into the world and creates defensiveness and intolerance among the very people harmed by racism. I am also angry with myself. I am angry with myself because I have just acted out of pure practicality, not out of morality. The moral act would have been to let Camera have her fun, because she was innocent of any wrongdoing. Instead, I had tampered with her innocence, her basic human right to act impulsively, to accept a gift from a friend in the same beautiful spirit in which it was given.

Deeply embarrassed now, I am ashamed at what I have done. I have made Camera adjust her behavior merely because of the likelihood that some people in the African American community would react to her innocence foolishly and perhaps even maliciously. I know I am not misreading the situation. I would have had telephone calls that very evening about the unsuitability of Camera's doll. Am I being a hypocrite? Yes, definitely, up to a point. I have allowed myself to give in to those people who say we must avoid even the slightest semblance of "Eurocentric" influence. But I also know what stands behind the entire situation. Racism ultimately created the state in which defensiveness and hypocrisy are our almost instinctive responses, and innocence and generosity are invitations to trouble.

This incident almost ruined the day for me. That night, when Jeanne and I talked about the excitement of the afternoon, and the money that would go to AIDS research and education because of the event, we nevertheless ended up talking mostly about the incident of dolls. We also talked about perhaps its most ironic aspect. In 1954, when the Supreme Court ruled against school segregation in *Brown v. Board of Education,* some of the most persuasive testimony came from the psychologist Dr. Kenneth Clark concerning his research on black children and their pathetic preference for white dolls over black. In 1992, the dolls are still a problem.

Once again, the shadow of race had fallen on me.

WHAT WILL MY MOTHER SAY

DYMPNA UGWU-OJU

Study Questions

1. Describe how American ideas of "Nigeria" affected the questions they asked Ugwu-Oju.
2. Describe Ugwu-Oju's knowledge of "black history" and why her knowledge was so limited.
3. Why did she have difficulty at first seeing racism in the United States?
4. What was the turning point for Ugwu-Oju?

John and Delia provided me the basic necessities for survival in America. But as my first weeks extended into months, they realized that New York City was *too* much America for me to survive on my own and that a less intimidating setting would provide an easier transition to the life I was determined to live. I applied to colleges in Westchester County in New York State, all of them women's colleges. America or not, I sought an environment that was at least familiar, a life I understood—I settled for an imitation convent.

Briarcliff promised to meet all my needs. It was extremely small (about four hundred students), and students received so much attention it would almost be like living with Mama. Every dorm had a "mother"—an elderly spinster who used her unspent maternal love on the students. These dorm mothers provided the girls everything, from extra blankets when they were cold to a hug or a sympathetic ear.

True enough, when I got to Briarcliff in the fall of 1975, my whole experience of America changed. I lived in the dorm with girls my age, who, though they had different orientations and concerns, drew me out of my lonely funk. Before I knew it, I was so immersed in college life—classes, perfecting my English, and Friday night mixers with cadets from West Point, undergraduates from Yale, and other neighboring co-eds—that I hardly remembered to miss home. My friendship with my suite-mates was as immediate as it was at the convent school at Nsukka. The relationships that I formed at Briarcliff went beyond the bounds of college; my friends were quite generous and invited me to their homes during the holidays, and we've stayed close to this day.

On the down side, my classmates at Briarcliff exhibited an unusual level of ignorance where Africa was concerned, and many of their questions were not only insensitive but downright humiliating.

"Don't you people go around naked in Africa? You must be really uncomfortable in your clothes."

"How does it feel to be in real clothes?"

"How did you all manage to sleep on tree tops without falling?"

Even some of the professors were no better. One actually commented after he ascertained I was from Nigeria, "Aren't you lucky to be here, with that ugly communist takeover of your emperor's power!"

"Emperor?" I wondered. What in the world is he referring to?

Others merely told me, "It's so sad to see all those starving kids in your country on television." What starving kids? Well, maybe during the Nigerian-Biafran war, which had ended several years before.

I quickly discovered that even the most intelligent Americans did not know the first thing about Africa. Their most common mistake was viewing Africa as a country or even a city instead of a continent, and erroneously believing that everyone knew everyone else there. With time, I was able to laugh at their gross inaccuracies and even give them a dose of their own medicine. Idi-Amin's reign of terror, for example, took place in Uganda, a country in East Africa more than a thousand miles away from Nigeria. But my American inquisitors thought it was the next town over.

"What a terror, that bully Idi-Amin, what he's doing to your people," I was told more times than I can recall. I accepted the concept of "my people," for I accepted all Africans as my brothers and sisters. But if only they had stopped there.

"Do you know him? I hope you're not related to him," others sympathized.

After explaining several times the geographical relation between Uganda and Nigeria, I decided to join them at their own game. With the help of one of my professors, I came up with responses to the most common questions about Africa. To Idi-Amin, I responded, "Yes, he's my uncle, from the bad side of the family, of course. Too bad, your own uncle, Anastasia Somoza, isn't doing much better!"

"What are you talking about?" My poor American acquaintances became so confused.

To questions about sleeping on tree tops, I answered, "But of course, if that's what you're raised with, you get used to it."

"But what about the children; how do they get up there?" my inquisitors would seek further clarification.

"Oh, they used elevators," I responded with a straight face.

"Ah, of course," they responded, probably thinking that anything was possible in Africa.

Unfortunately, I can't say that the situation has gotten any better, and although more than twenty years have passed since my first arrival to the United States, I find the questions no more enlightened than before.

My education was by no means limited to what I learned in undergraduate or graduate school. Delia continued to undo what Mama had spent a lifetime putting into place.

My sister-in-law became for me the symbol of American womanhood: fearless, determined, and aggressive. She taught me independence in my thinking and actions: that I, and I alone, should dictate what I wanted to do with my life. Delia invalidated almost everything Mama taught me about womanhood; to her, it was about speaking up for oneself, looking everyone straight in the eye, and following one's heart. I'm quite sure that without Delia's guidance, my American experience would not have been as rich and encompassing as it was. She became my primary educator, pushing me way beyond the bounds of academia.

Delia introduced me to writings of radical African Americans, especially the women's perspective, areas that my extensive education in predominantly white colleges had not touched. I studied Maya Angelou, Angela Davis, and others; Delia selected the books I read with as much care as she would her young daughters'. We moved from slavery to the Civil War to the reconstruction, from the civil rights movement to the women's movement. From there, I was guided to biographies of most American presidents as well as of other influential leaders, both national and international. I felt so deficient in knowledge, so unprepared for the world I was thrown into, that I read as fast as Delia could push the books my way. I had to write a summary of each book I read and present it to Delia before I could go on to another one.

Delia also opened my eyes to a part of life I never knew existed. She introduced me to Black America. On the day of my placement test as an incoming freshman at Malcolm-King College extension, as Delia drove me to the campus at 125th Street, we passed hordes of black people—men, women and children of all sizes and shades. In spite of my extensive study of America, I was surprised by the large number of blacks we saw.

"There are many, many Africans here in New York," I observed in a matter-of-fact way.

"They're not Africans, they're Americans," Delia replied, sounding indignant.

"But they look like Africans; where did they all come from?"

Delia looked at me as if I were an alien creature. "How can you not be aware of America's blacks?" she uttered in what I took to be disgust for my ignorance. How could any African not be aware of the existence of American blacks? The truth is that, my education about America notwithstanding, I believed (and I'm sure no one saw fit to contradict my erroneous assumptions) that all blacks, all descendants of American eighteenth-century slaves, were resettled in Liberia, Newfoundland, and the Caribbean countries. I was not aware that there were any blacks left in America; there was nothing in the textbooks—no pictures, no clues—that could have led me to that understanding.

Everything I thought I knew of America contradicted what I was seeing on the streets of New York. The history and geography texts had treated slavery as a historical issue; blacks were not mentioned or pictured in the books I had read in Nigeria. In addition, we were caught in our own civil war during America's civil rights movement, and much to my shame, I had never heard the name of Martin Luther King, Jr., or of other leaders of the black community until I came to America. I was not aware of the millions of Americans who have a common ancestry with me; I was completely oblivious to terms like racism. My ignorance stared me in the face, and there in the car with my sister-in-law, I had nowhere to hide.

Without Delia, the black experience would have remained remote and abstract. She brought it home for me. Before she embarked on her law career, she'd been a teacher of African-American history, a subject she knew inside and out. She herself had marched in Washington, D.C., on the day of Martin Luther King's "I Have a Dream" speech, and she already possessed most of the resources I needed to understand what it means to be black in America.

It took a while before it would all come together for me, and it was several years before I could begin to identify myself as a black person. It's strange but true. I must have felt some affinity with the blacks I saw on my first outing and subsequently, but there was nothing about their speech, their walk, the whining about "the system," the drunks who swaggered even in the mornings as I walked to school, with which I could identify. I saw American blacks from a distance, and with or without my sister-in-law's lessons, I was at a loss to find what I could really embrace. I thought racism was a figment of their collective imagination, and I never hesitated to point out to the few black girls at Briarcliff with me that "racism only exists in people's minds." I just didn't believe it.

I was probably one of ten blacks attending Briarcliff. I felt that I was treated as well as anyone else. I mixed well with the other students. In fact, I chose to live with white students and we became fast friends. I saw no difference in our lives. I got as many A's as my white friends. I simply did not see how my black skin had anything to do with my life.

On the other hand, I noticed that the other black students flocked together, as if separating from each other, even for one minute, would diminish their identity. They breathed, talked, walked their blackness and would not allow anyone who was different to come close to them. They dismissed me as not being one of them. "She acts white," they explained to those who asked why I was excluded from their group. If any of them received an undesirable grade, it was easily explained. "The professor hates blacks."

I argued with Yolanda, the leader of the black group, about why she missed more than half of the class meetings of an international relations course she took with me. "What difference would it make? The professor would still find a way to fail me," she said resignedly.

"How come he doesn't fail me?" I challenged her.

"Because you're African; you talk different. You don't rub them the wrong way."

"But I'm just as black," I threw back at her.

"You just don't understand," she said and walked away. As hard as I tried, I simply couldn't understand that mindset. How could they be so defeatist? How could they give up before trying? There was no room for self-pity where I was raised. No circumstance was deemed too hard to overcome, even when all doors were slamming in one's face. Even during the war, when our huts were razed to the ground and we had no more than the rags on our backs, we continued our struggle to survive; we had no time to point fingers at our persecutors. Hadn't I personally gone through worse adversities than any of them could possibly imagine? Hadn't I passed through a war and survived hunger, danger, and deprivation? Hadn't my own mother gone through worse, traded like an animal and passed from hand to hand until no one wanted her? Hadn't she also picked up the pieces when her husband died and left her with seven children? What could they have suffered that could be worse than I had? But as Yolanda told me, I simply didn't understand, and she was right. I couldn't then. It took many more years of living in America before I could see the debilitating effects of racism.

I discovered my blackness at Syracuse, well into my fifth year in America. Suddenly, in something of a blinding revelation, I saw myself as a black person for the very first time. Of course, I'd known I wasn't white, but I did not see myself as black either. It was as though I believed I belonged in a no-color zone. I don't know how that could have happened, except to attribute it to growing up in Nigeria, where black people were in the majority. I probably could not make the transition to being a member of a minority.

At Syracuse, there were many more black students and professors than at Briarcliff, but the only other black woman in the journalism masters program was forced to drop out because she could not maintain the required B average. So I alone was left to answer sometimes irritating or embarrassing questions about blacks. My colleagues, at times, boxed me into a stereotype that even after five years in the country was hard for me to comprehend.

The turning point took place at a lunch meeting I arranged to do a special feature article on students from countries with political instabilities. My partner in the assignment (Janelle, a white woman), two black Ethiopian students we were interviewing, and I were seated around a table at the College Center cafeteria, when another student in our program stopped by. "Janelle, you're outnumbered. There's only one of you to three blacks," he chuckled, before moving on.

My first reaction was that he had it wrong. "What in the world does he mean?" There were *two* black girls at the table, plus Janelle and me. "Who's the third black girl?"

Then it hit me. If felt like someone dropped a ton of bricks on my chest and knocked the wind out of me. For a few seconds, I was out of breath, was suffocating to death. "It's *me* he's talking about. I am the third black girl. I'm black, I'm black," I said over and over to myself, repeating what should have been obvious to me years ago. I don't remember much else of that meeting other than my sudden awareness of the color of my skin. And from that moment on, I began to see myself in a different light: as a black person in America. For the first time, I was aware of what others saw when they looked at me.

Armed with my new awareness, I no longer dismissed blacks' complaints of racism as groundless whining. I reinvestigated the plight of blacks, using Syracuse as my new laboratory. I truly began to understand how crippled they'd become as a result of institutionalized and internalized racism. I reviewed everything I came across for its black-white implications. I stared in every face I saw, looking for signs that they looked at me differently. I scrutinized every gesture, action, conversation, every nuance of friends, professors, and even strangers on the streets, for racial undertones. If I wrote a check at a store and was asked for an ID, even though my rational self understood the need for the ID, my first reaction was, "Did he do this because I'm black? Would he ask a white person for an ID?"

My black awareness was also the driving force behind my decision after I completed my master's program not to aggressively pursue a job with mainstream media organizations, but instead to accept a position as the editor of the *Syracuse Gazette,* the only weekly black newspaper in the central New York area. The job paid poorly but allowed me the independence to make the newspaper whatever I desired. It was also an excellent opportunity to explore the dimensions of being black in America. Each week, I built the newspaper around a major issue that I felt concerned blacks: issues of teenage parenting, feminism, poverty, more. I spent hour after hour interviewing disenfranchised blacks: black matrons in rundown public tenements, young black men in county holding cells awaiting arraignment, black teenage mothers battling welfare and child protective agency officers, black women in no-win relationships with their men. I was completely immersed, up to my elbows in it. By the time I left the paper, I thought I knew everything I needed to know.

Strangely, my new black solidarity did not cross over to my social life. I never once felt that I could relate to American blacks as anything other than colleagues or friends. I never dated a black American man, although I contemplated doing so from time to time. They were as strange to me as were Hausas and Yorubas. I felt their world too far removed from mine. They simply would not know my worth and would treat me as they treated their own women. When I considered serious relationships, especially marriage, it was always with an Ibo man. That never changed.

Choosing Up Sides

Judy Scales-Trent

Study Question

1. What does Judy Scales-Trent mean when she says, "We renounce the reality of our real families, and we embrace the unreal reality as a social construct"?

"**W**hatever he does, he had better not bring home a white girlfriend!" she exclaimed. We laughed. There were three of us, black women friends who had gotten together after a long absence, talking about our lives, our work, our men, and, of course, our children. Her son was not yet a teenager and would not be bringing anyone home for quite a while, but she was already clear about his choices.

I laughed too, but I sensed a vague discomfort at her words. It took me awhile to understand that feeling. But I finally understood that I was uneasy because she had rejected part of me, the white part, with her statement. And I was uncomfortable—fearful that my disguise might not hold, fearful that she might suddenly "see" that I was a white black woman. Michelle Cliff says it well: "She who was part-them felt on trembling ground." I also finally recognized that my laughter was dishonest: why laugh at my own rejection? But I did laugh, I laughed because, at that moment, my hunger to belong to that group of friends was stronger than my ability to be true to myself.

I thought about this for days. And what kept returning to my mind during that period were thoughts of Grandpa Tate, my father's maternal grandfather and the only white blood relative I ever heard of. I know little enough about him. I know that he was born sometime in the 1860s, and that he was a barber. I know that he married my great-grandmother Mary in 1886. I think he loved and respected her: I have a silver-plated dish inscribed "1886–1911" that he gave her on the occasion of their twenty-fifth anniversary. I know he made enough money investing in real estate to raise ten children in comfort and send them off to college. I have a picture of Grandpa Tate with his wife and children, taken around 1905. They all look healthy and well-dressed and well-groomed. It is clear that Grandpa Tate took good care of them. I know he was white, of Scottish origins. I also know that his wife, and therefore all of his children, were black. I think of the contribution Grandpa Tate made to my family, to me, and I am not willing to reject him. I respect and honor his memory and claim him as a cherished relative.

Racism is so deeply embedded in our consciousness that we don't often realize that society asks us, on a regular basis, to reject part of our family when we are required to take sides in this tragic war-game of race and color.

> "Which side are you on, black or white?
> There is a war going on.
> Allegiance must be clear.
> Choose!"

But choosing up sides means buying into the craziness of American-style racism. For there are many black Americans with white ancestors, and there are plenty of white Americans with black family members.

This is the way the American system works: if you have one parent or ancestor with African origins, you are black. You are not a member of the white family that might also claim you. That family must renounce you, and you must renounce it. You are in the black family, as will be all of your children and your grandchildren and your great-grandchildren. It is by thus redefining "family" to exclude their black family members that white Americans keep themselves and their "family" white. The notion of "family" in white America has very controlled borders: "family" stops where "black" begins.

The result is, then, that white people are all "white," and that black people are a wide range of colors—white, rosy, olive, tan, brown, reddish, black. We are forced to choose up sides, but the American rules dictate that choice. Real facts, like who your parents and grandparents were, don't matter: only social facts count.

Several years ago, a strange and sad incident took place at the law school. It involved a moot-court program sponsored by a national association of black law students. A young woman at the school who wanted to participate decided to join the local chapter of the association. But it was not as easy to join as she had expected, for although her father was black and she had African features, her mother was Puerto Rican. There was furious debate by the students in that chapter as to whether she could—or should—participate in a program for black students. Finally, they arrived at a solution. If she would renounce her Puerto Rican mother, she could join the association.

I hope this sounds as sick to you as it does to me. Renounce her mother? Were they all mad? And yet is this not what we all require of ourselves, of our children? We do it all the time. We renounce the reality of our real families, and we embrace the unreal reality of a social construct.

Think about it for a minute: whom have you renounced today? and why? Are we all mad?

There are two little girls whom I love. They are two years old. The world is theirs to explore, and they go at it full tilt. Anyone old enough to read these words would be hard-pressed to keep up with either of them for an afternoon. These little girls are sisters in the deepest sense of the word, for they are twins and have been together from their earliest watery memories. They speak their own language and giggle at their own secrets. But they are twins who do not look alike. One is brown, like her father; the other is fair, like her mother.

I once talked about the problems color would present them with their father, a nephew. And I wondered, would they too be forced to choose up sides? How would they choose? Whom would they renounce? How could they? And why should they be forced into such a cruel dilemma? Their father's family is from Africa and Scotland and other lands; their mother's family is from Scotland and other European lands. It is just as misleading to say that they are African American as it is to say that they are Scottish American, for their heritage is complicated and rich. And I wonder sadly if there is any chance that these little girls will ever be able to just be Americans.

Think about it, for it does not involve my family alone. It involves yours too. And we really should do better by our children.

Let me be clear. I am not claiming that I always see these complications. I often think and speak as if the categories "black" and "white" are real. I am just as hungry for a place to belong as anyone else. I am just as willing as others to choose up sides. But living on the margin forces me to live with, and therefore to see, the complications. And it is very complicated indeed. For the truth is that all Americans with some African ancestry are indeed "black," because that is how we are defined, and that in how white people treat us, and that is how we are raised. But the truth also is that "black" people are not *only* "black," since we also have ancestors who came from Europe and Asia and South America and the South Pacific; we have ancestors who were Cherokee, Choctaw, Lumbee.

I am torn by my understanding of both truths, which exist side by side at the same time, for it means that we both can and cannot choose up sides. It is holding both these truths in my hand at the same time that is so difficult—and so important—to do.

Identity Matters: The Immigrant Children

Marilyn Halter

Study Questions

1. How do the cases of Jack Custodio and Lucille Ramos support the argument that race is not a biological fact but a social construction?
2. What strategies did Jack Custodio employ to influence how others identified him? How does Custodio identify himself today?
3. Why did he "give-in" to the U.S. conception of race?
4. List the various racial identities Lucille Ramos and her family members took on. Which identity is the most accurate? Explain.

Vivid in the recollections of many of the men interviewed for this study was the jolt to their self-concept that was experienced during military service in World War II. For most Cape Verdean American male immigrants, joining the United States armed forces meant a first step out of the protective shelter of their enclave. This critical juncture in their lives brought them face to face with the existence of segregated troops and a wider society that did not know or care about the ethnic identity of a Cape Verdean. Most were sent to black regiments where they were forced to deal directly with the issue of race, both in terms of the racist treatment they received in the military and in having to confront the question of their own racial identification. As one Cape Verdean veteran said: "I grew up thinking of myself as brown-skinned Portuguese, not black at all. I remember telling this sergeant, a black guy, that I was Cape Verdean. He said, 'You ain't Portuguese nothing. You're a nigger.' It sounds incredibly naive, but I'd never thought of myself as black or white. I was both, and neither. I was Cape Verdean. America wants you to choose sides."[1]

Some were assigned to white units where they were not accepted either. Those Cape Verdean recruits who were sent with white regiments into the southern states found it especially painful to try to come to terms with the ambiguity of their own ethnic and racial background and the rigid racial barriers of their surroundings. The immigrants and their children had largely been raised to think of themselves as Portuguese, thus white, but once outside the ethnic community, they faced an indifferent, often hostile world that labeled them black. Interaction beyond the New England region became more problematic. Belmira Nunes Lopes sometimes handled it in this way:

> My trips south have been very interesting, but I must admit that every time I went south I always acted as if I wasn't too well acquainted with the English language because I didn't want to be discriminated against on the buses and the trains. I always put on a fake accent and I always managed to get away with it. I didn't want anybody to think I was an American black because I am darker than most so-called white persons. My mother had never been mistaken for a black woman. She had been taken sometimes for an Indian, but she could never speak English well. I decided that I was going to act as if I couldn't speak English well.[2]

The social and political events of the postwar era also penetrated the cocoon of the Cape Verdean enclave. Beginning with the civil rights movement, the 1960s were watershed years for Cape Verdean Americans as the rise of black nationalism and its attendant emphasis on pride in one's African heritage had a transformative effect on many. The domestic social changes coincided with the struggles for liberation from Portuguese colonialism on the continent of Africa as well. At the time, the Cape Verde islands in collaboration with Guinea-Bissau were engaged in a protracted armed conflict to procure their independence. They did find some support for their cause among Cape Verdean Americans but there was also much resistance to the idea of Cape Verde breaking its long-standing ties with Portugual and switching to an African-identified political and cultural ideology. The process of rethinking racial identifications touched most Cape Verdean families in this period, often creating intergenerational rifts between the parents and grandparents who were staunchly Portuguese and their children who were beginning to ally themselves with the African American struggle not only in political thought but also in cultural expression. Some, who could, would let their hair grow out into Afros; others may have dressed in colorful dashikis, much to the dismay of their Portuguese-identified parents. Writing about the 1960s, Belmira Lopes Nunes explained:

> At that time, our idea of Portuguese culture was Cape Verdean culture, and that was the thing that we really wanted to stress. To us, to be Portuguese was synonymous with being Cape Verdean. . . . The Cape Verdeans have been saying they were Portuguese all along. I was brought up to believe that I was Portuguese. My parents said they were Portuguese. Whenever anybody asked us what we were because we spoke a foreign language or because we looked different from any other

group, we always said that we were Portuguese. All of a sudden to be told that you are an African, I think, is a shock to most people, certainly to my generation and to many of those of this generation also, the children of Cape Verdean parents who have made their children feel that they had some reason to be proud of the Cape Verdean heritage.[3]

Perhaps the most graphic example I can give to illustrate Cape Verdean ambivalence concerning African origins is the anecdote reported to me about a woman, now middle-aged, whose Cape Verdean father, from the time she was a baby, would continually stroke her nose from the inner edges outward in a pointing motion in order to try to control its shape and development. The girl's mother was African American, and the father feared his daughter would grow up to have a nose of broad and flat contours.

Following are excerpts from the oral histories of two Cape Verdean Americans that cogently illustrate the multifarious and shifting nature of racial meanings. Both Joaquim A. "Jack" Custodio and Lucille Ramos were born in the United States, children of Cape Verdean immigrants and life-long residents in the New Bedford area. Each has a biography that has been punctuated by issues resulting from the ambiguity inherent in belonging to a nonwhite immigrant group. Both demonstrate how they and their families have been subjected to the arbitrary design of racial classification in the United States. In both accounts, the decade of the 1960s looms large. While each individual has a unique story to tell, I have selected these two life histories particularly for inclusion here because their experiences within the arena of racial-ethnic definitions have a universality among the Cape Verdean American population as I have understood it.

When I asked Jack Custodio in July of 1988, "What would you call yourself today in terms of identity?" he replied with his characteristic mixture of dead seriousness and ironic humor, "I'm black—I'm not beautiful, but I'm black. Positively black." How he arrived at this self-designation follows:

> The salient facts of my life are I was born September 6, 1914, a cold water flat, at home, as usual, all the births were in New Bedford. I was born to a Cape Verdean mother and a Cape Verdean father but it has to be noted that my mother was so fair that she could go any place whereas my father would have to get in the back of the bus. He's what we call in my own lingo, *besh roulade cavasa sec,* which means "thick lips and nappy hair" and that is still used by Cape Verdeans.
>
> The South End was the Cape Verdean ghetto but it has to be noted that in New Bedford you had the West End, which was another ghetto, these were Afro-Americans, for the most part, slaves who had migrated

north from the south, after the Civil War and there was *no* intermingling, there was no mixture, there was nothing. If you were in the West End that was it, if you were in the South End, you were in the South End. I grew up and my mother taught me to say, "Those damn niggers in the West End." I said it like any other little white boy.

This is where my identification dilemma was spawned. Because my mother always told me I was white. I went to a Cape Verdean school at which we were all treated as white officially but unofficially we got the worst teachers in regard to competence. The equipment, the material— all obsolete, the hand-me-downs from the other schools.

Now I can see it so clearly. There is a distinction. I have to bring in the white Portuguese here. The white Portuguese have been labeled *nhambobs* by Cape Verdeans. We never referred to ourselves as Portuguese in the context of the *nhambobs.* They were kept separate, not for definitions of race but that's because they were different, they were *nhambobs.* But it was a concession, I can see that so clearly now, to the fact that we, as Cape Verdeans were not white like the *nhambobs* were. Now that I look back on it, we professed to be white. If you asked me my race, I would tell you white, if you pin me down, I would tell you Cape Verdean or Portuguese. But I wouldn't do that until you pinned me down, and then, of course, I wouldn't be able to do that when I went to New Britain, Connecticut. I couldn't get away with saying Portuguese or Cape Verdean there because they didn't know either one.

But it raises the point now of identification which was, of course, cultivated by my own background and environment—I was not black. And when I went to New Britain, Connecticut, and got into fights with these Polish and Italian kids and whipped every one of them. When I left New Bedford and those kids in New Britain called me "nigger," I was outraged. How dare they call me "nigger." I know where the "niggers" are. The "niggers" are in the West End of New Bedford. And I plopped them one. That was it. And, of course, one of the advantages of growing up in the ghetto, you learned how to use your hands real quick. It's a question of survival more than anything else.

I was in the 8th grade. I must have been around 12 or 13 because I always kept pace with the norms. My mother had married again and my stepfather got a good job in Connecticut and he sent for us. I spent a year or two there and when things opened up here again in this area, we moved back because by that time my white aunt owned a house in Fairhaven [across the river from New Bedford] and she allowed us to move into the top floor of her house. I loved Fairhaven. At that time, Fairhaven was tolerant of particularly Cape Verdeans in the context of Portuguese.

Both my mother and father were born in São Vincent. My stepfather was from São Nicolau. But my stepfather could go anywhere. He and my mother made an ideal combination. They could go anywhere. My stepfather was the leader of the Cape Verdean band and they always thought that it was a *nhambob* leading the Cape Verdean band. He was a white man—every definition of the white race—the texture of his hair, the features, the coloring and he was white. I don't know anything about genetics but visibly there are a lot of Cape Verdeans that have been accepted by society as whites and once that happens then they don't want any black relatives. Both my mother and stepfather were firmly convinced in their own minds that they were white. This was not a question of passing. There was no need for them to masquerade.

There was no problem with the older people. The problem is with us who were born here. The dilemma—especially of looking black and being white. And, of course, if you looked white it was all right, but if you didn't look white, then forget about it.

So I grew up in New Bedford and when I went to New Bedford high school, I immediately found out that the cards were stacked against me. Number one, my ambition was to be an attorney. But I ended up in a commercial course. Now had my mother or my stepfather been aware of all these things, they could have advised me. Guidance counselor? I still don't know what a guidance counselor is—at my age. That was unheard of. So I ended up in a commercial course. I ended up typing, shorthand, bookkeeping, I was very good at it. I even took up French as an elective. And, you know, I did very well in French. I went through four years of high school and I didn't flunk a single subject. And I worked. If I hadn't been able to work at the Boys Club, I would never have been able to stay in high school.

Then I got out of high school—and lo and behold—talk about finding a job. That's when I began to have this dilemma of "What am I?" Because I'd call up and I'd make an appointment. I'd show up but I would never be hired. And inferior people were hired in regards to studies. And, of course, college was out of the question. I applied for a salesmen job. These magazines, you know, and they'd send me back a letter. This oil company wanted a salesman in this area. And I'll never forget the letter they sent me back. "Please send a photograph" and when I'd send a photograph and they'd send back a letter, "at this time we cannot consider hiring. We don't think your qualifications . . ."

I can't believe that. This is in the early 1930s. And it was a little more subtle but you couldn't get a job at the *Standard Times,* [the New Bedford daily newspaper]—all white. The banks—all white. I couldn't even get a job driving a cab. Do you know they didn't hire black cab drivers in those days? I tried to get a taxi driver's job in the fifties. Was already married with children. They wouldn't hire me. Union Street Railway. Safety Cab. Wouldn't hire me. And the theory behind this—white women aren't safe with black taxi drivers. Still prevails.

After I got out of high school, it was the usual series of cranberry picking, strawberries, for minimum, for non-existent wages—and dishwashing. All the chefs in this area were Cape Verdeans. That was a good job for us in that sense. We were allowed those jobs. Mills had gone out. Goodyear. Revere Copper and Brass. Even Chamberlain discriminated very blatantly against Cape Verdeans. After I left high school, I ran into all these problems. And, of course, what am I? The confusion was so disconcerting. Tell everybody I'm Cape Verdean and they'd put me in the back of the bus.

In the merchant marine in the early 30s, I was a mess boy. When I went on a ship, I found out that down south, if I were waiting for a trolley, there are two places. Colored and white. Well, I would speak Spanish, well my Portuguese, pidgeon Portuguese and Spanish, I would be with my *cumpads,* male *cumpads,* the firemen who was white, but the motor man would look at me and allow me to sit in front because I was still a Cape Verdean and I was not going to mix with quote "dem niggers." I wasn't going to do it that's all there was to it. They would view me with a suspicious eye, but they wouldn't throw me off the trolley. Then I'd get off the trolley car and I'd go uptown to a show in Newport News or Baltimore, mind you, this was in the early '30s. And they would not sell me an orchestra seat. You know, that's where I found out that that's where "Nigger Heaven" originated.

I've got to tell you this anecdote. In '38 and '39, I worked on this shrub as a relief fireman. And I had the car. And boy, it was a great thing to own a car in '38. All the other crewmen were dependent upon me for rides. From Bristol, Rhode Island, to New Bedford, we'd come home every other weekend. This was the lighthouse service, before it was taken over by the Coast Guard. Well, this guy, God bless his soul, Mach— Seraphim Olivera, Brava, typical Brava who would not identify. Strictly white. We made an agreement. We went to the show in Providence and the agreement was, use my car, my gas but he'd pay for the ticket. And he always prided himself on the fact that he was white. He used to tell me, "I won't go to the show with you—you're too black." He used to tell me this. Mind you, we were supposed to be friends. Of course, he resented the fact that—we had boxing gloves out there and every time we put on the gloves, I would kick the living daylights out of him. And I would do it deliberately, you see, because of his Brava feeling of being superior. We went to this show in Providence. Providence longshoremen told me this afterwards, but this show was notorious for not admitting blacks or Cape Verdeans downstairs. They still had the "nigger heaven" bit. So Mach went up—Mach was his nickname. *Mach* means male. Mach went up to the box and the woman didn't see me. And he asked for two orchestras. "Oh, no, no, no, there was vaudeville on. They're all sold out." So we went upstairs. Unknowing and innocent of the custom of the theater management. We get upstairs and lo and behold, downstairs is vacant. I told Mach, they won't let colored people sit downstairs. He says (all of this in *Crioulo*), "You are colored; I'm not colored." I says, "Well, you bought the tickets." He says, "Animal, the lady must have seen you. And refused to sell me the tickets." Now, I was out of the vision of the lady. I got hysterical. And all this was in his dialect. There he is, he bought the tickets but he's blaming me. He was so embarrassed and humiliated because they refused to accept him as white, which he was. That is a typical Cape Verdean story.

The feeling of animosity between the West End and the South End led to fights. The white Portuguese never, never accepted us in any way, shape or form except they'd do it on superficial basis. We had our own separate little areas. Cape Verdean Band Club, St. Vincent's Sporting Club. And if you weren't Cape Verdean. God forbid, if you married *American d'cor* [pejorative term for African American]. If my mother were alive right now knowing that both of my surviving daughters have married Afro-Americans, my mother would turn over in her grave.

You know, I had an inferiority complex when I was a kid. Of the three sisters' children, me and George were the ugly ones. It had nothing to do with shade. In fact some of my cousins were darker than me. We were nappy headed. It had nothing to do with color. My hair was considered *pret corvasa sec.* They had good hair and even though they may have been darker, their features were better. I was considered ugly and so was George—based on appearance and the texture of the hair.

So eventually, I lived in New Bedford. Public housing came into existence and I applied for it and was accepted. And Bay Village from Walnut Street right down to Canon Street was all Cape Verdean except for two Afro-American families. From Canon Street all the way down to Grinnell Street was all white. So then I found out, among other things that they violated the pact, which meant this was Cape Verdean, why did they have those two Afro-American families in there. Now, this was in the forties. Which goes to show you the feeling I still retained—this Cape Verdeanism—even then. In the 1940s, I had to be in my thirties. I still resented Afro-Americans being brought into my neighborhood. I still had that in-bred inferiority.

By the time of the "searing" sixties, I had started to change. By that time I had bumped into Duncan Dottin, a sociologist from Cambridge, an Afro-American who lived in the West End. He was fascinated. Here he is talking to me and I'm calling him a "nigger" and here I am telling him I'm white. One thing I've got to give Duncan credit for, Duncan has never, never held this against me. He knew my background. But God bless the man. He knew my potential. He was able to develop it. If I've got to the stage now where I'm fairly articulate and fairly knowledgeable, its due to the fact that Duncan was the springboard.

I'll never forget the time when he said something about Langston Hughes and I said to him, "Who's Langston Hughes?" He wanted to hit me. I began to recognize one thing, while I was not a "nigger" and I was Cape Verdean, they didn't accept Cape Verdeans and the more and more I looked around—you know the minute you hit School Street [the Cape Verdean neighborhood in New Bedford] you know where you are. I don't give a damn what they say, I don't give a damn if they speak a foreign tongue. You know they're not white. And if you're not white, man, in this country you've got to be black and when I say black—it is in the context of the oppression, the subjugation. So, who am I kidding?[4]

Lucille Ramos, mother of four and foster-mother of twenty-five children, has an intergenerational outlook on the Cape Verdean dilemma of social identity:

Being a Cape Verdean is special to me and to my children even more so—because we're a potpourri really, we're a mixture of people. I think we have both European and African influence. When I was younger our country was still ruled by the Portuguese government, we, we've gone through changes, you know. When we were young we were Portuguese because that was our mother country, and then we went through the Black part of our lives in the sixties. And now I think we finally know who and what we are, which is Cape Verdean, and it is something special. And we are different, we're different from the American Blacks and we're different from the Whites. We've taken from both cultures, and that makes us unique.

With the kids, I remember the first time I knew they were proud of being Cape Verdean was when they had clubs, in high school, like International Food and they would ask everyone for ethnic foods, and right away the kids wanted to bring in Cape Verdean dishes. When they were young it wasn't so important, but they began to have more pride as they grew older. When we were young we didn't really know that much about Cape Verdeanism. People just classified us as Portuguese because we were a Portuguese colony. Now since 1975 when Cape Verde gained its independence, I think it's become much more important to us, and in particular to our children.

Here in New Bedford, you know, we just kind of accepted the fact that we were Cape Verdean and that everybody knew what that meant. But when Cape Verdeans began to go away from the community, they began to have problems.

For instance, one of my sons was in the R.O.T.C. and they travel a lot. Everywhere he went he would say, "My name is Ramos," and everybody thought he was Spanish. And he would say, "No, I'm Cape Verdean." "What's a Cape Verdean?" they would all ask, so it became a thing to be able to tell them where the islands were, that we had our own language and dialect, had our own foods, music and culture.

The older people may still say "We're Portuguese." That is how they were raised. But I think the New Bedford Portuguese always objected to us saying we were Portuguese, because they felt we really weren't. . . .

In the sixties we had lots of problems here locally with the labels "Black" and "White." You see, up till then the kids identified themselves as Cape Verdean. But at that point they had to take a stand, especially in high school. You were either Black or you were White, there was no in-between. So you had to decide then, "Am I a Black or am I a White?" And nobody wanted to hear whether you were a Cape Verdean or not. It was just Black or White. The kids had a difficult time then because they had to make that decision.

People may not understand this, but it was very difficult because Cape Verdeans come in shades from pure white to ebony black. For instance when my kids were going to the Greene school [a New Bedford public school in the South End], the teacher would identify the child's race by looking at him. I had three sons all in the school at the same time. I was a carpet joke because I have three sons three shades; and one teacher identified one boy as Black, one teacher identified one as White, and one was identified as Mulatto. So I have three children identified as three different races.

But this kind of confusion was not unusual for me. I'm the fourth child in my family. I have three brothers older, and four of us were delivered by one doctor, and four of us delivered by another. In those days it was not the parent who determined the race—and you know how race goes on your birth certificate? Well, when my brothers went into the service their race was listed as Caucasian. So when I went for my marriage license, I remember the woman there said, "What is your race?" and I said "Caucasian," because I had just assumed I was listed Caucasian too. I remember this very distinctly because the place was crowded at the time, and she went and took out my birth certificate and said, in a very haughty voice "You're not Caucasian, you're colored!" and I said, "Whatever, my brothers were Caucasian." She said, "They must have had different fathers." I said, "No, we all have the same mother and father." She said, "That's impossible." But it was very true, and as far as I know, it is still true that the doctor who delivers the child names the child's race. And the amazing thing was the white doctor listed the children as Caucasian and the Cape Verdean doctor listed the children as Colored.

But my mother and father had no idea what we were listed as until we had to go and get our papers. My husband, who's half and half, was listed as Caucasian in the service. We married when he got out of the service. We went to Dartmouth for his papers, and they said, "What is your race?" and he said, "Caucasian," and they went and said, "You're a Mulatto, you're a mixed breed, your father is a Cape Verdean and your mother is White." So you know you run into these kinds of things.

I remember when my children were born that was a big thing for me. I told the doctor right at the beginning. "I will identify their race, not you." He said, "Fine, you do the whole thing," and it was funny because, with all the trouble my husband and I went through, we could now choose—and these were the choices—it was either Black, White, or Mulatto. We chose Mulatto. It became a crisis for them in the sixties, though, when they had to make a choice. Especially so when you had several kids in the family and one was light and one was dark, because—to us it meant nothing, but to the White person it meant something, or to the person who identified as Black it meant something.

I think the majority of the kids now are coming around to saying they are Cape Verdean. But if it is a choice of identifying White or Black, I think they would choose Black. I think it was more difficult for the older ones, the parents and the grandparents, to accept that their children identified as Black. Some of the kids were even dropping the Cape Verdean altogether and it was just Black. There was lots of peer pressure and they felt you couldn't be in-between, you had to be one or the other, and if the color of your skin wasn't pure white, that didn't give you much choice to begin with anyway.

But it was very difficult for the parents and grandparents to accept this. Take my father-in-law for instance. He is an extremely dark man, and looking at him there would be no doubt in your mind that this is a Black man. But he does not consider himself a Black man. He was born on the Cape Verdean islands. He is now in his eighties, and he considers himself Portuguese—he does not identify as Cape Verdean. He is Portuguese and Portuguese is White. Do you know the ridicule that a Black man faces when he says, "I'm White, I'm Portuguese."

But you see the kids were not going to be ridiculed that way. They knew what they were, and the thing is, they have been able to accept the pride in it, which is the important thing. Whereas for the older people being White meant being—special. They didn't want to be in the minority. But our kids don't feel that way, they're Black and they're proud. That came about in the sixties. And I think they realize that "Well, I may be Black but I am Cape Verdean and I have my own culture within the Black, and I can be as proud of that as being Black."

So they've gone through a lot of changes, which we have as well, as parents. So racially I think we've had our difficulties, and I think our children still have difficulties, although not so many now.

Notes

[1] Charles Andrade, Jr., quoted in Colin Nickerson, "Black, White or Cape Verdean?" *Boston Globe,* 29 Sept. 1983, p. 16.

[2] Maria Luisa Nunes, *A Portuguese Colonial in America: Belmira Nunes Lopes, the Autobiography of A Cape Verdean-American* (Pittsburgh: Latin American Literary Review Press, 1982), p. 193.

[3] Nunes, *A Portuguese Colonial in America,* pp. 144, 201.

[4] Interview with Joaquim A. Custodio, 28 July 1988.

[5] Lucille Ramos in *Spinner,* I, pp. 34–37.

How It Was for Me

Sarah Van't Hul

Study Questions
1. Van't Hul states "the racist attitude of whites was more inconspicuous than the overt anger from blacks, but both were equally powerful and disturbing." Give examples that support her generalization.
2. How did Van't Hul deal with her marginal status?

Nineteen seventy-two, the year abortion became legal, was the year of my birth. It was also the year that the Black Social Workers Association decided that white people should not be allowed to adopt black children. They said that it is more damaging for black children to be adopted by white parents than to be placed in foster care, because the adopted children would be stripped of their identity and culture. As a result of the BSWA's position, many black children have been left with no family and very likely a poor sense of identity.

When I was two months old I was adopted by a white family and brought from Toledo, Ohio, to Ann Arbor, Michigan, right around the time that the BSWA made its recommendation. There were few other black or biracial kids in the white middle-class community in which I was raised. Unsurprisingly, my first reaction toward white people was positive. I loved my parents, my sister, and my brothers. The friends I had were white, and if I didn't like somebody, I never associated my dislike of them with their appearance.

I distinctly remember when the difference in my appearance became an issue for me. On my first day of kindergarten all the other girls except me had on dresses and had long straight hair. I had on jeans and had a very short Afro. It was instant alienation and embarrassment. The girls didn't want to play with me; they told me I had fat lips and a big nose, and that my skin looked like "pooh." The only friend I had at first was a boy who was black like me, and he was just *as shy as I was.* We played with each other during recess because nobody else would play with us.

My first lasting friendship was with a girl named Laurie. I think part of what attracted us to one another was simply that we were the same color, and she had been adopted by a white family also. We were both different, and if one of us was teased by anyone for our color, we no longer had to bear it alone; they would have to deal with both of us.

It was in these early years that I heard one of my mother's friends say, "Oh, what a beautiful girl!" If she had only known know much I cringed when she said that! I though she was crazy, or just trying to be polite. Someone black can't be pretty. I thought; she should *know* that.

It wasn't long before I did have a lot of girlfriends, maybe just because I was friendly. But racism became a definite reality for me in the later years of grade school. I had a group of very close girlfriends and always seemed to get along with boys very well. Boys liked to play with me, because I was good at sports and didn't act "girlish." Wearing dresses was never my thing, and I was never afraid to fight. But when my girlfriends were beginning to date and have boys who had crushes on them, I found myself left out. The few boys that had the courage to date me soon let me know they didn't want to "go out with me," because I was black.

It took me a long time to feel comfortable about dating any boys, and I became the "feminist" amongst my friends. Girls began to see me as a source of strength, for I appeared confident and self-sufficient. What my friends never understood was that my so-called feminist strength was much less a choice on my part than a method of coping with prejudice.

Family outings, too, were often much more pain for me than pleasure. What I believed was my quirky family drawing so much attention in restaurants, I later realized was really subtle racism. Going out to dinner and on vacations was much like pulling teeth for me. In diners on the road (my father's favorite eating establishments) and in restaurants outside of Ann Arbor, I had to deal with seemingly endless silence, when my family of four white people and two black kids (one of my brothers is also black) entered a restaurant. Everything seemed to stop, except the music. The stares and the screaming silence filled me with shame and left a permanent scar.

When I was twelve years old, I lived in Switzerland for a year with my family. My self-consciousness hit its peak. Everybody stared at me. At least in Ann Arbor there were havens where I did not feel alienated. In Europe, it seemed like I was the only black person on the whole continent. I could not blend in. The school kids petted my skin and hair, as though I were an exotic creature. It was one of the most frightening experiences I have ever had.

The prejudice from white people was subtle, however, compared to the overt hostility that came from other blacks. My first exposure to groups of black people was in junior high, and, to my surprise, they completely rejected me. I quickly found that if the black kids have a problem with you, they will get in your face and tell you exactly what's wrong. They immediately let me know that my problem was that I thought I was white. Before I even opened my mouth, the black kids told me who I was: a "white wannabe." (This was kind of ironic, because *they* had bone-straight hair, and I had a natural.) I talked funny, I dressed funny, I thought I was better than anyone else, and why didn't I straighten that nappy do? Black girls frequently wanted to fight me for simply being me. They wanted me to be ashamed for being different and to hold my head down instead of up. My retaliation was verbal. I would try to show them that they were acting much worse than I was and it was stupid for them to want to fight me when I had done nothing to them.

L'Tonya was a big black girl who tormented me throughout junior high and until the eleventh grade in high school. Every time I walked down the hall, she loudly made fun of me—about everything, from my hair and clothes to the way I stood. Because I would never respond, teasing became unsatisfactory for her. One time when she and five of her friends caught me and one of my friends in the gym, she threw a basketball at my head, and then a chair. She called me all kinds of names and more than anything wanted to fight me. I told her I wouldn't fight her, and I didn't understand why she hated me so much. I don't remember everything I said, but I remember I left her speechless for the first time. She continued to harass me, but I began to recognize my strengths and her weaknesses, and I began not to cringe or care as much.

In the eleventh grade, I had to take the California Achievement Test; I was put in a room with the other black kids. I wasn't on my own turf, and I was awaiting the teasing and snickering. Instead, one black boy had the courage to approach and talk to me in front of the rest of the kids. L'Tonya was in the room, and she didn't look too happy, but after the boy walked away, she came up to me and, to my amazement, apologized for all the times she had made fun of me. I felt triumphant: for once I was appreciated just for being me. But I didn't say, "That's o.k."; I didn't say anything at all. For three years she had made me feel completely disowned and ugly, when I had given her nothing but respect. Now she wanted my respect, and I didn't have any for her.

Through all of this, I learned not to take my true friends for granted, for I knew they had to like me for me, and they often had to deal with name-calling from others just because they were friends with me.

Before I could even put into words what I felt, I knew I was different from other people who looked like me, and I struggled a lot with how to bridge the gap between me and them. I wondered what I had missed out on and what made me so different. I learned to accept the only position available to me when around other blacks—the observer. In that position I gained another kind of insight into black culture, one that has helped me become more understanding as to why I posed a threat to them and they to me.

It was the hostility of black kids that first made me conscious that being black means a lot more than having darker skin; it carries a whole history and anger. I resented those kids for punishing me for being black and confident, but I was also attracted to them for having more knowledge about black culture than I did.

In recent years, I have become very curious and interested in black awareness and identity. I have mainly taken the responsibility of educating myself both through reading and listening to others speaking about black issues.

Black history, past and present (in particular, the history of black women), has been one of my primary interests ever since I have been out of high school. I am starting to learn many of the answers to the "whys" I had growing up. It has been both a relief and empowering to learn about black culture. It is the whole other half of history I was never taught in school.

The racist attitude of whites was more inconspicuous than the overt anger from blacks, but they both were equally powerful and disturbing. Yet, since the rejection from blacks was obvious, I initially attached my immediate feeling of oppression to other blacks. As time has gone on, I have become more understanding (though not accepting) of the black kids' resentment and more aware and less tolerant of prejudice from whites.

Dancing saved my sanity. It has been my coping device. Often when I felt there was no one I could talk to or who would completely understand, dancing was the closest I could get to peace. I didn't start taking classes on a regular basis until late high school, but I would always dance in one of the free rooms of my house. My mother tells me that I started doing this as young as two years old.

As an aspiring dancer, I was not exposed to the latest moves in the black community, and although I would take classes in modern and ballet technique to strengthen myself, I never found a form of dance that I felt was completely my style. Instead I made up my own style and created movements that felt right for my body.

Now as a dance major at the University of Michigan, I don't just dance for pleasure, but with purpose. I find that through my choreography, I can finally speak and be heard. I have connected with black and white people (both in the audience and fellow dancers) at a level I could never reach verbally. Through my dance I found mutual respect.

One of the most significant questions I am frequently asked when people see me dance is where did I learn those moves, and if I could teach them. I tell them that I made them up. Although their interest is flattering, I have begun to realize that the real question they want to know the answer to, once again, is how to classify me. I believe I have started to define my own class, in dance and in the rest of my life, which grows out of both black culture and white culture.

Although I sometimes wish that I had been raised in a black community, I am still very grateful for having been raised as I was. Having a family at all, and especially one that loves and supports me, is far more important to me than being raised in a specific community.

I experienced some of the best and worst of both cultures, which has given me a wealth of insight that I only recently have begun to appreciate and hope that I can pass on to others. When I was growing up, I often felt like I had no place. Now I have come to realize that by not having a comfortable place, I had to create my own, which at times seems to serve as a bridge. In this world, full of so much hate, I believe we need all the bridges we can get.

MOJADO LIKE ME

JOSEPH TOVARES

Study Questions

1. How did Joseph Tovares and his colleagues "pass" as Mexican laborers? How did Tovares know he had "passed"?
2. Describe the life of a "Mexican laborer" as experienced by Tovares.
3. How does Tovares marginal status help us understand race in the United States?

Early last November I caught a radio news story about Latino support for California's Proposition 187, the bill that sought to deny educational, medical, and other benefits to undocumented immigrants. The report suggested that there was support for the measure among established Mexican Americans. Like a lot of people, I was stunned by what I heard. The "send them back to where they came from" attitude of some of my fellow Chicanos left me shaking my head in disbelief. It seems as though, in the span of one or two generations, many of us have become blind to the strife of our ancestors. How short can our collective memories be?

I am not pointing fingers. Although I find the very idea of Proposition 187 to be rooted in racism and find it abhorrent, I too have moments when I forget how I got here in the first place. I hadn't realized the extent of my memory lapses until I accepted an assignment that vividly reminded me of where I had once been.

The Mambo Kings. That's what we jokingly called ourselves as we drove across California shooting an undercover story for ABC's "Prime-Time Live." We were three college-educated, U.S.-born Latinos, but for this story we dressed as farm workers, spoke Spanish and broken English, and tried hard to look poor. There was Steve Blanco, a half Cuban American, half Puerto Rican from Miami and an ace freelance sound recordist; Gerardo Rueda, a first-generation Mexican American as well as a first-rate shooter and sound recordist; and me, a documentary producer, a Tejano/Chicano with roots in Texas stretching back to pre-Alamo days who just happens to be Jewish. As we traveled across the state in our beat-up Ford pickup, drawing nervous stares from shop owners and accusatory glances from policemen, I learned something about who I am and remembered much about who I used to be.

Back home in San Antonio and Miami, we led the good life. We worked for the networks, made good money, dressed well, and drove nice cars. We were living out our parents' dreams—the dreams of immigrants who longed for a better future for their children. Our folks had nothing to complain about—we were making good money and working for a prestigious show. "Nachas," the Jews call it. It's how old folks describe the pride and joy their children bring to them. For years we had brought our parents much "nachas."

But over the years, like most television veterans, I had picked up some bad habits. There is an "us and them" attitude that permeates our business. We're on the inside and everyone else is on the outside. Objectivity often forces journalists to put up walls, and Latino journalists are no different. A wall had developed between myself and almost everyone else, including other Chicanos. I somehow saw myself as different. After all, I was a freelance professional and I worked steadily. No one guaranteed me work; I worked because I was good and because I had paid my dues.

After much hard work, I had achieved a measure of success that I felt I had earned. I had been through what most professionals of color go through in this country. As a student I had put up with all the nonsense from white teachers, from first grade through graduate school. I had put up with all the snide remarks from co-workers who had never worked with a "Mexican." All that was behind me now. I didn't have to put up with anybody. In my mind I was a success. I had accomplished much more than I was supposed to. But with that success came the wall that divided me from my people and from my past.

I got the call from "PrimeTime Live" on a Sunday, and a few days later the job was set. Gerardo and I set out from San Antonio and Steve Blanco flew in from Miami a few days later. Susan Barnett, the producer, and Claudia Swift, the associate producer, had done their homework. Our job was to infiltrate work groups made up of Mexican workers, then determine their legal status and whether or not they were being exploited. Unconfirmed sources indicated that the workers were being illegally charged for transportation and tools. It was the old "company store" routine. In the end, the workers owed the boss money. If that wasn't bad enough, many workers were often forced to live in subhuman conditions deep inside our national forests. We suspected all of this was occurring under the watchful eye of the U.S. Forest Service, which awarded the contracts for reforestation. The scenario had the two most essential elements for a good story: clearly identifiable victims and bad guys.

We began our new, albeit temporary, life in old faded work pants, well worn flannel shirts, and dusty work boots. Susan and Claudia provided us with the proper vehicle—a 1979 Ford truck that had been in so many accidents it was now composed mostly of Bondo.

At first the job reminded me of *Black Like Me,* a sixties book by John Howard Griffin in which a white man foolishly thinks he can understand what it's like to be a black man in America by temporarily changing his skin color. A friend would later kid me about my adventure, referring to it as "Mojado Like Me." Mojado is a pejorative term, the Spanish equivalent of "wetback." But I didn't need to change my skin color; nor was I venturing into completely new territory.

We entered the town of Lindsay, California, anxiously looking for work. We walked the streets, chatting with everyone we could. On street corners, in restaurants, and in bars, we searched out employment in the sierra, the mountains. We only spoke Spanish—not the Spanish we learned in school but the language of the campesinos. By the end of the first day we knew we were "passing." We knew by the help we received from real farm workers and others we approached for information on jobs. Waitresses, barkeeps, and people on the streets would all refer us to contractors. But we also knew we were "passing" by the stares we received. Cops, shopkeepers, businesspeople would look at us with suspicion and speak to us in condescending tones. I had forgotten what that felt like, and it took me back to Michigan, to 1969 and to endless rows of Christmas trees.

It had been almost 25 years since that summer in Michigan. That was the last time I worked the fields. My mom and dad, my older brother Raul, and I worked long days trimming Christmas trees while my younger brothers played in the adjoining woods. Using machetes, we "formed" the trees, making sure they looked like Christmas trees should. All day long we would swing those machetes. Another crew followed closely behind, "painting" the mature trees with a green dye. After that summer, Christmas never seemed the same. Years later when my wife, Munya, and I were planning to marry, she asked if I would be willing to keep a Jewish home. I don't think she knows how easy it was for me to give up the Christmas tree.

A lot had changed in 25 years. I had gone from campesino child to East Coast-educated, hip (or so I thought) Latino. But like a lot of Latino professionals, there had developed a great distance between who I had once been and who I had become. I never forgot where I came from, but the memory had become fuzzier with time.

I had forgotten how much baggage poverty carries. Being without money is only part of the story. There is a side to poverty, exacerbated by race, that is much more difficult to understand. It is subtle yet oppressive. It is communicated by stares, gestures, and tone. Unless you've been there, you can't possibly understand. I had tried very hard to leave those feelings of inferiority far behind. I had graduated from high school, won a scholarship to college, and obtained a fellowship at graduate school. I thought I had come a long way. Yet, as I walked the streets looking for menial work, I realized that after all these years I had been only one change of clothes away from my past. A past I had tried to bury long ago.

The competition for jobs was stiff. There was a surplus of labor around, and it was hard to pin down the contratistas as to when they would get their contracts. We dogged one guy for days, hanging around his storefront office until he finally agreed to add us to his work crew. The entire time we were wired for video and sound, wondering if our mannerisms and movements would give us away and wondering what would happen if we were found out. After all, these were not Boy Scouts we were approaching for work. These were men who were accused of absconding with their workers' wages and abandoning them in the mountains without food or transportation. They would not take kindly to having their unethical behavior surreptitiously videotaped. Landing the job was a cause for some celebration—not only did we get work, we got it on tape. But the scope of the accomplishment was diminished by the severe reality of the work we were going to have to perform.

The work in the California mountains was more than hard—it was brutal. We left camp at six in the morning and returned around seven at night. The official term for the job is "manual release" but the other workers, all of whom were from Mexico and undocumented, simply called it "limpieza," or "cleaning." In "manual release," workers move along in a line, and with hoes, shears, and brute force, clear thick brush from around recently planted pine trees. Those little seedlings had value; in many ways they were much more valuable than we were. Lots of money went into planting those little trees, and we were there to protect them. The thick brush we were taking out had been robbing the pine trees of valuable nutrients and had to be removed. But it was no easy matter. Some bushes were bigger than we were and virtually impossible to completely take out. I hadn't worked that hard in a long time. There I was, my hands cut and scratched, my body completely covered in dirt, trying to chip away at thicket after thicket. We had no idea how much we would wind up being paid or when; no idea when we would eat lunch, no idea if we would get a break. Under the watchful eye of our patron, a fellow Chicano, we worked. At his request, several men sang old Mexican songs. The National Forest had been transformed into a hacienda.

The plan was for us to complete fourteen acres that first day of work, but we only finished six. Midway through the afternoon the boss gave us a pep talk. "The quicker we finish, the more money you make," he said. But the work was too much. The Mambo Kings were the first to quit. We got the pictures we needed and left.

Over the course of several days, we wandered among various work camps, taking more pictures and gathering information. Living in tents and working twelve hours a day proved too much of a strain for many of the laborers. Fresh workers were brought in to replace those who left. We were told that during a period of seven weeks more than 100 men had come and gone from the crew. Only two of the original fifteen men, a father and son, remained.

Their names were Gregorio and Pedro. Gregorio, the father, had been in the United States for a long time. Pedro, his son, had only just arrived. The boy claimed to be eighteen, but he had the face of a child. I was amazed as I watched Pedro work. His tools were not nearly as good as ours and the effort required to cut through the heavy bush and ground cover was taxing even for the grown men. But Pedro, who worked without gloves, never complained.

All day we would crawl to reach the trunks of the large and thorny bushes—constantly on the lookout for dangerous snakes. We were allowed fifteen minutes for lunch and given a ten-minute break in the late afternoon. As we worked side by side, Pedro told me of his solitary trek across Mexico and into the U.S. He had come to search for his father, hoping to land a job and assist him in supporting the family back in Oaxaca. The father and son expected to make about $6,000 between them, but after seven weeks of grueling work, all they received was $300 each. The last time I saw them was on television, several months after their job ended. They were still hoping to get paid.

Our job with ABC News lasted three weeks, but the memory will be with me forever. I can still remember the pain of the distrustful stares, the agony of watching men being treated like animals, and the anger of seeing Chicano contractors exploit Mexican workers. The lessons from those three weeks were startling. It didn't matter how different I thought I was from these men who hail from places like Oaxaca and Michoacan. To virtually all the people I met, I was one of them. The walls that I had built turned out to be made of paper, and they quickly crumbled.

Barely a month after the odyssey began, I was back home attending my twentieth high school reunion. There were doctors, lawyers, accountants, and businessmen—a dozen Hispanic success stories. Drinking and dancing at the San Antonio country club, we represented the new Chicano middle class. Part of me felt very much at home there, and the feeling troubled me. As I tried to make sense of my conflict, I glanced down and touched a small scar on my left hand. The scar had been left there by a careless boy trying to work as a man 25 years ago in Michigan. Day dreaming and machetes don't mix. Effortlessly the band segued from a rock tune to a Mexican polka, and the Chicanos shifted into barrio gear and slid across the dance floor with ease. As my wife and I danced, I realized that it is impossible to leave one life behind and simply begin another. Our lives are built on a series of experiences and, like it or not, even the difficult ones count.

So what started out as a good job with lots of overtime potential turned into a cathartic event that changed my life. I had tried for years to bury unpleasant memories, to deny they even existed. My career had made it easy to do. But during those three weeks in California I was forced into a deep reexamination of myself. The experience made me confront ugly realities about how this society treats a hidden underclass. Most important, it made me realize how easy it is for many of us who have escaped to simply forget.

Then Came the War

Yuri Kochiyama

Study Question

1. Describe the marginal status of Japanese-Americans during WWII. In particular list examples of how interned Japanese were still "Americans" even as they were isolated from the rest of the U.S. population.

I was red, white, and blue when I was growing up. I taught Sunday school, and was very, very American. But I was also very provincial. We were just kids rooting for our high school.

My father owned a fish market. Terminal Island was nearby, and that was where many Japanese families lived. It was a fishing town. My family lived in the city proper. San Pedro was very mixed, predominantly white, but there were blacks also.

I was nineteen at the time of the evacuation. I had just finished junior college. I was looking for a job, and didn't realize how different the school world was from the work world. In the school world, I never felt racism. But when you got into the work world, it was very difficult. This was 1941, just before the war. I finally did get a job at a department store. But for us back then, it was a big thing, because I don't think they had ever hired an Asian in a department store before. I tried, because I saw a Mexican friend who got a job there. Even then they didn't hire me on a regular basis, just on Saturdays, summer vacation, Easter vacation, and Christmas vacation. Other than that, I was working like the others—at a vegetable stand, or doing part-time domestic work. Back then, I only knew of two Japanese American girl friends who got jobs as secretaries—but these were in Japanese companies. But generally you almost never saw a Japanese American working in a white place. It was hard for Asians. Even for Japanese, the best jobs they felt they could get were in Chinatowns, such as in Los Angeles. Most Japanese were either in some aspect of fishing, such as in the canneries, or went right from school to work on the farms. That was what it was like in the town of San Pedro. I loved working in the department store, because it was a small town, and you got to know and see everyone. The town itself was wonderful. People were very friendly. I didn't see my job as work—it was like a community job.

Everything changed for me on the day Pearl Harbor was bombed. On that very day—December 7—the FBI came and they took my father. He had just come home from the hospital the day before. For several days we didn't know where they had taken him. Then we found out that he was taken to the federal prison at Terminal Island. Overnight, things changed for us. They took all men who lived near the Pacific waters, and had nothing to do with fishing. A month later, they took every fisherman from Terminal Island, sixteen and over, to places—not the regular concentration camps—but to detention centers in places like South Dakota, Montana, and New Mexico. They said that all Japanese who had given money to any kind of Japanese organization would have to be taken away. At that time, many people were giving to the Japanese Red Cross. The first group was thirteen hundred Isseis—my parent's generation. They took those who were leaders of the community, or Japanese school teachers, or were teaching martial arts, or who were Buddhist priests. Those categories which would make them very "Japanesey," were picked up. This really made a tremendous impact on our lives. My twin brother was going to the University at Berkeley. He came rushing back. All of our classmates were joining up, so he volunteered to go into the service. And it seemed strange that here they had my father in prison, and there the draft board okayed my brother. He went right into the army. My other brother, who was two years older, was trying to run my father's fish market. But business was already going down, so he had to close it. He had finished college at the University of California a couple of years before.

They took my father on December 7th. The day before, he had just come home from the hospital. He had surgery for an ulcer. We only saw him once, on December 13. On December 20th they said he could come home. By the time they brought him back, he couldn't talk. He made guttural sounds and we didn't know if he could hear. He was home for twelve hours. He was dying. The next morning, when we got up, they told us that he was gone. He was very sick. And I think the interrogation was very rough. My mother kept begging the authorities to let him go to the hospital until he was well, then put him back in the prison. They did finally put him there, a week or so later. But they put him in a hospital where they were bringing back all these American Merchant Marines who were hit on Wake Island. So he was the only Japanese in that hospital, so they hung a sheet around him that said, Prisoner of War. The feeling where he was was very bad.

You could see the hysteria of war. There was a sense that war could actually come to American shores. Everybody was yelling to get the "Japs" out of California. In Congress, people were speaking out. Organizations such as the Sons and Daughters of the Golden West were screaming "Get the 'Japs' out." So were the real estate people, who wanted to get the land from the Japanese farmers. The war had whipped up such a hysteria that if there was anyone for the Japanese, you didn't hear about it. I'm sure they were afraid to speak out, because they would be considered not only just "Jap" lovers, but unpatriotic.

Just the fact that my father was taken made us suspect to people. But on the whole, the neighbors were quite nice, especially the ones adjacent to us. There was already a six AM to six PM curfew and a five mile limit on where we could go from our homes. So they offered to do our shopping for us, if we needed.

Most Japanese Americans had to give up their jobs, whatever they did, and were told they had to leave. The edict for 9066—President Roosevelt's edict[1] for evacuation—was in February 1942. We were moved to a detention center that April. By then the Japanese on Terminal Island were just helter skelter, looking for anywhere they could go. They opened up the Japanese school and Buddhist churches, and families just crowded in. Even farmers brought along their chickens and chicken coops. They just opened up the places for people to stay until they could figure out what to do. Some people left for Colorado and Utah. Those who had relatives could do so. The idea was to evacuate all the Japanese from the coast. But all the money was frozen, so even if you knew where you wanted to go, it wasn't that simple. By then, people knew they would be going into camps, so they were selling what they could, even though they got next to nothing for it.

We were fortunate, in that our neighbors, who were white, were kind enough to look after our house, and they said they would find people to rent it, and look after it till we got back. But these neighbors were very, very unusual.

We were sent to an assembly center in Arcadia, California, in April. It was the largest assembly center on the West Coast, having nearly twenty thousand people. There were some smaller centers with about six hundred people. All along the West Coast—Washington, Oregon, California—there were many, many assembly centers, but ours was the largest. Most of the assembly centers were either fairgrounds, or race tracks. So many of us lived in stables, and they said you could take what you could carry. We were there until October.

Even though we stayed in a horse stable, everything was well organized. Every unit would hold four to six people. So in some cases, families had to split up, or join others. We slept on army cots, and for mattresses they gave us muslin bags, and told us to fill them with straw. And for chairs, everybody scrounged around for carton boxes, because they could serve as chairs. You could put two together and it could be a little table. So it was just makeshift. But I was amazed how, in a few months, some of those units really looked nice. Japanese women fixed them up. Some people had the foresight to bring material and needles and thread. But they didn't let us bring anything that could be used as weapons. They let us have spoons, but no knives. For those who had small children or babies, it was rough. They said you could take what you could carry. Well, they could only take their babies in their arms, and maybe the little children could carry something, but it was pretty limited.

I was so red, white, and blue, I couldn't believe this was happening to us. America would never do a thing like this to us. This is the greatest country in the world. So I thought this is only going to be for a short while, maybe a few weeks or something, and they will let us go back. At the beginning no one realized how long this would go on. I didn't feel the anger that much because I thought maybe this was the way we could show our love for our country, and we should not make too much fuss or noise, we should abide by what they asked of us. I'm a totally different person now than I was back then. I was naïve about so many things. The more I think about it, the more I realize how little you learn about American history. It's just what they want you to know.

At the beginning, we didn't have any idea how temporary or permanent the situation was. We thought we would be able to leave shortly. But after several months they told us this was just temporary quarters, and they were building more permanent quarters elsewhere in the United States. All this was so unbelievable. A year before we would never have thought anything like this could have happened to us—not in this country. As time went by, the sense of frustration grew. Many families were already divided. The fathers, the heads of the households, were taken to other camps. In the beginning, there was no way for the sons to get in touch with their families. Before our group left for the detention camp, we were saying goodbye almost every day to other groups who were going to places like Arizona and Utah. Here we finally had made so many new friends—people who we met, lived with, shared the time, and got to know. So it was even sad on that note and the goodbyes were difficult. Here we had gotten close to these people, and now we had to separate again. I don't think we even thought about where they were going to take us, or how long we would have to stay there. When we got on the trains to leave for the camps, we didn't know where we were going. None of the groups knew. It was later on that we learned so and so ended up in Arizona, or Colorado, or some other place. We were all at these assembly centers for about seven months. Once they started pushing people out, it was done very quickly. By October, our group headed out for Jerome, Arkansas, which is on the Texarkana corner.

We were on the train for five days. The blinds were down, so we couldn't look out, and other people couldn't look in to see who was in the train. We stopped in Nebraska, and everybody pulled the blinds to see what Nebraska looked like. The interesting thing was, there was a troop train stopped at the station too. These American soldiers looked out, and saw all these Asians, and they wondered what we were doing on the train. So the Japanese raised the windows, and so did the soldiers. It wasn't a bad feeling at all. There was none of that "you Japs" kind of thing. The women were about the same age as the soldiers—eighteen to twenty-five, and we had the same thing on our minds. In camps, there wasn't much to do, so the fun thing was to receive letters, so on our train, all the girls who were my age, were yelling to the guys, "Hey, give us your address where you're going, we'll write you." And they said, "Are you sure you're going to write?" We exchanged addresses and for a long time I wrote to some of those soldiers. On the other side of the train, I'll never forget there was this old guy, about sixty, who came to our window and said, "We have some Japanese living here. This is Omaha, Nebraska." This guy was very nice, and didn't seem to have any ill feelings for Japanese. He had calling cards, and he said "Will any of you people write to me?" We said, "Sure," so he threw in a bunch of calling cards, and I got one, and I wrote to him for years. I wrote to him about what camp was like, because he said, "Let me know what it's like wherever you end up." And he wrote back, and told me what was happening in Omaha, Nebraska. There were many, many interesting experiences too. Our mail was generally not censored, but all the mail from the soldiers was. Letters meant everything.

When we got to Jerome, Arkansas, we were shocked because we had never seen an area like it. There was forest all around us. And they told us to wait till the rains hit. This would not only turn into mud, but Arkansas swamp lands. That's where they put us—in swamp lands, surrounded by forests. It was nothing like California.

I'm speaking as a person of twenty who had good health. Up until then, I had lived a fairly comfortable life. But there were many others who didn't see the whole experience the same way. Especially those who were older and in poor health and had experienced racism. One more thing like this could break them. I was at an age where transitions were not hard—the point where anything new could even be considered exciting. But for people in poor health, it was hell.

There were army-type barracks, with two hundred to two hundred and five people to each block and every block had its own mess hall, facility for washing clothes, showering. It was all surrounded by barbed wire, and armed soldiers. I think they said only seven people were killed in total, though thirty were shot, because they went too close to the fence. Where we were, nobody thought of escaping because you'd be more scared of the swamps—the poisonous snakes, the bayous. Climatic conditions were very harsh. Although Arkansas is in the South, the winters were very, very cold. We had a pot bellied stove in every room and we burned wood. Everything was very organized. We got there in October, and were warned to prepare ourselves. So on our block, for instance, males eighteen and over could go out in the forest to chop down trees for wood for the winter. The men would bring back the trees, and the women sawed the trees. Everybody worked. The children would pile up the wood for each unit.

They told us when it rained, it would be very wet, so we would have to build our own drainage system. One of the barracks was to hold meetings, so block heads would call meetings. There was a block council to represent the people from different areas.

When we first arrived, there were some things that weren't completely fixed. For instance, the roofers would come by, and everyone would hunger for information from the outside world. We wanted to know what was happening with the war. We weren't allowed to bring radios; that was contraband. And there were no televisions then. So we would ask the workers to bring us back some papers, and they would give us papers from Texas or Arkansas, so for the first time we would find out about news from the outside.

Just before we went in to the camps, we saw that being a Japanese wasn't such a good thing, because everybody was turning against the Japanese, thinking we were saboteurs, or linking us with Pearl Harbor. But when I saw the kind of work they did at camp, I felt so proud of the Japanese, and proud to be Japanese, and wondered why I was so white, white when I was outside, because I was always with white folks. Many people had brothers or sons who were in the military and Japanese American servicemen would come into the camp to visit the families, and we felt so proud of them when they came in their uniforms. We knew that it would only be a matter of time before they would be shipped overseas. Also what made us feel proud was the forming of the 442 unit.[2]

I was one of these real American patriots then. I've changed now. But back then, I was all American. Growing up, my mother would say we're Japanese. But I'd say, "No, I'm American." I think a lot of Japanese grew up that way. People would say to them, "You're Japanese," and they would say, "No, we're Americans." I don't even think they used the hyphenated term "Japanese-American" back then. At the time, I was ashamed of being Japanese. I think many Japanese Americans felt the same way. Pearl Harbor was a shameful act, and being Japanese Americans, even though we had nothing to do with it, we still somehow felt we were blamed for it. I hated Japan at that point. So I saw myself at that part of my history as an American, and not as a Japanese or Japanese American. That sort of changed while I was in the camp.

I hated the war, because it wasn't just between the governments. It went down to the people, and it nurtured hate. What was happening during the war were many things I didn't like. I hoped that one day when the war was over there could be a way that people could come together in their relationships.

Now I can relate to Japan in a more mature way, where I see its faults and its very, very negative history. But I also see its potential. Scientifically and technologically it has really gone far. But I'm disappointed that when it comes to human rights she hasn't grown. The Japan of today—I feel there are still things lacking. For instance, I don't think the students have the opportunity to have more leeway in developing their lives.

We always called the camps "relocation centers" while we were there. Now we feel it is apropos to call them concentration camps. It is not the same as the concentration camps of Europe; those we feel were death camps. Concentration camps were a concentration of people placed in an area, and disempowered and disenfranchised. So it is apropos to call what I was in a concentration camp. After two years in the camp, I was released.

Going home wasn't much of a problem for us because our neighbors had looked after our place. But for most of our Japanese friends, starting over again was very difficult after the war.

I returned in October of 1945. It was very hard to find work, at least for me. I wasn't expecting to find anything good, just something to tide me over until my boyfriend came back from New York. The only thing I was looking for was to work in a restaurant as a waitress. But I couldn't find anything. I would walk from one end of the town to the other, and down every main avenue. But as soon as they found out I was Japanese, they would say no. Or they would ask me if I was in the union, and of course I couldn't be in the union because I had just gotten there. Anyway, no Japanese could be in the union, so if the answer was no I'm not in the union, they would say no. So finally what I did was go into the rough area of San Pedro—there's a strip near the wharf—and I went down there. I was determined to keep the jobs as long as I could. But for a while, I could last maybe two hours, and somebody would say "Is that a 'Jap'?" And as soon as someone would ask that, the boss would say, "Sorry, you gotta go. We don't want trouble here." The strip wasn't that big, so after I'd go the whole length of it, I'd have to keep coming back to the same restaurants, and say, "Gee, will you give me another chance." I figure, all these servicemen were coming back and the restaurants didn't have enough waitresses to come in and take these jobs. And so, they'd say "Okay. But soon as somebody asks who you are, or if you're a 'Jap,' or any problem about being a 'Jap,' you go." So I said, "Okay, sure. How about keeping me until that happens?" So sometimes I'd last a night, sometimes a couple of nights that no one would say anything. Sometimes people threw cups at me or hot coffee. At first they didn't know what I was. They thought I was Chinese. Then someone would say, "I bet she's a 'Jap'." And I wasn't going to say I wasn't. So as soon as I said "Yeah," then it was like an uproar. Rather than have them say, "Get out," I just walked out. I mean, there was no point in fighting it. If you just walked out, there was less chance of getting hurt. But one place I lasted two weeks. These owners didn't want to have to let me go. But they didn't want to have problems with the people.

And so I did this until I left for New York, which was about three months later. I would work the dinner shift, from six at night to three in the morning. When you are young you tend not to take things as strongly. Everything is like an adventure. Looking back, I felt the people who were the kindest to me were those who went out and fought, those who just got back from Japan or the Far East. I think the worst ones were the ones who stayed here and worked in defense plants, who felt they had to be so patriotic. On the West Coast, there wasn't hysteria anymore, but there were hostile feelings towards the Japanese, because they were coming back. It took a while, but my mother said that things were getting back to normal, and that the Japanese were slowly being accepted again. At the time, I didn't go through the bitterness that many others went through, because it's not just what they went through, but it is also what they experienced before that. I mean, I happened to have a much more comfortable life before, so you sort of see things in a different light. You see that there are all kinds of Americans, and that they're not all people who hate Japs. You know too that it was hysteria that had a lot to do with it.

All Japanese, before they left camp, were told not to congregate among Japanese, and not to speak Japanese. They were told by the authorities. There was even a piece of paper that gave you instructions. But then people went on to places like Chicago where there were churches, so they did congregate in churches. But they did ask people not to. I think psychologically the Japanese, having gone through a period where they were so hated by everyone, didn't even want to admit they were Japanese, or accept the fact that they were Japanese. Of course, they would say they were Japanese Americans. But I think the psychological damage of the wartime period, and of racism itself, has left its mark. There is a stigma to being Japanese. I think that is why such a large number of Japanese, in particular Japanese American women, have married out of the race. On the West Coast I've heard people say that sixty to seventy percent of the Japanese women have married, I guess, mostly whites. Japanese men are doing it too, but not to that degree. I guess Japanese Americans just didn't want to have that Japanese identity, or that Japanese part. There is definitely some self-hate, and part of that has to do with the racism that's so deeply a part of this society.

Historically, Americans have always been putting people behind walls. First there were the American Indians who were put on reservations, Africans in slavery, their lives on the plantations, Chicanos doing migratory work, and the kinds of camps they lived in, and even, too, the Chinese when they worked on the railroad camps where they were almost isolated, dispossessed people—disempowered. And I feel those are the things we should fight against so they won't happen again. It wasn't so long ago—in 1979—that the feeling against the Iranians was so strong because of the takeover of the U.S. embassy in Iran, where they wanted to deport Iranian students. And that is when a group called Concerned Japanese Americans organized, and that was the first issue we took up, and then we connected it with what the Japanese had gone through. This whole period of what the Japanese went through is important. If we can see the connections of how often this happens in history, we can stem the tide of these things happening again by speaking out against them.

Most Japanese Americans who worked years and years for redress never thought it would happen the way it did. The papers have been signed, we will be given reparation, and there was an apology from the government. I think the redress movement itself was very good because it was a learning experience for the Japanese people; we could get out into our communities and speak about what happened to us and link it with experiences of other people. In that sense, though, it wasn't done as much as it should have been. Some Japanese Americans didn't even learn that part. They just started the movement as a reaction to the bad experience they had. They don't even see other ethnic groups who have gone through it. It showed us, too, how vulnerable everybody is. It showed us that even though there is a Constitution, that constitutional rights could be taken away very easily.

Notes

[1] Executive Order No. 9066 does not mention detention of Japanese specifically, but was used exclusively against the Japanese. Over 120,000 Japanese were evacuated from the West Coast.

[2] American soldiers of Japanese ancestry were assembled in two units: the 442 Regimental Combat Team and the 100th Infantry Battalion. The two groups were sent to battle in Europe. The 100th Battalion had over 900 casualties and was known as the Purple Heart Battalion. Combined, the units received 9,486 purple hearts and 18,143 individual decorations.

PART·2

Classifying People by Race

On a variety of official documents, citizens are requested to state their race or ethnicity. In census tabulations, they are asked to respond, indeed, to confess to their race, to examine their skin color, the color of their blood, their type of hair, and the breadth of their nostrils to allocate themselves to racial groups.

Yehudi O. Webster
THE RACIALIZATION OF AMERICA (1993:44)

In Part 1, we examined the personal experiences of racial classification in the United States. While every person had a unique story, the stories cannot be separated from the prevailing system of racial classification and the conception of race that supports it. Whether people fit into a racial category or not, the categories remain central to how people think about their own and the racial identity of others. In this section, we describe and critique the system of racial classification in the United States.

Most people in the United States equate race with physical features. In their minds, the term *race* refers to a group of people who possess certain distinctive and conspicuous physical traits. Racial categories are assumed to represent "natural, physical divisions among humans that are hereditary, reflected in morphology, and roughly but correctly captured by terms like Black, White, and Asian (or Negroid, Caucasoid, and Mongoloid)" (Haney López 1994:6). This three-category classification scheme has many shortcomings, which immediately become evident when we imagine using it to classify the more than 5.6 billion people in the world. If we attempted this task, we would soon learn that three categories are not enough—especially when we consider that for the 1990 U.S. Census, respondents wrote in the names of 300 alleged races and 75 combinations of multiracial ancestry (Morganthau 1995).

The refusal on the part of the government of the United States to acknowledge the obvious conclusion that their categories only very poorly capture the range of human features is driven by long-standing historical and social reasons. "The idea that there exist three races, and that these races are 'Caucasoid', 'Negroid', and 'Mongoloid', is rooted in the European imagination of the Middle Ages, which encompassed only Europe, Africa and the Near East. . . . The peoples of the American continents, the

Indian subcontinent, East Asia, Southeast Asia, and Oceania—living out-side the imagination of Europe—are excluded from the three major races for social and political reasons, not for scientific ones. Nevertheless, the history of science has long been the history of failed efforts to justify these social beliefs" (Haney López 1994:13–14).

Adding more categories, however, would not ease the task of classifying the world's billions of people because racial classification rests on the fallacy that clear-cut racial categories exist. Why is this a fallacy? First, many people do not fit clearly into a racial category because no sharp dividing line distinguishes characteristics such as black skin from white skin or curly hair from wavy. This lack of a clear line, however, has not discouraged people from trying to devise ways to make the line seem clear-cut. For example, a hundred years ago in the United States there were churches that "had a pinewood slab on the outside door . . . and a fine tooth comb hanging on a string . . ." (Angelou 1987:2). People could go into the church if they were no darker than the pinewood and if they could run the comb through their hair without it snagging. At one time in South Africa, the state board that oversaw racial classification used a pencil test to classify individuals as white or black. If a pencil placed in the person's hair fell out, the person was classified as white (Finnegan 1986).

A second problem with the idea of clear-cut racial categories is that boundaries between races can never be fixed and definite, if only because males and females of any alleged race can produce offspring. Millions of people in the world have mixed ancestry and possess physical traits which make it impossible to assign them to any of the four narrow racial categories currently used by the U.S. government. The media often presents mixed ancestry as a recent phenomenon connected to the dismantling of laws forbidding interracial marriages in 1967 and a subsequent societal openness to interracial marriage (which produce mixed race children—*see* Beech 1996 as one example). Since colonial days in the United States, however, "there has been intermixture between White and Indian, between White and Negro, and between Negro and Indian. While the offspring of such unions could not be biologically classified (and by their very existence defy the popular meaning of race), many of them did undoubtedly become accepted and identified with one of the three recognized stocks" (Pollitzer 1972:720). Evidence of this intermixing before 1967 and of the fact that people become identified as belonging to one "racial" stock in spite of their mixed ancestry is reflected in 1929 and 1949 studies of the racial ancestry of college students attending historically black universities. In the 1929 study, 78% of Howard University students were of mixed "racial" ancestry. In the 1949 study, 84% of the college students studied were of mixed ancestry (Meier 1949). The widespread existence of intermixing, however, seemed to have little effect on dismantling beliefs that distinct racial categories exist.

A third shortcoming in systems of racial classification is that racial categories and guidelines for placing people in them are often vague, contradictory, unevenly applied, and subject to change. In the reading "'Indian' and 'Black' as Radically Different Types of Categories," Jack D. Forbes (1990:23–25) offers one example of how the rules of racial classification change depending on whether a person is of African or Native American ancestry.

As other examples of the arbitrary nature of classification rules, consider that for the 1990 Census coders were instructed to classify as white those who classified themselves as "white-black" and to classify as "black" those who classified themselves as "black-white" (U.S. Bureau of the Census 1994). Likewise the National Center for Health Statistics (1993) has changed the guidelines for recording race on birth and death certificates. Before 1989, a child born in the United States was designated as white if both parents were white; if only one parent was white, the child was classified according to the race of the nonwhite parent; if the parents were of different nonwhite races, the child was assigned to the race of the father.[1] If the race of one parent was unknown, the infant was assigned the race of the parent whose race was known. After 1989, the rules for classifying newborns changed: Now the race of the infant is the same as that of the mother (Lock 1993), as if identifying the mother's race would present no challenges. For more examples of the arbitrary nature of classification rules, refer to "Race" in Appendix A for the official statement on the meaning of race[2] (U.S. Bureau of the Census 1996).

Finally, in trying to classify people by race, we would find a tremendous amount of variation among people designated as belonging to a particular race. For example, people classified as Asian or Mongoloid include, among other groups, Chinese, Japanese, Malayans, Mongolians, Siberians, Eskimos, and Native Americans. Likewise, there is considerable heterogeneity within the population labeled as "black" in the United States. Green (1978) identified at least nine distinct "cultural-ecological areas" for the native-born black population including areas of Native American influence (Oklahoma and parts of Arkansas and Kansas) and French tradition (Louisiana, eastern Coastal Texas, and southwestern Mississippi). In addition,

> the black population includes immigrants from the Caribbean area and the African mainland. Almost half a million persons in the 1990 census indicated that they were of sub-Saharan African ancestry. The black population from the Caribbean basin countries is diverse and includes Spanish-speaking persons from Cuba, the Dominican Republic, and Panama;

French-speaking persons from Haiti and other French-speaking Caribbean areas; Dutch-speaking persons from the Netherlands Antilles; and English-speaking persons from the former British colonies. (Williams, Lavizzo-Mourey, and Warren 1994:33)

Perhaps the strongest evidence that race is not a biological fact but a social creation is the different rules for classifying people into racial categories across societies and the shifting rules for classifying people within a single society. In the United States, not only have the rules governing classification changed but so have the categories. For example, in the United States a question about race has appeared on every census since 1790, although it was not until 1850 that the government included a question that clearly attempted to distinguish the black population from the white. Prior to 1850, except for the category free whites, the other categories could include people of any race. Over the past 200 years, the U.S. Bureau of the Census has used as few as three racial categories and as many as 14. (See Table 1.) Although the rationale for determining the number and names of categories is the subject of a separate book, we can be sure that the various racial classification schemes reflect the prevailing ideologies of their times, and that to understand the various schemes and the changes in those schemes, one must place them in a larger social context.

Based on the information presented in Table 1, one can readily identify at least two themes. (1) There has only been one category reserved for the population classified as white. In other words, there has been no attempt to further subdivide this white population even though the majority of people in the United States are classified as such. (2) At various times in history, the federal government has been preoccupied with identifying subdivisions within one broad racial category. In 1890, for example, there was an unusual emphasis placed on categorizing people according to degree of blackness. Notice that half the categories listed are devoted to this task. In 1930, five subcategories of "other race" were designated for people of Asian heritage, which at that time constituted only less than one-quarter of one percent (.002%) of the population (Lee 1993).

Sharon Lee (1993) points out that although the classification schemes in the United States have changed in significant ways over time, four dominant themes prevailed:

1. *a pattern of separating the population into two groups: white and nonwhite*

The federal government's attempt to categorize people into two broad racial groups is the most enduring theme in the history of the United States. As mentioned above, there has been "a chronic concern with populations defined as non-White" (p. 82). As many as 13 categories have been

Table I Categories Used by the U.S. Bureau of the Census to Designate Race: 1790–1990

1790, 1800, 1810	
Free Whites	Slaves
All other Free	
Persons, except	
Indians not taxed	

1820, 1830, 1840	
Free Whites	Free Colored
Foreigners, not	Slaves
naturalized	

1850, 1860	
White	Mulatto
Black	Black slaves
	Mulatto slaves

1870, 1880, 1890, 1900, 1910, 1920	
White	Chinese
Black	Indian[3]
Mulatto	Quadroon*
	Octoroon*
	Japanese

1930	
White	All other
Negro	Indian
	Chinese
	Japanese
	Filipino
	Hindu
	Korean

1940	
White	Japanese
Negro	Filipino
Indian	Hindu
Chinese	Korean

1950	
White	Japanese
Negro	Chinese
American Indian	Filipino

1960	
White	Hawaiian
Negro	Part Hawaiian
American Indian	Aleut
Japanese	Eskimo
Chinese	

1970	
White	Chinese
Negro/Black	Filipino
Indian	Hawaiian
Japanese	Korean

1980	
White	Indian (American)
Black or Negro	Asian Indian
Japanese	Hawaiian
Chinese	Guamanian
Filipino	Samoan
Korean	Eskimo
Vietnamese	Aleut

1990	
White	Asian or Pacific
Black or Negro	Islander
Indian (American)	Chinese
Eskimo	Hawaiian
Aleut	Korean
	Vietnamese
	Japanese
	Asian Indian
	Samoan
	Guamanian
	Other API

*Category applied to 1890 Census only.
Source: U.S. Bureau of the Census (1989).

used to classify the numerically smaller population designated as nonwhite with no corresponding effort to do the same with the majority population classified as white. Although definitions of who belongs to white and non-white categories have shifted over time,[3] up until 1980, rules for the bureau of the census in classifying persons of mixed biological heritage had never specified the white category as an option. In other words, according to the bureau of the census "any mixture of white and nonwhite should be reported according to the nonwhite parent."

2. a belief in racial purity

The belief in the idea of racial purity is reflected in the absence of a mixed-race or multiracial category and in the absence of instructions to "check all that apply." In the United States, categories are treated as mutually exclusive—that is, it is not possible for someone to belong to more than one category. Even the 1990 Census asks respondents to "fill in ONE circle" for the race they consider themselves (and persons living within the same household) to be. If the person does not follow directions, census enumerators make every effort to assign people to one racial category even in instances where people give other kinds of responses.

Table 1 shows that there have been only a few attempts to identify multiracial populations. In 1890, the U.S. Bureau of the Census included the categories "Mulatto," "Quadroon," and "Octoroon"[4] in an attempt to identify the "partly Black" population and also gave special emphasis for identifying segments of the Native American population.[5] In the subsequent census, the categories "Quadroon" and "Octoroon" were dropped, never to appear again. The 1920 Census was the last time the term "Mulatto" appeared. Since 1920, with the exception of an attempt in 1950 to count "special communities"[6] and an attempt in 1960 to identify those who are "part Hawaiian," the U.S. government has not attempted to identify "partly white" or "mixed-race" populations. Such changes and omissions reflect the general acceptance of the "one-drop rule" in defining who is black or, for that matter, who is not white in the United States. These changes and omissions also reflect a belief in the idea of racial purity—that people can be, or rather are, assigned to one racial category no matter what the facts are with regard to ancestry. In the reading "Historical Origins of the Prohibition of Multiracial Legal Identity in the States and the Nation," Paul Knepper (1995) shows how this belief was incorporated into state and federal laws.

In making the decision to assign children of mixed parentage to the race the "nonwhite" parent has been assigned, the government asks people to accept the idea that one parent contributes a disproportionate amount of genetic material to the child, so large a genetic contribution that it negates the genetic contribution of the other parent. It also serves to establish the category "white" as the ideal/standard category. As one indicator that the category "white" has been treated as the ideal/standard by which all others are measured, consider that of the many court cases in U.S. history related to "wrongful classification," no persons have gone to court to prove they are something other than white.

The predominance of the one-drop rule in the United States suggests that other ideas about race were never considered or were dismissed as possibilities. Other ideas include assigning people of mixed "race" to the same race as the "white" parent,[7] creating new racial categories to accommodate mixed ancestry, dropping the idea of race as a valid way to categorize people (Scales-Trent 1995), and adopting the French and Spanish models.

> During the time Louisiana was a French or a Spanish colony—a time when liaisons between white men and black women were widespread and in some cases nearly formalized—the offspring was treated according to a Latin view of race that left room for a spectrum of colors between black and white. The French had eight terms to calibrate the spectrum—from "mulatre," for the product of a union between a black and a white, to words like "marabout" and "metis," to describe more complicated combinations. The Spanish managed to come with sixty-four terms. Then, in 1803, Louisiana was taken over by the Americans, who imposed what Edmonson refers to as a Germanic view of descent, common to Northern Europe and England: "When it comes to mixing between in-group and out-group, the offspring is flawed, and becomes a member of the out-group" (Trillin 1986:66–67)

3. a pattern of transforming many ethnic groups into one racial group

"Federal Statistical Directive No. 15," an Office of Management and Budget document issued in 1977 and still in use today, outlines the standards for recordkeeping, collection, and presentation of data on race and ethnicity. The directive names four official racial categories and two official ethnic categories (see Part 3). The four races are umbrella terms. That is, each is a supercategory under which aggregates of people who vary according to nationality, ethnicity, language, generation, social class, and time of arrival in the United States are forced into one category (Gimenez 1989). Those supercategories are listed below.

> *American Indian or Alaska Native* (any person having origins in any of the original peoples of North America which by some estimates includes more than 2000 distinct groups);
>
> *Asian or Pacific Islander* (any person having origins in any of the original peoples of the Far East, Southeast Asia, the Indian subcontinent, or the Pacific Islands;
>
> *Black* (any person having origins in the any of the black racial groups of Africa); and
>
> *White* (a person having origins in any of the original peoples of Europe, North Africa, or the Middle East).

It is significant that the definition of the Black category, unlike the definitions for the other three categories omits the words "original peoples" and substitutes "black racial groups of Africa."[8] If "original peoples" were included in the definition of black, every person in the United States would have to check this category. In the view of evolutionary biologists all people evolved from a common African ancestor. Moreover, how many people know enough about the original peoples of a geographic area to know whether they are descendants?

Judy Scales-Trent (1995) maintains that we are asking the wrong questions. The questions should not be where did your people originate? "but rather 'What countries did your people travel through on their way here from Africa?' Or maybe 'What was the most recent stop your people made on their trek to this place from Africa? Was it Denmark? Turkey? Bolivia? Vietnam?'" (p. 140).

4. no sharp distinction between race, ethnicity, and national origin

Sociologist Martha E. Gimenez (1989) points out that the race question is poorly constructed in that it offers respondents racial, ethnic, and national origin categories as possible responses. As one example, in the Asian or Pacific Islander category, the bureau of the census lists as examples eight national origin groups plus a category labeled Hawaiian, which gives the impression that race, country of birth, and/or national origin are one and the same. The national origin groups include Chinese, Filipino, Korean, Vietnamese, Japanese, Asian Indian, Samoan, and Guamanian. Consider the confusion these categories might pose for someone of Chinese ancestry who was born outside of China[9] (in Peru or Saudi Arabia, for example) and then immigrated to the United States. The point of these examples is to show that when a person checks "Chinese," we don't know if it is because he or she is of Chinese ancestry or because he or she was *born in* China (not everyone born in China is of Chinese ancestry). Does the word "Chinese" trigger in respondents associations of biological heritage or associations related to their country of birth or their ancestors' country of birth before their arrival to the United States? It is not clear whether respondents should think about race as something related to their ethnicity, physical appearance, biology, country of birth, or national origin.

This critique of the U.S. system of racial classification tells us that there is no such thing as race. Yet, the belief that physical appearance denotes one's race seems so obvious that it is difficult for us to accept this conclusion. "The central intellectual challenge confronting those who recognize that races are not physical fact [is]: Why do we easily recognize races when walking down the street if there is no morphological basis to race? Why does race seem obvious if it is only a fiction?" (Haney López 1994:19). Not knowing the details of other people's lives, we search a person's physical features looking for the telltale "Negroid," "Caucasian," or "Mongoloid" features and proceed to assign them to racial categories on the basis of their most superficial traits—skin color, hair texture, hair color, cheekbone structure, eye color, eyelids, and so on (Piper 1992). Given the importance of the idea of race as a fixed, objective phenomenon which dominates most people's thinking—what anthropologist Ashley Montagu (1964) called the "most dangerous myth of our time, and one of the most tragic" (p. 23)—it is appropriate that we review the evidence discrediting the idea that race is a biological fact. In the reading "Biology and the Social Construction of the 'Race' Concept," by Prince Brown, Jr. we learn why most biologists and social scientists have come to agree that race cannot be a biological fact. Further, we see clearly the systematic and persistent refusal of those assigned the task of racial classification in the United States to consider genetic reality. This failure to consider genetic reality is not unique to the United States. In "Comparing Official Definitions of Race in Japan and the United States," David M. Potter and Paul Knepper (1996) show that no scientific or logical basis exists for determining and assigning "race." Both societies nevertheless have an official ideology of "race" upon which they base their assumptions and practices. The United States claims to be a nation of distinct "racial" groups, while Japan describes itself as "racially pure." In both societies, powerful groups define the categories and make policies and laws to support their views.

Ian F. Haney López cautions that even if race has no biological basis, we cannot call it an hallucination. *Biological race* is the illusion; *social race* is not. Haney López (1994) defines race in social terms as "a vast group of people loosely bound together by historically contingent, socially significant elements of their morphology and/or ancestry" (p. 7). In evaluating this definition, we must keep in mind that a race is not created simply because a subset of people share just any characteristic (height, hand size, eye color or ancestry). It is the social significance ascribed to certain physical features and to certain ancestors, such as Africans, Europeans, or Asians, which define races. In "Passing for White, Passing for Black," Adrian Piper (1992) states, "What joins me to other blacks, then, and other blacks to another, is not a set of shared physical characteristics, for there is none that all blacks share. Rather, it is the shared experience of being visually or cognitively *identified* as black by a white racist[10] society, and the punitive and damaging effects of that identification" (pp. 30–31). If those physical features we associate with a specific race are *absent* in a person who claims to be of that race, or if those physical features are present in a person who claims *not* to be of that race, we accuse him or her of being "underhanded or manipulative, trying to hide something, pretending to be something [they were not]" (Piper 1992:23).

Even the U.S. Office of Management and Budget (OMB), which sets racial and ethnic classification policy and standard in the United States, acknowledged the social significance of race in *Federal Statistical Policy Directive No. 15*. The directive states that a person's mixed race or ethnic background was to be reported in a standard category which most closely reflects how others in the community recognize that person (Hunt 1993).

In the reading "The Mean Streets of Social Race," Ian F. Haney López (1994) expands on the social significance of race through the case of Piri Thomas, a Puerto Rican of mixed Indian, African, and European descent, who finds himself transformed into a Black person upon moving to the United States with his family. Haney López argues that race is *not* a fixed, inherited attribute, free of human intervention—something parents pass on to their offspring through their genes. Rather, race is a product of at least three overlapping and inseparable factors: chance (physical features and ancestry), context (historical, cultural, and social setting), and choice (everyday decisions).

In view of the shortcomings associated with the U.S. system of racial classification and the fact that race is not a fixed, inherited attribute, we should not be surprised to learn that the U.S. Office of Management and Budget is under pressure to modify the classification scheme outlined in *Federal Statistical Policy Directive No. 15*. The OMB has summarized the suggestions for changes drawn from public hearings and from literature and research reviews. These suggestions are presented in the reading "What Should the Specific Data Collection and Presentation Categories Be?" For your reference, see the race question (and accompanying instructions) for the 1990 Census on page 2 in the Introduction.

Notes

[1] There was one exception to this rule. If either parent was Hawaiian, the child was assigned to the Hawaiian category (National Center for Health Statistics 1993).

[2] The experiences of Minty Nelson who is of black, white, and Native American ancestry represents one example of the census bureau's persistent efforts to classify respondents into one racial category. In a 1996 interview with a *Seattle Times* staff reporter, Nelson said she checked three racial categories on the census forms. Within a few weeks a census bureau representative knocked on her door to ask which racial category was correct.

"All three," Nelson replied.

Can't be all three, the middle-aged woman told her, just one.

Back and forth they went, their patience ebbing. The woman rolled her eyes, sighing in gusts; Nelson spoke in monotones. Twenty minutes later, drained from the experience, Nelson stopped. She told the woman to pick a box, any box, herself. (Strickland 1996)

[3] Before 1980, Asian Indians were considered white. Mexicans were considered a separate race in 1930 but in the 1940 Census were classified as white.

[4] A *mulatto* is a person with one white and one Negro parent or any person with mixed Caucasian and Negroid ancestry. A *quadroon* is a person with one-quarter Negro ancestry. An *octoroon* is a person with one white parent and one parent who is one-eighth Negro.

[5] The 1880 and 1890 Censuses gave the following instuctions for coding responses related to Native American identity.

> If this person is of full-blood of this tribe, enter "/."For mixture with another tribe, enter name of latter. For mixture with white, enter "W.;" with black, "B,;" with mulatto, "Mu."
>
> If this is a white person adopted into the tribe, enter "W.A.;" if a negro or mulatto, enter "B.A."
>
> If this person has been for any time habitually on the reservation, state the time in years or fractions.
>
> If this person wears citizen's dress, state the time in years or fractions since he or she has habitually so worn it.
>
> If other than native language is spoken by this person, enter for English, "E.;" Spanish, "S.;" French, "F.;" &c.

[6] The 1950 Census instructed enumerators to "report persons of mixed white, Negro, and Indian ancestry living in certain communities in the Eastern United States in terms of the name by which they are locally known. The communities in question are of long standing and are locally recognized by special names, such as 'Croatan,' 'Jackson White,' 'We-sort,' etc. Persons of mixed Indian and Negro ancestry and mulattoes not living in such communities should be returned as 'Negro'" (p. 99).

[7] Beginning in 1989, the National Center for Health Statistics (1993) changed the rules for classifying mixed-race newborns so that this possibility existed. Prior to 1989, the child was assigned the same race as the nonwhite parent. In 1989, the baby was assigned to the same racial category as the mother, which means the baby was declared "white" even if the father was not. According to NCHC statistics, the majority of mixed race births were to mothers classified as white.

[8] This scheme also ignores the "original" black indigenous inhabitants of Tasmania, Australia, the Philippines, and the Melanesian Islanders of the Pacific.

[9] An estimated 32.3 million "Chinese" live outside of China in places like Peru (500,000), Saudi Arabia (769,000), and the former USSR (274,000) (Poston, Mao, and Yu 1994).

[10] By "a white racist society," Piper means the established and customary ways of doing things in society—the unchallenged rules, policies, and day-to-day practices that result in the oppression of people classified as nonwhites. Clearly the system of racial classification is an example of unchallenged rules, policies, and practices.

"Indian" and "Black" as Radically Different Types of Categories

Jack D. Forbes

Study Question

1. Summarize Forbes' argument that the categories "Indian" and "Black" are treated as radically different.

One of the strange things about the Americas is that ethnic and racial categories are extremely arbitrary and are unevenly applied. The same North American white writer who might regard every person with some degree of African ancestry as being "black" will *not* see every part-American as an "Indian" (as "red"). Of the 20 to 30 million persons in the United States who probably have American ancestry, only 1 to 2 million are regarded as "Indians."

But one who seeks to comprehend must first confront these strange mysteries: how can Africans always remain African (or black) even when they speak Spanish or English and serve as cabinet secretaries in the United States government or as trumpet players in a Cuban *salsa* group; yet "Indians" seem to be reclassified as "mestizos" (or "hispanics," etc.) the moment they leave a traditional way of life, with very few exceptions.

In short, "blacks" are always "blacks" even when mixed with white or American Indian. "Indians," however, exist as a sort of *cultural* category (or as a caste). They must remain unchanged in order to be considered "Indian."

Perhaps, then, in contrasting the two categories (in a loose way at first), we must bear in mind that "real Indians" are seen not exclusively or even primarily as a racial or ethnic category but as something more fluid, subject to change as the way of life changes. I am reminded of a Dutch book on "The Last Indians" featuring pictures *only* of traditional South American people still living a way of life which is stereotypically "Indian." Not a single picture of soldiers, factory-workers, or cowboys is presented, as if "the last Indians" will disappear when they put on pants (if they do) and thereby become less "exotic."

Blacks, on the other hand, are not seen *only* as traditional villagers in Africa. No one would dare to write a book on "The Last Blacks," with pictures of "tribesmen" in ceremonial costumes. So the category of "black" has a different quality than has that of "Indian," or so it would seem.

Of course, many anthropologists and historians are more sophisticated than is the popular media and are aware that "Indians" can change and still be "Indians." But even they do not equate the category "Indian" with that of "black." A "black" person may be an isolated individual, integrated into a white context, and still be "black," but an integrated "Indian" (having lost his "tribe" and language) is seldom regarded as an "Indian." He will be considered a "Ladino," "cholo," "mestizo," "caboclo," "Mexican," "Chicano," or whatever, but seldom will he be seen as an "Indian."

And with the mixture of bloods the "Indian" disappears. He is "blanched" out, becoming "white," or is darkened, becoming "black," or he is placed in a "Half-breed," non-Indian category.

Now, of course, this latter statement must be qualified for the United States, since mixed-bloods are sometimes regarded as "Indians" there, but usually only if they meet the same cultural criteria as are applied to unmixed "Indians."

The results of all of this are rather startling. One is told, for example, that there are no "Indians" left in most of the Caribbean, an assertion which leaves one rather surprised when people from Puerto Rico, Cuba, or the Dominican Republic—of obvious American ancestry—are met with.

One is told that the Sandinistas of Nicaragua are opposing the Miskito "Indians," and yet one looks in vain for any sharp racial differences between most "Nicaraguans" and Miskitos. Why aren't the Nicaraguans also called "Indians?"

Reports state that only about 250,000 "Indians" (or fewer) are left in Brazil; yet, one also reads of tens of millions of people starving in the dry northeast who are supposed to have been of "Indian" blood a little while back; one even reads of the *Mamalucos* (mamelucos) of southern Brazil and wonders where they have all disappeared to, after being so important not so very long ago.

Argentina is a "white" country we are told, with no "Indians" (or just a few thousands); yet, there were plenty of brown people there in 1890 (and no one mentions the "cabecitas negras" in the working class of Buenos Aires).

One can go on and on: One meets people who look "Indian" or part-"Indian" but they come from places where there are no reported "Indians." The "blacks" never have that problem! White writers are *always finding* "blacks" (even if they look rather un-African), and they are *always losing* "Indians."

Of course, all of the above is an oversimplification because North American and British-Canadian usage is somewhat different from that found in Francophone, Spanish-speaking, and Brazilian areas. No doubt North American racism has so thoroughly distorted discourse that one should not expect "logic" to operate there. The obsession with "black-ness" *as a genetic evil,* a product largely of the post-Civil War period and the early 20th century (but also found in the Iberian empires to some degree) has created a peculiar situation. American ancestry, on the other hand, has been viewed more as a *social or cultural evil.*

The "Indian," in short, is culturally a "savage" (or a backward rustle), but his blood can be "purified" by mixture with whites. It might have taken one or two generations in some areas, or four generations in others, but ultimately the "stain" could be removed. But African ancestry, while treated similarly in some cases, gradually came to be seen as "irre-deemable" in significant parts of North America at least.

The various barriers to interracial marriage, et cetera, which reflect the above, have been partially discussed in my recent book. In general, they tended to become evermore restrictive (and genetic) with the passage of time, but remained less restrictive for white-Native American marriages (in general). Doubtless this partially reflects the fact that many Native Americans are generally closer in appearance to Europeans than are West Africans, and that very few persons of less than one-quarter American ancestry can be distinguished from Europeans. However, some half-West Africans can also appear to be "white," and many one-quarter and even more one-eighth West Africans can "pass" as Europeans. Thus, the phenotypes of mixed-bloods do not entirely explain the differential treatment.

········ ········

Historical Origins of the Prohibition of Multiracial Legal Identity in the States and the Nation

Study Question

1. Explain the following statement: "The system of racial classification in place today results not from the desire of multiracial persons to identify with [a] particular racial [group], but from statutory and case law developed over more than 200 years of legal history."

The United States recognizes no legal concept of multiraciality. Multiracial offspring are assigned to the race of the mother or father, depending on the state, or to the parent with the lower ascribed social status according to the rule of hypodescent. While some states, such as Hawaii, do not strictly enforce hypodescent, no state permits an adult to change an incorrect racial status recorded at birth.[1]

The federal government prohibits multiracial identity as well. The law requires that all federal agencies (as well as state agencies which must comply with federal record-keeping requirements) place persons in one of four racial categories: "American Indian/Alaskan Native," "Asian/Pacific Islander," "Black," or "White." Reporting agencies must assign "persons who are of mixed racial and/or ethnic origins" to a single category; multiracial persons may neither choose their racial group nor retain their mixed status.[2]

The legal prohibition of multiracial identity is curious, especially since, biologically or ethnologically, no pure races of humankind exist.[3] In fact, many Americans could claim to be of mixed ancestry. The majority of American Indians, virtually all Latinos, and significant portions of African and European Americans are descended from documentable multiracial genealogies.[4]

Why do the state and national governments prohibit persons of multiracial parentage from reporting their true racial identity? Federal reporting guidelines imply that official categories merely reflect prevailing social definitions, namely, that multiracial persons choose to identify with one racial community or the other. This explanation, however, ignores the role of government in imposing the ideology of discrete races. When Hawaii became the fiftieth state, the United States Census Bureau imposed mutually exclusive racial categories on a population that had until then used categories consistent with the islands' multiracial reality. When ten million Americans marked "Other" on the 1990 census schedule rather than check one of the four races supplied, the Census Bureau reclassified them as Hispanic.[5]

Racial categorization is more political than the government's explanation suggests. Throughout American legal history, the states and the federal government have tended to impose a broad definition of "black" and a correspondingly narrow definition of "white." Both have countered pressures toward blurring racial distinctions with a greater delineation of racial lines.

The ideology of distinct races and legal efforts to support it began during the colonial period. Early lawmakers imposed mutually exclusive categories of race to sustain the distinction between master and slave. The Maryland Colonial Assembly, for example, enacted legislation in 1664 to clarify the position of persons identified as "Negro." The "Act Concerning Negroes and Other Slaves" stipulated that "all Negroes or other slaves already within the province, and all Negroes or other slaves to be hereafter imported into the province, shall serve *durante vita.*" While Africans in North America had formerly shared with other servants opportunities for eventual freedom, the Maryland law marked them unilaterally for lives of slavery.[6]

Maintenance of the institution of slavery required legal prohibitions of miscegenation and, not surprisingly, of attempts to determine the status of mixed offspring. Virginia enacted the first statute prohibiting all forms of miscegenation in 1661, providing that any white man or woman who married a "negro, mulatto, or Indian . . . bond or free" was liable to permanent banishment from the colony. The other colonies borrowed language from Virginia and, by the mid-eighteenth century, six of the thirteen colonies had enacted anti-miscegenation statutes.[7]

Colonial statutes classified multiracial persons or "mulattoes" with their black progenitors. In a departure from the normal doctrine of English law that the status of a child was determined by the status of the child's father, Virginia's 1662 law provided that "children got by an Englishman upon a Negro woman shall be bond or free according to the condition of the mother." Had Virginia followed English precedent, thousands of half-whites would have been free. A 1664 Maryland law held that any English woman who married a slave would be a slave herself during the life of her husband. The law had the consequence of encouraging exactly the unions that it sought to prevent. It was rewritten in 1681 to provide that, when instigated by the master, "the woman and her issue shall be free."[8]

The policy of classifying mulattoes as black was enforced unevenly by state courts. Prior to the Civil War, several states accorded light-skinned mulattoes who possessed requisite wealth and education "white" legal standing. The Supreme Court of Ohio in 1831 extended to a "quadroon" woman the "privileges of whites" partly because the judges were "unwilling to extend the disabilities of the statute further than its letter requires" and "partly from the difficulty of . . . ascertaining the degree of duskiness which renders a person liable to such disabilities." South Carolina's Court of Appeals adopted a similar position in 1846. The court recognized a third class of "negroes, mulattoes, and mestizos" in addition to "freemen" and "slaves." It noted "the constant tendency of this class to assimilate into the white" and found that the "question of the reception of colored persons into the class of citizens must partake more of a political than a legal character and, in the great degree, be decided by public opinion, expressed in the verdict of a jury."[9]

Other state courts insisted on a narrow and exclusive definition of white. In *People v. Hall* (1854), the California Supreme Court defined the words "Black, Mulatto, Indian and White person." The appellant, George W. Hall, a white man, was convicted of murder upon the testimony of Chinese witnesses. He challenged his conviction on the basis of a state statute providing that "[n]o Indian or Negro shall be allowed to testify as a witness in any action in which a white person is a party." The court cited the ethnological thinking of the day to indicate that "Indian" was a generic term for an Asiatic stock of humankind that included Chinese. "We are not disposed to leave this question in any doubt," the court concluded. "The word 'white' has a distinct signification, which *ex vi termini,* excludes black, yellow, and all other colors . . . The term 'black person' is to be construed as including everyone who is not of white blood."[10]

It was during the Jim Crow era, when white supremacists enacted a bewildering variety of laws requiring separations in public life, that racial categories acquired their modern rigidity. The United States Supreme Court's decision in *Plessy v. Ferguson* (1896) provided the legal rationale for discrimination based on race. It also determined the definition of race to be used.[11]

The *Plessy* case arose after a group of multiracial persons in New Orleans organized the Citizen's Committee to Test the Constitutionality of the Separate Car Law. The statute, Louisiana's Railway Accommodations Act (1890), required railway companies to provide "equal but separate accommodations for the white and colored races" and made it a misdemeanor for the conductor to seat members of different races in the same compartment. Homer Plessy, who appeared to be white, agreed to initiate the test. He then attempted to halt his trial with a writ of prohibition and argued that he was "of mixed descent, in the proportion of seven-eighths Caucasian and one-eight African blood," that "the mixture of colored blood was not discernable in him," and that he was entitled to the legal status of white citizens.[12]

Justice Henry Billings Brown, writing for the majority, acknowledged "a difference of opinion" among the states regarding the proportion of colored blood needed to create a colored person. The Court decided that legal definitions of race properly belonged to state governments and sustained the Louisiana law by finding that "the power to assign to a particular coach obviously implies the power to determine to which race the passenger belongs." The Court sympathized with railway employees who were compelled to sort out racial groups based solely on their appearance. "We are not prepared to say," Justice Brown wrote, "that the conductor, in assigning passengers to the coaches according to their race, does not act at his peril."[13]

Confusion over racial identity and the legal challenges that it presented continued throughout the Jim Crow period.[14] Whites, having been mistaken for blacks, brought considerable litigation against railway carriers required to seat them in separate cars. An Arkansas court ruled that a white woman forced to ride fifteen minutes in the "colored" section of a train coach was entitled to recover damages. In fixing the amount of the award, the court noted the absence of noise or misbehavior in the coach; the fact that other whites were riding with the sole black passenger; and the woman's age, degree of refinement, and her fear, nervous shock, and humiliation. In a 1912 Kentucky case, a woman won a $3,750 award for her shock and anguish because a conductor pushed her into a "colored" car and insulted her. White plaintiffs brought suit on similar grounds in Texas and Virginia.[15]

State legislatures responded with more stringent definitions of "whiteness." In constitutions, separate school laws, anti-miscegenation statutes, and other discriminatory legislation, state lawmakers institutionalized the "one-drop rule." Tennessee's segregation statutes defined "person of color" as "[a]ll negroes, mulattoes, mestizos, and their descendants, having any blood of the African race in their veins." Arkansas' prohibition of cohabitation of persons of "the Caucasian and of the negro race" defined "person of negro race" as "any person who has in his or her veins any negro blood whatever." Virginia's anti-miscegenation law limited "white person . . . only to such person as has no trace whatever of any blood other than Caucasian." Alabama unilaterally declared "negro" to include "mulatto" and mulatto to mean "a person of mixed blood descended on the part of the father or mother from negro ancestors, without reference to or limit of time or number of generations removed."[16]

State courts approved these definitions. The Supreme Court of Mississippi in 1917 decided that "colored," as used in the state constitution to provide for separate schools, included "not only Negroes but persons of mixed blood having any appreciable amount of Negro blood." Louisiana's court of last resort invoked a similar definition in reference to segregated railway cars. In *Lee v. New Orleans Great Northern R. Co.* (1910), the court held that the plaintiff, who argued that his children had been unlawfully assigned to the coach for "colored persons," had the burden of proof to establish that his children were "of the white race." The court acknowledged that "persons of color" may have descended from Indian parents, from a white parent, or from mulatto parents, but ruled that under the statute "colored persons" meant "all persons with any appreciable mixture of negro blood."[17]

The United States Supreme Court also approved. In *Rice v. Gong Lum* (1927), the Supreme Court of Mississippi prohibited a child of Chinese descent from attending the white school in her district. The court defined "white and colored races" as the "pure white or Caucasian race, on the one hand, and the brown, yellow and black races, on the other." The Supreme Court affirmed the *Rice* case the same year. Quoting the findings of the state supreme court, the Court declared that "the legislature is not compelled to provide separate schools for each of the colored races." Accordingly, the state had the authority to use "colored" in a broad rather than a restrictive sense in its social policy in order to preserve the purity of the white race.[18]

The federal judiciary supported the states' elastic definition of race in its interpretation of federal statutes, particularly immigration law. During the early decades of the twentieth century, Congress enacted immigration laws designed to restrict immigration of "inferior races." The Immigration Act of 1917 excluded immigration from Asia and the Pacific Islands. Immigration laws enacted during the 1920s further restricted immigration from Asia and established quota systems to reduce immigration from Southern and Eastern Europe.[19]

When challenged, federal courts supplied a narrow and exclusive definition of white. "White person" has been construed to exclude Afghans, Arabs, American Indians, Chinese, Filipinos, Hawaiians, Asian Indians, Japanese, and Koreans.[20]

Justice George Sutherland made explicit the federal judiciary's race definition policy in 1922. In *Ozawa v. United States,* the Court included persons of Japanese descent in the category of persons defined as "aliens ineligible for citizenship." Takao Ozawa, who had been born in Japan but had lived in California for 20 years, was not a "free white person" within the meaning of naturalization law. Ozawa argued that state courts had defined white as not black and, therefore, that "free white person" did not exclude Japanese. Justice Sutherland rejected Ozawa's contention and argued that state and federal courts had historically limited "white person" to "what is popularly known as the Caucasian race." Sutherland explained Congress's rationale: "The intention was to confer the privilege of citizenship upon that class of persons whom the fathers [framers] knew as white and to deny it to all who could not be so classified . . . The provision is not that Negroes and Indians shall be *excluded* but it is, in effect, that only free white persons shall be *included.*" Although Justice Sutherland admitted that racial distinctions possess "no sharp line of demarcation," he held that Ozawa was "clearly of a race which is not Caucasian."[21]

The Court further narrowed its definition of white in *United States v. Bhagat Singh Thind.* In this case, Justice Sutherland found that, although Thind, "of high caste Hindu stock, born in Punjab," had been classified by "scientific authorities" as a member of the "Caucasian or Aryan race," he was not a "white person" entitled to naturalization under the law. The Court subjected Thind to a "racial test" not based on "scientific terminology" but upon "understanding of the common man." "It may be true that the blond Scandinavian and the brown Hindu have a common ancestor in the dim reaches of antiquity," Justice Sutherland wrote, "but the average man knows perfectly well that there are unmistakable and profound differences between them today."[22]

The system of racial classification in place today results not from the desire of multiracial persons to identify with particular racial groups, but from statutory and case law developed over more than two hundred years of legal history. No legal concept of multiraciality emerged in the United States owing to the legacy of slavery. Colonial legislatures attempted to fix discrete categories of black and white. Both the federal and state courts secured these distinctions during the era of "separate but equal." The judiciary has refused to recognize the multiple and overlapping ancestry of the American people, but it has consistently upheld efforts to separate black from white.

It would seem that to acknowledge the reality of multiraciality would expose official racial categories as fluid and elastic, not discrete, mutually exclusive divisions of humankind determined by biology or social interaction. The legal prohibition of multiracial identity developed because no system of oppression based on ancestry can operate in a social environment in which people recognize their multiple heritages.

Notes

[1] Kathy Russell, Midge Wilson, and Ronald Hall, *The Color Complex* (New York: Anchor Books, 1992), pp. 78–79.

[2] U.S. Department of Commerce, Office of Federal Statistical Policy, "Directive No. 15: Race and Ethnic Standards for Federal Statistics and Administrative Reporting," *Statistical Policy Handbook* (Washington, DC: Government Printing Office, 1978). "Hispanic" is represented as an ethnic category; it was created by Congress in 1976 (P.L. 94–311, 90 Stat. 688). Essentially, "Hispanic" subdivides the "white race" into ethnic groups of "Hispanic Origin" and "White, Not of Hispanic Origin."

[3] See, for example, UNESCO's "Statement on the Nature of Race and Race Differences," *The Race Concept* (Westport, CT: Greenwood Press, 1951).

[4] Maria P.P. Root, "Within, Between and Beyond Race," in Maria P.P. Root, ed., *Racially-Mixed People in America* (Newbury Park, CA: Sage, 1992), p. 9.

[5] Felicity Barringer, "Ethnic Pride Confounds the Census," *New York Times,* May 9, 1993, p. E3.

[6] Assembly Proceedings (Maryland), 28–29 Liber WH & L (1664).

[7] 2 Laws of Va. 114–15 Hening (1823). *See also* George M. Fredrickson, *White Supremacy* (New York: Oxford University Press, 1981), p. 94.

[8] 2 Laws of Va. 170 Hening (1823). *See also* A. Leon Higginbotham, Jr., *In the Matter of Color* (New York: Oxford University Press, 1978), pp. 43–44; Fredrickson, *White Supremacy,* p. 101.

[9] *Gray v. Ohio,* 4 Ohio 353 (1831); *White v. Tax Collector of Kershaw District,* 3 S.C. 136 (1846). *See also Jeffries v. Ankeny,* 11 Ohio 372 (1842). Biracial persons were socially accepted as white in certain parts of the South as well. Virginia R. Dominquez, *White by Social Definition* (New Brunswick, NJ: Rutgers University Press, 1986).

[10] *People v. Hall,* 4 Cal. 399, 404 (1854). The early "one-drop rule,"—any known African ancestry and one is classified as black—is discussed in F. James Davis, *Who is Black?* (University Park, PA: Pennsylvania State University Press, 1991), pp. 35, 49.

[11] The classic account of the Jim Crow period is C. Vann Woodward, *The Strange Career of Jim Crow* (New York: Oxford University Press, 1972).

[12] *Plessy v. Ferguson,* 163 U.S. 537, 538 (1896).

[13] *Id.* at 548–549.

[14] Derrick Bell, *Race, Racism and American Law* (Boston: Little, Brown, 1980), p. 84, n.3. Bell notes this confusion, and he cites the cases which follow.

[15] *Chicago R.I.&P. v. Allison,* 120 Ark. 54, 178 S.W. 401 (1915); *Louisville and N.R.R. Co. v. Richtel,* 148 Ky. 701, 147 S.W. 411 (1912); *Missouri K.&T. Ry v. Ball,* 25 Tex. Civ. App. 500, 61 S.W. 327 (1901); *Norfolk and W. Ry. v. Stone,* 111 Va. 730, 69 S.E. 927 (1911).

[16] 8396 Tennessee Code 417a1 (1942); Acts [Arkansas] No. 320, s. 3 (1911); Virginia Code 5099A (1924); Code of Alabama, Title 1, s. 2 (1927). Portions of these are reprinted in Pauli Murray, *States' Laws on Race and Color* (Cincinnati, Oh.: Women's Division of Christian Service, 1951).

[17] *Moreau v. Grandich,* 114 Miss. 560, 75 So. 434 (1917); *Lee v. New Orleans Great Northern R. Co.,* 125 La. 236, 51 So. 182 (1910). See also *State v. Treadway,* 126 La. 300, 52 So. 500 (1910).

[18] *Rice v. Gong Lum,* 139 Miss. 760, 104 So. 105 (1927); *Gong Lum v. Rice,* 275 U.S. 73 (1927).

[19] Immigration Act of 1917, 39 Stat. 874, 8 U.S.C. 173; Immigration Act of 1924, 43 Stat. 153, 8 U.S.C. 201.

[20] 613 C.J.S. s. 94 White (1989).

[21] *Ozawa v. United States,* 260 U.S. 178 (1922).

[22] *United States v. Bhagat Singh Thind,* 261 U.S. 404 (1922).

Biology and the Social Construction of the "Race" Concept

Prince Brown, Jr.

Study Questions

1. From a biological point of view, why is it impossible to classify people by race?
2. What are the shortcomings associated with using skin color, inherited diseases, or blood type as criterion for categorizing people into clear-cut racial categories?

Most people assume, with little or no thought, that when observing various human physical traits they are seeing different types of human beings fundamentally different in their genetic makeup. They further assume that it is possible to take each human being and put that person in one of the several allegedly distinct categories that have been presented to them as different "races." In the United States, it has long been maintained that everyone could be classified using only three categories. A brief review of the history of the biological effort to explain variation in human characteristics will help us to understand why it is not possible to classify people by "race" (Diamond 1994; DOA 1986:238; Gould 1994; Livingstone 1962:279).

Current scientific investigations using genetic research and fossilized remains indicate that all modern humans evolved in Africa and migrated from there to the rest of the world (Stringer & Andrews 1988). Modern humans (*Homo sapiens*) include all of the people in the world today. All humans, regardless of their physical features readily exchange genes when they produce offspring. The variations in human traits (phenotype), evident when we look at each other, are anatomical and physiological adaptations which help humans to increase their chances of survival and extend longevity in a particular environment.

Genetic elasticity is the tendency of human beings to exhibit a wide range of physical traits which they readily exchange with each other when they mate and produce children. No particular set of traits is limited to any one group or "race." And all groups are able to produce children with members of any other group. For example, while grey eyes are associated with a light complexion, they do occur among dark-complexioned people—as do brown eyes and black eyes. In the same vein, curly hair is associated with dark skin, but we all know light-complexioned people who also have curly hair. These common sense illustrations help us to understand that no particular set of traits cluster together to form one group or "race."

Some people share similar traits (homogeneity) because they live in social isolation, which limits the availability of potential mates. Another reason why some people share similar traits is because the social rules (customs, laws) of their society (ideas about beauty, laws against interracial marriage[1]) prohibit them from mating with people whose features are different (Bell 1992:71–74). Of course we know that many people ignore the rules. When they do, we label their children "mixed-race" (Root 1992; Zack 1995).

Other words we use to label such children are Mulatto (one black and one white parent), Quadroon (one black grandparent and three white grandparents), and Octoroon (one black great grandparent and 7 white great grandparents). The features of children born from these relationships will not mirror those of any one parent, grandparent, or great grandparent but will appear as a blend of all of them (genetic elasticity). In biology we call the results of this blending and merging *heterogeneity*. It results from population contact and the preference[2] of people to mate with each other regardless of what rules are in place in society.

If human beings could be grouped into absolute "racial" categories, the differences should be evident at the most basic biological level—that of chromosomes or genes. What would we see if humans could be grouped into absolute "racial" categories? We would have groups of people unable to have children with any other groups. Each member of any one of the groups would be an exact duplicate of all of the other members of that same group. That is, there would not be any differences between people in the same group. Instead, what we find is that 75 percent of genes are identical (monomorphic) in all individuals regardless of the population to which they are socially assigned. The remaining 25 percent are genes which appear in more (polymorphic) than one form (Lewontin et al. 1984). A single gene, for example, produces blood. But this gene can take more than one form as is evident in the four (A, B, O, AB) different types of blood.

It has been shown that ". . . there is no gene known that is 100 percent of one form in one race and 100 percent of a different form in some other race" (Lewontin et al. 1984:122). That is, there is no gene for "race." Differences between people assigned to the same social group/"race" may be greater (eye color among whites) than those between individuals in two different groups (Nei & Roychoudhury 1972). In other words, if the genetic traits (blood type, inherited diseases) of a person are determined from a blood analysis, a geneticist would still not be able to say what that person's actual physical features (phenotype) will be. Likewise, when observing physical features it is not always possible to predict genetic composition. For example, being able to see the physical features of a person does not allow one to say specifically what a genetic analysis of his blood will tell us. There is no known direct relationship between genetic makeup and physical features. This explains how two humans can produce a child with traits not visible in either of the parents.

Three sets of traits have been used to try to separate humans into absolute categories: (1) internal physiological features (metabolic rate, genetic diseases); (2) blood type; and (3) anatomical features (skin color, hair texture) (Marger 1991:20). None of these, however, can be shown to clearly distinguish any one group of people from any other.

Inherited diseases result from mutations[3] and may occur with a higher frequency in some groups than in others—but is not exclusive to those groups. This can be demonstrated by looking at two such mutations: lactase deficiency (inability to break down lactose) and sickle-cell trait and anemia (anti-malaria). Lactase deficiency may be present in up to 100 percent of South American Indians and West Africans, 32 percent of people from England, and 90 and 86 percent of Japanese and Greeks, respectively. The sickling trait[4] is present in up to 16 percent of South American Indians, up to 34 percent of West Africans, absent in English and Japanese, and up to 32 percent of Greeks (Stein & Rowe 1989:186). If this criterion were used to assign "racial" status, some Greeks, some West Africans, and a smaller proportion of South American Indians would be placed in the same category. The refrain, again, is that inherited diseases do not enable the prediction of assigned "racial" status except within limits. Nor does assigned "racial" status enable us to predict the presence of inherited diseases.[5]

Lewontin et al. (1984) have reviewed the research literature relative to the feasibility of categorizing humans into absolute groups by blood type. If we know a person's blood type (A, B, O, or AB), we could not predict what "racial" group that person was assigned. Conversely, we could not predict blood type from observed physical features. While the proportion of a particular blood type differs for various groups . . . "no population was [is] exclusive of one blood type" (Lewontin et al. 1984:120). And of course, blood transfusions between alleged different "races" occur in hospitals all over the world every day.

The third set of traits, anatomical features, likewise, cannot be used to assign individuals to an alleged "racial" category. A range of colors, for example, can be found in all three socially constructed "racial" categories. East Indians (light tan to very dark), Europeans (very pale to amber), and Australians (tan to very dark) are all assigned to the "Caucasian/white" category. Straight hair is a characteristic of all three groups, as are grey, black, and brown eyes. Of course, possessing any of these traits does not prevent having children with people who do not possess them. Therefore, the term "race mixing" makes no sense—since distinct biological categories do not exist to begin with. Before we go further, it might help us to understand the wide range of human traits if we review some information about why some specific traits evolved.

Anatomical traits such as skin color, height, and lung capacity are all features which help individuals and groups to master their environment. Physical diversity (skin color, height) insures the success of humans by making it possible for us to exist in all known environmental zones (high and low elevation, cold and hot zones, etc.). Large lungs at higher elevations enable greater oxygen intake and more sustained physical activity. One of the features most often regarded as indicative of "race," skin color, has a complex evolutionary history (Wills 1994) and serves several different functions. Dark skin protects people from cancer by screening out the ultraviolet rays of the sun. It is logical, therefore, that people living along the Equator would be so complexioned.

What might appear to be distinctive "racial" traits are, in most cases, explainable by science. However, to fully appreciate the complexity of human morphology it should be noted that this rule does not explain the case of South American Natives living on the Equator who are light complexioned. Geneticists point out that multiple genetic, as well as, environmental and cultural factors affect skin color (Stein & Rowe 1989:168).

This brief review of the biological bases for classification schemes indicates that "The popular division of the human population into three major racial groupings—Caucasoid, Mongoloid, and Negroid—is thus imprecise and largely arbitrary" (Marger 1991:21). "Racial" classification schemes cause people to be overly impressed with what can be seen (physical features) and to simplify that which is invisible (genes) and equally not well understood. Scientifically and socially, the slightest hint of a specific physical trait (i.e., colored equals Black/Negroid (Trillin 1986) is used to assign a "racial" label. If we construct a table of "races" using the three "arbitrary" categories traditionally employed by anthropologists, Caucasoid, Mongoloid, and Negroid, it can be shown that in reality "The biological category of 'race' is virtually meaningless" (Wali 1992:7).

Table 1   Genetic Elasticity/Biological Amalgamation

		FEMALE		
		M	C	N
	M	MM- - - - - - - - - -	MC	MN
MALE	C	CM	- - - - - - - - CC- - - - - -	CN
	N	NM	NC	- - - - - -NN

M = Mongoloid, C = Caucasoid, N = Negroid.

Each cell in Table 1 represents a hypothetical person that almost everyone knows. The people *not* on the left-to-right diagonal are called "mixed race" or "interracial" (amalgamation). This simple table is much more representative of reality than the classification schemes people are socialized to carry around in their heads. It is at the same time deceptive. It would appear on first glance that there are nine different combinations of persons represented. A second look reveals six distinct combinations; NM and MN, MC and CM, and CN and NC are the same combinations. MM, CC, and NN would appear to represent "pure races." What the table shows, however, is that each can produce offspring with all of the other persons as well each other. Thus what are assumed to be "pure races" do not function genetically as mutually exclusive categories. As the review of anatomical, blood composition, and inherited diseases data indicated, individuals are more alike than they are different. If every "race" can reproduce any other "race"—then, what is "race"?

Now imagine what possibilities would exist when offspring of those in Table 1 pair off with the partners shown in Table 2 and produce offspring. Table 2 illustrates what the results would look like. What appears to make perfect biological sense is that every human being is potentially the source of any trait that characterizes any other human being.

If the 81 persons from Table 2 are used to make yet another table, the number of "races" could expand exponentially. We normally do not think in terms of multiple biological ancestries. But this is more so the rule than the exception. In the United States alone there are millions of people who share European, African, and Native American ancestries (Forbes 1993; Trillin 1986).

The method for determining "race" has been changed constantly (Norwood & Klein 1989) and, of course, no objective resolution is possible (Wright 1994). Both "race" and color have been used as criterion to type the American population. Table 2 makes clear why the U.S. Bureau of the Census has avoided trying to define so-called "multiracial" people[6] (Wright 1994). And, why, in Brazil more than 64 "racial" categories are

Table 2 Genetic Elasticity/Biological Amalgamation

		PARTNERS								
		MM	MC	MN	CM	CC	CN	NM	NC	NN
OFFSPRING FROM TABLE 1	MM	MMMM	MMMC	MMMN	MMCM	MMCC	MMCN	MMNM	MMNC	MMNN
	MC	MCMM	MCMC	MCMN	MCCM	MCCC	MCCN	MCNM	MCNC	MCNN
	MN	MNMM	MNMC	MNMN	MNCM	MNCC	MCCN	MNNM	MNNC	MNNN
	CM	CMMM	CMMC	CMMN	CMCM	CMCC	CMCN	CMNM	CMNC	CMNN
	CC	CCMM	CCMC	CCMN	CCCM	CCCC	CCCN	CCNM	CCNC	CCNN
	CN	CNMM	CNMC	CNMN	CNCM	CNCC	CNCN	CNNM	CNNC	CNNN
	NM	NMMM	NMMC	NMMN	NMCM	NMCC	NMCN	CMCM	CMNC	CMNN
	NC	NCMM	NCMC	NCMN	NCCM	NCCC	NCCN	NCNM	NCNC	NCNN
	NN	NNMM	NNMC	NNMN	NNCM	NNCC	NNCN	NNNM	NNNC	NNNN

employed (Marger 1991). This is the sense in which "race" is a social/legal construction. It is a function of language, rather than using language to describe an objective reality.

Given the facts cited in this essay, definitions of "race," such as that offered by Joseph Healy: "Biologically, a race is an isolated, inbreeding population with a distinctive genetic heritage" (1995:22), are simply another failed attempt at biological classification. Few populations in the world, any more, are truly isolated. Secondly, in the United States individuals who are socially assigned to one alleged "racial" group intermingle, mate with, and have children with persons who are assigned to another group every day. Finally, the critical point here biologically is that there is not a single known case of an isolated group not being able produce children with other people when they did come into contact. And, in fact, in every known case this is exactly what has happened. All human beings share a single gene pool with no known breeding restrictions under normal circumstances (Healy 1995, Montagu 1972). In fact, in Mexico and Brazil, where interbreeding has occurred for more than five centuries, the governments make little or no effort to classify people by race.

The development of the "race" doctrine is a social and political process (Hannaford 1994) that tells more about the history of relations between people who thought/think of—and define—themselves as different than it tells about what can be known using and practicing science. The majority of physical scientists (Wheeler 1995) are acknowledging this fact and are abandoning the term.

References

Bell, Derrick. 1992. *Race, Racism and American Law.* Boston: Little, Brown.

Diamond, Jared. 1994. Race Without Color. *Discover:* 82–89.

DOA (Dictionary of Anthropology). 1986. Boston: G.K. Hall.

Forbes, Jack D. 1993. *Africans and Native Americans.* Chicago: University of Illinois Press.

Gould, Stephen Jay 1994. "The Geometer of Race." *Discover* (November): 64–69.

Hannaford, Ivan. 1994. "The Idiocy of Race." *The Wilson Quarterly* (Spring): 8–35.

Healy, Joseph F. 1995. *Race, Ethnicity, Gender, and Class.* Thousand Oaks, CA: Pine Forge Press.

Lewontin, R.C., S.P. Rose, and L.J. Kamin. 1984. *Not in Our Genes.* New York: Pantheon.

Livingstone, Frank B. 1962. "On the Non-Existence of Human Races." *Current Anthropology* 3(3): 279.

Marger, Martin. 1991. *Race and Ethnic Relations: American and Global Perspectives.* Belmont, CA: Wadsworth.

Montagu, Ashley. 1972. *Statement On Race.* London: Oxford University Press.

Nei, Masatoshi and Arun K. Roychoudhury. 1972. "Gene Differences Between Caucasian, Negro, and Japanese Populations." *Science* 177: 434–35.

Norwood, Janet L. and Deborah P. Klein. 1989. "Developing Statistics to Meet Society's Needs." *Monthly Labor Review* (October): 14–19.

Root, Maria P. P., editor. 1992. *Racially Mixed People in America.* London: Sage.

Stein, Phillip L. and Bruce M. Rowe. 1989. *Physical Anthropology.* New York: McGraw-Hill.

Stringer, C.B. and P. Andrews. 1988. "Genetic and Fossil Evidence for the Origin of Modern Humans." *Science* 239: 1263–68.

Trillin, Calvin. 1986. "American Chronicles: Black or White." *The New Yorker* (April): 62–78.

Wali, Alaka. 1992. "Multiculturalism: An Anthropological Perspective." *Report from the Institute for Philosophy & Public Policy* 12(1): 6–8.

Wills, Christopher. 1994. "the skin we'in." *Discover:* 76–81.

Wright, Lawrence. 1994. "One Drop of Blood." *The New Yorker* (July 25): 46–55.

Wheeler, David L. 1995. "A Growing Number of Scientists Reject the Concept of Race." *The Chronicle of Higher Education* (February 17): A8–A9, A15.

Zack, Naomi. 1995. *American Mixed Race.* Lanham, MD: Rowman & Littlefield.

Notes

[1] Interracial marriages were illegal in some states in the U.S. until 1967. In 1967, in *Loving v. Virginia* (388 U.S.1) the Supreme Court finally declared such states' laws unconstitutional.

[2] Social preferences (in this context) are learned, and oftentimes legally enforced, conventions societies use when choosing intimate partners and making mate selections.

[3] *Webster's New World Dictionary* (1989) defines *mutation* as "a sudden variation in some inheritable characteristic in a germ cell of an individual animal or plant, as distinguished from a variation resulting from generations of gradual change."

[4] A disorder in individuals in which red blood cells will develop into a sickle shape which, in turn, will clog capillaries, resulting in anemia, heart failure, etc.

[5] Scientists know that some traits are determined by the environment. They do not always fully know the exact mechanism that is at work to produce the changes, however. *See* Stein & Rowe (1989:50–53).

[6] On the few occasions when such an attempt was made, it proved highly unsatisfactory and the rules for assigning "race" were constantly changed. Increasingly, however, persons who self-identify as "multiracial" are demanding that a category be created for them.

COMPARING OFFICIAL DEFINITIONS OF RACE IN JAPAN AND THE UNITED STATES

DAVID M. POTTER AND PAUL KNEPPER

Study Questions

1. How does the Japanese government "manipulate" data on its population to make it appear more monoracial than it is? Give examples.
2. How does the U.S. "manipulate" data on its population to make it appear as if people fit into clear racial categories? Give examples.
3. How is racial classification in each country used to marginalize some groups of people?

Official categories of race are powerful determinants of racial identity. The race that appears on people's birth certificates follows them throughout their lives and determines which box they check on government forms. To be "white" or "black" or "Asian/Pacific Islander," is to be a member of a racial group. Where do the official categories come from? Why does the government classify people by race anyway?

Comparing two nations' official racial classification policies will provide an answer. At first glance, Japan's and the United States' racial classification policies could not be more different. Japan insists on a monoracial ideology and so defines away those who do not fit. The United States divides its citizens into distinct categories according to its notion of a multiracial society. Yet a closer look reveals profound similarity. In both nations, the official policies work to the advantage of the majority and to the disadvantage of ethnic minorities. Although the two governments espouse different national ideologies concerning the concept of race, in both societies the impact is the same: the official definition of race strengthens the majority "race" and marginalizes ethnic populations. Further, we would argue that race is not a biological or social concept, but a political concept, which rests on the power of government to enforce and maintain it.

Specifically, we compare Japan and the United States on several aspects of racial definition. We begin with a look at *official ideologies* of race. Then, we look at the *elasticity* of official definitions—the way in which they are shaped by government for political purposes. Finally, we explore the creation of *racial identity* based on official classification. By examining these two nations' policies more closely, it becomes evident that both use similar processes of racial classification to achieve the same result. Both governments enforce policies of racial definition that shape racial identity.

Scientists' Views of Race

Before comparing official views of race in the United States and Japan, it is useful to examine the scientific definition of race, or rather, the absence of one. There is no scientific definition of race, only scientists' views of race. Although certain biologists, anthropologists, geneticists and zoologists and other scientists have devised various classification schemes for racial groups, there is no scientific way to divide human beings into discrete, mutually exclusive categories. As geneticist J.C. King explains, attempts to do so are arbitrary because, unlike the case for species, there are no objective boundaries for defining subspecies. Racial categories are "determined by the cultural practices of the classifiers, even," King adds, "sophisticated scientific classifiers".[1]

In the years immediately following the holocaust of European Jewish people, UNESCO sought to resolve some of the misunderstanding surrounding the idea of race and commissioned an international group of geneticists and physical anthropologists to give an exact meaning for the term. After much discussion, the conferees concluded that while some populations could be identified on the basis of nasal index, skin color, hair type, and so on, many others could not. They concluded that all members of the human species shared the same origin and that no "pure races" of humankind existed. The "races of mankind" amounted to statistically distinguishable groups only, since some biological differences within these groups were greater than those between groups. Skin color could not be used to identify racial groups, nor could geographical, linguistic, or cultural differences. Use of these criteria had resulted in harmful political and social consequences.[2]

Some members of the UNESCO conference, including Princeton anthropologist M. F. Ashley Montagu, recommended that the term "race" be abandoned altogether.[3] Accordingly, physical anthropologists have removed the concept entirely from their textbooks. In one current survey only two of twenty-two introductory physical anthropology textbooks used it to classify humans.[4] Some more recent approaches continue to make use of genes and geography to define statistically distinguishable groups or "breeding populations." However, breeding patterns between people change over time and they depend on the use of geographic boundaries, which are inherently arbitrary. "The extension of the concept of *race* to all magnitudes of populations, based on the concept of breeding," University of Toronto biologist Michael Levin concludes, "can be seen in retrospect as an attempt to preserve the concept by making it a synonym for population."[5]

From a scientific standpoint then, race is a meaningless concept. Despite popular thinking in North America about the white, black, red, and yellow races, these have no biological or anthropological validity. Nevertheless, the world's governments continue to identify people by race. Through official recognition of race in the USA, and through denial of ethnic differences in Japan, governments reinforce ideologies of race.

Official Ideologies of Race

The official ideologies of race in these two countries could not be more different. The United States government insists that its society consists of distinct races, while Japan sees itself as an ethnically pure society. The United States government divides persons into distinct categories, while the Japanese government defines society as monoracial.

In Japan, there is one official racial group, Japanese. The Japanese are noted for a strong sense of social and ethnic identity that does not permit assimilation by members of groups defined as non-Japanese. The sense of exclusiveness can be found throughout Japanese society, and it is argued by Japanese intellectuals as well. The idea that Japan is a monoracial society, that is has no problems with ethnic minorities because it has none, is frequently stated by political leaders who perceive the nation's ethnic homogeneity as a pillar of social stability. Most observers argue that the Japanese sense of exclusiveness is the product of social and cultural norms. Emiko Ohnuki-Tierney, for example, relates the marginalization of *burakumin* (outcast Japanese), despite formal emancipation, to social stratification and perceptions of insider-outsider status.[6] Foreigners are held to be "different" and therefore incapable of truly entering Japanese society for reasons that may have no objective behavioral basis.[7] One author links the persistence of discrimination to the failure to abolish the imperial system after World War II.[8] Michael Weiner argues that racial conceptions of Japaneseness underpinned the colonial relationship between Japan and Korea in the prewar period, but his essentially sociological approach does not distinguish state policy from private actions.[9] Wagatsuma and Yoneyama almost completely avoid the issue of racial discrimination domestically by dealing with Japanese attitudes toward whiteness and blackness.[10]

Despite official ideology, Japan does have ethnic minorities. The Ainu of Hokkaido are "culturally, linguistically and biologically" different from majority Japanese. Estimates of their numbers range from 20,000 to 300,000.[11] Resident Koreans and Chinese number about 700,000. Legal foreign workers are estimated at about 250,000; unofficial estimates increase this figure.[12] Some observers argue that Okinawans constitute an ethnic minority as well. Stephen Reed observes that the prewar Japanese empire was multiracial and that homogeneity today is simply the result of the loss of its colonial possessions in World War II.[13]

The Japanese government enforces its monoracial ideology by refusing to recognize ethnic minorities. Official statistics reinforce the notion that these groups do not exist in Japanese society by simply overlooking them. The census contains no data on racial or ethnic minorities. The number of resident Koreans and Chinese cannot be found in census publications, nor can the number of Ainu. *Burakumin* are similarly invisible. The national government has kept no official records on the number of Ainu in the postwar era. There is a separate category of "foreigners' vital statistics" which may include data on resident Koreans and Chinese, but there is no way from the census itself to test this. Similarly, annual crime statistics are not broken down by ethnic group, although crimes committed by foreigners list the numbers of offenders by nationality. Prison data show the prisoner's nationality, but not race.[14]

Koseki, family registers that function much as birth certificates do in the United States, do not include racial data either. Although the *koseki* do not list race or ethnic status, they operate as the primary instrument of defining Japanese nationality. As such, they serve as the official ethnic divider between Japanese (including Ainu and Okinawans, because they cannot be defined as "non-citizens") and other Asians, such as resident Koreans and Chinese. The *koseki* reifies the Japanese government's policy of exclusiveness because that government subscribes to the doctrine of *ius sanguinis:* nationality is acquired and passed by blood rather than by place of birth. The principle of *ius sanguinis* becomes operational through registration in *koseki.* Until recently, persons registered in *koseki* were Japanese, those not so registered were not. Because it is difficult to acquiring citizenship in Japan—the government has a clearly stated policy that it is not an immigrant nation—large numbers of non-Japanese are prevented from altering its population mix.

The government further promotes the notion of homogeneity by maintaining a policy of assimilation in which full membership in the Japanese polity comes as a tradeoff to the abandonment on one's native identity. In the case of the Ainu, this has meant legal proscription of that people's customs, religion, language, and economic practices. Ainu have been encouraged to marry majority Japanese and, as one Japanese legislator put it, to "self-awaken" to their Japanese identity.[15] For resident Koreans assimilation has meant naturalization, including the abandonment of non-Japanese names, customs, and identity. In some cases it has been averred that government inspectors have repeatedly visited applicants' homes to determine whether they live according to "Japanese" practice.[16]

Assimilation is reinforced by other government practices. The national government, for example, has no "minorities policy." The Ainu, who as a population live well below the national economic average, do not receive special assistance apart from the national welfare program. Rather, the government simply maintains a series of *ad hoc* policies toward various minority groups[17] that at once gives the lie to claims of a monoracial society yet refuses to recognize that reality. Moreover, because officially there are no minorities in Japan there is no need to ensure their representation in the government. As one scholar has pointed out, "no efforts are made to recruit minorities into the bureaucracy."[18]

The Japanese government's racial policy has been inconsistent—over time, across different agencies—in defining people as Japanese or not. Until the nineteenth century, the Ainu were not members of the Japanese polity. During the Tokugawa period (1600–1868), the military government in Edo and its vassals in northern Japan did not control the territory of Hokkaido; in fact, few majority Japanese resided on the northern island. As part of the process of assuming political control over the territory, the new Meiji government in the 1870s granted the Ainu citizenship with commoner status.[19] In so doing, the government introduced a racial minority into the Japanese polity and, therefore, the possibility of a "minority problem." Moreover, until the 1930s, the government maintained separate schools for Ainu despite its official policy of assimilation,[20] reinforcing that group's minority status.

The requirement for naturalization have shifted as well. Until 1986, Japanese nationality could be passed only through the paternal line. Children born to a Japanese mother and a non-Japanese father were automatically considered citizens of the father's country. Japanese women who married foreign men lost their citizenship and therefore their legal identity as Japanese. But the change that year allowed children of international marriages to obtain Japanese citizenship and permitted Japanese women to retain their citizenship even if they married non-Japanese men.

An excellent example of the flexibility of defining Japaneseness can be seen in the case of immigration. Despite an official policy that the country is not a final destination for refugees, Japan has witnessed a growing foreign population in recent years. In particular, the number of people seeking work in Japan has increased since the mid-1980s in the face of a labor shortage in that country. Most foreign workers are un-skilled or low-skilled, and many are willing to overstay their visas to se-cure work in positions most Japanese will no longer accept. Faced with the prospect of a permanent non-Japanese underclass in its midst, the government has sought alternately to stem and control the flow of work-ers into Japan. As part of the latter strategy, in 1989 it granted special res-idency status to *Nikkeijin,* descendants of Japanese emigrants, mostly from Peru and Brazil. That status is based in no small part on the as-sumption that these people will be able to assimilate into Japanese soci-ety more easily than other foreigners.[21] Whatever their actual cultural and linguistic backgrounds, the putative Japaneseness of *Nikkeijin* ren-ders them politically acceptable to a government concerned with its soci-ety's racial composition.

While the national government refuses to recognize the multiethnic character of its population, some local governments find themselves deal-ing with substantial groups of non-majority Japanese. The Hokkaido pre-fectural government keeps official statistics on the Ainu population be-cause of that group's concentration in that region.[22] In 1994 it opened the Hokkaido Ainu Culture Research Center with the mission of better under-standing the history of that officially overlooked people.[23] Local govern-ments have tended to recognize Ainu and in some cases have taken official measures to provide them the rights and benefits enjoyed by majority Japanese. The Osaka City and Nagano prefectural governments, within whose environs large Korean communities reside, has hired resident Kore-ans as public school teachers despite Ministry of Education proscription on full-time employment by non-citizens.

Racial Policy in the United States

Officially, four races of people live in the United States. There are the "white," "black," "American Indian or Alaskan Native," and "Asian or Pacific Islander" races.[24] "Hispanic" is officially defined as an "ethnic group." These categories were established by the Office of Federal Statisti-cal Policy and Standards, of the U.S. Department of Commerce, which is-sued Directive No. 15, known as "Race and Ethnic Standards for Federal

Statistics in Administrative Reporting," in 1977. All federal data-collection agencies, as well as all state agencies which must comply with federal record-keeping requirements, use these categories.[25]

These four categories coincide with popular thinking that people can be divided into four races: white, black, red, and yellow. They also represent the official ideology of race, and of discrete races. The government insists on dividing people into discrete groups despite the fact that people are multiracial. The majority of American Indians, virtually all Latinos, and significant portions of African and European Americans are descended from documentable multiracial populations.[26] Between seventy-five and ninety per-cent of those who check the "black" box on government forms, for instance, could check a "multiracial" box if available.[27]

The federal government has for years resisted recognition of Americans' multiracial reality. No "multiracial" box is available on government forms, not because nobody identifies as multiracial, but because the federal government insists that all persons must fit into one of the categories. When Hawaii became the fiftieth state, the U.S. Census Bureau imposed mutually exclusive categories on a population that had, until then, used categories consistent with the islands' multiethnic reality. When ten million Americans marked "other" on the 1990 census form rather than check one of the four official races supplied, the Census Bureau simply reclassified them. Most became "hispanic."[28] Officially, the *Statistical Policy Manual* stipulates that persons who claim "mixed racial and/or ethnic origins" be placed in "the category which most closely reflects the individual's recognition in his community."[29]

The four official categories of race in the United States are rather arbitrary. Practically speaking, a person's race is, officially, a matter of what appears on the birth certificate. One of the more outrageous examples is the case of three brothers from Dulac, Louisiana. All three were Houma Indians, of the same mother and father, with the same name. All three received their racial classification from medical people who assisted with their birth. The oldest brother, born at home without a doctor, was classified as negro because the state of Louisiana did not recognize Houma Indians before 1950. The second brother, born in a local hospital after 1950, received the designation Houma Indian. The third brother, born in a New Orleans hospital eighty miles away, received the white classification based on the family's French surname.[30]

Official classifications change over time. Consider, for example, the classification of Latinos. Protests by the Mexican government in the 1930s forced the U.S. Census Bureau to reclassify Mexicans as white for the 1940 census.[31] The Federal Bureau of Investigation in its *Uniform Crime Reports,* the nation's official crime statistics, listed Mexicans as a separate race in reporting crime figures until 1942, when they too reclassified Mexicans as white.[32] Mexican-Americans remained a part of the white racial category until 1980, when they were reclassified as "hispanic."[33]

State definitions of a nominally objective reality create interest groups based on race. In 1993, the House Committee on Census, Statistics and Postal Personnel concluded hearings on the racial categories to be used in the 2000 census. Various groups argued that the present racial classification was incorrect and needed to be changed. Senator Daniel K. Akaka of Hawaii, for example, argued that Native Hawaiians belonged in the American Indian category rather than the Asian category. The Arab American Institute asked that persons from the Middle East, now classified as white, be recognized with a separate category for Arabic peoples. The National Council of La Raza suggested that "hispanic" be classified as a race rather than an ethnic group. Significantly, representatives of various parts of the "hispanic" population offered different methods for classifying such people. The whole idea of changing the categories upsets the notion of fixed races, and it "raises the larger question of whether it is proper for the government to classify people according to arbitrary distinctions of skin color and ancestry."[34]

Elasticity of Definition

Official constructions of race are fluid and elastic, but not unsystematic. Governments alter and reformulate categories, but not at random. Racial definitions are always stretched a particular way. In both cases examined here, the category defining the dominant ethnic group is narrow and exclusive while the category defining the ethnic minority is broad and inclusive.

The issue of citizenship clearly shows the exclusiveness of Japanese racial ideology. Use of *koseki* to divide "Japanese" from "non-Japanese" has existed since the prewar period. As Japan added Taiwan and Korea to its empire, it introduced family registry systems for each, separate from the Japanese *koseki*. Korea presented a special problem for maintaining Japaneseness because it was treated as an integral part of Japan from its annexation in 1910. Indeed, where exactly colonial subjects fit into the racial hierarchy of the empire was a matter of considerable debate and elaboration by intellectual theorists and government officials alike.[35] Provisions allowing for transfer of individuals to the Japanese *koseki* through marriage and adoption, and hence into Japanese citizenship, were restricted in the case of Korea and therefore limited the ability of Koreans to acquire actual Japanese citizenship.[36]

Since the Occupation period, Koreans and Chinese who reside in Japan have been classified as resident foreigners. As early as 1948, the Census Bureau was determining who among formerly imperial citizens were to be Taiwanese and Korean citizens.[37] In April 1952, a Ministry of Justice circular declared that under the provisions of the 1951 San Francisco Peace Treaty, about to take effect, all Taiwanese and Koreans would lose their imperial citizenship. The circular took a typically narrow view of naturalization; foreigners who would have been registered in a Japanese *koseki* before the peace treaty took effect would retain their citizenship, while anyone registered after it took effect would not.[38] Because of the distinction between "Japanese" and "imperial" *koseki,* the effect was to remove a claim to Japanese citizenship from all former non-Japanese imperial subjects even if they lived in Japan. Subsequent court decisions have upheld this policy.[39]

That circular has been the basis of the Japanese government's policy toward Koreans ever since. In particular, it has served as the precedent for excluding the majority of resident aliens from citizenship and therefore full membership in Japanese society. The peace treaty between Japan and South Korea signed in 1965 provided for several categories of resident Koreans in Japan, but did nothing to alter the fundamental principle that members of that group would remain separate from Japanese society. Indeed, the Japanese government has avoided any action that might create a precedent for naturalizing any category of resident Koreans *en masse.* This includes second and third generation residents, most of whom were born in Japan. The government prefers to deal with resident aliens' applications for citizenship on a case-by-case basis. In practice, this means that individuals must file, or sue, for citizenship as individuals. In one recent case of two children born out of wedlock to a non-Japanese woman and a Japanese man, one child is officially Japanese and the other not simply because the father registered one at the ward office but not the other.[40] This allows governmental authorities maximum flexibility in deciding cases and, moreover, prevents any judicial or administrative decision to grant citizenship from establishing precedents for future cases. As a result, only about one-fifth of the Korean population has acquired citizenship.[41] The insistence on the outsider status of Koreans is well illustrated by the fact that the Japanese government formally has dealt with an ethnic problem by claiming it is a foreign policy issue with the government of South Korea, nominally the state of origin of that minority.

Implementors of state policy, including the police, deal with members of minority groups differently than majority Japanese. The special security police include "race" (*jinshu*) as one of forty-eight questions they ask of individuals under investigation.[42] In one port city, the security branch of the prefectural police, rather than the regular police force, had jurisdiction over resident Koreans, foreign sailors, and the local *burakumin*. Despite laws and regulations to the contrary, the police displayed discriminatory attitudes concerning the acceptability of recruiting police from other minority communities. Police relations with the Korean community were more hostile than with majority Japanese.[43]

The whole enterprise of classifying individuals by race on public documents would seem to be out-of-place in the United States, a society which professes to be colorblind. The very act of classifying individuals by race violates the "equal protection clause" of the fourteenth amendment to the U.S. constitution.[44] Or, as the Supreme Court put it in *Anderson v. Martin* (1964), a case concerning a Louisiana statute requiring that ballots designate the race of candidates for political office, there is a "vice" in "placing the power of the state behind a racial classification that induces racial prejudice at the polls." Racial categorization operated as a vice because "by directing the citizen's attention to the single consideration of race or color, the state indicates that a candidate's race or color is important—perhaps paramount—in the citizen's choice."[45]

Historically, the American judiciary has pursued a broad and inclusive definition of blackness. Persons who identified themselves as more white than black in ancestry, appearance, or both, have been generally classified as black in court. Some states placed the proportion of African blood necessary for membership in the black race at one-fourth, others one-eighth. Still others have defined "negro" as a person with "any visible mixture." Ohio's Supreme Court, for example, put the issue this way: "In affixing 'colored', we do not ordinarily stop to estimate the precise shade, whether light or dark, though where precision is desired they are sometimes called 'light-colored' or 'dark-colored'. There is no margin between white and colored, and all that are non-white are colored."[46]

As a means of enforcing this definition, courts have shifted the criteria on which racial definitions are based. In defining white, courts have relied on a geographic conception of race. "White person" means "primarily the European peoples," more specifically "migrants from the British Isles and Northwestern Europe . . . and later migrants from Eastern, Southern and Middle Europe." While courts have invoked the pseudo-scientific concept of "Caucasian" it is noteworthy that this term is itself derived from geography. On the other hand, black is defined using physical features. One court specified that "negro" is defined as a "black man, especially one of the race who inhabit tropical Africa, and who are distinguished by crisped or curly hair, flat noses and protruding lips."[47]

Shifting the criteria, using physical appearance rather than geographical origin, has allowed the definition of black to be broadly conceived. Persons of mixed African and European ancestry are classified as black, not white, according the "one drop rule": a person with any trace of African ancestry is classified as black. Persons who were born in Europe, but "appear" black, are classified as black according to their appearance, not according to place of origin. When delineating the black race, the judiciary has used a broad brush; when describing the white race, the court has used a very fine one.

The Politics of Racial Identity

What determines a person's racial identity? In the United States, legal race identity is determined by what is written on the birth certificate. In Japan, the *koseki* does much the same thing. Race is less obvious in Japan because of the presumption that that society has only one ethnic identity. One is either Japanese or a foreigner. That an Ainu is physically distinct from a majority Japanese is not an issue because most Japanese simply ignore the presence of that group within their society. As one government official put it at a United Nations conference on indigenous peoples, the Ainu are not a minority because they are not treated as such.[48] Official ideology overlooks reality's messiness. Interestingly, like its American counterpart, the Japanese government does not accept mixed race as an official category. *Konketsu,* or mixed blood, is a term used popularly to refer to the children of international or Korean-Japanese marriages, but it has no official meaning. One is Japanese or not for government purposes, depending on whether and how one is registered on a *koseki.*

Race is a significant tool for marginalizing populations. Residents in Japan to whom the family registration law does not apply, for example, may not vote or run for office in public elections, nor may they hold public sector jobs or pursue careers in the law.[49] Until 1982, Koreans could not be employed as university professors. Their ownership of certain economic resources is also restricted.[50] At the same time, however, such residents are subject to the same tax burden as citizens. The designation of "foreigner," moreover, lumps dissimilar populations together. Police crime statistics also show high arrest rates for Korean and Chinese "foreigners."[51] The designation "foreigner" implies that the higher crime rates among these populations are attributable to the activities of Japanese-born Koreans and Chinese rather than to recent immigrants or transitory crime rings. In fact, it obliterates any distinction between these minorities in Japan whose ancestors were denied the possibility of naturalization during the Occupation or by people of the same ethnic or national groups who normally reside abroad. By being classified as foreigners, they may be tainted by the perceptions of increasing crime among "foreigners" in recent years. This designation and its association with deviant behavior is especially invidious when it become clear that the most common crime among "foreigners" is violation of visa and residency restrictions.

The Hitachi case of 1971 exemplifies the use of state definition as a tool of discrimination. The case involved a resident Korean who had applied for a position with the Hitachi Corporation. He had the appropriate level of education, had passed the company entrance examination at the top of the pool of applicants, and had been hired. Because he had not listed his *koseki* identity, the fact of his ancestry did not become known to company officials until he had been employed. When company officials found out his identity, however, the company fired him. He sued for breach of contract and won in 1974. The incident has been discussed as an example of the employment discrimination resident foreigners face,[52] yet it is important to understand that the fact of his ancestry registered in his *koseki* provided the mark that identified him as foreign and therefore "unemployable" by the company.

Despite what many Americans believe, the United States government claims no biological or anthropological basis for its system of racial categories. The *Statistical Policy Manual* specifically states that the racial and ethnic categories "should not be interpreted as being scientific in nature."[53] Rather, the government insists, the categories merely reflect prevailing social definitions. Nampeo McKenney, chief of racial and ethnic statistics at the Census Bureau, explains that the categories depend on "social identity, what's commonly accepted by the public. Not science."[54]

The claim that official categories merely reflect social definitions denies the role of the American government in creating and enforcing definitions. It was the government, after all, that *created* racial categories in the first place. As historian Lerone Bennett explains, "the first white colonists had no concept of themselves as *white* men." White men are identified on legal documents from the period as Englishmen or Christians. The word "white" did not come into usage until later in the seventeenth century.[55] "Blacks and whites had to be taught the meaning of blackness and whiteness."[56] People had to be taught to sustain the system of slavery, which was based on distinctions between master and slave, between white and black.

As Susan Guillory Phipps discovered in 1983, the legal definitions of race established during the antebellum period remain. Phipps, who thought she was white, lived as white, and twice married as white, had been denied a passport because she checked white on her application when her birth certificate showed the race of both of her parents as "colored." She sued the State of Louisiana to change her parents birth certificates to white so that she and her brothers and sisters—some of whom were blue-eyed blondes—could be designated white. In district court, counsel for the state claimed to have proof that she was three thirty-seconds black because her great-great-great-great grandmother had been. Because the Louisiana legislature had defined a black person as any person whose ancestry was greater than one thirty-second black, Phipps' "trace of ancestry" was enough for the court to declare her legally black.[57]

Phipps used her socially-defined white racial status to challenge her black legal status, and the court ruled that she and her children would remain black. Although publicity surrounding the case led the legislature to give parents the right to designate the race of their children, the "traceable amount rule" and its judicial precedent remain. Louisiana's Fourth Circuit Court of Appeals affirmed the district court's decision on the grounds that the fact "that appellants might today describe themselves as white does not prove error in a document which designates their parents as colored."[58] Both the Louisiana Supreme Court and the U.S. Supreme Court have declined to review the decision. The nation's highest court refused to disturb the slavery-based system of racial classification "for want of a substantial federal question."[59]

Conclusion

Each nation examined here espouses different assumptions about the racial character of its national identity. In each, the state maintains an official racial ideology that reinforces these assumptions. Japan sees itself as racially pure while the United States subscribes to the idea of a nation peopled with distinct racial groups. In this paper, we do not argue that state policies in each case are identical. For example, the federal structure of the American political system allows state governments to define racial identities independently of the national government in ways that the Japanese government's unitary structure does not. The Phipps case provides an excellent example of the ability of the Louisiana legislature to define blackness down to a specific percentage of ancestry regardless of federal or other state policy. In Japan, prefectural and municipal governments simply react to national policy by complying or not. Nevertheless, we find striking similarities in the process of racial identification and the preservation of consequent distinctions. Moreover, both sets of official ideologies function to preserve the position of the "majority race." Whether the official myth espouses a community based on racial purity or a polity composed of distinct races, government activities reinforce political arrangements which marginalize minority populations.

In each case, the government is not simply following biological or social definitions of race. There are no pure races of humankind, no distinctive racial characteristics that divide humans into distinct, mutually exclusive groups. There is no scientific classification scheme for identifying races that transcends government policy. At the same time, neither government is merely responding to prevailing social definitions. Citizens do not have the power to determine their own racial identity. Persons or groups who, because of their social status, challenge their official classification are redefined or defined out of existence.

In each case government creates racial identities. Racial identity is determined, according to official ideology, at birth on legal documents. These official definitions of race become powerful tools for imposing and maintaining race as a means of inclusion in, or exclusion from, the majority. The concept grew out of governmental activities and is used by governments to reinforce particular political arrangements. Administrative and legal decisions about how to categorize members of a population have a significant impact on images of that population. Elasticity of racial definitions does not serve the interests of minorities but rather eases the process of denying them equal place in society. Both the United States and Japan marginalize ethnic minorities. And in both nations, citizens learn to adopt a particular racial identity based on their government's ideology and classification practices.

References

Ames, Walter. 1981. *Police and Community in Japan.* Berkeley: University of California Press.

Baba Yuko. 1980. "A Study of Minority-Majority Relations: The Ainu and Japanese in Hokkaido." *Japan Interpreter* (1):60–92.

Barringer, Felicity. 1993. "Ethnic Pride Confounds Census." *New York Times* (May 19): E3.

Befu, Harumi. 1971. *Japan: an Anthropological Introduction.* New York: Harper and Row.

Bennett, Lerone F. 1993. *The Shaping of Black America.* New York: Penguin Books.

Campbell, John C. 1989. "Democracy and Bureaucracy in Japan," in Ellis Krauss and Takeshi Ishida, eds., *Democracy in Japan.* Pittsburgh: Pittsburgh University Press.

Davis, James F. 1991. *Who is Black? One Nation's Definition.* University Park, PA: Pennsylvania State University Press.

Diamond, Raymond T. and Robert J. Cottrol. 1993. "Codifying Race: Louisiana's Racial Classification Scheme and the Fourteenth Amendment." *Loyola Law Review* 29(2):255–85.

Ebitsubo Isamu and Nakamura Tokuji. 1994. "Chronology." *Japan Quarterly* (September–December): 522–23.

Federal Bureau of Investigation. 1984. *Crime in the United States. Uniform Crime Reports.* Washington, DC: Government Printing Office.

Herzog, Peter. 1993. *Japan's Pseudo-Democracy.* New York: New York University Press.

Hirowatari Seigo. 1993. "Foreigners and the 'Foreigners Question' under Japanese Law." *Annals of the Institute of Social Science* (35):91–122.

Human Rights Watch Prison Project. 1995. *Prison Conditions in Japan.* New York: Human Rights Watch.

Iwasawa Yuji. 1986. *Legal Treatment of Koreans in Japan: The Impact of International Human Rights Law on Japanese Law.* Washington, DC: International Human Rights Law Group.

Keisatsu Hakusho. Annual. Tokyo: Keisatsucho.

Kim, Hong Nack. 1990. "The Korean Minority in Japan." *Korea and World Affairs* (Spring): 111–136.

King, James C. 1981. *The Biology of Race.* Berkeley: University of California Press.

Komatsu Sueo. 1986. *Sabetsu to Tennosei.* Tokyo: Shiraishi Shoten.

Lee, Changsoo and George deVos. 1981. *Koreans in Japan: Ethnic Conflict and Accommodation.* Berkeley: University of California Press.

Levin, Michael D. 1991. *Population Differentiation and Racial Classification,* in Encyclopedia of Human Biology, Vol. 6. New York: Academic Press.

Mizuno Takaaki. 1987. "Ainu: The Invisible Minority." *Japan Quarterly* 34 (April–June): 142–48.

Montagu, M. F. Ashley. 1952. *Man's Most Dangerous Myth: The Fallacy of Race.* New York: Harper.

Morris-Suzuki, Tessa. 1993. "Rewriting History: Civilization Theory in Contemporary Japan." *Positions,* (Fall).

Office of Federal Statistical Policy. 1978. *Statistical Policy Manual.* Washington, DC: U.S. Department of Commerce.

Ohnuki-Tierney, Emiko. 1987. *The Monkey as Mirror.* Princeton, NJ: Princeton University Press.

Public Offices Election Law. 1958. EHS Law Bulletin Series, No. 1110.

Reed, Stephen. 1993. *Making Common Sense of Japan.* Pittsburgh: Pittsburgh University Press.

Root, Maria P. P. 1992. "Within, Between and Beyond Race," in Maria P. P. Root, ed., *Racially Mixed People in America.* Newbury Park, CA: Sage.

Sjoberg, Katarina. 1993. *The Return of the Ainu: Cultural Mobilization and the Practice of Ethnicity in Japan.* Chur, Switzerland: Harwood Academia Publishers.

Sorifu Tokeikyoku. 1948. *Waga Kuni Jinko no Gaiyo.* Tokyo: Nihon Hyoronsha.

Spickard, Paul. 1992. "The Illogic of American Racial Categories," in Maria P. P. Root, ed., *Racially Mixed People in America.* Newbury Park, CA: Sage.

Trillin, Calvin. 1986. "American Chronicles: Black or White." *The New Yorker* (April 14).

United Nations Educational, Scientific and Cultural Organization. 1970. *The Race Concept: Results of an Inquiry. Statement on the Nature of Race and Race Differences 1951.* Westport, CT: Greenwood Press.

Usdansky, Margaret L. "California's Mix Offers a Look at the Future." *USA Today* (December 4): 8A.

Van Wolferen, Karel. 1989. *The Enigma of Japanese Power.* London: MacMillan.

Wagatsuma Hiroshi, and Yoneyama Toshinao. 1967, 1994. *Henken no Kozo.* Tokyo: NHK Books.

Wheeler, David L. 1995. "A Growing Number of Scientists Reject the Concept of Race." *Chronicle of Higher Education* (February 17): A8–9, A15.

Weiner, Michael. 1994. *Race and Migration in Imperial Japan.* London: Routledge.

White Papers of Japan, 1985–86. 1986. Tokyo: Japan Times, 1986.

Wright, Lawrence. 1994. "One Drop of Blood." *The New Yorker* (July 25): 46–55.

Yamanaka Keiko. 1993. "New Immigration Policy and Unskilled Foreign Workers in Japan." *Pacific Affairs* 66:1 (Spring): 72–90.

Yanagi Daion. 1992. *Sabetsu to Kanshi no Naka de.* Tokyo: Gendaishi Shuppankai.

Notes

[1] James C. King, *The Biology of Race* (Berkeley: University of California Press, 1981), p. 157. For a discussion of the difficulties of specifying those characteristics that define even a homogeneous "race" such as the Japanese, see Wagatsuma Hiroshi and Yoneyama Toshinao, *Henken no Kozo* (*The Structure of Discrimination*) (Tokyo: NHK Books, 1994), pp. 141–60.

[2] United Nations Educational, Scientific, and Cultural Organization, *The Race Concept: the Results of an Inquiry, 1951* (Westport, CT: Greenwood Press, 1970), pp. 11–16.

[3] Ashley M. F. Montagu, *Man's Most Dangerous Myth: The Fallacy of Race* (New York: Harper, 1952).

[4] David Wheeler, "A Growing Number of Scientists Reject the Concept of Race," *Chronicle of Higher Education,* February 17, 1995, p. A9.

[5] Michael Levin, "Population Differentiation and Racial Classification," in *Encyclopedia of Human Biology,* vol. 6 (New York: Academic Press, 1991), p. 101.

[6] Emiko Ohnuki-Tierney, *The Monkey as Mirror* (Princeton: Princeton University Press, 1987). The notion of insider and outsider is widely used to describe and explain behavior in Japanese groups.

[7] Harumi Befu, *Japan: an Anthropological Introduction* (New York: Harper and Row, 1971), p. 125.

[8] Komatsu Sueo, *Sabetsu to Tennosei* (*Discrimination and the Emperor System*) (Tokyo: Shiraishi Shoten, 1986).

[9] Michael Weiner, *Race and Migration in Imperial Japan* (London: Routledge, 1994).

[10] Wagatsuma and Yoneyama, *Henken no Kozo.*

[11] Katerina Sjoberg, *The Return of the Ainu: Cultural Mobilization and the Practice of Ethnicity in Japan* (Chur, Switzerland: Harwood Academia Publishers, 1993), pp. 2, 131.

[12] Hirowatari Seigo, "Foreigners and the 'Foreigners Question' under Japanese Law," *Annals of the Institute of Social Sciences* 35 (1993), p. 91.

[13] Stephen Reed, *Making Common Sense of Japan* (Pittsburgh: University of Pittsburgh Press, 1993).

[14] Human Rights Watch Prison Project, *Prison Conditions in Japan* (New York: Human Rights Watch, 1995), p. vi.

[15] Sjoberg, 1993, pp. 9, 130.

[16] Iwasawa Yuji, *Legal Treatment of Koreans in Japan: The Impact of International Human Rights Law on Japanese Law.* Washington, DC: International Human Rights Law Group, 1986, pp. vii–ix.

[17] Sjoberg, *Return of the Ainu,* pp. 129–30.

[18] John C. Campbell, "Bureaucracy in Japan," in Ellis Krauss and Takeshi Ishida, eds., *Democracy in Japan* (Pittsburgh: University of Pittsburgh Press, 1989), p. 116.

[19] Baba Yuko, "A Study of Minority-Majority Relations: The Ainu and Japanese in Hokkaido," *Japan Interpreter,* 1980, No. 1, pp. 61–63.

[20] Sjoberg, *Return of the Ainu,* pp. 128–29.

[21] Yamanaka Keiko, "New Immigration Policy and Unskilled Foreign Workers in Japan," *Pacific Affairs* 66 (Spring, 1993), pp. 72–90.

[22] Sjoberg, *Return of the Ainu,* p. 131.

[23] Ebitsubo Isamu and Nakamura Tokuji, "Chronology," *Japan Quarterly,* September–December, 1994, p. 522.

[24] Since it is our contention that racial categories are arbitrarily maintained by governments, we have decided to put all racial designations in lower case unless they are recognized proper nouns (e.g., "Japanese") or are capitalized in quotations from cited sources.

[25] Office of Federal Statistical Policy, *Statistical Policy Manual* (Washington, DC: United States Department of Commerce, 1978).

[26] Maria Root, "Within, Between, and Beyond Race," in Maria Root, ed., *Racially Mixed People in America* (Newbury Park, CA: Sage, 1992), p. 9.

[27] James Davis, *Who Is Black? One Nation's Definition* (University Park, PA: Pennsylvania State University Press, 1991), p. 21.

[28] Felicity Barringer, "Ethnic Pride Confounds the Census," *New York Times,* May 9, 1993, p. E3.

[29] Office of Federal Statistical Policy, *Statistical Policy Manual,* p. 37.

[30] Paul Spickard, "The Illogic of American Racial Categories," in Root, ed., *Racially Mixed People,* p. 23.

[31] Margaret Usdansky, "California's Mix Offers a Look at the Future," *USA Today,* December 4, 1992, p. 8A.

[32] Federal Bureau of Investigation, *Crime in the United States: Uniform Crime Reports* (Washington, DC: Government Printing Office, 1942), p. 46.

[33] Federal Bureau of Investigation, *Crime in the United States: Uniform Crime Statistics* (Washington, DC: Government Printing Office, 1984), p. 58.

[34] Lawrence Wright, "One Drop of Blood," *The New Yorker,* July 25, 1994, p. 46.

[35] Weiner, *Race and Migration.*

[36] Iwasawa, *Legal Treatment of Koreans,* p. 15; Hirowatari, "Foreigners and the 'Foreigners Question'," pp. 100–101.

[37] Sorifu Tokeikyoku, *Waga Kuni Jinko no Gaiyo (Outline of Japan's Population)* (Tokyo: Nihon Hyoronsha, 1948), pp. 56–59.

[38] Hirowatari, "Foreigners and the 'Foreigners Question'," pp. 101–104.

[39] Iwasawa, *Legal Treatment of Koreans,* pp. 15–17.

[40] *Asahi Shinbun,* August 6, 1995, p. 31.

[41] Hong Nack Kim, "The Korean Minority in Japan," *Korea and World Affairs* (Spring, 1990), pp. 131–32.

[42] Yanagi Daion, *Sabetsu to Kanshi no Naka de (Discrimination and the Inside of Investigation)* (Tokyo: Gendai Shuppankai, 1992), p. 29.

[43] Walter Ames, *Police and Community in Japan* (Berkeley: University of California Press, 1981), pp. 97–99, 145, 163.

[44] Raymond Diamond and Robert Cottrol, "Codifying Race: Louisiana's Racial Classification Scheme and the Fourteenth Amendment," *Loyola Law Review* 29:2 (1983), pp. 255–85.

[45] *Anderson v. Martin,* 375 U. S. (1964), 399, 402.

[46] *Van Camp v. Board of Education of Village of Logan,* 9 Ohio State, pp. 406, 411.

[47] *State v. Treadway,* 52 So., pp. 500, 511. Johann Friedrich Bluemenbach, a German physician, coined the term "Caucasian" in 1795. He defined four races—Mongolian, Ethiopian, American, and Malay—on the basis of hair, skin, eye color, skull shape, and other features of the head. Caucasian, the original variety whence the others appeared through a process of "degeneration," was defined based on the place of origin. This "most beautiful race of men" had first appeared on the slopes of Mt. Caucasus, so he gave them the name Caucasian. See King, *The Biology of Race,* p. 123.

[48] Mizuno Takaaki, "Ainu: The Invisible Minority," *Japan Quarterly,* April–June, 1987, p. 145.

[49] *Public Offices Election Law* (EHS Law Bulletin Series, No. 1110, 1958), p. 189; Changsoo Lee and George deVos, *Koreans in Japan: Ethnic Conflict and Accommodation* (Berkeley: University of California Press, 1981), pp. 278–80.

[50] Iwasawa, *Legal Treatment of Koreans,* pp. 36–37.

[51] See *Keisatsu Hakusho (Police White Paper)* (Tokyo: Keisatsucho, selected years).

[52] See, for example, Tanaka Hiroshi, *Zainichi Gaikokujin (Foreigners Residing in Japan)* (Tokyo: Iwananmi Shoten, 1995), pp. 130–35: Kim, "Korean Minority," p. 121.

[53] Office of Federal Statistical Policy, *Statistical Policy Manual,* p. 37.

[54] Usdansky, "California's Mix," p. 8A.

[55] Lerone Bennett, *The Shaping of Black America* (New York: Penguin Books, 1993), p. 17.

[56] Ibid., p. 69.

[57] Davis, *Who Is Black?,* pp. 8–11.

[58] 479 So. 2d, p. 371.

[59] Davis, *Who Is Black?,* p. 107; 107 S. Ct., p. 638.

Federal Statistical Directive No. 15: Race and Ethnic Standards for Federal Statistics and Administrative Reporting

(as adopted on May 12, 1977)

The U.S. Office of Management and Budget

Study Questions

1. What is the minimum number of acceptable (a) race categories, (b) ethnic categories, (c) combined race and ethnic categories specified in Directive No. 15?
2. Does the Directive limit the collection of race and ethnic data to the categories identified in that document?
3. What kinds of reporting tasks require that Directive No. 15 be followed?

This Directive provides standard classifications for recordkeeping, collection, and presentation of data on race and ethnicity in Federal program administrative reporting and statistical activities. These classifications should not be interpreted as being scientific or anthropological in nature, nor should they be viewed as determinants of eligibility for participation in any Federal program. They have been developed in response to needs expressed by both the executive branch and the Congress to provide for the collection and use of compatible, nonduplicated, exchangeable racial and ethnic data by Federal agencies.

1. **Definitions**

   The basic racial and ethnic categories for Federal statistics and program administrative reporting are defined as follows:

   a. American Indian or Alaskan Native. A person having origins in any of the original peoples of North America, and who maintains cultural identification through tribal affiliations or community recognition.

b. Asian or Pacific Islander. A person having origins in any of the original peoples of the Far East, Southeast Asia, the Indian sub-continent, or the Pacific Islands. This area includes, for example, China, India, Japan, Korea, the Philippine Islands, and Samoa.

c. Black. A person having origins in any of the black racial groups of Africa.

d. Hispanic. A person of Mexican, Puerto Rican, Cuban, Central or South American or other Spanish culture or origin, regardless of race.

e. White. A person having origins in any of the original peoples of Europe, North Africa, or the Middle East.

2. **Utilization for Recordkeeping and Reporting**

To provide flexibility, it is preferable to collect data on race and ethnicity separately. If separate race and ethnic categories are used, the minimum designations are:

a. Race:
   American Indian or Alaskan Native
   Asian or Pacific Islander
   Black
   White

b. Ethnicity:
   Hispanic origin
   Not of Hispanic origin

When race and ethnicity are collected separately, the number of White and Black persons who are Hispanic must be identifiable, and capable of being reported in that category.

If a combined format is used to collect racial and ethnic data, the minimum acceptable categories are:
   American Indian or Alaskan Native
   Asian or Pacific Islander
   Black, not of Hispanic origin
   Hispanic
   White, not of Hispanic origin

The category which most closely reflects the individual's recognition in his community should be used for purposes of reporting on persons who are of mixed racial and/or ethnic origins.

In no case should the provisions of this Directive be construed to limit the collection of data to the categories described above. However, any reporting required which uses more detail shall be organized in such a way that the additional categories can be aggregated into these basic racial/ethnic categories. The minimum standard collection categories shall be utilized for reporting as follows:

a. Civil rights compliance reporting. The categories specified above will be used by all agencies in either the separate or combined format for civil rights compliance reporting and equal employment reporting for both the public and private sectors and for all levels of government. Any variation requiring less detailed data or data which cannot be aggregated into the basic categories will have to be specifically approved by the Office of Management and Budget (OMB) for executive agencies. More detailed reporting which can be aggregated to the basic categories may be used at the agencies' discretion.

b. General program administrative and grant reporting. Whenever an agency subject to this Directive issues new or revised administrative reporting or recordkeeping requirements which include racial or ethnic data, the agency will use the race/ethnic categories described above. A variance can be specifically requested from OMB, but such a variance will be granted only if the agency can demonstrate that it is not reasonable for the primary reporter to determine the racial or ethnic background in terms of the specified categories, and that such determination is not critical to the administration of the program in question, or if the specific program is directed to only one or a limited number of race/ethnic groups, e.g., Indian tribal activities.

c. Statistical reporting. The categories described in this Directive will be used at a minimum for federally sponsored statistical data collection where race and/or ethnicity is required, except when: the collection involves a sample of such size that the data on the smaller categories would be unreliable, or when the collection effort focuses on a specific racial or ethnic group. A repetitive survey shall be deemed to have an adequate sample size if the racial and ethnic data can be reliably aggregated on a biennial basis. Any other variation will have to be specifically authorized by OMB through the reports clearance process. In those cases where the data collection is not subject to the reports clearance process, a direct request for a variance should be made to OMB.

3. Effective Date

The provisions of this Directive are effective immediately for all new and revised recordkeeping or reporting requirements containing racial and/or ethnic information. All existing recordkeeping or reporting requirements shall be made consistent with this Directive at the time they are submitted for extension, or not later than January 1, 1980.

4. Presentation of Race/Ethnic Data

Displays of racial and ethnic compliance and statistical data will use the category designations listed above. The designation "nonwhite" is not acceptable for use in the presentation of Federal Government data. It is not to be used in any publication of compliance or statistical data or in the text of any compliance or statistical report.

In cases where the above designations are considered inappropriate for presentation of statistical data on particular programs or for particular regional areas, the sponsoring agency may use:

(1) The designations "Black and Other Races" or "All Other Races," as collective descriptions of minority races when the most summary distinction between the majority and minority races is appropriate;

(2) The designations "White," "Black," and "All Other Races" when the distinction among the majority race, the principal minority race and other races is appropriate; or

(3) The designation of a particular minority race or races, and the inclusion of "Whites" with "All Other Races," if such a collective description is appropriate.

In displaying detailed information which represents a combination of race and ethnicity, the description of the data being displayed must clearly indicate that both bases of classification are being used.

When the primary focus of a statistical report is on two or more specific identifiable groups in the population, one or more of which is racial or ethnic, it is acceptable to display data for each of the particular groups separately and to describe data relating to the remainder of the population by an appropriate collective description.

·················
····················

THE MEAN STREETS OF SOCIAL RACE

IAN F. HANEY LÓPEZ

Study Questions
1. Haney López identifies three factors which determine a person's race: chance (morphology and ancestry), context (social setting), and choice (everyday, ordinary decisions). Expand on the meaning of each factor.
2. Give examples from Piri Thomas's life to illustrate the role of each factor in determining race.

The literature of minority writers provides some of the most telling insights into, and some of the most confused explorations of, race in the United States.[150] Piri Thomas's quest for identity, recorded in *Down These Mean Streets*,[151] fits squarely within this tradition of insight and confusion. Thomas describes his racial transformation, which is both willed and yet not willed, from a Puerto Rican into someone Black.[152] Dissecting his harrowing experiences, piercing perceptions, and profound misapprehensions offers a way to disaggregate the daily technology of race. To facilitate this discussion, I employ the terms of chance, context, and choice: chance refers to morphology and ancestry, context to the contemporary social setting, and choice to the quotidian decisions of life. In the play of race, chance, context, and choice overlap and are inseverable. Nevertheless, I distinguish among these neologisms to focus on key aspects of how race is created, maintained, and experienced. Drawing upon these terms and using the ordeals Thomas recorded in *Down These Mean Streets* as a foil, I return to the definition proffered at the beginning of this essay, that a race is best thought of as a group of people loosely bound together by historically contingent, socially significant elements of their morphology and/or ancestry.

Chance

The first terms of importance in the definition of race I advance are "morphology" and "ancestry." These fall within the province of chance, by which I mean coincidence, something not subject to human will or effort, insofar as we have no control over what we look like or to whom we are born. Chance, because of the importance of morphology and ancestry, may seem to occupy almost the entire geography of race. Certainly for those who subscribe to notions of biological race, chance seems to account for almost everything: one is born some race and not another, fated to a particular racial identity, with no human intervention possible. For those who believe in biological race, race is destiny. However, recognizing the social construction of race reduces the province of chance. The role of chance in determining racial identity is significantly smaller than one might initially expect.

The random accidents of morphology and ancestry set the scene for Piri Thomas's racial odyssey. Seeking better prospects during the depression, Thomas's parents moved from Puerto Rico to Spanish Harlem, where Piri and his three siblings were born. Once in the United States, however, the family faced the peculiar American necessity of defining itself as White or Black. To be White would afford security and a promising future; to be Black would portend exclusion and unemployment. The Thomas family—hailing from Puerto Rico of mixed Indian, African, and European antecedents—considered themselves White and pursued the American dream, eventually moving out to the suburbs in search of higher salaries and better schools for the children. Yet in their bid for Whiteness, the family gambled and lost, because even while the three other children and Piri's mother were fair, Piri and his father were dark skinned. Babylon, Long Island proved less forgiving of Piri's dark skin than Spanish Harlem. In the new school, the pale children scoffed at Piri's claim to be Puerto Rican rather than Black, taunting Piri for "passing for Puerto Rican because he can't make it for white,"[153] and proclaiming, "[t]here's no difference . . . [h]e's still black."[154] Piri's morphology shattered not only the family's White dream, but eventually the family itself.

While the family insisted on their own Whiteness as the crucial charm to a fulfilling life in the United States, Thomas, coming of age amid the racial struggles of the 1950s and himself the victim of White violence, fought the moral hypocrisy he saw in their claim to Whiteness.[155] Piri unyieldingly attacked the family's delusion, for example challenging with bitterness and frustration the Whiteness of his younger brother José:

> José's face got whiter and his voice angrier at my attempt to take away his white status. He screamed out strong: "I ain't no nigger! You can be if you want to be. . . . But—I—am—*white!* And you can go to hell!"

But Piri persisted in attacking the family, one at a time:

> "And James is *blanco,* too?" I asked quietly.

"You're damn right."

"And Poppa?"

. . . "Poppa's the same as you," he said, avoiding my eyes, "Indian."

"What kinda Indian," I said bitterly. "Caribe? Or maybe Borin-quen? Say, José, didn't you know the Negro made the scene in Puerto Rico way back? And when the Spanish spics ran outta Indian coolies, they brought them big blacks from you know where. Poppa's got *moyeto* [Black] blood. I got it. Sis got it. James got it. And, mah deah brudder, you-all got it. . . . It's a played-out lie about me—us—being white."[156]

The structure of this painful exchange casts a bright light on the power that morphology and ancestry wield in defining races. In the racially charged United States, skin color or parentage often makes one's publicly constructed race inescapable.

Piri's dark features and José's light looks are chance in the sense that neither Piri nor José could choose their faces, or indeed their ancestry. Yet, two important qualifications about chance should be made. The most important of these, that morphology and ancestry gain their importance on the social and not the physical plane, is the subject of the next part. The second caveat bears mention here. Upon reflection, what we look like is *not* entirely accident; to some extent looks can be altered in racially significant ways. In this respect, consider the unfortunate popularity of hair straightening,[157] blue contact lenses, and even facial surgery.[158] Or consider that in 1990 alone approximately $44 million was spent on chemical treatments to literally lighten and whiten skin through the painful and dangerous application of bleach.[159] It seems we minorities do not leave our looks to chance, but constantly seek to remake them, in tragic obeisance to the power of racial aesthetics in the United States.[160] Though morphology and ancestry remain firmly in the province of chance, that province daily suffers incursions of the will.

Context

Given Piri's status as a Puerto Rican with ancestral ties to three continents, there is a certain absurdity to his insistence that he is Black. This absurdity highlights the importance of context to the creation of races. Context is the social setting in which races are recognized, constructed, and contested; it is the "circumstances directly encountered, given and transmitted from the past."[161] At the meta level, context includes both ideological and material components, such as entrenched cultural and customary prejudices, and also maldistributed resources, marketplace inequalities, and skewed social services. These inherited structures are altered and altered again by every-thing from individual actors and community movements to broad-based changes in the economic, demographic, and political landscape. At the same time, context also refers to highly localized settings. The systems of meaning regarding morphology and ancestry are inconstant and unstable. These systems shift in time and space, and even across class and educational levels, in ways that give to any individual different racial identities depending upon her shifting location.[162] I refer to context in order to explain the phrases "historically contingent" and "socially significant" in the proffered definition of race.

The changes in racial identity produced by the shifting significance of morphology and ancestry are often profoundly disconcerting, as Piri Thomas discovered. In Puerto Rico, prevailing attitudes toward racial identity situated the Thomases, as a family not light enough to be Spanish but not so dark as to be black, comfortably in the mainstream of society.[163] They encountered no social or economic disadvantages as a result of their skin color, and were not subjected to the prejudice that usually accompanies rigid racial constructs. However, the social ideology of race in the United States—more specifically, in New York in the late 1950s—was firmly rooted in the proposition that exactly two biological races existed. Such an ideology forced the Thomas family to define themselves as either White or Black. In the context confronting Piri, "[i]t would seem indeed that . . . white and black represent the two poles of a world, two poles in perpetual conflict: a genuinely Manichean concept of the world . . . ."[164] Once in the United States, Thomas came to believe that he and his family were Black as a biological fact, irrespective of their own dreams, desires, or decisions. Yet, Thomas was not Black because of his face or parents, but because of the social systems of meaning surrounding these elements of his identity.

Consider how Thomas came to believe in his own Blackness. In a chapter entitled "How to be a Negro Without Really Trying," Thomas recalls how he and his fair-skinned Puerto Rican friend Louie applied for a sales job. Though the company told Thomas they would call him back, they hired Louie to start Monday morning. Thomas's reflections bear repeating:

> I didn't feel so much angry as I did sick, like throwing-up sick. Later, when I told this story to my buddy, a colored cat, he said, "Hell, Piri . . . a Negro faces that all the time."
>
> "I know that," I said, "but I wasn't a Negro then. I was still only a Puerto Rican."[165]

Episodes of discrimination drove Piri towards a confused belief that he was Black.[166] Aching to end the confusion, Piri traveled to the South, where he hoped to find out for sure whether his hair, his skin, and his face somehow inextricably tied him, a Puerto Rican, to Black America. Working in the merchant marine between Mobile, New Orleans, and Galveston, Piri experienced firsthand the nether world of White supremacy, and the experience confirmed his race; bullied by his White bosses, insulted by White strangers, confronted at every turn by a White racial etiquette of violence, Thomas accepted his own Blackness. "It was like Brew said," he reflected after his time in the South, "any language you talk, if you're black, you're black."[167] Suffering under the lash of White racism, Thomas decided he was Black. Thomas's Blackness did not flow from his morphology but from traveling the mean streets of racial segregation. His dislocations suggest a spatial component to racial identities, an implication confirmed in Thomas's travel from Spanish Harlem, where he was Puerto Rican, to Long Island, where he was accused of trying to pass, to the South, where he was Black.[168]

Piri and his family were far from the first to face the Manichean choice between White or Black. The Chinese, whose population in the United States rose fifteenfold to 105,465 in the twenty years after 1850, were also initially defined in terms of Black and White. Thus in Los Angeles circa 1860 the Chinese area downtown was called "Nigger Alley."[169] During their first years in the United States, as Ronald Takaki observes, "[r]acial qualities that had been assigned to blacks became Chinese characteristics."[170] Not only were the supposed degenerate moral traits of Blacks transferred wholesale to the Chinese, but in a fascinating display of racist imagination, Whites also saw a close link between Black and Chinese morphology. Takaki cites a commentator who argued that Chinese physiognomy indicated "but a slight removal from the African race,"[171] and he reprints a startling cartoon contrasting Anglo Uncle Sam with a Chinese vampire replete with slanted eyes, but also with very dark skin, woolly hair, a flat nose, and thick lips.[172]

In California, where the racial imagination included Mexicans and Indians as well as Blacks, the racial categorization of the Chinese involved their construction not only in terms of Blackness but also in terms of every non-White race, every rejected and denigrated Other. This point furnishes yet more evidence for the theory that racial identity is defined by its social context. Consider the 1879 play *The Chinese Must Go* by Henry Grimm of San Francisco. Notice the language Grimm ascribes to the Chinese characters, discussing, predictably, their nefarious Anti-American plot to destroy White labor through hard work:

> AH CHOY: By and by white man catchee no money; Chinaman catchee heap money; Chinaman workee cheap, plenty work; white man workee dear, no work—sabee?
> SAM GIN: Me heep sabee.[173]

The Chinese in this Grimm play speak in the language that Whites associated with Indians and Mexicans, making Sam Gin sound remarkably like Tonto playing out the Lone Ranger's racial delusions. Thus, the Chinese were assigned not only their own peculiar stereotypes, like a fiendish desire to work for low wages, but also the degenerate characteristics of all the minorities loathed by Whites. Not coincidentally, three years after Grimm's play, the United States passed its first immigration law: The 1882 Chinese Exclusion Act.[174] In a telling example of law reifying racist hysteria, the Supreme Court upheld the Chinese Exclusion Act in part by citing the threat posed by the Chinese to White labor.[175] The first Chinese, like the Thomas family nearly a century later, entered a society fixated on the idea of race and intent on forcing new immigrants into procrustean racial hierarchies.

The racial fate of Piri and the Chinese turned to a large extent on the context into which they immigrated. Context provides the social meanings attached to our faces and forbears, and for this reason I write that races are groups of people bound together by *historically contingent, socially significant* elements of their morphology and/or ancestry. A race is not created because people share just any characteristic, such as height or hand size, or just any ancestry, for example Yoruba or Yugoslav. Instead, it is the social significance attached to certain features, like our faces,[176] and to certain forebears, like Africans, which defines races. Context superimposed on chance largely shapes races in the United States.

Choice in Context

Piri's belief that he is Black, and his brother José's belief in his own Whiteness, can in some sense be attributed to the chance of their respective morphology and the context of their upbringing. Yet, to attribute Thomas's racial identity only to chance and context grossly oversimplifies his Blackness. Thomas's father shared not only his social context, but his dark looks as well, making context and chance equal between them. Nevertheless, his father insisted on his Whiteness, and explained this decision to Piri as follows:

> I ain't got one colored friend . . . at least one American Negro friend. Only dark ones I got are Puerto Ricans or Cubans. I'm not a stupid man. I saw the look of white people on me when I was a young man, when I walked into a place where a dark skin isn't supposed to be. I noticed how a cold rejection turned into an indifferent acceptance when they heard my exaggerated accent. I can remember the time when I made my accent heavier, to make me more of a Puerto Rican than the most Puerto Rican there ever was. I wanted a value on me, son.[177]

Thomas's father consciously exaggerated his Puerto Rican accent to put distance between himself and Black Americans. Thomas himself also made conscious and purposeful decisions, choices that in the end made him Black. As Henry Louis Gates argues, "one must *learn* to be 'black' in this society, precisely because 'blackness' is a socially produced category."[178]

Choice composes a crucial ingredient in the construction of racial identities and the fabrication of races. Racial choices occur on mundane and epic levels, for example in terms of what to wear or when to fight; they are made by individuals and groups, such as people deciding to pass or movements deciding to protest; and the effects are often minor though sometimes profound, for instance, slightly altering a person's affiliation or radically remaking a community's identity. Nevertheless, in every circumstance choices are exercised not by free agents or autonomous actors, but by people who are compromised and constrained by the social context. Choice, explains Angela Harris, is not uncoerced choice, "freely given, but a 'contradictory consciousness' mixing approbation and apathy, resistance and resignation."[179] Nevertheless, in racial matters we constantly exercise choice, sometimes in full awareness of our compromised position, though often not.[180]

Perhaps the most graphic illustration of choice in the construction of racial identities comes in the context of passing. Passing—the ability of individuals to change race—powerfully indicates race's chosen nature. Not infrequently someone Black through the social construction of their an-cestry is physically indistinguishable from someone White.[181] Consider Richard Wright's description of his grandmother in *Black Boy:* "My grandmother was as nearly white as a Negro can get without being white, which means that she was white."[182] Given the prevalent presumption of essential, easily recognized phenotypical differences, light-skinned Blacks exist at an ambiguous and often unacknowledged racial border between White and Black.[183] Those in this liminal space often respond along a range from some few who cross the established color line by "passing" to those who identify strongly with their Black status.[184]

For most people, the pervasive social systems of meaning that attach to morphology ensure that passing is not an option.[185] Moreover, for those who do jump races, the psychological dislocations required—suspending some personal dreams, for example childbirth; renouncing most family ties, for instance foregoing weddings and funerals; and severing all relations with the community, for example, ending religious and civic affiliations—are brutal and severe.[186] In addition, because of the depth of racial animosity in this society, passing may only succeed in distancing one from her community, not in gaining her full acceptance among Whites. In this sense, recall the words of Thomas's father: "I noticed how a cold rejection turned into an indifferent acceptance when they heard my exaggerated accent."[187] Nevertheless, some people do choose to jump races, and their ability to do so dramatically demonstrates the element of choice in the micromechanics of race.

It also demonstrates, however, the contingency of the choices people make, and reinforces the point that choices are made in specific contexts. Choices about racial identity do not occur on neutral ground, but instead occur in the violently racist context of American society. Though the decision to pass may be made for many reasons, among these the power of prejudice and self-hate cannot be denied. Thomas's younger brother José reveals the racist hate within him in the same instant that he claims to be White. José shouts at Piri: "I ain't black, damn you! Look at my hair. It's almost blond. My eyes are blue, my nose is straight. My motherfuckin' lips are not like a baboon's ass. My skin is white. White, goddamit! White!"[188] José's comments are important, if painful to repeat, because they illustrate that a person's choice in the matter of race may be fatally poisoned by ambient racist antipathies. Nevertheless, notice that the context in which passing occurs constantly changes. For example, it may be that in the contemporary context passing as White increasingly does not in fact require that one *look* White. Recently, many Anglos, committed to the pseudo-integrationist idea that ignoring races equals racial enlightenment, have seemingly adopted the strategy of pretending that the minorities they are friendly with are White. Consider the words of a White Detroit politician: "I seldom think of my girlfriend, Kathy, as black. . . . A lot of times I look at her and it's as if she is white; there's no real difference. But every now and then, it depends on what she is wearing and what we're doing, she looks very ethnic and very Black. It bothers me. I don't like it. I prefer it when she's a regular, normal, everyday kind of person."[189] Even so, passing may be far less common today than it was a hundred years ago. One observer estimates that in the half-century after the Civil War, as many as 25,000 people a year passed out of the Black race.[190] The context in which passing occurs constantly changes, altering in turn the range of decisions individuals face.

Despite the dramatic evidence of choice passing provides, by far the majority of racial decisions are of a decidedly less epic nature. Because race in our society infuses almost all aspects of life, many daily decisions take on racial meanings. For example, seemingly inconsequential acts like listening to rap and wearing hip hop fashions constitute a means of racial affiliation and identification. Many Whites have taken to listening to, and some to performing, rap and hip hop.[191] Nevertheless, the music of the inner city remains Black music.[192] Rapping, whether as an artist or audience member, is in some sense a racial act. So too are a myriad of other actions taken every day by every person, almost always without conscious regard for the racial significance of their choices. It is here, in deciding what to eat, how to dress, whom to befriend, and where to go, rather than in the dramatic decision to leap races, that most racial choices are rendered. I do not suggest that these common acts are racial choices because they are taken with a conscious awareness of their racial implications. Rather, these are racial choices in their overtones or sub-text, because they resonate in the complex of meanings associated with race. Given the thorough suffusion of race throughout society, in the daily dance of life we cannot avoid making racially meaningful decisions.

Notes

[Notes 24, 92, 120, 129 are included here because they are referred to in subsequent notes.]

[24] Masatoshi Nei & Arun K. Roychoudhury, *Genetic Relationship and Evolution of Human Races,* in 14 EVOLUTIONARY BIOLOGY 1, 11 (1982)

[92] For a powerful critique of the model minority line, see RONALD TAKAKI, IRON CAGES: RACE AND CULTURE IN 19TH CENTURY AMERICA 298–302 (1990). If Asians are held up to Blacks as indictments by comparison, then for Latinos, Cubans serve that role. Cubans, particularly those who arrived here prior to the 1981 Marielos exodus, are relatively prosperous, well-educated, and politically powerful. The success of Cubans as recent immigrants, therefore, is often brandished as evidence of community guilt or cultural shortcomings in debates on the economic plight of Chicanos, Puerto Ricans, and Central Americans. On occasion, those who tout Cuban success concede that as immigrants they often possessed considerable education, business experience, professional training, and wealth, prior to their arrival in the United States. Far less frequently mentioned is that the federal government, in its ideologically inspired desire to embarrass Fidel Castro, undertook to ensure the economic well-being of Cuba's emigres by providing them with $957 million in aid in the years between 1961 and 1974. *See* GASTON FERNÁNDEZ, BEVERLY NAGEL, & LEON NARVÁEZ, HISPANIC MIGRATION TO THE UNITED STATES 80 (1987). *See also* Lisa Otero & Juan Zúñiga, *Latino Identity and Affirmative Action: Is There a Case for Hispanics* (1992) (unpublished manuscript, on file with author); *see generally* ELEANOR ROGG, THE ASSIMILATION OF CUBAN EXILES: THE ROLE OF COMMUNITY AND CLASS (1974). This aid took the form of re-settlement assistance, job training, professional recertification, job search assistance, special research and teaching grants for Cuban scholars, funding for public school bilingual education programs, and assistance to the public schools for the extra costs incurred by the rapid influx of Cuban children. FERNÁNDEZ ET AL., at 80. *See also* Migration and Refugee Assis-

tance Act, Pub. L. No. 87-510 (1962). I await, though in vain, a similar commitment to other Latinos, and all racial minorities generally.

[120] Notice that the racial and sexual construction of Mexican women as European, refined, and eligible for marriage differs markedly from the construction historically accorded Black women, which has emphasized sexual availability and condoned rape while stigmatizing marriage. It should be emphasized that this view of Mexican women applied only to some, in particular to those of the elite class with significant European antecedents, and began to wane towards the end of the 19th century as more Anglo women moved into the Southwest. Nevertheless, the different social-sexual-racial identity accorded Mexican and Black women at virtually the same historical and geographical moment is remarkable. This may reflect the absence of a rule of racial construction as applied to Mexicans similar to the one-drop rule prevalent in the reigning U.S. mythology concerning Blacks. *See* F. JAMES DAVIS, WHO IS BLACK: ONE NATION'S DEFINITION 168 (1991) (Davis argues, perhaps overbroadly, that "racially visible minority groups other than blacks in the United States . . . are not subject to a one-drop rule, and those persons whose ancestry is one-fourth or less from one of those groups are able to become fully assimilated by intermarrying with whites.").

[129] Because the identities of Whites and Blacks (and other minorities) are constructed in dualistic opposition to each other, the rehabilitation of minorities implies a more honest appraisal of the characteristics of Whites. More pointedly, challenging the stereotype that Blacks are evil challenges the myth that Whites are innocent.

> [The] three unarmed Black men [who became lost in Howard Beach] threatened to undo the very concept of white that so occupies the imagination of Europe and America that it blots out everything else. The threat that the Black Other brings to white space is not that more houses will be robbed but that the crime rate will *not* rise with their presence—that they will actually come and go peacefully and without incident. This would be the greatest catastrophe because then it would be inescapably revealed that whites rob the homes of other whites, that white men rape white women, that the evils of white society are attributable to whites, and ultimately that whites do not exist because the defining characteristics of whiteness—innocence and purity—is a phantasm.

Richard Ford, *Urban Space and the Color Line: The Consequences of Demarcation and Disorientation in the Postmodern Metropolis,* 9 HARV. BLACKLETTER J. 117, 138 (1992) (citation omitted).

[150] Black literature is replete with powerful examples. For two classic considerations of race by Black authors, see RALPH ELLISON, INVISIBLE MAN (1947) and JAMES WELDON JOHNSON, AUTOBIOGRAPHY OF AN EX-COLORED MAN (1960). For important explorations of race and identity by Asian authors, see e.g., CARLOS BULOSAN, AMERICA IS IN THE HEART (1943); CYNTHIA KADOHATA, THE FLOATING WORLD (1989); and DAVID MURA, TURNING JAPANESE; MEMOIRS OF A SANSEI (1991). On Asian American literature, see generally READING THE LITERATURES OF ASIAN AMERICA (Shirley Geok-lin Lim & Amy Ling eds., 1992). For investigations of these same themes by Latino authors, see, e.g., JULIA ALVÁREZ, HOW THE GARCÍA GIRLS LOST THEIR ACCENT (1992); JOSÉ ANTONIO VILLAREAL, CLEMETE CHACÓN (1984). For first-rate commentary on Chicano literature, see JUAN BRUCE-NOVOA, RETROSPACE: COLLECTED ESSAYS ON CHICANO LITERATURE (1990). For a Native American's literary reflections on identity in modern America, see JIM NORTHRUP, WALKING THE REZ ROAD (1993).

151 PIRI THOMAS, DOWN THESE MEAN STREETS (1967).

152 The reformulation of questions of identity into questions of race is a common theme in Latino literature, though often the conflict plays out in nationalistic terms. *See, e.g.,* OSCAR ACOSTA, THE AUTOBIOGRAPHY OF A BROWN BUFFALO (2d ed. 1989) and THE REVOLT OF THE COCKROACH PEOPLE (2d ed. 1989) (author rejects an individually American or Mexican identity before embarking on a journey of self-creation as a Chicano).

153 THOMAS, *supra* note 151, at 90.

154 *Id.* at 91.

155 I say what Piri "saw" as moral hypocrisy because for my part I want to warn against facile condemnations of those who, in the context of a violently racist society, strive to envelop themselves and their loved ones in the protective mantle of Whiteness. *See, e.g.,* JOHNSON, *supra* note 150. Johnson's ex-colored man chose to pass as White in order to spare his children the depredations of being Black in the United States.

156 THOMAS, *supra* note 151, at 145.

157 For an enlightening discussion of the politics of hair among African Americans, as well as a trenchant analysis of the unfortunate and ill-conceived distinction in antidiscrimination jurisprudence between "immutable" and "cultural" characteristics—where employers can discriminate on the basis of the latter but not the former—see Paulette Caldwell, *A Hair Piece: Perspectives on the Intersection of Race and Gender,* 1991 DUKE L.J. 365.

158 For a compilation of interesting but poorly analyzed anecdotes concerning the politics of appearance in the Black community, see KATHY RUSSELL, MIDGE WILSON & RONALD HALL, THE COLOR COMPLEX: THE POLITICS OF SKIN COLOR AMONG AFRICAN AMERICANS (1992). It bears mention that not only Blacks seek to whiten their features. Eyelid surgery among Asians and blue contact lenses and bleached hair among Latinos are all too common.

159 *Id.* at 51.

160 "So we rub ointments on our skin and pull our hair and wrap our bodies in silk and gold. We remake and redo and we sing and we pray that the ugliness will be hidden and that our beauty will shine through like light and be accepted. And we work and we work and we work at ourselves. Against ourselves. In spite of ourselves, and in subordination of ourselves." Patricia J. Williams, *The Obliging Shell: An Informal Essay on Formal Equal Opportunity,* 87 MICH L. REV. 2128, 2141 (1989).

161 KARL MARX, THE EIGHTEENTH BRUMAIRE OF LOUIS BONAPARTE (1963), *quoted in* RENATO ROSALDO, CULTURE AND TRUTH: THE REMAKING OF SOCIAL ANALYSIS 105 (1989).

162 As Law Professor Deborah Waire Post relates: "People are often misled by the context in which they find me, and I find their confusion funny. When I worked for Margaret Mead, students who asked me ['What are you?'] always assumed the answer would be 'Samoan.' When I lived in Texas, there were those who assumed the answer would be 'Hispanic' and others who just knew I had to be Creole from Louisiana." Deborah Waire Post, *Reflections on Identity, Diversity and Morality,* 6 BERKELEY WOMEN'S L.J. 136 (1991).

163 *See* Melvin M. Tumin & Arnold Feldman, *Class and Skin Color in Puerto Rico, in* COMPARATIVE PERSPECTIVES ON RACE RELATIONS 197 (Melvin M. Tumin ed., 1969).

[164] Frantz Fanon, Black Skin, White Masks 44–45 (1967).

[165] Thomas, *supra* note 151, at 108.

[166] Thomas might have agreed with Adrian Piper's sense that "[w]hat joins me to other blacks, then, and other blacks to another, is not a set of shared physical characteristics, for there is none that all blacks share. Rather, it is the shared experience of being visually or cognitively *identified* as black by a white racist society, and the punitive and damaging effects of that identification." Adrian Piper, *Passing for White, Passing for Black,* 58 Transition 30, 31 (1992).

[167] Thomas, *supra* note 151, at 187–88.

[168] The role of spatial demarcation in determining racial identity produces strange results: "Persons in Virginia who are one-fourth or more Indian and less than one-sixteenth African black are defined as Indians while on the reservation but as blacks when they leave." Davis, *supra* note 148, at 9 (citing Brewton Berry, Race and Ethnic Relations 26 (3d ed. 1965)). For a first-rate discussion of the spatial elements of race, see Ford, *supra* note 129.

[169] Richard Griswold Del Castillo, The Los Angeles Barrio, 1850–1890: A Social History 141 (1979).

[170] Takaki, Iron Cages, *supra* note 92, at 217.

[171] *Id.*

[172] *Id.* at 218.

[173] *Id.* at 221.

[174] 22 Stat. 58 § 14 (1882).

[175] The Chinese Exclusion Case: Chae Chan Ping v. United States, 130 U.S. 581, 595 (1889). The Chinese, the Court wrote, "were generally industrious and frugal. Not being accompanied by families, except in rare instances, their expenses were small; and they were content with the simplest fare, such as would not suffice for our laborers and artisans. This competition between them and our people was for this reason altogether in their favor, and the consequent irritation, proportionately deep and bitter, was followed, in many cases, by open conflicts, to the great disturbance of the public peace." *Id.*

[176] "The erection of racial classification in man based upon certain manifest morphological traits gives tremendous emphasis to those characters to which human perceptions are most finely tuned (nose, lip and eye shapes, skin color, hair form and quantity), precisely because they are the characters that men ordinarily use to distinguish individuals." Richard C. Lewontin, *The Apportionment of Human Diversity,* 6 Evolutionary Biology 381, 382 (1972).

[177] Thomas, *supra* note 151, at 152.

[178] Henry Louis Gates, Jr., Loose Canons: Vol. 101 Notes on the Culture Wars (1992).

[179] Angela Harris, *Race and Essentralism in Feminist Legal Theory,* 42 Stan L. Rev. 581, 614 (quoting T.J. Jackson Lears, *The Concept of Cultural Hegemony: Problems and Possibilities,* 90 Am. Hist. Rev. 567, 570 (1985).

[180] Consider as an example of racial choice exercised in the full recognition of context Deborah Waire Post's self-identification as Black:

> My decision to identify myself as black person is not exclusively a matter of descent, although my father's grandfathers were a runaway slave and a free black man who fought in the Civil War. Nor is it simply a matter of residence, although the fact that I grew up in a black neighborhood surely played a part in the creation of my sense of identity. It is not a matter of skin color, although there has

never been a question about the fact that I am a person of color. Some might argue that I am black because whites will not let me be anything else. I prefer to believe I am who I am, a black woman, because I made an ethically and morally correct choice with respect to my identity.

Post, *supra* note 162, at 137.

[181] Notice, of course, that under the prevalent social rules governing racial identity the opposite is not true. Any Black ancestry makes one Black. The "one-drop rule" or the "rule of hypodescent," as this phenomenon is sometimes called, is discussed in Neil Gotanda, *A Critique of "Our Constitution is Color-blind,"* 44 STAN. L. REV. 1, 24–26 (1991). *See also,* DAVIS, *supra* note 120, at 4–16 (explaining the "one-drop rule"). There may be light-skinned Blacks, but there are no dark-skinned Whites.

[182] RICHARD WRIGHT, BLACK BOY 48 (1966). Nei and Roychoudhury state that "about 20% of the gene pool of American Negroid is known to have been derived from Caucasoid by recent racial admixture." Nei & Roychoudhury, *supra* note 24 at 11 (citing T. Edward Reed, *Caucasian Genes in American Negroes,* 165 SCIENCE 762 (1969)). Notice that again Nei and Roychoudhury, by referring to the "gene pool" of the "American Negroid" and "Caucasoid" populations, cannot free themselves from language that strongly insinuates the existence of distinct biological races. We can presume that Nei and Roychoudhury are in fact referring to the gene pool of those peoples socially defined as Black, which reveals intermixture with those peoples socially defined as White. This intermingling occurs despite pronounced social taboos. Opposition to miscegenation remains very strong among Whites. In 1972, nearly two out of five Whites (39%) not only objected to interracial marriage, but thought such marriages should be illegal. In 1991, a sad and startling 17% of Whites continued to support the criminalization of interracial marriage. *See* RUSSELL ET AL., *supra* note 158, at 116.

Nei & Roychoudhury are not the first to recognize the small proportion of genetic difference attributable to race. Richard Lewontin reached similar conclusions in 1972. See Richard C. Lewontin, *The Apportionment of Human Diversity,* 6 EVOLUTIONARY BIOLOGY 381, 397 (1972). *See generally,* L.L. Cavalli-Sforza, *The Genetics of Human Populations,* 231 SCI. AM. 80 (Sept. 1974). Lewontin argued that biologists should abandon all talk of biological races. "Since such racial classification is now seen to be of virtually no genetic or taxonomic significance . . . no justification can be offered for its continuance." Lewontin at 397. Nei & Roychoudhury agree that talk of biological races should be abandoned, but point out that there remains statistically significant differences between smaller population groups that justify the continued scientific division of humans by gene type. Nei & Roychoudhury, *supra* note 24 at 41.

> The key prerequisite for differentiation of any animal population into races is some kind of separation of groups that prevents interbreeding. In man's development separation must have been achieved mainly by geography . . . Geographic distance favors local differentiation even where there are no major barriers to movement. Unless there are strict barriers of some kind, however, the differences are not sharp but gradual, continuous rather than discontinuous. This kind of gradation is characteristic of most human racial differentiation.

In *Human Races,* Nei & Roychoundhury present their findings in dendrograms, horizontal branching trees that compare genetic variation among populations. The "Dendrogram for representative human populations of the world" demonstrates the gradual gene frequency shifts as one moves through the following groups: Lapp, English, Italian, Iranian, Northern Indian, Malay, Chinese, Japanese, Polynesian, Micronesian, South Amerind (American Indian), Eskimo, Alaskan Indian, Australian Aborigine, Papuan, Nigerian, Bantu, and Bushman (Khoi). Nei & Roychoudhury, *supra* note 24, at 38.

Unfortunately, in presenting their evidence Nei and Roychoudhury seem to reinscribe racial hierarchies. They present nine separate dendrograms. Because the dendrogram is horizontal, the compared populations appear listed vertically at the ends of the branches. Of the nine dendrograms, eight roughly but unquestionably list the different populations in a literal hierarchy ranging downward from the most fair-skinned groups. For example, the hierarchy of African populations places Italians at the top of the tree, "as a reference population," and then starts down: North African, Beja, Sandawe, Bantu, Yoruba, Dama, Pygmy, Bushman, and Hottentot. *Id.* at 22. At the top are the Italians, followed by the North Africans, who are "Caucasoids," *Id.* at 18, below them are the Beja, who "seem to have had gene admixture with eastern Mediterranean Caucasoids," *Id.* at 19. Skipping the Sandawe, the next major group includes the Bantu, Yoruba, and Dama. The Bantu "are morphologically similar to the Yoruba"; the Yoruba "are classic Negroes"; and the Dama are similar to the Bantu and Yoruba. Finally, the hierarchy reaches the pygmies (who call themselves Babinga), the Bushman (San), and the Hottentot (Khoi), all of whom are "short-statured" or "middle-sized." This ordering is not dictated by geographic proximity, nor does it reflect a simple, North-South bias. While the North African and Beja populations are from the North, the Sandawe from Tanzania are ranked above the Yoruba from Nigeria, and the Bantu and the Dama from South Africa are listed above the Babinga of Central Africa and the Khoi and San of Namibia. Nor is the ranking dictated by genetic closeness. Because a dendogram measures genetic distance among populations, there is little scientific advantage to start with any one particular group. For examples of dendrograms that do not reflect racial hierarchies, see Cavalli-Sfroza, at 87. Nei and Roychoudhury install Italians at the apex and arrange the ranking of African populations so that the fairest-skinned groups are at the top, and the "classic" African populations below, but still above—literally and figuratively—the shorter Babingas, San, and Khoi. Nei and Roychoudhury reflexively fall into the comfortable habit of White supremacy in science.

[183] Looking White but being Black comes with a host of painful experiences. For a law professor's take on the confusions induced by white skin and Black identity, see Judy Scales-Trent, *Commonalities: On Being Black and White, Different and the Same,* 2 YALE J.L. & FEM. 305 (1990). *See also* Piper, *supra* note 166.

[184] Some prominent Black leaders have had predominantly White ancestors. Walter White, for example, served as president of the National Association for the Advancement of Colored People (NAACP) from 1931 to 1955 and clearly identified himself as Black, though at least one scholar estimates that he was likely not more than one-sixty-fourth African by ancestry. DAVIS, *supra* note 120, at 7. Interestingly, White did occasionally pass as White, but only in order to investigate lynchings in the South. *Id.* at 56. Adrian Piper evokes the choice between being White or Black in the title of her piece on passing, *Passing for White, Passing for Black.* Piper, *supra* note 166.

[185] "There are groups to which we belong or, perhaps more descriptively, into which we are thrown. A mere act of will cannot disaffiliate us from these groups. Even our attempt to hold ourselves apart merely reconfirms our membership." Gerald Torres, *Critical Race Theory: The Decline of the Universalist Ideal and the Hope of Plural Justice—Some Observations and Questions of an Emerging Phenomenon,* 75 MINN. L. REV. 993, 1005 (1991).

186 *See* DAVIS, *supra* note 120, at 143 ("Those who pass . . . must give up all family ties and loyalties to the black community in order to gain economic and other opportunities.").

187 THOMAS, *supra* note 151, at 152. *See supra* note 177.

188 THOMAS, *supra* note 151, at 144.

189 RUSSELL ET AL., *supra* note 158, at 120. For a collection of essays on racial assimilation, see LURE AND LOATHING: ESSAYS ON RACE, IDENTITY, AND THE AMBIVALENCE OF ASSIMILA-TION (Gerald Early ed., 1993).

190 DAVIS, *supra* note 120, at 22 ("The peak years for passing as white were probably from 1880 to 1925, with perhaps 10,000 to 25,000 crossing the color line each year, although such estimates are most likely inflated. By 1940 the annual number had apparently declined to no more than 2,500 to 2,750. . . . At least since the 1920s, apparently, most mulattoes who could pass have remained in the black population.").

191 *See* Ford, *supra* note 129, at 128 (commenting on the "refreshing if at the same time disquieting subversion of racial identity" implicit in the emergence of White rappers).

192 Some commentators read a bit more into rap. For example, one suggests that "rap is the voice of alienated, frustrated, and rebellious black youth who recognize their vulnerability and marginality in post-industrial America." Clarence Lusane, *Rhapsodic Aspirations: Rap, Race and Politics,* 23 THE BLACK SCHOLAR 37 (1993). My claim is more limited. I posit only that rap has a racial character to it, and that that character is Black.

193 *See, e.g.,* Toni Morrison, *On the Backs of Blacks,* TIME, Fall 1993, at 57 ("It is a mistake to think that Bush's Willie Horton or Clinton's Sister Souljah was anything but a candidate's obligatory response to the demands of a contentious electorate unable to understand itself in terms other than race."). *See generally* Thomas B. Edsall, *Clinton Stuns Rainbow Coalition: Candidate Criticizes Rap Singer's Message,* WASH. POST, June 14, 1992, at A1.

194 U.S. BUREAU OF THE CENSUS, CONSISTENCY OF REPORTING OF ETHNIC ORIGIN IN THE CURRENT POPULATION SURVEY, TECHNICAL PAPER NO. 31 (1979) at 61, *quoted in* David Hayes-Bautista & Jorge Chapa, *Latino Terminology: Conceptual Bases for Standardized Terminology,* 77 AM. J. PUB. HEALTH 61 (1987) at 64. Few Mexican Americans saw themselves as Anglo-Saxons. Most, however, did consider themselves *Hispanos,* people of Spanish descent, emphasizing their European heritage over their indigenous roots.

195 Guillermo Fuenfrios, *The Emergence of the New Chicano,* in AZTLÁN: AN ANTHOLOGY OF MEXICAN AMERICAN LITERATURE 288 (Luis Valdez & Stan Steiner eds., 1973).

196 For a powerful critique of the male-dominant gender hierarchy in the Chicano movement, *see* Angie Chabram-Dernersesian, *I Throw Punches for My Race, but I Don't Want to Be a Man: Writing Us—Chica-nos (Girl Us)/Chicanas—into the Movement Script,* in CULTURAL STUDIES 81 (Lawrence Grossberg, Cary Nelson & Paula Treichler eds., 1992).

197 "The postwar black movement, later joined by other racially based minority movements, sought to transform dominant racial ideology in the United States, to locate its elements in a more egalitarian and democratic framework, and thereby to reconstruct the social meaning of race." MICHAEL OMI & HOWARD WINANT, RACIAL FORMATION IN THE UNITED STATES: FROM THE 1960S TO THE 1980S 63 (1986).

198 Renato Rosaldo, *Others of Invention: Ethnicity and It's Discontent,* 35 VILLAGE VOICE Feb. 13, 1990, at 27.

199 "[Deconstructing races] does open new avenues for understanding the technologies of race so that racial meaning and identity can in some sense be chosen by individuals and

groups themselves. . . . Deconstruction leaves us free to reject those manifestations of the broad, totalizing, trans-cultural concept of race that continue to marginalize, stigmatize, and brutalize human beings, while we retain those definitions of race that reflect positive lived realities."

Ford, *supra* note 129, at 121 (citations omitted).

[200] Barbara Jeanne Fields, *Slavery, Race and Ideology in the United States of America,* 181 NEW LEFT REV. 95, 118 (1990).

What Should the Specific Data Collection and Presentation Categories Be?

The U.S. Office of Management and Budget

Study Questions

1. Look over the race question from the 1990 Census in Table 2 of the Introduction before you read "What Should the Specific Data Collection and Presentation Categories Be?" and consider how you might revise the questions and accompanying instructions.
2. Based on the public suggestions and review of the literature, describe how you would rewrite the race question for the 2000 Census.

There are no clear, unambiguous, objective, generally agreed-upon definitions of the terms, "race" and "ethnicity." Cognitive research shows that respondents are not always clear on the differences between race and ethnicity. There are differences in terminology, group boundaries, attributes, and dimensions of race and ethnicity. Historically, ethnic communities have absorbed other groups through conquest, the expansion of national boundaries, and acculturation.

Groups differ in their preferred identification. Concepts also change over time. Research indicates some respondents are referring to the national or geographic origin of their ancestors, while others are referring to the culture, religion, racial or physical characteristics, language, or related attributes with which they identify. The 1977 Directive No. 15 categories are a mix of these. The categories do not represent objective "truth" but rather, are ambiguous social constructs and involve subjective and attitudinal issues.

Some said the categories should reflect ancestry or cultural affiliation rather than skin color. Some wanted to indicate they were "American" and had ancestry from a particular geographic region ("hyphenated Americans") while others opposed this ("we are all Americans"). Cognitive research indicated that some people use race and ethnic origin interchangeably; they see little difference between the two concepts. Most people do understand the concept of ancestry.

Some groups stated that their preference was for standard categories that would maximize the size of their population because they believed larger numbers provide importance in society and greater political leverage.

In short, groups differed in what they considered the most desirable standard. It is impossible to satisfy every request for racial and ethnic categories that OMB received; such a list would be both lengthy and contradictory. Some persons requested religious identification; this option is not discussed below because the Federal collection of religious affiliation has been interpreted as possibly violating the separation of church and state.

Below is a discussion of public comment with regard to the current broad [racial] categories of "White," "Black," "Asian or Pacific Islander," "American Indian or Alaskan Native." Part **(e)** below discusses options with respect to classification of persons of multiple races, a category that does not exist in the current standards.

(a) White

In Directive No. 15, the "White" category includes persons having origins in any of the original peoples of Europe, North Africa, or the Middle East. The public comment included suggestions for subcategories and related changes in terminology to collect more detailed information on White ethnic groups according to the geographic region of their ancestors. This summary reports only on options proposed during public hearings and in the public comment period. Inclusion in the summary does not reflect OMB endorsement of the comments or suggestions. Requests included:

Options Suggested in Public Comments

1. Collect data for White ethnic groups according to the country of ancestral origin (for example, German, Scottish, or Irish). Some prefer other terms such as "European-American," or "German-American" and some requested that "European" be further subcategorized into "Western European" and "Eastern European." Some suggested subcategories for identifying the original peoples of Europe, North Africa, and Southwest Asia (Middle East).

2. Create a separate category for Arabs/Middle Easterners (currently included as part of the "White" category) in order to distinguish this population from persons of European descent in the "White" category. The public comment offered different suggestions for the name of the category and how to define the population group it would be intended to cover. Some comments supported a separate category for the decennial census enumeration, but not necessarily adding a separate category to the minimum set of racial and ethnic categories in Directive No. 15. These suggestions included:

   • Create a geographically oriented category called "Middle Eastern" (based not on race but on region of origin) for persons from the Middle East/North Africa and West Asian region, regardless of their race, religion, or language group. It would include Arab states, Israel, Turkey, Afghanistan, and Iran. Some suggested also including Pakistanis and Asian Indians in their geographic definition of the term. Data availability on subsets of the Middle Eastern regional category was also requested. Some comments referred to the "Middle Eastern" category as an ethnic identifier; some favored the addition of a "Middle Eastern" category to the list of basic racial and ethnic categories; and others suggested a "Middle Eastern" subcategory be created within the "White" category. Those preferring a "Middle Eastern" to an "Arab" category felt that the category would build on the other regionally defined categories, consolidate people from different countries but with similar cultural/geographic experiences regardless of race, and distinguish them from persons of European descent in the "White" category.

   • Add an ethnic category called "Arab-American" based on a linguistic and cultural approach to the minimum set of categories in Directive No. 15. Those who preferred the term, "Arab" said Arabs, like Hispanics, are an ethnic group of mixed race and have a shared language and culture. They would make "Arab" a separate category rather than part of the "White" category; they would leave North Africans, who are not Arabs, as part of the "White" category.

   • Reclassify "Muslim West Asians" as part of the "Asian or Pacific Islander" category.

3. Alternative words suggested for "White" include "Caucasian" and "Anglo."

Past research results/literature review. Some object to the term "White" (for example, in cognitive research one said, "white is the color of paint" and in a letter another said, "I am not the color of this paper").

Some preferred the term, "Caucasian." Ethnicity is largely symbolic or optional for many Whites. Whites often reported inconsistently, as "American," or not at all in response to the 1990 census ancestry question. A significant number of Whites do not strongly identify with a specific European ethnicity. This has been the case for decades. For example, only about 55 percent of matched persons who reported English, Scottish, or Welsh in the March 1971 Current Population Survey (CPS) reported the same origin in March 1972. The "example effect" is very strong for White ancestry groups. For example, in two surveys held five months apart, 40 million people reported English as their ancestry and in the other, nearly 50 million said they were English. The only difference was placement of a question on language use in their home (English for 90 percent of the population) after the ancestry question in the second survey and farther apart in the first survey. "German" was the first example in the 1990 census ancestry question and, as a result, the German population appeared to grow very rapidly. Some Whites, however, do identify strongly with their ancestry and were confused by the 1990 census race question which listed nationality groups for Asians and Hispanics but not for Whites.

(b) Black

The term "Black" in Directive No. 15 refers to a person having origins in any of the Black racial groups of Africa. There were suggestions to change the definition to "persons having origins in any of the Black peoples of Africa," or to define the term to include all Black persons regardless of country of origin or country of citizenship. Requests were made to identify Blacks according to the geographic region of their ancestors. "African-American" and "Black African-American" were suggested as names for the category [the suggestions of "Black American" and "Amerofian" (described as Blacks who are American Natives, European, and West African) are not discussed below]. This summary reports only on options proposed during public hearings and in the public comment period. Inclusion in the summary does not reflect OMB endorsement of the comments or suggestions. Requests included:

Options Suggested in Public Comments

1. Collect data for Black ethnic groups according to geographic origin of Black ancestors (African, Haitian, Jamaican, Caribbean, West Indian, Brazilian, Ethiopian, etc.).

2. Create a separate category for Louisiana (French) Creoles. They objected to categorization with Blacks as they are a multi-racial/ethnic group (African, French, American Indian, and Hispanic).

3. Use the alternative term, "African American" or "Black, African-American."

4. Provide a separate category for Cape Verdeans (Portuguese and African ancestry from Cape Verde on the western tip of Africa. This is mostly a multiracial population. "Cape Verdean" is generally considered a national, ethnic and linguistic designation rather than a racial designation). The category could be an ethnic category rather than a racial category as is the case for persons of Hispanic origin.

Past research results/literature review. In surveys from 1989 to 1991, more Blacks said it did not matter if they were called "Black" or "African American" than said they preferred one over the other. Among those with a preference, the ratio choosing "Black" over "African-American" was 1.2 to 1. In a 1993 survey in the Chicago area, a majority of Blacks preferred "African American" for their ethnicity and "Black" for their race but the proportion had declined since 1991.

Several studies of Blacks with roots in the Caribbean or Africa show they do not feel they share a common history or culture with American-born Blacks and distinguish themselves from this population. Further research is needed on the terminology that is generally understood or most acceptable. In the 1990 census, about 370,000 persons wrote in an entry classified as "Black"; about three-fourths of these were ethnic subgroups such as Jamaican and Haitian. Cognitive research suggests that many foreign-born Blacks interpreted the race question in terms of national origin rather than race.

(c) Asian or Pacific Islander

The definition used for "Asian or Pacific Islander" in Directive No. 15 refers to a person having origins in any of the original peoples of the Far East, Southeast Asia, the Indian subcontinent, and the Pacific Islands. This area includes, for example, China, India, Japan, Korea, the Philippine Islands, the Hawaiian Islands, and Samoa. Public comment indicated confusion about which countries are included in this definition, particularly for "Indian subcontinent" and whether the aboriginal peoples of Australia are included in this category. Requests were made to have separate categories for Asians and Pacific Islanders and to provide additional subcategories under "Asians" to describe better this diverse population; to move Native Hawaiians, American Samoans, and Chamorros to either a separate category or to the "American Indian or Alaskan Native" category. This summary reports only on options proposed during public hearings and in the public comment period. Inclusion in the summary does not reflect OMB endorsement of the comments or suggestions. Requests included:

Options Suggested in Public Comments

1. Make two categories, one for "Asians" and one for "Pacific Islanders." Pacific Islanders include indigenous populations from American Samoans, Carolinians and Chamorros, and Native Hawaiians, as well as other population groups in the Pacific Islands. Native Hawaiians have a specific legal status in Federal statutes different from other indigenous Pacific Islanders.
2. Specify major Asian nationality groups.
3. Develop a new category for original peoples of acquired American lands ("indigenous" populations). This would include persons having origins in any of the original peoples of North America who maintain cultural identification through tribal affiliation or community recognition (American Indians, Alaskan Indians, Aleuts, and Eskimos); the Hawaiian Islands; American Samoa; Guam and the Northern Marianas. Some suggested this be a "Native American" category. Refer also to category **(d)** (2).
4. Have a separate category for Native Hawaiians (defined as individuals who are descendants of the aboriginal people who, prior to 1778, occupied and exercised sovereignty in the area that now constitutes the State of Hawaii). Change "Hawaiian" to "Hawaiian, part-Hawaiian," because most Native Hawaiians are part Hawaiian and many, in the past, have categorized themselves as "White."

Past research results/literature review. The proportion of Asian and Pacific Islanders such as Cambodians and Laotians (groups not listed separately) reporting in the "other race" response circle to the 1990 census race item may be due to question design. Additionally, persons who were not Asians or Pacific Islanders marked the circle for "Other Asian or Pacific Islander." Of persons marking the "Other Asian or Pacific Islander" circle in the 1990 census, 54 percent of the write-ins were not consistent with the marked circle and nearly 40 percent were Hispanic group write-ins.

(d) American Indian or Alaskan Native

The category of American Indian or Alaskan Native in Directive No. 15 includes persons having origins in any of the original peoples of North America and who maintain cultural identification through tribal affiliations or community recognition. This summary reports only on options proposed during public hearings and in the public comment period. Inclusion in the summary does not reflect OMB endorsement of the comments or suggestions. Requests included:

Options Suggested in Public Comments

1. Suggestions for change in category title include: "American Indian, Alaskan Indian, Eskimo, and Aleut"; "American Indian, Alaskan Indian, Aleut, or Eskimo"; "Federally Recognized American Indian and Alaskan Native"; and "Native American." Some prefer "Alaska Native" to "Alaskan Native." Suggestions also include collecting information on Tribal enrollment.
2. Change the category to include Native Hawaiians and other indigenous populations. Suggested category names include: "American Indian, Alaskan Native, or Native Hawaiian"; "American Indian, Alaskan Native, Native Hawaiian, and American Samoan"; "aboriginal population"; "indigenous populations"; and "Indigenous/Aboriginal People" (also see discussion under (c) (3).
3. Collect information on specific tribal affiliation and distinguish between Federally-recognized tribes and State-recognized tribes (Tribal affiliation is based on criteria established by the tribe, not self-identification.).

Past research results/literature review. Of persons reporting as "American Indian" in the 1990 census, 13 percent did not specify a tribe; this was an improvement from the 1980 census results.

There was higher than expected growth rate of American Indians from 1980 to 1990 (as well as from 1970 to 1980) which raises questions about what the census race question is measuring for this population. Some of the change is attributed to growth and improvements in the census and outreach programs, some to misreporting (for example, some Asian Indian parents reported their children as American Indian), and some to shifts in self-identification from White to American Indian. The quality of the data for the American Indian population is of concern since it is a relatively small population (about 2 million in 1990) and the data are used to disburse Federal program funds to American Indian tribal and Alaska Native

Village governments. About 2 million persons said they were American Indian in the race question of the 1990 census; however, 8.7 million included American Indian in their response to the ancestry question.

(e) Multiracial

How to classify persons who identify with more than one race is perhaps the issue that has engendered the most controversy in the present review. For the most part, the public comment used the term "multiracial" to refer to persons of two or more races. A variety of options were suggested in public comment for how to collect racial data from multiracial persons. They are shown below, followed by pros and cons cited for each option. Table 1 summarizes the options. This summary reports only on options proposed during public hearings and in the public comment period. Inclusion in the summary does not reflect OMB endorsement of the comments or suggestions.

In Latin America, a racially mixed society, there is an array of terms to describe gradations of skin color. This has not been the history of the United States in this century where the terminology implies "pure" races such as White or Black, rather than biracial or multiracial categories. In 1960, there were about 150,000 interracial marriages compared with 1.5 million in 1990. In the 1990 census, about 4 percent of couples reported they were of different races or one was of Hispanic origin. Such households had about 4 million children.

Directive No. 15 says that persons of mixed racial and ethnic origins should use the single category which most closely reflects the individual's recognition in his or her community. The public comments indicate that

Table I	Summary of Options for Identification of Multiracial Persons
(e) (1)	**Multiracial identification not allowed (must pick one broad category):**
(aa)	Individual chooses the one with which he or she most closely identifies
(bb)	Mother's category is designated
(cc)	Father's category is designated
(dd)	Race of minority-designated parent (if one is White)
(e) (2)	**Multiracial identification allowed:**
(aa)	"Multiracial" category—self-identification (SI) or observer identification (OI)
(bb)	"Mark all that apply" from list of specific categories—SI only
(cc)	Open-ended question—SI or OI
(dd)	"Other"—SI only
(ee)	Mother's and father's geographic ancestry—SI only
(ff)	Skin-color gradient chart—SI or OI

multiracial persons objected to this instruction. The commenters indicate that a single category does not reflect how they think of themselves. From their perspective, the instruction requires them to deny their full heritage and to choose between their parents. They feel they are being required to provide factually false information. They maintain that the current categories do not recognize their existence. They say they could mark "Other" where that category is provided but they feel it is demeaning. They want to identify their multiple races, but say that those who prefer to choose one of the existing broad categories could do so.

One concern of those who oppose a category for multiracial persons is that it will reduce the count for persons in the basic categories. Organizations representing multiracial persons disagree. They say minority groups could gain numbers as some persons are now classified as "White" under the "choose one" rule. As reflected in the options listed below, there was disagreement as to whether identification should include specific races. If specific races are identified, there might be some flexibility in how users could tabulate data. For some, this is seen as an advantage. For others, it is seen as a disadvantage because different tabulation rules would result in different counts of groups.

Some asked how far back in one's ancestry respondents should go in deciding to identify multiple races. Most who commented meant only the race or Hispanic origin of parents. This would require additional instructions and may not be acceptable to those who wish to identify their earlier ancestry. Presumably, persons would be instructed to list all races if the parent(s) were also of multiple races; this concerned those who oppose a multiracial category.

The discussion below refers to "race" but some respondents suggested multiple "ancestry" (listing both parents) should be the focus instead. Asking about ancestry focuses the questions back in time and conveys an historical and geographic context which some feel is clearer than the ambiguity of "race" or "ethnicity."

Past research results/literature review on a multiracial category. Some persons of mixed parentage or parents of interracial children who want to report more than one race are unsure how to respond. In the 1990 census, 98 percent of the population identified in one category; only 2 percent provided write-in multiple responses to the race question despite the instruction to mark one race only. Developing instructions for who should and who should not mark a "multiracial" category is difficult; in a 1994 pretest of the Census Bureau's redesigned Survey of Income and Program Participation, some persons thought they were being asked what race they would like to be if they could be multiracial even though their parents were from the same racial group.

PART·3

Ethnic Classification

Because of the problematic nature of the "race" concept and difficulties associated with racial classification, many social scientists have suggested that the term be abandoned. They argue that "ethnicity" is a concept which more meaningfully captures important human attributes and should be used instead. In this section, we examine the concept of ethnicity and the system used in the United States for ethnic classification. In addition, we ask whether it is possible to classify people according to ethnicity.

Social scientists use the term *ethnicity* very broadly. It can refer to people who share (or believe they share) a national origin; a common ancestry; a place of birth; distinctive and visible social traits such as religious practice, style of dress, body ornaments, or language; and/or socially important physical characteristics such as skin color, hair texture, and/or physical build. This broad definition suggests that a person's ethnicity can be based on almost countless number of traits.

The U.S. Bureau of the Census asks respondents at least six questions to determine their ethnicity. It asks about race, Hispanic origin, ancestry, place of birth, and language, including a self-rating of ability to speak English (see reading "Questions Related to Ethnicity"). These questions tell us nothing about the meaning a specific ethnicity holds for respondents, about the forces that have shaped respondents' senses of their ethnic identities, or the importance of ethnicity to their lives.

Federal Statistical Directive No. 15 (see reading in Part 2) names two official ethnic categories into which all people in the United States must be placed: (1) Hispanic/Spanish origin and (2) non-Hispanic/Spanish origin. The directive defines Hispanic/Spanish as a person of Mexican, Puerto Rican, Cuban, Central, or South American, or other Spanish culture or origin, regardless of race (see Table 1). Although federal agencies may collect information on other ethnic groups, those groups must ultimately fall under the two official categories.

In determining whether someone is Hispanic or non-Hispanic, census bureau coders consider the answers respondents give to the six ethnicity questions. If respondents give inconsistent answers to these questions, coders are directed to assign the "correct" ethnic identity. In many cases, census coders assigned an ethnicity that did not match the respondents'

Table 1   United States: Hispanic Origin by Race

HISPANIC ORIGIN BY RACE (UNIVERSE: PERSONS)	
Not of Hispanic origin:	
White	188,424,773
Black	29,284,596
American Indian, Eskimo, or Aleut	1,866,807
Asian or Pacific Islander	69,943
Other race	239,306
Hispanic origin:	
White	11,402,291
Black	645,928
American Indian, Eskimo, or Aleut	148,336
Asian or Pacific Islander	232,684
Other race	94,708

Source: U.S. Bureau of the Census (1996a).

answers. For example, 40 percent of those whom the census bureau classified as "Hispanic" on the basis of their answers to the place of birth, ancestry, and language questions answered "no" to the Hispanic origin question.

Census coders and other researchers blamed these inconsistencies on "response error"—on respondent misunderstanding, ignorance, ambivalence about their "real" ethnic identity, or a desire to hide their "true" ethnic identity (Gimenez 1989). Figure 1 shows the flowchart census bureau interviewers and coders use to make decisions about the category in which to place respondents who give complex answers to the ethnicity questions. Notice how the flowchart directs interviewers to classify the "problem" respondents as belonging to one ethnic group.

Sociologist Martha Gimenez (1989) argues that the source of inconsistencies in answers given to the six ethnicity questions lies not with the respondents but with the concept of Hispanic/Spanish origin. It "forces respondents to agree to having 'Spanish/Hispanic' origin; something which for a substantial number of people makes no sense, both in terms of their actual ancestry and/or in terms of their historical sense of who they are and/or (in the case of Latin Americans) their nationalistic allegiance to their country of origin" (p. 566).

In the readings "A View From the South" by Peter Winn (1995) and "Directive No. 15 and Self-Identification" by Luis Angel Toro (1995), we gain insights about why the label "Hispanic" is confusing to the many people the U.S. government eventually labels as such. In order to show why this approach is so confusing, Winn reviews the history of the countries labeled as "Latin American." We learn that Latin America is a land of immigrants

Figure I   Procedures for Recording Ethnic Origin for Problem Cases

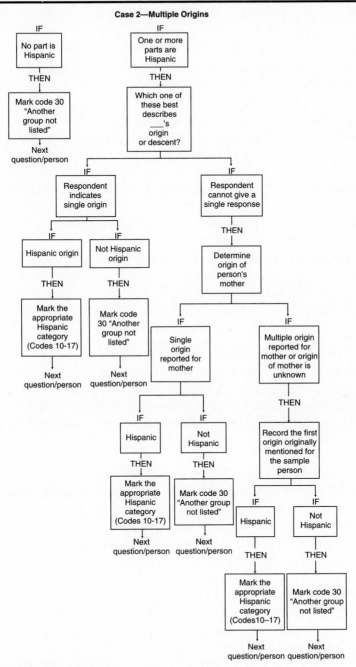

Source: U.S. Bureau of the Census 1994.

just like the United States and the rest of the Americas. In fact, the history of Latin America is intertwined with that of Asia, Europe, the Middle East, and Africa. As a result of this interconnected history, the countries of Latin America are not populated by a homogeneous group known as "Hispanics," but by native- and foreign-born persons, immigrants and nonimmigrant residents, and persons from every conceivable ancestry (not just Spanish ancestries). Toro offers four case studies of people whose lives reflect the history of intermixing that Winn describes. These cases show that for many people, "answering the racial and ethnic identity questions involves considerable guesswork as to what the government is asking" (Toro 1995:1260). In spite of the confusing facts, many people continue to use "Hispanic" to describe themselves or others, as if the label provides meaningful information about a person. (See "When Is Ethnicity Relevant in a Case Report?") We fail to realize that the category "Hispanic" is an artificial population—"a statistical construct formed by aggregates of people who differ greatly in terms of national origin, language, race, time of arrival in the United States, culture, minority status, social class, and socioeconomic status" (Gimenez 1989:559).

The difficulties associated with simply defining and determining who is of "Hispanic/Spanish" ethnicity leaves us with some nagging questions about the nature of ethnicity such as the following:

- Who belongs to an ethnic group?
- What characteristics distinguish one ethnic group from others (i.e., Is eating rice for breakfast a behavior which makes someone Japanese? Is the ability to speak French a behavior that makes someone French?)
- Is it possible to describe what it means to be a member of a particular ethnic group?

Cynthia K. Mahmood and Sharon Armstrong's (1989) research shows that these questions are not easy to resolve. For their research, Mahmood and Armstrong traveled to Eastermar, a village in the Netherlands province of Friesland, to study the Frisian people's reactions to a book published about them. They found that the Frisian people were unable to agree on a single "truth" about them as described in that book. At the same time, Frisian villagers could not come up with a list of features that would apply to all Frisian people and distinguish them from other people living in Eastermar. Yet, the Frisians were "convinced of their singularity" and the villagers reacted emotionally to the suggestion that perhaps they did not constitute a distinct culture.

The Frisian situation captures the conceptual challenges associated with the idea of identifying an ethnic group: the paradox of recognizing an ethnic group but being unable to define its *boundaries,* the characteristics which mark some people off from others as unified and distinct. In other

When Is Ethnicity Relevant in a Case Report?

To the Editor:—With reference to a recently published case report of a 29-yr-old woman with a bronchial trifurcation at the carina, we fail to understand the medical or epidemiologic relevance of describing the patient as "Hispanic"[1] The term Hispanic refers to a cultural group, not a racial group. Hispanics may be white, black, Asian, or any other race.[2] The 1990 Census considers persons to be of Spanish Hispanic origin if the person's origin or ancestry is Mexican, Mexican-American, Chicano, Puerto Rican, Cuban, Argentinean, Colombian, Costa Rican, Dominican, Ecuadorian, Guatemalan, Honduran, Nicaraguan, Peruvian, Salvadoran; from other Spanish-speaking countries of the Caribbean or Central or South America; or from Spain.[3] In fact, the only real prerequisite for being Hispanic is self-identification. For federal data collection purposes, Hispanic persons are those who say they are Hispanic. A large number of Hispanics in the United States are bilingual. Thus, this classification does not necessarily mean that the individual cannot speak English. The term Hispanic has caused controversy in the past and has been associated with derogatory remarks. A number of alternative terms have been used by Hispanic-Americans to name themselves, including Spanish or Latino.

Our comments should not be interpreted as excessive sensitivity nor to suggest that the term "Hispanic" should not be used. We suggest avoiding labeling patients in a scientific publication, unless the description adds relevant, pertinent, and useful information.

Rafael Ortega, M.D.
Assistant Professor of Anesthesiology
Marcelle M. Willock, M.D.
Professor and Chairman
Department of Anesthesiology
Boston University Medical Center
88 East Newton Street
Boston, Massachusetts 02118

References

1. Stene R, Rose M, Weinger MB, Benumof JL, Harrell J: Broch trifurcation at the carina complicating use of a double-lumen tracheia tube. ANESTHESIOLOGY 80:1162–1164, 1994

2. Garwood AN: Hispanic Americans: A Statistical Source book Boulder, Numbers and Concepts, 1991

3. Schick FL, Schick R: Statistical Handbook on U.S. Hispanics Phoenix, The Oryx Press, 1991

(Accepted for publication June 26, 1994.)

Anesthesiology
81:1082, 1994

In Reply:—Ortega and Willock make several excellent and thoughtful points. The use of the adjective "Hispanic" has no useful medical or epidemiologic purpose in our article that I know of. I thank Ortega and Willock for their culturally sensitive comments.

Jonathan L. Benumof, M.D.
Professor of Anesthesia
Department of Anesthesiology, 0801
University of California, San Diego
9500 Gilman Drive
La Jolla, California 92093

words, there is no easy formula that can be used to clearly classify people into distinct ethnic categories (Nathan 1993).

To further illustrate the difficulties of conceptualizing ethnicity and placing people into ethnic categories, consider that when Raymond Breton and his colleagues (1990) studied ethnicity in Toronto, they asked respondents 167 questions to determine their ethnicity. They found no single question could be used as a mark of membership in an ethnic group. Likewise, when Mary C. Waters (1990) studied the process by which people reach an answer to the question "What is your ethnic origin (ancestry)?", she asked subjects at least 83 follow-up questions to determine how they came up with an answer.

Breton and Waters asked such a large number of questions because membership in an ethnic group involves more than sharing a language, a national origin, or distinctive physical features. Membership involves social demands. Consider Merry White's (1988) discussion about what it means to be Japanese in Japan.

> The simplest definition of being Japanese is to be born in Japan, to be of Japanese parents, to live in Japan, and to speak Japanese. As we have seen, a person is Japanese not only because he or she speaks Japanese, likes raw fish, and carries a Japanese passport, but because he or she is an active participant in relationships with clearly drawn lines of responsibility and loyalty. (p. 110)

Breton and Waters' research challenges the common practice of using the most visible biological markers such as eye shape and color, hair texture and color, and skin color to determine ethnicity. The problem with biological markers is that our genetic endowment gives us human and physical traits, not an ethnic culture or identity. Anthropologist Dorrinne Kondo (1990) recalls that most of the people she encountered while doing fieldwork in Japan found it difficult to accept the idea that biological markers are not an accurate predictor of ethnicity.

> As a Japanese American, I created a conceptual dilemma for the Japanese I encountered. For them, I was a living oxymoron, someone who was both Japanese and not Japanese. Their puzzlement was all the greater since most Japanese people I knew seemed to adhere to an eminently biological definition of Japaneseness. Race, language, and culture are intertwined, so much so that any challenge to this firmly entrenched conceptual schema—a white person who speaks flawlessly idiomatic and unaccented Japanese, or a person of Japanese ancestry who cannot—meets with what generously could be described as unpleasant reactions. . . .
>
> Indeed, it is a minor miracle that those first months [in Japan] did not lead to an acute case of agoraphobia, for I knew that once I set foot outside the door, someone somewhere (a taxi driver? a salesperson? a bank clerk?) would greet one of my linguistic mistakes with an astonished 'Eh?' I became all too familiar with the series of expressions that would

flicker over those faces: bewilderment, incredulity, embarrassment, even anger, at having to deal with this odd person who looked Japanese and therefore human, but who must be retarded, deranged, or—equally un-desirable in Japanese eyes—Chinese or Korean. Defensively, I would mull over the mistake-of-the-day. I mean, how was I to know that in or-der to 'fillet a fish' you had to cut it 'in three pieces'? Or that opening a bank account required so much specialized terminology? Courses in liter-ary Japanese at Harvard hadn't done much to prepare me for the realities of everyday life in Tokyo. Gritting my teeth in determination as I groaned inwardly, I would force myself out of the house each morning. (p. 11)

One reason there are no markers that can be used to clearly classify people into distinct ethnic categories is that most people have mixed an-cestry and possess a blend of physical and cultural traits. The case of culi-nary artist and chef Jeannette Holley, featured in *American Visions,* shows that ethnic categories can never be clear cut.

The 37-year-old chef is thin and tall, with taffy-colored skin and sculp-tured black hair. Her deep, almond eyes allow only momentary glimpses into her private world of inner connections. Her father is African-American, her mother, Japanese, and Holley has spent much of her life in Asia, first outside Tokyo and later in Seoul, Korea. "I was raised an American. I lived in Asia for 17 years. I spoke English at home, although it wasn't my first language. Language itself becomes a property of who you are. The less Japanese I speak, the less Japanese I feel." (Burns 1993:36)

Depending on the marker one chooses to use—skin color, national origin, territory, ancestry, eye structure, language—Jeannette Holley could be classified as a member of any number of ethnic groups. Yet, because Hol-ley has no single ethnic identity, we cannot say that she lacks an ethnicity.

The Holley case suggests that if we try to determine objectively what constitutes membership in an ethnic group, we introduce the issue of au-thenticity or the question of who is more African-American, Japanese, Ital-ian, and so on. Salman Rushdie (1991) makes this point in *Imaginary Home-lands* when he argues that there are many ways to be Indian in England.

England's Indian writers are by no means the same type of animal. Some of us, for instance, are Pakistani. Others Bangladeshi. Others West, or East, or even South African . . . This word "Indian" is getting to be a pretty scattered concept. Indian writers in England include political ex-iles, first-generation migrants, affluent expatriates whose residence here is frequently temporary, naturalized Britons, and people born here who may never have laid eyes on the subcontinent. Clearly nothing that I say can apply across all these categories. (pp. 16–17)

Charles Hirschman (1993) points out that there is no such thing as mutu-ally exclusive or clear-cut ethnic categories. There has always been *ethnic blending*—"inter-ethnic unions (interbreeding) and shifts in ethnic affiliation" (p. 549)—such that "most ethnic communities are either amalgams of different peoples or have absorbed significant numbers of other groups through conquest, the expansion of national boundaries, or acculturation" (p. 550). The reading "The Mingling of Alaska Natives with 'Foreigners': A Brief Historical Overview" by Julie E. Sprott (1994) illustrates Hirschman's point.

If people possessed complete information related to their ancestry, practically everyone in any society would belong to multiple ethnic categories. Hirschman suggests that the ambiguity of ethnicity would seem to minimize the importance of ethnicity in people's lives. Yet, based on a casual reading and viewing of the news, exactly the opposite seems to be true. Hirschman believes this is the case because in most societies the politics of ethnicity are based on notions of inclusion and exclusion (or the idea that clear boundaries separate outsiders from insiders), which discourage people from claiming multiple ethnic identifications. Thus Hirschman argues that the questions we ask about ethnicity should reflect a social and political reality in the United States which assumes that *one* ethnicity dominates.

Hirschman's argument may be true with regard to the politics of ethnicity (see the reading "Ethnicity as Explanation, Ethnicity as Excuse" by Paul A. Goble (1994) for more on the politics of ethnicity). It does not seem to apply to self-identification. The majority of respondents who participated in the 1990 Census, when asked about their ancestry or ethnic origin, listed multiple ancestries. If anything, the census bureau codes the ancestry data in such a way to make it appear as if people have only one ancestry or ethnicity (see Table 2 and the reading "Ancestry" from the U.S. Bureau of the Census (1996b)).

Because there are no clear markers which can be used to classify people into ethnic groups, perhaps the best way to determine someone's ethnicity is to rely on self-identification. Self-identification can prove to be problematic because people's sense of ethnic identification "can range from nonexistent to levels so high that the fate of the group is experienced as the fate of the self" (Verkuyten 1991:286). In addition, everyone has different criteria—some more stringent than others—for claiming membership in an ethnic group. For example, as sociologist Anny Bakalian (1991) remarks in her research on Armenian identity, "One can say he or she is an Armenian without speaking Armenian, marrying an Armenian, doing business with Armenians, belonging to an Armenian church, joining Armenian voluntary associations, or participating in the events and activities sponsored by such organizations" (p. 13). The basis for such a claim may be "a nostalgic allegiance to the culture of the immigrant generation, or that of the old country; a love for and pride in a tradition that can be felt without having to be incorporated in everyday behavior" (Nagel 1994:154).

Table 2   Ancestry in the United States

REPORTED SINGLE ANCESTRY (000–862, 900–994, 998):

Arab (400–415, 417–418, 421–430, 435–481, 490–499)	557,232
Austrian (003–004)	263,593
Belgian (008–010)	129,901
Canadian (931–934)	254,262
Czech (111–114)	601,499
Danish (020, 023)	456,876
Dutch (021, 029)	1,456,886
English (015, 022)	11,455,445
Finnish (024–025)	259,731
French (except Basque) (000–001, 016, 026–028, 083)	2,262,836
French Canadian (935–938)	1,708,273
German (032–045)	22,673,935
Greek (046–048)	632,540
Hungarian (125–126)	596
Irish (050, 081, 099)	12,300,701
Italian (030–031, 051–074)	7,299,048
Lithuanian (129)	327,393
Norwegian (082)	1,359,789
Polish (142–143)	3,834,659
Portuguese (084–086)	666,515
Romanian (144–147)	160,947
Russian (148–151)	1,210,323
Scotch-Irish (087)	2,972,113
Scottish (088)	1,518,108
Slovak (153)	811,461
Subsaharan African (500–599)	430,796
Swedish (089–090)	1,338,964
Swiss (091–096)	241,423
Ukrainian (171–174)	356,386
United States or American (939–994)	13,051,601
Welsh (097)	4,147
West Indian (excluding Hispanic origin groups) (300–359)	987,399
Yugoslavian (152, 154, 176–177)	248,755
Race or Hispanic origin groups (200–299, 900–928)	45,823,082
Other groups (002, 005–007, 011–014, 017–019, 049, 075–080, 098)	10,172,861
Reported multiple ancestry (000–998)	73,771,307
Unclassified or not reported (863–899, 995–997, 999)	26,101,626

Continued

Then there are those who simplify their ethnicity by a process sociologist Mary C. Waters (1990) calls "selective forgetting." In the reading "Choosing an Ancestry" Waters describes how people she interviewed chose to reorganize only some of their ancestries and forget or discount the others and are uncertain about whether they actually belong to a particular

Table 2 *Continued*

REPORTED MULTIPLE ANCESTRY

First ancestry reported (000–999):

Arab (400–415, 417–418, 421–430, 435–481, 490–499)	716,391
Austrian (003–004)	545,856
Belgian (008–010)	248,075
Canadian (931–934)	361,612
Czech (111–114)	10,125
Danish (020, 023)	980,868
Dutch (021, 029)	3,475,410
English (015, 022)	21,836,397
Finnish (024–025)	465,070
French (except Basque) (000–001, 016, 026–028, 083)	6,204,184
French Canadian (935–938)	2,296,123
German (032–045)	45,583,932
Greek (046–048)	921,782
Hungarian (125–126)	997,545
Irish (050, 081, 099)	22,721,252
Italian (030–031, 051–074)	11,286,815
Lithuanian (129)	526,089
Norwegian (082)	2,517,760
Polish (142–143)	6,542,844
Portuguese (084–086)	900,060
Romanian (144–147)	235,774
Russian (148–151)	2,114,506
Scotch-Irish (087)	43,341
Scottish (088)	3,315,306
Slovak (153)	1,210,652
Subsaharan African (500–599)	469,285
Swedish (089–090)	2,881,950
Swiss (091–096)	607,833
Ukrainian (171–174)	514,085
United States or American (939–994)	13,052,178
Welsh (097)	1,038,603
West Indian (excluding Hispanic origin groups) (300–359)	1,058,345
Yugoslavian (152, 154, 176–177)	361,190
Race or Hispanic origin groups (200–299, 900–928)	49,556,818
Other groups (002, 005–007, 011–014, 017–019, 049, 075–080, 098)	11,716,884
Unclassified or not reported (863–899, 995–997, 999)	26,101,626

Continued

ethnic group, in what respect they belong, and to what degree (see also In-field 1951). The uncertainty may stem from a wide range of experiences. For example, people may become uncertain about their ethnic identity when the professed identity does not correspond to what others believe someone claiming that identity should be. Conversely, what others believe

Table 2 *Continued*

REPORTED MULTIPLE ANCESTRY

Second ancestry reported (000–999):

Arab (400–415, 417–418, 421–430, 435–481, 490–499)	1,543
Austrian (003–004)	324,675
Belgian (008–010)	146,580
Canadian (931–934)	199,279
Czech (111–114)	602,901
Danish (020, 023)	653,801
Dutch (021, 029)	2,751,679
English (015, 022)	10,819,382
Finnish (024–025)	193,800
French (except Basque) (000–001, 016, 026–028, 083)	4,133,216
French Canadian (935–938)	539,275
German (032–045)	12,401,663
Greek (046–048)	188,591
Hungarian (125–126)	584,757
Irish (050, 081, 099)	16,047,948
Italian (030–031, 051–074)	3,428,124
Lithuanian (129)	285,776
Norwegian (082)	1,351,635
Polish (142–143)	2,823,262
Portuguese (084–086)	2,532
Romanian (144–147)	129,770
Russian (148–151)	836,867
Scotch-Irish (087)	1,283,576
Scottish (088)	2,078,275
Slovak (153)	672,245
Subsaharan African (500–599)	36,903
Swedish (089–090)	1,798,913
Swiss (091–096)	437,662
Ukrainian (171–174)	226,718
United States or American (939–994)	99
Welsh (097)	995,290
West Indian (excluding Hispanic origin groups) (300–3)	97,145
Yugoslavian (152, 154, 176–177)	136,494
Race or Hispanic origin groups (200–299, 900–928)	5,377,404
Other groups (002, 005–007, 011–014, 017–019, 049, 075–080, 098)	1,779,925
Unclassified or not reported (863–899, 995–997, 999)	1,749,386

Source: U.S. Bureau of the Census (1996b).

a person should be may not fit with that person's conception of himself or herself. For example, novelist and critic Ilan Stavans (1995), grew up "in Mexico's capital, a secure, self-imposed Jewish ghetto" (p. 195). He spoke Spanish, took vacations to Disney World in Florida, went to Texas on shopping sprees, watched "Star Trek" on television, ate junk food and yet considered himself Mexican. "What makes me Mexican? It's hard to know: language and the air I breathed" (p. 195). As a foreign student on scholarship in the United States, Stavans "ceased to be Mexican and became, much to my surprise, a Latino—what's worse, a white Latino, something most people have difficulty understanding" (p. 196).

It is important to recognize that self-identification is not simply a matter of individual choice but it is affected by larger societal, historical, and political constraints. Some kinds of people have more freedom than others in claiming an ethnic identity. For example, people classified in racial terms as "white" have a great deal of freedom in determining their ethnic identity; those defined in 'nonwhite,' especially those defined as black, have much less choice. Black Americans, whether they be native born or immigrants from Haiti, Jamaica, Trinidad, Germany, or Kenya experience considerable social pressure to identify as black "even when they know or believe they have many "nonblack" ancestors (Waters 1994, 1990). Then there is the phenomenon of *involuntary ethnicity*. In this situation, a dominant group defines others in racial and ethnic terms, thus forcing the latter to become, appear, and/or feel more ethnic than they might otherwise be. Some ethnic groups, such as Hispanic, are an artificial product of government classification. Other ethnic groups such as the Punjabi Mexicans emerge as a result of immigration laws, the system of racial and ethnic classification, and anti-miscegenation laws. Pujabi Mexicans are the offspring of unions between Mexican women, who immigrated to the United States in the wake of the Mexican Revolution, and Pujabi men, who immigrated from India to the United States at the turn of the twentieth century without wives. At that time, U.S. immigration laws established an annual quota allowing only 100 men from India into the country each year and prevented those men from bringing wives. The Pujabi men's "choice of wives was strongly affected by the anti-miscegenation laws in effect at the time. Asian Indians were technically Caucasians, but [because of their skin color] they were not generally regarded as 'white' and this meant that they were prohibited from marrying 'white' women" (Leonard 1993:4).

Even when people are free to define their ethnicity, we must remember that people's sense of their ethnic identity is not static. It may shift over time. Joane Nagel (1995b) writes about the phenomenon of ethnic renewal on an individual and collective level. On an individual level, *ethnic renewal* occurs when a person takes on or asserts a new ethnic identity. Ethnic renewal can take many forms including reclaiming a discarded identity (as when an adopted child learns about and identifies with biological relatives), discovering a new side of the family, or learning about and reviving lost traditions. (See "Shifts in Self-Identification".)

Ethnic renewal can also be a collective phenomenon as when an organization forms or plans strategies to restore and/or revive institutions, cul-

Shifts in Self-Identification

"When I was a kid, I and the young fellows I ran around with couldn't have cared less about our Indian background," he said. "We never participated in any of the tribal ceremonies, we didn't know how to dance, and we wouldn't have been caught dead in regalia. We thought anyone who made a fuss about our heritage was old-fashioned, and we even used to make fun of the people who did. Well, when I came back from the Army, in 1948, I had a different outlook on such matters. You see, there happened to be two other Indians in my basic-training company at Fort Dix. One of them was an Iroquois from upper New York State, and the other was a Chippewa from Montana. I was nineteen years old, away from Mashpee for the first time in my life, and, like most soldiers, I was lonely. Then, one night, the Iroquois fellow got up and did an Indian dance in front of everybody in the barracks. The Chippewa got up and joined him, and when I had to admit I didn't know how, I felt terribly ashamed. During the next two years, I had the recurring feeling of not really knowing who or what I was, and I decided that when I got out of the service I would find out and do something about it. So one of the first things I did after I got back home was go and see Mabel Avant, who I heard was trying to interest the townspeople in restoring the old meetinghouse. When she saw that I really wanted to help out, she told me things about my people and our history that I had had no idea of. She got me so worked up about it all that I went straightaway to my father and asked him to show me how to make Indian baskets. Was he surprised! He had learned basketry as a young man from old Eben Queppish, who was the last master basketmaker in Mashpee. Nobody in Mashpee had made baskets in years, and my father was very pleased to find that I wanted to keep the art alive. What with soaking and stripping maplewood and weaving the bark into baskets, we both kept busy for several months."

Source: Brodeur (1978:103).

ture, history, or traditions. One striking example of ethnic renewal can be found by comparing the 1980 and 1990 census findings on the number of Native American ethnic groups. In Table 3, we see that overall the number of Native Americans increased by 458,868 or 31 percent, an increase that cannot possibly be explained by new births alone. For one Native American ethnic group, the numbers increased by as much as 248 percent.

The point is that ethnicity cannot be accommodated by a simple mark-box on a census form. As Mary C. Waters (1990) argues in *Ethnic Options: Choosing Identities in America,* "[k]nowledge of one's ethnic ancestry is the result of sifting, simplifying, and distorting the knowledge one has about it in interaction with the labels others attach to it" (p. 26). In fact one might

Table 3 Top 25 American Indian Tribes for the United States: 1990 and 1980 (Data are based on a sample)

TRIBE	1990 CENSUS		1980 CENSUS	
	NUMBER	PERCENT	NUMBER	PERCENT
All American Indians	1,937,391	100.0	1,478,523	100.0
Cherokee	369,035	19.0	232,080	15.7
Navajo	225,298	11.6	158,633	10.7
Sioux[1]	107,321	5.5	78,608	5.3
Chippewa	105,988	5.5	73,602	5.0
Choctaw	86,231	4.5	50,220	3.4
Pueblo[2]	55,330	2.9	42,552	2.9
Apache	53,330	2.8	35,861	2.4
Iroquois[3]	52,557	2.7	38,218	2.6
Lumbee[4]	50,888	2.6	28,631	1.9
Creek	45,872	2.4	28,278	1.9
Blackfoot[2]	37,992	2.0	21,964	1.5
Canadian and Latin American	27,179	1.4	7,804	0.5
Chickasaw	21,522	1.1	10,317	0.7
Tohono O'Odham	16,876	0.9	13,297	0.9
Potawatom	16,719	0.9	9,715	0.7
Seminole[2]	15,564	0.8	10,363	0.7
Pima	15,074	0.8	11,722	0.8
Tlingit	14,417	0.7	9,509	0.6
Alaskan Athabaskans	14,198	0.7	10,136	0.7
Cheyenne	11,809	0.6	9,918	0.7
Comanche	11,437	0.6	9,037	0.6
Paiute[2]	11,369	0.6	9,523	0.6
Osage	10,430	0.5	6,884	0.5
Puget Sound Salish	10,384	0.5	6,591	0.4
Yaqui	9,838	0.5	5,197	0.4

TRIBE	CHANGE	
	NUMBER	PERCENT
All American Indians	458,868	31.0
Cherokee	136,955	59.0
Navajo	66,665	42.0
Sioux[1]	28,713	36.5
Chippewa	32,386	44.0
Choctaw	36,011	71.7
Pueblo[2]	12,778	30.0
Apache	17,469	48.7
Iroquois[3]	14,339	37.5
Lumbee[4]	22,257	77.7
Creek	17,594	62.2
Blackfoot[2]	16,028	73.0
Canadian and Latin American	19,375	248.3

Continued

Table 3   *Continued*

| | CHANGE | |
TRIBE	NUMBER	PERCENT
Chickasaw	11,205	108.6
Tohono O'Odham	3,579	26.9
Potawatomi	7,004	72.1
Seminole[2]	5,201	50.2
Pima	3,352	28.6
Tlingit	4,908	51.6
Alaskan Athabaskans	4,062	40.1
Cheyenne	1,891	19.1
Comanche	2,400	26.6
Paiute[2]	1,846	19.4
Osage	3,546	51.5
Puget Sound Salish	3,793	57.5
Yaqui	4,641	89.3

[1] Any entry with the spelling "Siouan" in the 1990 Census was miscoded to Sioux in North Carolina.

[2] Reporting and/or processing problems in the 1980 Census have affected the data for this tribe.

[3] Reporting and/or processing problems in the 1990 Census have affected the data for this tribe.

[4] Miscoding of entries in the 1980 Census for "Lummee," "Lummi," "Lumbee," or "Lumbi" have affected the data for this tribe.

The data in this table are consistent with those published in 1990 CP-3-7, *1990 Census of Population,* "Characteristics of American Indians by Tribe and Language," issued July 1994. The report is available from the Government Printing Office (GPO) for $51.00. The GPO stock number for the report is 003-024-08700-6. The GPO telephone number is (202) 512-1800.

The Subject Summary Tape File (SSTF) 13, "Characteristics of American Indians by Tribe and Language," can be ordered from the Census Bureau's Customer Service Office, (301) 457-4100 or FAX (301) 457-3842. Also, a CD-ROM presenting these data is available from the Customer Services Office.

Source: U.S. Bureau of the Census (1996a).

argue that the individual process Waters describes mirrors the popular sifted, simplified, distorted versions of U.S. history many people hold which assumes every ethnic group has a separate history and that the most important story is the settling of the frontier or westward migration of English-speaking people. In "Reflections on American Ethnicity" David Steven Cohen (1991) argues that "Ethnicity has been an important factor from the beginning. In a sense ethnicity is a better explanation than the frontier of the shaping of American culture" (p. 320). But the ethnicity Cohen describes is dynamic, emerging, changing, not static, unvarying, or constant.

In the reading "Resource Competition Theories," Joane Nagel (1995a) explains how the concept of resource competition helps us to understand the conditions under which ethnicity becomes a collective phenomenon.

Questions Related to Ethnicity

The U.S. Bureau of the Census

Study Question

1. Look over the questions from the U.S. Bureau of the Census that are related to ethnicity." Think of three scenarios in which respondents would be classified as "Hispanic" but in which that classification does not capture the complexity of respondents' "ethnic" backgrounds.

1. Race (Question 4 was asked of all respondents).

   Instructions for Question 4

   Fill ONE circle for the race each person considers himself/herself to be.

   If you fill the "Indian (Amer.)" circle, print the name of the tribe or tribes in which the person is enrolled. If the person is not enrolled in a tribe, print the name of the principal tribe(s).

   If you fill the "Other API" circle [under Asian or Pacific Islander (API)], only print the name of the group to which the person belongs. For example, the "Other API" category includes persons who identify as Burmese, Fijia Hmong, Indonesian, Laatian, Bangladeshi, Pakistani, Tongan, Thai, Cambodian, Sri Lankan, and so on.

   If you fill the "Other race" circle, be sure to print the name of the race.

   If the person considers himself/herself to be "White," "Black or Negro," "Eskimo," or "Aleut," fill one circle only. Do not print the race in the box.

Figure I   Race Question for the 1990 Census

4. Race Fill ONE circle for the race that the person considers himself/herself to be. If Indian (Amer.), print the name of the enrolled or principal tribe.→	○ White ○ Black or Negro ○ Indian (Amer.) (Print the name of the enrolled or principal tribe.) [ ]
	○ Eskimo ○ Aleut Asian or Pacific Islander (API)
If Other Asian or Pacific Islander (API), print one group, for example: Hmong, Fijian, Laotian, Thai, Tongan, Pakistani, Cambodian, and so on. →	○ Chinese ○ Japanese ○ Filipino ○ Asian Indian ○ Hawaiian ○ Samoan ○ Korean ○ Guamanian ○ Vietnamese ○ Other API↓ [ ]
If Other race, print race.→	○ Other race (Print race.)↑

The "Black or Negro" category also includes persons who identify as African-American, Afro-American, Haitian, Jamaican, West Indian, Nigerian, and so on.

All persons, regardless of citizenship status, should answer this question.

2. Hispanic origin (Question 7 was asked of all respondents).

   Instructions for Question 7

   A person is of Spanish/Hispanic origin if the person's origin (ancestry) is Mexican, Mexican-Am., Chicano, Puerto Rican, Cuban, Argentinian, Colombian, Costa Rican, Dominican, Ecuadoran, Guatemalan, Honduran, Nicaraguan, Peruvian, Salvadoran; from other Spanish-speaking countries of the Caribbean or Central or South America; or from Spain.

   If you fill the Yes, other Spanish/Hispanic circle, print one group.

   A person who is not of Spanish/Hispanic origin should answer this question by filling the No (not Spanish/Hispanic) circle. Note that the term "Mexican-Am." refers only to persons of Mexican origin or ancestry.

Figure 2   Hispanic Question for the 1990 Census

7. **Is this person of Spanish/Hispanic origin?**
Fill ONE circle for each person.
 	
If **Yes, other Spanish/Hispanic,**
print one group. →
	○ No (not Spanish/Hispanic)
	○ Yes, Mexican, Mexican-Am., Chicano
	○ Yes, Puerto Rican
	○ Yes, Cuban
	○ Yes, other Spanish/Hispanic
	   (Print one group, for example:
	   Argentinean, Colombian, Dominican,
	   Nicaraguan, Salvadoran, Spaniard,
	   and so on.)↓

All persons, regardless of citizenship status, should answer this question.

3. Ancestry (Question 13 was asked of a sample of the population).

Instructions for Question 13

Print the ancestry group. Ancestry refers to the person's ethnic origin or descent, "Roots," or heritage. Ancestry also may refer to the country of birth of the person or the person's parents or ancestors before their arrival in the United States. All persons, regardless of citizenship status, should answer this question.

Persons who have more than one origin and cannot identify with a single group may report two ancestry groups (for example, German-Irish).

Be specific. For example, print whether West Indian, Asian Indian, or American Indian. West Indian includes persons whose ancestors came from Jamaica, Trinidad, Haiti, etc. Distinguish Cape Verdean from Portuguese; French Canadian from Canadian; and Dominican Republic from Dominica Island.

A religious group should not be reported as a person's ancestry.

4. Place of Birth (Question 8 was asked of a sample of the population).

Instructions for Question 8

For persons born in the United States:

Print the name of the State in which this person was born. If the person was born in Washington, D.C., print District of Columbia.

Figure 3   Ancestry Question for the 1990 Census

> **13. What is this person's ancestry or ethnic origin?**↓
> (See instruction guide for further information.)
>
> ```
> [                                  ]
> ```
>
> (For example: German, Italian, Afro-Amer., Croatian,
> Cape Verdean, Dominican, Ecuadoran, Haitian, Cajun,
> French Canadian, Jamaican, Korean, Lebanese,
> Mexican, Nigerian, Irish, Polish, Slovak, Taiwanese, Thai,
> Ukranian, etc.)

If the person was born in U.S. territory or commonwealth, print Puerto Rico, U.S. Virgin Islands, Guam, American Samoa, or Northern Marianas.

For persons born outside the United States:

Print the name of the foreign country or area where the person was born. Use current boundaries, not boundaries at the time of the person's birth. Specify whether Northern Ireland or the Republic of Ireland (Eire); East or West Germany; North or South Korea; England, Scotland or Wales (not Great Britain or United Kingdom). Specify the particular country or island in the Caribbean (not, for example, West Indies).

5. Language (Question 15 was asked of a sample of the population).

Instructions for Question 15

Mark Yes if the person sometimes or always speaks a language other than English at home.

Figure 4   Place of Birth Question for the 1990 Census

> **8. In what U.S. state or foreign country was this person born?** ↓
>
> ```
> [                                  ]
> ```
>
> (Name of state or foreign country; or Puerto Rico, Guam
> etc.)

Figure 5   Language and Ability to Speak English Questions for the 1990 Census

---

15a. Does this person speak a language other than English at home?

    ○ Yes   ○ No - Skip to 16

---

b. What is this language?↓

    (For example: Chinese, Italian, Spanish, Vietnamese)

---

c. How well does this person speak English?

    ○ Very well   ○ Not well
    ○ Well   ○ Not at all

Do not mark Yes for a language spoken only at school or if speaking is limited to a few expressions or slang.

Print the name of the language spoken at home. If this person speaks more than one non-English language and cannot determine which is spoken more often, report the first language the person learned to speak.

Source: U.S. Bureau of the Census (1994).

A View From the South: Lands of Immigrants

Peter Winn

Study Questions

1. List the national origin and ancestry groups Winn names as figuring into the history of Latin America.
2. Can you see why the question about Hispanic origin would be confusing to U.S. immigrants from Latin America? Explain.

Alfredo Jaar, the artist who created "This Is Not America," is a Chilean of Dutch descent. He was shocked to be regarded as a "Hispanic" in the United States, a complaint echoed by Brazilians, who do not even speak Spanish. One of the misconceptions that many North Americans have about Latin America and the Caribbean is that it is a homogeneous region, whose people "all look alike." On the contrary, the diversity of its population, the result of immigration patterns as complex as those that formed the United States and Canada, is what gives the region its unique character. Most are of European descent, although roughly one quarter have Indian ancestors and perhaps an equal number African roots.

We think of Latin America as an area of Iberian* colonization, but this is a simplification of its history and heritage, as a partial list of recent heads of state makes clear. Guatemala's Kjell Lagerud's Scandinavian heritage is evident in his name, as are the Slavic roots of Brazil's Kubitschek or the Italian and German lineages of his military successors, Médici and Geisel. Chile's Aylwin has British forebears, his predecessor Pinochet French origins. Nor are all of the region's heads of state of European descent. Argentina's Menem is of Arab ancestry. Peru's Fujimori campaigned for president dressed as a Japanese samurai. Yet names can also be deceiving. The roots of Grenada's Maurice Bishop

---

*In this context, Iberian refers to Spain and Portugal.

and Trinidad's Eric Williams lie in Africa, not England, as do those of Haiti's francophone Duvaliers and Jean-Bertrand Aristide. Their names are a reflection of the colonial powers that brought their ancestors to the Caribbean.

Like the United States, the rest of the Americas are lands of immigrants. The first "Americans" were Asian hunters who crossed the Bering land bridge at the dawn of hemispheric prehistory and gradually made their way south. In time they evolved into the peoples Columbus mistakenly called "Indians," a name that has stuck even among many of these indigenous peoples. In 1492 there may have been sixty million of them, ranging from nomadic hunters and gatherers in the Amazon rain forest to the sophisticated urban civilizations of the Andes and Mesoamerica, where their more than 125 million descendants are still concentrated today. Most are now mestizos, people of mixed Amerindian and European ancestry, and anthropologists insist that only some twenty-five million are culturally "Indians"—a claim that prompted Francisco Calí, a Guatemalan Mayan leader, to retort: "Who are these foreigners to tell *us* who is an Indian?"

Europeans came next, beginning in 1492, to exploit the wealth of America: Spaniards pursuing gold and glory; Portuguese looking for tropical luxuries and elusive El Dorados; Northern Europeans seeking Iberian treasure and fertile lands; Catholic friars in search of heathen souls and American utopias. By 1800 some two million Europeans had migrated to Latin America and the Caribbean.

From the start, the Europeans brought enslaved Africans with them, first as personal servants, then increasingly as field hands to work the tropical plantations and mines of the Caribbean and Brazil. This wave of forced migration grew with time, cresting in the eighteenth century. Some ten million enslaved Africans were taken across the Atlantic in chains before this inhuman traffic was finally ended in the mid-nineteenth century. They are the ancestors of the more than one hundred million people of African descent who inhabit Latin America and the Caribbean today. Many of these are mulattos, people of mixed African and European origin, a separate racial category in Latin America and the Caribbean that is ignored in North America. Perhaps half of Brazil's 150 million citizens have African roots, as do most Caribbean islanders and many Panamanians and Venezuelans.

The late nineteenth century witnessed another massive influx of seven to nine million Europeans in search of land, jobs, and opportunities. Most were from Italy, Spain, and Portugal, but many were Germans and Slavs, and some were Britons and French. These European immigrants settled mostly in southern South America, changing the face of Argentina and Uruguay, as well as parts of Brazil and Chile. Asians came, too, during this

DIRECTIVE NO. 15 AND SELF-IDENTIFICATION

LUIS ANGEL TORO

Study Question

1. What do the four examples in this reading say about the category "Hispanic"?

Heavy public criticism of Directive No. 15 reveals another primary consideration when thinking about governmental racial and ethnic classification schemes: the issue of self-identification. Persons with many different cultural identifications find that Directive No. 15 badly misconceptualizes their identity.[1] The poor fit between Directive No. 15 and the society it attempts to describe has practical as well as ethical implications. As a practical matter, confusing, indecipherable, or inaccurate classifications will result in an inaccurate picture of the population being measured. Ethically, it is difficult to justify imposing a racial classification system reflecting theoretically discredited white supremacist ideals[2] on the very people whom civil rights laws were meant to protect and assist. For most Chicanos,[3] Directive No. 15 presents no right answer. Instead, Chicanos must choose some formula that misstates their identity or be forced into the statistical limbo of the "Other" classification.[4]

While Directive No. 15 purports to embrace the idea that people should be allowed to declare their own identity, it permits such expression only within the confines of the racial world view it embodies. For persons whose upbringing did not inculcate them with the view of race embodied in the Directive, answering the racial and ethnic identity questions involves considerable guesswork as to what the government is asking. Consider these hypothetical examples of its application. These are not likely to be hypothetical in a strict sense; evidence suggests that all of the examples in the following sections have actually occurred.

Two Chicano Examples

A Mexican couple immigrates to the United States and has children. They receive a Census form in the mail and set about determining their own and their children's racial identity. Looking at the racial categories, the couple sees none that describe them. They do not view themselves as American Indians but as *mestizos,* persons of mixed European and indigenous heritage. They are not enrolled members of a recognized tribe, nor are they identified as Indians in the community in which they live.[5] By the same token, neither are they identified as whites.[6] In the "Hispanic origin" question, the couple sees "Mexican, Mexican-American or Chicano" specifically listed as a "Hispanic" group. They identify themselves as part of that group and as being of "Other" race on the race question.

This couple might identify their children in the same manner. Alternatively, they might believe that a "Mexican or Mexican-American" is only someone who was born in Mexico. As immigrants, they may not be familiar with the north of the border term "Chicano." Since their children were born in the U.S., they answer the Hispanic origin question in the negative. Knowing that there are millions of people like their children in this country, and believing that there must be some place on the Census form for them, they think again about the race question. Obviously, their children are not white: Every day they face the avoidance behaviors and "microaggressions" exhibited by whites, designed to remind them that they are not part of that group.[7] They do not believe that their children are part of the "Black" or "Asian/Pacific Islander" groups, so they think again about the American Indian category. Perhaps aware of the one drop rule that, at least culturally, defines as Black any person with any known African ancestor or trace of apparent African ancestry,[8] they conclude that "community recognition" as Indian means being treated as nonwhite on the basis of apparent indigenous ancestry. Therefore, they mark their children as members of the "American Indian or Alaskan Native" race.[9]

Now, suppose that a fourth generation Chicano is filling out a Census form. Spiritually uplifted by the cultural pride inherent in the concept of Aztlán, he identifies himself racially as "American Indian" but answers "yes" to the Hispanic origin question, marking the "Mexican, Mexican-American, or Chicano" box. To the respondent, this seems like a decent reflection of his *mestizo* identity. To the Census Bureau, it is a wrong answer.

Suppose now that this same fourth generation Chicano is responding to a question under the combined race/ethnic short format permitted under Directive No. 15. Choosing between the selections, "White, Hispanic" and "American Indian" is easy. The respondent selects "American Indian" as the response, because he has never been treated as a white person in his community, because "Hispanic" seems an inaccurate description of a Chicano culture that has a strong indigenous influence,[10] and because in physical appearance, i.e., "racially," the respondent is far closer to being a Native American than a European.

Two Filipino Examples

Now, let us imagine that a Filipina with a Spanish surname is filling out the Census form. She was born to parents who moved to the United States shortly after World War II. She is aware that "Spanish surname" used to be the name of today's "Hispanic" classification, and that the Philippines were a Spanish colony for centuries before becoming a U.S. dependency after the Spanish-American War in 1898.[11] She is a Catholic, but neither she nor any member of her family speaks Spanish. She knows some Chicanos at work, but her close friends are all Filipino.

Examining the "race" question, she faces little difficulty. The Philippines are Pacific islands, and "Filipino" is specifically listed as a subgroup of the designation "Asian/Pacific Islander." She identifies herself "racially" as "Filipino." The next question asks her if she is of "other Spanish origin or culture." She seems to fit under this broad categorization. Her name, like that of many Filipinos, is Spanish, and the Roman Catholic religion was brought to the Philippine Islands by Spanish conquistadors.[12] She feels that this satisfies the "other Spanish culture or origin" criterion, so she indicates that she is also of "Hispanic origin," selecting the "Other Hispanic" box.

Her brother lives nearby and receives a Census form. He works at a place with many Chicanos and spends a great deal of time socializing with them. Like his sister, he identifies himself "racially" Filipino. Turning to the "Hispanic origin" question, he perceives that this question is designed to capture persons like his coworkers who identify as Mexican-American, and not persons from the Philippines. He therefore answers "no" to the Hispanic origin question.

This hypothetical is not offered to imply that Filipinos are responsible for the gap between "Hispanic" and Chicano achievement.[13] Certainly Filipinos are a racialized minority group in the United States with a long history of oppression.[14] This hypothetical does reveal, however, that the decision whether to answer the "Hispanic origin" question affirmatively may not relate at all to the question of whether the person is a member of one of the groups the classification is meant to capture. For both Chicanos and Filipinos, responding to Directive No. 15 requires guessing how a white person would classify them rather than exercising the power of self-definition.

Even for a Filipino, however, the decision whether or not to claim "Hispanic origin" might be tactical under the combined format. If the person feels that being identified as "Hispanic" might be more advantageous than being identified as an "Asian/Pacific Islander," for example, because affirmative action is being used as an excuse to cap Asian/Pacific Islander admissions to a university,[15] the decision to claim "Hispanic origin" might allow the person a competitive advantage, secured, of course, at the expense of the Chicano community. At least in this instance, the person could claim that switching categories did not detract from the overall goal of affirmative action—to assist racially subordinated minorities in a racist society. The same cannot be said of whites who employ the same device to help their careers and defeat the goals of affirmative action as they relate to the Chicano community.

Notes

[1] In a series of hearings in Boston, Denver, San Francisco, and Honolulu, OMB officials heard criticisms from, among others, Native Hawaiians who felt they should be grouped as indigenous Americans rather than as a subgroup of the Asian/Pacific Islander classification; children of mixed-culture marriages who resented being forced to select one cultural identity: Arab-Americans who felt that being described as part of the white majority inaccurately reflected their position in society; and persons, including this author, who criticized the "Hispanic" classification on a number of grounds. *See* Tony Bizjak, *Speakers Voice Varied Views on Race Classification,* (SACRAMENTO BEE, July 15, 1994, at B4); Steven A. Holmes, *U.S. Urged to Reflect Wider Diversity In Racial and Ethnic Classifications,* (N.Y. TIMES, July 8, 1994, at 18); Gregory Lewis, *Census Racial Designations Slammed in S.F.,* (SAN FRANCISCO EXAMINER, July 15, 1994, at A-1).

[2] *See supra* notes 70 and 141–43 and accompanying text.

[3] I use the terms "Mexican-American" and "Chicano" interchangeably, recognizing that a considerable difference of opinion exists within the community about the appropriateness of either term. As one historian has noted, the terms used to describe members of this group have varied over time and have depended largely on who was doing the describing. *See* RODOLOFO ACUÑA, *Occupied America: A History of Chicanos* ix (3d ed. 1988). I also do not assume that immigrants from Mexico form a distinct community from Chicanos. To the contrary, I argue that immigrants merge into the existing community. *See infra* notes 148–95 and accompanying text.

[4] *See* Richard Reinhold, *Others (Among Others) Play Havoc With Census,* (N.Y. TIMES, Oct. 11, 1981, at 8).

[5] Directive No. 15, *supra* note 11, at 19.269.

[6] *Id.*

[7] *See* Peggy Davis, *Law as Microaggression,* 98 YALE L.J. 1559, 1565–68 (1989).

[8] While most likely the one drop rule was accepted in the lives of most white Americans, it rarely constituted the legal definition of Blackness. Finkelman, *Crime of Color, supra* note 4, at 2110 n. 240.

[9] A significant number of households had parents who marked themselves as "Hispanics," or Mexicans of "Other" race, while listing their children as racially American Indian. *Hearings, supra* note 146, as 10 (statement of Harry A. Scarr, Acting Director, Bureau of the Census).

[10] *See* Anzaldúa, *supra* note 115, at 1–6, 27–39, 65–91.

[11] See The Diamond Rings, 183 U.S. 176, 178 (1901).

[12] See Phillipines: A Country Study 5–6 (Ronald E. Dolan ed., 1993).

[13] Some 57,000 persons described themselves in the 1990 Census as "Hispanic, Asian/Pacific Islander." Alternative Comparison Groups, *supra* note 30, at 3.

[14] See Chang, *supra* note 18, at 1291–92 (noting that despite early efforts to portray themselves as more "Western" than other "Asian-American" groups, Filipinos have been treated as part of a "yellow peril").

[15] On the use of affirmative action as a method to secure a permanent majority quota of white men, see Derrick Bell, And We Are Not Saved: The Elusive Quest for Racial Justice 140–61 (1987): Richard Delgado, *Affirmative Action as a Majoritarian Device: Or, Do You Really Want to be a Role Model?* , 89 Mich. L. Rev. 1222 (1991).

THE MINGLING OF ALASKA NATIVES WITH "FOREIGNERS": A BRIEF HISTORICAL OVERVIEW

JULIE E. SPROTT

Study Questions
1. What three characteristics define the history of contact between groups of white Russo-Euro-American origin and Alaska
   natives?
2. Make a chart showing the major waves of migration and the moti-
   vating factors behind each wave.

Mixed-blood ancestry for some Native groups of Alaska has a long history.
Before the modern era, population admixture took place within specific lo-
cales where foreign visitors were concentrated. Today the process is more
nearly ubiquitous, played out largely through migration of Natives to urban centers. In some situations, a great power imbalance in favor of the
visitors tempered the intimate interaction of the foreign men with Native
women, characteristic, for example, in the early Russian period. What admixture "meant" for identity or social status of Natives has been variably
depicted in the literature as a negative influence, an advantage, or without
social significance.

For the purposes of this article, I will ignore the intermingling of
Alaska Natives with other ethnic populations and concentrate on relationships between Alaska Natives and groups of white Russo-Euro-American
origin. Three features of the history of contact are pertinent: (1) the vast
majority of visitors were male; (2) foreigners typically came to Alaska in cycles or "waves"; (3) the motivation for new arrivals involved exploitation
of one or more natural resources that afforded monetary or strategic advantage. Once those resources fell in price, became depleted, or lost strategic edge, the bulk of the visitors left. There were, on the other hand, many
examples of non-Natives such as trappers and traders who stayed to work
and raise families in rural regions. Some were missionaries who attempted

to convert the Natives to Christianity, to provide medical care, and to educate the populace (VanStone 1964). Though not properly depicted as coming in "waves," traders and missionaries were significant agents of sociocultural change, a topic that falls outside the scope of this article.

Another caveat to the idea of recurring waves of migration is the phenomenon of "bureaucratization of the north" that has accelerated in the most recent period. Jobs have burgeoned as a result of federal, state, and local government-related activities in Alaska particularly since World War II and the enactment of statehood in January, 1959. This trend is shown, for example, in census data. In 1939, the distribution of the population between Natives (45%) and non-Natives (54%) was almost equal: by 1950, close to a decade later, whites consisted of 72% of the population (Levin 1991:17). At present, 36.1% of Alaska's work force is employed in government-sector jobs, including military personnel (ADL 1993a, 1993b).

The date usually cited for the official arrival of foreigners to Alaska and the beginning of colonization is 1741, the year of the Russian Vitus Bering's sighting of the southern coast of Alaska and his crew's wintering over on Bering Island (Fisher 1990:17). In the first 50 years of contact, Russians brutalized peoples of the southwest and southcentral areas of Alaska populated by Aleut, Koniag, and Chugach Natives (summarized by VanStone 1984). Military men and traders who followed the early explorers virtually enslaved the population and compelled Native men to hunt for seal and otter pelts; many Native women became wives or concubines of the intruders (Oleska 1990:178). Population decline among Natives in the southwest during that time has been estimated between 80–90% (Smith and Barnett 1990:14, Veltre 1990:181). A class designation for mixed-blood children called Creoles developed in subsequent generations.

The Russians expanded their range of influence further to the south, founding a fur-trading post that later became the colonial capital of Sitka in 1806. Tlingit who lived nearby showed their displeasure by attacking the fort several times (Antonson 1990:165) and were never fully subdued by the Russians (Fedorova 1975:17). By 1799, a gentler, less interfering policy toward Natives was adopted after the Russian-American Company began administering the territory through an Imperial Charter, renewed twice until the sale of Alaska to the US in 1867.

Contact with the more northerly and interior Native groups was effected primarily through fur trading, fishing, and mission activities that accompanied the establishment of outposts by the Russian-American Company. From the early 1800s, these efforts were concentrated around Bristol Bay, the Yukon-Kuskokwim Delta, the Copper and Nushagak River regions, and Norton Sound. The Inupiat, residents of the northern coastal regions, had minimal contact until the search for the Franklin expedition and whaling began in the 1840s (Arndt 1990, Fortuine 1989:25). Most of the more interior-dwelling Athapaskan Indians encountered few outsiders until the end of the nineteenth century.

The Creoles—An Historical Example of a Socially Recognized Mixed-Blood Class

By the time of the signing of the Second Charter for the Russian-American Company in 1821, mixed-blood Natives were common, although they never exceeded an estimated 1,900 (Black 1990:152). Both the second and third charters specified a status estate for the new Creole class. Creoles received the right to obtain a formal education in exchange for service to the Company, becoming free men when this service ended (Fedorova 1975:12–13).

Not all of Creole status were mixed bloods, because some "islanders" who pledged political allegiance to Russia were also joined to the Creole class (Oleska 1990:185). Nevertheless, the enumeration of Creoles is considered a fair indication of the numbers born to intermixed couples in the region (Black 1990:146). It is well documented that many creoles held respected positions as explorers, traders, priests, and health care personnel (Arndt 1990:95, Fortuine 1990:127–128). For example, as many as half the Company ships in the 1860s were under the command of Creoles (Fedorova 1975:14).

What the Creole estate meant in relation to ethnic identity compared to other status groups in Russian America is difficult to discern from the literature, as mentioned earlier. Some historians argue that Creoles maintained their aboriginal cultural identity and embraced the best of both worlds (Oleska 1990), but others voice the opposite—that they belonged to neither culture and were despised by both (Fedovora 1975:14). Oleska (1987, 1990) contends that Creoles became key culture-bearers in the region, because it was through literary traditions of the Creole Russian Orthodox priests that aspects of Aleut culture survived to the present. No other Native groups in Alaska suffered as great a population loss and deprivation as did the early contacted groups, and in no other region was there a formally recognized mixed-blood class like the Creoles.

Other "Waves" of Contact: Whalers, Gold Seekers, the Military, and Oilmen

The whaling enterprise in the latter half of the nineteenth century and the brief but intensive Gold Rush of 1898 and 1899 massively impacted Eskimo populations of the Bering Strait and north coast, bringing them into contact with men from many different countries. As many as 232 vessels came in search of whales in that region in 1854 (Ray 1975:198). Seventy ships were seen in Point Hope alone in 1884 (Milan 1978). It has been estimated by Foote (1964:18) that "from 1848 to 1885 about 3,000 American whaling ships carrying approximately 90,000 men passed northward through Bering Strait." During the wintering-over period that became common later in the whaling era, Natives were hired as cabin boys, cooks, hunters, and seamstresses. Whole families set up residence close to the ships and as a result, increased the potential of intercourse between whalers and Native women (Stefansson 1913:202–203). An observer at Saint Michael in 1898, for example, wrote that mixed bloods outnumbered full bloods in the village (Ray 1975:245).

The Gold Rush of 1898–1899 created more disruption, particularly in the Saint Michael and Nome areas. Each region received "from ten to twelve times the population of the entire Bering Strait in the space of a year"; some 30,000 non-Natives flocked to the Seward Peninsula (Ray 1975:204, 246, 251). Following the initial rush, less intense, but nevertheless ongoing mineral exploration took miners into the interior via major routes along the Yukon and Kuskokwim Rivers up through the 1920s (Oswalt 1990:100–106). Oswalt relates that there was a general silence in the newspapers of the time about the interaction of goldseekers with Natives, though some missionaries wrote of their concerns, and one in particular from Bethel was found by Oswalt (1990:106) to have written: "It is gravely true that many of the white men now here do create serious difficulties in the uplift of the natives. Profanity and basest animal lust are either openly practiced or hidden beneath a much scratched veneer of politeness." Jenness (1957:165) said of the North Slope region that "by 1914 half or more of the Eskimos around Barrow and Point Barrow were of 'foreign' extraction; and twenty years later not more than fifteen Mackenzie natives could claim descent from the original population." As Ray (1975:159, 170–171) indicates, many non-Native men took Native women as wives, and often, the white man who became a permanent resident was viewed positively by villagers, although this attitude is largely undocumented in the literature. Similar to Burch's opinion cited in the introduction of this article, Ray (1975:252) depicts a predominance of Native cultural values and norms in the village setting:

> When a white man remained, he became a member of the Eskimo community. If he married an Eskimo woman, his children were looked upon as Eskimo; and though he usually did not learn the language, he often preferred to adopt Eskimo values and way of life . . . Life resolved culturally and genetically to the Eskimo.

The next large influx of non-Natives to Alaska occurred during the Second World War and subsequent Cold War period with the construction and maintenance of the DEW Line radar stations dotting the Arctic Circle. The Aleuts again suffered extreme hardship and population losses, this time as a result of relocation away from their natal villages during the War. For other Native groups living near military installations, the effect of the military presence was a double-edged sword—more money flowed into villages as jobs increased, but culture change intensified as well. Hughes (1960) outlined changes that accompanied the military base on Saint Lawrence Island, including electrification of the village, construction of mainland-style housing, and considerable out-migration during the mid-1940s to mid-1950s. Men joined the National Guard and were trained or served in the "Lower 48." He noted that at least six women in the village married whites and moved to the mainland; a number of other young women said they wished to do likewise (Hughes 1960:284).

Oil exploration in the Cook Inlet and the North Slope regions and subsequent construction of the TransAlaska oil pipeline in the 1960s and 1970s brought a new wave of migrants from the Lower 48. Resulting oil revenues to Alaska transformed its politics, economics, and sociocultural milieu, all of which is beyond the scope of this article to detail. Changes accompanying the oil wealth have not all been positive. For example, in a household survey of residents of North Slope villages completed in 1977, more than one-third of adults were ambivalent about their quality of life. Some saw development from oil revenues as "good" and cited increases in available jobs; others decried development, citing the ill effects on the environment (Kruse, Kleinfeld, and Travis 1980:80). Jorgensen (1990) suggests that windfalls from oil development have resulted in a deepening of economic dependence in Native villages. During 1982–1987, the years of his study, he noted an increase in the cost of living and more reliance on welfare by families (Jorgensen 1990:305).

The literature yields few clues about the interaction of Native families with oil workers. The north coast Prudhoe Bay facilities are remote, and staff rotate work in shifts for several weeks at a time. Contact could perhaps take place between workers who maintain the pipeline along its corridor and Natives living nearby, but whatever the effects of this interchange, the vastly greater impact has occurred indirectly as a byproduct of the oil wealth. Purchasing power has effected increased intrusion of popular culture, as, for example, through the medium of television. Practically every village home contains a television set and many homes are connected to cable TV. Desire for amenities of the city, and education and job opportunities account in part for the increasing out-migration of villagers to the city. As a concomitant circumstance, many date and marry non-Natives.

Indicators of Admixture and Intermarriage in the Contemporary Era

The history of contact for Alaska Natives has varied by region and Native subgroup. Population admixture began intensively more than 200 years ago. Contemporary empirical research offers little information about this melding, with a few exceptions. Research conducted by the International Biological Program in the late 1960s used a genealogical methodology to estimate admixture among adults of five north coastal villages. Results showed that 25–37% of the population pool had non-Eskimo genes primarily of western European origin, with additional heritage from Africans, Asians, and Polynesians (Milan 1978, Szathmary 1984).

Another study determined the extent of European-related genetic markers in red blood cells and sera of Saint Lawrence Islanders and residents of Wales. No greater than 9% of admixture was found for any village group, touted by the authors as evidence for geographic isolation even to the near present (Crawford, et al. 1981), although the discussion by Hughes (1960) presented earlier suggests that this low percent of admixture was probably a function of significant out-migration of ethnically mixed couples.

These studies aside, little is known about the current ancestral makeup of Alaska Native subgroups as a whole. According to the 1990 Census, 85,698 Alaska Natives comprised 15.6% of the state's population (ADL 1991:9). About 44% of Alaska Natives live in urban settings, with a little less than 40% of this group residing in Anchorage, dubbed "the largest Native village." The Alaska data mirror trends in the lower 48: approximately 49% of Native Americans lived in cities in 1980 (Thornton 1987:227).

Migration away from rural villages in Alaska has steadily increased since the 1950s, with more women leaving villages than men (Bureau of the Census 1983, Kruse and Foster 1986). Urban-based studies on Alaska Natives that contain marital data show high percentages of Native women married to non-Native men, 47% from a sample in Anchorage (Dubbs 1975), and 40% from a Fairbanks sample (Milan and Pawson 1975). Extrapolating from 1980 census data, Levin (1991:141) found that regardless of residential location, Athapaskan women and Southeast Indian women were more likely to marry non-Native men than Native men. A 1988–89 survey study of 1,237 households of North Slope Inupiat showed a similar trend. Forty percent of the 25 married women between 18 and 24 years of age had non-Native spouses (Kruse 1991:323). Moreover, according to birth records of Native infants born in Anchorage in 1977, only 85 of the 430 births were of a Native father and mother; 144 were of a Native mother and white father, and 81 had a white mother and Native father (Ender 1980). Data on marriages in 1990 for Alaska residents indicate that about 50% of Native brides married white men; a third of the brides of Native men were white (ABVS 1993:132). Taken together, these data confirm significant increases in intermarriage and a rise in the number of Alaska Native infants of multiple ancestry in the most recent era.

ETHNICITY AS EXPLANATION, ETHNICITY AS EXCUSE

PAUL A. GOBLE

Study Questions
1. Why has there been a new surge in ethnonationalism? What factors hold a check on nationalism?
2. List the five types of ethnonationalism and give examples of each type.
3. Why isn't ethnonationalism a sufficient explanation for major conflicts around the world?

Ethnicity—or more precisely, its political expression, ethnonationalism—has become an all-purpose explanation for analysts who seek to comprehend post-Cold War conflicts under a single rubric. And it has become an all-purpose excuse for political elites who, reflecting to the wishes of populations eager to rid themselves of foreign commitments, seek to justify a retreat from the world by suggesting that ethnic conflicts are by their very nature insoluble.

Neither of these uses of the term is justified. Ethnonationalism certainly does not explain all the conflicts in the world. In many cases, it is not involved; and even where it is, it is never the only factor. And it does not excuse Western governments from action because ethnic conflicts, like all other kinds, can be ameliorated or even ended by various mechanisms that already exist.

To say this is not to argue for intervention in any particular conflict or in any particular way, but rather to suggest that until we understand both the nature of ethnicity and its role in conflicts, we will remain handicapped in both our analyses and our choices about actions. The purpose here is not to provide any final set of guidelines but rather to advance the discussion by focusing on three main issues: first, the nature and variety of the latest flowering of ethnonationalism; second, the kinds of ethnic conflict such ethnic assertiveness can lead to; and third, the likely outcomes of such conflicts and, in particular, the role of third parties in promoting their resolution.

A New Age of Nationalism?

During the Cold War, Western and Soviet analysts assumed that the world—or at least Europe—had moved beyond nationalism, that ethnicity was a "survival of the past" that would soon be overcome.[1] But the dramatic role of nationalism, both in the destruction of the Soviet monolith and in the conflicts that have followed, has led many who denied any role for ethnonationalism in the past to make the equal and opposite error that ethnonationalism is the only force worth speaking about in the current environment. To get beyond such simplistic and extreme judgments, we need to consider why there has been this new upsurge in nationalism, why it may be more limited than many people now assume, and what forms of ethnonationalism are in fact out there now.[2]

Perhaps the best explanation for the new rise of nationalism—the notion that a human community defined by actual or assumed primordial ties must be recognized as deserving special treatment, autonomy or even independence—is that many of the forces which led to a rise of nationalism in the 18th and 19th centuries have exact and even more powerful analogues in the current environment:

- First, nationalism, both then and now, represents an effort to replace a discredited alternative model of political integration, in this case, the collapse of Marxism.
- Second, the vast expansion of media penetration across state borders reduces the legitimacy of any stratum between the community and its participation in the international media—in the 18th century because of the rise of public education and the penny press; now, by the globalization of CNN.
- Third, the increasing importance of the state to society makes control of the state an ever more important issue to the various population groups under its control. The 18th century saw a dramatic expansion in the state sector: so did the late 20th century.
- Fourth, the increasing internationalization of economic life produces migration flows that create new minorities and greater cross-cultural awareness of differences in status and economic position. Both periods saw increasing contacts and comparisons between groups: no one wants to live in a hovel once someone else has built a palace.
- Fifth, the increasing rapidity of social change has increased the level of alienation among virtually all populations. That, in turn, has spurred the search for new communities, the most available and apparently stable of which are primordial ones that we usually group under the rubric "ethnic."

Because these forces already affect much of the world, there has been growing concern that they and the ethnonationalism they produce will soon overwhelm the capacity of the international system to cope. But there are three good reasons to assume that this will not happen. First, most of the world's 6,500 ethnic communities are too small or are too satisfied to engage in political life to become politicized. Second, the power of ethnicity is undercut by other group loyalties which in many cases are far stronger than ethnic ones. Thus, while my ethnic attachment may be very important to me, my political or professional identities may override it in my choice of action. And third, the place where ethnicity has exploded the most is precisely where the state manipulated ethnicity for so long, namely the former Soviet Union and the former Yugoslavia.

This last point is particularly important. The Soviets and, following their lead, the Yugoslavs, politicized, territorialized and arranged into a hierarchy the ethnic groups under their control, thus increasing the salience of ethnicity and decreasing the importance of other collective memberships of the populations under their control. Thus, it should come as no surprise that in these two regions, there is a general confusion about the difference between ethnicity and citizenship and even between language and ethnicity.[3] Consequently, we should stop blaming the victims of this policy and recognize that this peculiar pattern is unlikely to be repeated elsewhere.

Because these impulses have affected a variety of communities whose current status, size and location vary enormously, they have produced a wide variety of ethnonationalisms. Perhaps the following groupings can organize our thinking before we turn to the relationship between ethnonationalism and ethnic conflict. In the European context, there are five obvious types of ethnonationalism:

- Classical nationalism, the striving of a previously submerged community to achieve state independence;[4]
- Irredentist nationalism, the demand that borders be rectified to take into account ethnic or cultural divisions;[5]
- Unexpected nationalism, the use of ethnic symbols to build political authority in a state whose independence occurred independently of the efforts of its elites and populations;[6]
- Xenophobic nationalism, the attacks against ethnically differentiated groups who may live within a larger community in order to relieve tensions and to reinforce the psychic borders of the larger group;[7] and
- Retrenchment nationalism, the articulation of an identity for a group that has lost its imperial possessions and is unsure of its psychological barriers. The model is post-Ottoman Turkey; the current problem is Russia.[8]

In all these cases, it should be noted, ethnicity serves as an instrumental value, as a resource used by elites and masses to advance their interests, and not simply as a source of virtual identity. And to the extent that this is true, ethnic mobilization and countermobilization should be analyzed just as other mobilization and countermobilization tools routinely are. Unfortunately, that has seldom been the case to date.

Conflict Classifications

Before attempting to classify ethnic conflicts, three preliminary observations are in order. First, not all ethnic assertiveness leads to ethnic conflict—most, but not all. Moreover, in some cases, it may even lead to the amelioration of conflicts, ethnic and otherwise, by resolving issues that had agitated society. Second, ethnicity is in no case the only issue involved in such conflicts—it may frame them, power them and even justify them, but ethnicity is about access to resources, psychic and otherwise—and it is not necessarily divorced from the state. (Indeed, much of the discussion about ethnic conflict is actually about the deterioration of state authority rather than about ethnonationalism per se. This is particularly the case in discussions about Bosnia and about several of the former Soviet republics.) In that sense, it is a filter as well as a weapon. And third, ethnic conflicts are even more varied than the kinds of ethnic groups described above.

Among the ways that ethnic conflicts can be classified are by the following criteria:[9]

- Goals of the group involved: irredentism, state independence, domestic stability through the creation or maintenance of ethnic solidarity, mobilization of populations for national efforts including war, conflicts over resources, expulsion of minorities, and assertion of a comfort level for members of the in-group;
- Kinds of participants in the conflicts: communal, individual, state vs. minority, state vs. state, and by whether outside groups are involved, either in order to use the competitors as proxies for larger goals or to end the conflict; and
- Intensity of the conflict, ranging from latest interpersonal hostility to communal violence to interstate war.

Cutting across all these divisions is the issue of the importance of the conflict to outsiders. Sometimes a conflict may be important because of who is involved; at other times because of the potential role of other outsiders; and at still other times, because of its intensity or propensity to spill over or snowball into other, potentially more serious conflicts. In discussing any particular ethnonational conflict, we need to be extremely precise as to what we mean and what we care about—just as we would for conflicts of any other type.

Outcomes and Strategies

These observations about the nature of ethnicity and the nature of ethnonational conflict allow us to confront the question of how we should react. Before doing that we need to make yet again three preliminary observations. First, ethnic conflicts are not by their nature either rational or irrational, and nonethnic conflicts are not necessarily rational. Irrational behavior can be driven by nonethnic means, and rational behavior may be dictated by ethnic considerations. Second, ethnonational conflicts are never simply the result of "ancient ethnic animosities." This phrase may please editorialists and pundits, but it seriously distorts reality. Anyone who asserts that a conflict is the product of these must explain why there has not always been fighting at a particular level of intensity. Once that explanation is made, it becomes obvious that ethnonational conflicts are powered by immediate as well as longstanding feelings and conclusions. Third, precisely because both ethnic and nonethnic issues are invariably involved, outsiders considering what to do should not forget all the means that have worked on past conflicts that were traditionally if not always accurately described as nonethnic.

Because we can assume that we will seek to get involved only in those conflicts that we deem for our own reasons to be significant, we can usefully group them into the following four-part schema:

- Conflicts where ethnic involvement is low relative to the importance of other factors and the intensity of the conflicts is also low. In such cases, we would generally look to the local authorities to act.
- Conflicts where ethnic involvement is high relative to the importance of other factors and the intensity of the conflicts is low. In such cases, we would also tend to rely on local authorities or international human-rights organizations.
- Conflicts where ethnic involvement is low relative to the importance of other factors and the intensity of the conflicts is high. In such cases, our strategies should be chosen primarily from those used for conflicts we would describe as nonethnic.

- Finally, conflicts where ethnic involvement is high relative to other factors and the intensity of the conflict is high as well. In these cases—which are usually the ones we are referring to when we speak of ethnonational conflicts—we must employ strategies drawn up for other kinds of conflicts and specific strategies for ethnonational conflicts.

There are five important categories of strategy that can be employed to deal with the ethnic dimension of conflicts of the last type:

- *Changing international support of and tolerance for ethnic assertiveness.* One of the major reasons for greater amounts of ethnic assertiveness in the period after the collapse of the Soviet Union and Yugoslavia is that the international community dramatically changed its approach for rewarding ethnic assertiveness. Prior to that time, the West's approach to such conflicts was to oppose secession, as in Biafra, and that opposition by itself sent a signal that ethnic assertiveness would not pay. This observation also applies to irredentism, communal violence and other forms of ethnonational conflict. Sanctions may or may not work, but a clear statement that such actions will not be rewarded will serve as a constraint.
- *Using countermobilization techniques.* This can involve providing supports for other kinds of identities in the situation or introducing a new outside threat that will dwarf existing divisions. An example is economic aid: If it is carefully targeted, it can reduce ethnic conflict; otherwise, it will only make the situation worse.
- *Removing irritants or making compromises.* Some conflicts can be resolved by doing one or the other. Ethnic conflicts are not forever. They emerge, intensify and disappear. All the resolutions may not be pretty, and they are certainly not what everyone would like, but the conflicts themselves will eventually disappear.
- *Containing the conflict and letting the two or more sides wear themselves out.* Perhaps the most important strategy in dealing with ethnic conflicts is to prevent outsiders from becoming involved, either through alliances or the supply of arms and other aid, thus making the conflicts more serious.
- *Using military force.* In many ethnic conflicts, this is the ultimate answer. Sometimes, as when the conflict is communal, military force must do more than end the conflict, it must engage in state-building. Other times, when the conflict is state-to-state, this need not be the case. Sometimes limited force can provide the breathing room for the other strategies outlined above to work.

Obviously, ameliorating or ending ethnic conflicts is not going to be easy, but neither is this task beyond our means. We may decide that any particular conflict is unimportant, and we may be right. But in thinking about such conflicts, especially in Europe, we should remember Winston Churchill's description of the world following World War I:

> To the faithful, toil-burdened masses the victory was so complete that no further effort seemed required. Germany had fallen, and with her the world combination that had crushed her. Authority was dispersed; the world unshackled; the weak became the strong; the sheltered became the aggressive; the contrast between victors and vanquished tended continually to diminish. A vast fatigue dominated collective action. Though every subversive element endeavored to assert itself, revolutionary rage like every other form of psychic energy burnt low. Through all its five acts the drama has run its course; the light of history is switched off, the world stage dims, the actors shrivel, the chorus sinks. The war of the giants has ended; the quarrels of the pygmies have begun.[10]

Churchill's words were written in 1929. They capture as in a distant mirror our own mood and inclinations now. They were written only four years before Hitler came to power and a decade before the world was plunged into general war.

Notes

[1] On these assumptions and their limitations, see Susan Olzak, "Contemporary Ethnic Mobilization," *Annual Review of Sociology,* 9 (1983):355–374; and Francois Nielsen, "Toward a Theory of Ethnic Solidarity in Modern Societies," *American Sociological Review* 50 (1985):133–149.

[2] For a fuller discussion of the issues raised in this section, see Paul A. Goble, "A New Age of Nationalism," in Bruce Seymour II. ed., *The Access Guide to Ethnic Conflicts in Europe and the Former Soviet Union* (Washington, D.C., 1994), pp. 1–8, and the recommended readings on pp. 9–16.

[3] For an especially egregious example of this, see the report of the Gorbachev Foundation, "Russkie v 'blizhnem zarubezh'e.'" *Nezavisimaya gazeta,* 7 September 1993. Cf. the analysis of it in Paul A. Goble, "Can We Help Russia to be a Good Neighbor?" *Demokratizatsiya,* forthcoming. On the broader process of politicization of ethnicity and the creation of nationality in the Soviet case, see Paul A. Goble, "Gorbachev and the Soviet Nationality Problem," in Maurice Friedberg and Heyward Isham, eds., *Soviet Society Under Gorbachev* (Armonk, N.Y., 1987), pp. 76–100.

[4] For a useful discussion of this kind, see Isaiah Berlin, "Nationalism: Past Neglect and Present Power." *Partisan Review* 46 (1979):337–358.

[5] See J. Gottmun, *The Significance of Territory* (Charlottesville, Va., 1973).

[6] See Paul A. Goble, "The 50 Million Muslim Misunderstanding." *Chanteh* 1 (1993):36–39.

[7] On this phenomenon, see Group for the Advancement of Psychiatry, *Us and Them: The Psychology of Ethnonationalism* (New York, 1987), esp. p. 87 ff.

[8] See Paul A. Goble, "Russia's Extreme Right," *The National Interest* 33 (Fall 1993): 93–96.

[9] See the various works of Horowitz, Rothschild and Royce for surveys of the various ways ethnic activism can be categorized.

[10] Winston Churchill, *The Aftermath* (New York: Charles Scribner's Sons, 1929), p. 17.

ANCESTRY

THE U.S. BUREAU OF THE CENSUS

Study Question
1. Identify the strategies that the U.S. Bureau of the Census uses to simplify complex answers respondents give to the ancestry question.

The data on ancestry were derived from answers to the Census questionnaire item 13, which was asked of a sample of persons. The question was based on self-identification; the data on ancestry represent self-classification by people according to the ancestry group(s) with which they most closely identify. Ancestry refers to a person's ethnic origin or descent, "roots," or heritage or the place of birth of the person or the person's parents or ancestors before their arrival in the United States. Some ethnic identities, such as "Egyptian" or "Polish" can be traced to geographic areas outside the United States, while other ethnicities such as "Pennsylvania Dutch" or "Cajun" evolved in the United States.

The intent of the ancestry question was not to measure the degree of attachment the respondent had to a particular ethnicity. For example, a response of "Irish" might reflect total involvement in an "Irish" community or only a memory of ancestors several generations removed from the individual.

The Census Bureau coded the responses through an automated review, edit, and coding operation. The open-ended write-in ancestry item was coded by subject-matter specialists into a numeric representation using a code list containing over 1,000 categories. The 1990 code list reflects the results of the Census Bureau's own research and consultations with many ethnic experts. Many decisions were made to determine the classification of responses. These decisions affected the grouping of the tabulated data. For example, the "Assyrian" category includes both responses of "Assyrian" and "Chaldean."

The ancestry question allowed respondents to report one or more ancestry groups. While a large number of respondents listed a single ancestry, the majority of answers included more than one ethnic entry. Generally, only the first two responses reported were coded in 1990. If a response was in terms of a dual ancestry, for example, Irish-English, the person was assigned two codes, in this case one for Irish and another for English.

However, in certain cases, multiple responses such as "French Canadian," "Scotch-Irish," "Greek Cypriote," and "Black Dutch" were assigned a single code reflecting their status as unique groups. If a person reported one of these unique groups in addition to another group, for example, "Scotch-Irish English," resulting in three terms, that person received one code for the unique group ("Scotch-Irish") and another one for the remaining group ("English"). If a person reported "English Irish French," only English and Irish were coded. In certain combinations of ancestries where the ancestry group is a part of another, such as "German-Bavarian," the responses were coded as a single ancestry using the smaller group ("Bavarian"). Also, responses such as "Polish-American" or "Italian-American" were coded and tabulated as a single entry ("Polish" or "Italian").

The Census Bureau accepted "American" as a unique ethnicity if it was given alone, with an ambiguous response, or with State names. If the respondent listed any other ethnic identity such as "Italian American," generally the "American" portion of the response was not coded. However, distinct groups such as "American Indian," "Mexican American," and "African American" were coded and identified separately because they represented groups who considered themselves different from those who reported as "Indian," "Mexican," or "African," respectively.

In all tabulations, when respondents provided an unacceptable ethnic identity (for example, an uncodeable or unintelligible response such as "multi-national," "adopted," or "I have no idea"), the answer was included in "Ancestry not reported."

The tabulations on ancestry are presented using two types of data presentations—one used total persons as the base, and the other used total responses as the base. The following are categories shown in the two data presentations:

Presentations Based on Responses

Total Ancestries Reported. Includes the total number of ancestries reported and coded. If a person reported a multiple ancestry such as "French Danish," that response was counted twice in the tabulations—once in the "French" category and again in the "Danish" category. Thus, the sum of the counts in this type of presentation is not the total population but the total of all responses.

First Ancestry Reported. Includes the first response of all persons who reported at least one codeable entry. For example, in this category, the count for "Danish" would include all those who reported only Danish and those who reported Danish first and then some other group.

Second Ancestry Reported. Includes the second response of all persons who reported a multiple ancestry. Thus, the count for "Danish" in this category includes all persons who reported Danish as the second response, regardless of the first response provided.

The Census Bureau identified hundreds of ethnic groups in the 1990 census. However, it was impossible to show information for every group in all census tabulations because of space constraints. Publications such as the 1990 CP-2, Social and Economic Characteristics and the 1990 CPH-3, Population and Housing Characteristics for Census Tracts and Block Numbering Areas reports show a limited number of groups based on the number reported and the advice received from experts. A more complete distribution of groups is presented in the 1990 Summary Tape File 4, supplementary reports, and a special subject report on ancestry. In addition, groups identified specifically in the questions on race and Hispanic origin (for example, Japanese, Laotian, Mexican, Cuban, and Spaniard), in general, are not shown separately in ancestry tabulations.

Limitation of the Data. Although some experts consider religious affiliation a component of ethnic identity, the ancestry question was not designed to collect any information concerning religion. The Bureau of the Census is prohibited from collecting information on religion. Thus, if a religion was given as an answer to the ancestry question, it was coded as an "Other" response.

Comparability. A question on ancestry was first asked in the 1980 census. Although there were no comparable data prior to the 1980 census, related information on ethnicity was collected through questions on parental birthplace, own birthplace, and language which were included in previous censuses. Unlike other census questions, there was no imputation for nonresponse to the ancestry question.

In 1990, respondents were allowed to report more than one ancestry group; however, only the first two ancestry groups identified were coded. In 1980, the Census Bureau attempted to code a third ancestry for selected triple-ancestry responses.

New categories such as "Arab" and "West Indian" were added to the 1990 question to meet important data needs. The "West Indian" category excluded "Hispanic" groups such as "Puerto Rican" and "Cuban" that were identified primarily through the question on Hispanic origin. In 1990, the ancestry group "American" is recognized and tabulated as a unique ethnicity. In 1980, "American" was tabulated but included under the category "Ancestry not specified."

A major improvement in the 1990 census was the use of an automated coding system for ancestry responses. The automated coding system used in the 1990 census greatly reduced the potential for error associated with a clerical review. Specialists with a thorough knowledge of the subject matter reviewed, edited, coded, and resolved inconsistent or incomplete responses.

Source: U.S. Bureau of the Census (1996b)

CHOOSING AN ANCESTRY

MARY C. WATERS

Study Questions
1. How did Mary Waters come to learn about "hidden ancestries"?
2. Why do you think many people selectively forget or dismiss some parts of their ethnic heritage?

In my interviews I explored the issue of how people decide how to answer a question about ethnic origin in a census or survey. I began each interview by showing people the census ancestry question and asking how they would answer it. Then I immediately asked the reason for that particular answer. The ways in which people described their family histories and the ways in which they came to their answers reveal just how much sifting and sorting occurs *even* before they consider the question. The complex interplay among the different aspects of an individual's ethnic identification was an overriding theme in the interviews.

Very often over the course of an interview, individuals remembered an ancestry that was not even consciously a part of what they believed their ethnic origins to be. This selective forgetting is illustrated in the case of Laurie Jablonski, a 29-year-old social worker. Laurie reported at the beginning of the interview that she was fourth-generation Polish-German. Her great-grandparents on her mother's side had been German immigrants, her father's grandmother was German, and her father's grandfather was Polish. Laurie discussed at length the various elements that she thought made up her Polish and German heritage. Even though culturally her family observes many German customs and is very German-identified, Laurie often gives her ethnic identity simply as Polish when asked. She said this was because her last name was Polish, and that is often how others identify her. Thus though her self-identification in private and with her family is German-Polish, and she believes that her origin is more than three-quarters German, her self-identification to others is often only Polish.

However, a much more extreme example of simplification and "selective forgetting" became clear at the end of the interview. At the end of an hour-and-a-half interview, when the tape recorder was turned off, Laurie said that she had just remembered that she had some English in her too, that her grandmother had told her five years ago that one of her ancestors, she does not know which one, had been married to an English person. She recalled being really annoyed when her grandmother told her this and remembered thinking, "I am already this mishmash, don't tell me that I am anything else too."

Ted Jackson, a 27-year-old office worker, also reported feeling annoyance when he discovered that he really had more ancestral elements in his background than he had originally thought. He said he was of Irish, French, German, English, and Scottish ancestry: "I didn't even know I was Scottish until I got interested in my roots and I went over to my grandmother's. I didn't know I was English. I thought I was only a couple of things, but then she really made me feel like a dirt ball—throw everything else in there too."

Further probing in many of the interviews revealed ancestries in the histories of these people that were just deemed too inconsequential to mention. A respondent who seemed on the verge of forgetting an ancestry was Mike Gold, a 54-year-old lawyer, who reported that he would have answered English and French on the census form, and that he was fourth-generation American. When I asked why he would have answered English and French, he answered:

A: Well, my mother was English and my father was French and Polish.
Q: Then why would you not answer English, French, and Polish?
A: I don't know. I guess I just never think about the Polish.

The unimportance of certain ancestries to people is clear in the ways in which they naturally describe these ancestries as part of their origin immediately after giving themselves an ethnic label that does not include them. For instance, Bill Kerrigan, a 19-year-old college student:

Q: What is your answer to the census question?
A: I would have put Irish.
Q: Why would you have answered that?
A: Well, my dad's name is Kerrigan and my mom's name is O'Leary, and I do have some German in me, but if you figure it out, I am about 75 percent Irish, so I say I am Irish.
Q: You usually don't say German when people ask?
A: No, no, I never say I am German. My dad just likes being Irish . . . I don't know, I guess I just never think of myself as being German.
Q: So your dad's father is the one who immigrated?
A: Yes. On this side it is Irish for generations. And then my grandmother's name is Dubois, which is French, partly German, partly French, and then the rest of the family is all Irish. So it is only my maternal grandmother who messes up the line.

Thus in the course of a few questions Bill labeled himself Irish, admitted to being part German but not identifying with it, and then as an afterthought added that he was also part French. His identification as Irish was quite strong, both culturally and socially, which explains his strong self-labeling. Further in the interview, however, he described a strong German influence as he was growing up. His mother's first husband, who died before she married his father, had been a German immigrant, and he had spoken German with her. Bill's half brothers and sisters from that marriage were apparently quite German-identified, and Bill himself was quite knowledgeable about his German maternal grandmother. He reported that his mother was strongly committed to her German ancestry and would definitely have mentioned it along with her Irish ancestry on the census form. He said he never thought of himself as German, however.

Another example is a 46-year-old manager, Rose Peters, who chose between her Italian and Irish ancestries based on the ideas she got about both from her parents:

Q: When you were growing up did you consider yourself ethnic?
A: Yes, I was very strongly Italian, because the Irish . . . whenever I was in a bad mood, that was the Irish in me. So I always related the Irish with the bad things and the Italian with all of the good things.
Q: Why?
A: I guess because every time I would do something bad, my mother would say, "Oh, that's those Irish eyes. That's the Irish from your father." The good things, like if I cleaned my room, she would say, "Oh, look, you are a Rosio," which was the Italian. So I thought all the Irish were hotheads and all the Italians had clean houses and good food.

People contradicted themselves frequently in the interviews because they had become so used to the simplifications of their ancestors' backgrounds that they did not even notice that their first answer to the question was incomplete. Notice how Betty O'Keefe, a 60-year-old housewife, did not even notice that she was telling me about a French part to her ancestry:

Q: Ancestry?
A: Irish.
Q: Why?
A: Because the majority, the great majority, of my ancestors were Irish.
Q: Do you know anything about the immigrants?
A: It wasn't my father and it wasn't my grandfather. I met my great-grandmother, and she didn't have an Irish accent, so it must have been like in the 1840s with the famine Irish, I presume. That's my father's side. They have a branch that were French too, but mostly Irish.

There were many other cases in which other ancestries would "pop up" in the course of an interview. And these "hidden ancestries" were often present in people who had very strong identifications with only those parts of their identities they "claimed" or recognized. Of course, the selective identification described here is not just the choice of the individual. A large part of this simplification occurs when parents decide what they will tell their children about who they are and who their ancestors were.

REFLECTIONS ON AMERICAN ETHNICITY

DAVID STEVEN COHEN

Study Question
1. List some of the popular misconceptions about the role of ethnicity in shaping U.S. history. Explain why these ideas can be classified as misconceptions.

. . . **E**thnicity has been an important factor from the beginning. In a sense, ethnicity is a better explanation than the frontier of the shaping of American culture. The frontier, conceived as either a line moving westward or as an area of supposed free land, is ethnocentric to a fault. It is limited to an Anglo-American perspective on history. The frontier may more accurately be seen as the place where Europeans, African-Americans, and Native Americans came into contact in the Americas. Many of the cultural traits associated with the frontier were in fact ethnic culture traits. Three examples are the log cabin, the covered wagon, and the cowboy. Research by folklorists and cultural geographers has shown that the log cabin was not an indigenous product of the American frontier. It was an adaptation of Scandinavian and German log construction techniques to floorplans that were English and Scotch-Irish. First introduced in the Delaware Valley, this construction technique diffused throughout the Appalachian Valley and into the Trans-Appalachian West, following the routes of migration.[1] The covered wagon, or Conestoga wagon, as it was sometimes called, is derived from northern European freight and farm wagons found in western Germany and the Netherlands. The English adopted these wagons from the Netherlands. Thus, there were German, Dutch, and English prototypes for these wagons that became the famed "prairie schooners" of the American West.[2] And what could be more American than the cowboy? But, the cowboy was in fact an Anglo-American adaptation of ranching techniques introduced to the Americas by the Spaniards. The cowboy was known by different names in different countries—the *gauchos* of Argentina, the *llaneros* of western Venezuela and eastern Colombia, and the *vaqueros* of Mexico— but they were all part of the same Spanish ranching complex.[3]

Instead of viewing the settling of North America in the ethnocentric terms of the western migration of English-speaking people, the frontier may better be visualized as the boundary between settlements of several European ethnic groups (the French in Canada, the Spaniards in New Spain, the Dutch in New Netherland, the Swedes in New Sweden, the English in the British colonies), several Native-American culture groups (the eastern woodland, the southeastern, the plains, the southwestern, and the Pacific northwestern), and several West African culture groups (the Yoruba, the Kongo, the Dahomean, the Mande). The interaction among these peoples resulted, in the words of one historian, in a "Columbian exchange" that reshaped the diet, the language, the music, the dance—not just of America, but of the world.[4]

Before proceeding, we might distinguish between immigration and ethnicity. Immigration is one of several ways that an ethnic group comes to reside in a particular place. It refers to the voluntary act of leaving one's country of birth and moving to another country to live and work. The immigration model does not apply to most African-Americans and Native Americans. With the exception of those people of African ancestry who have immigrated from South America, the Caribbean, or Africa (whom the census incidentally lists as black, but not African-American) most African-Americans were brought to America involuntarily as slaves. Native Americans, of course, were here when the first Europeans arrived. The current theory is that their ancestors migrated from Asia to the Americas about 15 thousand years ago across a land bridge that once spanned the Bering Straits. Thus, Native Americans exemplify two other processes by which an ethnic group might come into existence; that is, by migration and by conquest.

There are those who argue that African-Americans and Native Americans should not be considered ethnic groups, but racial groups. Through the 1930s sociologists continued to use the terms "race" and "immigrant" synonymously. It wasn't until World War II, in reaction to Nazi racial theories about the so-called "Aryan master race," that scholars began to distinguish between race, linguistic group, and ethnic group.[5] Furthermore, the *Harvard Encyclopedia of Ethnic Groups* includes within its definition of ethnicity, regional groups (Southern Appalachian Mountain People, Southerners, Yankees) as well as religious groups (Jews, Eastern Catholics, Eastern Orthodox, Mormons, Muslims).[6] I would argue that race, language, region, or religion may help define an ethnic group, but they are not synonymous with ethnicity. Blacks may be African-American, Afro-Cuban, Jamaican, or Haitian; Southern Mountain People may be German, Scotch-Irish, or English; Jews may be Sephardic or Ashkenazic; Hispanics may be Cuban, Colombian, or Puerto Rican; and so on.

Ethnicity is dynamic. Ethnic identities emerge and change. Immigrants become ethnics, a process which is manifested in the emergence of a sense of group identity. Many nineteenth-century immigrants identified with the town or region from which they came, not the country. In fact, the country may not have existed when they left. The Poles identified with Warsaw or Galicia, the Italians with Sicily or Naples, the Germans with Hanover or Bavaria. Once they settled in America, the group identity emerged. For some, like the Ukrainians, the name of the ethnic group did not even exist until the twentieth century. Previously, they were known as Ruthenians or Little Russians, terms which they dislike today. Often the identity that emerged in this country was a composite of traits from different regions of the old country. For example, the Ukrainian-American ethnic identity combines the woodcarving tradition from the Carpathian Mountains, the music and dance tradition of the Cossacks, and the embroidery and costumes of the eastern province of Poltava.[7] Ethnic boundaries have not been water-tight. Some individuals and groups have changed their ethnic identity. My own research indicates that more than half the Dutch settlers in New Netherland were not from the Netherlands. But they became Dutch, because this was the dominant culture in the region. And my work with the Ramapo Mountain People underlines the fact that a group that originated as free blacks who were culturally Dutch is in the process of becoming recognized by their neighbors and the newspapers, if not the Bureau of Indian Affairs, as an Indian tribe.[8]. . .

Some historians and sociologists see ethnic groups as subcultures in a predominantly White Anglo Saxon Protestant America. They use the term ethnic to mean "minority" as distinct from a vague construct called "mainstream" American culture. While it is true that there is a popular culture that cuts across regional, class, religious, racial, and ethnic divisions, this popular culture is not necessarily the culture of a single ethnic group, even though certain individuals have tried to define American culture in terms of their own region, class, religion, or ethnic group. For example, the frontier thesis may be considered the result of Frederick Jackson Turner's effort to define America in terms of the region from which he came.

It has been customary to refer to the United States as predominantly WASP, because American institutions were derived from our experience as British colonies. Historian David Hackett Fischer argues that the population of the United States in 1790 was also predominantly British.[9] There are two problems with this notion. First, it is derived from the total white population, excluding African-Americans, who constituted approximately 19.3 percent of the population in 1790. Second, it presumes that the English, the Scots, and the Irish were a single ethnic group. When you factor out these non-English people who also came from the British Isles, but who had different languages and cultures, the English population of the United States in 1790 was only about 49.2 percent of the total population, including African-Americans. Thus, the English were the largest single ethnic group—as compared to African-Americans (19.3 percent), Irish, both Ulster and Erie (7.8 percent), Germans (7 percent), Scots (6.6 percent), and Dutch (2.6 percent)—but they were a plurality rather than a majority of the total population.[10] This is an important point in understanding American ethnicity.

Some historians also persist in distinguishing between the so-called "old" immigrants (that is, the Irish, Germans, and Chinese who came to the United States in great numbers between 1840 and 1880) and the "new" immigrants (the eastern and southern Europeans who came between 1880 and 1930).[11] There are several problems with this periodization, but most notable is defining what constitutes "new" immigration. To term an immigration that ended in 1930 as "new" may have made sense at one time, but certainly not today. The period since World War II has seen a whole new wave of immigration from different parts of the world. The immigrants who have come since the immigration act of 1965 may be the real "new" immigrants, but so may those who have come since 1980, which also represents a shift in countries of origin. The problem will not go away as long as the terms "old" and "new" are used.

I would like to suggest a different periodization, one not based solely on immigration, but which deals with the "peopling" not just of *British* North America, but of North America in general.[12] I suggest four major periods: (1) the pre-Columbian migration of the ancestors of Native Americans across the Bering Straits and their dispersal throughout North America, (2) the migration of Europeans and Africans, mostly as indentured servants and slaves, during the colonial period from about 1500 to the end of the slave trade in the United States in 1808, (3) the period between 1820 and 1930, during which European immigrants were attracted to the United States by the related developments of industrialization and urbanization, and (4) the period between World War II and the present, during which suburbanization and a post-industrial economy combined with a shift in immigration sources to Latin America, the Caribbean, and Asia. . . .

Ethnicity has had an important impact on the local, regional, and national levels of American culture and society. The ethnic neighborhood is one of the most visible signs of ethnicity in America, as was noted by Robert E. Park, his students, and colleagues at the University of Chicago during the 1920s. They noted that immigrants in Chicago tended to cluster together in "colonies" or "ghettos," which were segregated, residential enclaves. These ethnic neighborhoods underwent a process which the University of Chicago sociologists termed "succession," as more recent immigrant groups replaced earlier immigrant groups.[13] However, as historian

Humbert S. Nelli has shown, despite the high visibility of one ethnic group in these neighborhoods, rarely was the neighborhood the residence of a single ethnic group nor did a single ethnic group even constitute a majority of the population. Often remnants of earlier immigrant groups that resided in the neighborhood remained. One or two of the largest ethnic groups composed a plurality of the population and stamped its identity on the neighborhood.[14]

This pattern can be seen in the Ironbound or Down Neck neighborhood of Newark, New Jersey. The names derive from the fact that the neighborhood is bounded by railroad trestles and by a necklike curve in the Passaic River. In 1860, 37 percent of its population was born in Ireland, 20 percent in Germany, and 23 percent in other foreign countries. By 1910, the population make-up of the neighborhood had changed. In that year, 11.7 percent of the population was born in Italy, 11.3 percent in Russia, and 7.7 percent in Austria. The 1980 census, which listed ethnic identity rather than foreign birth, showed that 36.6 percent of the population was Portuguese, 14.7 percent Spanish, and 9.8 percent Puerto Rican. There were still small Italian and Polish populations, 8 percent and 4.4 percent respectively.[15]

The one major exception to this pattern is African-Americans. For them, residential segregation in northern urban neighborhoods has been increasing progressively.[16] In the city of Newark, in 1850 blacks constituted only 5 percent of the population of the Third Ward. By 1940, in the midst of the Great Migration of African-Americans from the South to northern cities, which commenced during World War I, blacks constituted 63.2 percent of the population of the Third Ward. By the 1980 census, in 15 of Newark's census tracts, blacks constituted 75 percent or more of the population, and in 7 census tracts they were 90 percent or more of the total population. This unprecedented degree of urban, residential segregation is unmatched by any other ethnic group, including Hispanics.[17]

Not only are different ethnic groups clustered within cities, cities have different ethnic make-ups, which is one factor that has given these cities their distinct identities. For example, the largest foreign-born population in Milwaukee in 1920 was German (33.1 percent of the total foreign-born population), in Boston it was Irish (23.5 percent of the foreign-born), and in New York it was Russian and Lithuanian (24 percent), approximately 80 percent of which was Jewish.[18] Thus, the association of Boston with the Irish, Milwaukee with the Germans, and New York with the Jews, has some basis in the distribution of ethnic populations.

Ethnicity is not solely an urban phenomenon. One of the lesser explored dimensions of American ethnic history has been rural ethnicity. In 1911, the report of the United States Senate's Immigration Commission on

Recent Immigrants in Agriculture noted that in 1900, 21.7 percent of all foreign-born breadwinners were employed in agriculture. The largest number of foreign-born farmers were German, but there were also Norwegians, Swedes, Italians, Poles, Portuguese, Bohemians, and Japanese. In New Jersey alone, there were significant South Jersey agricultural populations of Germans in Egg Harbor City, Italians in Vineland, and eastern European Jews in the so-called Jewish agricultural colonies.[19] Many Italians continue to be engaged in agriculture in South Jersey.

Contrary to the positions of some sociologists, such as Herbert J. Gans and Will Herberg, who argued in the 1950s and 1960s that class or religious identities eclipsed ethnic identity in the suburbs, the overall pattern that has emerged since then clearly shows that ethnicity continues strong in suburbia.[20] The 1980 census shows that, like urban ethnic neighborhoods, certain suburban communities have become associated with particular ethnic groups. For example, in New Jersey the largest suburban concentration of Italians was in Belleville (a suburb of Newark), where people of Italian and Italian mixed with some other ancestry constituted 52 percent of the total population. The largest suburban concentration of Poles was in South River with a total Polish and Polish mixed with other ancestry constituting 31 percent of the population. In the Jersey Shore resort community of Spring Lake, Irish and Irish mixed with other ancestry constituted 48.3 percent. Middle-class blacks also have moved out of the inner cities into the suburbs. The largest suburban black concentration in 1990 was in Plainfield, where they constituted 63 percent of the total population 18 years or older. In the post-World War II suburban community of Willingboro, which was the Levittown studied by Herbert Gans, blacks constituted 52.4 percent of the 18-or-older population in 1990.[21]

The differential distribution of ethnic groups has also influenced regional identities. In 1860, two-thirds of the Irish in the United States lived in New England or the Mid-Atlantic States, mostly in cities, and about half the Germans in the country lived in the Midwest, mainly on farms. The 1980 census showed that 79 percent of Poles live in the Northeast and Midwest in what some people have termed the "Polka Belt," 53 percent of African-Americans live in the South, 77 percent of the Japanese in the West, and 73 percent of Puerto Ricans live in the Northeast.[22]

On the national level, changes in the sources of immigration have changed the overall make-up of the American population. According to the 1990 Census, the total population of the United States was 248.7 million. Of this total, 12.1 percent listed themselves as black, 9 percent as Hispanic, 2.9 percent as Asian or Pacific Islander, and 0.8 percent as American Indian, Eskimo, or Aleut. At this time the breakdown of the white European population by ethnic group is not yet available for the 1990 census, but in 1980 was as follows: of a total population of 226.5 million, only 21.9 percent listed themselves as English, 21.7 percent as German, 17.7 percent as Irish, and 4.4 percent as Scottish.[23] Thus, American pluralism continues to mean that no one ethnic group composes more than a plurality of the population.

Certain ethnic traits have become part of our national popular culture. I already have mentioned the log cabin, the covered wagon, and the cowboy, all of which have ethnic origins. Much of the American diet has ethnic origins as well. Consider such Native American foods as corn (maize), the tomato, and chili peppers, the German sausage (which became the American hot dog), the Italian pizza, the Jewish bagel, and the Mexican taco, all of which have been adopted into the American diet, as seen by their appearance on the menus of franchise restaurants around the country. The American language has incorporated words and expressions from the great variety of languages spoken by American ethnic groups. Consider the African-American expressions "boogie-woogie," "jive," "jazz," "rock and roll," "rap"; the Dutch "stoop," "cookey," and "hook" (for a point of land); the Spanish "vamoose," "calaboose," "buckeroo" (from *vaquero*); the German "kindergarten," "delicatessen," and "nix" (for veto); the Chinese "kowtow"; the Yiddish "klutz," and so on.[24] American music has also been shaped by ethnic traditions, from the African-American blues and spirituals to the Scotch-Irish ballads and fiddle tunes, which together represent the twin fountainheads of American popular music. To this mix have been added Cajun, Tex-Mex, polka, salsa, and zydeco music, all of which are ethnic. In dance, there is African-American buck dancing, Celtic-American step dancing (which is the grandparent of square dancing and clog dancing), as well as the numerous dance traditions that have come from Latin America (tango, samba, mambo, cha-cha, and conga). And finally, there are the ethnic festivals, including both single group festivals like Saint Patrick's Day, which is celebrated by Irish and non-Irish alike, and the ubiquitous multi-ethnic festivals that have become so popular since the ethnic revival of the 1970s.

I am not suggesting that ethnicity is the only, or even the most important, factor in American history. It is only one factor—along with race, class, religion, gender, and region—all of which are related to ethnicity, yet are independent from it. Certain topics in American history, such as the Civil War, for example, may best be explained by factors other than ethnicity, such as race or region.

Whether or not one approves of ethnic diversity, it is a fact of life in America and has been from the beginning. But what is the future of ethnicity in America? As the world enters a post-Cold-War era, and ethnic conflict in eastern Europe and the Middle East seems to be tearing nations apart, what will be the effect of ethnic diversity in the United States? I don't adhere to the Pollyanna view of cultural pluralists who think that all one has to do is to attend a multi-ethnic festival and everyone will get along with one other. There has been too much ethnic conflict in the United States to think that ethnic diversity is always a force for peace and understanding. However, what makes ethnicity different in the United States than in some other countries are the facts that no ethnic group constitutes more than a plurality of the total population and that, despite the clustering of ethnic populations, no ethnic group completely dominates any particular state or region. In the last analysis, James Madison's insight about American government applies to American ethnicity; namely, that this nation is sufficiently large and sufficiently diverse that no one ethnic group can have its way all the time. To rephrase Madison's dictum, in America we behold a pluralistic remedy for the diseases most incident to pluralistic society.

Notes

[1] Henry Glassie, "The Types of the Southern Mountain Cabin," in Jan Harold Brunvand, *The Study of American Folklore: An Introduction* (New York: W. W. Norton, 1968), 338–370; Henry Glassie and Fred Kniffen, "Building in Wood in the Eastern United States: A Time-Place Perspective," *The Geographical Review* 56 (1966), 40–66; Harold R. Shurtleff, *The Log Cabin Myth* (Gloucester, Mass.: Harvard University Press, 1939); C. A. Weslager, *The Log Cabin in America, From Pioneer Days to the Present* (New Brunswick: Rutgers University Press, 1969).

[2] J. Geraint Jenkins, *The English Farm Wagon: Origins and Structure* (Lingfield, England: The Oakwood Press for the Museum of English Rural Life, 1961); John Omwake, *The Conestoga Six-Horse Bell Teams of Eastern Pennsylvania* (Cincinnati: Ebbert and Richardson, 1930); George Schumway and Howard C. Frey, *Conestoga Wagon, 1750–1850; Freight Carrier for One Hundred Years of America's Westward Expansion* (n.p.: George Schumway, 1968).

[3] Charles Julian Bishko, "The Peninsular Background of Latin American Cattle Ranching," *The Hispanic American Historical Review* 32 (1952), 491–515; Fred Kniffen, "The Western Cattle Complex: Notes on Differentiation and Diffusion," *Western Folklore* 12 (1953), 179–185: Peter Riviere, *The Forgotten Frontier: Ranchers of Northern Brazil,* Case Studies in Cultural Anthropology (New York: Holt, Rinehard, and Winston, 1972).

[4] Andrew W. Crosby, Jr., *The Columbian Exchange: Biological and Cultural Consequences of 1492.* Contributions in American Studies, no. 2 (Westport, Conn: Greenwood Press, 1972).

[5] Ruth Benedict, *Race, Science, and Politics* (New York: Viking Press, 1945), 11–12.

[6] Stephen Thernstrom, ed., *Harvard Encyclopedia of American Ethnic Groups* (Cambridge and London: Belknap Press of Harvard University Press, 1980).

[7] Robert B. Klymaaz, "Ukrainian Folklore in Canada: An Immigrant Complex in Transition" (Ph.D. diss., Indiana University, 1971); Robert B. Klymaaz, *Continuity and Change: The Ukrainian Folk Heritage in Canada* (Ottowa: Canadian Centre for Folk

Culture Studies, the National Museum of Man, and the National Museums of Canada, 1972); Paul Robert Magocsi, "Ukrainians," in Thernstrom, *Harvard Encyclopedia of American Ethnic Groups,* 200–210; David S. Cohen, *Ukrainian-Americans: An Ethnic Portrait,* photographs by Donald P. Lokuta (Trenton: New Jersey Historical Commission, 1982).

8 Fredrik Barth, ed., *Ethnic Groups and Boundaries* (London and Bergen-Oslo: George Allen & Unwin, Universitets Forlager, 1969); David S. Cohen, "How Dutch Were the Dutch of New Netherland?" *New York History* 62 (1981), 43–60; David S. Cohen, *The Romapo Mountain People* (New Brunswick: Rutgers University Press, 1974).

9 David Hackett Fischer, *Albion's Seed: Four British Folkways in America* (New York: Oxford University Press, 1989).

10 Thomas J. Archdeacon, *Becoming American: An Ethnic History* (New York and London: Macmillan, 1983), 25. These figures computed by Archdeacon are based on estimates in American Council of Learned Societies, "Report of the Committee on Linguistic and National Stocks in the United States," *Annual Report of the American Historical Association for the Year 1931* (Washington: Government Printing Office, 1932). These figures have been slightly revised by Thomas L. Purvis, "The European Ancestry of the United States Population, 1790," *William and Mary Quarterly* 41 (1984), 85–135.

11 Leonard Dinnerstein and David M. Reimers, *Ethnic Americans: A History of Immigration and Assimilation* (New York: Dodd, Mead and Co., 1975), 10–55.

12 Bernard Bailyn, *The Peopling of British North America: An Introduction* (New York: Alfred A. Knopf, 1986).

13 Robert E. Park, Ernest W. Burgess, and Roderick D. McKenzie, *The City* (London: University of Chicago Press, 1967), 9–12, 50–53, 142–155.

14 Humbert S. Nelli, *Italians in Chicago, 1880–1930: A Study in Ethnic Mobility* (New York: Oxford University Press, 1970), 22–54.

15 Raymond Michael Ralph, "From Village to Industrial City: The Urbanization of Newark, New Jersey, 1930–1860" (Ph.D. diss., New York University, 1978), 157; U.S. Census, 1910. Population, 3: 152; U.S. Census, 1980. Newark SMSA. Tracts 68–79.

16 William Julius Wilson, *The Truly Disadvantaged: The Inner City, the Underclass, and Public Policy* (Chicago and London: University of Chicago Press, 1987).

17 Ralph, "From Village to Industrial City," 157; Clement A. Price, "The Beleaguered City as Promised Land: Blacks in Newark, 1917–1947," in William C. Wright, ed., *Urban New Jersey Since 1870* (Trenton: New Jersey Historical Commission, 1975): U.S. Census, 1980. Newark SMSA, PHC 80-2-261, P-7.

18 U.S. Census, 1920. Population, 2: 738, 745, 747, 1008–1009. The figure of 80 percent of New York City population born in Lithuania and Russia as Jewish is based on the relative numbers of Lithuanian, Russian, and Yiddish and Hebrew speakers in the city's population.

19 U.S. Senate Immigration Commission, *Immigrants in Industries,* Part 24 *Recent Immigrants in Agriculture* (1911), 1: 3–9, 47 ff.; 2: 89ff; Emily Fogg Meade, "The Italian on the Land: A Study in Immigration." U.S. Bureau of Labor, *Bulletin* no. 70 (1907), 473–533; Dieter Cunz, "Egg Harbor City: New Germany in New Jersey," New Jersey Historical Society, *Proceedings* 73 (1955), 89–123; Joseph Brandes, *Immigrants to Freedom: Jewish Communities in Rural New Jersey Since 1882* (Philadelphia: University of Pennsylvania, 1971); Rita Zorn Moonsammy, David S. Cohen, and Lorraine E. Williams, eds.

[20] Herbert J. Gans, *The Levittowners: Ways of Life and Politics in a New Suburban Community* (New York: Random House, 1967); Will Herberg, *Protestant, Catholic, Jew: An Essay in American Religious Sociology* (1955: Reprint, Garden City: Doubleday, 1960).

[21] U.S. Census, 1990. Reapportionment/Redistricting Data. PL-94, 171.

[22] Leonard Dinnerstein and Frederic Cople Jaher, *Uncertain Americans: Readings in Ethnic History* (New York: Oxford University Press, 1977), 72; U.S. Bureau of the Census. *Statistical Abstract of the United States* (1989), 41.

[23] "Census Shows Profound Changes," *New York Times,* March 11, 1991, pp. A1, B4: U.S. Census, 1910. Supplementary Report, Ser. PC80-S1-10.

[24] H. L. Mencken, *The American Language: An Inquiry into the Development of English in the United States* (New York: Alfred A. Knopf, 1921), 51–55, 100–109, 197–205.

RESOURCE COMPETITION THEORIES

JOANE NAGEL

Study Questions
1. Define "resource competition."
2. Under what conditions is resource competition likely to be organized along ethnic lines?
3. Under what conditions is resource competition likely to increase?

The concept of competition in interpersonal and intergroup relations occupies a central role in classical and contemporary social theory. Marx (1957, 1959) located the competition over control of resources and surplus value at the core of the capitalist system, predicting class formation, conflict, and ultimately revolutionary change from the contradictions and tensions it produced. While acknowledging the contest of material interests, Weber (1964) added the notion of competition for status honor as a basic dimension of social stratification systems. Simmel (1968) identified the patterns of alliances and oppositions based on conflict and competition over diverse interests at the center of the web of group affiliations. Competition for scarce resources is a basic assumption in many more recent theories as well: game-theoretic models of international relations (Brams & Kilgour, 1988; Myerson, 1991), human ecology (Hannan & Carroll, 1992; Hawley, 1986), and rational choice theory (Banton, 1983, 1985; Hechter, 1987, 1992).

The contemporary application of the notion of resource competition to ethnic relations can be traced to the influential work of Fredrik Barth (1969) and his associates, who argue that ethnicity is best conceived as a system of intergroup boundaries whose strength and salience in interaction are determined, in part, by the extent of contact and resource competition among ethnic groups. According to this view, ethnicity is a variable rather than a fixed or immutable group characteristic. An individual's ethnic identification is thus seen as situational (depending on the competitive utility of ethnic identification in different settings) and, to some extent, volitional (permitting some degree of choice among available ethnicities).

Several propositions about the nature of ethnicity and the structure of interethnic relations are basic to this line of argument:

1. Ethnicity is a problematic social category, the boundaries and meaning of which are negotiated by in-group and out-group members.
2. To the extent that resource competition in a society is organized along ethnic (rather than class, gender, age, etc.) lines, increased competition increases the likelihood of
   a. ethnic identification (strengthened ethnic boundaries);
   b. racism and prejudice (discrimination and hatred against ethnic competitors);
   c. interethnic conflict (interpersonal and intergroup violence); and
   d. ethnic mobilization (movements and collective action).
3. Increased interethnic contact (integration) in the presence of ethnic resource competition increases the likelihood of
   a. ethnic identification;
   b. racism and prejudice;
   c. interethnic conflict; and
   d. ethnic mobilization.

These preliminary propositions identify several aspects of ethnicity that are affected by resource competition: *ethnic identification,* the importance of ethnicity as an organizing principle of daily life; *racism and prejudice,* the extent of negative stereotypes and evaluations of ethnic outgroups; *interethnic conflict,* the likelihood of violent conflict among ethnic groups; and *ethnic mobilization,* the pursuit of ethnic group interests through ethnic organizations and activism.

Central to these propositions are the questions. When will resource competition be organized along ethnic lines, and What are the conditions under which competition increases? The following sections address these questions, defining two major forms of resource competition—economic and political—and examining the support in the social science literature for the stated propositions.

Ethnicity and Resource Competition

Ethnicity refers to differences of language, religion, color, ancestry, and/or culture to which social meanings are attributed and around which identity and group formation occurs. According to Barth (1969), ethnicity can be the result of self-identification or ascription. In the self-identification case, ethnicity is determined (selected) by the individual: Shall I be Mexican, Latino, Irish, White, Cherokee, Indian, Chinese, Asian, or simply American? In the ascription case, ethnicity is determined (assigned) by the larger society: You shall be Black, Indian, Chinese, or Jewish. Thus ethnicity involves an element of choice, but only to the extent that the choice is socially (or politically) allowed.

The range of ethnic choices is different for different people. Waters (1990) discusses the wide array of "ethnic options" available to White Americans, noting that a much narrower set of choices is available to Americans of color. Indeed, while documenting the changing definitions of *Who Is Black?* in the United States, Davis (1991) acknowledges the powerful ascriptive character of the Black ethnic label in American society. Harris (1964) labels the American racial typing system "hypodescent," whereby any African ancestry results in the social designation of Black.[1] Ethnicity, then, is the combined result of individual choice and social designation.

Ethnic choices and designations are generally organized around historical differences in ancestry, religion, language, and the like. However, the extent of ethnic self-awareness and the level of external ascription can vary a great deal over time, with ethnic differences quite prominent at some points in history and relatively unimportant at others. For instance, the extensive linguistic and cultural diversity of African countries is well documented (Morrison, Mitchell, & Paden, 1989). Yet the level of interethnic conflict and the number of African subnationalist movements (e.g., in Biafra, in Eritrea, and in the Ogaden, among others) increased greatly in the wake of the state formation processes (and the associated political competition) following World War II (see Paden, 1980). The reasons for this epidemic of African ethnic violence centered mainly on the restructuring of African polities and economies following the breakdown of colonial rule. The competition by mainly (ethno)regional contenders for control of newly independent African central governments[2] and the easy availability of arms supplied by Eastern and Western bloc powers[3] escalated and militarized ethnic conflict all over the continent.

A similar process of increasing ethnic nationalist mobilization (following decades of quiet ethnic relations) occurred in the former Soviet Union and Eastern Europe during the state-making period of the late 1980s and 1990s. We need not infer from these variations in African and Eastern European ethnic conflict that ethnic divisions or ethnic animosity actually disappeared during periods of low conflict. But these cases remind us that there is much variation in the level of ethnic self-awareness, ethnic political mobilization, and interethnic conflict in even the most ethnically fractionalized regions of the world.

Even in instances of apparently more consistent patterns of ethnic mobilization, there is notable variation in the degree of identification and conflict. For example, the Basque nationalist movement is a highly organized, often violent movement that stretches back well into the last century, with goals ranging from regional autonomy to independence from Spain. Yet even here the degree of Basque nationalist identification and the level of violent and nonviolent activism have varied considerably during its history (Clark, 1984).

In the United States, the long record of oppression and discrimination against Native Americans and African Americans has also seen variations in terms of the level of violence directed against these groups by the White majority (Olzak, Shanahan, & West, 1994; Olzak & West, 1991; Thornton, 1987) as well as variations in the degree of mobilization by Indians and Blacks in response to majority domination (Josephy, 1971; McAdam, 1982; Morris, 1984; Nagel, 1994). The history of ethnic relations in most countries shows similarly variable patterns of conflict and mobilization (see Horowitz, 1985).

Not only does ethnicity wax and wane in its strength of identification, degree of violence, and level of mobilization, there is also variation in the bases on which ethnic boundaries are constructed. Language, religion, culture, and the like are the building blocks of ethnicity. Which of these differences will be activated and transformed into mobilized ethnic differences can vary greatly over time. For instance, religion has receded as a major basis for ethnic discrimination or conflict in contemporary United States.[4] This has not always been the case (see Higham, 1988), and religion serves as a basis of conflict in many parts of the world—for example, Northern Ireland, the Middle East, and the Indian subcontinent (Young, 1976, 1986, 1993; See, 1986a, 1986b).

Similarly, language differences are important sources of mobilization and conflict in many countries (e.g., Canada, Spain, Belgium). Yet in numerous other countries with much greater linguistic diversity (e.g., much of multilingual Africa and Asia), ethnic conflict is framed not as a language dispute but more in religious or cultural terms. Interestingly, and despite strong evidence that English remains unchallenged as the dominant American language, in certain regions of the United States ethnic tensions have become focused on language. Examples are the "English First" organizations, activism, and referenda in Florida and the Southwest during the 1980s (Baron, 1990; Barringer, 1990; Crawford, 1992a, 1992b).

An important lesson to be gained from historical and international comparisons of ethnicity is that variations in language, religion, or culture do not necessarily tell us which of these differences, if any, will result in strong ethnic divisions (e.g., closed ethnic communities), which of these divisions will produce interethnic conflict (e.g., attacks or pogroms against ethnic minorities), or which will promote ethnic mobilization (e.g., minority rights or secessionist movements). We can see that such differences *can be-*

come the basis for ethnic identification, the rationale for interethnic conflict, or the logic of ethnic collective action. Nevertheless, the question remains, *When* will ethnicity become a major division in society, one characterized by group formation, conflict, and mobilization? Resource competition theories of ethnicity look for the answer to this question in patterns of economic and political competition in societies.

Causes of Ethnic Competition

Competition theories of ethnicity stress the role of resource competition as a basis for ethnic group formation, interethnic conflict, and the formation of ethnic social and political movements. Few would argue against the notion that competition for scarce economic (jobs, markets) or political (elected or appointed offices, distribution of tax dollars) resources is a powerful force in society. Such competition causes contenders to organize themselves (sometimes into interest groups, formal associations, social movements), to develop ideologies (sometimes constructive, such as political platforms; sometimes critical, such as stereotyping or denigrating opposition groups), and to engage in conflict (sometimes through institutionalized channels, such as the ballot box or the marketplace; sometimes through illicit means, such as street violence or criminal intimidation). But there are many bases along which groups compete for resources in society: age, class, gender, region, political party, to name but a few. The question is, When will competition and competitors be organized along *ethnic* lines?

Researchers identify a number of situations and conditions that tend to promote distinctly ethnic competition in society. One set of such situations is *historical,* based in past and present ideologies, institutions, and social organization. The other set of situations and conditions that produces ethnic competition is *emergent,* growing out of ongoing demographic, political, and economic processes.

Historical Factors Promoting Ethnic Competition

An important form of social organization with the capacity to generate ethnic conflict and ethnic movements is what many researchers call the "cultural division of labor" (Hechter, 1978; Hechter & Levi, 1979). Cultural divisions of labor are more than economically segregated workforces. Such segregated social systems are generally characterized as systems of "internal colonialism," representing historical patterns of political domination, economic exploitation, and social denigration of minority ethnic groups by one or more dominant groups. Cultural divisions of labor tend to produce segregated ethnic communities characterized by great inequalities of wealth, power, and status. They also tend to be ethnoregional, organized into core and periphery areas where disadvantaged minorities occupy peripheral geographical regions distinct from those occupied by dominant ethnic groups, although minority laborers often migrate into core regions for work.

Cultural division of labor theorists argue that when conflict occurs in these societies, it tends to be organized along ethnic rather than class or political ideological lines.[5] There is some disagreement among researchers concerning the conditions under which ethnic conflict or mobilization will occur in cultural divisions of labor. For instance, Hechter (1975) argues that ethnic solidarity in the British Celtic fringe grows out of growing class awareness by exploited peripheral ethnic groups; thus the conditions of ethnic mobilization arise out of peripheral isolation. Ragin (1986), however, finds little evidence that ethnic party support results simply from the persistence of inequalities between the Celtic states of Scotland and Wales on the one hand and England on the other, but instead requires a shifting of political alignment that opens the door to ethnic parties. Nielsen (1986) identifies a similar role played by the availability of political opportunity (what he calls "structural conduciveness") in the emergence of Flemish party support in Belgium. Together, Ragin's and Nielsen's work suggests that increases in opportunities for political competition raise the likelihood of ethnic party formation and electoral support.

Another structural facilitator of ethnic competition is the split labor market. Bonacich and her associates have documented the existence and operation of split (and enclave) labor markets and their links to ethnic conflict or "antagonism" (Bonacich, 1972, 1973, 1979; Bonacich & Modell, 1980; Light & Bonacich, 1988). Split labor markets occur when two ethnic groups compete with one another for employment and when one group is paid a lower wage. The competition for jobs reinforces the ethnic boundary dividing the group and increases the likelihood of intergroup conflict. Belanger and Pinard (1991) conditionalize the role of competition in interethnic hostility. They find that interethnic competition for jobs in Quebec increased support for the (separatist) *Parti Quebecois* only when French-speaking respondents reported a perception that job competition was unfair.

A variation of the split labor market, closer to but distinct from the notion of an ethnic enclave, can be found in studies of ethnic entrepreneurs—that is, ethnic small business owners who sell to a different ethnic clientele (Light & Bonacich, 1988). Ethnic entrepreneurs are distinguished from ethnic enclave business owners in that there is an ethnic difference between the entrepreneur and his or her clients. An example would be Korean business owners operating in African American neighborhoods and selling to Black customers. By contrast, buyers and sellers in ethnic enclaves tend to be coethnics (Portes & Manning, 1986). Both types of ethnic economies tend to produce interethnic conflict for somewhat similar reasons. Competition and conflict between ethnic entrepreneurs and their customers result from the tendency of ethnic entrepreneurs to hire coethnics rather than local workers and from the perception that entrepreneurs are somehow prospering at the expense of their ethnically different customers. Competition and conflict between members of ethnic enclaves and outside ethnic groups result also from enclave employment patterns, which are seen as ethnically exclusionary, and from enclave success, which is seen as unfair or exploitative. For instance, Morgan (1978) reports that the 19th- and early 20th-century movement to restrict Chinese immigration to the United States, although rooted in labor force competition, tended to be phrased in moral ethnic terms stressing the clannish and "un-American" willingness of Chinese workers to work as "slave" laborers, living on less than their White counterparts.

Contemporary Factors Promoting Ethnic Competition

Historical divisions of labor and patterns or perceptions of exploitation are not the only ways that resource competition becomes organized along ethnic lines in societies. Many factors promoting ethnic competition for societal resources emerge from ongoing social, economic, and political processes. One of the most powerful forces generating interethnic competition is immigration.

Immigration is an engine that constructs new ethnic groups. Whether they are sojourners who intend to return to their countries of origin, refugees who are temporarily or permanently exiled from their homeland, or immigrants who plan to permanently relocate in the host country, foreign migrants are often seen by members of the host society as competitors for jobs, housing, social services, and educational opportunities. Ethnic distinctiveness of immigrant communities can be enhanced when immigrants cluster together in ethnic neighborhoods or enclaves. Such communities may provide many services to immigrants: assistance in finding jobs, housing, loans, ethnic foods, foreign-language newspapers, social contacts, and cultural events (Cohen, 1974). As discussed previously, these ethnic enclaves can exacerbate ethnic competitive tensions when they are seen as successful and exclusionary (see the work of Portes and his associates on ethnic enclaves: Portes & Bach, 1985; Portes & Manning, 1986; Portes & Rumbaut, 1990).

In societies with prior ethnic tensions, these new immigrant ethnic groups fit easily into the existing ethnic stratification system and can quickly become integrated into the patterns and ideology of ethnicity and ethnic competition already institutionalized in the society. For instance, in the United States, African Americans feel both solidarity with and competitive antagonism toward dark-skinned Caribbean immigrants of African descent (e.g., Cubans, Dominicans, Haitians). Solidarity stems from the fact that Caribbean immigrants must confront the same patterns of discrimination faced by all Blacks in American society; antagonism arises from the perceived advantages some immigrants receive because of their political refugee status or their connection to economically successful enclave communities or from the disdain immigrants might display toward African Americans (Massey & Denton, 1989; Waters, [1994]).

Even in countries with no significant history of ethnic division or competition, during times of economic contraction, immigrant groups can become targets for racist attacks, political mobilization for their expulsion, or restrictions on their rights or entry. For instance, in many ethnically homogeneous European countries (e.g., Sweden, Denmark, Germany), guest workers from less developed regions of Europe (e.g., Greece, Turkey, Yugoslavia), who were welcomed during the 1970s when they were needed to fill labor shortages, became targets of anti-immigrant mobilization by White hate groups (skinhead, Nazi) during the more economically austere 1980s (Louis & Prinaz, 1990).

Politics and political policies comprise another category of factors that can promote ethnic competition in society. The power of the state as the dominant institution in society has evolved during the last century (Evans, Rueschemeyer, & Skocpol, 1985), particularly since the end of World War II. During this past half century, the number of sovereign states has more than doubled around the world, growing from approximately 75 on the eve of World War II to more than 170 today (Crawford, 1979). This growth in the number of states and in the centrality of government as the institution controlling major societal resources makes politics an extremely important factor in shaping patterns of ethnic competition in two related ways: access to political office and control over political policies.

Access to Political Office Governments themselves are often the prizes in ethnic competition (Brass, 1985) because the group(s) that controls the state also controls state resources and future access to those resources. Contenders for political power organize themselves along ethnic lines for a variety of reasons: ethnicity is a convenient basis for political organizers due to the commonality of language and culture and the availability of ethnic organizations with their ready-made leadership and membership (Bates, 1983); ethnoregional resource deposits (oil, natural gas, minerals, water) reinforce ethnic self-awareness and sensitize ethnic groups to the possibility of exploitation by other groups (Nafziger, 1983); historical patterns of ethnic political domination—for example, by a group preferred or advantaged by a colonial ruler such as the Igbos in Nigeria (Laitin, 1986) or the Sikhs in India (Schermerhorn, 1978)—can mobilize ethnic opposition groups; where there are ethnically distinct regions, regional representation arrangements can encourage the formation of ethnoregional political parties (Horowitz, 1985; Young, 1976).

Control Over Political Policies   Governments regulate ever greater areas of social life; thus political policies become objects of ethnic and other intergroup competition for control of politically regulated resources. Ethnic competition increases to the extent that political policies acknowledge or regulate ethnicity as a basis for access to political and economic resources. The role of political policy in ethnic competition appears somewhat tautological on its face: Political policies that allocate resources on the basis of ethnicity will result in ethnic competition for political resources. However, when viewed in historical perspective, we can see that political policies can exert an independent influence on ethnic competition. An example is affirmative action policies in two very different settings: India and the United States. In both countries, political policies were used to provide some reparation for historically exploited and disadvantaged groups, untouchables in India and African Americans in the United States (Schermerhorn, 1978; Simmons, 1982). In both countries, these affirmative action policies promoted ethnic mobilization among other non-designated minorities who wished to receive similar treatment: religious and linguistic minorities in India; Latinos, Native Americans, and Asian Americans in the United States (Darnell & Parikh, 1988; Lopez & Espiritu, 1990; Schermerhorn, 1978). In both countries, these political reparation policies promoted a backlash movement by the dominant majority: upper caste Hindus in India and White, in the United States (Burstein, 1991; Desai, 1992).

Factors Increasing the Level of Ethnic Competition

As we have seen, a variety of historical and contemporary factors tend to promote competition for political and economic resources in society along ethnic lines. Historical divisions of labor and patterns of exploitation and incorporation tend to become institutionalized into ongoing political and economic relations, promoting ethnic identification and ethnic mobilization as a strategy for attaining rights and resources. Immigration creates new ethnic groups that can be defined as economic and/or political competitors: Political policies that acknowledge ethnic differences or attempt reparations for past discrimination can promote parallel or oppositional mobilization by groups attempting to compete in the political arena.

Given these various factors directing competition along ethnic channels, there remains the question about the level of competition among groups already inclined to compete in ethnic terms. In other words, in some societies at some points in history, there is a great deal of ethnic competition, sometimes leading to high rates of ethnic conflict, which can take extreme forms such as internment, expulsion, or genocide. Yet at other moments in time, ethnic competition appears to be nonexistent—ethnic relations are placid and ethnic boundaries are permeable (intermarriage, religious conversion, language loss). In some cases, these two extremes can be temporally quite proximate. An example is Yugoslavia during the 1980s.

From the end of World War II and prior to the recent disintegration of the Soviet Union and its loosened control over the Eastern bloc states, which included Yugoslavia, the ethnically fractious Balkan region of Yugoslavia remained quiet, exhibiting many signs of ethnic integration (intermarriage, ethically mixed political representation, ethnic migration and settlement outside home regions). Many observers attributed this ethnic affability to former leader Tito's strong-handed government and to Soviet intolerance of ethnic conflict (McFarlane, 1988; Rusinow, 1988). No doubt repression played an important role in Yugoslavia's ethnic honeymoon. However, at least as important as repression was the lack of reward for ethnic competition in Yugoslavian economics or politics. The structure of the Yugoslav state did not permit advantage on the basis of ethnicity. There was no rationale for ethnic competition.

The decline of Soviet hegemony, particularly Mikhail Gorbachev's announcement in 1989 that he would not intervene in the internal affairs of Eastern bloc states, which quickly led to the dismantling of the Berlin Wall in November, set in motion a process that reshaped the calculus underlying Yugoslavian political competition. The Serbian majority became a dominant force that threatened to occupy the political center and to disadvantage permanently the various Yugoslavian religious, linguistic, and regional minorities (Croats, Bosnians, Muslims, Montenegrans, etc.). One after another of these minorities decided to secede from Yugoslavia and seek independent recognition from the international state system. The Serbian response was, first, to attempt their forced repatriation through military action by the Serbian-controlled Yugoslav army and, second, to create ethnically "cleansed" Serbian regions. The disintegration of Yugoslavia was not due simply to the lifting of repression, but also the result of political competition generated by the move toward democratic government. In Yugoslavia (and perhaps in many other cases as well), democracy was impossible when one ethnic competitor was seen as unfairly advantaged.[6]

Political change is not the only condition under which competition can shake up formerly quiescent, if not congenial, ethnic relations. Olzak (1986, 1992) finds that two kinds of economic change can produce ethnic conflict: economic contractions, when jobs and markets become more (ethnically) competitive; and ethnic integration, when formerly economically segregated societies begin to integrate and thus introduce ethnic competition for jobs and markets. Although Olzak's research focuses mainly on economic integration, her argument is extended to include social and political integration.

Not all instances of competition for jobs or sales markets that occur during times of economic contraction are organized into *ethnic* competition. However, research suggests that there are many instances in which economic competition becomes "ethnicized." One such case is when employers use minority workers to undermine wages or to break unions. For instance, Higgs (1977) and Wilson (1978) report on the historical practice by American employers of hiring immigrant and African American workers to weaken labor union organization efforts or work actions such as strikes. In such cases, interethnic antagonism can rise. For instance, Olzak (1989, 1992) finds that turn-of-the-century labor strike activity in the United States is associated with increased attacks by Whites on these two groups. Moreover, recent studies of the emergence of "invention" of Whiteness as an ethnic category in the United States stress the importance of labor and resource competition with African Americans and Native Americans in the construction of White identity (Allen 1994; Roediger 1991, 1994; Saxton, 1990).

Economic competition can also become ethnically organized when formerly segregated labor markets begin to integrate. This can occur as a result of the migration of lower-paid ethnic workers into new labor markets. Examples include the internal migration of African American workers from the rural South into southern and northern cities during the early 20th century (Lemann, 1991; Marks, 1989) or the international immigration (legal and illegal) of Latin American workers into the United States during the decades following World War II (Portes & Bach, 1985; Portes & Rumbaut, 1990). In her investigations into American ethnic violence during the period from 1880 to 1914, Olzak (1989, 1992) reports that both immigrant and Black migration into urban labor markets were associated with increased attacks on both groups but particularly on African Americans, even when Blacks were not directly included in labor force competition with native-born Whites.

Social and political integration can also bring formerly isolated groups into contact and competition with each other and can spark increased ethnic identification, conflict, and mobilization. Political policies fostering ethnic and racial desegregation are generally intended to equalize access to economic and political resources (jobs, education, housing, political agency posts and offices). Because such desegregation undermines the monopoly of control over such resources by dominant groups, desegregation tends to result in interethnic competition and thus to produce interethnic hostility and conflict.

The heightened racial conflict surrounding the use of busing to achieve public school integration in the United States represents an example of this process. Although many White objections to busing were phrased in the discourse of racism that typically characterizes American race relations, it was not merely racialistic sensibilities that were offended by school busing. White parents were afraid their children would receive an inferior education in poorer quality, formerly Black schools (Olzak et al., 1994; Rubin, 1972).[7]

Consequences of Ethnic Competition

The propositions listed earlier identified at least four consequences of ethnic competition: increased ethnic identification and group formation, increased racism and prejudice, increased interethnic conflict, and increased ethnic mobilization and activism. The social science literature provides a number of examples of how competition leads to these various outcomes.

Before reviewing some of this literature, it is important to note that much of this research rests on the notion that ethnicity is a variable. In other words, ethnicity can be increased or decreased in terms of individual ethnic self-awareness or identity in the physical, social, and cultural markers that become the bases for ethnic differences; in the number of ethnic groups in existence at any point in time; in the extent to which ethnicity organizes social interaction; and in the amount of conflict associated with ethnic differences. Competition is a major factor in shaping such variations in ethnicity and ethnic relations.

One major form of competition is international conflict, particularly war. American involvement in various international wars during the 20th century resulted in an increase of ethnic awareness and interethnic conflict on the homefront. For instance, Petonito (1991, 1992) reports that both American and Japanese ethnicity were reconstructed and enhanced during World War II when the United States and Japan were adversaries. Although German Americans were also targets of official and informal suspicion in the United States during the 1940s, it was during World War I that German American ethnicity was under greatest attack, with the result that German language usage by German Americans virtually disappeared (Wittke, 1974). More recently, the 1991 Gulf War between Iraq and an American-led alliance increased anti-Arab sentiment in the United States, creating fear of attack among many Arab Americans (Applebome, 1991). Even civil wars can activate ethnic differences and spark a resurgence in ethnic identification abroad. For instance, Kelly (1993, 1995) argues that Lithuanian American ethnic identification in the United States increased as a result of the Lithuanian independence movement in the former Soviet Union.

The whole question of ethnic conflict—when will attacks on ethnic minorities occur?—has important links to intergroup competition. For instance, Olzak and her associates (Olzak, 1992; Olzak et al., 1994; Olzak & West, 1991) find that attacks against immigrants and African Americans (including lynchings) in the United States during the late 19th century and at various points during the 20th century are linked to labor force competition and to the desegregation (and thus increased competition) of American economic and political institutions.

"Ethnogenesis," or the creation of new ethnic groups, can also be prompted by competition (see Despres, 1975). For instance, prior to the mobilization for independence from British colonial rule during the 1950s, Nigerians, although linguistically and religiously quite diverse, did not have a history of extensive internal ethnic animosity or conflict. The British blueprint for independent Nigerian government was organized around regional representation in a central government. Because the regions tended to be ethnically distinct, the organization of regional political organizations and parties tended to be along ethnic lines. The result of this political competition for control of the central government and the resources it commanded was an ethnicization of Nigerian politics, which ultimately led to the secession of the eastern region ("Biafra") and a civil war during the late 1960s (Kirk-Greene, 1971; Sklar, 1963).

Ethnogenesis in the United States is also tied to politics and the competition for politically controlled resources. Padilla (1985, 1986) describes the emergence of Latino ethnic identity, organization, and activism in Chicago's Mexican American and Puerto Rican communities. The shift in ethnic identification from Mexican or Puerto Rican to the broader ethnic category, "Latino," is tied to the strategic utility of Latino ethnicity in the competition for city-controlled affirmative action resources and jobs. Indeed, the emergence of panethnic organizations and movements in the United States (Latinos, Indo-Americans, Asian Americans, Native Americans) is seen by researchers as a strategy used by disadvantaged groups to compete in American political and economic spheres (Espiritu, 1992; Lopez & Espiritu, 1990; Nagel, 1982, 1996; Wei, 1993).

Conclusion

Competition can be seen as a driving force underlying patterns of ethnic identification, ethnic group formation, ethnic conflict and antagonism, and ethnic movements. The conditions that generate ethnic, as opposed to some other form of, competition seem to depend on the degree of institutionalization of ethnicity into social, economic, and political life. Once society is organized along ethnic lines, competition similarly tends to be ethnically organized.

The tenacity of ethnicity as an organizing principle in social life can be seen in the vast amount of ethnic violence and ethnic nationalist mobilization occurring around the world at the close of the 20th century. Despite decades of efforts at nation building, subnationalist identification and the mobilization for political independence remain a dominant force in world politics. There are several reasons for the durability of ethnicity as a basis for social organization. First is the history of ethnic discrimination and domination that characterizes most of the world's states. This historical pattern of ethnic competition heightens the awareness of both dominant and subordinate groups of the potential disadvantages of enclosure in a multiethnic state. Second is the advantage to be gained in the modern world by sovereignty and political independence. The structure of supranational organizations such as the United Nations or the European Community tend to favor and advantage sovereign states over the ethnic components of multiethnic states. Thus the emergence of these suprastate structures adds a competitive rationale to pressures toward Balkanization (see Nagel & Olzak, 1982). Finally, the structure of the world state system rests on an ideological foundation of home-rule, representative government, and self-determination. All of these themes resonate with ethnonationalism and undermine the moral legitimacy of denying minorities expanded rights, autonomy, or independence. Indeed, the move to democratic government may contain within it the seeds of ethnic conflict as political participation, formerly denied by one-party or authoritarian rulers, increases and becomes organized along ethnic (often ethnoregional) lines because of the successful efforts of ethnic political entrepreneurs to fan minority fears of majority domination or because of long-held ethnic dreams of a national homeland. Although not all ethnic minorities enclosed in multiethnic states will be successful in their competition for home rule,[8] ethnicity remains a viable and dynamic force in societies around the world.

References

Allen, T. W. (1994). *The invention of the White race: Racial oppression and social control.* London: Verso.

Applebome, P. (1991, February 20). Arab-Americans fear a land war's backlash. *New York Times,* p. A1.

Banton, M. (1983). *Racial and ethnic competition.* New York: Cambridge University Press.

Banton, M. (1985). Mixed motives and the processes of rationalization. *Ethnic and Racial Studies, 8,* 534–547.

Baron, D. E. (1990). *The English-only question: An official language for Americans?* New Haven, CT: Yale University Press.

Barringer, F. (1990, February 6). Judge nullifies law mandating use of English. *New York Times,* pp. A1, A17.

Barth, F. (1969). *Ethnic groups and boundaries.* Boston: Little, Brown.

Bates, R. H. (1983). Modernization, ethnic competition, and the rationality of politics in contemporary Africa. In D. Rothchild & V. Olorunsola (Eds.), *State versus ethnic claims: African policy dilemmas* (pp. 152–171). Boulder, CO: Westview.

Belanger, S., & Pinard, M. (1991). Ethnic movements and the competition model: Some missing links. *American Sociological Review, 56,* 446–457.

Bonacich, E. (1972). A theory of ethnic antagonism: The split labor market. *American Sociological Review, 37,* 547–559.

Bonacich, E. (1973). A theory of middleman minorities. *American Sociological Review, 38,* 583–594.

Bonacich, E. (1979). The past, present, and future of split labor market theory. *Research in Race and Ethnic Relations, 1,* 17–64.

Bonacich, E., & Modell, J. (1980). *The economic basis of ethnic solidarity: Small business in the Japanese-American community.* Berkeley: University of California Press.

Botev, N. (1994). Where East meets West: Ethnic intermarriage in the former Yugoslavia, 1962–1989. *American Sociological Review, 59,* 461–480.

Brams, S. J., & Kilgour, M. (1988). *Game theory and national security.* New York: Basil Blackwell.

Brass, P. (1985). Ethnic groups and the state. In P. Brass (Ed.), *Ethnic groups and the state* (pp. 1–56). London: Croom Helm.

Burstein, P. (1991). "Reverse discrimination" cases in the federal courts: Legal mobilization by a countermovement. *Sociological Quarterly, 32,* 511–528.

Clark, R. (1984). *The Basque insurgents: ETA, 1952–1980.* Madison: University of Wisconsin Press.

Cohen, A. (1974). *Urban ethnicity.* New York: Harper & Row.

Crawford, J. (1979). *The creation of states in international law.* Oxford: Clarendon.

Crawford, J. (1992a). *Hold your tongue: Bilingualism and the politics of English only.* New York: Addison-Wesley.

Crawford, J. (1992b). *Language loyalties: A source book on the official English controversy.* Chicago: University of Chicago Press.

Darnell, A., & Parikh, S. (1988). Religion, ethnicity, and the role of the state: Explaining conflict in Assam. *Ethnic and Racial Studies, 11,* 263–281.

Davis, J. F. (1991). *Who is Black? One nation's definition.* University Park: Pennsylvania State University.

Desai, M. (1992, April). *The demise of secularism and the rise of majority communalism in India.* Paper presented at the annual meeting of the Midwest Sociological Society, Kansas City, MO.

Despres, L. (1975). Toward a theory of ethnic phenomena. In L. Despres (Ed.), *Ethnicity and resource competition* (pp. 186–207). The Hague, Netherlands: Mouton.

DeVise, P. (1978). *The anti-redlining campaign: Three perspectives on its origins, meanings, and results.* Chicago: University of Illinois at Chicago Circle, School of Urban Sciences.

Espiritu, Y. (1992). *Asian American panethnicity: Bridging institutions and identities.* Philadelphia: Temple University Press.

Evans, P., Rueschemeyer, D., & Skocpol, T. (Eds.). (1985). *Bringing the state back in.* New York: Cambridge University Press.

Glenny, M. (1992). *The fall of Yugoslavia.* New York: Penguin.

Gold, D. E. (1980). *Housing market discrimination: Causes and effects of slum formation.* New York: Praeger.

Hannan, M. T., & Carroll, G. R. (1992). *Dynamics of organizational populations: Density, legitimation, and competition.* New York: Oxford University Press.

Harris, M. (1964). *Patterns of race in the Americas.* New York: Norton.

Hawley, A. (1986). *Human ecology: A theoretical essay.* Chicago: University of Chicago Press.

Hechter, M. (1975). *Internal colonialism.* Berkeley: University of California Press.

Hechter, M. (1978). Group formation and the cultural division of labor. *American Journal of Sociology, 84,* 293–318.

Hechter, M. (1987). *Principles of group solidarity.* Berkeley: University of California Press.

Hechter, M. (1992). The dynamics of secession. *Acta Sociologica, 35,* 267–283.

Hechter, M., & Levi, M. (1979). The comparative analysis of ethnoregional movements. *Ethnic and Racial Studies, 2,* 260–274.

Higgs, R. (1977). *Competition and coercion: Blacks in the American economy, 1865–1914.* New York: Cambridge University Press.

Higham, J. (1988). *Strangers in the land: Patterns of American nativism* (2nd ed.). New Brunswick, NJ: Rutgers University Press.

Hodson, R., Sekulic, D., & Massey, G. (1994). National tolerance in Yugoslavia. *American Journal of Sociology, 99,* 1534–1558.

Horowitz, D. (1985). *Ethnic groups in conflict.* Berkeley: University of California Press.

Josephy, A. M., Jr. (1971). *Red power.* New York: McGraw-Hill.

Kelly, M. (1993). The re-emergence of ethnic identity among third and fourth generation Lithuanian-Americans in Kansas City. *Sociologija Lietuvoje: Praeitis ir Dabartis* (Kaunas Technological University, Lithuania), *3,* 162–165.

Kelly, M. (1995). *Born again Lithuanians: Ethnic pilgrimages and conversions.* Ph.D. dissertation, University of Kansas, Department of Sociology.

Kirk-Greene, A. (1971). *Crisis and conflict in Nigeria* (2 vols.). London: Oxford University Press.

Laitin, D. D. (1986). *Hegemony and culture: Politics and religious change among the Yoruba.* Chicago: University of Chicago Press.

Lemann, N. (1991). *The promised land: The Great Black Migration and how it changed America.* New York: Alfred A. Knopf.

Louis, P., & Prinaz, L. (1990). *Skinheads, Taggers, Zulus, and Company.* Paris: La Table Ronde.

Light, I., & Bonacich, E. (1988). *Immigrant entrepreneurs: Koreans in Los Angeles, 1965–1982.* Berkeley: University of California Press.

Lopez, D., & Espirito, Y. (1990). Panethnicity in the United States: A theoretical framework. *Ethnic and Racial Studies, 13,* 198–224.

Mandela, N. (1990). *Nelson Mandela's speeches, 1990: Intensify the struggle to abolish Apartheid.* New York: Pathfinder.

Marks, C. (1989). *Farewell—We're good and gone: The Great Black Migration.* Bloomington: Indiana University Press.

Marx, K. (1957). *Capital* (Vol. 2). Moscow: Foreign Languages.

Marx, K. (1959). *Capital* (Vols. 1, 3). Moscow: Foreign Languages.

Massey, D., & Denton, N. (1989). Hypersegregation in U.S. metropolitan areas: Black and Hispanic segregation along five dimensions. *Demography, 26,* 373–392.

McAdam, D. (1982). *Political process and the development of Black insurgency, 1930–1970.* Chicago: University of Chicago Press.

McFarlane, B. J. (1988). *Yugoslavia: Politics, economics, and society.* New York: Pinter.

Melson, R., & Wolpe, H. (Eds.). (1971). *Nigeria: Modernization and the politics of communalism.* East Lansing: Michigan State University Press.

Morgan, P. (1978). The legislation of drug laws: Economic crisis and social control. *Journal of Drug Issues, 9,* 53–62.

Morris, A. (1984). *The origins of the Civil Rights Movement.* New York: Free Press.

Morrison, D., Mitchell, R. C., & Paden, J. N. (1989). *Black Africa: A comparative handbook* (2nd ed.). New York: Paragon House, Irvington.

Myerson, R. B. (1991). *Game theory: Analysis of conflict.* Cambridge, MA: Harvard University.

Nafziger, E. W. (1983). *The economics of political instability: The Nigerian-Biafran War.* Boulder, CO: Westview.

Nagel, J. (1982). The political mobilization of Native Americans. *Social Science Journal, 19,* 37–46.

Nagel, J. (1994). U.S. Indian activist movements. In D. Champagne (Ed.), *Native America: Portrait of the peoples* (pp. 1–20). Detroit: Visible Ink.

Nagel, J. (1996). *American Indian ethnic renewal: Red power and the resurgence of identity and culture.* New York: Oxford University Press.

Nagel, J., & Olzak, S. (1982). Ethnic mobilization in new and old states: An extension of the competition model. *Social Problems, 30,* 127–143.

Nagel, J., & Whorton, B. (1992). Ethnic conflict and the world system: International competition in Iraq (1961–1991) and Angola (1974–1991). *Journal of Political and Military Sociology, 20*(1), 1–35.

Nielsen, F. (1986). Structural conduciveness and ethnic mobilization: The Flemish movement in Belgium. In S. Olzak & J. Nagel (Eds.), *Competitive ethnic relations* (pp. 173–198). New York: Academic Press.

Olzak, S. (1986). A competition model of ethnic collective action in American cities, 1877–1889. In S. Olzak & J. Nagel (Eds.), *Competitive ethnic relations* (pp. 17–46). New York: Academic Press.

Olzak, S. (1989). Labor unrest, immigration, and ethnic conflict: Urban America 1880–1915. *American Journal of Sociology, 94,* 1303–1333.

Olzak, S. (1992). *The dynamics of ethnic competition and conflict.* Stanford, CA: Stanford University Press.

Olzak, S., & West, E. (1991). Ethnic conflict and the rise and fall of ethnic movements. *American Sociological Review, 56,* 458–474.

Olzak, S., Shanahan, S., & West, E. (1994). School desegregation, interracial exposure, and antibusing activity in contemporary urban America. *American Journal of Sociology, 100,* 196–241.

Paden, J. (Ed.). (1980). *Values, identities, and national integration: Empirical research in Africa.* Evanston, IL: Northwestern University Press.

Padilla, F. (1985). *Latino ethnic consciousness: The case of Mexican Americans and Puerto Ricans in Chicago.* Notre Dame, IN: University of Notre Dame Press.

Padilla, F. (1986). Latino ethnicity in the city of Chicago. In S. Olzak & J. Nagel (Eds.), *Competitive ethnic relations* (pp. 153–171). New York: Academic Press.

Petonito, G. (1991, August). *Racial discourse, claims making and Japanese internment during World War II.* Paper presented at the annual meeting of the American Sociological Association, Cincinnati, OH.

Petonito, G. (1992). Constructing "Americans": "Becoming American," "Loyalty" and Japanese internment during World War II. In G. Miller & J. Holstein (Eds.), *Perspectives on social problems* (pp. 93–108). Greenwich, CT: JAI.

Portes, A., & Bach, R. (1985). *Latin journey: Cuban and Mexican immigrants in the United States.* Berkeley: University of California Press.

Portes, A., & Manning, R. (1986). The immigrant enclave: Theory and empirical examples. In S. Olzak & J. Nagel (Eds.), *Competitive ethnic relations* (pp. 47–68). New York: Academic Press.

Portes, A., & Rumbaut, R. (1990). *Immigrant America: A portrait.* Berkeley: University of California Press.

Ragin, C. (1986). The impact of Celtic nationalism on class politics in Scotland and Wales. In S. Olzak & J. Nagel (Eds.), *Competitive ethnic relations* (pp. 190–220). New York: Academic Press.

Roediger, D. R. (1991). *The wages of Whiteness: Race and the making of the American working class.* London: Verso.

Roediger, D. R. (1994). *Towards the abolition of Whiteness: Essays on race, politics, and working class history.* London: Verso.

Rubin, L. B. (1972). *Busing and backlash: White against White in a California school district.* Berkeley: University of California Press.

Rushow, D. (Ed.). (1988). *Yugoslavia: A fractured federalism.* Washington, DC: Wilson Center.

Saxton, A. (1990). *The rise and fall of the White republic: Class politics and mass culture in nineteenth-century America.* London: Verso.

Schermerhom, R. A. (1978). *Ethnic plurality in India.* Tucson: University of Arizona Press.

See, K. O. (1986a). *First World nationalisms.* Chicago: University of Chicago Press.

See, K. O. (1986b). For God and Crown: Class, ethnicity, and Protestant politics in Northern Ireland. In S. Olzak & J. Nagel (Eds.), *Competitive ethnic relations* (pp. 221–246). New York: Academic Press.

Sekulic, D., Massey, G., & Hodson, R. (1994). Who were the Yugoslavs? Failed sources of a common identity in the former Yugoslavia. *American Sociological Review, 59,* 83–97.

Simmel, G. (1968). *The conflict in modern culture, and other essays* (K. P. Ktzkom, Trans.). New York: Teachers College.

Simmons, R. (1982). *Affirmative action: Conflict and change in higher education after Bakke.* Cambridge, MA: Schenkman.

Sklar, R. (1963). *Nigerian political parties.* Princeton, NJ: Princeton University Press.

Thornton, R. (1987). *American Indian holocaust and survival.* Norman: University of Oklahoma Press.

Waters, M. (1990). *Ethnic options: Choosing identities in America.* Berkeley: University of California Press.

Waters, M. (in press). Ethnic and racial identities of second generation Black immigrants in New York City. *International Migration Review.*

Weber, M. (1964). *The theory of social and economic organization.* New York: Free Press.

Wel, W. (1993). *The Asian American movement.* Philadelphia: Temple University Press.

Wilson, W. J. (1978). *The declining significance of race.* Chicago: University of Chicago Press.

Wittke, C. F. (1974). *German-Americans and the World War.* New York: J. S. Ozer.

Young, C. (1976). *The politics of cultural pluralism.* Madison: University of Wisconsin Press.

Young, C. (1986). Cultural pluralism in the Third World. In S. Olzak & J. Nagel (Eds.). *Competitive ethnic relations* (pp. 113–122). New York: Academic Press.

Young, C. (1993). *The rising tide of cultural pluralism.* Madison: University of Wisconsin Press.

Notes

[1] This "one drop" rule, where one drop of African blood results in the individual being labeled Black, stands in contrast to the more flexible ethnic labeling system in many Latin American countries (e.g., Brazil, Mexico), where there is a broad array of ethnic choices available to many individuals of Indian, European, and African mixed ancestry. Harris (1964) designates this type of ethnic labeling system "amalgamation."

[2] The organization of ethnically distinct regions into contenders for political power was often the result of colonial policies that created regions as legal, political, educational, administrative units that were then slated to compete against each other in independent electoral systems (see Laitin, 1986; Melson & Wolpe, 1971; Young, 1976).

[3] These powers were themselves engaged in the competitive relations of the cold war (see Nagel & Whorton, 1992).

[4] This is not to say that religious identification in the United States is waning but that it is not as important a basis of ethnic identification as race, ancestry, or language.

[5] Although conflict in cultural divisions of labor tends to be organized along ethnic lines, with movements built out of ethnic organizations, the conflict can be framed in both ethnic and nonethnic ideological terms with objectives of transforming society, not simply benefiting a particular ethnic group. For instance, in South Africa, the African National Congress's platform embraces a nonracialistic society, not the domination of Whites by Blacks (Mandela, 1990).

[6] For discussions of ethnicity in pre- and post-1989 Yugoslavia, see Botev, 1994; Glenny, 1992; Hodson, Sekulic, & Massey, 1994; and Sekulic, Massey, & Hodson, 1994.

[7] The integration of neighborhoods had a similar competitive dimension—fear of declining housing values should Blacks move in due to bank and insurance company redlining practices (DeVise, 1978; Gold, 1980).

[8] For example, the former components of the Soviet empire are faring considerably better in achieving sovereignty than did many of those groups enclosed in African and Asian states formed out of the European colonial empire at the end of World War II.

PART·4

The Persistence, Functions, and Consequences of Social Classification

"Sir! Observing from left to right, You will notice a short, stout dark-complected man; that is Mayor LaGuardia. Seated next to him, you will see another man of swarthy complexion; and he is commissioner Newbold Morris. They may look like colored men from here, but they are, in fact, both white men. Now, on the other side of the platform you will observe the presence of two men of very fair complexion. The one at which I point is Congressman A. C. Powell, Jr., and the gentleman seated next to him is Mr. Walter White, the secretary of the National Association for the Advancement of Colored People. Though these two gents look like white men, they are actually Negroes."

John G. Jackson
MAN, GOD, AND CIVILIZATION (1972:207)

In this part, we address the broad question of why the idea of race, and formal and informal efforts to categorize and classify people by "race," persist and continue when they have no logical scientific basis. In particular, attention is given to the manner in which the legal system supports classification, the relationship between classification schemes and educational theory and practice, and how each of these reinforces the other. The prefaces and readings so far make the point that the categories created in the past appear logical even today because they match what people already think and believe.

There are several related answers to the question of why the idea of "race" and racial classification persists. One answer is that the schemes reflect the desires, interests, and needs of people who have the power to make laws which define self and others. Legal rulings, in turn, legitimate the exploitation and control of less powerful groups by more powerful ones (Bell nd). Consider the following cases that have made classification schemes an integral and enduring part of social relations in the United States.

- In 1830, the Congress of the United States authorized the negotiated removal of Native Americans to what was then Oklahoma territory. "The Indian Removal Act" was supposedly based on consent, but in fact many groups were forcibly removed by the military (Hazel 1985). What was at work was the power of the people who made the laws to enforce them. In this case, the law restricted most Native Americans to life on a reservation and made them, in essence, wards of the federal government. This third-class citizenship status is a condition from which many Native Americans have still not been able to extricate themselves.

- In *People v. Hall,* 1854, the California Supreme Court legally defined the meaning of the terms: "Black, Mulatto, Indian and White Person." It declared that the phrase "White Person" applied to a single, fixed category. The other terms applied in a generic sense to all categories of persons labeled non-white regardless of their specific features. The effect of the decision was to add people of Asian descent to the list of persons legally barred from testifying against whites in court.

  > . . . In using the words, "No Black, or Mulatto person, or Indian shall be allowed to give evidence for or against a White person," the Legislature, if any intention can be ascribed to it, adopted the most comprehensive terms to embrace every known class or shade of color, as the apparent design was to protect the White person from the influence of all testimony other than that of persons of the same caste. The use of these terms must, by every sound rule of construction, exclude every one who is not of white blood. . . . (cited in Rothenberg 1988:202)

- In 1636, Colonists in the Caribbean declared that Indians and Negroes could be sold for life. In 1640, four years later, the colony of Virginia sentenced a black indentured servant who had runaway along with two whites to "serve his said master or his assigns for the rest of his natural life here or else where" (Jordan 1974:42). The two white servants were sentenced to serve an additional four years each. These decisions signaled the beginning of the association of the color "black" with the status "slave" and the color "white" with "privileged status" in the United States.

What is to be noted about these cases is that there is no attempt to hide the intent here. The language speaks directly to the prejudice of white lawmakers as they created color/race-based classification systems to their advantage and to the disadvantage of everyone else. How does one group come to possess the kind of power that allows it to categorize other people and to construct legal systems to support what they do.

A necessary condition for the emergence of groups with varying degrees of wealth, power, and unequal privilege is a society characterized by extreme inequality. Sociologists have identified five patterns of contact between different groups that seem to lead to conditions of dominance and subordination. In each of these cases, inequality is a significant factor in the initial contact phase and tends to intensify over time. Martin Marger (1991, 54–56) have labeled the five patterns as follows:

1. *Annexation.* A process that leads to the incorporation of all or part of one nation into an adjacent, more powerful nation. The annexation may be negotiated (as in the Louisiana Purchase from the French by the United States) or attained through military action (as in the ceding of the Southwestern Territories to the United States at the close of the war with Mexico). Mexicans living in these areas immediately took on a subordinate status set apart by their physical features, language, and traditions.

2. *Voluntary Immigration.* The process whereby people living in one country elect to move to another country. Push factors (economics, political conditions, natural disasters) and pull factors (political and religious freedom, jobs, higher pay) induce people to emigrate. Voluntary immigration is well-known and is the most common pattern of contact. The best example is the voluntary movement of thousands of people from Ireland to the United States in the 1840s and 1850s motivated in part by a potato famine. The low social standing given the Irish by European society followed them to the United States where they found themselves on the bottom of the white class structure.

3. *Involuntary Immigration.* This involves the forced transfer of people from one society to another. The best known example is the transfer of millions of Africans to the Americas over a more than 400-year period. They were set apart by physical features, language, religion, and cultural traditions most divergent from that of the Europeans. All these factors, in the minds of their captors, made them ideal candidates for slavery. Indentured servants also fit the category of involuntary immigrants.

4. *Conquest/Colonialism.* This is a form of domination in which an external country imposes its political, economic, social, and cultural institutions on an indigenous people. Using superior military force, the European countries controlled parts of Asia, Africa, Australia, and the Americas for hundreds of years. Puerto Rico and the Virgin Islands are present-day examples of American colonies. A special case of colonialism is termed *internal colonialism.*

5. *Internal Colonialism.* When relations that mirror those in classical colonialism exist among ethnic groups in the same country, it is called internal colonialism. The concept is normally used to explain

the situation of disadvantaged groups involuntarily subjugated in newly independent nations that emerged following the era of European colonialism. The relations of African, Asian, Hispanic, and Native Americans to white Americans in the United States is an example of this.

Bonnie C. Freeman (1978) defined the following characteristics as "essential to a colonial relationship, and especially to the colonial educational process":

1. The colonized group is assumed to be intellectually, morally, and physically inferior
2. The colonial educational system is controlled by the dominant group and is detached from the culture of the colonized and colonizer as well
3. The history of the colonized is either denied or reinterpreted in such a fashion that colonial education constitutes a fundamental assault on the identity of the colonized group
4. The substance of the colonial education is different from that given the colonizer
5. A plausible outcome of the colonial situation is that the colonized began to identify with their oppressor, to assume the superiority of his values and knowledge, to see themselves as weak and ignorant, and, finally, to depend on the colonizer for a definition of the situation, "protection," and other resources (208–209)

Conflict emerges as a central and defining feature in the relationships between "racial and ethnic" groups in all of the above contact patterns. As dominant groups take steps to make permanent and institutionalize their advantage, they develop an ideology of "difference," or "classification" to rationalize and justify their treatment of less-powerful groups, hence, "the Other." The first public school in the country opened its doors exclusively to white males in 1821 (Pulliam 1968). The privileged status of white males in America today is due almost exclusively to the fact that they alone benefited from this early access to education. In societies like the United States where inequality was/is the foundation of its construction, it should not be surprising that classification schemes that function to maintain differences (Kozol 1992) would be an integral part of the formal education system.

It has been emphasized that categories which are illogical or without biological foundation maintain significance because powerful people benefit materially from their existence. The phrase "the Other" appears repeatedly in legal documents constructed by ruling class whites in the system devised to control, dominate, and exploit nonwhite peoples. A 1712 South

Carolina law used the term in a legal document enslaving African Americans, Native Americans, and their descendants.[1] This law no doubt served as a partial model for the inclusion of the phrase in the Constitution of the United States.

> Representatives and direct Taxes shall be apportioned among the several States which may be included within this Union, according to their respective Numbers, which shall be determined by adding to the whole Number of free Persons, including those bound to Service for a Term of Years, and excluding Indians not taxed, three fifths of all other Persons.[2]

"Those bound to Service" is a reference to indentured servants. ". . . three-fifths of all other persons," included all those persons legally declared slaves (chattel property). This is known as the "three-fifths compromise." Slaves, of course, were not allowed to vote. Nevertheless, they could be counted as three-fifths of a person, which had the effect of increasing the number of representatives from slave-holding states in the Congress. The ratification of the Constitution had the effect of raising "inequality" to the level of a formal value in a society supposedly based on an unswerving commitment to "equality."

The idea that Africans were only three-fifths of a human being is reflected in the popular characterization of them as "mules" in Southern culture. Judy Scales-Trent (1995) addresses this question in the reading "On Being Like a Mule." The term whites used to classify the off-spring of a "white" and a "black" person is *mulatto*. The word mulatto is full of symbolisms that help whites to rationalize the classification and abuse of "the other"; in this case, the Negro slave, who is, somehow, "less than a human being." ". . . Negro slaves and their descendants," are "chattel property—as, that is to say, an automatically inferior form of humanity, a kind of two-legged domestic animal" (Pope-Hennesy 1969:47). You do not have to treat an animal the way you would treat a full human being.

A mule is a work animal. It is used to carry heavy burdens and as a draft (plow) animal in farming. To liken enslaved Africans to a mule then is to objectify and give concrete meaning to the often-heard expression among white Southerners that the slaves were "beasts of the field." Scales-Trent also suggests that the analogy is intended to make the case for "racial purity" since the mule is a sterile animal and cannot reproduce. This is an interesting argument because during and after slavery most children with African and European ancestry were born to white fathers and African or Native American mothers. And, in fact, throughout colonial America, classification systems were devised that were intended to specify the exact proportion of African blood a person carried (Marger 1991). As Scales-Trent makes clear, the mule analogy represents the extreme form of "the other."

Many states, as one part of the effort to control slaves, made it illegal to teach them to read and write. The primary purpose of such laws was to prevent slaves from reading and understanding abolitionist newspapers, and in general, knowing too much.[3] A North Carolina law had the following title: "An Act to Prevent All Persons from Teaching Slaves to Read and Write, the Use of Figures Excepted." Why do you think it was acceptable to teach slaves elementary arithmetic but not other forms of literacy? The answer is simply that plantation owners wanted to be sure that their slaves could keep an accurate count of the number of bales of cotton and barrels of rice being shipped to market. The denial of the right to an education along with that of the right to vote, more so than their actual enslavement, explains the lack of educational achievement of African Americans. The legacy of these forms of legal discrimination was to relegate the slaves and their descendants to a lower-than-average standard of living.

The reading "Article XIX, Chinese: Constitution of the State of California" exemplifies several aspects of the purpose and function of classification and how dominant groups use it to their advantage. For example, Asian-Americans, like African and Native Americans, are treated like an internally (Blauner 1969, 1972) colonialized group. The Ruling:

1. *Set limits on non-white voluntary immigration.* Asian immigration was always very rigidly controlled. The major restrictions were not removed until the 1960s. Most Hispanics became U.S. citizens by virtue of the annexation of what had been parts of Mexico. African voluntary immigration has been virtually non-existent.
2. *Legally protected jobs for whites by limiting opportunities for non-white employment.* This has been a constant feature of American society since the end of the Civil War. Nonwhites could be used as slaves or as forced laborers as needed. In all other instances they were not wanted.
3. *Reinforced in the popular mind (socialization) the idea of the significance of color classification in American society.*
4. *Highlighted the fact that "race" in the United States is defined by the legal system in the absence of any clear biological basis for doing so.* This is another example of "racial" ideology being confused with what is assumed to be fact.
5. *Stigmatized Asian-Americans and assigned them to the status of "the Other," while institutionalizing and upholding white supremacy.*

The important thing to understand about all these cases is that they were never intended to reduce group boundaries (classification/categories) leading to the full integration of various ethnic groups into the mainstream of society. Its purpose has always been to maintain existing relations of inequality (Altbach and Kelly 1987, Carnoy 1974). The first objective of classification is social control; another is to produce docile, hardworking categories of persons (indentured servants, Asian coolies, black sharecroppers, Hispanic farm workers) who know and stay in their place (Altbach and Kelly 1978).

In the reading "Persons of Mean and Vile Condition," Howard Zinn offers insights into the "origin of the color line" and the manner in which classification schemes functioned to control people in the early history of the United States. For the elite in the American colonies, the greatest fear was that discontented whites, especially indentured servants who were treated like slaves, would join blacks and overthrow the existing order. Laws were passed to segregate and encourage animosity between blacks and whites. For example, if a white servant and a slave escaped together and were captured, the white servant would have to serve time beyond that of his contract. The black slave would be beaten and dismembered in some way. There were also laws forbidding interracial marriage (whites were banished; blacks beaten) and laws preventing blacks from striking whites (blacks could have their ears cut off for retaliating in this way).

Other strategies colonial officials used to promote division included (1) monopolizing the eastern seaboard land, forcing landless whites to move into the frontier placing the frontiersman in direct conflict with the Indians; (2) passing laws prohibiting free blacks from traveling through Indian country; (3) signing treaties with Indians requiring them to return fugitive slaves; and (4) declaring all "interracial" children "black," thereby reducing the number of persons labelled "white" and, therefore, privileged.

The idea of "race" and the belief that people can be classified according to "racial" schemes finds support in the work of formal educators and scientists precisely because they profess objective and disinterested neutrality in the outcomes they report. In other words, what they report supposedly reflects the application of the scientific method to whatever is being studied. In fact, more often than not, what they conclude, report, and teach is not without ideological bias. Educators and scientists appear to the general public as all-knowing experts, committed to understanding and explaining cultural and physical reality. Because basic scientific and research principles are either not taught very well or are not sufficiently retained, most people are not prepared to critically assess and analyze what researchers report.

Further, researchers are not immune to ideological currents that are of long-standing duration and have powerfully impacted the values, norms, and social arrangements of a culture. Too often science simply reflects and reinforces popular opinion. Science, to be sure, is a powerful tool when properly applied. But much of it is still largely trial and error and one cannot declare 100 percent confidence in the research methods being employed. What is considered a tentative conclusion by most researchers is too often taken as an absolute truth by the general public. In their urge to classify people, for example, scientists have generally ignored those persons they label "mixed race." In fact, the classification schemes they use follow popular opinion that there are clear-cut "racial" categories. These same popular views, when embraced by scientists, receive official sanction and are used by the Federal government as guidelines for "racial" classification.

Stephen Jay Gould (1981a) has described several instances in which so-called scientists have misused science to claim that the "racial" classification schemes they use are valid and accurate. In an article entitled "The Politics of Census," Gould (1981b) showed how the Census of 1840 was used to justify the institution of slavery. Dr. Edward Jarvis, a medical statistician, reviewed census tables for that year and showed that "one in 162 blacks was insane in free states, but only one in 1,558 in slave states" (Gould 1981b:20). Taken on face value, the census tables showed that insanity among blacks increased as one moved from the North to the South. Location, however, did not impact insanity among whites. The implication of the census figures was that: "The slaves actually benefitted from not having many of the hopes and responsibilities which the free, self-thinking and self-acting enjoy and sustain, for bondage saves him from some of the liabilities and dangers of active self-direction" (Gould 1981b:20). Upon further investigation, Jarvis was actually able to show that there were many errors in collecting the data. In one case, it was reported that 133 out of 156 blacks were insane. It turned out that the figure actually referred to the number of whites in the local state mental hospital. Despite Jarvis's efforts, he was unable to have the data corrected, and it was allowed to stand as fact. As recently as 22 years ago, social scientists like Eugene Genovese (1974) were still using racist ideology to argue that blacks actually benefitted from what he described as the paternalistic nature of American slavery.

The reading "Science and Jewish Immigration" by Gould (1983) is yet another example of the misuse of science. It helps us to understand that self-identifying as white, and being so regarded even by the dominant group, is not always enough to keep people from being negatively classified and suffering the consequences. Traditionally, immigration officials with the support of scientists had been able to use general measures of dullness and lack of intelligence to exclude Italians, Greeks, Turks, and Slavic immigrants from the United States. When they found that these measures could not be used to exclude most Jews, they decided to make the test "more sophisticated." A study by H. H. Goddard, one of the leaders of the Eugenics movement in the United States, and one by Karl Pearson, an English scientist and Eugenicist credited with having invented statistics, was used to make the claim that Jews, too, were stupid.

Goddard claimed, at first, that he could identify mentally defective people simply from their facial features. He later turned to a form of the IQ test developed at Stanford University. Pearson claimed that his use of a biased "cold statistic" controlled for bias and thus proved the mental inferiority of Jews. To measure and predict intelligence, he used such variables as (a) cleanliness of hair and (b) teachers' judgments to try to predict Jewish intelligence. In this case, the statistical technique (correlation) proved only as good as the data it was used to analyze. Both researchers used faulty operational definitions of intelligence, violating basic research principles.

This example is a classic case of the use of the self-fulfilling prophecy and the misuse of science to support what the researchers had already concluded. As a result of these highly biased studies by "reputable" researchers, immigration restrictions were put in place in 1924. The quotas resulting from this act reduced Eastern European and Jewish immigration to a trickle. The author suggests that the climate created by these activities in England and America helped to prepare the world to "turn the other cheek" to Hitler's racist assault on Jews, homosexuals, and gypsies in World War II. Some studies of prejudice and discrimination claim that the traits are real symptoms of lower, working class beliefs and behaviors. However, scientists and intellectuals are the sources of the various systems of classification and of the rationalizations and justifications that support them.

In "Remarks on the First Two Volumes of *Sex and Race,*" world historian (labeled black historian) J. A. Rogers describes how mainstream scholars and others "who didn't want the present knowledge in their heads disturbed" (1972:6), dismissed his work as biased and irrelevant without, in most cases, reading what he had written. Rogers' experiences offer insights into how certain accounts of the past do not become part of the school curriculum. It does not seem to matter that Rogers loathes "racial propaganda" and was committed to avoiding it. Likewise, it does not matter that Rogers' historical accounts are the result of tens of thousands of miles of travel at home and abroad and that he has

> consulted books and printed matter so vast in number that were I to try to say how many I would sound like a Munchausen; visited the leading museums of many of the civilized lands, and engaged in research in their libraries and ever going to great pains to get my facts as humanly correct as possible. In short, I felt I have looked into books and dug up buried knowledge that many college professors or doctors of philosophy do not

know exist, because just as there is a life in the deeper depths of the ocean of which the average fisherman knows nothing so there are depths in the ocean of research of which some of the most learned have never dreamed. (Rogers 1972:vi)

What Rogers does in the three-volume work entitled *Sex and Race* is effectively destroy the "myth" of "racial purity," an idea which serves as the cornerstone of social relations in colonial and ex-colonial societies.

"Why 'Race' Makes No Scientific Sense: The Case of Africans and Native Americans" by Prince Brown, Jr. illustrates why the idea of "racial purity" is in fact a myth. The article is an historical account of unions and relationships between Native Americans and African slaves and the emergence of a people known as the "Black Indians." It is a powerful example of the fact that race is a social construction. As you read this article, consider that by social convention the people we call Indians are classified as Mongoloid and that the people we call African Americans are classified as belonging to the Negroid/Negro[4] "race." Katz reminds us that when slaves ran away, they often ran to Native American villages where they formed unions with those who took them in. Exposure to this historical fact leaves us with many questions and highlights the weaknesses of the various classification schemes employed in the United States: To which "racial" category do the offspring of Native Americans and Africans belong? How do we describe the American experience so that it reflects the contributions of Native Americans and African Americans? How does the fusion of African and Native American culture affect our ideas of "American culture?"

In the reading "Science, Pseudo-science and Racism," Albert Jacquard presents Unesco's position on the current state of biological understanding about the concept of "race." It makes clear that the view emerging from current scientific research is poorly understood (racial classification is not biologically possible) and is not a part of what most people think about the concept.

Given the questionable nature of classification schemes and the fact that even the most well-meaning researchers are influenced by the beliefs and values in their cultural milieu caution must be utilized when interpreting and using social science research findings in a social policy context (Merton 1970; 1976). Of particular concern are those cases in which findings are consistent with what many people claim to have understood intuitively even before the research was conducted.[5] Consider, for example, that most of the research does not support long-standing beliefs about "racial" differences with regard to education and achievement. Nevertheless, the small percentage of research that supports the beliefs gets the widest popular dissemination (Herrnstein and Murray 1994). What we mean to suggest is that through covert and overt ways, biased research findings, offered as objective science, help to support beliefs about differences and classification that people hold as a result of their everyday, normal, socialization. Social scientists call this *selective perception*—given two or more alternatives, people select the one that is consistent with what they already believe (Vidmar and Rokeach 1974) regardless of the evidence presented.

We are now ready to offer a sociological explanation to this question: Why do classification schemes persist given the numerous critiques of them that undermine their validity? "The ideology of race is a system of ideas which interprets and defines the meaning of racial differences, real or imagined, in terms of some system of *cultural values*"[6] (Nash 1962:285). One way in which sociologists study cultural values in society is by using what is called the *functionalist perspective.* Sociologist Richard T. Schaefer writes:

> In the view of a functionalist, a society is like a living organism in which each part contributes to the survival of the whole. Therefore, the *functionalist perspective* emphasizes how the parts of society are structured to maintain its stability. According to this approach, if an aspect of social life does not contribute to a society's stability or survival—if it does not serve some identifiably useful function—it will not be passed on from one generation to the next. It would seem reasonable to assume that bigotry between races offers no such positive function, and so why, we ask, does it persist? The functionalist, although agreeing that racial hostility is hardly to be admired, would point out that it does serve some positive functions from the perspective of racists. (1995:13)

What powerful whites in the United States, who are able to define/label others and have their definitions become widely accepted, understand is that (racial) classification serves their purpose and interest; albeit, at the expense of others. Much widespread discrimination in the United States is rationalized as just good business practice.

Based on his review of the research literature Manning Nash formulates "four functions that racial beliefs [values] have for the dominant group":

1. Racist ideologies provide a moral justification for maintaining a society that routinely deprives a group of its rights and privileges. Southern whites justified slavery by believing that Africans were physically and spiritually subhuman and devoid of souls.

2. Racist beliefs discourage subordinate people from attempting to question their lowly status, for to do so is to question the very foundations of the society.

3. Racial beliefs provide a cause for political action and focus social uncertainty on a specific threat. Racial ideologies not only justify existing practices but serve as rallying points for social movements, as seen in the rise of Nazi party.

4. Racial myths encourage support for the existing order by introducing the argument that if there were any major societal change, the subordinate group would suffer even greater poverty and the dominate group would suffer lower living standards (1962: 286–87).

Thus a racial ideology evolves when a set of values, such as those which support a system of oppression (i.e., internal colonialism), is challenged or threatened (Nash 1962). According to functionalist theory, classification schemes persist because they function to help support and preserve arrangements which benefit powerful people in society. Dysfunctional aspects of classification are harmful to both the dominant and subordinate groups but have the greatest negative impact on the subordinate groups. Arnold Rose (1951:19–24) has identified some of the dysfunctional factors.[7] They continue to be the source of major social problems in the United States.

We shall now turn to brief introductions of the other articles in this part. They were selected to help make clearer how classification schemes were created, what their functions are, and how they were institutionalized. ". . . we must be prepared to find that discrimination is in part sustained by a socialized reward system" (Merton 1976:201).

The term *institutionalization* means that beliefs and behaviors that reflect the values of a society's dominant group have become widely accepted, and have become a part of the personality of the majority of persons as they are socialized. Further, social arrangements/structures within the society are organized in accordance with the values, and societal behavior reflects the beliefs. The values, beliefs, and behaviors exist at the center of the cultural ethos[8] of the society. Because people accept certain definitions for race, derive from their values as real/true, they practice and view as normal, behaviors which they argue are a logical extension of these alleged facts. Sociologist, W. I. Thomas calls this "the definition of the situation . . . if men define situations as real, they are real in their consequences" (Thomas and Thomas 1928:572).

For example, after African Americans were declared slaves, and along with Native Americans labeled "the Other" in the U.S. Constitution, parallel but unequal social institutions such as segregated schools were created to reflect the fact of these definitions. In order to justify these behaviors, white Americans argued that persons of African descent lack the intellect for formal education and that it would be a waste of resources to attempt to do so. Rules that called for separate public drinking fountains for blacks and whites were largely followed by members of both groups. This is a stage in the process of the institutionalization of an idea/practice that sociologists call *accommodation* (Park 1950).[9] Violation of the rules resulted in mild social rebuke for whites (from other whites) and severe legal sanctions for blacks (many were actually charged with a crime). Thus, something is institutionalized when it is the (sometimes unconscious) normal, everyday, expected mode of interaction between individuals in a society. "Racial" tension arises, and conflict erupts when subordinate group individuals challenge the institutionalized conventions and attempt to change them. This last point (nonwhite challenges to institutionalized white privilege) is the central theme in the summations of the two readings that follow.

"White Reconstruction in the University," by Charles A. Gallagher, deals with the "ideology of race" (racism) at the individual and group level. It shows just how intertwined the lives of people who live in "racially" classified cultures have become. Some "white" students, at last, are beginning to understand that the status "white" can be socially reconstructed such that it carries a strong negative "stigma." Many are being forced to deal with this question: What does it mean to be white? Gallagher studied white students at a large urban university in order to address this issue.

As transformative academic awareness (Banks 1993) ever so slowly begins to penetrate the education canon, whites are being forced to reexamine the assumption that "Whiteness" was/is sacrosanct. They are having to deal with charges of racism every day of their lives, a situation from which they have been shielded by the historical segregation in American society. They are frustrated by the fact that now integration had been forced upon them, they cannot totally control the nature of the interaction. Witness the complaint about blacks segregating themselves on university campuses which means in turn that whites are also segregating themselves; a fact which does not lead to complaints.

Many white students still, mistakenly so, believe that the United States is a "colorblind" society; most say that they believe the maxim "all men are created equal." They also just happen to believe that most black students are admitted to the university because of affirmative action, and that most others are admitted based on merit. White students feel threatened by the new Multicultural and Afrocentric perspectives, and are beginning to circle the wagons and demand "White Studies and White Holidays," never comprehending that this is what they have always had. They are beginning to consciously develop a "white identity." As members of the dominant group, they did not have to do this in the past because non-whites lacked the power to question who and what they are; why they are more deserving than others; and what makes them think they are superior?

Unlike blacks, white students have no experience being asked such questions let alone having to try to answer them. As Toni Morrison writes: "The trauma of racism is, for the racist and the victim, the severe fragmentation of the self" (1989:16). Given their normative socialization—more specifically their mis-education in a racist culture—some whites do not perceive or understand institutionalized racism. White students are being forced to endure the mental and psychological turmoil that has always been the lot of internally colonized peoples, and they do not like it. Being classified "white" no longer guarantees one safe passage through America's troubled "racial" waters. The response of the students in Gallagher's study reveals the first signs of a crack in the white monopoly on defining perception and what is regarded as "real" in American society.

The next reading "Taking Back the Center" by Trina Grillo and Stephanie M. Wildman builds further on one of the points raised by Gallagher: white angst resulting from the non-white challenge to white dominance in all aspects of American institutional life. According to these authors, white supremacy has resulted from their expectation that they and their concerns will occupy center stage in any and all discussions. People who benefit from white privilege perceive it as normative and implicit. Their socialization has not prepared them to have it challenged by its victims.

Many whites resent, and respond with anger and disrespect, when they are not the presenters or the subject of presentations. They do not know how to deal with the fact that they have not had to compete. That is, until the 1950s and 1960s white privilege was protected by law and since that time by custom and tradition. This resentful behavior is evident even when non-white scholars are interpreting their own history and planning their self-help efforts. Toni Morrison explains why the African Americans' reach to share center stage is so bothersome to some whites:

> Now that Afro-American artistic presence has been "discovered" actually to exist, now that serious scholarship has moved from silencing the witnesses and erasing their meaningful place in and contribution to American culture, it is no longer acceptable merely to imagine us and imagine for us. We have always been imagining ourselves . . . We are the subjects of our

own narrative, witnesses to and participants in our own experience, and, in no way coincidentally, in the experience of those with whom we have come in contact. We are not, in fact, "other." We are choices. (1989:8–9)

Whites rightly perceive that African Americans are transforming the academic canon and redistributing the privilege and power that has been associated with the white monopoly of it.

Some white professors and administrators who feel pressure to attend Black History month presentations usually only do so when the presenters are white. The culture of denial that has developed around the "racial" history of the United States leads them to prefer not to hear Black interpretations of it. White women relate to such presentations more so than do males due to their own second-class-status, and likewise try to steer the discussion to issues of concern to themselves. Because they too experience discrimination at the hands of white males, they tend not to see themselves as part of the white cycle of oppression. In meetings of black and white women, white women tend to want to make sexual discrimination the major discussion, while "racial" issues are of equal or greater concern to black women. The reading by Grillo and Wildman helps us to understand how classification makes it more unlikely that similarly oppressed groups will develop cooperative relations in multiethnic societies.

Plessy v. Ferguson (1896) is the best-known, and perhaps the most infamous, legal decision rendered by the U.S. Supreme Court in the post-slavery period. In 1891, Homer A. Plessy challenged a Louisiana law that required him to ride in a segregated railway car. In 1896, the U.S. Supreme Court ruled against him, making segregation in public places the law of the land. Interestingly, segregation emerged as a general feature of American society as a way of controlling African Americans after slavery was declared illegal. The first article is the actual text of the decision rendered by the Court. Speaking for the majority, Mr. Justice Brown puts forth the "rationale" offered to assert and legally institutionalize white supremacy. That is, a rationale is a reason or list of reasons that does not have to be consistent with any facts. Mr. Justice Harlan's dissenting opinion is, on the other hand, a "rational" act consistent with or based on reason or fact. The decision of the majority shows how classification schemes were used to rationalize inequality—even when information existed that should have dictated another outcome.

The second article on the case by Cheryl I. Harris is a law review essay that makes several noteworthy points. Usually not reported when this case is cited is the fact that Plessy's physical features were such that he easily could, and often did, pass for "white." The fact that he had "African blood" had to be brought to the attention of the court. So, one of the things that the court was deciding was Plessy's "race." Again, "race" is not a self-evident biological fact. Nevertheless, the court's decision carried consequences for Plessy that he would not have had to endure had the court not been informed of his African ancestry.

A second point made by Harris is that the court gave voice to the idea that "whiteness" was an implicit quality, a property, that had "an actual pecuniary value" (Harris 1993). This was not true for "blackness" and therefore, whites and blacks could not ride in the same railroad car since this would have the effect of equating the two and not recognizing the privilege that was implicit in being white. At the same time, the court decided that requiring segregated railroad cars did not amount to discrimination against blacks, it was only that blacks chose to interpret it that way. The effect of the ruling was to legalize what had become the custom of white supremacy and to uphold "race" subordination.

We have argued the scientific view that "racial" classification is not possible and has a hard time competing with the popular (ideologically constructed) view of "race." The experience of one teacher dramatizes this reality. Eloise Hiebert Meneses, who teaches a class on Anthropology of Race and Ethnicity, explains that:

> . . . I spend three weeks providing students with the scientific data on biological interrelatedness and discover, in the end, that I have convinced very few of them that race (as a set of discrete biological characteristics) does not exist. Their daily experience of interaction with people of other "races" convinces them I have some abstract, nitpicking theory that doesn't fit the real evidence, easily obtained by their own eyes. Furthermore, it is clear that neither I nor other scientists are going to find it easy to convince people anywhere that "there is no such thing as race." If those in the biological sciences are right, whence this firm commitment to folk theory of race?" (Meneses 1994:139)

Dr. Meneses' perception is confirmed by another astute observer, "You can just look around and see how the world is split up—black people sitting over there at that table, white people walking down the hall, maybe a table with black people and white people sitting together. Our eyes tell us the truth" (Scales-Trent 1995:2). These views make clear how difficult it is to change beliefs resulting from socialization that are centered at the core of the personality. The reading by Dr. Albert Jacquard and "The Declaration of Athens" are intended to help people understand the difference between what Nash (1962) has labeled "race and the ideology of race." It is the ideology and not the fact that drives society's preoccupation with the concept.

Further, as Nash and Jacquard make clear, while researchers may continue to study what some call "race," it is not possible to show any relationship between it and traits like intelligence and morality. Such traits are heavily influenced by the cultural experiences that people have.

The readings reflect the consequences of social classification. They do not, as some would argue, reflect the objective practice of science or rational, logical thought. Science can tell us how to perform an abortion; it cannot, and does not, tell us whether we should do so. That decision reflects the general social situation and prevailing values. We must address not only what value will prevail but also—whose values. The values at work when some people are oppressed are those of the people who have the power to impose their will on others. They do so by dominating and controlling mainstream societal institutions (political, legal, economic, military, education, political, etc.), and by socially creating and misusing specious and nonscientific classification systems.

Notes

[1] Thomas Cooper and David J. McCord, eds., *Statutes at Large of South Carolina* (10 vols., Columbia, 1836–1841), VII, 352–7.

[2] The U.S. Constitution, Article I, Section 2. P5 in *The United States Government Manual 1996/1997.* Washington, DC: United States Government Printing Office.

[3] Laws such as these expose the contradictory nature of much proslavery logic. If, as one of the arguments go (an argument made by no less an American personage than Thomas Jefferson), slaves were biologically incapable of learning and thinking abstractly, why the great concern about them reading, understanding, and acting on it?

[4] A term, by the way, that means absolutely nothing to continental Africans and has been largely rejected by diasporan Africans. The word was coined and used almost exclusively by Europeans as a negative and derogatory term for Africans. *See* John B. Opdycke, 1950. Pp. 241–42 in *The Opdycke Lexicon of Word Selection.* New York: Funk & Wagnalls.

[5] This is not to argue that all such findings are automatically without foundation, but that one needs here to exercise special caution and vigilance in interpreting and explaining conclusions.

[6] Italics added for emphasis.

[7] (1) A society that practices discrimination fails to use the resources of all individuals. Discrimination limits the search for talent and leadership to dominate the group. (2) Discrimination aggravates social problems such as poverty, delinquency, and crime and places the financial burden of alleviating these problems on the dominant society. (3) Society must invest a good deal of time and money to defend it's barriers to the full participation of all members. (4) Goodwill and friendly diplomatic relations between nations are often undercut by racial prejudice and discrimination. (5) Communications between groups is restricted. Little accurate knowledge of the minority and its culture is available to the society at large. (6) Social change is inhibited since it may contribute to assisting the minority. (7) Discrimination promotes disrespect for law enforcement and the peaceful settlement of disputes.

[8] The disposition, character, or fundamental values peculiar to a specific people, culture, or movement. *The American Heritage Dictionary,* 2nd College Edition, 1985.

[9] While all such laws were declared unconstitutional in the mid 1960s, it should be understood that changing a law does not change attitudes and only changes public behavior that can readily be observed and monitored. Today, African Americans are still refused service in some public facilities in the United States.

ON BEING LIKE A MULE

JUDY SCALES-TRENT

Study Questions

1. Given that the person labeled a "mulatto" has one white and one black ancestor, how would you classify him or her? What would be the basis of your classification of that person?
2. How do you think European Americans who parented children with African Americans perceived themselves since it was their direct offspring who were labelled as "mules"?

It is impossible to look on a man and pretend that this man is a mule. It is impossible to couple with a Black woman and describe the child you have both created as a mulatto—either it's your child, or a child, or it isn't.

—James Baldwin

It wasn't until very recently, as I was looking up the spelling of the word "mulatto" in the dictionary, that I inadvertently discovered its derivation: "From the Spanish 'mulato', young mule." Transfixed by those words on the page, I looked slowly down the column of words to find the definition of "mule":

"(myōōl), n.
1. The sterile offspring of a female horse and a male donkey, valued as a work animal, having strong muscles, a body shaped like a horse, and donkeylike large ears, small feet, and sure-footedness . . . .
2. Any hybrid between the donkey and the horse.
3. *Informal.* A very stubborn person.
4. *Bot.* any sterile hybrid . . . ."

"Sterile hybrid." What a ghastly term to apply to a person. It describes the result of a sexual union so unnatural, by species so unlike, that this creature is unable to meet one of the basic criteria of a species—the ability to reproduce. It describes a creature that will, happily, *not* be able to continue its unnatural line—a being that will die without offspring, so that the categories "horse" and "donkey" ("white," "black") will return to their former state of purity.

Sexual license across boundaries, with no social consequences—this is the dream of America.

I struggle to get a feeling for my namesake, the mule. My first thought is of Zora Neale Hurston's description of the black woman as "de mule uh de world"—the one who has to pick up the load and carry it for everyone else, white people and black men alike. I think of the mules in the Arizona copper mines who walked slowly down into the pitch-black mines, then slowly back up, laden with ore, year after year, never seeing the world outside of the mine, never seeing the light, until they went blind. A beast of burden. Slave-like. And stupid enough to accept slave treatment.

It is hard to think of anything positive about mules. They are not noble like horses, loyal like dogs, elegant like the lion. It was not mules who crossed the Alps to win a war for Hannibal. Mules are just there, stolid and stupid, strange-looking horses with ill-fitting ears.

Names are important. What people call us is important. Sometimes, when we name ourselves, the name says something about the person wearing the name. But, more often, we are named by others, and the name tells us something valuable about the namer.

In this case, the namer, America, calls me "mulatto," "like a mule." What does this tell us about America? What is gained by comparing those with ancestors from both Europe and Africa to a mule, a "sterile hybrid"? Actually, quite a lot. First of all, it makes clear that people from Africa and people from Europe are two different animal species, species that should lead separate lives, species that cannot be family. It also emphasizes the notion of hierarchy, for it seems obvious to me that our culture values horses more than donkeys. There are legends, poems, movies about horses; they are swifter, more lovely than donkeys. It is horses that are the superior creature in this unnatural couple. And what happens when this superior animal violates the normal order of things, transgresses strict boundaries to have sexual union with an inferior being, a creature of another species? Nature herself is offended, and condemns this union by presenting it with a deformed offspring—one that cannot reproduce. Thus, the image of the "sterile hybrid"—the mule, the mulatto—has enormous value. It teaches the lesson that America wants us all to remember. It reminds us of concepts of difference and opposition between African American and European American. It reinforces our understanding of the hierarchy of racial power and the importance of racial purity. And it tells us once again that sexual union between the two groups will not go unpunished.

In a country that considered it important to divide people by ancestry, in a country that decided to create a special name for those children born of the union of people from different lands, think of all the *other* words that could have been used! Imagine what new name could have been created if, instead of seeing this union as an attack on the dream of racial purity, America saw it as an opportunity to join two groups, much as royalty has used marriage to symbolize and consolidate the union of different groups of people. America could have then created a name to celebrate this union:

"people-who-link-us-together"
"people-who-join-our-families"
"people-who-bind-us-in-friendship"

Or, America could have seen these people as the forerunners of a new world, a world where all are linked through kinship:

"new people"
"people-of-the-future"

Or indeed, America could have looked at all the new, glorious skin colors created through the union of so many different kinds of people and celebrated this display of beauty:

"people-of-the-rainbow"

It would make me think of Joseph's coat of many colors. It would make me think of children returning home. It would make me think of God.

But no, we have only the mule, and the word "mulatto." We have only messages of opprobrium, disdain, ridicule—images of stupidity, slavery, and powerlessness. The young woman startled me with her rage. A European American with an African American child, she rejected the term out-right. "I *hate* that word! It is so ugly. I will *not* use it for my child." She's right, of course. She doesn't have to use that word. Ever. None of us do.

I recently attended a conference at which African American scholars from many disciplines came together to discuss issues of ethnicity, color, and gender as they pertain to African American identity. How exciting to be part of a group that finally wanted to address these hard, hard questions within our community! Because the discussion concerned color, there was some debate during the sessions about the use of the word "mulatto." Some refused to use it, noting its insulting connotations. Others used it, but pointed out that they did so only because it was an important historical word that had been used extensively in the literature of race and color: they could not address that literature without using that term. This all seemed thoughtful and well-reasoned to me.

But it was there, for the first time, that someone named me "a hankety-haired yellow heifer." Well, no—not me directly, but it *felt* direct, because the dark-skinned scholar who made the reference in her presentation was angry when she made it. She was angry because a white black woman—a nineteenth-century writer—had made derogatory comments in her writing about black Americans with dark skin. Now this scholar laughed when she said the words, as if to diminish their force. She also apologized before using it, and called it "a phrase from my youth," as if it was really not her using those words that day. But it was. It was a phrase she used to wound, and she meant it for that moment and for the pain she felt that day.

I have decided not to travel down the path of trying to figure out all that she meant by naming me after yet another farm animal: a heifer, a "hankety-haired yellow heifer." I know enough. It sure wasn't good.

Article XIX, Chinese: Constitution of the State of California

Repealed. Nov. 4, 1952

Study Question

1. Codes enacted in 1872 to the California Constitution placed tight controls on Asian Americans living in that state. What is different about their status and that of African Americans during slavery?

Historical Note

Article XIX was repealed at the general election of November 4, 1952. Prior to its repeal, the article read as follows:

Section 1. Undesirable aliens; protection from. The Legislature shall prescribe all necessary regulations for the protection of the State, and the counties, cities, and towns thereof, from the burdens and evils arising from the presence of aliens who are or may become vagrants, paupers, mendicants, criminals, or invalids afflicted with contagious or infectious diseases, and from aliens otherwise dangerous or detrimental to the well-being or peace of the State, and to impose conditions upon which persons may reside in the State, and to provide the means and mode of their removal from the State, upon failure or refusal to comply with such conditions; provided, that nothing contained in this section shall be construed to impair or limit the power of the Legislature to pass such police laws or other regulations as it may deem necessary.

Sec. 2. Corporations; employment of Chinese prohibited. No corporation now existing or hereafter formed under the laws of this State, shall, after the adoption of this Constitution, employ directly or indirectly, in any capacity, any Chinese or Mongolian. The Legislature shall pass such laws as may be necessary to enforce this provision.

Sec. 3. Public work; employment of Chinese prohibited. No Chinese shall be employed on any State, county, municipal, or other public work, except in punishment for crime.

Sec. 4. Foreigners Ineligible to citizenship; coolieism; segregation of Chinese. The presence of foreigners ineligible to become citizens of the United States is declared to be dangerous to the well-being of the State, and the Legislature shall discourage their immigration by all the means within its power. Asiatic coolieism is a form of human slavery, and is forever prohibited in this State, and all contracts for coolie labor shall be void. All companies or corporations, whether formed in this country or any foreign country, for the importation of such labor, shall be subject to such penalties as the Legislature may prescribe. The Legislature shall delegate all necessary power to the incorporated cities and towns of this State for the removal of Chinese without the limits of such cities and towns, or for their location within prescribed portions of those limits, and it shall also provide the necessary legislation to prohibit the introduction into this State of Chinese after the adoption of this Constitution. This section shall be enforced by appropriate legislation.

PERSONS OF MEAN AND VILE CONDITION

HOWARD ZINN

Study Question

1. How does Howard Zinn's presentation of the interaction among Europeans, Native Americans, and Africans add to your understanding of race relations in colonial America? Does it cause you to re-examine what you believed before reading the article? Explain.

In the 1600s and 1700s, by forced exile, by lures, promises, and lies, by kidnapping, by their urgent need to escape the living conditions of the home country, poor people wanting to go to America became commodities of profit for merchants, traders, ship captains, and eventually their masters in America. Abbot Smith, in his study of indentured servitude, *Colonists in Bondage,* writes: "From the complex pattern of forces producing emigration to the American colonies one stands out clearly as most powerful in causing the movement of servants. This was the pecuniary profit to be made by shipping them."

After signing the indenture, in which the immigrants agreed to pay their cost of passage by working for a master for five or seven years, they were often imprisoned until the ship sailed, to make sure they did not run away. In the year 1619, the Virginia House of Burgesses, born that year as the first representative assembly in America (it was also the year of the first importation of black slaves), provided for the recording and enforcing of contracts between servants and masters. As in any contract between unequal powers, the parties appeared on paper as equals, but enforcement was far easier for master than for servant.

The voyage to America lasted eight, ten, or twelve weeks, and the servants were packed into ships with the same fanatic concern for profits that marked the slave ships. If the weather was bad, and the trip took too long, they ran out of food. The sloop *Sea-Flower,* leaving Belfast in 1741, was at sea sixteen weeks, and when it arrived in Boston, forty-six of its 106 passengers were dead of starvation, six of them eaten by the survivors. On another trip, thirty-two children died of hunger and disease and were thrown into the ocean. Gottlieb Mittelberger, a musician, traveling from Germany to America around 1750, wrote about his voyage:

> During the journey the ship is full of pitiful signs of distress—smells, fumes, horrors, vomiting, various kinds of sea sickness, fever, dysentery, headaches, heat, constipation, boils, scurvy, cancer, mouth-rot, and similar afflictions, all of them caused by the age and the high salted state of the food, especially of the meat, as well as by the very bad and filthy water. . . . Add to all that shortage of food, hunger, thirst, frost, heat, dampness, fear, misery, vexation, and lamentation as well as other troubles. . . . On board our ship, on a day on which we had a great storm, a woman about to give birth and unable to deliver under the circumstances, was pushed through one of the portholes into the sea. . . .

Indentured servants were bought and sold like slaves. An announcement in the *Virginia Gazette,* March 28, 1771, read:

> Just arrived at Leedstown, the Ship Justitia, with about one Hundred Healthy Servants, Men Women & Boys. . . . The Sale will commence on Tuesday the 2nd of April.

Against the rosy accounts of better living standards in the Americas one must place many others, like one immigrant's letter from America: "Whoever is well off in Europe better remain there. Here is misery and distress, same as everywhere, and for certain persons and conditions incomparably more than in Europe."

Beatings and whippings were common. Servant women were raped. One observer testified: "I have seen an Overseer beat a Servant with a cane about the head till the blood has followed, for a fault that is not worth the speaking of. . . ." The Maryland court records showed many servant suicides. In 1671, Governor Berkeley of Virginia reported that in previous years four of five servants died of disease after their arrival. Many were poor children, gathered up by the hundreds on the streets of English cities and sent to Virginia to work.

The master tried to control completely the sexual lives of the servants. It was in his economic interest to keep women servants from marrying or from having sexual relations, because childbearing would interfere with work. Benjamin Franklin, writing as "Poor Richard" in 1736, gave advice to his readers: "Let thy maidservant be faithful, strong and homely."

Servants could not marry without permission, could be separated from their families, could be whipped for various offenses. Pennsylvania law in the seventeenth century said that marriage of servants "without the consent of the Masters . . . shall be proceeded against as for Adultery, or fornication, and Children to be reputed as Bastards."

Although colonial laws existed to stop excesses against servants, they were not very well enforced, we learn from Richard Morris's comprehensive study of early court records in *Government and Labor in Early America*. Servants did not participate in juries. Masters did. (And being propertyless, servants did not vote.) In 1666, a New England court accused a couple of the death of a servant after the mistress had cut off the servant's toes. The jury voted acquittal. In Virginia in the 1660s, a master was convicted of raping two women servants. He also was known to beat his own wife and children; he had whipped and chained another servant until he died. The master was berated by the court, but specifically cleared on the rape charge, despite overwhelming evidence.

Sometimes servants organized rebellions, but one did not find on the mainland the kind of large-scale conspiracies of servants that existed, for instance, on Barbados in the West Indies. (Abbot Smith suggests this was because there was more chance of success on a small island.)

However, in York County, Virginia, in 1661, a servant named Isaac Friend proposed to another, after much dissatisfaction with the food, that they "get a matter of Forty of them together, and get Gunnes & hee would be the first & lead them and cry as they went along, 'who would be for Liberty, and free from bondage', & that there would enough come to them and they would goe through the Countrey and kill those that made any opposition and that they would either be free or dye for it." The scheme was never carried out, but two years later, in Gloucester County, servants again planned a general uprising. One of them gave the plot away, and four were executed. The informer was given his freedom and 5,000 pounds of tobacco. Despite the rarity of servants' rebellions, the threat was always there, and masters were fearful.

. . . Escape was easier than rebellion. "Numerous instances of mass desertions by white servants took place in the Southern colonies," reports Richard Morris, on the basis of an inspection of colonial newspapers in the 1700s. "The atmosphere of seventeenth-century Virginia," he says, "was charged with plots and rumors of combinations of servants to run away." The Maryland court records show, in the 1650s, a conspiracy of a dozen servants to seize a boat and to resist with arms if intercepted. They were captured and whipped.

The mechanism of control was formidable. Strangers had to show passports or certificates to prove they were free men. Agreements among the colonies provided for the extradition of fugitive servants—these became the basis of the clause in the U.S. Constitution that persons "held to Service or Labor in one State . . . escaping into another . . . shall be delivered up. . . ."

Sometimes, servants went on strike. One Maryland master complained to the Provincial Court in 1663 that his servants did "peremptorily and positively refuse to goe and doe their ordinary labor." The servants responded that they were fed only "Beanes and Bread" and they were "soe weake, wee are not able to perform the imploym'ts hee puts us uppon." They were given thirty lashes by the court.

More than half the colonists who came to the North American shores in the colonial period came as servants. They were mostly English in the seventeenth century, Irish and German in the eighteenth century. More and more, slaves replaced them, as they ran away to freedom or finished their time, but as late as 1755, white servants made up 10 percent of the population of Maryland.

What happened to these servants after they became free? There are cheerful accounts in which they rise to prosperity, becoming landowners and important figures. But Abbot Smith, after a careful study, concludes that colonial society "was not democratic and certainly not equalitarian; it was dominated by men who had money enough to make others work for them." And: "Few of these men were descended from indentured servants, and practically none had themselves been of that class."

. . . By the years of the Revolutionary crisis, the 1760s, the wealthy elite that controlled the British colonies on the American mainland had 150 years of experience, had learned certain things about how to rule. They had various fears, but also had developed tactics to deal with what they feared.

The Indians, they had found, were too unruly to keep as a labor force, and remained an obstacle to expansion. Black slaves were easier to control, and their profitability for southern plantations was bringing an enormous increase in the importation of slaves, who were becoming a majority in some colonies and constituted one-fifth of the entire colonial population. But the blacks were not totally submissive, and as their numbers grew, the prospect of slave rebellion grew.

With the problem of Indian hostility, and the danger of slave revolts, the colonial elite had to consider the class anger of poor whites—servants, tenants, the city poor, the propertyless, the taxpayer, the soldier and sailor. As the colonies passed their hundredth year and went into the middle of the 1700s, as the gap between rich and poor widened, as violence and the threat of violence increased, the problem of control became more serious.

What if these different despised groups—the Indians, the slaves, the poor whites—should combine? Even before there were so many blacks, in the seventeenth century, there was, as Abbot Smith puts it, "a lively fear that servants would join with Negroes or Indians to overcome the small number of masters."

There was little chance that whites and Indians would combine in North America as they were doing in South and Central America, where the shortage of women, and the use of Indians on the plantations, led to daily contact. Only in Georgia and South Carolina, where white women were scarce, was there some sexual mixing of white men and Indian women. In general, the Indian had been pushed out of sight, out of touch. One fact disturbed: whites would run off to join Indian tribes, or would be captured in battle and brought up among the Indians, and when this happened the whites, given a chance to leave, chose to stay in the Indian culture. Indians, having the choice, almost never decided to join the whites.

Hector St. Jean Crevecoeur, the Frenchman who lived in America for almost twenty years, told, in *Letters from an American Farmer,* how children captured during the Seven Years' War and found by their parents, grown up and living with Indians, would refuse to leave their new families. "There must be in their social bond," he said, "something singularly captivating, and far superior to anything to be boasted among us; for thousands of Europeans are Indians, and we have no examples of even one of those Aborigines having from choice become Europeans."

But this affected few people. In general, the Indian was kept at a distance. And the colonial officialdom had found a way of alleviating the danger: by monopolizing the good land on the eastern seaboard, they forced landless whites to move westward to the frontier, there to encounter the Indians and to be a buffer for the seaboard rich against Indian troubles, while becoming more dependent on the government for protection. Bacon's Rebellion was instructive: to conciliate a diminishing Indian population at the expense of infuriating a coalition of white frontiersmen was very risky. Better to make war on the Indian, gain the support of the white, divert possible class conflict by turning poor whites against Indians for the security of the elite.

Might blacks and Indians combine against the white enemy? In the northern colonies (except on Cape Cod, Martha's Vineyard, and Rhode Island, where there was close contact and sexual mixing), there was not much opportunity for Africans and Indians to meet in large numbers. New York had the largest slave population in the North, and there was some contact between blacks and Indians, as in 1712 when Africans and Indians joined in an insurrection. But this was quickly suppressed.

In the Carolinas, however, whites were outnumbered by black slaves and nearby Indian tribes; in the 1750s, 25,000 whites faced 40,000 black slaves, with 60,000 Creek, Cherokee, Choctaw, and Chickasaw Indians in the area. Gary Nash writes: "Indian uprisings that punctuated the colonial period and a succession of slave uprisings and insurrectionary plots that were nipped in the bud kept South Carolinians sickeningly aware that only through the greatest vigilance and through policies designed to keep their enemies divided could they hope to remain in control of the situation."

The white rulers of the Carolinas seemed to be conscious of the need for a policy, as one of them put it, "to make Indians & Negros a checque upon each other lest by their Vastly Superior Numbers we should be crushed by one or the other." And so laws were passed prohibiting free blacks from traveling in Indian country. Treaties with Indian tribes contained clauses requiring the return of fugitive slaves. Governor Lyttletown of South Carolina wrote in 1738: "It has allways been the policy of this government to create an aversion in them [Indians] to Negroes."

Part of this policy involved using black slaves in the South Carolina militia to fight Indians. Still, the government was worried about black revolt, and during the Cherokee war in the 1760s, a motion to equip five hundred slaves to fight the Indians lost in the Carolina assembly by a single vote.

Blacks ran away to Indian villages, and the Creeks and Cherokees harbored runaway slaves by the hundreds. Many of these were amalgamated into the Indian tribes, married, produced children. But the combination of harsh slave codes and bribes to the Indians to help put down black rebels kept things under control.

It was the potential combination of poor whites and blacks that caused the most fear among the wealthy white planters. If there had been the natural racial repugnance that some theorists have assumed, control would have been easier. But sexual attraction was powerful, across racial lines. In 1743, a grand jury in Charleston, South Carolina, denounced "The Too Common Practice of Criminal Conversation with Negro and other Slave Wenches in this Province." Mixed offspring continued to be produced by white-black sex relations throughout the colonial period, in spite of laws prohibiting interracial marriage in Virginia, Massachusetts, Maryland, Delaware, Pennsylvania, the Carolinas, Georgia. By declaring the children illegitimate, they would keep them inside the black families, so that the white population could remain "pure" and in control.

What made Bacon's Rebellion especially fearsome for the rulers of Virginia was that black slaves and white servants joined forces. The final surrender was by "four hundred English and Negroes in Armes" at one garrison, and three hundred "freemen and African and English bond-servants" in another garrison. The naval commander who subdued the four hundred wrote: "Most of them I persuaded to goe to their Homes, which accordingly they did, except about eighty Negroes and twenty English which would not deliver their Armes."

All through those early years, black and white slaves and servants ran away together, as shown both by the laws passed to stop this and the records of the courts. In 1698, South Carolina passed a "deficiency law" requiring plantation owners to have at least one white servant for every six male adult Negroes. A letter from the southern colonies in 1682 complained of "no white men to superintend our negroes, or repress an insurrection of negroes. . . ." In 1691, the House of Commons received "a petition of divers merchants, masters of ships, planters and others, trading to foreign plantations . . . setting forth, that the plantations cannot be maintained without a considerable number of white servants, as well to keep the blacks in subjection, as to bear arms in case of invasion."

A report to the English government in 1721 said that in South Carolina "black slaves have lately attempted and were very near succeeding in a new revolution . . . and therefore, it may be necessary . . . to propose some new law for encouraging the entertainment of more white servants in the future. The militia of this province does not consist of above 2000 men." Apparently, two thousand were not considered sufficient to meet the threat.

This fear may help explain why Parliament, in 1717, made transportation to the New World a legal punishment for crime. After that, tens of thousands of convicts could be sent to Virginia, Maryland, and other colonies. It also makes understandable why the Virginia Assembly, after Bacon's Rebellion, gave amnesty to white servants who had rebelled, but not to blacks. Negroes were forbidden to carry any arms, while whites finishing their servitude would get muskets, along with corn and cash. The distinctions of status between white and black servants became more and more clear.

In the 1720s, with fear of slave rebellion growing, white servants were allowed in Virginia to join the militia as substitutes for white freemen. At the same time, slave patrols were established in Virginia to deal with the "great dangers that may . . . happen by the insurrections of negroes. . . ." Poor white men would make up the rank and file of these patrols, and get the monetary reward.

Racism was becoming more and more practical. Edmund Morgan, on the basis of his careful study of slavery in Virginia, sees racism not as "natural" to black-white difference, but something coming out of class scorn, a realistic device for control. "If freemen with disappointed hopes should make common cause with slaves of desperate hope, the results might be worse than anything Bacon had done. The answer to the problem, obvious if unspoken and only gradually recognized, was racism, to separate dangerous free whites from dangerous black slaves by a screen of racial contempt."

There was still another control which became handy as the colonies grew, and which had crucial consequences for the continued rule of the elite throughout American history. Along with the very rich and the very poor, there developed a white middle class of small planters, independent farmers, city artisans, who, given small rewards for joining forces with merchants and planters, would be a solid buffer against black slaves, frontier Indians, and very poor whites.

The growing cities generated more skilled workers, and the governments cultivated the support of white mechanics by protecting them from the competition of both slaves and free Negroes. As early as 1686, the council in New York ordered that "noe Negro or Slave be suffered to work on the bridge as a Porter about any goods either imported or Exported from or into this Citty." In the southern towns too, white craftsmen and traders were protected from Negro competition. In 1764 the South Carolina legislature prohibited Charleston masters from employing Negroes or other slaves as mechanics or in handicraft trades.

Science and Jewish Immigration

Stephen Jay Gould

Study Questions

1. How does "Science and Jewish Immigration" help you to understand that the practice of science is a social process and that attitudes and values effect the outcome of research?

In April 1925, C. B. Davenport, one of America's leading geneticists, wrote to Madison Grant, author of *The Passing of the Great Race,* and the most notorious American racist of the genteel Yankee tradition: "Our ancestors drove Baptists from Massachusetts Bay into Rhode Island, but we have no place to drive the Jews to." If America had become too full to provide places of insulated storage for undesirables, then they must be kept out. Davenport had written Grant to discuss a pressing political problem of the day: the establishment of quotas for immigration to America.

Jews presented a potential problem to ardent restrictionists. After 1890, the character of American immigration had changed markedly. The congenial Englishmen, Germans, and Scandinavians, who predominated before, had been replaced by hordes of poorer, darker, and more unfamiliar people from southern and eastern Europe. The catalog of national stereotypes proclaimed that all these people—primarily Italians, Greeks, Turks, and Slavs—were innately deficient in both intelligence and morality. Arguments for exclusion could be grounded in the eugenic preservation of a threatened American stock. But Jews presented a dilemma. The same racist catalog attributed a number of undesirable traits to them, including avarice and inability to assimilate, but it did not accuse them of stupidity. If innate dullness was to be the "official" scientific rationale for excluding immigrants from eastern and southern Europe, how could the Jews be kept out?

The most attractive possibility lay in claiming that the old catalog had been too generous and that, contrary to its popular stereotype, Jews were stupid after all. Several "scientific" studies conducted between 1910 and 1930, the heyday of the great immigration debate, reached this devoutly desired conclusion. As examples of distorting facts to match expectations or of blindness to obvious alternatives, they are without parallel. This essay is the story of two famous studies, from different nations and with different impact.

H. H. Goddard was the director of research at the Vineland Institute for Feebleminded Girls and Boys in New Jersey. He viewed himself as a taxonomist of mental deficiency. He concentrated upon "defectives of high grade" who posed special problems because their status just below the borderline of normality rendered their identification more difficult. He invented the term "moron" (from a Greek word for "foolish") to describe people in this category. He believed at the time, although he changed his mind in 1928, that most morons should be confined to institutions for life, kept happy with tasks apportioned to their ability, and above all, prevented from breeding.

Goddard's general method for identifying morons was simplicity itself. Once you had enough familiarity with the beast, you simply looked at one, asked a few questions, and drew your evident conclusions. If they were dead, you asked questions of the living who knew them. If they were dead, or even fictitious, you just looked. Goddard once attacked the poet Edwin Markham for suggesting that "The Man with the Hoe," inspired by Millet's famous painting of a peasant, "came to his condition as the result of social conditions which held him down and made him like the clods that he turned over." Couldn't Markham see that Millet's man was mentally deficient? "The painting is a perfect picture of an imbecile," Goddard remarked. Goddard thought he had a pretty good eye himself, but the main task of identifying morons must be given to women because nature had endowed the fair sex with superior intuition:

> After a person has had considerable experience in this work, he almost gets a sense of what a feeble-minded person is so that he can tell one afar off. The people who are best at this work, and who I believe should do this work, are women. Women seem to have closer observation than men.

In 1912, Goddard was invited by the U.S. Public Health Service to try his skill at identifying morons among arriving immigrants on Ellis Island. Perhaps they could be screened out and sent back, thus reducing the "menace of the feebleminded." But this time, Goddard brought a new method to supplement his identification by sight—the Binet tests of intelligence, later to become (at the hands of Lewis M. Terman of Stanford University), the Stanford-Binet scale, for the conventional measure of IQ. Benet had just died in France and would never witness the distortion of his device for identifying children who needed special help in school into an instrument for labeling people with a permanent stamp of inferiority.

Goddard was so encouraged by the success of his preliminary trials that he raised some money and sent two of his women back to Ellis Island in 1913 for a more thorough study. In two and a half months, they tested four major groups: thirty-five Jews, twenty-two Hungarians, fifty Italians, and forty-five Russians. The Binet tests produced an astounding result: 83 percent of the Jews, 87 percent of the Russians, 80 percent of the Hungarians, and 79 percent of the Italians were feebleminded—that is, below mental age twelve (the upper limit of moronity by Goddard's definition). Goddard himself was a bit embarrassed by his own exaggerated success. Weren't his results too good to be true? Could people be made to believe that four-fifths of any nation were morons? Goddard played with the numbers a bit, and got his figures down to 40 or 50 percent, but he was still perturbed.

The Jewish sample attracted his greatest interest for two reasons. First, it might resolve the dilemma of the supposedly intelligent Jew and provide a rationale for keeping this undersirable group out. Second, Goddard felt that he could not be accused of bias for the Jewish sample. The other groups had been tested via interpreters, but he had a Yiddish-speaking psychologist for the Jews.

In retrospect, Goddard's conclusions were far more absurd than even he allowed himself to suspect in anxious moments. It became clear, a few years later, that Goddard had constructed a particularly harsh version of the Binet tests. His scores stood well below the rankings produced by all other editions. Fully half the people who scored in the low, but normal, range of the Stanford-Binet scale tested as morons on Goddard's scales.

But the greater absurdity arose from Goddard's extraordinary insensitivity to environmental effects, both long-term and immediate, upon test scores. In his view, the Binet tests measured innate intelligence by definition, since they required no reading or writing and made no explicit reference to particular aspects of specific cultures. Caught in this vicious circle of argument, Goddard became blind to the primary reality that surrounded his women on Ellis Island. The redoubtable Ms. Kite approaches a group of frightened men and women—mostly illiterate, few with any knowledge of English, all just off the boat after a grueling journey in steerage—plucks them from the line and asks them to name as many objects as they can, in their own language, within three minutes. Could their poor performance reflect fear, befuddlement, or physical weakness rather than stupidity? Goddard considered the possibility but rejected it:

> What shall we say of the fact that only 45 percent can give sixty words in three minutes, when normal children of 11 years sometimes give 200 words in that time! It is hard to find an explanation except lack of intelligence. . . . How could a person live even 15 years in any environment without learning hundreds of names of which he could certainly think of 60 in three minutes.

Could their failure to identify the date, or even the year, be attributed to anything other than moronity?

> Must we again conclude that the European peasant of the type that immigrates to America pays no attention to the passage of time? That the drudgery of life is so severe that he cares not whether it is January or July, where it is 1912 or 1906? Is it possible that the person may be of considerable intelligence and yet, because of the peculiarity of his environment, not have acquired this ordinary bit of knowledge, even though the calendar is not in general use on the continent, or is somewhat complicated as in Russia? If so what an environment it must have been!

Goddard wrestled with the issue of this moronic flood. On the one hand, he could see some benefits:

> They do a great deal of work that no one else will do. . . . There is an immense amount of drudgery to be done, an immense amount of work for which we do not wish to pay enough to secure more intelligent workers. . . . May it be that possibly the moron has his place.

But he feared genetic deterioration even more and eventually rejoiced in the tightening of standards that his program had encouraged. In 1917, he reported with pleasure that deportations for mental deficiency had increased by 350 percent in 1913 and 570 percent in 1914 over the average for five preceding years. Morons could be identified at ports of entry and shipped back, but such an inefficient and expensive procedure could never be instituted as general policy. Would it not be better simply to restrict immigration from nations teeming with morons? Goddard suggested that his conclusions "furnish important considerations for future actions both scientific and social as well as legislative." Within ten years, restriction based upon national quotas had become a reality.

Meanwhile, in England, Karl Pearson had also decided to study the apparent anomaly of Jewish intelligence. Pearson's study was as ridiculous as Goddard's, but we cannot attribute its errors (as we might, being unreasonably charitable, in Goddard's case) to mathematical naïveté, for Pearson virtually invented the science of statistics. Pearson, the first Galton Professor of Eugenics at University College, London, founded the *Annals of Eugenics* in 1925. He chose to initiate the first issue with his study of Jewish immigration, apparently regarding it as a model of sober science and rational social planning. He stated his purpose forthrightly in the opening lines:

> The purport of this memoir is to discuss whether it is desirable in an already crowded country like Great Britain to permit indiscriminate immigration, or, if the conclusion be that it is not, on what gounds discrimination should be based.

If a group generally regarded as intellectually able could be ranked as inferior, then the basic argument for restriction would be greatly enhanced, for who would then defend the groups that everyone considered as stupid? Pearson, however, loudly decried any attempt to attribute motive or prior prejudice to his study. One can only recall Shakespeare's line, "The lady doth protest too much, methinks."

> There is only one solution to a problem of this kind, and it lies in the cold light of statistical inquiry. . . . We have no axes to grind, we have no governing body to propitiate by well advertised discoveries; we are paid by nobody to reach results of a given bias. We have no electors, no subscribers to encounter in the market place. We firmly believe that we have no political, no religious and no social prejudices. . . . We rejoice in numbers and figures for their own sake and, subject to human fallibility, collect our data—as all scientists must do—to find out the truth that is in them.

Pearson had invented a statistic so commonly used today that many people probably think it has been available since the dawn of mathematics—the correlation coefficient. This statistic measures the degree of relationship between two features of a set of objects: height versus weight or head circumference versus leg length in a group of humans, for example. Correlation coefficients can range as high as 1.0 (if taller people are invariably heavier to the same degree) or as low as 0.0 for no correlation (if an increase in height provides no information about weight—a taller person may weigh more, the same, or less, and no prediction can be made from the increase in height alone). Correlation coefficients can also be negative if increase in one variable leads to decrease in the other (if taller people generally weigh less, for example). Pearson's study of Jewish immigration involved the measurement of correlations between a large and mental array of physical and mental characters for children of Jewish immigrants living in London.

Pearson measured everything he imagined might be important in assessing "worthiness." He established four categories for cleanliness of hair: very clean and tidy, clean on the whole, dirty and untidy, and matted or verminous. He assessed both inner and outer clothing on a similar scale: clean, a little dirty, dirty, and filthy. He then computed correlation coefficients between all measures and was generally disappointed by the low values obtained. He could not understand, for example, why cleanliness of body and hair correlated only .2615 in boys and .2119 in girls, and mused:

> We should naturally have supposed that cleanliness of body and tidiness of hair would be products of maternal environment and so highly correlated. It is singular that they are not. There may be mothers who consider chiefly externals, and so press for tidiness of hair, but it is hard to imagine that those who emphasize cleanliness of body overlook cleanliness of hair.

Pearson concluded his study of physical measures by proclaiming Jewish children inferior to the native stock in height, weight, susceptibility to disease, nutrition, visual acuity, and cleanliness:

> Jewish alien children are not superior to the native Gentile. Indeed, taken all round we should not be exaggerating if we asserted that they were inferior in the great bulk of the categories dealt with.

The only possible justification for admitting them lay in a potentially superior intelligence to overbalance their physical shortcomings.

Pearson therefore studied intelligence by the same type of short and subjective scale that had characterized his measures of physical traits. For intelligence, he relied upon teachers' judgments rated from A to G. Computing the raw averages, he found that Jewish children were not superior to native Gentiles. Jewish boys ranked a bit higher, but the girls scored notably lower than their English classmates. Pearson concluded, with a striking analogy:

> Taken on the average, and regarding both sexes, this alien Jewish population is somewhat inferior physically and mentally to the native population. . . . We know and admit that some of the children of these alien Jews from the academic standpoint have done brilliantly; whether they have the staying power of the native race is another question. No breeder of cattle, however, would purchase an entire herd because he anticipated finding one or two fine specimens included in it; still less would he do it, if his byres and pastures were already full.

But Pearson realized that he was missing one crucial argument. He had already admitted that Jews lived in relative poverty. Suppose intelligence is more a product of environment than inborn worth? Might not the average scores of Jews reflect their disadvantaged lives? Would they not be superior after all if they lived as well as the native English? Pearson recognized that he had to demonstrate the innateness of intelligence to carry his argument for restricted immigration based on irremediable mediocrity.

He turned again to his correlation coefficients. If low intelligence correlated with measures of misery (disease, squalor, and low income, for example), then an environmental basis might be claimed. But if few or no correlations could be found, then intelligence is not affected by environment and must be innate. Pearson computed his correlation coefficients and, as with the physical measures, found very few high values. But this time he was pleased. The correlations produced little beyond the discovery that intelligent children sleep less and tend to breathe more through their nose! He concluded triumphantly:

There does not exist in the present material any correlation of the slightest consequence between the intelligence of the child and its physique, its health, its parents' care or the economic and sanitary conditions of its home. . . . Intelligence as distinct from mere knowledge stands out as a congenital character. Let us admit finally that the mind of man is for the most part a congenital product, and the factors which determine it are racial and familial. . . . Our material provides no evidence that a lessening of the aliens' poverty, an improvement in their food, or an advance in their cleanliness will substantially alter their average grade of intelligence. . . . It is proper to judge the immigrant by what he is as he arrives, and reject or accept him then.

But conclusions based upon negative evidence are always suspect. Pearson's failure to record correlations between "intelligence" and environment might suggest the true absence of any relationship. But it might also simply mean that his measures were as lousy as the hair in his category 4. Maybe a teacher's assessment doesn't record anything accurately, and its failure to correlate with measures of environment only demonstrates its inadequacy as an index of intelligence. After all, Pearson had already admitted that correlations between physical measures had been disappointingly small. He was too good a statistician to ignore this possibility. So he faced it and dismissed it with one of the worst arguments I have ever read.

Pearson gave three reasons for sticking to his claim that intelligence is innate. The first two are irrelevant: teachers' assessments correlate with Binet test scores, and high correlations between siblings and between parents and children also prove the innateness of intelligence. But Pearson had not given Binet tests to the Jewish children and had not measured their parents' intelligence in any way. These two claims referred to other studies and could not be transferred to the present case. Pearson appreciated this weakness and therefore advanced a third argument based upon internal evidence: intelligence (teachers' assessment) failed to correlate with environment but it did correlate with other "independent" measures of mental worth.

But what were these other independent measures? Believe it or not, Pearson chose "conscientiousness" (also based on teachers' assessments and scored as keen, medium, and dull), and rank in class. How else does a teacher assess "intelligence" if not (in large part) by conscientiousness and rank in class? Pearson's three measures—intelligence, conscientiousness, and rank in class—were redundant assessments of the same thing: the teachers' opinion of their students' worth. But we cannot tell whether these opinions record inborn capacities, environmental advantages, or teachers' prejudices. In any case, Pearson concluded with an appeal to bar all but the most intelligent of foreign Jews:

> For men with no special ability—above all for such men as religion, social habits, or language keep as a caste apart, there should be no place. They will not be absorbed by, and at the same time strengthen the existing population; they will develop into a parasitic race.

Goddard's and Pearson's studies shared the property of internal contradictions and evident prejudice sufficient to dismiss all claims. But they differed in one important respect: social impact. Britain did not enact laws to restrict immigration by racial or national origin. But in America, Goddard and his colleagues won. Goddard's work on Ellis Island had already encouraged immigration officials to reject people for supposed moronity. Five years later, the army tested 1.75 million World War I recruits with a set of examinations that Goddard helped write and that were composed by a committee meeting at his Vineland Training School. The tabulations did not identify Jews per se but calculated "innate intelligence" by national averages. These absurd tests, which measured linguistic and cultural familiarity with American ways, ranked recent immigrants from southern and eastern Europe well below the English, Germans, and Scandinavians who had arrived long before (Gould 1981a). The average soldier of most southern and eastern European nations scored as a moron on the army tests. Since most Jewish immigrants arrived from eastern European nations, quotas based on country of origin eliminated Jews as surely as collegiate quotas based on geographical distribution once barred them from elite campuses.

When quotas were set for the Immigration Restriction Act of 1924, they were initially calculated at 2 percent of people from each nation present in America at the census of 1890, not at the most recent count of 1920. Since few southern and eastern Europeans had arrived by 1890, these quotas effectively reduced the influx of Slavs, Italians, and Jews to a trickle. Restriction was in the air and would have occurred anyway. But the peculiar character and intent of the 1924 quotas were largely a result of propaganda issued by Goddard and his eugenical colleagues.

What effect did the quotas have in retrospect? Allan Chase, author of *The Legacy of Malthus,* the finest book on the history of scientific racism in America, has estimated that the quotas barred up to six million southern, central, and eastern Europeans between 1924 and the outbreak of World War II (assuming that immigration had continued at its pre-1924 rate). We know what happened to many who wanted to leave but had no place to go. The pathways to destruction are often indirect, but ideas can be agents as surely as guns and bombs.

Remarks on the First Two Volumes of Sex and Race

J. A. Rogers

Study Questions

1. What is the central message in J. A. Rogers' remarks on Volumes I and II of *Sex and Race?*
2. Given the problems described by Rogers, what would you suggest be done to ensure that a wide variety of views are included in school curriculum?

Our race is essentially slavish; it is the nature of all of us to believe blindly in what we love, rather than that which is most wise. We are inclined to look upon an honest, unshrinking pursuit of truth as something irreverent. We are indignant when others pry into our idols and criticize them with impunity, just as a savage flies to arms when a missionary picks his fetish to pieces . . . .

Sir F. Galton III

Certain orthodox scholars, white and colored, have not liked the history as given in the two preceding volumes of "Sex and Race," as well as in my earlier books. One English editor after reading the "100 Amazing Facts About the Negro," wrote me that it made him feel as if the white race had never accomplished anything. Others said that I claim everybody who has ever done anything as Negro, nevertheless, I had never said, or dreamed of saying, that Homer, or Pericles, or Aeschylus, or Julius Caesar, or Alfred the Great, Shakespeare, Milton, Michael Angelo, Bach, Handel, Wagner, Washington, Lincoln, Edison, Franklin D. Roosevelt, Einstein or thousands of other noted white men were of Negro ancestry; nor did I attribute to Negroes any role of any importance in Europe, itself, from say the sixteenth century onwards. Yet because I mention a few individuals, whom they had all along believed to be of unmixed white strain, I have been called "fantastic" and "credulous!"

And I have been ridiculed not on the result of research, not on examination of the sources which I have given abundantly, but on sheer belief. These scholars did not happen to run across such facts in their reading, in a word, the research I had done was off the beaten track of the college curriculum, therefore, it did not exist.

Perhaps I exaggerate, perhaps I am really being fantastic when I say this of the orthodox scholars, well, I shall give a not uncommon illustration and let the reader judge for himself.

In 1943, Gunnar Myrdal, noted economist of the University of Stockholm, Sweden, aided by 75 experts, working for five years, completed for the Carnegie Corporation at a cost of $209,000, a work on the race problem entitled "An American Dilemma" and published by Harper and Brothers. On page 1393 of this book (1st ed.) I am listed as an example of those who write "pseudo-history, fantastically glorifying the achievements of Negroes."

On what grounds was this judgment arrived at? On anything I had written? No, I was judged on a non-existent book—a book that no mortal could ever have seen.

Here are the facts: In 1927, I finished a manuscript entitled "This Mongrel World, A Study of Negro-Caucasian Mixing In All Ages and All Countries." At about that time I was asked to fill out a blank for "Who's Who in Colored America," and intending to publish the manuscript soon I listed it as being published. However, circumstances prevented my doing so. Thirteen years later, due to the much greater research I had done on the subject, I changed the title to "Sex and Race." Parts of the manuscript I used in Volumes One and Two of that work and discarded most of the rest. In short, when "An American Dilemma" was published not even the manuscript of "This Mongrel World" existed. Nevertheless this *non-existent manuscript* is listed as a *published book* in Myrdal's bibliography. What had happened? In reading through my biographical sketch in "Who's Who in Colored America," Myrdal, or some of his assistants, saw the title and on that alone condemned me. Not a word was said of any of my published books. They probably didn't take the trouble to look into any of them.

Now what is the difference between an attitude of this sort and that of any uneducated man, or any bigot, who would similarly condemn Myrdal's work, or that of any other scientist in such off-hand manner? So far as I am concerned, none whatever.

Furthermore, though I have no philanthropist or foundation, or staff of experts behind me, I go to as great pains as any of the most conscientious of these experts to get my facts straight, checking and re-checking, and travelling hither and yon to see with my own eyes whenever possible what I am writing about; and quoting only from the original sources and from those I have reason to believe are the most reliable. One can do no more. Of course, there will always be errors, but when seventy-six experts, working with unlimited funds as in "An American Dilemma," make errors surely a lone worker, like myself, might be forgiven a few.

Another reason why some object to the facts as given in my books is that they feel that their own learning is being impeached. If such facts were true, why, they certainly would have known them. One able Negro musician, who had a fine education in England, admitted to me later that when he heard me say for the first time that Beethoven was colored, he was "offended." Had he not long been acquainted with Beethoven?

In 1930 while I was carrying in the Negro press a series of articles on great Negroes, an Aframerican, studying in Germany, and now a college professor, wrote the Pittsburgh Courier, leading Negro weekly, that my stories were dubious even though I had included Bilal, Dumas, Pushkin, General Dodds, Chevalier de St. George, Henri Diaz, and others who are very plainly mentioned in biographies as being of Negro ancestry. The simple truth is that he didn't know the first thing of the true ancestry of these individuals but never having heard it, why, that alone made what I said false. As for my statement that the Virgin Mary and Christ were once worshipped as black and that at the present time pilgrimages are made to the shrines of the Black Virgins in France, Spain, and even in Germany, that seemed a veritable Munchausen tale, One Negro columnist, a Catholic, actually resented the idea that the Madonna could have been black. Had he not all his life seen her depicted as white?

Still another reason for their rejecting my researches is that they didn't want the present knowledge in their brains disturbed. They had been taught that the Negro's position in history had been that of a slave and it was much more pleasant to go on believing that than to investigate.

Race prejudice is responsible too, in part. There are those who at the merest mention that this or that noted person was, or might have been, of Negro ancestry, at once set their backs up like an angry cat. So racial are such people that when one attributes Negro ancestry even to an ancient Greek or Egyptian it is "social equality"—a lowering of their own personal dignity. One white woman angrily resented the idea that Alexander Dumas, the great novelist, could possibly have been of Negro ancestry.

The classic example of this sort, however, is Mary Preston, a Southern white woman, whose readings on Shakespeare were popular in her day. Miss Preston twisted "Othello" to suit herself. While admitting that Shakespeare did make Othello "black," that was positively not what Shakespeare meant so far as she was concerned. She said (italics hers): "In studying the play "Othello" I have always *imagined* its hero a *white man*. It is true the dramatist paints him black, but this shade does not suit the man. It is a stage decoration which *my taste discards;* a fault of color from an artistic point of view. I have, therefore, as I before stated in my *readings* of this play, dispensed with it. Shakespeare was too correct a delineator of human nature to have colored Othello *black* if he had personally acquainted himself with the idiosyncracies of the African race. We may regard, then, the daub of black upon Othello's portrait as an *ebullition* of fancy, a *freak* of imagination—the visionary concept of an ideal figure . . . Othello *was a white* man."[1]

Wherein we ask does such an attitude differ from that of any blind believer in revealed religion?

Of course this attitude is hugely amusing. It is one of a piece, too, with the feeling of certain Gentiles when they take up a book on Jewish biography and see for the first time that this or that great pioneer, scientist, or soldier whom they had all along fancied to be non-Jewish was a Jew.

The result of this attitude toward "Negro" history is that the better-known historians, sociologists, and anthropologists, with few exceptions, have been great claimers of Negroid peoples as white. The idea has been to maintain white supremacy. Pick up any national or world history and you'll find even the Ethiopians, who such early writers as Xenophanes, Aristotle, Herodotus and Strabo, tell us were black and wooly-haired, that is, the type now called Negro, are white. They still say the Ethiopians are white though they are uniformly blacker and more wooly-haired than the American Negroes.

Whenever, too, Negroes are mentioned as having appeared anywhere, whether in prehistoric America, the Caucasus, or Albania, they are invariably spoken of as "slaves." For instance, Ignatius Donnelly in trying to prove that the so-called New World was known to the people of the Old reproduces from the ancient Mexican monuments certain portraits of Negroes which he calls "idols."[2] But in the same breath he says they were "slaves" who "were brought to America at a very remote epoch." (Please note the contradiction: "slaves" who were "idols!") His reason for saying they were slaves is that "Negroes have never been a sea-going race," for which statement he hasn't a shred of evidence. Of course, the "slave" had to be brought in to square with white imperialism and the exploitation of the darker peoples even though what he mentions occurred in prehistoric times. The Negro must always be marked down so that his labor can be had in the cheapest market.

The motive for this twisting of history is that white imperialism must be shown as being of old, aristocratic ancestry. This imperialism was built upon the backs of the darker races. A noted example was the British empire, of whose 500,000,000 people, eighty percent are colored. Now some of these colored people as the Ethiopians, Egyptians, East Indians, and Moors were the originators of Western civilization; they were highly civilized when the Europeans were savages[3]—a fact that cannot be denied as long as the works of Julius Caesar and Tacitus exist. But it would never do to show that the lord and master once had very humble beginnings so it must be shown that the originators of civilization were white—that the white has always been on top. Therefore, for the purposes of adding lustre to white imperialism, the Ethiopians, Egyptians and the others are called "white" but for the purposes of profit they are treated as colored. Thus the white imperialist eats his cake and has it too.

It is a blow to the pride of certain white Americans, Englishmen, and Germans to hear it said that peoples and individuals they had all along fondly believed to be "pure" white were not so. Because I said on the testimony of white people who knew Beethoven, as well as on reports of his ancestry by German scholars, that he showed evidence of Negro strain, I have received letters as cross as if I had attacked the writers themselves.

Any talk of Negro progress angers many. If the blacks advance who will they have to be better than? There will go their splendid isolation of fancied superiority. Even worse, they already see themselves losing out, a state of mind expressed by Bacon when he said, "Men of noble birth are noted to be envious towards new men when they arise for the distance between them is altered and it is like a deceit of the eye that when others come on they think themselves go back."

So thorough has been the penetration of white imperialist propaganda that only a small percentage of the white or the colored in any part of Western civilization today have any idea that any other than white people had a hand in the origin of civilization. Although I had been an omnivorous reader from my earliest years I was well past twenty before it began to dawn upon me that the darker peoples could have had a part in it. Even now I can recall my astonishment when this occurred to me.

Even as the white manufacturers have bleached out our salt, sugar, flour, so the white historian has bleached out world history. The dark or mineral portion has been rejected. Of course this process has produced a product beautifully pleasing to the eyes of those who have been psychologized to admire it, but which, nevertheless, is constipative and harmful to the mental digestion.

But as there are those who, realizing the value of the minerals that have been rejected from our foods, have placed them in again, thereby increasing the health value, as say how bran has been restored to the bleached, starved-out white bread, so in like manner I have attempted to gather up the Negro, or dark, rejected portion of history in the hope that some day they will be restored to world history, thereby permitting a less clogging effect on the mind.

Such being my purpose I do not ever claim that I am writing world or national history. Call it the bran of history if you will. As for those who will regard this "bran" as proving that the white race has never accomplished anything and that the Negro did everything. I can do nothing about it.

I can say, in addition, that I dislike too much the whitening of history; I have too great a loathing for racial propaganda, even knowingly to indulge in it. Moreover, the facts I have given have been culled nearly always from white writers, some of them very ancient, who related facts as they saw them, and who did not worship at the shrine of white imperialism, or did not think of the effect of what they said would have in later years.

To get those little known facts I have travelled tens of thousands of miles in many lands; consulted books and printed matter so vast in number that were I to try to say how many I would sound like a Munchausen; visited the leading museums of many of the civilized lands, and engaged in research in their libraries and ever going to great pains to get my facts as humanly correct as possible. In short, I felt I have looked into books and dug up buried knowledge that many college professors or doctors of philosophy do not know exist, because just as there is a life in the deeper depths of the ocean of which the average fisherman knows nothing so there are depths in the ocean of research of which some of the most learned have never dreamed. For instance, it is estimated that in the National Library of France alone there are 8,000,000 books and pieces of printed matter. How much does the most educated man now alive know of the totality of knowledge in these books? Very, very little. One is ever learning. Truly, as Sir Isaac Newton once said as he looked out on the ocean that there he was picking up pebbles on the beach as it were while the vast ocean of unexplored knowledge lay before him.

Those who will forget their orthodoxy for a while and read my books might not find them so fantastic after all. And even should they reject them they might still profit to the extent of knowing the arguments on the other side and thus be able to refute them, not by denunciation, but in a manner more compatible with common sense.

I hasten to add that I am not accusing all the leading historians of catering to white imperialism. Some as H. G. Wells, Hendrik Van Loon, and Arnold J. Toynbee, have made striking utterances against race prejudice. I believe that these latter accepted the popular white view of history without thinking that there was another side. As the New World was not on the charts of the scholars prior to Columbus so the achievements of the Negro and Negroid peoples were not on theirs.

Furthermore, there are white writers as Volney, Godfrey Higgins, Gerald Massey, Henry M. Stanley, David Livingstone, and Frobenius, greatest of all the Africanologists, who gave a perspective of Negro history that is increasingly found to be the truth. Why, we ask, were the works of these men by-passed by Wells and Toynbee? Were what they said of the Negro in history too fantastic to be considered?

For instance, Toynbee, who is one of the most unprejudiced of historians, attributes a civilization even to the Polynesian but denies any to the Negro. He says, "When we classify Mankind by color, the only one of the primary races . . . which has not made a creative contribution to any of our twenty-one civilizations is the Black Race . . .

"The Black Race has not helped to create any civilization while the Polynesian White Race has helped to create one civilization, the Brown Race two, the Yellow Race three, the Red Race and the Nordic White Race four apiece, the Alpine White Race nine, and the Mediterranean White Race ten."[4]

What is the Polynesian White Race? There is no such people. The Polynesians, prior to the migration of white people to their islands, were chiefly of mixed Negro and Mongolian strain, with probably a slight admixture of white strain from Asiatic Russia. The Paris Museum of Ethnology in the Jardin des Plantes has what is, without a doubt, the most comprehensive collection of casts of Polynesian types from nearly all the islands and they are shown to be what would be loosely called Negroes in the United States. Of course, much white "blood" has been mixed in with the South Sea islander since these casts were made over a century ago. Gobineau calls the Polynesians black and he was right at the time he wrote.

Let me express here once again my theory of so-called race. It is this: There is a single human race, which by imperceptible degrees shades from the blond of the Scandinavian to the blackness of the Senegambian or the Solomon Islander with the Sicilian or the Maltese somewhere in the centre. Some peoples as the Portuguese are nearer to the blond, while others as those of Mauretania or Southern India are nearer to the black, therefore, when I see anywhere, no matter where, an individual whose appearance is Negroid, that it, if his facial contour, his lips, nose, hair, present what a lifetime of observation has taught me are signs of Negro inheritance, I say that that person had a Negro ancestor near or distant according to the Negroid signs he presents. One's ancestry, I know, does not come out of the air, but is a reality of realities.

Similarly, if I see anywhere an individual whose appearance is Caucasian, that is, his lips, nose, hair, etc., present what a lifetime of observation has taught me are signs of "unmixed" Caucasian inheritance, I set that person down as white. If it is logical to speak of Caucasian strain among Negroes it is just as logical to speak of Negro strain among Caucasians. In this latter respect the Nazi anthropologists are at least right.

For instance, I once attended a reception given to an American Negro publisher and his wife in London. The latter was very fair and in her evening gown looked whiter in skin and more regular in profile than some of the Englishwomen present. If I attributed Negro ancestry to the publisher's wife, whose mother was undoubtedly colored, what should I have said of these Englishwomen who were more colored than she is in appearance?

One may sometimes find Negro ancestry where one least expects it. Take Colette, France's leading woman writer. She is blonde and to all appearances a European. Only a very experienced eye would discover signs of a strain not "pure" Nordic in her. Yet she had a Negro ancestor. When I said that in 1930, I was again charged with claiming all noted white persons as Negroes. But who said it first? Colette, herself.[5] The European, unlike the American, is not inclined to hide his Negro strain, if any. Also J. Larnac in his biography of her says that she inherited some Negro strain from her grandfather ("tenant de son grandpère un peu de sang coloré"). Her mother, "Madame Colette," he says, "is the daughter of Sophie Celeste Chatenay and a colored man with violet fingernails, who manufactured chocolates in Belgium, Henri Marie Landay."[6] If Colette, who is so blonde, has a Negro strain, I fail to see where the same would be impossible in the case of Beethoven, who did show Negro ancestry.

Again, there are those dear souls who will say that I exaggerate when I call these apparently white persons "Negroes." Would such kindly address themselves to the United States Census Bureau which decrees that if one has a known Negro ancestor, he is a Negro. The wife of the Negro editor mentioned above, was listed as a Negro. And the unwritten law is that if one is known to be of such ancestry, however distant, he is at once marked down. As long as this "one drop" theory remains refutation of alleged Negro inferiority must follow the arbitrary lines set by the Bureau of the Census.

However, no one can possibly know what so-called racial elements enter into his make-up. O. A. Wall estimated that the total number of one's ancestors since the time of Christ was around 144 quadrillions, and said that if one did not count the intermarriage of relatives the figure would be 288,230,376,151,711,742.[7] Thus since life goes back at least a million years the ancestors of any individual would be as many as the sands of the sea or the stars of the firmament.

Talk of a pure race after that!

I, furthermore, visualize changes in human types as I visualize changes in cosmography, that is, as land that was once at the bottom of the sea now rears lofty peaks among the Alps and the Himalayas and vice versa; and as lands that were once tropical are now frigid, all due to the eternal change in Nature, so peoples who were once black are now white, and the opposite. Or to use a symbol: As parts of the earth are white or black or intermediate tints depending on whether such parts are facing, or are behind, or are sideways to the sun, so, in cosmic time it is with the coloring of the human race.

That humanity is one, that the earliest human beings were of a single color, is evident to even the Australian Bushman, supposedly the lowest in intelligence on earth. Dr. Berkeley Hill says they believe "that a white man is only one of themselves re-born. 'Tumble-down black fellow, jump up white fellow', is the common phrase among them "to express this belief," he says.

There are two principal sides to every question both of which when mixed together go to form the truth as oxygen and hydrogen to form water. My aim is to glean from both sides, using experience and an open mind as my guide. Because one is definitely opposed to our theory, he is not necessarily wrong, and because one favors us, neither does that make him right.

Everything that is, is truth by sheer force of its existence. Therefore by truth I mean that principle, which, at every moment, upholds the right of each individual, regardless of whoever or whatever he may be, to equality of dignity and opportunity, in short, equal justice.

As regards the term, Nature, I use it in no anthropomorphic sense. I do not think of it as a deity but as meaning the totality of all things—that unknown Force which is forever being unfolded, and within which lies the destiny of all things. The term, Nature, is inadequate of course, but since it is impossible to find a correct name that seems to me as good as any other.

I have also tried to get away from the crass materialism of Western civilization, which because of its eagerness to get hold of material things is forever rending itself and bringing untold misery on itself and all mankind. Three appallingly catastrophic wars in a quarter of a century!

Happily, there is a certain trend in the West today towards the animism of the East and of Africa, to explore into and to make one's self a part of the great inner forces of Nature. For the really cultured Western thinker of today, a bit of board is no longer just board but a segment of the universe seething with the life of the atom; trees are no longer just trees but breathing organisms, marvellous with their own psychology, their own loves and aversions; bees, insects, spiders, animalculae are discovered to have histories almost as intricate and hardly less interesting than those of man; cats, dogs, apes, elephants are discovered to have intelligence which has been cut out of the same cloth, so to speak, as man's. Though its reach is far lower, it operates essentially the same, all intelligence, human and animal, being but a part of the Great Whole.

Finally, as regards human beings, we are getting farther and farther away from the old "science" of physiognomy, and are appraising individuals, not on their looks, but on their acts. We are learning that to gauge intelligence by skull measurement, size of brain, skin color and hair are the sheerest infantilism, no matter how high the reputation of the scientist who advances such theories.

Let not those who think they are up be jealous of those who have been down and are rising. Let them rather rejoice that the human race, of which we are all part, is advancing. Let the thrill of feeling superior come not as the result of looking down on others but in seeing them rise, and in knowing that we are in a position to help them to do so.

To love one's fellow-man is the beginning of all true wisdom and the end of war, the greatest of all insanities.

In the better days that are coming it will be immaterial what color or what race of human beings did this or that great thing. This insanity of color fastened on us by the Virginia slaveholder and the New England slave-dealer will pass as other fantastic theories have passed. In the meantime the reciting of Negro accomplishment, past and present, will be necessary to counteract anti-Negro propaganda even as the reciting of Jewish accomplishment is a foil to anti-Semitism.

Notes

[1] *Studies in Shakespeare,* p. 71, 1869. Apropos of this a noted psychoanalyst once objected to my saying during a discussion period that when Shakespeare said, "Black men are pearls in beauteous ladies eyes," he actually meant black men. No, he said, there were no Negroes in England in Shakespeare's time, and he was positive about it. I informed him that there was not only Negro slavery in England at the time but that G. B. Harrison, an Elizabethan authority, thinks that Shakespeare, himself, had a Negro sweetheart. (For sources see Sex and Race, Vol. I, p. 201, 1941, and Vol. II, p. 400.)

[2] Donnelly, I. *Atlantis,* pp. 174–5, 1882.

[3] Julian Huxley and A. C. Haddon say, "It is asserted vociferously in certain quarters that the Nordic 'race' is gifted above all others with initiative and originality and that the great advances in civilization have been due to Nordic genius.

"What are the facts? The fundamental discoveries on which civilization is built are the art of writing, agriculture, the wheel and building in stone. All these appear to have originated in the Near East, among peoples who by no stretch of the imagination could be called Nordic or presumed to have but the faintest admixture of Nordic or proto-Nordic genes." (*We, Europeans,* p. 94, 1935.)

[4] Toynbee, A. J. *A Study of History,* Vol. I, p. 234, 1934.

[5] *La Maison de Claudine,* p. 99, 1922.

[6] *Colette,* pp. 11, 17, 18, 1927. See also *Sex and Race,* Vol. I, p. 240, 1941.

[7] *Sex and Sex Worship,* pp. 304–06, 1992. I do not see, however, where the intermarriage of relatives would affect the computation of one's ancestors except in the cases of those who are the product of incest, and that only in the case of where brother weds sister. Even if a man cohabited with his mother and had children by her as the ancient Britons used to do (at least that is what I infer from Caesar when he said that fathers and sons had the same wives), it seems to me something else would enter into the ancestry of the child. And there is no doubt of it when first cousin marries first cousin. The uncle or the aunt of the latter would have wed someone not related to the family, thus creating new combinations of genes. One has, it is true, only eight great-grandparents but we must not forget that behind each one of these stood enough millions of ancestors probably to go around the world several times. Truly, as Einstein has said, the number of one's ancestors is "astronomical."

Caesar's statement on incest among the ancient Britons reads, "Groups of ten or twelve men have wives together in common and particularly brothers along with brothers and fathers with sons." (*Gallic Wars,* Bk. V, 14.)

WHY "RACE" MAKES NO SCIENTIFIC SENSE: THE CASE OF AFRICANS AND NATIVE AMERICANS

PRINCE BROWN, JR.

Study Question

1. Based on the information presented in "Why 'Race' Makes No Scientific Sense: The Case of African and Native Americans," why do you think scientists and other researchers have ignored the complex biological reality in favor of the idea that people can be classified in a single racial category?

In the futile efforts to create "racial" classification schemes, people born to the combination of African and Native American parents have been overlooked. Examining this particular case of the fusion of biology and culture assists understanding of human variation and makes clear that fixed, distinct, and exclusive categories for races, never have existed and do not now exist.

Everywhere ships anchored in the Americas, Asia, Africa, and the various islands there was immediate exchange and sharing of human genes. In the case of Africans and Native Americans, this process was set in motion more than 500 years ago and continues unabated. Hence, many persons labeled African American have Native American ancestry, and the reverse is true. According to the African American historian Carter G. Woodson, the history of the relationship between Africans and Native Americans is long, deeply intertwined, and largely unwritten (Woodson 1920, p. 45).

In this reading the term *Native American* shall be used to refer to the native inhabitants of North, Central, and South America and the Caribbean Islands. *African* shall be used to refer to people descendant from the African continent; *European* shall, in the same manner, be used to reference people from Europe.

Conventional history teaches that Native American–African contact commenced with Columbus's arrival in the Americas in 1492. We may start then by calling attention to the physical characteristics of the Spanish and

ples in the Americas were replaced [killed off or died out] and the area re-populated by Europeans and Africans is erroneous. Rather, he suggests that

> [Native] American survivors and African survivors (because huge numbers of Africans also died in the process) have merged together to create the basic modern populations of much of the Greater Caribbean and adjacent mainland regions. (1993, p. 270)

The case of African and Native Americans makes clear that the label *race*, when assigned to a particular set of observable human features, is socially derived. The categories widely used to denote "race" are inappropriate since they do not capture "real" biological distinctions (Levin, 1991) but rather reflect social and cultural conventions. The point is that it is not possible to identify biological ancestry simply by referencing physical features. Indeed, from the perspective of evolutionary biology we are all Africans—sharing common ancestors who evolved first in Africa.

References

Campbell, Mavis. 1990. *The Maroons of Jamaica 1655–1796.* Trenton NJ: Africa World Press.

CKSSG Chodorow, S., M. Knox, C. Schirokauer, J. Strayer, and H. Gatzke. 1989. *The Mainstream of Civilization to 1715.* Orlando, FL: Harcourt Brace Jovanovich.

Forbes, Jack D. 1993. *Africans and Native Americans.* Urbana and Chicago: University of Illinois Press.

hooks, bell. 1992. *Black Looks: Race and Representation.* Boston: South End Press.

Johnston, James H. 1929. "Documentary Evidence of the Relations of Negroes and Indians." *Journal of Negro History* Vol. 14 (1).

Katz, William L. 1986. *Black Indians.* New York: Macmillan.

———. 1987. *The Black West.* Seattle, WA: Open Hand Publishing.

Levin, Michael D. 1991. "Population Differentiation and Racial Classification." *Encyclopedia of Human Biology* Vol. 6. Academic Press.

Mullin, Michael. 1992. *Africa in America.* Chicago: University of Illinois Press.

Porter, Kenneth W. 1932. "Relations Between Negroes and Indians Within the Present Limits of the United States." *Journal of Negro History* Vol. XVII, No. 3 (July).

Rogers, J. A. 1984. *Sex and Race,* Vol. 2. St. Petersburg FL: Helga M. Rogers.

Strickland, Rennard. 1980. *The Indians in Oklahoma.* Norman, OK, and London: University of Oklahoma Press.

Woodson, Carter G. 1920. "The Relations of Negroes and Indians in Massachusetts." *Journal of Negro History* Vol. 5 (1).

Science, Pseudo-science and Racism

Albert Jacquard

Study Question

1. Does the Jacquard article help you to understand why "race" is a social construction and not a biological fact? Why or why not?

Organized by Unesco at the invitation of the Foundation for Human Rights of Athens, a symposium devoted to a critical review of the pseudo-scientific theories invoked to justify racism and racial discrimination was held in the Greek capital from 30 March to 3 April 1981.

Since those who attempt to impose the notion that some kind of "natural hierarchy" exists between different populations or between different individuals often invoke science in support of their theories, it was necessary for Unesco to clarify the situation by making the true standpoint of scientists widely known. Twenty-three distinguished personalities from eighteen countries, representing the various disciplines involved—geneticists, biologists, anthropologists, sociologists, psychologists, historians, etc.—spent a week analysing the most up-to-date findings of science and drawing from them the arguments with which to counter the affirmations of the neo-racists.

The collective statement of their conclusions known as The Declaration of Athens *and drawn up by the scientists gathered at Athens and addressed to all the peoples of the world is published following this article. The article below, by French geneticist Albert Jacquard, rapporteur at the Athens symposium, highlights the main themes of the debate.*

Man's spontaneous and apparently natural reaction to a setback is to find the culprit, who necessarily has to be someone else, or "other" people. In a similar situation a group will react by attributing its misfortunes to some other group or, preferably, to a sub-group of its own kind.

These instinctive, infantile, cowardly reactions bear no relation to a reasoned analysis of events in the real world and their causes, but they seem to be so widespread and so persistent that there are few grounds to hope that they can be made to disappear. If, in spite of everything, we must keep this hope alive, we can only to do so through "science", a somewhat solemn name for the efforts of the human mind to understand the real world.

326

Strangely, it is in the name of science that overtly racist attitudes are beginning to re-emerge in certain Western societies. People refer to "recent biological discoveries" or to "the latest genetic research" as justification for their attempts to classify men in certain categories or "races", and above all to compare these races according to various criteria and to rank them in hierarchies.

However, what scientists are actually saying, especially those working in genetics, the discipline most directly concerned, runs counter to any such claim. Any attempt to make biology serve as a basis for elitist theories is rooted in a fundamental misconception, whether the "elite" consists of certain individuals within each group, or of certain groups in themselves.

It is essential, therefore, that scientists should in the present circumstances speak out, for it is their duty to describe clearly and publicize the discoveries made in their disciplines. Reasoned arguments, unswayed by sentiment, are needed to combat the different forms of racism. For this, clarity is vitally important, so we must carefully define the terms we use.

To be "racist" is to despise someone else simply because he belongs to a group. This group may be defined by many different criteria: colour of skin, language, religion, genetic inheritance or cultural heritage. And so it is more realistic to talk of racisms rather than racism. The first requisite of each form of racism is a definition, firstly of how to classify people into relatively homogeneous and distinct categories, and secondly, of how to establish a scale of values applicable to these categories. In other words, the different "races" must first be defined, and then ranked in a hierarchy.

In the case of a species which has gradually become differentiated into definitively and strictly separate populations as a result of a series of separations, the gap between the genetic or cultural structures of two populations widens as they move further in time from the initial split. It is thus possible to attempt to reconstitute the genealogy of these successive separations, taking as a starting point the structures which can be observed today.

On the other hand, when the history of a species does not take the form of a tree which has become progressively differentiated, resembling instead a network of amalgamations and exchanges between distinct populations (i.e. migrations), this attempted reconstitution is doomed to failure, save in exceptional cases. Our knowledge of the present state of the groups does not allow the steps which have led to this state to be retraced. In the case of the human species, which is remarkable for its nomadism, this difficulty is particularly great.

To be sure, geographical distance has prevented exchanges between populations living on opposite sides of the globe; migrations have come up against sometimes insuperable natural obstacles; cultural differences have raised barriers and isolated certain groups genetically. But the history of human populations is so intertwined that none can be described without reference to its exchanges with many others. Little by little, each has come to be related to the others. At the same time, natural processes (the foremost being that of sexual reproduction) have given rise to and sustained a remarkable degree of diversity within each population.

Mankind is an aggregate of persons, families, ethnic groups, and nations, all of them different. But these differences can only be classified at the cost of an arbitrary impoverishment of our view of individuals and groups. The most rigorous form of classification concerns genetic inheritances: the degree of frequency with which various genes occur in each of two populations being seen as a token of the degree of dissimilarity between these populations.

If confined to a small number of genes, the attempt at classification will soon produce results, but they will vary from one group of genes to another. If, for example, we take the genes responsible for the synthesis of melanin, a pigment which accumulates in the skin and gives it a dark colouring, we find that, where these genes are concerned, blacks differ very greatly from yellow or white people.

As for the genes responsible for the activity of lactase, the enzyme which makes it possible to digest milk, they are very frequent among North European populations, slightly less so in the Mediterranean region, but very rare in Asia and Africa. The classification of people into two groups, based on the frequency of these genes, would set the Europeans apart from people from the other continents.

In the case of two biological characteristics whose genetic mechanism is well known, the Rhesus blood system and the HL-A immunological system, both result in a classification of people into two groups, with Asiatics and Eskimos on one side, and Indo-Europeans and Black Africans on the other.

Depending upon the criteria selected—skin colour, persistence of lactase, or immunological "systems"—our view of the relations between the three major human groups classically referred to alters completely: it may arbitrarily be claimed that the populations of Europe resemble those of Africa more closely than those of Asia, or the reverse.

This is because the history of humanity cannot be expressed in the form of a progressively ramified tree. Instead, it consists in a network of exchanges, mergers and separations. It is therefore a mistake to try to devise a classification that can have no global validity.

The impossibility of devising such a classification is confirmed by research which is not based on some arbitrarily selected characteristics, but on a synthesis of information concerning all the different characteristics studied.

Where many sets of genes are involved, it is possible to express the various resemblances and differences between the genetic structures of two populations in terms of "distance". The definition of race here means attributing populations with small distances between them to the same group, and populations separated by a large distance to two distinct groups. In the case of human populations, this method cannot be conclusive.

Basing his research on the best-known blood systems, the Harvard geneticist R. Lewoutin has shown that the distance between two populations belonging to different "races" is, on average, not more than 7 or 8 per cent higher than the distance between two populations of the same race.

In other words, if belonging to a given race or a given nation is not without significance as regards genetic structure, its consequences are very limited; an Eskimo or an African could well be closer to me genetically than the policeman in my village. This is not to deny the differences between the various human groups. But the web of similarities and dissimilarities is so intricate that the picture becomes blurred as soon as an attempt is made to incorporate all the available data.

So the geneticist's answer, when asked about the meaning of the word "race", is categorical; insofar as the human species is concerned, there can be no objective and stable definition of this concept.

Experience shows that the classification of humanity into more or less distinct groups usually goes hand in hand with a value judgement distinguishing the "good" from the "bad". Thousands of examples could be cited of writers who are convinced that they are not racists and yet take it for granted that their own group is the best. A book read by several generations of French children, *Le Tour de la France par Deux Enfants,* presents stereotyped portraits of Whites, Blacks, Yellow people and redskins, and affirms that "the white race is the most perfect."

Current attempts to establish a hierarchy of races seek to envelop themselves with an aura of scientific respectability by making reference to research in a variety of disciplines, notably those concerned with explaining the evolution of species and those that study the various manifestations of intellectual activity.

For over a century, explanations of evolution have been dominated by Darwinism. The key concept of this theory is that of the survival of the fittest; those individuals best fitted for the "struggle for life" have the best chances of surviving and transmitting their genetic inheritance to the next generation. According to this theory, the biological structure of the population undergoes transformation as a result of this inequality of individual capacities, desirable characteristics spread, and undesirable ones gradually die out.

When, thanks to the Austrian botanist Gregor Mendel, it was understood that sexed beings transmit not their characteristics but the genes governing these characteristics, it became necessary to modify this theory and to attribute a "selective value" not to the individuals or to their characteristics but to the genes they possess. Darwinism was supplanted by neo-Darwinism whose approach is basically the same.

However, the attribution of a "value" to people or to genes can be highly misleading. By definition, this value corresponds exclusively to the gene's ability to transmit its biological inheritance, i.e. to procreate children. Individuals who die without offspring are thus "of no selective value". To classify them as "inferior beings" is to confuse their selective value and their value as human beings.

This blunder has been made many times by those who have extrapolated a social Darwinism from the original biological Darwinism, and have advocated a type of society in which the powerful must "naturally" prevail over the weak. Contemporary Western thought has been deeply influenced by this kind of reasoning, which many regard as dictated by "the laws of nature". The fact is, however, that nature really teaches us the exact opposite of this hierarchical vision.

One of the consequences of natural selection ought apparently to be the gradual standardization of populations. Since the "good" drive out the "bad", in due course only the best genes remain, and there is less diversity. Now, analysis of the genetic inheritance of various species shows, on the the contrary, that this diversity is maintained. One unexpected discovery made by biologists, which has gradually been confirmed over the last ten or fifteen years, is the extent of "polymorphism", the existence of a wide field of variation within a given population.

This discovery has led to a fundamental revision of neo-Darwinism. This revision has taken two directions: certain scientists are developing a "neutralist" theory, from which the concept of selective value has been eliminated; others retain the concept but give it a much more complex definition, giving weight to the interaction of several genes on a single characteristic. In either case, this revision renders obsolete all reasoning based on the existence of a scale of values according to which individuals, characteristics or genes may be set in a hierarchy.

The mechanisms at work in nature do not select the best and weed out the less good: they preserve the sustained coexistence of a wide variety of characteristics. If we are to learn from nature, then we ought to rank groups not according to the *quality* of their characteristics, but according to the *variety* of these characteristics. The "best" group is the one that has managed to preserve the greatest diversity, whatever the content of this diversity.

Our judgments on our fellow men often concern their psychological rather than their physical characteristics. It is the role of the psychologist to define with greater precision the various traits of the personality, and for nearly a century now, Western psychologists have sought to turn their discipline, with all its nuances and subtle distinctions, into a "scientific" discipline.

For this, they have introduced quantitative criteria. In particular, they have popularized the intelligence quotient, or IQ, a parameter that supposedly measures the activity of our intelligence. Admittedly, psychologists themselves denounce the abuses that have arisen in connexion with the cult of IQ. Even so, this quotient figures prominently in many misconceived arguments; it serves to justify often harsh decisions concerning children's school careers, and it has been the crux of the controversy provoked in the United States by the revival of a certain kind of racism.

This is not to deny the usefulness of the concept of IQ. But it is necessary to define the limits of its significance: IQ indicates the position of an an individual on an arbitrarily defined scale of reference within a given population, at a specific moment in time. This indicator is extremely imprecise, and its stability is little-known and probably low.

Despite these limitations, certain scientists have used IQ to compare human populations. The most famous study is the one conducted by the American psychologist Arthur Jensen, who in 1969 compared Blacks and Whites in the United States and concluded that there was a 15-point differential in favour of the latter.

This conclusion depends upon the factors to which the observed difference is attributed. This involves a delicate genetic concept known as inheritability. Certain psychologists have totally misunderstood this concept: they have forgotten that the inheritability of IQ merely measures a resemblance and have used it to attribute IQ differentials between populations to genetic factors.

This is not to deny the influence of genetic inheritance on a characteristic such as intellectual activity. Clearly, the medium for this activity, namely the central nervous system, is produced from the genetic inheritance, but its ontogenesis also requires the intervention of the environment. The outcome will depend upon the way they interact. But to try to measure the relative influence of each is meaningless.

Thus it is impossible to base a classification of the "intellectual potential" of different human groups on observable intellectual performance, or even to ascribe observed variations, as certain doctrinaire thinkers have tried to do, to genetic differences.

The very concept of intellectual potential is indefinable. Attempts to establish a hierarchy of races on the basis of this criterion are not just mistaken: they are absurd. Experience unfortunately shows that it is harder to combat an absurdity than to clear up a mistake.

The chief lesson to be learned from genetics is that the groups to which we belong do indeed differ from each other, but that the individuals within each of these groups are even more different still.

The only value judgement with any scientific backing concerns the importance of differences for their own sake, without attaching a plus or a minus sign to these differences. I am neither superior nor inferior to anybody else; I am different from everybody; the more different we are, the more I give to my neighbour and the more I receive from him in return.

This is not an assertion dictated by a moral system; it is the central lesson of genetics. It is a serious matter that this lesson should have been distorted to justify racist doctrines. It would be easier to combat this kind of perversion of the truth if communication between scientists and public opinion were better organized. In this field, the activities of Unesco could prove decisive for the future of us all.

THE DECLARATION OF ATHENS
Scientists Speak Out Against Racism

Study Question
1. List at least two reasons why "race" is not a biological reality.
2. Why has racism persisted?

The scientists brought together by Unesco appeal to the peoples of the world and to all individuals everywhere to base their attitudes, behaviour and statements on the following conclusions, which represent the present state of scientific knowledge on the racial question.

1. The latest anthropological discoveries confirm the unity of the human species.
2. The geographical dispersion of the human species has favoured its racial differentiation but has not affected its basic biological unity.
3. All attempts to classify the human species so as to give objective content to the concept of race have been based on visible physical characteristics. In fact, the concept of race can only be based on transmissible characteristics, that is to say, not on visible physical features but on the genetic factors that govern them.
4. Modern biological techniques have made it possible to study these factors. They reveal a far greater genetic diversity than had been imagined.
5. It has been found that the difference between the genetic structures of two individuals belonging to the same population group can be far greater than the differences between the average genetic structures of two population groups. This finding makes it impossible to arrive at any objective and stable definition of the different races and consequently deprives the word "race" of much of its biological meaning.
6. Whatever the differences observed, biology can in no way serve as the basis for a hierarchy between individuals or population groups, since no human group possesses a consistent genetic inheritance. In any event, one is never justified in proceeding from observation of a difference to the affirmation of a superiority-inferiority relationship.
7. In fact, each human being possesses a genetic combination that is unique among the countless possible combinations.
8. Man has developed culture, which has enabled the human race to adapt itself to different ecological environments and to transform them according to its needs.

9. The pre-eminence of culture makes the human species unique and invalidates any explanations of human behaviour based solely on the study of animal behaviour. There are no grounds for explaining variations in group behaviour in terms of genetic differences.

10. Intellectual activity constitutes one of the most striking characteristics of man. Certain disciplines have developed techniques for measuring this activity.

11. These techniques are designed to compare individuals within a given population group and cannot, by definition, be used for the purpose of comparing different population groups.

12. It follows, *a fortiori,* that any value judgement on the intellectual capacities of a given group based on such measurements is completely without foundation.

13. Indeed, the complexity of the interaction between biological and cultural factors makes any attempts to establish the relative importance of innate and acquired characteristics completely meaningless.

14. It is unacceptable and scientifically unjustifiable to use the results of psychological tests and the intelligence quotient in particular to promote social ostracism and racial discrimination.

15. The social sciences provide no support for the view that racism is a collective form of behaviour that inevitably arises when certain kinds of social relationship predominate between different ethnic groups. On the other hand, the plurality and coexistence of cultures and races that characterize many societies constitute the most felicitous form of mutual enrichment between peoples.

16. Racism, which takes a number of forms, is in reality a complex phenomenon involving a whole range of economic, political, historical, cultural, social and psychological factors. Effective action to combat racism must necessarily address itself to all these factors.

17. Racism is generally a tool used by certain groups to reinforce their political and economic power, the most serious cases being those involving apartheid and genocide.

18. Racism also takes the form of denying that certain peoples have a history and of underrating their contribution to the progress of mankind.

19. While the quantitative analysis of social phenomena can help to elucidate sociological and economic issues, it can also be used to promote exclusion and segregation. The application of quotas, tol-

erance thresholds and numerical stipulations for educational purposes based on ethnic or racial criteria should be denounced when it violates the basic principles of human rights. However, legitimate measures can be taken to redress the wrongs inflicted on certain underprivileged groups.

20. Those engaged in scientific activity bear a major responsibility for the social future of their contemporaries. Where racism is concerned, this responsibility involves political and ethical choices. Scientific research, particularly in the field of the human and social sciences, should always be based on respect for human dignity.

21. Recognition of the risks to mankind implicit in certain applications of science should lead not to a rejection of science but rather to the fostering among the public at large of a genuinely scientific attitude, that is, an attitude based not on an accumulation of certainties but on the cultivation of a critical spirit and the continual challenging of accepted views. The struggle against racism in all its forms calls for the extensive involvement of scientists in the fostering of these attitudes, making use in particular of education systems and the media.

22. There is a need therefore for scientists, whatever their differences or divergencies of viewpoint, to strive to maintain the objectivity that will ensure that their work and conclusions cannot be used as the basis for falsifications and interpretations detrimental to mankind.

Signatories

A. C. Bayonas (Greece), historian and philosopher;
T. Ben Jelloun (Morocco), philosopher and writer;
J. Björnebye (Norway), philologist;
A. Bouhdiba (Tunisia), sociologist;
H. Condamine (France), geneticist;
E. Czeizel (Hungary), geneticist;
M. Diabate (Ivory Coast), ethno-sociologist;
C. A. Diop (Senegal), anthropologist;
R. Droz (Switzerland), psychologist;
M. Fraginal (Cuba), ethnologist;
S. Genoves (Mexico), anthropologist;
A. Jacquard (France), geneticist and mathematician;
J. Ki-Zerbo (Upper Volta), historian;
C. B. Krimbas (Greece), geneticist;

E. Nevo (Israel), geneticist;

H. Tawa (Lebanon), historian and mathematician;

D. Trichopoulos (Greece), professor of medicine;

T. Tsunoda (Japan), professor of medicine;

P. Vegleris (Greece), lawyer and professor of law;

L. P. Vidyarthi (India), anthropologist;

G. Wald (U.S.A), Nobel Prize for medicine;

A. Yotopoulos Marangopoulos (Greece), President of the Athens Human Rights Foundation;

I. M. Zolotareva (USSR), anthropologist.

WHITE RECONSTRUCTION IN THE UNIVERSITY

CHARLES A. GALLAGHER

Study Questions

1. In terms of your own personal experiences, do you think Gallagher is correct in arguing that white students are experiencing a "white" identity/racial crisis in the United States?
2. Do you think white students are justified in responding to discussions about racism in America today with anger and resentment? Why or why not?
3. Do discussions about "race," integration, affirmative action, and interracial dating lead to tensions in your family? Explain.

I mean, before, if I were filling out some type of application, you just put white, you know, that's the only time I really had to think about it. You know what I mean. I mean now I really have to think about it. Like now I feel white. I feel white. I feel different. I feel really different compared to other people.

Elise, a 19-year-old college student[1]

Like, everything was white, like white, white, white, but now everything is black, black, black, and I don't think it's helping anything. I don't know. Are there any clubs, like the white pre-law society?

Marianne, a junior from a working-class neighborhood

KIM: Like one of my girlfriends is always saying that when she's rich and famous she's going to start herself a white scholarship fund.

BARBARA: Or a white college fund. Yes!

KIM: I mean a white mind is a terrible thing to waste, too. As she always says.

Kim and Barbara, lamenting over problems paying tuition

The quotes typify the sentiments of white working- and middle-class students at a large urban university in the United States. Drawn from an extensive research project on white identity conducted in the spring of 1993, they reveal how being white is an explicit, meaningful part of how students construct their social identities. The students I interviewed experience their whiteness as a "real" social category that intrudes on most of their everyday activities. Race matters for these students because they have been weaned on a brand of racial politics and media exposure that has made whiteness visible as a racial category while simultaneously transforming whiteness into a social disadvantage.

"Being" white in the 1990s, however, is far from straightforward. It is riddled with ambiguity and marked by a general sense of racial angst as to what it means to be white. What, for instance, does Elise mean when she explains that she "feels white?" Is feeling white situational and fleeting, or is it more akin to a dull constant pain? Does whiteness only exist in opposition to nonwhites? Is it merely a "politically constructed category parasitic on blackness," as Cornel West suggests?[2] Or is white identity being reconstructed as an explicit, salient category of self-definition emerging in response to the political and cultural challenges of other racialized groups?[3] Is it possible to evoke white collective interests, history, and culture in a nonracist manner, and if so, how would this be articulated or accomplished?

By examining processes and events that have influenced the construction of whiteness, this essay will consider some of the ways it becomes both visible and meaningful to whites, particularly young white college students. First, I want to lay to rest the notion that all whites see themselves as colorless or racially transparent. While this may have been the case at one time, contemporary racial politics and the effect of the media have made it practically impossible for many whites not to think about themselves as occupying a racial category. Second, I discuss the influence of identity politics on the raising of whites' consciousness. I argue that the political and cultural mobilization of racially defined minorities has forced, perhaps inadvertently, young whites to think about who they are racially in relation to other racial groups. Third, I contend that the decline of ethnicity among later-generation whites has created an identity vacuum, which has been at least partially replaced by an identity centered around race. Finally, I want to connect these trends to the right's attempt to reconstruct "white" as a nonracist cultural identity. Students' recognition of whiteness is not solely a reactionary response to challenges from nonwhites; it is also a reflection of the need to provide oneself with a narrative of whiteness that does not demonize white as a racial category. As expressed by many students, young whites are in the midst of constructing an identity and cultural space centered around a white experience that they believe is ostensibly nonracist.

I draw on information from two sources: first, the over 40 hours of focus-group discussions and interviews that I conducted with 75 randomly selected white students and a survey of 514 students (65 percent white) at a large urban university with a primarily working- and middle-class student population;[4] second, the debates and concerns voiced in the popular and academic press illustrating how whiteness is currently defined.

The Erosion of White Invisibility

An underlying theoretical supposition of the current work on white racial identity is the belief that white racial hegemony has rendered whiteness invisible or transparent, functioning elusively as the racial norm and as the baseline to which all other racial groups are compared. The result of this racial dominance, as it is often argued, is that whites do not have to think about being white because white privilege and white standards are so culturally embedded that whiteness has been "naturalized." As the racial norm, being white or acknowledging one's whiteness need never be recognized or analyzed by whites because whites generally view themselves as the racial yardstick with which other racial groups are compared.

Many identity theorists and cultural critics argue that whites routinely see the "other" as a racialized subject but view themselves as colorless. Robert Terry, in perhaps the most straightforward explanation of white invisibility, argues that "to be white in America is not to have to think about it. Except for hard core racial supremacists, the meaning of being white is having the choice of attending to or ignoring one's own whiteness."[5]

In a recent article "White is a Color!" Leslie Roman argues that the word "race" has become a "reified synonym" for racially subordinate groups; in other words, whites need not think of themselves as a race because they are the "racial norm" in the United States.[6] From this perspective, whites are viewed as simultaneously being privileged by their skin color yet unable or unwilling to recognize the cultural and institutional conventions and practices that continue to normalize white invisibility. For bell hooks, this tendency among her white students is "their absence of racial recognition."[7] Richard Dyer argues that as a category, "white," in contrast to the many ways in which "blackness" is marked off culturally, "is not anything really, not an identity, not a particularizing quality, because it is everything."[8]

These reflections on white invisibility miss the contemporary process of white reconstruction taking place among a sizable part of the white population, particularly among young people. Whiteness is no longer invisible or transparent as a racial category because it is in crisis. Whiteness as the "normalizing" center with which other racial categories must be referenced and compared is no longer defensible or sustainable in the face of multiple attacks on white privilege by racially defined minorities. Russell Ferguson contends that as the socially constructed white center is challenged by groups historically pushed to margins, "the invisibility of the so-called center becomes harder to sustain."[9] It would be difficult to argue that the socially constructed white center has not been contested to varying degrees in most social spheres. Recently *Newsweek* and *Business Week* ran front-page feature articles on white men's "paranoid" worries about multiculturalism and on business efforts to diversify offices that historically have been completely white. The mainstream press would have its readers believe that the majority of white men feel they are under attack by anyone who is not white and male, even though the 47 percent of white males in the labor force account for almost 92 percent of corporate officers and 88 percent of corporate directors.[10] These facts, however, are often completely ignored, as illustrated by the comment of a retired business executive to a *Newsweek* reporter: "The white male is the most persecuted person in the United States." Another man, quoted in the *Business Week* story, was clearer about the reasons for his persecution: his crime was that he had the "wrong pigment, wrong plumbing."[11]

That many whites see themselves as victims of the multicultural, PC, feminist onslaught would be laughable if not for the sense of mental crisis and the reactionary backlash that underpin these beliefs. Nowhere has this backlash been more vicious than in academia. During the last four years universities have been embroiled in a divisive battle over what intellectual works define the collegiate canon. The movement to build an inclusive, multicultural, multiracial curriculum that reflects scholarship outside the traditional Western canon was met with fervent hostility and resistance as neoconservatives countered with the PC debate. The PC movement spawned conservative and partially legitimating organizations like the National Association of Scholars and Accuracy in Academia. What has been lost in the huge and continuing debate between liberal and conservative academics is the influence these campus curriculum wars have had on the white student population. Many white students did not experience these debates as a series of internecine pedagogical battles over political ideology or what authority will determine intellectual standards. Instead, these debates were interpreted by many as an economic burden, an attack on whiteness, and a form of punitive therapy.

Rather than embracing the values behind multiculturalism, many white students wanted to know if any race classes would become an additional requirement necessary for graduation. One white student explained to me that he would need to work more hours every week to take a class so he could be told that white people are racists. Viewed as a form of academic punishment for, as one student put it, "the sins of our grandfathers," new requirements addressing issues of race raise concerns of fairness, relevance, and the broader (and naive) charge that the "new" curriculum is politically biased. It is commonly assumed among many white students that any class that addresses issues of race or racism must necessarily be antiwhite. More specifically, students believe that the instructors of these classes will hold individual white students accountable for slavery, lynching, discrimination, and other heinous acts. Although these concerns may appear particular to the racial politics of an integrated college campus, I would argue that at least to some degree, they are distillations of what might be occurring outside the university. The Black Caucus, the NAACP, La Raza, the Racial Justice Act, issues of affirmative action, immigration, and the countless other race-based groups take on an antiwhite taint for many whites.

Many other students questioned the relevance of classes addressing issues of race. As one student put it, "It's bad enough I have to take American history, I don't want to have to take black history or black women's history because I don't see it's necessary for me. I mean, I'm just tired of hearing about it."

This student, and many others, were "tired of hearing about" the role whites have played in American racial history. Interviewees were also tired of the discomfort they experience when discussing these issues with nonwhites seated next to them in the classroom. When presented with the ugly details of white history, a common strategy was to ignore, or at least discount, past wrongs and dwell on the more egalitarian aspects of contemporary race relations. Luke, a sophomore, feels that race classes are no longer "necessary" in the 1990s: "Why is it still such a problem when everything is like over and done with since the sixties?"

It is a small leap from viewing university-sanctioned race-based curricula and social clubs as biased against whites to whites viewing themselves as targets because of their skin color. As Shannon explained,

> [Many blacks] don't want to talk to me because I'm white. They think that I'm racist. They are prejudging me. And I feel I have to be extra nice to them because I feel I am doing something wrong by being white. I feel like I am being racist because I am white. . . . I want them to know that I'm not racist because I don't want them to have to feel uncomfortable. But they make me feel uncomfortable because I think that they think I'm a racist.

Shannon's last line betrays an assumption that was expressed several times in different ways throughout my interviews. Many white students explained that they think about "being" white because, in their eyes, many blacks automatically see them as racist because they are white. In this way, whites could turn the tables on blacks by viewing them as racist, because, they believe, whites are being "prejudged" based on their skin color.[12] The tendency of many white students to blindly impute racist inclinations to other racial groups is sadly ironic. Many see themselves as being victimized by black racists when in reality they have constructed their own racist projections about what blacks think about whites. These projections are typically not based on firsthand accounts of social interaction with blacks; they are, for the most part, racist fantasies.

White Recognition

In such a racially charged environment it is difficult not to think about individual racial identity. As the first student quoted in this essay made clear, interacting in a multiracial environment has forced her to think about the relational nature of her racial identity. Elise, like the majority of students I surveyed, grew up and went to a high school in a neighborhood that was overwhelmingly white.[13] Part of her "feeling white" no doubt reflects the culture shock that indirectly results from the extensive residential segregation in the United States.[14]

This culture shock is intensified by Urban University's location in a poor, black section of the city, which has been ravaged by state neglect and deindustrialization. White students find themselves parking their cars in or emerging from public transportation into a neighborhood that is socioeconomically and racially quite different from what they are accustomed to. This racial disorientation explains, at least in part, the distorted view white students have of the size of racial groups on campus. In the survey portion of my project, white students described, on average, the racial distribution on campus as being 48 percent white, 31 percent black, 14 percent Asian, and 8 percent "other." Nearly 1 in 5 white students (19 percent) described

Urban University as being 70 percent or more nonwhite. In fact, Urban University is close to 70 percent white, not the other way around. The racial angst of being in a black section of the city seems to result in white students doubling and tripling the count of the nonwhite population. But commuting to campus cannot completely explain the hypervisibility of nonwhites. White students overestimated the percentage of the US population that is black, Asian, and "other" as well. The Census Bureau found that the "average American" (no doubt white) also overestimates the non-white proportion of the US population (Jews are also overestimated).[15] Race politics on campus might bring issues of white racial identity to the fore, but the college experience does not create racial identity out of whole cloth. The construction and acknowledgment of racial identity exist in many malleable, inchoate, and dynamic forms prior to a white student's arrival on campus. Perceiving whites as a smaller group and cultivating a sense of social vulnerability connotes one such social construction formed prior to the college experience.

One of the social-psychological results of segregated lives outside the university and integrated ones within it is that the majority of white students feel unsure of how to act around nonwhites. James put the dilemma this way:

> Walking across campus or, like if you're in a room someplace and it's mostly black, I just start to feel really nervous for no apparent reason. I mean, I start thinking, I'm white, and they're black. I will probably say something stupid and I'll slip—in the back of your mind that's always coming through—what to say and what not to say. It's almost like you can't talk to them honestly half the time because anything you might say might be taken up and turned around and stereotyped.

James's comments not only reflect the racial angst he experiences when in a multiracial environment but also provide evidence of the cultural baggage he has brought with him to campus. He says he feels "nervous for no apparent reason," although at the end of this quote he reveals the grounds for his fears; he must closely monitor what he says in black company for fear of being misinterpreted. James's racial anxiety stands in stark contrast to bell hooks's comment that in a racist society "white people can 'safely' imagine that they are invisible to black people."[16] The above remarks are not the ruminations of someone who sees himself as racially invisible but of someone who feels branded by his whiteness.

Contrary to hooks's views on the white imagination, Ruth Frankenberg's analysis of how race and gender intersect in the lives of white women seems more accurate to the situational and contradictory process of white racialization experienced by many white college students.

Frankenberg explains that "white people are 'raced' just as men are gendered."[17] After listening to white students voice the varied ways they get "raced," the explanatory powers of the invisibility thesis seem simplistic and anachronistic. There is also an inherent danger in believing whites can be racially invisible. As Coco Fusco points out, "Racial identities are not only Black, Asian American, and so on; they are also white. To ignore white ethnicity is to redouble its hegemony by naturalizing it."[18]

Identity Politics and White Consciousness

Lack of exposure to nonwhites only partially explains white identity and its de novo construction. Elise's acknowledgment of her whiteness is not just predicated on not being black or Asian—though clearly that is part of it. Whiteness understood through a dichotomy with what it is not glosses over the meanings that whites construct of and attach to "being" white.

The central question, then, is "How is whiteness as a social identity understood and constructed?" Are whites constructing an "essence," or, to borrow again from Dyer, developing their own "particularizing quality" as a racial category? Or is acknowledging whiteness, "feeling white," simply the antithesis of not being the racial "other"?

What seems to be taking place is a complex amalgamation of two often contradictory depictions of how whiteness is understood and articulated by white students. It is clear that racial identity politics has forced white students to think about their race and about what being white means culturally. Whiteness is unquestionably emerging, or more accurately mutating, in response to challenges from racially defined minorities.

In this way, the current construction of whiteness, at least among the young whites I talked with, can be viewed as being based on both a perception of current and future material deprivation and the need to delineate white culture in a nondemonized fashion. At the material level, the erosion of and challenge to white privilege and the status associated with those privileges by racially defined minorities has created an economic defensiveness on the part of whites. At the cultural level, many whites have reconstructed a white history and a set of interests that mark whiteness off as not something invisible, bland, or inherently evil but as a visible social category complete with its own sublime past and list of contemporary grievances. In this process, whiteness becomes acknowledged and reified as a positive social category, existing outside any specific historical or social context. White essentialism, the "particularizing quality" of what it means to be white, seems to be emerging among many white students in reaction to the contestation of white privilege and through the use of cultural stereotypes of nonwhites to point out what whites are not.[19] Below I address both the status threat to whites and the production of white culture.

Feeling Threatened, Becoming White

Much of the anger white students expressed stems from their belief that in a "colorblind" society, where maxims like "all men are created equal" are sacrosanct, race-based organizations are racist and "discriminatory" toward whites. The bifurcated white consciousness forged from the contradictions between ideal and real cultural expectations raises a troubling question for many whites: If the socioeconomic playing field has been leveled between whites and nonwhites, why must the majority of social interactions revolve around racial identity, and why should whites be the "new" losers in these exchanges? The cost of being white, at least for many white students I interviewed, was that the deck was now stacked against them in the labor market. Henry Louis Gates Jr. points out how racial consciousness and economic competition are inextricably linked. He explains that "race has become a trope of ultimate, irreducible difference between cultures, linguistic groups, or practitioners of specific belief systems, who more than not have fundamentally opposed economic interests."[20]

The view that there is now a social cost to being white was evident whenever issues of affirmative action on and off campus were discussed. The majority of white students believe affirmative action is unfair today because issues of overt racism, discrimination, and equal opportunity were addressed by their parents' generation in the 1960s. A majority of white students argued that we live in a meritocracy where nonwhites have every advantage whites do and, in some cases, more opportunity because of affirmative action. As Dolly told me about her job prospects, "White men are a dime a dozen, but to be a minority is gonna be—is—great right now." This zero-sum game mentality implies that what is "great" for minorities must be a handicap for whites.

Charlie summed up the whiteness-as-liability and the equal opportunity perspectives in this short statement:

> I don't know why they have to keep bringing it up, you know, keep causing stuff—well, we were slaves. You weren't a slave. Your great, great, great, great, great, great, great-grandparents were slaves. There is no reason to cause a fight now. You know like Michael Jordan is like one of the highest paid athletes in the sports business. . . . He gets paid more than the president. Michael Jackson. Look at his house. You know. You're black, you're white, you're Hispanic, you're Asian. You can do it, too.

Like so many other students, Charlie wants to believe the United States is an egalitarian, colorblind society because to think otherwise would raise the irritating issue of white privilege. The working- and middle-class students I interviewed do not see themselves as privileged or benefiting from their skin color. It becomes difficult for working-class college students to think about white privilege when they are accumulating college debt, forced to live with their parents, working 25 hours a week, and concerned that K-Mart or the Gap may become their future employer.

The perception that a racial double standard exists on campus is commonplace. In the majority of my interviews and focus groups, white students asserted that race-based organizations on Urban University's campus are a form of reverse discrimination. Last academic year, 29 out of 119 student organizations on campus used race as their primary organizing principle. Mainly cultural and political, these organizations encourage an affirmation of racial identity and provide a safe, supportive space for students of color to develop social and professional networks. However, the latent effect of these organizations is that they may transform and contribute to redefining the meaning of racial identity for whites on campus. When they are excluded from these organizations, white students get a taste of what it is like to be reduced to a racial category. They are generally unnerved by this experience and quickly slip into reactionary, defensive postures. The resentment, anger, and frustration that white students express at being excluded provide the foundation for a white identity based on the belief that whites are now under siege.

Student organizations like the Black Pre-Law Society or the Korean Cultural Club were sanctioned by the university, but, as was said many times in my interviews, if whites tried to establish an organization and it had "white" in the title, a major controversy would ensue and the group and its members would be labeled racist.[21] The resentment that results from a sense of exclusion was voiced by these two students in a focus group:

> TOM: But it's not like they're discriminated anymore, it's like the majority is now the minority because we are the ones being discriminated against because we are boxed in. We can't have anything for ourselves anymore that says exclusively white or anything like that. But everyone else can.
> KIA: Can't we have the United Caucasian College Fund?

The Political Construction of White Culture

For many of the white students I interviewed, "being" white requires a raison d'être that eschews both the idea of white privilege and identification as the oppressor group. Finding a legitimate, positive narrative of one's own whiteness was accomplished by constructing an identity that negated white oppressor charges and framed whiteness as a liability. This inversion involved a description of the United States as the land of equal opportunity, especially for nonwhites. As the argument was given, being white—historically unproblematic—has now become a general liability in various social settings, particularly the labor market. The whiteness-as-liability perspective was characterized as affecting material circumstances, but many white students also felt the "ability" to be white was being silenced.

The majority of students seldom had to negotiate being white on a daily basis until they found themselves in a multiracial environment. Within this setting, white consciousness was raised only to be perceived by many white students as being repressed by campus racial politics. One student summed up her frustration with what she viewed as the double standard of race-based groups on campus by explaining, "You're not allowed to be white." Another student commented, "You can be proud of your religion but you can't be proud [she pauses], you can't be like I'm white and I'm proud, I'm white." Unfortunately, for many white students the sense that their racial identity is being repressed in some conspiratorial way is channeled into intense resentment toward other racial groups on campus. Perhaps more importantly, it also appears to be leading to the development of a white consciousness complete with its own interests and agenda.

Suppression of the ability to "be" white has raised group consciousness among many young whites in ways that mirror the coalition building that has historically taken place among nonwhites. Culturally distinct groups have been galvanized politically around racial categories through a mobilization Yen Le Espiritu describes as "panethnicity," which refers to a political and cultural "collectivity made up of peoples of several, hitherto distinct, tribal or national origins."[22] The "racial lumping" that occurs from outside and within these ethnic collectives is the essence of race-based identity politics. Political mobilization of racial minorities in the last two decades has produced hundreds of race-based organizations, which, according to Todd Gitlin, have resulted in a "thickening" of identity politics. Gitlin's description of why identity politics is important to young people at this particular moment is instructive, because it identifies politics as being instrumental in the forging of ethnic and racial identities. He suggests that "identity politics presents itself as—and many students and other young people experience it as—the most compelling remedy for the anonymity in an otherwise impersonal world."[23]

Gitlin's critique that "anatomy becomes destiny" on university campuses and in the political sphere raises several troubling questions about the future of race politics as they pertain to the development of white identity. Many young whites refuse to feel in any way responsible for the role whites have played in US race relations. The common response "I don't feel responsible for my father's sins" reflects this sentiment. Or as another student put it, "The slavery thing happened so long ago, they can't keep prosecuting us—I don't even know if my ancestors were here then, so I'm kind of sick of keeping that held against me."

Perhaps more troubling than their denial of US racial history is white students' belief that they in no way benefit from their skin color. This was not, however, considered a form of racism among white students. The idea that things are rough for everyone allowed white students to equate their life chances with those of racial minorities. It seems that for much of the Woodstock '94 generation, white guilt about the state of race relations has given way to white stigmatization for both white privilege and its loss. Believing, to quote another student, that "opportunity is equal for everyone" allows white guilt to be removed from any analysis of race relations.

The generation of students who were just starting elementary school when Reagan took office in 1980 are now in college, rejecting any stigma associated with being white. The racial logic of a colorblind society promoted by the Reagan and Bush administrations helps white students espouse an ideology that appears race-neutral but maintains the racial status quo. Embracing a colorblind view of race relations enables a retreat from issues that have their roots in racial inequality while allowing white students to benefit from, as Du Bois put it, the additional "public and psychological" wages that accrue to whites because of their skin color. With anxieties similar to those experienced by many southern whites during Reconstruction, many white students today view the contestation of white privilege as having resulted in a decline in their "public and psychological" wages, which once took the form of complete social and economic deference by nonwhites to even the poorest whites.[24] The "white man's burden" has been resurrected for the turn of the twentieth century, only now it is whites claiming the status of victim.

Perhaps ironically, a common reaction of white students, which may be simultaneously defensive, posturing, and yearning for a more positive articulation of whiteness, came through in what I call "immigrant tales."[25] For the majority of the subjects in my study, little is left in the way of ethnic solidarity, ethnic identity, or even symbolic nostalgia for the ethnic traditions of their older kin. When asked to define themselves in ethnic or racial terms (or both), the majority of students labeled themselves as white or Caucasian, ignoring labels such as Italian American. Like most whites their age, these students have undergone such extensive generational assimilation and convergence of cultural experiences that a few chose to describe themselves as "plain old American," "mutt," or "nothing." The young whites I interviewed are so removed from the immigrant experience that even the small minority who defined themselves in ethnic terms acknowledged that their ethnicity is in name only. As one student remarked, he thinks of his mixed Polish heritage only when he eats kielbasa at Christmas. Ethnicity is a subjective series of choices or, as Mary Waters writes, an "option" in constructing an identity. However, the majority of white students I interviewed and surveyed come from families where very little in the way of "ethnic options" exists because the symbolic ethnic practices have all but died out.[26]

Interestingly, the only reference to personal histories with ethnic character occurred when questions about affirmative action were raised. White students have heard stories of struggling grandparents or great-grandparents and, as a defense mechanism, tap their experiences to suggest that no single group has a monopoly on being a victim. In this way young whites selectively resurrect their ethnicity through "immigrant tales" when they believe white privilege is being contested, even though their perceived ethnic history does not necessarily originate from Poland, Italy, or Ireland, for instance, but from a generalized idea of Europe.[27]

This common, yet fuzzy, connection to the European "old country" provides the historical backdrop and cultural space for the construction of white identity, or as Bob Blauner points out, "a yearning for a usable past."[28] As the importance of ethnicity wanes in the lives of young whites, the immigration experience of older (or dead) kin becomes a mythological narrative providing a historical common denominator of passage, victimization, and assimilation. As white students often tell it, blacks can point to the middle passage and slavery, the Japanese and Chinese can speak of internment and forced labor, respectively, and whites have the immigrant experience. Insofar as past group victimization or hardship is part of the American experience, young whites, when confronted by real or perceived charges of racism, can point to the mistreatment of their older relatives when they were newly arrived immigrants to the United States.

Many white ethnics did experience prejudice and discrimination when they arrived in the United States, but it is unlikely that young whites today experience anything remotely similar. Despite the white ethnic revival movement of the 1960s and 1970s, it is impossible to politically mobilize young whites around their ethnicity because, unlike their parents or their grandparents, they no longer possess an ethnic identity.

The choice of *white* or *Caucasian* as a social label for the majority of white students in my survey also points to a fundamental questioning of what being *American* now means. Toni Morrison argues that, unlike in other countries where both race and nation need to be articulated (for example, by white South Africans), in the United States being "American means white."[29] The majority of students in my survey labeled themselves white or Caucasian, not American. The students that did use *American* in their self-descriptions were more likely to use it as part of a longer title, such as white Italian American or Caucasian Irish American. Bob Blauner sees *American* as no longer being the linguistic property of whites, because the term *white* is too stigmatized for everyday use. He contends that "'white' itself is a racial term and thereby inevitably associated with our nation's legacy of social injustice." If whites view *American* and *white* as interchangeable, it seems *American* as a label would have been a common response. It was not. Moreover, the perception of lost status and racial persecution now allows white students to use the term *white* without mustering up any historical baggage. The small but visible gains racial minorities have made politically and economically require whites to broaden their definition of who is American. Perhaps the statement "American used to mean white" might better reflect the mythological white halcyon days many whites wish to return to and the angst many whites feel about their current status relative to other racial groups.

Smells Like White Essence

Like all racial categories, whiteness is capable of being "created, inhabited, transformed and destroyed."[30] Yet until quite recently, the multiple ways in which whiteness has been politically manipulated, culturally mediated, and historically constructed have in large part been ignored.[31]

Ignoring the ways in which whites "get raced" has the makings of something politically dangerous. A fundamental transformation of how young whites define and understand themselves racially is taking place. The white students I interviewed have generally embraced the belief that the US class system is fair and equitable. Most students argued that individuals who delay gratification, work hard, and follow the rules will succeed, irrespective of their color.[32] Black TV stars, the media's treatment of the black middle class, and stereotypes of Asians as model minorities have provided young whites with countless nonwhite success stories. For many whites the leveled playing field argument has rendered affirmative action policies a form of reverse discrimination and source of resentment. White students who believe social equality has been achieved are able to assert a racial identity without regarding themselves as racist, because they see themselves as merely affirming their identity through language and actions—something racially defined groups do frequently. On the individual level, the racism most prevalent in my interviews was not the cultural stereotypes some white students used to counter charges of white privilege but the racist projections many made about how blacks perceive whites.

White identity is not only a reaction to the entrance of historically marginalized racial and ethnic groups into the political arena and the ensuing struggle over social resources. Whiteness as an explicit cultural product may be taking on a life of its own, developing its own racial logics and essences as it is molded by the political right. The rhetoric of neoconservatives serves to legitimate the benefits that accrue to whites based on skin color. Starting with the false premise of social equality and equal opportunity, conservatives can speak of America's Western roots and traditions in racial terms but not appear racist. This ostensibly nonracist white space being carved out of our cultural landscape allows whites to be presented as just another racial contender in the struggle over political and cultural resources and self-definition. When George Will explained that a Eurocentricity should be the cultural norm "in American curricula and consciousness, because it accords with the facts of our history,"[33] he could argue he was not being racist, but defending the place of white "values" and whites' contributions in the shaping of "our" history. As a key speaker at the 1992 Republican National Convention, Patrick Buchanan could argue he was defending the values of the "average American," who just happens to be Christian, heterosexual, middle-class, and white. David Duke was able to capture 55 percent of the white vote in his race for governor of Louisiana by ditching his Ku Klux Klan hate rhetoric and reinventing himself as someone who understood the economic plight of the white "everyman."

If, as the argument goes, Latinos, blacks, and Asians can fight for their roots and voice in American history, why can't whites? The history of the West and whites' place in that history are being sanitized and rewritten as a palatable "best-of-whites" anthology. In a recent interview, James Q. Wilson picks through a long history of Western colonialism and terror only to tell his readers it was the West that "provided the principal basis for attacking slavery."[34]

The explicit reinsertion of whiteness into politics is possible only by creating the illusion that being white is no different than belonging to any other racial group in the United States. If that illusion can be maintained, a white identity and white culture modeled on a Disney America theme park, with its purified historic revisionism, will allow whites to reinvent a cultural history that does not evoke such matters as the Ku Klux Klan or Japanese internment during World War II but instead is synonymous with egalitarianism, rugged individualism, and democracy.

Not fathoming the privileges accorded to white skin in the United States is quite different from being invisible or colorless. No doubt many whites do not think about their whiteness, but I would argue that they are increasingly in the minority. Whiteness must be addressed because the politics of race, from campus clubs to issues of crime to representation in the statehouse, permeate almost every social exchange.[35] I do not share the sanguine projections recently raised by Michael Omi and Howard Winant in this journal about the future of white identity.[36] They suggest that as whiteness becomes more visible, this need not result in a "reactionary" form of social identity. Quite the contrary: many young whites, particularly those in the working classes, are anxious. They believe the American dream of social mobility has stopped or at least stalled with their generation. They have heard countless times that their generation will be the first not to replicate, let alone surpass, their parents' class position. There is no "left" left that has been able to reach out and satisfactorily address young whites' insecurities regarding their future. Nor has the left been able to successfully challenge the racially coded and divisive rhetoric of the neoconservatives. Given the right's cynical manipulation of racial anxieties and the sheer ubiquitousness of race in the American psyche, the next generation of white adults may choose, or feel forced, to develop solidarity in their whiteness.

Notes

[1] All names have been changed to ensure students' confidentiality.

[2] Cornel West, "The New Cultural Politics of Difference," in *The Cultural Studies Reader,* ed. Simon During (New York: Routledge, 1993), p. 212.

[3] I employ Omi and Winant's term of "racialization" to mean the political and social construction of racial categories and racial meaning where none had previously existed (Michael Omi and Howard Winant, *Racial Formation in the United States: From the 1960's to the 1980's,* 2d ed. (New York: Routledge, 1994).

[4] The limits of this essay should be made clear at the start. I have not addressed how gender and students' class backgrounds affect the construction of whiteness. This is not an oversight but reflects the point I have reached in my research. It should also be noted that most of the comparisons are black/white. White students had much more to say about blacks than they did about other racial groups. These issues will be addressed in future writings.

[5] Robert W. Terry, "The Negative Impact on White Values," in *Impacts of Racism on White Americans,* ed. Benjamin P. Bowser and Raymond G. Hunt (Beverly Hills, CA: Sage, 1981), p. 120.

[6] Leslie G. Roman, "White is a Color! White Defensiveness, Postmodernism, and Anti-Racist Pedagogy," in *Race, Identity and Representation in Education,* ed. Cameron McCarthy (New York: Routledge, 1993), p. 72.

[7] bell hooks, *Black Looks: Race and Representation* (Boston: South End, 1992), p. 167.

[8] Isaac Julien and Kobena Mercer, "Introduction: De Margin and De Center," *Screen* 29, no. 4 (autumn 1988): p. 6.

[9] Russell Ferguson, "Introduction: The Invisible Center," in *Out There: Marginalization and Contemporary Cultures,* ed. Martha Gever, Russell Ferguson, Trinh T. Minh-ha, and Cornel West (Cambridge: MIT Press, 1990), p. 10.

[10] David Gates, "White Male Paranoia," *Newsweek,* Mar. 29, 1993, pp. 48–53; Michelle Green and Ann Palmer, "White, Male, and Worried," *Business Week,* Jan. 31, 1994, pp. 50–55.

[11] Ibid.

[12] In its broadest sense, racism refers to the assigning of attitudes, behaviors, and abilities to individuals or groups based on skin color and includes the institutional arrangements that privilege one group over another and the ideological apparatus that perpetuates and makes those arrangements possible.

[13] Of the students I surveyed, 65 percent grew up in neighborhoods that were at least 95 percent white. Another 24 percent lived in neighborhoods that were 65 to 94 percent white.

[14] See Douglas S. Massey and Nancy A. Denton, *American Apartheid: Segregation and the Making of the Underclass* (Cambridge, MA: Harvard University Press, 1993).

[15] Richard Nadeau, Richard Niemi, and Jeffrey Levine, "Innumeracy about Minority Populations," *Public Opinion Quarterly* 57: pp. 332–347.

[16] hooks, p. 168.

[17] Ruth Frankenberg, *White Women, Race Matters: The Social Construction of Whiteness* (Minneapolis: University of Minnesota Press, 1993), p. 1.

[18] Cited in David Roediger, *The Wages of Whiteness* (New York: Verso, 1991), p. 6.

[19] Omi and Winant define essentialism as "the belief in real, true human essences, existing outside or impervious to social and historical context" (p. 187 n. 57).

[20] Henry Louis Gates Jr., *Loose Canons: Notes of the Cultural Wars* (New York: Oxford University Press, 1992), p. 49.

[21] A White Student Union was briefly formed on campus but quickly folded.

[22] Yen Le Espiritu, *Asian American Panethnicity: Bridging Institutions and Identities* (Philadelphia: Temple University Press, 1993), p. 2.

[23] Todd Gitlin, "From Universality to Difference: Notes on the Fragmentation of the Idea of the Left," *Contention* 2, no. 2 (winter 1993): p. 18.

[24] W. E. B. Du Bois, *Black Reconstruction in America, 1860–1880* (New York: Atheneum, 1975), p. 700.

[25] I am indebted to Kevin Delaney for suggesting this term and allowing me to claim it as my own.

[26] Mary Waters, *Ethnic Options: Choosing Identities in America* (Berkeley: University of Califorinia Press, 1990).

[27] Richard Alba explores the idea of "European American" in *Ethnic Identity: The Transformation of White America* (New Haven, CT: Yale University Press, 1990). In a discussion I had with Professor Alba, he suggested that "white" as a label carries with it too much stigma. This may be true for the older white ethnics, but it may not represent the way young whites construct their identity.

[28] Bob Blauner, "Talking Past Each Other: Black and White Languages of Race," in *Race and Ethnic Conflict,* ed. Howard J. Ehrlich and Fred L. Pincus (New York: Westview, 1994), p. 27.

[29] Toni Morrison, *Playing in the Dark: Whiteness and the Literary Imagination* (Cambridge, MA: Harvard University Press, 1992), p. 47.

[30] Omi and Winant, p. 55.

[31] See Roediger, *The Wages of Whiteness* and *Towards the Abolition of Whiteness* (New York: Verso, 1994); Alexander Saxton, *The Rise and Fall of the White Republic* (New York: Verso, 1990); and Frankenberg.

[32] James R. Kluegal and Eliot R. Smith, *Beliefs about Inequality: Americans' Views of What Is and What Ought to Be* (New York: Aldine, 1986).

[33] Cameron McCarthy, "After the Canon: Knowledge and the Ideological Representation in the Multicultural Discourse on Curriculum Reform," in *Race, Identity and Representation in Education,* ed. Warren Crichlow and Cameron McCarthy (New York: Routledge, 1993), p. 294.

[34] James Q. Wilson, "The New Old Fashioned Morality: Eurocentric and Proud," *National Times,* Jan. 1994, p. 69.

[35] Thomas Edsall and Mary Edsall, *Chain Reaction: The Impact of Race Rights and Taxes on American Politics* (New York: Norton, 1991).

[36] Michael Omi and Howard Winant, "Responses," *Socialist Review* 23, no. 3 (1994): p. 131.

Taking Back the Center

Trina Grillo and Stephanie M. Wildman

Study Question

1. Would you say that the tactics "white" people are using in their efforts to "take back the center" help or hurt the progress toward integration?

White supremacy creates in whites the expectation that issues of concern to them will be central in every discourse. Analogies serve to perpetuate this expectation of centrality. The center-stage problem occurs because dominant group members are already accustomed to being on center-stage. They have been treated that way by society; it feels natural, comfortable, and in the order of things.

The harms of discrimination include not only the easily identified disadvantages of the victims (such as exclusion from housing and jobs) and the stigma imposed by the dominant culture, but also the advantages given to those who are not its victims. The white, male, heterosexual societal norm is privileged in such a way that its privilege is rendered invisible. As Kimberlé Crenshaw explained:

> According to the dominant view, a discriminator treats all people within a race or sex category similarly. Any significant experiential or statistical variation within this group suggests . . . that the group is not being discriminated against. . . . Race and sex, moreover, become significant only when they operate to explicitly *disadvantage* the victims; because the *privileging* of whiteness or maleness is implicit, it is generally not perceived at all.[1]

Because whiteness is the norm, it is easy to forget that it is not the only perspective. Thus, members of dominant groups assume that their perceptions are the pertinent perceptions, that their problems are the problems that need to be addressed, and that in discourse they should be the speaker rather than the listener.[2] Part of being a member of a privileged group is being the center and the subject of all inquiry in which people of color or other non-privileged groups are the objects.[3]

So strong is this expectation of holding center-stage that even when a time and place are specifically designated for members of a non-privileged group to be central, members of the dominant group will often attempt to take back the pivotal focus. They are stealing the center[4]—usually with a complete lack of self-consciousness.[5]

This phenomenon occurred at the annual meeting of Law and Society, where three scholars, all people of color, were invited to speak to the plenary session about how universities might become truly multicultural. Even before the dialogue began, the views of many members of the organization were apparent by their presence or absence at the session. The audience included nearly every person of color who was attending the meeting, yet many whites chose not to attend.

When people who are not regarded as entitled to the center move into it, however briefly, they are viewed as usurpers. One reaction of the group temporarily deprived of the center is to make sure that nothing remains for the perceived usurpers to be in the center of. Thus, the whites who did not attend the plenary session, but who would have attended had there been more traditional (i.e., white) speakers, did so in part because they were exercising their privilege not to think in terms of race, and in part because they resented the "out groups" having the center.

Another tactic used by the dominant group is to steal back the center, using guerilla tactics where necessary. For example, during a talk devoted to the integration of multicultural materials into the core curriculum, a white man got up from the front row and walked noisily to the rear of the room. He then paced the room in a distracting fashion and finally returned to his seat. During the question period he was the first to rise, leaping to his feet to ask a lengthy, rambling, question about how multicultural materials could be added to university curricula without disturbing the "canon"—the exact subject of the talk he had just, apparently, not listened to.

The speaker answered politely and explained how he had assigned a Navajo creation myth to accompany St. Augustine, which highlighted Augustine's paganism and resulted in each reading enriching the other. He refrained, however, from calling attention to the questioner's rude behavior during the meeting, to his asking the already-answered question, or to his presumption that the material the questioner saw as most relevant to his own life was central and "canonized," while all other reading was peripheral, and, hence, dispensable.

Analogies offer protection for the traditional center. At another gathering of law professors—the annual meeting of the American Association of Law Schools—issues of racism, sexism, and homophobia were the focus of the plenary session for the first time in the organization's history. Again at this session, the number of white males present was far fewer than would ordinarily attend such a session. After moving presentations by an African-American woman, an Hispanic man, and a gay white man who each opened their hearts on these subjects, a question and dialogue period began.

The first speaker to rise was a white woman, who, after saying that she did not mean to change the topic, said that she wanted to discuss another sort of oppression—that of law professors in the less elite schools. As professors from what is perceived by some as a less-than-elite school, we agree that the topic is important and it would have interested us at another time, on another day. But this questioner had succeeded in depriving the other issues of time devoted (after much struggle) specifically to them, and turned the spotlight once again onto her own concerns. She did this, we believe, not out of malice, but because she too had become a victim of analogical thinking.

The problem of taking back the center exists apart from the issue of analogies; it will be with us as long as any group expects, and is led to expect, to be constantly the center of attention.

Notes

[1] Crenshaw, *supra* note 7, at 150–51.

[2] *See* Wildman, *The Question of Silence: Techniques to Ensure Full Class Participation,* 38 J. LEGAL EDUC. 147, 149–50 (1988).

[3] *See* HOOKS, *supra* note 3, at 43 (discussing liberation struggles initiated when people seen as objects "assert that they are subjects").

[4] Parents of young children who try to have a telephone conversation will easily recognize this phenomenon. At the sound of the parent's voice on the phone, the child materializes from the far reaches of the house to demand attention.

[5] For an interesting discussion of how law contributes to our vision of reality and our self-consciousness, *see* Reich, *Law and Consciousness,* 10 CARDOZO L. REV. 77 (1988).

PLESSY V. FERGUSON

May 18, 1896
163 U.S. 537 (1896)

THE U.S. SUPREME COURT

Study Questions

1. One of Plessy's attorneys, Albion Tourgee, argued "Probably most white persons if given a choice, would prefer death to life in the United States *as colored persons*." What does this say about the status "white" relative to the status "color/black" in the United States in 1896?
2. What do you think other people should think and understand when they learn that Plessy's African heritage (physically he appeared to be white) had to be brought to the attention of the court?

MR. JUSTICE BROWN, after stating the case, delivered the opinion of the court.

This case turns upon the constitutionality of an act of the General Assembly of the State of Louisiana, passed in 1890, providing for separate railway carriages for the white and colored races. Acts 1890, No. 111, p. 152.

The first section of the statute enacts "that all railway companies carrying passengers in their coaches in this State, shall provide equal but separate accommodations for the white, and colored races, by providing two or more passenger coaches for each passenger train, or by dividing the passenger coaches by a partition so as to secure separate accommodations: *Provided,* That this section shall not be construed to apply to street railroads. No person or persons, shall be admitted to occupy seats in coaches, other than, the ones, assigned, to them on account of the race they belong to."

By the second section it was enacted "that the officers of such passenger trains shall have power and are hereby required to assign each passenger to the coach or compartment used for the race to which such passenger belongs; any passenger insisting on going into a coach or compartment to which by race he does not belong, shall be liable to a fine of twenty-five dollars, or in lieu thereof to imprisonment for a period of not more than twenty days in the parish prison, and any officer of any railroad insisting on assigning a passenger to a coach or compartment other than the one set aside for the race to which said passenger belongs, shall be liable to a fine of twenty-five dollars, or in lieu thereof to imprisonment for a period of not more than twenty days in the parish prison; and should any passenger refuse to occupy the coach or compartment to which he or she is assigned by the officer of such railway, said officer shall have power to refuse to carry such passenger on his train, and for such refusal neither he nor the railway company which he represents shall be liable for damages in any of the courts of this State."

The third section provides penalties for the refusal or neglect of the officers, directors, conductors and employés of railway companies to comply with the act, with a proviso that "nothing in this act shall be construed as applying to nurses attending children of the other race." The fourth section is immaterial.

The information filed in the criminal District Court charged in substance that Plessy, being a passenger between two stations within the State of Louisiana, was assigned by officers of the company to the coach used for the race to which he belonged, but he insisted upon going into a coach used by the race to which he did not belong. Neither in the information nor plea was his particular race or color averred.

The petition for the writ of prohibition averred that petitioner was seven eighths Caucasian and one eighth African blood; that the mixture of colored blood was not discernible in him, and that he was entitled to every right, privilege and immunity secured to citizens of the United States of the white race; and that, upon such theory, he took possession of a vacant seat in a coach where passengers of the white race were accommodated, and was ordered by the conductor to vacate said coach and take a seat in another assigned to persons of the colored race, and having refused to comply with such demand he was forcibly ejected with the aid of a police officer, and imprisoned in the parish jail to answer a charge of having violated the above act.

The constitutionality of this act is attacked upon the ground that it conflicts both with the Thirteenth Amendment of the Constitution, abolishing slavery, and the Fourteenth Amendment, which prohibits certain restrictive legislation on the part of the States.

1. That it does not conflict with the Thirteenth Amendment, which abolished slavery and involuntary servitude, except as a punishment for crime, is too clear for argument. Slavery implies involuntary servitude—a state of bondage; the ownership of mankind as a chattel, or at least the control of the labor and services of one man for the benefit of another, and the absence of a legal right to the disposal of his own person, property and services. This amendment was said in the *Slaughter-house cases,* 16 Wall. 35, to have been intended primarily to abolish slavery, as it had been previously known in this country, and that it equally forbade Mexican peonage or the Chinese coolie trade, when they amounted to slavery or involuntary servitude, and that the use of the word "servitude" was intended to prohibit the use of all forms of involuntary slavery, of whatever class or name.

It was intimated, however, in that case that this amendment was regarded by the statesmen of that day as insufficient to protect the colored race from certain laws which had been enacted in the Southern States, imposing upon the colored race onerous disabilities and burdens, and curtailing their rights in the pursuit of life, liberty and property to such an extent that their freedom was of little value; and that the Fourteenth Amendment was devised to meet this exigency.

So, too, in the *Civil Rights cases,* 109 U.S. 3, 24, it was said that the act of a mere individual, the owner of an inn, a public conveyance or place of amusement, refusing accommodations to colored people, cannot be justly regarded as imposing any badge of slavery or servitude upon the applicant, but only as involving an ordinary civil injury, properly cognizable by the laws of the State, and presumably subject to redress by those laws until the contrary appears. "It would be running the slavery argument into the ground," said Mr. Justice Bradley, "to make it apply to every act of discrimination which a person may see fit to make as to the guests he will entertain, or as to the people he will take into his coach or cab or car, or admit to his concert or theatre, or deal with in other matters of intercourse or business."

A statute which implies merely a legal distinction between the white and colored races—a distinction which is founded in the color of the two races, and which must always exist so long as white men are distinguished from the other race by color—has no tendency to destroy the legal equality of the two races, or reestablish a state of involuntary servitude. Indeed, we do not understand that the Thirteenth Amendment is strenuously relied upon by the plaintiff in error in this connection.

2. By the Fourteenth Amendment, all persons born or naturalized in the United States, and subject to the jurisdiction thereof, are made citizens of the United States and of the State wherein they reside; and the States are forbidden from making or enforcing any law which shall abridge the privileges or immunities of citizens of the United States, or shall deprive any person of life, liberty or property without due process of law, or deny to any person within their jurisdiction the equal protection of the laws.

The proper construction of this amendment was first called to the attention of this court in the *Slaughter-house cases,* 16 Wall. 36, which involved, however, not a question of race, but one of exclusive privileges. The case did not call for any expression of opinion as to the exact rights it was intended to secure to the colored race, but it was said generally that its main purpose was to establish the citizenship of the negro; to give definitions of citizenship of the United States and of the States, and to protect from the hostile legislation of the States the privileges and immunities of citizens of the United States, as distinguished from those of citizens of the States.

The object of the amendment was undoubtedly to enforce the absolute equality of the two races before the law, but in the nature of things it could not have been intended to abolish distinctions based upon color, or to enforce social, as distinguished from political, equality, or a commingling of the two races upon terms unsatisfactory to either. Laws permitting, and even requiring, their separation in places where they are liable to be brought into contact do not necessarily imply the inferiority of either race to the other, and have been generally, if not universally, recognized as within the competency of the state legislatures in the exercise of their police power. The most common instance of this is connected with the establishment of separate schools for white and colored children, which has been held to be a valid exercise of the legislative power even by courts of States where the political rights of the colored race have been longest and most earnestly enforced.

One of the earliest of these cases is that of *Roberts v. City of Boston,* 5 Cush. 198, in which the Supreme Judicial Court of Massachusetts held that the general school committee of Boston had power to make provision for the instruction of colored children in separate schools established exclusively for them, and to prohibit their attendance upon the other schools. . . .

Similar laws have been enacted by Congress under its general power of legislation over the District of Columbia, Rev. Stat. D.C. §§ 281, 282, 283, 310, 319, as well as by the legislatures of many of the States, and have been generally, if not uniformly, sustained by the courts. *State v. McCann,* 21 Ohio St. 198; *Lehew v. Brummell,* 15 S. W. Rep. 765; *Ward v. Flood,* 48 California, 36; *Bertonneau v. School Directors,* 3 Woods, 177; *People v. Gallagher,* 93 N.Y. 438; *Cory v. Carter,* 48 Indiana, 327; *Dawson v. Lee,* 83 Kentucky, 49.

Laws forbidding the intermarriage of the two races may be said in a technical sense to interfere with the freedom of contract, and yet have been universally recognized as within the police power of the State. *State v. Gibson,* 36 Indiana, 389.

The distinction between laws interfering with the political equality of the negro and those requiring the separation of the two races in schools, theatres and railway carriages has been frequently drawn by this court. Thus in *Strauder v. West Virginia,* 100 U.S. 303, it was held that a law of West Virginia limiting to white male persons, 21 years of age and citizens of the State, the right to sit upon juries, was a discrimination which implied a legal inferiority in civil society, which lessened the security of the right of the colored race, and was a step toward reducing them to a condition of servility. Indeed, the right of a colored man that, in the selection of jurors to pass upon his life, liberty and property, there shall be no exclusion of his race, and no discrimination against them because of color, has been asserted in a number of cases. *Virginia v. Rives,* 100 U.S. 313; *Neal v. Delaware,* 103 U.S. 370; *Bush v. Kentucky,* 107 U.S. 110; *Gibson v. Mississippi,* 162 U.S. 565. So, where the laws of a particular locality or the charter of a particular railway corporation has provided that no person shall be excluded from the cars on account of color, we have held that this meant that persons of color should travel in the same car as white ones, and that the enactment was not satisfied by the company's providing cars assigned exclusively to people of color, though they were as good as those which they assigned exclusively to white persons. *Railroad Company v. Brown,* 17 Wall. 445.

Upon the other hand, where a statute of Louisiana required those engaged in the transportation of passengers among the States to give to all persons travelling within that State, upon vessels employed in that business, equal rights and privileges in all parts of the vessel, without distinction on account of race or color, and subjected to an action for damages the owner of such a vessel, who excluded colored passengers on account of their color from the cabin set aside by him for the use of whites, it was held to be so far as it applied to interstate commerce, unconstitutional and void. *Hall v. De Cuir,* 95 U.S. 485. The court in this case, however, expressly disclaimed that it had anything whatever to do with the statute as a regulation of internal commerce, or affecting anything else than commerce among the States.

In the *Civil Rights case,* 109 U.S. 3, it was held that an act of Congress, entitling all persons within the jurisdiction of the United States to the full and equal enjoyment of the accommodations, advantages, facilities and privileges of inns, public conveyances, on land or water, theatres and other places of public amusement, and made applicable to citizens of every race and color, regardless of any previous condition of servitude, was unconstitutional and void, upon the ground that the Fourteenth Amendment was prohibitory upon the States only, and the legislation authorized to be adopted by Congress for enforcing it was not direct legislation on matters respecting which the States were prohibited from making or enforcing certain laws, or doing certain acts, but was corrective legislation, such as might be necessary or proper for counteracting and redressing the effect of such laws or acts. In delivering the opinion of the court Mr. Justice Bradley observed that the Fourteenth Amendment "does not invest Congress with power to legislate upon subjects that are within the domain of state legislation; but to provide modes of relief against state legislation, or state action, of the kind referred to. It does not authorize Congress to create a code of municipal law for the regulation of private rights; but to provide modes of redress against the operation of state laws, and the action of state officers, executive or judicial, when these are subversive of the fundamental rights specified in the amendment. Positive rights and privileges are undoubtedly secured by the Fourteenth Amendment; but they are secured by way of prohibition against state laws and state proceedings affecting those rights and privileges, and by power given to Congress to legislate for the purpose of carrying such prohibition into effect; and such legislation must necessarily be predicated upon such supposed state laws or state proceedings, and be directed to the correction of their operation and effect."

Much nearer, and, indeed, almost directly in point, is the case of the *Louisville, New Orleans & c. Railway v. Mississippi,* 133 U.S. 587, wherein the railway company was indicted for a violation of a statute of Mississippi, enacting that all railroads carrying passengers should provide equal, but separate, accommodations for the white and colored races, by providing two or more passenger cars for each passenger train, or by dividing the passenger cars by a partition, so as to secure separate accommodations. The case was presented in a different aspect from the one under consideration, inasmuch as it was an indictment against the railway company for failing to provide the separate accommodations, but the question considered was the constitutionality of the law. In that case, the Supreme Court of Mississippi, 66 Mississippi, 662, had held that the statute applied solely to commerce within the State, and, that being the construction of the state statute by its highest court, was accepted as conclusive. "If it be a matter," said the court, p. 591, "respecting commerce wholly within a State, and not interfering with commerce between the States, then, obviously, there is no violation of the commerce clause of the Federal Constitution. . . . No question arises under this section, as to the power of the State to separate in different compartments interstate passengers, or affect, in any manner, the privileges and rights of such passengers. All that we can consider is, whether the State has the power to require that railroad trains within her limits shall have separate accommodations for the two races; that affecting only commerce within the State is no invasion of the power given to Congress by the commerce clause."

A like course of reasoning applies to the case under consideration, since the Supreme Court of Louisiana in the case of the *State ex rel. Abbott v. Hicks, Judge, et al.,* 44 La. Ann. 770, held that the statute in question did not apply to interstate passengers, but was confined in its application to passengers travelling exclusively within the borders of the State. The case was decided largely upon the authority of *Railway Co. v. State,* 66 Mississippi, 662, and affirmed by this court in 133 U.S. 87. In the present case no question of interference with interstate commerce can possibly arise, since the East Louisiana Railway appears to have been purely a local line, with both its termini within the State of Louisiana. Similar statutes for the separation of the two races upon public conveyances were held to be constitutional in *West Chester &c. Railroad v. Miles,* 55 Penn. St. 209; *Day v. Owen,* 5 Michigan, 520; *Chicago & c. Railway v. Williams,* 55 Illinois, 185; *Chesapeake &c. Railroad v. Wells,* 85 Tennessee, 613; *Memphis &c. Railroad v. Benson, 85 Tennessee,* 627; *The Sue,* 22 Fed. Rep. 843; *Logwood v. Memphis &c. Railroad,* 23 Fed. Rep. 318; *McGuinn v. Forbes,* 37 Fed. Rep. 639; *People v. King,* 18 N.E. Rep. 245; *Houck v. South Pac. Railway,* 38 Fed. Rep. 226; *Heard v. Georgia Railroad Co.,* 3 Int. Com. Com'n, 111; *S.C.,* 1 Ibid. 428.

While we think the enforced separation of the races, as applied to the internal commerce of the State, neither abridges the privileges or immunities of the colored man, deprives him of his property without due process of law, nor denies him the equal protection of the laws, within the meaning of the Fourteenth Amendment, we are not prepared to say that the conductor, in assigning passengers to the coaches according to their race, does not act at his peril, or that the provision of the second section of the act, that denies to the passenger compensation in damages for a refusal to receive him into the coach in which he properly belongs, is a valid exercise of the legislative power. Indeed, we understand it to be conceded by the State's attorney, that such part of the act as exempts from liability the railway company and its officers is unconstitutional. The power to assign to a particular coach obviously implies the power to determine to which race the passenger belongs, as well as the power to determine who, under the laws of the particular State, is to be deemed a white, and who a colored person. This question, though indicated in the brief of the plaintiff in error, does not properly arise upon the record in this case, since the only issue made is as to the unconstitutionality of the act, so far as it requires the railway to provide separate accommodations, and the conductor to assign passengers according to their race.

It is claimed by the plaintiff in error that, in any mixed community, the reputation of belonging to the dominant race, in this instance the white race, is *property,* in the same sense that a right of action, or of inheritance, is property. Conceding this to be so, for the purposes of this case, we are unable to see how this statute deprives him of, or in any way affects his right to, such property. If he be a white man and assigned to a colored coach, he may have his action for damages against the company for being deprived of his so called property. Upon the other hand, if he be a colored man and be so assigned, he has been deprived of no property, since his is not lawfully entitled to the reputation of being a white man.

In this connection, it is also suggested by the learned counsel for the plaintiff in error that the same argument that will justify the state legislature in requiring railways to provide separate accommodations for the two races will also authorize them to require separate cars to be provided for people whose hair is of a certain color, or who are aliens, or who belong to certain nationalities, or to enact laws requiring colored people to walk upon one side of the street, and white people upon the other, or requiring white men's houses to be painted white, and colored men's black, or their vehicles or business signs to be of different colors, upon the theory that one side of the street is as good as the other, or that a house or vehicle of one color is as good as one of another color. The reply to all this is that every exercise of the police power must be reasonable, and extend only to such laws as are enacted in good faith for the promotion for the public good, and not for the annoyance or oppression of a particular class. Thus in *Yick Wo v. Hopkins,* 118 U.S. 356, it was held by this court that a municipal ordinance of the city of San Francisco, to regulate the carrying on of public laundries within the limits of the municipality, violated the provisions of the Constitution of the United States, if it conferred upon the municipal authorities arbitrary power, at their own will, and without regard to discretion, in the legal sense of the term, to give or withhold consent as to persons or places, without regard to the competency of the persons applying, or the propriety of the places selected for the carrying on of the business. It was held to be a covert attempt on the part of the municipality to make an arbitrary and unjust discrimination against the Chinese race. While this was the case of a municipal ordinance, a like principle has been held to apply to acts of a state legislature passed in the exercise of the police power. *Railroad Company v. Husen,* 95 U.S. 465; *Louisville & Nashville Railroad v. Kentucky,* 161 U.S. 677, and cases cited on p. 700; *Daggett v. Hudson,* 43 Ohio St. 548; *Capen v. Foster,* 12 Pick. 485; *State ex rel. Wood v. Baker,* 38 Wisconsin, 71; *Monroe v. Collins,* 17 Ohio St. 665; *Hulseman v. Rems,* 41 Penn. St. 396; *Orman v. Riley,* 15 California, 48.

So far, then, as a conflict with the Fourteenth Amendment is concerned, the case reduces itself to the question whether the statue of Louisiana is a reasonable regulation, and with respect to this there must necessarily be a large discretion on the part of the legislature. In determining the question of reasonableness it is at liberty to act with reference to the established usages, customs and traditions of the people, and with a view to the promotion of their comfort, and the preservation of the public peace and good order. Gauged by this standard, we cannot say that a law which authorizes or even requires the separation of the two races in public conveyances is unreasonable, or more obnoxious to the Fourteenth

Amendment than the acts of Congress requiring separate schools for colored children in the District of Columbia, the constitutionality of which does not seem to have been questioned, or the corresponding acts of state legislatures.

We consider the underlying fallacy of the plaintiff's argument to consist in the assumption that the enforced separation of the two races stamps the colored race with a badge of inferiority. If this be so, it is not by reason of anything found in the act, but solely because the colored race chooses to put that construction upon it. The argument necessarily assumes that if, as has been more than once the case, and is not unlikely to be so again, the colored race should become the dominant power in the state legislature, and should enact a law in precisely similar terms, it would thereby relegate the white race to an inferior position. We imagine that the white race, at least, would not acquiesce in this assumption. The argument also assumes that social prejudices may be overcome by legislation, and that equal rights cannot be secured to the negro except by an enforced commingling of the two races. We cannot accept this proposition. If the two races are to meet upon terms of social equality, it must be the result of natural affinities, a mutual appreciation of each other's merits and a voluntary consent of individuals. As was said by the Court of Appeals of New York in *People v. Gallagher,* 93 N.Y. 438, 448, "this end can neither be accomplished nor promoted by laws which conflict with the general sentiment of the community upon whom they are designed to operate. When the government, therefore, has secured to each of its citizens equal rights before the law and opportunities for improvement and progress, it has accomplished the end for which it was organized and performed all of the functions respecting social advantages with which it is endowed." Legislation is powerless to eradicate racial instincts or to abolish distinctions based upon physical differences, and the attempt to do so can only result in accentuating the difficulties of the present situation. If the civil and political rights of both races be equal one cannot be inferior to the other civilly or politically. If one race be inferior to the other socially, the Constitution of the United States cannot put them upon the same plane.

It is true that the question of the proportion of colored blood necessary to constitute a colored person, as distinguished from a white person, is one upon which there is a difference of opinion in the different States, some holding that any visible admixture of black blood stamps the person as belonging to the colored race, (*State v. Chavers,* 5 Jones, [N.C.] 1, p. 11); others that it depends upon the preponderance of blood, (*Gray v. State,* 4 Ohio, 354; *Monroe v. Collins,* 17 Ohio St. 665); and still others that the predominance of white blood must only be in the proportion of three fourths. (*People v. Dean,* 14 Michigan, 406; *Jones v. Commonwealth,* 80 Virginia, 538.) But these are questions to be determined under the laws of each State and are not properly put in issue in this case. Under the allegations of his petition it may undoubtedly become a question of importance whether, under the laws of Louisiana, the petitioner belongs to the white or colored race.

The judgment of the court below is, therefore, *Affirmed.*

MR. JUSTICE HARLAN dissenting.

By the Louisiana statute the validity of which is here involved, all railway companies (other than street-railroad companies) carrying passengers in that state are required to have separate but equal accommodations for white and colored persons, "by providing two more passenger coaches for each passenger train, or by dividing the passenger coaches by a partition so as to secure separate accommodations." Under this statute, no colored person is permitted to occupy a seat in a coach assigned to white persons; nor any white person to occupy a seat in a coach assigned to colored persons. The managers of the railroad are not allowed to exercise any discretion in the premises, but are required to assign each passenger to some coach or compartment set apart for the exclusive use of his race. If a passenger insists upon going into a coach or compartment not set apart for persons of his race, he is subject to be fined, or to be imprisoned in the parish jail. Penalties are prescribed for the refusal or neglect of the officers, directors, conductors, and employés of railroad companies to comply with the provisions of the act.

Only "nurses attending children of the other race" are excepted from the operation of the statute. No exception is made of colored attendants traveling with adults. A white man is not permitted to have his colored servant with him in the same coach, even if his condition of health requires the constant personal assistance of such servant. If a colored maid insists upon riding in the same coach with a white woman whom she has been employed to serve, and who may need her personal attention while traveling, she is subject to be fined or imprisoned for such an exhibition of zeal in the discharge of duty.

While there may be in Louisiana persons of different races who are not citizens of the United States, the words in the act "white and colored races" necessarily include all citizens of the United States of both races residing in that state. So that we have before us a state enactment that compels, under penalties, the separation of the two races in railroad passenger coaches, and makes it a crime for a citizen of either race to enter a coach that has been assigned to citizens of the other race.

Thus, the state regulates the use of a public highway by citizens of the United States solely upon the basis of race.

However apparent the injustice of such legislation may be, we have only to consider whether it is consistent with the constitution of the United States. . . .

In respect of civil rights, common to all citizens, the constitution of the United States does not, I think, permit any public authority to know the race of those entitled to be protected in the enjoyment of such rights. Every true man has pride of race, and under appropriate circumstances, when the rights of others, his equals before the law, are not to be affected, it is his privilege to express such pride and to take such action based upon it as to him seems proper. But I deny that any legislative body or judicial tribunal may have regard to the race of citizens when the civil rights of those citizens are involved. Indeed, such legislation as that here in question is inconsistent not only with that equality of rights which pertains to citizenship, national and state, but with the personal liberty enjoyed by every one within the United States. . . .

The white race deems itself to be the dominant race in this country. And so it is, in prestige, in achievements, in education, in wealth, and in power. So, I doubt not, it will continue to be for all time, if it remains true to its great heritage, and holds fast to the principles of constitutional liberty. But in view of the constitution, in the eye of the law, there is in this country no superior, dominant, ruling class of citizens. There is no caste here. Our constitution is color-blind, and neither knows nor tolerates classes among citizens. In respect of civil rights, all citizens are equal before the law. The humblest is the peer of the most powerful. The law regards man as man, and takes no account of his surroundings or of his color when his civil rights as guarantied by the supreme law of the land are involved. It is therefore to be regretted that this high tribunal, the final expositor of the fundamental law of the land, has reached the conclusion that it is competent for a state to regulate the enjoyment by citizens of their civil rights solely upon the basis of race.

In my opinion, the judgment this day rendered will, in time, prove to be quite as pernicious as the decision made by this tribunal in the Dred Scott Case.

It was adjudged in that case that the descendants of Africans who were imported into this country, and sold as slaves, were not included nor intended to be included under the word "citizens" in the constitution, and could not claim any of the rights and privileges which that instrument provided for and secured to citizens of the United States; that, at the time of the adoption of the constitution, they were "considered as a subordinate and inferior class of beings, who had been subjugated by the dominant race, and, whether emancipated or not, yet remained subject to their authority, and had no rights or privileges but such as those who held the power and the government might choose to grant them" 17 How. 393, 404. The recent amendments of the constitution, it was supposed, had eradicated these principles from our institutions. But it seems that we have yet, in some of the states, a dominant race,—a superior class of citizens,—which assumes to regulate the enjoyment of civil rights, common to all citizens, upon the basis of race. The present decision, it may well be apprehended, will not only stimulate aggressions, more or less brutal and irritating, upon the admitted rights of colored citizens, but will encourage the belief that it is possible, by means of state enactments, to defeat the beneficent purposes which the people of the United States had in view when they adopted the recent amendments of the constitution, by one of which the blacks of this country were made citizens of the United States and of the states in which they respectively reside, and whose privileges and immunities, as citizens, the states are forbidden to abridge. Sixty millions of whites are in no danger from the presence here of eight millions of blacks. The destinies of the two races, in this country, are indissolubly linked together, and the interests of both require that the common government of all shall not permit the seeds of race hate to be planted under the sanction of law. What can more certainly arouse race hate, what more certainly create and perpetuate a feeling of distrust between these races, than state enactments which, in fact, proceed on the ground that colored citizens are so inferior and degraded that they cannot be allowed to sit in public coaches occupied by white citizens? That, as all will admit, is the real meaning of such legislation as was enacted in Louisiana.

The sure guaranty of the peace and security of each race is the clear, district, unconditional recognition by our governments, national and state, of every right that inheres in civil freedom, and of the equality before the law of all citizens of the United States, without regard to race. State enactments regulating the enjoyment of civil rights upon the basis of race, and cunningly devised to defeat legitimate results of the war, under the pretense of recognizing equality of rights, can have no other result than to render permanent peace impossible, and to keep alive a conflict of races, the continuance of which must do harm to all concerned. This question is not met by the suggestion that social equality cannot exist between the white and black races in this country. That argument, if it can be properly regarded as one, is scarcely worthy of consideration; for social equality no more exists between two races when traveling in a passenger coach or a public highway than when members of the same races sit by each other in a street car or in the jury box, or stand or sit with each other in a political assembly, or when they use in common the streets of a city or town, or when they are in the same room for the purpose of having their names placed on the registry of voters, or when they approach the ballot box in order to exercise the high privilege of voting. . . .

The arbitrary separation of citizens, on the basis of race, while they are on a public highway, is a badge of servitude wholly inconsistent with the civil freedom and the equality before the law established by the constitution. It cannot be justified upon any legal grounds.

If evils will result from the commingling of the two races upon public highways established for the benefit of all, they will be infinitely less than those that will surely come from state legislation regulating the enjoyment of civil rights upon the basis of race. We boast of the freedom enjoyed by our people above all other peoples. But it is difficult to reconcile that boast with a state of the law which, practically, puts the brand of servitude and degradation upon a large class of our fellow citizens,—our equals before the law. The thin disguise of "equal" accommodations for passengers in railroad coaches will not mislead any one, nor atone for the wrong this day done. . . .

I am of opinion that the statute of Louisiana is inconsistent with the personal liberty of citizens, white and black, in that state, and hostile to both the spirit and letter of the constitution of the United States. If laws of like character should be enacted in the several states of the Union, the effect would be in the highest degree mischievous. Slavery, as an institution tolerated by law, would, it is true, have disappeared from our country; but there would remain a power in the states, by sinister legislation, to interfere with the full enjoyment of the blessings of freedom, to regulate civil rights, common to all citizens, upon the basis of race, and to place in a condition of legal inferiority a large body of American citizens, now constituting a part of the political community, called the "People of the United States," for whom, and by whom through representatives, our government is administered. Such a system is inconsistent with the guaranty given by the constitution to each state of a republican form of government, and may be stricken down by congressional action, or by the courts in the discharge of their solemn duty to maintain the supreme law of the land, anything in the constitution or laws of any state to the contrary notwithstanding.

For the reason stated, I am constrained to withhold my assent from the opinion and judgment of the majority.

PLESSY

CHERYL I. HARRIS

Study Questions

1. How does knowing Plessy's physical appearance change your thinking about and understanding of the court case *Plessy v. Ferguson?*

Plessy arose at a time of acute crisis for Blacks. The system of legalized race segregation known as Jim Crow[1] and heightened racial violence[2] had reversed the minimal gains attained by Blacks during Reconstruction.[3] Against a background of extreme racial oppression, the Supreme Court's opinion in *Plessy* rejecting thirteenth and fourteenth amendment challenges to state enforced racial segregation was consonant with the overall political climate.

The case arose in 1891, as one of a series of challenges to a Louisiana law that required racial segregation of railway cars, and was brought after Homer A. Plessy attempted to board a coach reserved for whites and was arrested for violating the statute.[4] Because, according to the plea filed on Plessy's behalf, "the mixture of African blood [was] not discernable in him,"[5] it is evident that Plessy's arrest was arranged as part of a strategy that included the tacit cooperation of railway officials, many of whom were displeased with the separate car law due to the increased expense of operation.[6] The Court dismissed Plessy's claim that legalized racial separation produced racial subordination because

> [T]he underlying fallacy of the plaintiff's argument consists in the assumption that the enforced separation of the two races stamps the colored race with a badge of inferiority. If this be so, it is not by reason of anything found in the act but solely because the colored race chooses to put that construction on it.[7]

Plessy's claim, however, was predicated on more than the Equal Protection Clause of the Fourteenth Amendment. Plessy additionally charged that the refusal to seat him on the white passenger car deprived him of property—"this reputation [of being white] which has an actual pecuniary value"—without the due process of law guaranteed by the amendment.[8] Because phenotypically Plessy appeared to be white,[9] barring him from the

371

railway car reserved for whites severely impaired or deprived him of the reputation of being regarded as white.[10] He might thereafter be regarded as or be suspected of being not white[11] and therefore not entitled to any of the public and private benefits attendant to white status.

The brief filed on Plessy's behalf advanced as its first argument that, because "the reputation of belonging to the dominant race . . . is property, in the same sense that a right of action or inheritance is property," empowering a train employee to arbitrarily take property away from a passenger violated due process guarantees.[12] Because of white supremacy, whiteness was not merely a descriptive or ascriptive characteristic—it was property of overwhelming significance and value. Albion Tourgée, one of Plessy's attorneys, pointedly argued that the property value in being white was self-evident:

> How much would it be *worth* to a young man entering upon the practice of law, to be regarded as a *white* man rather than a colored one? Six-sevenths of the population are white. Nineteen-twentieths of the property of the country is owned by white people. Ninety-nine hundredths of the business opportunities are in the control of white people. . . . Probably most white persons if given a choice, would prefer death to life in the United States *as colored persons.* Under these conditions, is it possible to conclude that *the reputation of being white* is not property? Indeed, is it not the most valuable sort of property, being the master-key that unlocks the golden door of opportunity?[13]

Moreover, Tourgée noted that, in determining who was white, not only were there no national standards, there were also conflicting rules that, by definition, incorporated white domination:

> There is no law of the United States, or of the state of Louisiana defining the limits of race—who are white and who are "colored"? By what rule then shall any tribunal be guided in determining racial character? It may be said that all those should be classed as colored in whom appears a visible admixture of colored blood. By what law? With what justice? Why not count everyone as white in whom is visible any trace of white blood? There is but one reason to wit, the domination of the white race.[14]

The Court ignored Tourgée's argument, and asserted simply that, although the statute obviously conferred power on the train conductor to make assignments by race, no deprivation of due process had resulted because the issue of Plessy's race did not "properly arise on the record."[15] Because there was nothing to indicate that Plessy had been improperly classified under any operative racial definition, no claim for a lack of judicial process in reviewing an improper classification would lie.

The opinion, however, inexplicably proceeded to consider whether Plessy had suffered damage to his property in the form of his reputation, a question dependent on the issue of racial classification that the Court had previously declined to address. The Court simply concluded that, if Plessy were white, any injury to his reputation would be adequately compensated by an action for damages against the company, given that counsel for the state had conceded that the statute's liability exemption for conductors was unconstitutional.[16] The Court stated:

> If he be a white man and assigned to a colored coach, he may have his action for damages against the company for being deprived of his so-called property. Upon the other hand, if he be a colored man and be so assigned, he has been deprived of no property, since he is not lawfully entitled to the reputation of being a white man.[17]

At one level, the Court's opinion amounted to a wholesale evasion of the argument that, as a matter of federal constitutional law, Plessy's assignment to a railway car for Blacks, in the absence of a clear standard defining who was white, was an arbitrary and unauthorized taking of the valuable asset of being regarded as white. At another level, the Court's decision lent support to the notion of race reputation as a property interest that required the protection of law through actions for damages. It did not specifically consider any particular rule of race definition, but it protected the property interest in whiteness for all whites by subsuming even those like Plessy, who phenotypically appeared to be white, within categories that were predicated on white supremacy and race subordination. Officially, the court declined to consider whether Plessy met any statutory definition of whiteness, but deferred to state law as the legitimate source of racial definitions.[18] Although the opinion rhetorically signaled some qualifications about the existence of the property right in whiteness,[19] in fact, the Court protected that right by acknowledging that whites could protect their reputation of being white through suits for damages and by determining that Plessy would be subject to rules that continued white privilege. *Plessy* demonstrated the Court's chronic refusal to dismantle the structure of white supremacy, which is maintained through the institutional protection of relative benefits for whites at the expense of Blacks. In denying that any inferiority existed by reason of de jure segregation, and in denying white status to Plessy, "whiteness" was protected from intrusion and appropriate boundaries around the property were maintained.

Notes

[1] *See generally* C. VANN WOODWARD, THE STRANGE CAREER OF JIM CROW *passim* (1974) (describing the American system of legally mandated race segregation).

[2] Lynching, an extreme form of social control designed to contain or obliterate potential economic and political challenges posed by Blacks, rose during the ten-year period between 1890 and 1900. In 1892 alone, over 255 Black men, women, and children were lynched. *See* GIDDINGS, *supra* note 37, at 26.

[3] Some historians have argued that the actual material conditions of Blacks deteriorated in the last two decades of the nineteenth century as they were squeezed out of the core of the labor force. *See* MYRDAL, *supra* note 4, at 222 (arguing that, after Emancipation, "no . . . proprietary interest [of slaveowners] protected negro laborers from the desire of white workers to squeeze them out of skilled employment[,] [t]hey were gradually driven out and pushed down into 'Negro jobs', a category which has been more and more narrowly defined").

[4] *See* CHARLES LOFGREN, THE PLESSY CASE 41 (1987).

[5] *Id.* at 41.

[6] *See id.* at 32.

[7] *Plessy v. Ferguson,* 163 U.S. 537, 551 (1896).

[8] Brief for Plaintiff in Error at 8, *Plessy* (No. 210) [hereinafter Brief for Homer Plessy].

[9] *See* LOFGREN, *supra* note 173, at 41.

[10] Albion Tourgée, attorney for Plessy, had specifically sought a fair-skinned plaintiff in order to raise this argument, over vigorous opposition from organized Black leadership. Although Tourgée was seeking a narrower ground for the Court to rule upon, as he was very pessimistic about overturning Jim Crow in the hostile political climate, Black leadership objected that such a strategy, even if successful, would mitigate conditions only for those Blacks who appeared to be white. Legally sanctioning the privilege of fair skin over dark would only serve to reinforce the legitimacy of the race hierarchy that kept white over Black. Nevertheless, Tourgée prevailed in his efforts to pursue this strategy and Homer A. Plessy was chosen because phenotypically he appeared to be white. *See* JACK GREENBERG, LITIGATION FOR SOCIAL CHANGE: METHODS, LIMITS AND ROLE IN DEMOCRACY 13–15 (1974). Greenberg notes that one of the benefits of Tourgée's approach was that, had it been accepted by the Court, it might have, in time, made Jim Crow laws extremely difficult to administer. Thus, states might simply have abandoned them. *See id.* at 14.

[11] *See* Brief for Homer Plessy, *supra* note 177, at 9–10.

[12] *Id.* at 8.

[13] *Id.* at 9.

[14] *Id.* at 11. Although from a very different perspective and analysis, Tourgée's attack on the arbitrariness of racial categories presaged the full-blown assault on the illusion of color-blindness offered by Neil Gotanda's insight that recognition of race in this society involves race subordination. Gotanda states:

> Under hypodescent [the rule governing race in the United States], Black parentage is recognized through the generations. . . . Black ancestry is a contaminant that overwhelms white ancestry. Thus, under the American system of racial classification, claiming a white racial identity is a declaration of racial purity and an implicit assertion of racial domination. . . .

... [T]he moment of racial recognition is the moment in which is *reproduced* the inherent asymmetry of the metaphor of racial contamination and the implicit impossibility of racial equality.

Gotanda, *supra* note 24, at 26–27 (footnotes omitted).

[15] *Plessy v. Ferguson,* 163 U.S. 537, 549 (1896). The information filed against Plessy had failed to specify his race. *See* Lofgren, *supra* note 173, at 154. However, Plessy's petition for writs of prohibition and certiorari had alleged that he was seven-eighths white. *See id.* at 55. Attached to the petition was the affidavit of the arresting officer who had identified Plessy as a "passenger of the colored race." *Id.* Notwithstanding the court's demurral, there was thus little doubt that the record contained facts pertaining to Plessy's race.

[16] *See Plessy,* 163 U.S. at §49.

[17] *Id.*

[18] The Court validated, as acceptable norms, state law requirements including, presumably, all common law regarding the proportion of "colored blood necessary to constitute a colored person." The Court stated:

> It is true that the question of the proportion of colored blood necessary to constitute a colored person, as distinguished from a white person, is one upon which there is a difference of opinion in the different states. . . . But these are questions to be determined under the laws of each state and are not properly put in issue in this case.

[19] *Id.* at 552 (citations omitted).

Obviously, state law also would control the federal due process claim. This fact invites speculation that had Plessy been on a train in a different state with different laws defining whiteness, the case might have gone the other way, although on the narrower basis of the deprivation of due process.

PART · 5

Toward a New Paradigm: Transcending Categories

> I am not under the illusion that changing habits and emotions is easy. Even when one has been persuaded by reason and swears off the practice of race-thinking, one must be continually on guard against betrayal by words and especially by thought-clichés. The power of superstition is that it speaks in the tones of common sense.
>
> Jacques Barzun
> *RACE: A STUDY IN SUPERSTITION* (1965:xvii)

In this book, we have presented evidence to support the argument that there is no such thing as race. We have shown that racial classification is based on at least two false assumptions: (1) that people can be divided into clear-cut categories so that everyone fits into one category only and (2) that each category tells us something meaningful about the people assigned to it that differentiates them from people assigned to other categories. As stated in the Introduction, our goal in critiquing classification schemes was not to create "better" categories with clearer dividing lines but to show the futility of trying to classify people in this matter. Our goal was to explore how people come to define arbitrary categories as clear-cut and the mechanisms by which they maintain the illusion of independent or pure categories.

If we have succeeded in showing there is no such thing as race, it would seem that the only logical recommendation we can make is to abandon the practice of classifying people by race. Such a solution, however, ignores a critical moral question: How do we deal with the legacy of racial classification? Keep in mind that the racial categories in place today did not come into being because multiracial people chose to identify with one particular racial group over others. The system of racial classification is the result of more than 200 years of laws and practices enforcing categorization (Knepper 1995), beginning with the 19th century vision of a hierarchy of the races with Europeans on top supported by the assumption that physical, mental, moral, and aesthetic attributes are biologically determined. This ranking and classification system was used to justify colonialism, slavery, and other forms of imperialism "as a moral necessity because the original inhabitants were seen as less than human and did not deserve the land they inhabited" (Mirza and Dungworth 1995:347).

The idea of "race" and, by extension, racial classification have been challenged for some time. As noted in the Preface, *Race: A Study in Modern Superstition* by Jacques Barzun was published in 1937 and reissued in 1965. In the preface to the 1965 edition, Barzun states "This book is coming back into print because the idea [of race] it treats of, although repeatedly killed, is nevertheless undying" (p. ix). However, it is only recently that these challenges have begun to reach mainstream audiences. Hundreds of articles and books have been written in the 1990s on this subject. As well, a significant number of authors have written autobiographical accounts describing what it means to fit no one racial category. Examples include *Life on the Color Line: The True Story of a White Boy Who Discovered He Was Black* by Gregory Howard Williams (1995), *Notes of a White Black Woman* by Judy Scales-Trent (1995), and *The Color of Water: A Black Man's Tribute to His White Mother* by James McBride (1996). In addition, the U.S. Bureau of Census is reviewing the literature and research findings related to racial classification and is evaluating the adequacy of current racial and ethnic categories specified in Federal Statistical Directive No. 15. The census bureau is also asking interested individuals and groups for specific suggestions about how to revise race questions. All of this attention to the meaning of race suggests that we are in the midst of a paradigm shift. Still, as the comments from students in a recent Race and Gender class at Northern Kentucky University make clear, the process by which the old paradigm loosens its grip on thinking is a slow one (see "Conversations About the Meaning of Race").

Thomas Kuhn (1975) wrote about paradigm shifts in *The Structure of Scientific Revolutions.* According to Kuhn, paradigms are the dominant and widely accepted theories and concepts which are used to comprehend and explain events in the world. In the reading "The Anthropology of Race: A Study of Ways of Looking at Race," Vivian J. Rohrl (1995) offers a brief historical overview of the so-called scientific paradigms related to race beginning with those of the late 18th and early 19th century (phase 1), which assumed for the most part the existence of clear-cut racial categories. She ends with the 1960s and early 1970s (phase 6)—the years in which the anthropologist Ashley Montagu (a person ahead of his time) puts forth the paradigm that "there is no such thing as race." Rorhl traces how the meaning of race has evolved from clear-cut divisions of humanity to "a way in which one group designates itself as 'insider' and other groups as 'outsiders' to reinforce or enforce its wishes and/or ideas in social, economic, and political realms" (p. 96).

Paradigms gain their status not because they explain everything, but because they seem to be the "best" way of looking at the world for the time being. On the one hand, paradigms are important because

Conversations About the Meaning of Race

At the end of the spring 1996 semester, I asked students in my Race and Gender class if any of them had tried to tell a relative, friend or acquaintance that "there is no such thing as race." Out of the 80 students in the class, 78 had tried to explain this idea to someone. A sample of their experiences are listed below.

- I mentioned to a friend of mine when a golf tournament was on that Tiger Woods was not "black". My friend looked at me blankly and said "he looks black to me." I tried to explain that each of his parents were "mixed race," so therefore Tiger could not be one race. I don't think my friend was convinced.

- I tried to discuss this idea with my parents. They were open to the idea that people of different "races" can have children. Yet they still believe that if a baby looks "black" (or Asian, or Native American, or Hispanic) it is black regardless of its genetic heritage. The conversation seemed very futile because they had no real concept of different ethnic groups among the races. They are educated people but these ideas didn't seem to make sense to them.

- I had a short conversation with a person classified as "black". I kept it short because I didn't want to offend him. But now I know him a little bit better and I don't think he would be offended since I learned that he grew up among whites most of his life. He pretty much knew where I was coming from on this issue. I can't quite remember exactly what specific issues we talked about but I do remember that he was very open-minded about it.

- I have discussed these ideas with my parents and husband. The immediate reaction from my husband was "that's why I hate those classes, they try to brainwash you to socialist thinking." Now, my husband is not racist but he could not understand the concept of race as a myth. I gave up on him. My parents laughed and thought it was a waste of time to study such matters and I gave up trying to convey the message. Actually I had the same kind of reaction on the first day of class, but after studying the readings, viewing photographs, and discussing these ideas everything seemed to make sense.

- I have discussed this class with many people. I actually talked about Tiger Woods to my parents as we were watching a golf tournament. I told them he wasn't "black". They said, "well, what is he?" I tried to tell them and they did not believe me. This topic came up the following Sunday only this time with my parents and grandparents. One of my parents announced to everyone there, "Kim said Tiger Woods isn't black." I tried to explain it again but everyone said "he looks black to me and so do his parents." Then I used examples to explain how physical characteristics do not tell the whole genetic story. After I explained this idea they believed me a little bit but not fully.

- I have tried several times to try and explain the idea of racial classification to my boyfriend John. I told him that race doesn't really exist. Our conversations did not last very long because he couldn't understand what I was trying to say. I tried to tell him

Continued

about the articles we read and that helped a little. He basically said that I was probably right that people created the idea of race, but there was nothing we could do about it now. I think he wanted to understand, but did not know how to make himself.

- Since I started this class, I've discussed some of the ideas with my parents. My parents are golfers so I told them about Tiger Woods. They are very open minded and are just intrigued by this "new" interpretation of race as I am. This is a topic people need to know about. Ignoring it will only cause more problems.

- I have discussed the idea that race doesn't exist with a friend at work. At first she thought I was really strange, but as I spoke more on the subject she started to understand and get the meaning of what I was saying. I gave several examples of how the idea of race has been embedded in our minds from a very young age, and even in our textbooks at school. It didn't take too much convincing on my part to get my friend to understand what I was saying.

- I have talked about the idea of "race" with my district manager at work for about five hours. I told him how I used to believe in race but that I no longer do. At first he was very surprised by my comments but as I explained the different things we have learned in class he somehow started to believe me. He very much enjoyed talking about "race" because his mother is "black" and his father is "white."

- I told my great-uncle, who is racist, that I was taking this course and about the ideas we were learning. He asked me why I was taking such

a course. At first, I considered saying "Because I have to" but instead I said "it seemed interesting." He asked me more questions about the content of the course. He seemed to think it was some kind of plot against America's youth. I asked why and he said "Everyone knows that 'niggers' are different."

- A friend of mine and I spent probably 2 hours talking about this topic. She seemed very receptive to the idea. It wasn't that hard to get my point across to her. On the other hand, I tried discussing it with my parents and they looked at me like I was crazy. They were not very interested in even trying to understand. I think they are set in their ways and don't want to be open to new ideas. I really think it is a generation thing. I think it is so hard for them to be open-minded because of the way they were raised to see race. They don't understand me when I talk about it. I told my dad, an avid golfer, about Tiger Woods. He seemed to understand that Tiger's genetic heritage is complex but he still refers to him as the "black golfer."

- I was at work, (UPS) one night when management asked us to fill out an employee survey. One of the questions was, "what race are you?" There were four choices (Black, White, Asian/Pacific Islander, and Native American) but there was also a fifth choice—"Hispanic." I told my co-workers that Hispanic wasn't a race, but they asked me "how come?" I tried to explain that Hispanics can be of any race, but it wasn't getting through. We talked about it for at least 5 minutes.

they serve a unifying function offering a common vocabulary by which to think about the world, about themselves, and others. For example, most people in the United States, even "mixed-race" people, think of themselves and others in terms of race. "[T]hey go along with the idea that they are members of one of the races recognized by the government. In fact, they often identify with a traditional race that represents only a small fraction of their genetic heritage" (Earnest 1989:182). While paradigms impose an order on the world and people's relationships with each other, they act as blinders, severely limiting the kinds of questions that people ask, the observations they make, and the actions they take.

The explanatory value, and hence the status, of a paradigm is threatened by *anomaly,* an observation or observations that it cannot explain. Anomalies confront us with the fact that the "old" paradigm is not relevant. In the case of the idea of race, those persons who are products of sexual unions between two individuals classified as belonging to different races are the anomalies who challenge the paradigm which directs us to think about race in terms of clear boundaries and distinct differences. Obviously, the existence of anomalies alone is not enough to cause people to abandon a particular paradigm. Otherwise, racial classification would have been abandoned long ago, and we would laugh and shudder at the thought that people once believed in the idea of race (Barzun 1965). Consider that W.E.B. Du Bois' writing alerted us to this anomaly at the turn of the twentieth century.

Du Bois was preoccupied with the "strange meaning of being black here in the dawning of the Twentieth Century."[1] His preoccupation was no doubt affected by the fact that his father was a Haitian of French and African descent and his mother was an American of Dutch and African descent (Lewis 1993). Historically, in the United States a "black" person is a black even when their parents are of different "races." In order to accept this idea, we act as if white and blacks do not marry and/or produce offspring, and we act as if one parent, the "black" one, contributes a disproportionate amount of genetic material—so large a genetic contribution that it negates the genetic contribution of the other parent. In *The Philadelphia Negro: A Social Study,* originally published in 1899, Du Bois wrote about popular ideas of race and reality (see the reading "The Intermarriage of the Races"). Ironically, almost 100 years after this book was published the flaws of the U.S. system of racial classification are just now becoming a standard topic in many sociology texts. Yet, Du Bois documented that blacks and whites married and paired off, despite laws prohibiting marriage, and that they did have children. He reminded us that race amalgamation took place "largely under the institution of slavery and for the most part, though not wholly, outside the bonds of legal marriage" (1996 reprint: 359). It is this kind of data which Du Bois painstakingly collected that is used today to discredit the idea of race as a valid way of categorizing humanity and to remind us that a "multiracial" people is not a recent phenomenon.

We have learned, however, that even when the evidence supporting the myth of race is right before our eyes, we have glossed over the stubborn facts and dismissed them or explained them away (see the reading "Letter from Thomas Jefferson"). Barzun (1965) wrote about this resistance in the preface to *Race: A Study in Modern Superstition:*

> The present book attempted a modest beginning of persuasion, having in view the adult educated reader to whom it showed in some detail the inconsistent racial fantasies developed in civilized Europe during the last 180 years. Men of good will, men of honor, scholars and scientists in the several branches of learning, have been the authors of these theories and the apologists of this superstition. They have argued on every conceivable premise of physique, language, temperament, moral character, coloring, shape of skull, and political belief, to establish the reality and the ranking of dozens, of hundreds, of supposed races. To each race they have ascribed traits that explained why the world was as it was and whither it was going. They have struggled to gloss over stubborn facts or to dismiss them; they have argued with the fanatics of rival theories or despised them. Encased in verbal armor, they have fought sham fights with real emotions and on real issues within and across national boundaries. Their labor has been great, and in the aggregate self-destructive, for their 'facts' cancel one another and their habits of thought only prove to the detached observer that here are men of one culture, cast in the same intellectual mold, and unfortunately not graced with simple judgement. (pp. xx–xxi)

In the face of such resistance, under what conditions do paradigms shift? According to Kuhn, before people abandon old paradigms, someone must articulate an alternative paradigm that accounts convincingly for the anomaly. A scientific revolution occurs when enough people in the community *hear* the critique, break from the old paradigm, and change the nature of their research or thinking in favor of a new paradigm. The new paradigm "changes some of the field's most elementary theoretical generalizations" (Kuhn 1975:85). The new paradigm causes converts to see the world in an entirely new light and to wonder how they could possibly have taken the old paradigm seriously. "[W]hen paradigms change, the world itself changes with them" (p. 111). The story of how people come to hear the ideas which discredit dominant paradigms is obviously a complicated one. Clearly, most people have failed to hear ideas expressed by Du Bois and Barzun. Du Bois (1868–1963) was not confident that his ideas would be heard or taken seriously as is clear from what he wrote in "The After-

Thought" to his book *The Souls of Black Folk:* "Hear my cry, O God the Reader; vouchsafe that this my book fall not still-born into the world wilderness. Let there spring, Gentle One, from out leaves vigor of thought and thoughtful deed to reap the harvest wonderful."

Law professor Cruz Reynoso (1992) offers some insights about the slow process by which many people in the United States have come to change their views about race and ethnicity. In the reading "Ethnic Diversity: Its Historical and Constitutional Roots," Reynoso describes some major events and court cases which show that the United States has struggled to accommodate diversity and has made fundamental changes in thought and practice. He does not argue that the changes have been perfect or fast. In fact, history shows that change has been slow and laborious, but it has occurred.

The struggle we face today can be stated in question form: How do we begin to dismantle racial classification without abdicating a responsibility to correct its legacy? This is an especially difficult question because today the major justification for collecting data on race and ethnicity is to monitor and enforce civil rights laws (see Appendix B: "Federal and Program Uses of the Data Derived from Race and Ethnicity Questions"). If we abandon racial classification, we lose an important mechanism through which we can appraise the success or failure of efforts to combat discrimination. The reading "One Drop of Blood" by Lawrence Wright (1994) addresses this dilemma of abandoning a classification system many now recognize as unworkable while still using it as a monitoring device. In view of this dilemma, we offer some modest suggestions to continue the process of change.

Suggestion 1. Carefully consider every situation where racial classification occurs and ask this question before making a decision about whether to abandon classification in that setting: Is this instance of racial classification satisfying an obligation to correct past injustices or is it contributing to further injustice? In the reading "Perceptions and Misperceptions of Skin Color" by Stephen H. Caldwell and Rebecca Popenoe (1995a), the authors give us one example of a situation where knowing someone's race is of limited value to accomplishing the task at hand. Caldwell and Popenoe argue that clinicians should consider dropping any reference to the race of their patients during case presentations because, in most cases, knowing their race does not improve diagnostic and therapeutic decisions. In fact, knowing someone's race can introduce bias and even obscure an accurate appraisal of a patient's genetic and cultural background. Caldwell and Popenoe (1995b) maintain that the clinicians must recognize the limited scientific meaning of the terms "black" or "white" "Indian" and "Asian."[2] They suggest that clinicians drop references to race and ask patients about their ethnic history when they suspect that cultural factors or geographic origin may offer clues about the diseases to which a patient may be inherently prone and about the ways in which he or she may react to both illness and treatment (1995b).

In the reading "Identifying Ethnicity in Medical Papers," Edward J. Huth (1995) reacts to Caldwell and Popenoe's recommendation and argues that assigning an ethnicity to patients is not an easy task, but if clinicians and epidemiologists[3] consider ethnicity to be an important factor they should state clearly why they think it is important and explain the criteria they used to place patients in particular ethnic categories.

While it might be useful to limit references to race and ethnicity in case presentations and epidemiological research, keeping track of the race and ethnicity of patients is essential to monitoring whether equality exists with regard to access to health and treatment outcomes. If people classified as "Black" or "Native American" have less access to certain treatments (i.e., organ transplants or kidney dialysis) or if they have less favorable health outcomes than people classified as "White," then we have an obligation to investigate the possibility that people may have been treated differently because of their race or because of the race others perceive them to be. The reading "Selected Discrimination Cases Handled by the U.S. Department of Justice in 1996" shows that both individual and institutional discrimination exist and must be held in check. Individual discrimination is any overt action by an individual that depreciates someone from the outgroup, denies outgroup opportunities to participate, or is violent toward others' lives and property. Institutionalized discrimination, on the other hand, is the established and customary way of doing things in society—the challenged and unchallenged rules, policies, and day-to-day practices that impede or limit minority members' achievements and keep them in a subordinated and disadvantaged position. It is "systematic discrimination through the regular operations of societal institutions" (Davis 1978:30). Institutional discrimination can be overt or subtle. It is overt when laws and practices are designed with the clear intention of keeping minorities in subordinate positions as in the 1831 Act Prohibiting the Teaching of Slaves to Read. Institutionalized discrimination is subtle when the discriminatory consequences of a practice are neither planned nor intended.

Suggestion 2. Develop the intellectual discipline to recognize *race-thinking,* a habit of thought where "people permit themselves to think of human groups without the vivid sense that groups consist of individuals and that individuals display the full range of human differences" (Barzun 1965:ix). Race-thinking is evident when people engage in *selective perception,* a thought process in which people notice only those behaviors or events that support their stereotypes about a race or ethnic group. For example, while watching the Olympics a spectator notices that "blacks" are concentrated in sports such as basketball and certain track events (sprints). He or she uses

people. These categories are supposedly based partially on skin color and partially on such factors as occupation and education. As a result, two children in the same Brazilian family can be classified in different "racial" categories from their parents and from each other. Furthermore, Brazilians don't completely agree on the features in their categories, for example, whether *moreno claro* was lighter or darker than *mulato blanco.* Thus, there is no segregation of races in Brazil, and there is no concept of *hypodescent* such as exists in the northern hemisphere. What this means is that in the United States, if a person was known to have a drop of African blood, that person was considered African, while in Brazil people were put on a continuum, in which one group graded into the next. Thus, social definitions have nothing to do with genes. It is easy to attribute significance on a physiological feature when one wants to (Alland 1967; Mead 1971).

In the United States, there are at least three ways of claiming American Indian, or Native American, ancestry. There is the legal Indian, a reservation member, who maintains this identity as long as she or he lives on the reservation. Secondly, there is the person with the Indian phenotype, who may not be considered Indian in certain times and places. Thirdly, there is the person who claims Indian ancestry (Alland 1967). All of these classifications may not have much to do with genetic composition of the person.

What About Race and Intelligence?

Although some scientists have tried to correlate race with intelligence, there is no such thing as fixed races or immutable intelligence. Among most anthropologists, and many other persons, this almost doesn't need to be said. In order to explore this further, let us actually see what "intelligence" consists of. Scales that we use in our society, including the "Stanford-Binet 60," the Wechsler scales, and the Guilford model of intellect use such concepts as "verbal," "memory," "spatial relations," and "abstractive abilities" as partial measures of intelligence. So, if a group of people emphasizes abilities associated with reading and modern mathematics, we might see abstractive abilities valued and exercised, while in cultures without a written tradition, memory-related tasks would make the people seem superior to the average as measured in Anglo-American tests of memory. Among societies that do not emphasize verbal or rhetorical skills and where the children learn by watching and copying, spatial relations abilities may be more highly developed. And this survey of test elements does not even take into account the effect on the brain of good nutrition and emotional well being, both of which, in an urban environment, are usually accessible to privileged socio-economic groups and raise performances on intelligence measures (Rohrl 1979).

Intelligence tests measure culturally patterned experience. Thus, for young elementary school children, a test was devised in which the children were asked to write the first letter of a word that describes a given picture. Needless to say, when seeing a picture of snow for the first time, California children proved "dumber" than their more northerly counterparts.

There are also cultural differences in the way people react to test-taking. For example, when Porteus, a psychologist, in the early 1900s, gave his Porteus Maze Test—a pencil-and-paper maze—to Australian aborigines, they were unaccustomed to paper and pencil and unaccustomed to answering questions alone as individuals rather than as a group. Consequently, they fared less well "intelligence"—wise than a comparable group of Europeans or Anglo-Americans while, on the other hand, the aborigines in a real situation could find their way around the woods much faster than the average Western "civilized" person (Porteus 1931).

There is also no correlation between brain size and intelligence. The Neandertals, as I already mentioned, had, on the average, a larger head and brain case than many modern humans. Culture itself, being learned behavior, is not correlated with size or shape of the brain or any other physiological feature (Boas 1940; Montagu 1965). Our measures of intelligence tell us more about our own culture—the measurers and creators of tests—than about the people we are measuring. Now, let's talk about:

The Trouble with Ethnicity

These days, all too frequently, people confuse race and culture, even after the strictures of Boas and his students, colleagues, and followers. Just to add to the confusion, I will briefly take us back to earlier days, before industrialization, to see how human groups thought of themselves, as reflected in what they called themselves. Some groups of human beings had either never seen outsiders or didn't associate much with them, had lived in small bands that were accustomed to one familiar territorial range and had a culture, a life style, in common. Their name for their own people frequently translates simply as "people" or "human beings." Thus, the Navajo Indians, of the American Southwest, called themselves *diné,* which means "people." The Cheyenne Indians of the American Central Great

Plains called themselves, in their own language, *Tsis-tsis-tas,* which also means "people." The Ojibwa of the North Central Lakes region of North America called themselves *Anish-a-nah-be,* which also means "the original people" (Rohrl 1981).

This range of self-labels simply reflects the fact that we all tend to think of our own nature as human nature. On seeing other cultural types, we tend to assume that we have reached the best style of living and adapting. The best way to express this would be by describing the encounter between the governor of Virginia and the Six Nations Indians who resided there, in 1744 (Franklin 1784): the Government of Virginia has made an offer to the Indian Chiefs that if they would send six youths from the Six Nations to Williamsburg, the college there would take care of them, feed and provide for them, and instruct them in all the learning of the white people. The Indian spokesman replied:

> We know that you highly esteem the kind of learning taught in those colleges, and that the maintenance of our young men, while with you, would be very expensive to you. We are convinced, therefore, that you mean to do us good by your proposal and we thank you heartily.
>
> But you, who are wise, must know that different nations have different conceptions of things; and you will not therefore take it amiss, if our ideas of this kind of education happen not to be the same with yours. We have had some experience of it; several of our young people were formerly brought up at the colleges of the northern provinces; they were instructed in all your sciences; but when they came back to us, they were bad runners, ignorant of every means of living in the woods, unable to bear either cold or hunger, knew neither how to build a cabin, take a deer, nor kill an enemy, spoke our language imperfectly, were therefore neither fit for hunters, warriors, nor counselors; they were totally good for nothing.
>
> We are however not the less obligated by your kind offer, though we decline accepting it; and to show our grateful sense of it, if the gentlemen of Virginia will send us a dozen of their sons, we will take care of their education, instruct them in all we know, and make men of them.

Not only did these 18th-century Indians of the Six Nations have a well-developed style of living, they also were aware of the bicultural standards, the standard of the "sciences" and the standards of the well-adapted hunter and food-grower. If we return to the origin of the definition of "intelligence," meaning the ability to understand relationships and differentiate or choose between the forms and styles around us to enhance our survival, the Six Nations of the 18th century possibly demonstrated more of it.

Even the most well-meaning policies can overlook the large variability of people within one designated group. In one instance, the (ethnic) category "Asian" designated who would live in a government-assisted housing project for newly arrived immigrants to the United States. Immediately, differences arose between two Southeast Asian neighbors, a Laotian and a Cambodian family, who spoke different languages and had different—in some ways, almost opposite—social and family structures (Rohrl, n.d.).

Conclusion

Getting back to our main subject, examples of the bicultural or multicultural encounters illustrate that intelligence and culture are not determined by any biologically inherited features. If the native Indian youths had accepted the offer of the Virginian government, they would simply have acquired a new language and culture adapted to an alien life style. So, the questions really get down to "ours and yours" or the differences between "selves" and "others." Race is simply a way in which one group designates itself an "insider" and other groups as "outsiders" to reinforce or enforce its wishes and/or ideas in social, economic, and political realms. Furthermore, even "scientifically determined" microraces are not constant and are related to ecological and cultural factors. This is why most physical anthropologists no longer use even the concept of "microrace." In fact, for the past twenty years, the concept of races has been considered no longer valid in anthropology. Anthropologists do study individual genetic mechanisms for specific studies, for example adaptability to certain ecological environmental features, such as the sickle cell that is found mainly in populations that carry a large potential for malarial infection, in Africa south of the Sahara, especially in a belt of agricultural societies including the Central Sudan, Nigeria, Ghana, and Gambia. The sickling gene increases where malaria is widespread. However, currently, with hardly any threat of malaria in the United States, the number of African Americans with the sickle cell trait in this country is much smaller than in malaria-infested areas of Africa. Thus, human populations are, even biologically, in constant flux. This is why in physical/biological anthropology the concept of human variation replaces the former idea of "race" as a biological entity (Lasker 1976). The variability within any one so-called "race" is greater than the variability between the specified ethnic groups or races. These are some reasons why the concept of "race" is at best controversial, and why most social scientists of the 90s believe that, in general, the concept has neither usefulness nor validity (Wolf 1994). Perhaps in the future we will look back at the ways in which people have used the term "race" as just another step in our continuing enlightenment. At the moment, the conflation of community with heredity is still one of the most dangerous fallacies of modern times.

References

Alland, A. 1967. *Evolution and Human Behavior.* New York: Natural History Press.

Bellah, R. N., R. Madsen, W. M. Sullivan, A. Swidler, and S. M. Tipton. 1985. *Habits of the Heart: Individualism and Commitment in American Life.* New York: Harper & Row.

Boas, F. 1940. *Race, Language, and Culture.* New York: The Free Press.

Franklin, B. 1784. "The Indian's Refusal," in *Remarks Concerning the Savage of North America.*

Garn, S. M. 1974. "Races of Mankind" in *The New Encyclopædia Brittannica.* Chicago: Encyclopædia Brittanica, Inc., Vol. 15, pp. 348–357.

Gould, S. J. 1981. *The Mismeasure of Man.* New York: W. W. Norton.

Lasker, G. W. 1976. *Physical Anthropology.* New York: Holt, Rinehart & Winston.

Mead, M. and J. Baldwin. 1971. *A Rap on Race.* Philadelphia: J. B. Lippincott.

Montagu, A., Editor, 1964. *The Concept of Race.* New York: The Free Press.

———. 1965. *The Idea of Race.* Lincoln, Nebraska: University of Nebraska Press.

———. 1971 (1951). *Statement on Race.* New York: Oxford University Press.

———. 1982 (1964). *Man's Most Dangerous Myth: The Fallacy of Race.* Cleveland: World.

Porteus, S. D. 1931. *The Psychology of a Primitive People.* New York: Longmans, Green and Company.

Rohrl, V. 1979. "Culture, Cognition, and Intellect: Towards a Cross-cultural View of 'Intelligence'" in *The Journal of Psychological Anthropology,* Vol. 2 No. 3, pp. 337–364.

———. 1981. *Change for Continuity: The People of a Thousand Lakes.* Washington, D.C.: University Press of America.

———. n.d. "Field Notes of a Community Mediator," unpublished manuscript.

Shanklin, Eugenia. 1994. *Anthropology and Race.* Belmont, Ca: Wadsworth.

Stocking, G. W. 1982. *Race, Culture, and Evolution.* Chicago: University of Chicago Press.

Varenne, Herve. 1993. "American Race Through the News," paper presented at the annual meetings of the American Anthropological Association, Washington, D.C.

Wolf, Eric. 1994. "Perilous Ideas: Race, Culture, People," in *Current Anthropology,* Vol. 35 (1), pp. 1–12.

THE INTERMARRIAGE OF THE RACES

W. E. B. Du Bois

Study Questions

1. Distinguish between the theory and practice with regard to the intermarriage between the "races."
2. Given that Du Bois was writing in 1899, how do you think the lives of "mixed-race" couples were affected by the larger societal context?

For years much has been said on the destiny of the Negro with regard to intermarriage with the whites. To many this seems the difficulty that differentiates the Negro question from all other social questions which we face, and makes it seemingly insoluble; the questions of ignorance, crime and immortality, these argue, may safely be left to the influence of time and education; but will time and training ever change the obvious fact that the white people of the country do not wish to mingle socially with the Negroes or to join blood in legal wedlock with them? This problem is, it must be acknowledged, difficult. Its difficulty arises, however, rather from an ignorance of surrounding facts than from the theoretic argument. Theory in such case is of little value; the white people as members of the races now dominant in the world naturally boast of their blood and accomplishments, and recoil from an alliance with a people which is to-day represented by a host of untrained and uncouth ex-slaves. On the other hand, whatever his practice be, the Negro as a free American citizen must just as strenuously maintain that marriage is a private contract, and that given two persons of proper age and economic ability who agree to enter into that relation, it does not concern any one but themselves as to whether one of them be white, black or red. It is thus that theoretical argument comes to an unpleasant standstill, and its further pursuit really settles nothing, nay, rather unsettles much, by bringing men's thoughts to a question that is, at present at least, of little practical importance. For in practice the matter works itself out: the average white person does not marry a Negro; and the average Negro, despite his theory, himself marries one of his race, and frowns darkly on his fellows unless they do likewise. In those very circles of

Negroes who have a large infusion of white blood, where the freedom of marriage is most strenuously advocated, white wives have always been treated with a disdain bordering on insult, and white husbands never received on any terms of social recognition.

Notwithstanding theory and the practice of whites and Negroes in general, it is nevertheless manifest that the white and black races have mingled their blood in this country to a vast extent. Such facts puzzle the foreigner and are destined to puzzle the future historian. A serious student of the subject gravely declares in one chapter that the races are separate and distinct and becoming more so, and in another that by reason of the intermingling of white blood the "original type of the African has almost completely disappeared;"[1] here we have reflected the prevailing confusion in the popular mind. Race amalgamation is a fact, not a theory; it took place, however, largely under the institution of slavery and for the most part, though not wholly, outside the bonds of legal marriage. With the abolition of slavery now, and the establishment of a self-protecting Negro home the question is, what have been the tendencies and the actual facts with regard to the intermarriage of races? This is the only question with which students have to do, and this singularly enough has been the one which they, with curious unanimity, have neglected. We do not know the facts with regard to the mingling of white and black blood in the past save in a most general and unsatisfactory way; we do not know the facts for to-day at all. And yet, of course, without this knowledge all philosophy of the situation is vain; only long observation of the course of intermarriage can furnish us that broad knowledge of facts which can serve as a basis for race theories and final conclusions.[2]

The first legal obstacle to the intermarriage of whites and blacks in Pennsylvania was the Act of 1726, which forbade such unions in terms that would seem to indicate that a few such marriages had taken place. Mulattoes early appeared in the State, and especially in Philadelphia, some being from the South and some from up the State. Sailors from this port in some cases brought back English, Scotch and Irish wives, and mixed families immigrated here at the time of the Haytian revolt. Between 1820 and 1860 many natural children were sent from the South and in a few cases their parents followed and were legally married here. Descendants of such children in many cases forsook the mother's race; one became principal of a city school, one a prominent sister in a Catholic church, one a bishop, and one or two officers in the Confederate army.[3] Some marriages with Quakers took place, one especially in 1825, when a Quakeress married a Negro, created much comment. Descendants of this couple still survive. Since the War the number of local marriages has considerably increased.

In this work there was originally no intention of treating the subject of intermarriage, for it was thought that the data would be too insignificant to be enlightening. When, however, in one ward of the city thirty-three cases of mixed marriages were found, and it was known that there were others in that ward, and probably a similar proportion in many other wards, it was thought that a study of these thirty-three families might be of interest and be a small contribution of fact to a subject where facts are not easily accessible.

The size of these families varies, of course, with the question as to what one considers a family; if we take the "census family," or all those living together under circumstances of family life in one home, the average size of the thirty-three families of the Seventh Ward in which there were intermarried whites was 3.5. If we take simply the father, mother and children, the average size was 2.9. There were ninety-seven parents and children in these families, and twenty other relatives living with them, making 117 individuals in the families.

Notes

[1] Hoffman's "Race Traits and Tendencies," etc., pp. 1 and 177.

[2] Hoffman has the results of some intermarriages recorded, but they are chiefly reports of criminals in the newspapers, and thus manifestly unfair for generalization.

[3] From a personal letter of a lifelong Philadelphian, whose name I am not at liberty to quote.

LETTER FROM THOMAS JEFFERSON: VIRGINIA'S DEFINITION OF A MULATTO

Study Question

1. Reread Jacques Barzun's account on page 382 of one way in which the myth of race is perpetuated. How does Thomas Jefferson's equation for determining "race" support Barzun's argument?

March 4, 1815   *Monticello*

You asked me in conversation, what constituted a mulatto by our law? And I believe I told you four crossings with the whites. I looked afterwards into our law, and found it to be in these words: "Every person, other than a Negro, of whose grandfathers or grandmothers anyone shall have been a Negro, shall be deemed a mulatto, and so every such person who shall have one-fourth part or more of Negro blood, shall in like manner be deemed a mulatto;" L. Virgà 1792, December 17: the case put in the first member of this paragraph of the law is *exempli gratiâ*. The latter contains the true canon, which is that one-fourth of Negro blood, mixed with any portion of white, constitutes the mulatto. As the issue has one-half of the blood of each parent, and the blood of each of these may be made up of a variety of fractional mixtures, the estimate of their compound in some cases may be intricate, it becomes a mathematical problem of the same class with those on the mixtures of different liquors or different metals; as in these, therefore, the algebraical notation is the most convenient and intelligible. Let us express the pure blood of the white in the capital letters of the printed alphabet, the pure blood of the Negro in the small letters of the printed alphabet, and any given mixture of either, by way of abridgment in MS. letters.

Let the first crossing be of *a,* pure Negro, with A, pure white. The unit of blood of the issue being composed of the half of that of each parent, will be $a/2 + A/2$. Call it, for abbreviation, *h* (half blood).

Let the second crossing be of h and B, the blood of the issue will be $h/2 + B/2$ or substituting for $h/2$ its equivalent, it will be $a/4 + A/4 + B/2$ call it q (quarteroon) being $\frac{1}{4}$ Negro blood.

Let the third crossing be of q and C, their offspring will be $q/2 + C/2 = a/8 + A/8 + B/4 + C/2$, call this e (eighth), who having less than $\frac{1}{4}$ of a, or of pure Negro blood, to wit $\frac{1}{8}$ only, is no longer a mulatto, so that a third cross clears the blood.

From these elements let us examine their compounds. For example, let h and q cohabit, their issue will be $h/2 + q/2 = a/4 + A/4 + a/8 + A/8 + B/4 = {}^3a/8 + {}^3A/8 + B/4$ wherein we find $\frac{3}{8}$ of a, or Negro blood.

Let h and e cohabit, their issue will be $h/2 + e/2 = a/4 + A/4 + a/16 + A/16 + B/8 + c/4 = {}^5a/16 + {}^5A/16 + B/8 + c/4$, wherein $\frac{5}{16}$ a makes still a mulatto.

Let q and e cohabit, the half of the blood of each will be $q/2 + e/2 = a/8 + A/8 + B/4 + a/16 + A/16 + B/8 + C/4 = {}^3a/16 + {}^3A/16 + {}^3B/8 + C/4$, wherein $\frac{3}{16}$ of a is no longer a mulatto, and thus may every compound be noted and summed, the sum of the fractions composing the blood of the issue being always equal to unit. It is understood in natural history that a fourth cross of one race of animals with another gives an issue equivalent for all sensible purposes to the original blood. Thus a Merino ram being crossed, first with a country ewe, second with his daughter, third with his granddaughter, and fourth with the great-granddaughter, the last issue is deemed pure Merino, having in fact but $\frac{1}{16}$ of the country blood. Our canon considers two crosses with the pure white, and a third with any degree of mixture, however small, as clearing the issue of the Negro blood. But observe, that this does not re-establish freedom, which depends on the condition of the mother, the principle of the civil law, *partus sequitur ventrem,* being adopted here. But if e emancipated, he becomes a free *white* man, and a citizen of the United States to all intents and purposes. So much for this trifle by way of correction.

ETHNIC DIVERSITY: ITS HISTORICAL AND CONSTITUTIONAL ROOTS

CRUZ REYNOSO

Study Questions
1. List the various historical and constitutional events that show the struggle in the United States to accommodate diversity.
2. Evaluate the process of change.

I want to talk with you about the law and ethnic diversity in our country. Since the birth of our nation, we Americans have been in an evolutionary process of defining who we are as Americans, what the American community is, and who belongs to it. In that regard, the American experience has been a great historical experiment, successful sometimes, but not successful other times. The experience we have had as a people is intertwined with our Constitution and the principles that the Constitution has established. The basic question we have to ask ourselves is the following: How can we as a people, or as peoples of diverse religions, races and ethnicities live together and prosper together?

Before the birth of our nation, and sadly it continues today, some of the great wars in this world have come about due to the hatred toward those who are different—by religion, race or ethnicity. We see what is happening in the former Soviet Union, Eastern Europe, the Middle East, Africa and even such places as South America. These hatreds are live issues, traumatic issues that have brought a great deal of suffering to the human family. When we as Americans came together to form our nation, I think we asked the same basic question: Can we have a nation, can we have a people, who can live together and consider themselves as one, and yet be as different as the peoples of this world?

One of America's experiments was in religion. Even though the Constitution declares that the federal government shall not establish religion, we understood early that the essence of that constitutional mandate was a concern about our right, as individual Americans, to practice our own religion. Those who penned the Constitution had in mind the great wars of Europe and the Middle East which had killed so many and had brought so much suffering. So they concluded that the new country had to be one in which folk of different religions could live together. The living together by those who practice different religions has not been all that easy. Books have been written about the "other Americans," Americans who were not of European, Protestant ancestry. Fred Hart, former Dean of the University of New Mexico, and still a professor there, tells that his dad remembers when they were growing up in Boston. Signs in some establishments that hired workers would read something like, "Help wanted: Irish and Dogs need not apply." That reaction of prejudice and hatred by some of the owners of those plants was based on religion as well as ethnicity. Indeed, it was not until John Kennedy's presidential campaign that the nation said, "We have matured enough that we can see a Catholic in the White House." That is a long time—from the inception of our country until 1960.

We have succeeded in creating an American culture wherein folk of different religions can live together and consider themselves one people. We appear to have reached a relatively satisfactory solution, at least for a while, because the issue of religion does not come up all the time. There is a fellow you may have heard of by the name Pat Buchanan. He is described by some as a conservative, a right winger, a racist, and by others as a great American. Never is he described as "the Catholic candidate." Yet he is a Catholic, and he often cites his Catholicism to reject the accusation that he is a racist. To me, it is an evolution in the public life of our country that we have a person running for president whose Catholicism hardly gets mentioned.

Others have also suffered. Non-Christians, particularly Jewish people, as well as Hindus and Native Americans have suffered from exclusion. A few years ago, the Alaska Supreme Court issued, I thought, a moving opinion about the rights of a Native American to kill a moose because it was part of the religion of that particular tribe.[1] The Alaska Supreme Court was balancing the right of the state to protect the environment with the right of that particular tribe to exercise its own religion, and, in a sensitive opinion, tried to balance those interests. Thus, the historic process continues.

Issues of religion will always be with us, because who we are religiously is so important to each of us. Yet, we have made so much progress. That is our success story. In America we have been able to live together and consider ourselves as one people, though a people of great religious diversity.

The next area in which we as a nation have worked so hard has been that of race, particularly pertaining to African-Americans. We succeeded so poorly that we experienced here what had happened in other countries—a great war, a great civil war. A larger percentage of Americans were killed and maimed during that war than any other war, over something called race. The Civil War is just a reminder of how important and divisive issues of diversity can be. But from the suffering of this nation in that great war, which pitted brother against brother and sister against sister, came an important amendment to the Constitution—the Fourteenth Amendment. Some post-Civil War amendments, like the Thirteenth, are easily understood. The more difficult Fourteenth Amendment provided the source for a redefinition of who we are as Americans. The constitutional notions of equality and due process found within the pre-Civil War Fifth Amendment were incorporated into the post-Civil War amendments. With the Fourteenth Amendment our country was saying, "We meant what we said in the original Ten Amendments." We redefined ourselves as a people to include African-Americans, including former slaves. While many African-Americans had lived as freed men and women before the Civil War we had not previously succeeded in dealing with the issue of race.

You recall that in the Lincoln-Douglas debates Abraham Lincoln argued that the Constitution set forth the ideal of equality. Those who signed the Constitution understood that we would not meet that ideal immediately, but that we as Americans had a duty to work day in and day out to get the reality of our country a little bit closer to that ideal. To me, and this may sound strange to you, we reached a new public understanding of the reality that we as Americans are of many races, when we built the Vietnam Veterans Memorial in Washington, D.C., and included a black soldier among the soldiers represented. I think we recognized publicly that all races have sacrificed to make this nation great.

Native Americans, like African-Americans, have suffered because of race. Our country originally dealt with Native Americans through the War Department. We viewed Native Americans as the enemy—they were to be killed or captured. Since then American history has evolved to a better understanding between the Indian and non-Indian.

In recent years, the issue of ethnicity and language has come into the forefront. Ethnicity and language, like religion and race, define us. Are we as Americans, or should we be, a people of one language and one ethnicity? In many states there is what is called the English-only movement. A friend of mine from New England, with whom I have served on several committees of the American Bar Association, came up to me one day and said, "Cruz, I know an elderly couple, friends of mine, who went from New England to Florida, and when they came back they said that they were taken aback. They found portions of Miami where everybody spoke Spanish. Only when the couple explained that they did not speak Spanish was English spoken." My friend said, "Cruz, we must do something about this; we must have one language for all of us." I responded: "You are absolutely right. When are you learning Spanish?"

We have struggled with the issue of language and ethnicity throughout our national life. I do not think that we have yet decided what our national ideal is in that regard. My own view is that we Americans are now, and have historically always been, a people of many languages and many ethnic groups. I mentioned the Native Americans, who were here before the European-Americans, and who enjoyed great civilizations and who created marvelous works of art. Somehow we look at the Native Americans of Mexico and the Latin Americans as being those who created great civilizations and great art. The reality is that Native Americans who have lived in what we now call the United States also had that great creativity. We can look to the great irrigation system constructed in New Mexico, or we can look to the political organization of the Navajo nation. Other ethnic groups, such as the Spanish-speaking, came to this land over a hundred years before the English-speaking. Travel in New Orleans or Florida, certainly in Puerto Rico and the Southwest, demonstrates their influence. Sante Fe, New Mexico claims to be the longest standing city that has been a seat of government in what is now the United States. It goes back to the mid-sixteenth century. So folk of different languages and different ethnics groups have been here for a long time.

In the seventeenth century, when the English-speaking Europeans came to the eastern shores of the United States, so did those who spoke French and German and other languages. Indeed, in his autobiography, Benjamin Franklin spoke about how the United States Constitution was translated into the German language during the political debates about whether or not the Constitution should be approved by the people of this country. It seems to me that we have always recognized the importance of people who are of different ethnic groups and tongues.

Take a look at the history of my own state of California. While I spent four years in New Mexico, and I tell folks that I consider myself part manito (a New Mexican is a manito), I was born in California. First came the Native Americans, then the Mexicans and Spaniards who came and settled that land well before the Americans got there. Then came groups from South America, particularly the Chilean community in San Francisco, in large parts because they were fishermen and traders who sailed up and down the Pacific coast. In the middle of the last century, the Americans came to California, and about the same time came many Chinese, followed by Japanese and Filipinos. Currently we have great influxes of people from Southeast Asia and Central America. In Los Angeles, I see whole communities change in a matter of few years. I used to stay in a certain part of Los Angeles which a few years ago was mostly Mexican-American (Chicano) and Anglo-Americans. Now it is mostly Central Americans.

We have seen these great historical changes in our country. It seems to me that we have the political foundation and the ideals of our Constitution to help us meet those realities. Those ideals will help us craft a country in which we consider ourselves as one people, while continuing to enjoy the strength which comes from different religions, races, languages and ethnicities.

We start with basics. The Constitution states that all of us, all the "persons" in this country, enjoy constitutional protections; it is not "citizens," the "English-speaking" or the "Spanish-speaking," who are protected, but all of us as "persons." The United States Supreme Court had occasion to deal with the issue of ethnicity and language in a case that came before it in 1923. You may have read about it in your Constitutional Law classes, *Meyer v. Nebraska.*[2] You may remember that it is a case that dealt with a state statute enacted around 1919 during the First World War.[3] There was a strong anti-German feeling during that time in America. I recall older persons I knew, who were adults during that war, telling me that in their schools, German books and music were destroyed. If they were German, they could not be good. At the time, the Nebraska legislature enacted a criminal statute that prohibited the teaching of German to youngsters before they had graduated from the eighth grade.[4] There was a parochial school in Nebraska called the Zion Parochial School where youngsters were taught in English and in German.[5] A young teacher by the name of Meyer, despite the law, continued to teach in German. He was arrested and convicted.[6] Here is what the statute said:

> No person individually or as a teacher, shall, in any private, denominational, parochial or public school, teach any subject to any person in any language other than the English language. . . . Languages, other than the English language, may be taught as languages only after a pupil shall have attained and successfully passed the eighth grade as evidenced by a certificate of graduation issued by the county superintendent of the county in which the child resides.[7]

Meyer appealed his conviction, but the courts in Nebraska upheld the constitutionality of the statute.[8] Interestingly, court decisions in Nebraska excluded the "dead languages,"—Latin, Greek and Hebrew—from this statute.[9] The legislature, according to the state supreme court, did not mean that students could not study dead languages, only that they could not study certain "live" languages.[10] Eventually the case reached the United States Supreme Court, and the Court looked at the facts and asked itself whether the statute could be constitutional. The Court tried to define what "liberty" meant under the Fourteenth Amendment.[11]

Although the Justices did not talk about it, I think they were also concerned about the Ninth Amendment. When the first Ten Amendments were introduced, an important political debate took place regarding the question of whether those protections that we receive from the first ten amendments were exclusive. In many states, many people said, "No, we want to make clear that those protections are by way of description, for there are many other rights that we have as Americans that government does not have the right to take away." That conclusion was echoed in the *Meyer* case:

> While this Court has not attempted to define with exactness the liberty thus guaranteed [by the Fourteenth Amendment], the term has received much consideration and some of the included things have been definitely stated. Without a doubt, it denotes not merely freedom from bodily restraint but also the right of the individual to contract, to engage in any of the common occupations of life, to acquire useful knowledge, to marry, to establish a home and bring up children, to worship God according to the dictates of his own conscience, and generally to enjoy those privileges long recognized at common law as essential to the orderly pursuit of happiness by free men.[12]

Notice that none of these protections mentioned are found in the Constitution. The Court was saying that surely the right to marry, the right to have children, the right to bring up your family have to be so fundamental that Congress and the states cannot monkey around, if you will, with those rights. Those unstated rights include the right to worship God according to the dictates of a person's own conscience, and generally to enjoy those privileges long recognized at common law as essential to the orderly pursuit of happiness by free men and women. The Court then went on to discuss the importance of language to an individual.[13] The Court ruled that the Nebraska statute was unconstitutional, and that the state had to have an overwhelmingly important reason to prohibit a youngster from learning German, or a teacher from teaching German.[14] The state, the Court wrote, clearly may go very far in order to improve the quality of its citizens, physically, mentally and morally.[15] The individual, however, has certain fundamental rights which must be respected and that includes the right of languages.[16] It seems to me that such a right includes the right of ethnicity. The right to one's own language was recognized as fundamental within our constitution.

The Court had another occasion to look at the issue of ethnicity in a case from the state of California. We produce a great deal of constitutional law from the state of California. A case came up in 1947, if I remember correctly, called *Oyama v. California*.[17] California had passed a statute that prohibited aliens from owning land in California.[18] The breadth of the statute had been narrowed by court decisions; by the 1940s the statute had been interpreted to mean that Japanese could not own land in California. A Japanese immigrant had bought and paid for some land and then put the title in the name of his son, so the son was the legal owner.[19] The father then filed in court to become the guardian, and, in fact, was the child's actual guardian.[20] The statute declared that if a person, who could not legally become a citizen, paid for the land, it would be presumed that such payment was an effort to get around the statute.[21] In that event, the land would escheat to the state.[22] Interestingly, it was the Attorney General of California who brought the action against Mr. Oyama. The only person who testified was the person in charge of the land.[23] The Oyamas did not testify because the hearing took place during the Second World War, when the Oyamas were confined in a concentration camp.[24]

The trial court decided against the Oyamas, and the case was appealed in the California courts.[25] The courts found that the father had paid for the land, and that the Oyamas were clearly trying to get around the statute, and, therefore, the land properly escheated to the state.[26]

The United States Supreme Court looked at the case from the point of view of the little boy, Fred Oyama, and said, "Wait a minute. We are looking at the rights of a citizen, Fred Oyama."[27] Another contemporaneous statute in California permitted parents to make a gift of land to a child by paying for the land.[28] The Court underscored that an American citizen, the child, was being treated differently because of who his parents were.[29] This case presented a conflict between a state's right to formulate a policy in land holding within its boundaries and the right of American citizens to own land anywhere in the United States.[30] The Court concluded that when these two rights clash, the rights of a citizen may not be subordinated merely because of his father's country of origin (that is, the ethnicity of the citizen).[31]

So we start to see a constitutional pattern which protects persons from discrimination on the basis of ethnicity. And I just want to remind us that the Constitution so often deals in the negative, that is, "You can't do A, B, and C," but what it really means is that people have certain rights. While the Court ruled that the Constitution provided protection from discrimination, it really was defining the right of Americans to their own language and ethnicity.

When I was a youngster in Orange County, California, we still had segregated schools. For several years I was sent to a public grammar school referred to as "The Mexican School." There were other schools called "The American Schools." I was born in the then-little town of Brea; Orange County was rural in those pre-Disneyland days. I had gone to school in

Brea for a couple years and then my family moved to the nearby community of La Habra. There were a lot of folks in La Habra of Mexican ancestry. When September came, we looked for a school and found a place that looked like a school we were used too—it was built with bricks, it was two stories and had a playground in the back. My brothers and I went there to sign up, and the school officials said, "No, you don't go to this school, you go to another, the Wilson School." So we went to Wilson School. We noticed that all the youngsters there were Latinos and Chicanos, and we asked why we were being sent to this school. We were told that we were being sent to this school to learn English. Since my brothers and I already knew English, we were a little bit suspicious that maybe that was not the reason. After a few months a black family with two youngsters moved into our barrio. They did not speak a word of Spanish; they only spoke English. Nonetheless, they were sent to our school. So we got doubly suspicious. Incidentally, educationally-speaking, it was not a lost cause at all. You may have heard of the "immersion system" of learning a language other than your own; those black youngsters were speaking Spanish as well as we in about six months. Meanwhile, we noticed that there were Anglo-American families whose houses literally abutted on Wilson School, and they were being sent to distant schools. After a while we recognized that, in fact, ours was a segregated school.

A few years after I "graduated" from Wilson (grades kindergarten through sixth), the school was integrated. A lawsuit was filed challenging the segregation of Mexican-American school children in a nearby school district. A federal judge ruled that under California law, school segregation was unlawful.

Related issues reached the United States Supreme Court. It was in a different context that the case of *Hernandez v. Texas*[32] came before the high Court in 1954. A Texan who was Mexican-American had been convicted of murder and appealed.[33] He was unhappy that there had been no Latinos, Chicanos or Mexican-Americans on the jury.[34] The county in Texas where he was tried was fourteen percent Mexican-American, yet for twenty-five years there had not been one Latino on a jury commission, a grand jury or a petit jury.[35] During that time apparently 6,000 persons had been called to serve on one of those commissions or juries and not one had a Spanish surname.[36] Indeed, the Court also pointed out that there were some suspicious matters in that community. In the courthouse, there were two bathrooms, one unmarked, and the other with a sign that read "Colored Men" and then below it "Hombres Aqui" (Men Here). That made the Court a little bit suspicious.[37] There was at least one restaurant in town, the Court said, that had a sign in front that read, "No Mexicans Served."

Until very recently the public schools had been segregated.[38] There was extensive testimony in the record by the authorities arguing that they had never discriminated against Latinos; all they tried to do was to find the best possible people to serve.[39] The Supreme Court concluded that despite the generalized denial, it was very difficult to believe that out of 6,000 people, they had not been able to find one qualified Latino.[40] The Court noted that "[t]he state of Texas would have us hold that there are only two classes— white and Negro—within the contemplation of the Fourteenth Amendment,"[41] even as late as 1954. Incidentally, you will find *Hernandez v. Texas* reported just before a case that may sound familiar to you, *Brown v. Board of Education of Topeka*.[42] The Court was busy in those days. The Court rejected the Texas notion out of hand. "The Fourteenth Amendment," the Court said, "is not directed solely against the discrimination due to a 'two-class theory'—that is, based upon differences between 'white' and Negro."[43] The Court went on to say that the Constitution indeed protects everybody:

> The exclusion of otherwise eligible persons from jury service solely because of their ancestry or national origin is discrimination prohibited by the Fourteenth Amendment. The Texas statute makes no such discrimination, but the petitioner alleges that those administering the law do.[44]

And, in fact, the Court was convinced that that is exactly what had happened. So again we have a confirmation by the Court that ethnicity is protected.

For those of you who might be concerned about the current Supreme Court, I just want to tell you that the following is written by a distinguished observer of the court:

> Even Justice Rehnquist, the modern Justice who takes the least interventionist view of equal protection and who is the strongest opponent of the expansion of "suspect classification" jurisprudence, acknowledged in *Trimble v. Gordon* . . . that classifications based on "national origin, the first cousin of race" . . . were areas where "the Framers obviously meant [equal protection] to apply."[45]

So apparently even those who take lightly the post-Civil War amendments are convinced that in this area, in the area of ethnicity, there is no question that it is protected by the Constitution.

Finally, I want to mention a case decided by the California Supreme Court called *Castro v. California*.[46] It is one of my favorite cases, maybe because I was the director of a legal services group called California Rule Legal Assistance (CRLA) which filed this action on the behalf of its clients.

The challenged California constitutional provision read: "[N]o person who shall not be able to read the Constitution in the English language, and write his or her name, shall ever exercise the privileges of an elector in this State."[47] That constitutional provision was passed in 1891, and I will come back to that fact in a few minutes.[48]

Our clients were able to show that in Los Angeles County where they lived, there were seventeen newspapers published in Spanish, eleven magazines, many radio and television stations, and through these, they were able to know exactly what the public issues of the day were and were able to cast a vote that was educated.[49] The California Supreme Court, analyzing the state constitutional provision by the standards of the federal Constitution, said, in essence, "It cannot stand. We consider the right of citizens. The right to vote is very important." The court determined that the state could not take away the right to vote unless there was a very important reason to do so, and here the court simply did not find that reason. These voters, by reading and hearing, could, in fact, educate themselves.[50] Then, at the end of the opinion, the court added one of my favorite paragraphs in American jurisprudence. Writing for the court, Justice Raymond Sullivan said:

> We add one final word. We cannot refrain from observing that if a contrary conclusion were compelled it would indeed be ironic that petitioners, who are the heirs of a great and gracious culture, identified with the birth of California and contributing in no small measure to its growth, should be disenfranchised in their ancestral land, despite their capacity to cast an informed vote.[51]

So we have come a long way—in California and in the nation.

In *Castro,* the court reviewed the history of constitutional and statutory changes in California, and in one of the footnotes it cited to a case called *People v. Hall.*[52] It is one of my favorite cases in California jurisprudence for a reason opposite that of *Castro v. California.* Let me tell you about the *Hall* case. When California was first formed into a state, the English-speaking and the Spanish-speaking worked cooperatively. They got together in the constitutional convention of 1849 and agreed upon a constitution, even though some who were at that convention spoke no English, and others spoke no Spanish. Yet they got together and created a constitution that was published in both English and Spanish.

But then, sadly, the atmosphere started changing in California, and the case of *People v. Hall,*[53] decided in 1854, gives you a sense of how much change had come about. The legislature had passed a statute that prohibited any testimony against a white person in court if the testimony came from a black, mulatto or an American Indian.[54] A white man was convicted of murder by the testimony of a Chinese man.[55] At that time we had no intermediate court, so the lawyers for the convicted appealed directly to the California Supreme Court.

The California Supreme Court was composed of three members at that time, and it wrote an opinion that is great fun to read in its historical context. The court pointed out that the Native Americans are part of the Mongoloid races and that eons ago, the Mongoloid races from Asia had travelled over the Bering Straits and through Alaska. In the course of many thousands of years these migrants ended up in the lands we now call the United States. The Indians and the Chinese were of the Mongoloid race. When the legislature said Indians could not testify, it obviously meant to include anybody of the Mongoloid race.[56] Since Chinese belong to the Mongoloid race, the court reasoned, they obviously cannot testify against a white man, and so the court reversed the murder conviction.

The *Hall* court described the Chinese people as a "distinct people . . . whose mendacity is proverbial; a race of people whom nature has marked as inferior, and who are incapable of progress or intellectual development beyond a certain a point, as their history has shown. . . ."[57] This quote does not include another discussion in which the court noted that if allowed to testify against a white person, the Chinese would soon want to vote, want to be lawyers, and would even want to sit on the bench.[58] The court ruled on the basis of clear statutory construction. The court seemingly asked, "How could anybody disagree that Indian means Chinese." Indeed, the court wrote: "[E]ven in a doubtful case we would be impelled to this decision on the grounds of public policy."[59]

Sadly, just a few years thereafter, Manuel Dominguez, who had been at the California constitutional convention, and had signed the constitution, was not permitted to testify in a court of law in San Francisco in 1857 because he was of Indian ancestry. That is part of the history of California. To look at the *Castro* decision and see how the law has evolved is a matter of great satisfaction to me.

Incidentally, I have always been interested in Los Angeles. If you visit Los Angeles, go down to the area where Los Angeles was first founded, La Placita (the little plaza). There is a plaque there which has the names of all of the people who helped found Los Angeles. The Spaniards were great record keepers. The records identify people by race and by occupation as well as other characteristics. That plaque identifies the race of the original settlers. I have a book here[60] which published a census taken about the time Los Angeles was founded. Let me just go down the line; you will see the great variety of people that founded California. The reality contrasts with the early romanticized movies that came out of Hollywood portraying Spanish vaqueros as typical. Here are the real Californios: Josef de Lara, Spaniard; his wife Maria, india sabina; Josef Navarro, mestizo; his wife Maria, mulata; Basil Rosas, indian; a husband, indian; his wife, indian; another husband Alejandro Rosas, indian; his wife Juana, coyote indian—mixture of pure Indian and mestizo; Pablo Rodriguez, indian; wife Maria Rosalia, indian; Manuel Camero, mulato; his wife Maria Tomasa, mulata; Luis Quintera, negro; his wife Maria Petmulata; Jose Moreno, mulato; Antonio Rodriguez, chino (Chino—a person who has negroid features, but was born of white parents).[61] That is the real mixture of Los Angeles from whence many of us come.

Let me just read you a passage from that same book. A very distinguished early Californio, Pablo de la Guerra, who was late as state senator, is quoted. The title of the book was FOREIGNERS IN THEIR NATIVE LAND, taken from a speech he delivered in the California legislature in 1856:

> It is the conquered who are humble before the conqueror asking for his protection, while enjoying what little their misfortune has left them. It is those who have been sold like sheep—it is those who were abandoned by Mexico. They do not understand the prevalent language of their native soil. They are *foreigners in their own land.* I have seen seventy and sixty year olds cry like children because they have been uprooted from the lands of their fathers. They have been humiliated and insulted. They have been refused the privilege of taking water from their own wells. They have been denied the privilege of cutting their own firewood.[62]

This is our history.

Yet we have struggled. As the cases from the California and the United States Supreme Courts indicate, we have indeed made a great deal of progress. The struggles continue. Issues like education and political empowerment create conflict. As we all know, progress does not come overnight. My hope is that as we struggle with these issues, we will also struggle with that notion of how can we be diverse and yet be one people.

For myself, I have enjoyed that diversity. I have a friend by the name of Bill Ong Hing, a professor at Stanford. He invited my family and me to go to his church where a Chinese play was presented. We enjoyed tremendously seeing a culture that my family and I had not seen before. I remember walking down the streets of San Francisco and a gentleman coming up to Bill. The two of them chatted for a couple of minutes in Chinese and then spoke in English. I did not feel that they were talking about me during that time. So often we reject folk who speak a language other than our own, because we think, "Well, they must be talking about me." I never thought that any one person was that important. I would hope that we learn to enjoy the reality that other people are different and that they have a language, a cultural richness, if you will, that we can enjoy. Indeed, I really do give thanks for the fact that we have people in this country who speak different languages and come from different cultures who will make our country far stronger economically and far stronger politically.

I always think of the advertising that we as Americans do. I am told that there was a time when General Motors was advertising in Latin America for their then-new car called the Nova. Apparently nobody had told them that "Nova" in Spanish is "Nova," which means "It won't go." It was not a successful advertising campaign. Or another time when my former colleague, Justice Joseph Groden of the California Supreme Court, came back from a long trip in China, and he told me there were Coca-Cola signs all over China. I asked about Pepsi-Cola because I had read that Pepsi had a contract with the Chinese government. At that time Pepsi-Cola had a little ditty, you may remember many years ago, that went something like, "Pepsi, come alive with Pepsi." Unfortunately, it had been mistranslated in Chinese to read, "Pepsi brings your ancestors back to life," and the Chinese, with their respect for their ancestors, were not amused. Pepsi apparently lost its contract.

I also remember reading an article by a German industrialist who said basically, "You know, I speak English, and I go to all of these gatherings where folk come from all over the world selling their high-tech equipment. I go and look at all that and I see that the Americans make very good equipment, and the Japanese have very good equipment, as do other nationals. They all look very good. Then afterwards, though I speak English, I socialize with folks generally in the German language, because I feel more comfortable in German. All I can tell you is that in Germany, you'll sell in the German language."

I think that our diversity will indeed bring strength to us, and I think that we can profit from it. But more importantly, we need to continue working with the reality that we are a very diverse people, ethnically and linguistically. Despite those differences, as with differences of race and religion, we ought to look at what unites us, what makes us all Americans. We need to look at our history, at the land, at the suffering we have been through as a people. We need to examine the ideals that we find in the Constitution, those very ideals that have brought the California and the United States Supreme Courts to declare that there are those rights so important that government can not take them away from us. If nobody can take those rights away from us, we need to rejoice in those rights, to rejoice in our differences, to appreciate those differences, and to profit one from another.

Notes

[1] Frank v. State of Alaska, 604 P.2d 1068 (Ala. 1979).

[2] 262 U.S. 390 (1923).

[3] *Id.* at 397 (citing NEB LAWS 1919, ch. 249 (entitled "An act relating to the teaching of foreign languages in the State of Nebraska" (approved April 9, 1919))).

[4] *Id.* (citing NEB. LAWS 1919, ch. 249, § 2).

[5] *Id.* at 396–97.

[6] *Id.* at 396.

[7] *Id.* at 397 (quoting NEB. LAWS 1919, ch. 24, §§ 1–2).

[8] *Id.*

[9] *Id.* at 400–01.

[10] *Id.* at 401.

[11] The Fourteenth Amendment states, in pertinent part: "No State shall . . . deprive any person of life, liberty, or property, without due process of law; nor deny to any person within its jurisdiction the equal protection of the laws." U.S. CONST. amend. XIV, § 1.

[12] *Meyer,* 262 U.S. at 399.

[13] *Id.* at 400–03.

[14] *Id.* at 402–03.

[15] *Id.* at 402.

[16] *Id.* at 400–01.

[17] 332 U.S. 633 (1948).

[18] *Id.* at 635–36 & nn. 1 & 3 (citing Alien Land Law, 1 CAL. GEN. LAWS, Act 261 (Deering 1944 & Supp. 1945)).

[19] *Id.* at 636–37.

[20] *Id.*

[21] *See id.* at 636 (citing Alien Land Law, 1 CAL. GEN. LAWS, Act 261, § 9(a)).

[22] *Id.*

[23] *Id.* at 638. The witness, John Kurfurst, had been left in charge of the Oyama property when the Oyama family was evacuated in 1942 as part of the evacuation of persons of Japanese descent during World War II. *Id.* at 637–38.

[24] *See id.* at 638.

[25] *See id.* at 639.

[26] *Id.* at 639–40.

[27] *See id.* at 640.

[28] *Id.* at 640 & n. 16 (citing CAL. PROB. CODE ANN. § 1407).

[29] *Id.* at 640–41.

[30] *Id.* at 647.

[31] *See id.* at 646–47.

[32] 347 U.S. 475 (1954).

[33] *Id.* at 476.

[34] *Id.* at 476–77.

[35] *Id.* at 480–81 & n. 12.

[36] *Id.* at 482.

[37] *Id.* at 479–80.

[38] *Id.* at 479.

[39] *Id.* at 481.

[40] *Id.* at 482.

[41] *Id.* at 477.

[42] 347 U.S. 483 (1954).

[43] *Hernandez,* 347 U.S. at 478.

[44] *Id.* at 479.

[45] CONSTITUTIONAL LAW 624 n.3 (Gerald Gunther ed., 11th ed. 1985) (citing Trimble v. Gordon, 430 U.S. 762, 777 (1977) (Rehnquist, J., dissenting)).

[46] 466 P. 2d 244 (Cal. 1970).

[47] *Id.* at 245 (quoting CAL. CONST. art. 2, § 1).

[48] *Id.* The English literacy requirement was proposed in 1891 by a California state assemblyman, A.J. Bledsoe, who in 1886 had been part of a committee that expelled all persons of Chinese ancestry from Humboldt County, California. *Id.*

[49] *Id.* at 254–55.

[50] *See, e.g., id.* at 254–57.

[51] *Id.* at 259.

[52] *Id.* at 248 n.11 (citing People v. Hall, 4 Cal. 399 (1854)).

[53] 4 Cal. 399 (1854).

[54] *Id.* at 399 (quoting Act of April 16, 1850 (regulating California criminal proceedings)).

[55] *Id.*

[56] *Id.* at 400–04.

[57] *Castro,* 466 P.2d at 248 n.11 (quoting *Hall,* 4 Cal. at 404–05).

[58] *Hall,* 4 Cal. at 404–05.

[59] *Id.* at 404.

[60] FOREIGNERS IN THEIR NATIVE LAND 33 (David J. Weber ed., 1st ed. 1973).

[61] *Id.* at 34–35.

[62] *Id.* at vi (quoting Pablo de la Guerra, Speech to the California Senate (1856)).

ONE DROP OF BLOOD

LAWRENCE WRIGHT

Study Questions
1. Describe the gap between self-perceived membership in a racial category and independent observer assessments.
2. Describe the pros and cons associated with dismantling racial classification.
3. What are some arguments against adding a multiracial category?

Whatever the word "race" may mean elsewhere in the world, or to the world of science, it is clear that in America the categories are arbitrary, confused, and hopelessly intermingled. In many cases, Americans don't know who they are, racially speaking. A National Center for Health Statistics study found that 5.8 per cent of the people who called themselves Black were seen as White by a census interviewer. Nearly a third of the people identifying themselves as Asian were classified as White or Black by independent observers. That was also true of seventy per cent of people who identified themselves as American Indians. Robert A. Hahn, an epidemiologist at the Centers for Disease Control and Prevention, analyzed deaths of infants born from 1983 through 1985. In an astounding number of cases, the infant had a different race on its death certificate from the one on its birth certificate, and this finding led to staggering increases in the infant-mortality rate for minority populations—46.9 per cent greater for American Indians, 48.8 per cent greater for Japanese-Americans, 78.7 per cent greater for Filipinos—over what had been previously recorded. Such disparities cast doubt on the dependability of race as a criterion for any statistical survey. "It seems to me that we have to go back and reëvaluate the whole system," Hahn says. "We have to ask, 'What do these categories mean?' We are not talking about race in the way that geneticists might use the term, because we're not making any kind of biological assessment. It's closer to self-perceived membership in a population—which is essentially what ethnicity is." There are genetic variations in disease patterns, Hahn points out, and he goes on to say, "But these variations don't always correspond to so-called races. What's really important is, essentially, two things. One, people from different ancestral backgrounds have different behaviors—diets, ideas about what to do when you're sick—that lead them to

422

different health statuses. Two, people are discriminated against because of other people's perception of who they are and how they should be treated. There's still a lot of discrimination in the health-care system."

Racial statistics do serve an important purpose in the monitoring and enforcement of civil-rights laws; indeed, that has become the main justification for such data. A routine example is the Home Mortgage Disclosure Act. Because of race questions on loan applications, the federal government has been able to document the continued practice of redlining by financial institutions. The Federal Reserve found that, for conventional mortgages, in 1992 the denial rate for blacks and Hispanics was roughly double the rate for whites. Hiring practices, jury selection, discriminatory housing patterns, apportionment of political power—in all these areas, and more, the government patrols society, armed with little more than statistical information to insure equal and fair treatment. "We need these categories essentially to get rid of them," Hahn says.

The unwanted corollary of slotting people by race is that such officially sanctioned classifications may actually worsen racial strife. By creating social-welfare programs based on race rather than on need, the government sets citizens against one another precisely because of perceived racial differences. "It is not 'race' but a *practice* of racial classification that bedevils the society," writes Yehudi Webster, a sociologist at California State University, Los Angeles, and the author of "The Racialization of America." The use of racial statistics, he and others have argued, creates a reality of racial divisions, which then require solutions, such as busing, affirmative action, and multicultural education, all of which are bound to fail, because they heighten the racial awareness that leads to contention. Webster believes that adding a Multiracial box would be "another leap into absurdity," because it reinforces the concept of race in the first place. "In a way, it's a continuation of the one-drop principle. Anybody can say, 'I've got one drop of *something*—I must be multiracial.' It may be a good thing. It may finally convince Americans of the absurdity of racial classification."

In 1990, Itabari Njeri, who writes about interethnic relations for the Los Angeles *Times,* organized a symposium for the National Association of Black Journalists. She recounts a presentation given by Charles Stewart, a Democratic Party activist: "If you consider yourself black for political reasons, raise your hand." The vast majority raised their hands. When Stewart then asked how many people present believed they were of pure African descent, without any mixture, no one raised his hand. Stewart commented later, "If you advocate a category that includes people who are multiracial to the detriment of their black identification, you will replicate what you saw—an empty room. We cannot afford to have an empty room."

Njeri maintains that the social and economic gap between light-skinned blacks and dark-skinned blacks is as great as the gap between all blacks and all whites in America. If people of more obviously mixed backgrounds were to migrate to a Multiracial box, she says, they would be politically abandoning their former allies and the people who needed their help the most. Instead of draining the established categories of their influence, Njeri and others believe, it would be better to eliminate racial categories altogether.

That possibility is actually being discussed in the corridors of government. "It's quite strange—the original idea of O.M.B. Directive 15 has nothing to do with current efforts to 'define' race," says Sally Katzen, the director of the Office of Information and Regulatory Affairs at O.M.B., who has the onerous responsibility of making the final recommendation on revising the racial categories. "When O.M.B. got into the business of establishing categories, it was purely statistical, not programmatic—purely for the purpose of data gathering, not for defining or protecting different categories. It was certainly never meant to *define* a race." And yet for more than twenty years Directive 15 did exactly that, with relatively little outcry. "Recently, a question has been raised about the increasing number of multiracial children. I personally have received pictures of beautiful children who are part Asian and part black, or part American Indian and part Asian, with these letters saying, 'I don't want to check just one box. I don't want to deny part of my heritage.' It's very compelling."

This year, Katzen convened a new interagency committee to consider how races should be categorized, and even whether racial information should be sought at all. "To me it's *offensive*—because I think of the Holocaust—for someone to say what a Jew is," says Katzen. "I don't think a government agency should be defining racial and ethnic categories—that certainly was not what was ever intended by these standards."

Is it any accident that racial and ethnic categories should come under attack now, when being a member of a minority group brings certain advantages? The white colonizers of North America conquered the indigenous people, imported African slaves, brought in Asians as laborers and then excluded them with prejudicial immigration laws, and appropriate Mexican land and the people who were living on it. In short, the nonwhite population of America has historically been subjugated and treated as second-class citizens by the white majority. It is to redress the social and economic inequalities of our history that we have civil-rights laws and affirmative-action plans in the first place. Advocates of various racial and ethnic groups point out that many of the people now calling for a race-blind society are political conservatives, who may have an interest in undermining the advancement of nonwhites in our society. Suddenly, the conservatives have adopted the language of integration, it seems, and the left-leaning racial-identity advocates have adopted the language of separatism. It amounts to a polar reversal of political rhetoric.

Jon Michael Spencer, a professor in the African and Afro-American Studies Curriculum at the University of North Carolina at Chapel Hill, recently wrote an article in *The Black Scholar* lamenting what he calls "the postmodern conspiracy to explode racial identity." The article ignited a passionate debate in the magazine over the nature and the future of race. Spencer believes that race is a useful metaphor for cultural and historic difference, because it permits a level of social cohesion among oppressed classes. "To relinquish the notion of race—even though it's a cruel hoax— at this particular time is to relinquish our fortress against the powers and principalities that still try to undermine us," he says. He sees the Multiracial box as politically damaging to "those who need to galvanize peoples around the racial idea of black."

There are some black cultural nationalists who might welcome the Multiracial category. "In terms of the African-American population, it could be very, very useful, because there is a need to clarify who is in and who is not," Molefi Kete Asante, who is the chairperson of the Department of African-American Studies at Temple University, says. "In fact, I would think they should go further than that—identify those people who are in interracial marriages."

Spencer, however, thinks that it might be better to eliminate racial categories altogether than to create an additional category that empties the others of meaning. "If you had who knows how many thousands or tens of thousands or millions of people claiming to be multiracial, you would lessen the number who are black," Spencer says. "There's no end in sight. There's no limit to which one can go in claiming to be multiracial. For instance, I happen to be very brown in complexion, but when I go to the continent of Africa, blacks and whites there claim that I would be 'colored' rather than black, which means that somewhere in my distant past—probably during the era of slavery—I could have one or more white ancestors. So does that mean that I, too, could check Multiracial? Certainly light-skinned black people might perhaps see this as a way out of being included among a despised racial group. The result could be the creation of another class of people, who are betwixt and between black and white."

Whatever comes out of this discussion, the nation is likely to engage in the most profound debate of racial questions in decades. "We recognize the importance of racial categories in correcting clear injustices under the law," Representative Sawyer says. "The dilemma we face is trying to assure the fundamental guarantees of equality of opportunity while at the same time recognizing that the populations themselves are changing as we seek to categorize them. It reaches the point where it becomes an absurd counting game. Part of the difficulty is that we are dealing with the illusion of precision. We wind up with precise counts of everybody in the country, and they are precisely wrong. They don't reflect who we are as a people. To be effective, the concepts of individual and group identity need to reflect not only who we have been but who we are becoming. The more these categories distort our perception of reality, the less useful they are. We act as if we knew what we're talking about when we talk about race, and we don't."

Perceptions and Misperceptions of Skin Color

Stephen H. Caldwell and Rebecca Popenoe

Study Question

1. Explain why knowledge of a patient's race has little diagnostic or therapeutic utility.

Case presentations are part of many clinicians' daily routines. The format for such presentations often involves stating the age, sex, and race of the patient in the opening description. However, although single-word racial labels such as "black" or "white" are of occasional help to the clinician, they are of limited diagnostic and therapeutic help in many routine cases. Because of their broad scope and lack of scientific clarity, these terms often poorly represent information—for example, about genetic risks and perceptions of disease—that they are supposed to convey. In many instances, they are superficial and potentially misleading terms that fail to serve the patient's medical needs. Demoting these terms from the opening line of routine case presentations shows a recognition of their limitations as scientific labels. Our patients will be better served by more detailed explorations of ethnicity, when germane, in the History of Present Illness or Social History sections of the case presentation in question.

The presentation of a case history has a traditional format that has evolved over centuries (1). In many institutions, medical students are routinely taught to begin their case presentations with a statement describing the age, sex, and "race" of the patient. In regions of the United States such as ours, where the population is predominantly of European-American or African-American descent, the description of race is often distilled down to "black" or "white." Thus, in our institution and in those with similar demographics, the fourth spoken word of many case presentations broadly describes the patient as black or white. Exactly when and how this form of introduction became common is unclear. French physician Louis Martinet (1795–1875) described the importance of stating "the name, sex, age, and occupation of the patient. . . . In some cases it becomes necessary to state the country or district from which the patient comes and the diseases which prevail there" (2). In the United States, the format of the opening line seems to have been established a priori in case reports in the early and mid-20th century. Since then, the actual utility or validity of these terms has seldom been discussed. We hope to show that the diagnostic and therapeutic utility of the terms "black" and "white" is limited. We contend that the use of these terms in the opening statements of routine, day-to-day case presentations implies that the terms have an importance and a scientific validity beyond their real merit. If ethnicity is thought to be pertinent to the case in question, the patient will be better served if the physician replaces these terms with more detailed comments in the History of Present Illness, the Social History, or the Physical Examination sections of the report. When broadly and routinely applied, as they often are, racial labels such as "black" and "white" can actually obscure an accurate appraisal of a patient's genetic and cultural backgrounds, both of which may significantly affect the patient's health risks and outcomes for various diseases. A similar argument may be made for other traditional racial terms, such as Hispanic, Asian, or Native American. Because most of our experience has been with patients of European-American and African-American descent, we focus primarily on this area.

Case Presentations

Several examples will serve to illustrate the superficiality of racial divisions in day-to-day medical parlance. Recently, a 24-year-old "white" female presented in our clinic with, among other problems, α-thalassemia trait. A thorough social history later revealed that one of the patient's parents was of Mediterranean ancestry, a point obscured by the patient's married name and fair complexion and the clinician's use of the label "white." Similarly, a middle-aged, "white" male presented with recurring fever and abdominal pain. He was eventually diagnosed with familial Mediterranean fever. A careful social history revealed the patient's Greek ancestry. In short, the term "white" encompasses a diversity of genetic backgrounds that the term poorly represents.

The label "black" may also be misleading in predicting diagnoses among African-American patients. Although we are not aware of any studies of specific prevalences, auto-immune hepatitis is perceived to be more common in patients of European descent than in others, and indeed it may be more common because it is associated with inherited histocompatibility antigens. However, we have encountered the disorder not infrequently in patients of African-American descent. A recent published case report described a "black" female with autoimmune hepatitis and a poor response to steroid therapy that may have been due to carriage of α-1-antitrypsin (3), which has also been reported to occur less frequently in patients of African descent (4). As in the cases of "white" patients mentioned above, the notation "black" in the opening description of this patient was potentially misleading if her diagnoses were to be based on suspected prevalences. The authors of the report were obviously unimpressed with the likelihood of either disorder based on the patient's stated race, and they rightly pressed ahead to arrive at their diagnosis.

The terms "race" and "ethnicity" are often used interchangeably, but they are in fact far from synonymous: "Race" refers to differences of biology, "ethnicity" to differences of culture and geographic origin. We contend that ethnic differences, rather than distinctions between black and white, more accurately convey information potentially relevant to a particular case. For instance, a Kenyan, a Haitian, and an African-American would be considered racially identical—"black"—according to current practice, but they do not share nutritional habits, attitudes and beliefs about medical care, or even biological inheritance.

Webster's Dictionary defines race as "any of the major biological divisions of mankind, distinguished by color and texture of hair, color of skin and eyes, stature, bodily proportions, etc." But are the crucial differences among human beings really those of superficial appearance? Is it scientifically justified to assume that these outer traits indicate inner biological differences among humans?

By using the terms "black" and "white," the medical community purports to refer to real biological divisions within our species, and yet a closer look at the data shows that these divisions do not fall as neatly as our terms for skin color suggest. For instance, persons from Papua New Guinea, although "black"-skinned, are genetically more closely related to Asians than to "black" Africans.

In addition, numerous studies (5) of human physical variation within populations show that traits that are often lumped together as definitive of a race do not in fact vary as a group. When population geneticist Richard Lewontin measured the degree of population differences in gene frequencies for 17 polymorphic traits, he found that only 6.3% of all variation could be accounted for at the level of major geographic race (6). The visible characteristics of "race" were unreliable indicators of genotypic variation.

This is not to argue that regional genetic variation does not exist. As Pat Shipman has recently pointed out (7), the fact that the lines of classification are so difficult to draw and necessarily so imprecise (one reason for this is constant mating across established group lines) does not refute the existence of regional variants of our species. Future researchers could explore more medically relevant differences among groups of *Homo sapiens* that have occupied different regions over time. At the present stage of knowledge, however, the division of the world's population into perceived races lacks scientific clarity and legitimacy.

Anthropologists have long recognized that the racial lines drawn by a society are cultural rather than scientific constructions (8, 9). Within the international medical community, therefore, racial divisions may not even be perceived in the same way. What is black to someone from the United States, for example, may be white to a Brazilian or a Caribbean Islander. The terms "black" and "white" say more about how U.S. society has been structured than about medically relevant, biological realities.

Webster's Dictionary defines the term "ethnic" as "designating or of any of the basic divisions or groups of mankind, as distinguished by customs, characteristics, language, etc." Social scientists accept "ethnicity" as a term that refers to the cultural distinctions that persons make themselves—their identities. Reductionist racial labels often obscure rather than illuminate ethnic differences. Ideas about medical care, nutrition, and disease that bear on treatment are better provided by giving information about ethnic identity and background in the Social History section of the case presentation.

The medical community is increasingly aware of the ways in which cultural practices influence a person's health (10). The various persons grouped as black and white, however, are often widely divergent in beliefs, habits, reactions to illnesses, and perceptions of the medical community. The terms "black" and "white" do not impart the type of information implied by their continued use in the introductions to routine case presentations.

Genetic Background of the U.S. Population

In the United States, 350 years of interaction has led to considerable mixing between persons of various geographic origins (11). Although the evidence of such diverse ancestry is at least implicitly acknowledged in the African-American community by attention to gradations of skin color, it is less frequently acknowledged that many "whites" have African and other non-"white" ancestors. However, a recent highly acclaimed autobiography by Shirlee Taylor Haizlip (12), a "black" woman, calls attention to the prevalence of such cases. Haizlip recounts her discovery of her own "white" relatives who had split off from the "black" side of her family a generation earlier. As for the African-American population in the United States, geneticist Luigi Cavalli-Sforza (13) has estimated that 30% of their genes derive from "white" sources.

These facts suggest that the traditional racial divisions used in the United States are of questionable utility and accuracy. This issue has recently earned the attention of U.S. government demographers. According to news accounts (14), the current official categories used in the U.S. Census and other documents are presently being reviewed by the Office of Information and Regulatory Affairs in the Office of Management and Budget. The debate within the government treats issues of ethnic and racial identity that are beyond the scope of this paper, but it supports our contention that the use of racial labels is burdened by inaccuracies. This seems especially true at the level of the routine case presentation.

Does Bias Become an Issue?

Numerous reports about the course and optimal treatment of many diseases have been based on perceived racial groupings. We do not dispute that racial or ethnic categories sometimes have important epidemiologic implications. However, the division into "black" and "white" in routine, day-to-day presentations is often irrelevant and potentially misleading.

Do these terms engender bias? One study (15), which examined the way in which "black" and "white" patients are presented at morning report, suggests that they do. Black patients were far more likely than whites to be identified by a racial label, and yet that label was considered relevant in only 2 of 18 cases. The authors perceived the presentations of black patients to be unflattering more often than the presentations of white patients.

To the extent that the terms "black" and "white" often needlessly separate persons in a clinical setting, their use may sometimes be construed as pejorative, whether this is intended or not. In most cases, racial monikers simply represent a long-followed tradition. We submit that many clinicians who work in settings in which these terms are routinely used may be surprised at their own reactions when the terms are deleted from day-to-day presentations.

Published Case Reports and Current Practice

Although our emphasis is on the routine "workday" oral case presentation, we reviewed case reports or clinical pathological conference reports from

Table 1   Statements of Case Reports or Clinical Pathologic Conference Reports Published in Medical Journals*

Journal	Type of Report	Racial Description Used in 1994	Racial Description Used in 1984
American Journal of Cardiology	Case	Varied	No
American Journal of Gastroenterology	Case	No	Varied
American Journal of the Medical Sciences	Case	No	Varied
Chest	Case	Varied	Varied
Circulation	CPC	Yes	No reports available
Gastroenterology	Case	Yes	No reports available
Mayo Clinic Proceedings	Case	No	No
Medicine	Case	Varied	Varied
New England Journal of Medicine	CPC	No	No

*The May or June issues of the journals were reviewed. Most issues had more than one case report; two issues had one clinical pathologic conference report each. CPC = clinical pathologic conference reports.

current and past issues of nine medical journals to assess the ways in which these reports have been presented over the past 10 years. Overall, most of the journals varied considerably in their use of racial labels in the opening lines of case reports. In general, this seemed to be less the result of editorial policy than of individual authors' styles (Table 1).

In addition, we informally surveyed the clerkship directors of 48 U.S. medical schools using a brief written questionnaire that asked specifically whether medical students were taught by oral or written example to use the terms "black" or "white" in the introductory statements of routine case presentations. Four responses were possible ("yes," "no," "variable," and "don't know") and allowance was made for qualifying comments.

Thirty-seven (77%) clerkship directors responded (7 from the Northeast, 15 from the South, 12 from the Midwest, and 3 from the West). Twenty-two of the 37 (59%) answered "yes" and 12 (32%) answered "variable." Only one answered "no," and he added that students are expressly taught to not use the terms unless they think them relevant. Two directors answered "don't know," and occurs by "osmosis" from the resident housestaff to the students.

Many of those who responded with "yes" or "variable" also commented that this practice is taught to students passively, by the oral example of residents. Thus, as experience with residents and clinicians from numerous medical schools might suggest, describing race in the opening line seems to be common in U.S. medical schools. This practice is either passed along as oral tradition or formally taught. We could not detect a significant regional variation in this small survey (6 of 7 directors from the Northeast and 9 of 15 directors from the South answered "yes" and the remainder from these regions answered "variable" or "don't know").

Conclusions

Most physicians would agree that both the genetic constitution and the cultural background of a person predisposes him or her to various diseases and may modulate responses to certain therapies. An accurate social history can, in many cases, provide invaluable information about a patient's ethnic background and possible risks for certain diseases. However, labels such as "black" or "white" in the opening line of case histories poorly represent this important information. The same may be said of other broad, superficial terms, such as Hispanic or Asian, that inadequately address attributes that should be dealt with in a more meaningful way when thought to be pertinent to patient care.

In many routine cases, such terminology serves as little more than a "jog" to the memory of busy clinicians. The costs, however, may be to engender the perception of bias, to miss clinically relevant information, and to assume the presence or absence of genetic or cultural factors that, in fact, may or may not be present. Demoting these labels from the opening line of our day-to-day presentations shows a recognition of their limitations as scientific terms and a commitment to representing pertinent ethnic variations in an accurate, relevant, and ultimately more helpful manner.

References

1. Stoeckle JD, Billings JA. A history of history-taking: the medical interview. *J Gen Intern Med.* 1987;2:119–27.
2. Walker HK. The origins of the history and physical examination. In: Walker HK, Hall DW, Hurst JW, eds. *Clinical Methods: The History, Physical, and Laboratory Examinations.* Boston: Butterworths; 1990:17.
3. Lok AS, Ghany MG, Gerber MA. A young woman with cirrhosis: autoimmune hepatitis vs. alpha 1-antitrypsin deficiency [Clinical Conference]. *Hepatology.* 1994;19:1302–6.
4. Wulfsberg EA, Hoffmann DE, Cohen MM. Alpha 1-antitrypsin deficiency. *JAMA.* 1994;271:217–22.

5. Molnar S. *Human Variation: Races, Types, and Ethnic Groups.* 2d ed. Englewood Cliffs, New Jersey: Prentice-Hall; 1983:128–46.
6. Lewontin RD. Human Diversity. In: Nelson H, Jurmain R, eds. *Introduction to Physical Anthropology.* St. Paul: West Publishing; 1982:203.
7. Shipman P. *The Evolution of Racism: Human Differences and the Use and Abuse of Science.* New York: Simon and Schuster; 1994.
8. Boas F. The Mind of Primitive Man: A Course of Lectures Delivered before the Lowell Institute, Boston, Mass., and the National University of Mexico, 1910–1911. New York: Macmillan; 1911.
9. Gould SJ. *The Mismeasure of Man.* New York: W. W. Norton; 1981.
10. Pachter LM. Culture and clinical care. Folk illness beliefs and behaviors and their implications for health care delivery. *JAMA.* 1994;271:690–4.
11. Buckley TE. Unfixing race. *The Virginia Magazine of History and Biography.* 1994;102:349–80.
12. Haizlip ST. *The Sweeter the Juice.* New York: Simon and Schuster; 1994.
13. Shipman P. Facing racial differences together. *The Chronicle of Higher Education.* 3 Aug 1994;40:B-1.
14. Holmes SJ. Federal government is rethinking its system of racial classification. *New York Times* 1994 8 July.
15. Finucane TE, Carrese JA. Racial bias in presentation of cases. *J Gen Intern Med.* 1990;5:120–1.

Identifying Ethnicity in Medical Papers

Edward J. Huth

Study Questions

1. What tentative conclusion does the author make about the utility of ethnic identification in epidemiological research and about how it may be properly applied in clinical trials?
2. Based on the information presented in Part 3, what recommendations would you make about how to use ethnicity in research and case presentation?

"**B**e not the first by whom the new are tried. Nor yet the last to lay the old aside." Pope aimed his couplet (1) at literary criticism in the 18th century, but it makes sense for medicine in the 20th century. Be not the first to recommend to patients a new treatment with value not established by a rigorous clinical trial. Be not the last to discard antique habits of practice. An example of this second fault is the subject of the "Perspective" essay by Caldwell and Popenoe (2). For years, medical students have been taught, with good reason, to systematically record every fact ascertainable from a patient, no matter its final relevance or irrelevance to deducing the diagnosis or selecting treatment. To show their thoroughness in history taking and physical examination, they have generally been expected to trot out all of these details when presenting cases. Among these details has often been a term for the patient's "race." Hence, a case presentation would typically open with a description like "This 69-year-old black male came to the clinic with a chief complaint of. . . ." As Caldwell and Popenoe point out, what is the listener to make of the statement, as in this example, of "black"? What value does such "racial" designation have for diagnostic analysis in most cases? In rare instances, it might be a clue to the genetic determinant of a disease, as with sickle cell anemia, but even in such cases, far more convincing markers than skin color for genetically determined diseases are now likely to be available. Perhaps more frequently, a "racial" term might be a clue to some nongenetic risk factor for a disease. In such cases, specific inquiries into potential risk factors are much more likely to be fruitful. Caldwell and Popenoe emphasize this point by recommending that simplistic "racial" terms such as "black" and "white" be dropped and that more attention be paid to detailed history taking that can yield "invaluable information" on "ethnic background and possible risks for certain diseases" and "potentially important cultural information."

Caldwell and Popenoe's analysis is just as relevant to case reports for publication as to oral presentations. Efficient and effective scientific prose proceeds with "precision and brevity," a phrase coined in another field (3) but relevant to medical writing. Readers of case reports wish to have only what they need to know and no more. They need a presentation of the facts that were efficiently relevant to diagnostic analysis of the case or to therapeutic decisions. They do not need details that simply represent old habits in the ritualistic presenting of cases. A case report properly prepared for publication will not open with a "racial" or ethnic term unless a fact represented by that term was crucial to decisions in the case. Facts representing apparent influences on the patient's problems from genetic or cultural factors related to the patient's ethnic background will be stated as specific facts and not left to be possibly inferred from an ethnic term.

You may be asking, why quotation marks around *race* and *racial* and not around *ethnicity* and *ethnic?* The concept "race" was derived from taxonomic concepts long applied in botany and zoology. As one medical dictionary (4) puts it, a "race" is "a subspecies or other division of a species." But taxonomic assignments require precise and detailed descriptions that justify creating taxonomic categories. Three longstanding traditional categories of "race" (4) have been "Caucasoid (white), Negroid (black), and Mongoloid (yellow)." Unfortunately, as the same dictionary points out, "a limited range of visible characteristics [of "races"] tends to oversimplify and distort the picture of human variation." The concept of "race" implied a degree of genetic homogeneity among persons designated as members of a "race." Modern genetics has trashed that view (5). As one detailed discussion (6) concludes, "Although estimates of [the amount of genetic variation in human populations] vary, all agree that the amount of variation within any ethnic group is much greater than the difference between groups."

From these and related considerations, thoughtful judgments (5–8) have concluded that "race" has little or no utility in careful medical thinking. In contrast, *ethnicity* represents a concept that makes no claims to biological precision and that reflects a broader view of factors that may influence the susceptibility of individuals to etiologic agents and the ways in which they may respond to those agents. Senior and Bhopal (7) summarize the concept thus: ". . . [ethnicity] implies one or more of the following: shared origins or social background; shared culture and traditions that are distinctive, maintained between generations, and lead to a sense of identity and group; and a common language or religious tradition." But for reasons advanced by Caldwell and Popenoe, ethnic identifications in single-case reports are not likely to be any more useful for diagnostic analysis than "racial" identifications.

The question of the utility of ethnic identifications is more complex for reports of epidemiologic research (7–10) or clinical trials. Genetic and cultural characteristics of ethnic groups could be determinants of disease or its severity (7) in at least some members. The finding of a higher prevalence or incidence of a disease in one ethnic group than in another could be a valuable clue to an etiologic agent. The finding of a different response to, or a different frequency of an adverse effect from, a drug in one ethnic group compared with another (11) could be a valuable guide to decisions on dosage or a clue to mechanisms affecting a drug's mechanism of action or metabolism. The practical difficulties in ascertaining all potentially relevant genetic and cultural characteristics of individual subjects in epidemiologic research and clinical trials may force investigators to rely simply on ethnic-group designations of persons for assessing how those characteristics might account for findings. Hence, identifying the ethnicity of persons covered by an epidemiologic study or treated in a clinical trial may be a legitimate part of study designs for such research.

Designers of an epidemiologic study or clinical trial should know explicitly, however, why they include ethnic identifications in their research. Some antecedent findings may form a reasonable basis for identifying ethnicity to test a hypothesis about an ethnic influence on the variables to be measured. The other possible use of ethnic identifications is in heuristic efforts (also known as "fishing expeditions") to find factors that could account for variances in measured values. But with either approach, investigators should be clear in their minds and in published reports about how they justified identifying ethnicities.

The problem of defining an ethnicity is not an easy one, whether in medical research or for much wider applications. In the United States, the most conspicuous example is the classifications for the decennial national census. As preparations for the year 2000 census begin, pressures (12) on the Census Bureau for reclassifications and new categories of ethnic groups are mounting. These pressures may arise in part from emotional needs for ethnic identity, but even stronger pressures are those arising from the economic advantages for ethnic groups defined in various government programs. In the far smaller field of clinical trials, there are pressures to adequately represent ethnic groups that can legitimately wish to know whether trial results found with persons from one ethnic group are more widely applicable. At least one analysis (13) has led to doubts that important ethnic (and gender) differences in the way the body handles drugs are more than rare, but the questions of possible differences may have to be considered for new drugs or reexamined for drugs studied mainly in a single ethnic (or gender) group. If answers to such questions are going to be sought by designers of clinical trials, how should ethnic groups be designated?

Substantial effort (7–10) has already gone into considering this and related questions for epidemiologic research. One clear conclusion (7) is that epidemiologic reports "should state explicitly how [ethnic group] classifications were made." These and other conclusions (7–10) are also relevant to the design and reporting of clinical trials. Clinical-trials research has in common with epidemiology the sampling of populations that may be diverse in geographic origin and cultural customs. Hence, subjects in clinical trials (14) may differ in their genetic determinants of responses to external agents and in their dietary patterns and other cultural influences on responses to drugs. Designers of clinical trials, as well as epidemiologists, must, however, keep clearly in mind that even within properly defined ethnic groups social, cultural, and economic characteristics may differ widely. One Euro-American may be living in poverty and malnourished; another may be a highly paid, well-fed executive in a major corporation. Hence, designers of trials must not rely simply on ethnic identifications if more specific variables covered by *ethnicity* can be defined for the research design.

These tentative conclusions on ethnic identifications and how they may be properly applied in clinical trials probably also have implications for editors' and readers' expectations of reports on clinical trials. A few months ago, this journal published a position paper (15) proposing the kinds of information that should be included in the introductions, methods and results sections, and discussions of papers reporting trial results. This paper calls for details on "planned study population," "inclusion and exclusion criteria," "planned subgroup analyses," and "demographics . . . of the study population." For reports of trials that identify the ethnicities of persons, those details could be expected to include statements on whether the investigators categorized persons according to ethnicity and on the definitions that were used, or on whether persons categorized themselves using their own terms or terms supplied by the investigators. Such information could be crucial for scientifically sound judgments about apparent ethnic differences and the generalizability of results from clinical trials.

References

1. Pope A. An essay on criticism. In: Bartlett J. *Familiar Quotations: A Collection of Passages, Phrases, and Proverbs Traced to Their Sources in Ancient and Modern Literature.* 16th ed. Boston: Little, Brown; 1992.
2. Caldwell SH, Popenoe B. Perceptions and misperceptions of skin color. *Ann Intern Med.* 1995;122:614–7.
3. Schoenberg A. *Style and Idea: Selected Writings of Arnold Schoenberg.* Berkeley: Univ California Pr; 1984:415.
4. Becker EL. *International Dictionary of Medicine and Biology:* in Three Volumes. New York: J Wiley; 1986:2376.
5. Cruickshank JK, Beevers DG, eds. *Ethnic Factors in Health and Disease.* Boston: Wright; 1989:vii.
6. Hill AV. Molecular markers of ethnic groups. In: Cruickshank JK. Beevers DG, eds. *Ethnic Factors in Health and Disease.* Boston: Wright; 1989:25–31.
7. Senior PA, Bhopal R. Ethnicity as a variable in epidemiological research. *BMJ.* 1994;309:327–30.
8. McKenzie KJ, Crowcroft NS. Race, ethnicity, culture, and science [Editorial]. *BMJ.* 1994;309:286–7.
9. Centers for Disease Control and Prevention. Use of race and ethnicity in public health surveillance. Summary of the DC/ATSDR workshop. Atlanta, Georgia. March 1–2, 1993. *MMWR Morb Mortal Wkly Rep.* 1993;42:1–16.
10. Centers for Disease Control and Prevention. Limitations of concepts, measures, and uses. In: Centers for Disease Control and Prevention. Use of race and ethnicity in public health surveillance. Summary of the DC/ATSDR workshop. *MMWR Morb Mortal Wkly Rep.* 1993;42:1–16, p. 12–6.
11. Balant L, Gex-Fabry M, Balant-Gorgia A. Implications for the design and interpretation of phase III clinical trials. In: Walker S. Lumley C, McAuslane N. eds. *The Relevance of Ethnic Factors in the Clinical Evaluation of Medicines.* Boston: Kluwer Academic: 1994:201–17.
12. Wright L. One drop of blood. *The New Yorker.* 25 Jul 1994;25:46–55.
13. Edwards LD. A survey of current practices in the U.S. regarding minorities and gender. In: Walker S. Lumley C, McAuslane N. eds. *The Relevance of Ethnic Factors in the Clinical Evaluation of Medicines.* Boston: Kluwer Academic; 1994:107–14.
14. Spilker B. *Guide to clinical trials.* New York: Raven; 1991:150, 621.
15. Call for comments on a proposal to improve reporting of clinical trials in the biomedical literature. Working Group on Recommendations for Reporting of Clinical Trials in the Biomedical Literature. *Ann Intern Med.* 1994;121:894–5.

:::::::::::::::::::

SELECTED DISCRIMINATION CASES HANDLED BY THE U.S. DEPARTMENT OF JUSTICE IN 1996

Study Questions
1. Determine whether each case is an example of institutional discrimination or individual discrimination.
2. List some of the ways discrimination is institutionalized.

Justice Department Sues Montgomery Real Estate Firm for Refusing to Show African Americans Rental Properties Located in White Areas

WASHINGTON, D.C.—The Justice Department today sued a Montgomery, Alabama real estate firm that allegedly refused to refer African Americans to properties in predominantly white parts of town.

The suit is the 31st stemming from a nationwide Justice Department fair housing program to detect discrimination. Under the program trained pairs of African-Americans and whites posing as prospective tenants inquire about the availability of rental units. By comparing the experiences of the testers, investigators discover whether minorities were treated less favorably than whites.

Today's complaint, filed in the U.S. District Court in Montgomery, accused the Hamilton Realty Company, its owner, and an agent of engaging in a pattern of discrimination against African Americans who asked about rental properties listed with the company.

It alleged that Hamilton Realty rental agents did not tell African Americans about properties located in predominantly white areas of Montgomery, while whites were told. It also claimed that agents would steer African Americans toward properties located in predominantly minority areas of Montgomery and whites toward predominantly white areas.

"All Americans should have the chance to live in the neighborhood of their choice," said Assistant Attorney General for Civil Rights Deval L. Patrick. "Real estate agents who restrict housing opportunities based on race are segregating our nation."

Patrick noted that "steering" occurs when a rental agent discloses different properties to applicants with the intent to concentrate people in separate areas according to race or national origin.

"There is a broad consensus in our society that equal rights in housing for all people is a basic right of citizenship," said Redding Pitt, U.S. Attorney in Montgomery. "It is our intention in filing this action to ensure that these fundamental rights are sustained in this instance, and to demonstrate our determination to vindicate the principle of justice for all."

Patrick noted that with today's cases, the testing program has produced 31 suits in eight states, including Ohio, Michigan, California, South Dakota, Indiana, Missouri and Florida. Currently, the Justice Department is conducting testing in about a dozen cities.

Today's suit seeks a court order preventing Hamilton Realty from engaging in further discriminatory practices and requiring the defendants to pay monetary damages to any identified victims of discrimination. Under the Fair Housing Act, a court may also require each defendant to pay a civil penalty of up to $50,000 for the first violation and $100,000 for a subsequent violation.

"Today's action should warn all housing providers that housing discrimination is not immune to detection," added Patrick.

Individuals who believe they may have been the victims of housing discrimination at Hamilton Realty should call the Housing Section of the Civil Rights Division of the Justice Department at 202-514-4713 or the U.S. Attorney's Office at 334-223-7280.

96-014

***

Justice Department Sues Phoenix for Allegedly Suspending Parks Worker Who Helped Civil Rights Investigators

WASHINGTON, D.C.—The Justice Department today sued the City of Phoenix for allegedly suspending a Parks Department worker because he helped federal authorities who were investigating allegations of discrimination lodged by a co-worker.

The suit, filed in U.S. District Court in Phoenix, alleged that the City of Phoenix violated Title VII of the Civil Rights Act of 1964 by retaliating against Thomas R. Ivan, a mechanic in the City's Department of Parks, Recreation and Library.

Assistant Attorney General Deval L. Patrick noted that the suspension occurred after Ivan provided information to the Equal Employment Opportunity Commission (EEOC). The EEOC was investigating a complaint filed by another City employee who had alleged discrimination on the basis of national origin.

Following his suspension and other retaliatory measures, Ivan informed the Equal Employment Opportunity Commission ("EEOC") of the City's actions. After investigating Ivan's allegations and concluding there was reasonable cause to believe the city had discriminated, the EEOC referred the matter to the Justice Department. The Justice Department conducted its own investigation and reached a similar conclusion. When efforts to settle the case were unsuccessful, the Justice Department decided to file the suit.

Today's suit seeks a court order requiring the City to pay compensatory damages to Ivan, as well as back pay and related benefits.

96-018

***

Justice Department Sues New York City for Allegedly Discriminating Against Qualified Minority Custodians

WASHINGTON, D.C.—The Justice Department today sued New York City for using an allegedly discriminatory test in hiring and promoting minorities who wanted to be custodians and custodian engineers. The City could not show that the tests measured the skills needed to succeed on the job.

Although nearly half of the qualified labor force is comprised of minorities, the City school system has hired whites for 92 percent of its custodian positions.

The suit, filed today in U.S. District Court in Brooklyn, accuses the City, its Board of Education and its Department of Personnel of violating Title VII of the Civil Rights Act of 1964.

"We are committed to seeing an American workplace free of discrimination," said Assistant Attorney General for Civil Rights Deval L. Patrick. "When unreasonable and unnecessary hurdles knock out qualified minorities, we will take all steps to eliminate them and to compensate any victims."

Patrick claimed that the entry-level and promotional written examinations used by the City in 1985, 1989 and 1993 unlawfully discriminated against qualified black and Hispanic test-takers in part because they cannot be shown to measure how well individuals would perform on the job.

To become a custodian, which is a supervisory position, one must have a high school diploma and two years experience or education in engineering or in cleaning and maintaining buildings. Each school has one custodian who is responsible for hiring individuals to clean and maintain the schools.

The custodian engineer position is essentially the same as the custodian position, except that to qualify for this position an individual must have a high pressure boiler operating engineer license and previous experience as a custodian or five years experience in the supervision of cleaning or maintaining buildings.

The median annual salaries for the custodian and custodian engineer positions are approximately $51,000 and $58,000 respectively.

- The complaint seeks a court order requiring the City to: stop using unlawfully discriminatory selection procedures, including written examinations;
- engage in recruitment efforts aimed at attracting qualified black, Hispanic, Asian and female candidates for the jobs; and,
- award appropriate make-whole relief, including job offers, back pay, pension benefits and retroactive seniority to identified victims of the unlawful written exams.

Finally, the complaint also called upon the city to bolster its efforts to recruit Asian and female employees, who are also significantly underrepresented in relation to their share of the qualified work force.

***

Two Louisiana Nightclubs Agree with Justice Department to Open Their Doors to African Americans

WASHINGTON, D.C.—A Louisiana nightclub that was sued for refusing to admit an African American prosecutor and a Louisiana bar that denied service to an African American teacher each agreed today to end their discriminatory policies.

In two separate agreements reached today with the Justice Department, the owners of La Poussiere in Breaux Bridge and the C'est Ma Vie Lounge in Broussard admitted to unlawfully refusing to serve African Americans because of their race.

"Some people believe blatant discrimination is a thing of the past. It isn't. These cases serve as a reminder that the fight for simple justice is not yet over," said Assistant Attorney General for Civil Rights Deval L. Patrick. "America must have zero tolerance for racial discrimination."

La Poussiere

Last April, the Justice Department alleged the owners of La Poussiere violated Title II of the Civil Rights Act of 1964 by turning away a black prosecutor, Zaldwaynaka (Zee) Scott, and her white colleagues, Helene Greenwald and Matthew Bettenhausen.

According to the agreement, filed today in U.S. District Court in Lafayette, the three prosecutors with the U.S. Attorneys office in Chicago, who had been attending a conference in New Orleans, visited the Lafayette area to listen to Cajun music. When they arrived at La Poussiere on April 16, 1994, two of the prosecutors remained in the car as Greenwald walked to the entrance to see if the club was open. The person admitting people to the club said that it was, and that there was a two dollar cover charge.

When Greenwald returned with Scott, a Shreveport native who prosecutes criminal and civil rights cases, the woman at the door said they could not enter because the club was hosting a private party. After Greenwald confronted her, the woman admitted that they were not allowed inside because of Scott's race.

The government subsequently sent two pairs of FBI agents, one white couple and one black couple, to the nightclub the following July and found that the black couple was denied entry while the white couple was admitted after paying a nominal cover charge.

Under the agreement, the owners of La Poussiere:

- admit they have unlawfully excluded African Americans, including the three Assistant U.S. Attorneys;
- will no longer discriminate;
- will undergo training on civil rights issues; and,
- will publish an advertisement in a local newspaper and post a sign outside its door emphasizing that the nightclub is open to all members of the public.

Patrick noted that the three victims, who filed a separate suit, are negotiating a separate monetary settlement with the nightclub owners.

C'est Ma Vie

In the second agreement, filed together with a lawsuit today in U.S. District Court in Lafayette, the owner of the C'est Ma Vie Lounge in Broussard agreed to stop discriminating against African Americans, train its staff about civil rights law, and advertise that it is open to everyone.

According to the agreement, the owner of the bar, Dennis Broussard, admitted he had denied service to an African-American teacher at a local school because of her race. Patrick noted that the teacher, Carmen West, was visiting the lounge last March 25 with two other teachers following a parent-faculty volleyball tournament.

Upon arriving at the bar, the owner informed the three that they could only get drinks to go because he did not serve "colored people". After West complained to the local police, the town's police chief, Irving Flugence, who is also African American, returned to the club with West. At that time, Broussard confirmed his policy and acknowledged that West's race was the reason he had not served her and her companions.

"While most bars and nightclubs in this area serve people regardless of their skin color, unfortunately some do not," said Michael D. Skinner, U.S. Attorney in Lafayette. "Our office will continue to vigorously enforce the civil rights laws."

West did not file a separate private suit in the case.

The agreements must be approved by the U.S. District Court.

95-048

***

Justice Department Sues Nebraska Bank for Allegedly Charging Native Americans Higher Interest Rates

WASHINGTON, D.C.—A northwest Nebraska bank that allegedly charged Native Americans higher interest rates on consumer loans than other equally-qualified applicants was sued today by the Justice Department.

The case was referred to the Justice Department last year after an examination by the Office of the Comptroller of the Currency (OCC). The Justice Department conducted a subsequent investigation. No non-racial business explanation to justify the price differences was found.

The complaint, filed today in U.S. District Court in Rapid City, South Dakota, alleged that the First National Bank of Gordon engaged in a pattern of discrimination. It claimed that the one-branch bank charged Native Americans higher interest rates for consumer loans than those charged to whites, in violation of the Equal Credit Opportunity Act and the Fair Housing Act.

"It's unfair and illegal to make Native Americans pay more," said Assistant Attorney General for Civil Rights Deval L. Patrick. "Every American deserves a fair chance at credit which can make a difference in improving their lives."

The bank, which is situated in Gordon approximately 25 miles from the South Dakota border, includes the Pine Ridge Indian Reservation in its service area. The reservation, located in South Dakota, is home to the Oglala Sioux Tribe, where the victims are located.

Patrick noted that the difference in interest rates between the loans made to Native American borrowers and those made to similarly situated white borrowers could not have occurred by chance and cannot be explained by factors unrelated to race or national origin.

"By working together with the lending industry we are making access to credit more available for all Americans," added Patrick.

Patrick noted that today's complaint seeks an order requiring the bank to stop discriminating against Native Americans, pay compensatory and punitive damages to the victims, adopt a plan to remedy the bank's discriminatory practices, and pay a civil penalty of up to $50,000 to the U.S. treasury.

"Native Americans throughout the region should have the same access to credit as all other applicants," said Karen E. Schreier, U.S. Attorney in Sioux Falls, South Dakota. "We will not tolerate banks treating Native Americans differently than other customers."

Patrick noted that over the past four years the Justice Department has reached settlements with eight other financial institutions.

In January 1994, it sued the Blackpipe State Bank in Martin, South Dakota for allegedly charging Native Americans higher interest rates than other equally qualified applicants, and for refusing to make loans when the collateral was located on reservations. Under a settlement, the bank agreed to create a $125,000 fund to compensate victims of its discriminatory conduct.

96-165

***

Michigan Athletic Conference to Invite High Schools with Significant Black Student Populations

WASHINGTON, D.C.—A Michigan high school athletic league that failed to admit certain school districts with significant black student enrollments will invite six of the schools into their league, under an agreement reached today with the Justice Department. The agreement will ensure that the once excluded schools will be able to compete with the other conference schools in all sports and extracurricular activities.

The agreement requires 18 public school districts located outside of Detroit, which founded the Michigan Mega Conference Athletic League, to invite previously excluded schools into the league.

"This is a victory for the students. Now everyone will be able to compete on the same playing field," said Assistant Attorney General for Civil Rights Deval L. Patrick. "We hope all the Mega schools will begin next year not only as competitors but also as partners."

Mega, an interscholastic high school athletic and extra-curricular league, did not offer invitations to certain schools when it was formed in 1992 even though the schools were located in the same geographic area. When Mega was formed, the proportion of black students in the Mega schools was less than 5% overall, while the proportion in each of the formerly excluded schools ranged from 32 percent to 99 percent.

In 1993, two school districts filed a complaint with the Office of Civil Rights (OCR) at the U.S. Department of Education. Each alleged that the founding schools discriminated in the formation and operation of the league.

After determining that the Mega school districts violated Title VI of the Civil Rights Act of 1964 and its implementing regulations, OCR tried to negotiate a resolution with the founding school districts. When the efforts failed, OCR referred the matter to the Justice Department last summer. After further investigation, the Justice Department entered into negotiations with the founding Mega districts, which produced today's agreement.

Romulus, one of the two districts that filed complaints with OCR, was invited to join Mega after it filed its complaint. Other high schools that were not invited to join, but will now receive invitations, include Robichaud, which filed the other complaint, Ypsilanti, Willow Run, River Rouge, Inkster and Highland Park high schools.

Patrick expressed his appreciation for the cooperation and assistance provided by OCR to the Justice Department in reaching the agreement.

96-151

***

Inspector General Announces Arrest of INS Official in Alien Smuggling Ring

Michael R. Bromwich, Inspector General for the U.S. Department of Justice, today announced the arrest by Hong Kong authorities of Jerry Wolf Stuchiner, a 19 year employee of the Immigration and Naturalization Service (INS) and current Officer in Charge of INS interests in Honduras.

Stuchiner was arrested by the Hong Kong Independent Commission Against Corruption (ICAC) as he arrived in Hong Kong Monday evening, using a United States diplomatic passport and carrying 5 fraudulent Honduran passports. Also arrested was an El Salvadoran woman traveling with Stuchiner. They were arrested and detained under a Prevention of Bribery Ordinance and will be formally charged by the ICAC with passport related fraud later this week.

The arrests culminate a cooperative investigation conducted by the OIG and ICAC into allegations that Stuchiner facilitated the sale of fraudulent Honduran passports and visas to Chinese immigrant smugglers. According to Hong Kong authorities, Stuchiner was part of a scheme that involved Chinese citizens endenturing themselves to smugglers in return for passports, travel identities, and airline tickets to Central America where they would then be smuggled into the United States.

Hong Kong resident Dickson Yao was also arrested at the airport by the ICAC, and Honduran Consulate General Herby Weizenblut was briefly detained and questioned. Five additional Hong Kong residents were detained on Monday by the ICAC for their suspected involvement in the alien smuggling ring.

Mr. Bromwich stated that OIG agents were on hand at the Hong Kong airport when Stuchiner arrived and served as a liaison between the ICAC and Department of Justice. Mr. Bromwich commended the ICAC and the Immigration & Naturalization Service for their cooperation with the Office of Inspector General.

96-339

***

Teachers Who Were Discriminated Against Can Receive Funds Under Justice Department Settlement with Northern Mariana School System

WASHINGTON, D.C.—One hundred and seventy Filipino school teachers in the public school system on the Northern Mariana Islands who received lower salaries and less favorable benefits than state-side American teachers can now receive their share of a $2.1 million settlement reached with the Justice Department.

Judge Alex R. Munson, of the U.S. District Court on Saipan, on Friday approved the distribution of the funds to 170 former and current employees of the school system. The court has already begun allocating the funds provided under the agreement—the second largest obtained by the Justice Department in an employment discrimination case based on national origin.

The agreement reached in August 1994, resolved a 1992 Justice Department suit alleging that the Commonwealth violated Title VII of the Civil Rights Act by engaging in a pattern of discrimination against Filipino public school teachers.

The suit alleged, among other things, that the Commonwealth paid Filipinos less than similarly qualified American teachers recruited from the continental United States and Hawaii, known as state-siders, refused to provide housing and transportation benefits to Filipino teachers, and provided less favorable conditions of employment to Filipino teachers than state-siders.

Under the settlement, the Commonwealth, Board of Education, Public School System, and Commissioner of Education agreed to pay back wages and other benefits to those victims of the discrimination; develop a written policy prohibiting discrimination; establish guidelines to ensure equal pay for equal education and experience; and adjust existing housing and salary disparities for teachers.

The school system also agreed to submit reports on its employment patterns to the Justice Department until September 1997, and allocate an additional $150,000 to be used to fund an Equal Employment Opportunity specialist position and related employment awareness programs.

"We will continue to monitor the Commonwealth's Public School System to ensure it complies with the requirements of Title VII and treats all its employees fairly," said Assistant Attorney General for Civil Rights Deval L. Patrick.

Claimants who wish to pick up their awards in the Commonwealth can do so by presenting positive identification to the Clerk of the U.S. District Court, on the 2nd floor of the Horiguchi Building on Saipan. The Philippine Consulate and the U.S. Embassy in Manila have agreed to help distribute checks to claimants who currently reside in the Philippines. Claim checks will be mailed to claimants who live in places other than the Commonwealth or the Philippines.

96-326

***

Two Texas Men Plead Guilty to Burning Down a House Belonging to a Black Family

WASHINGTON, D.C.—Two Texas men pled guilty today to attempting to intimidate an African-American family by burning down the house where the family planned to move, the Justice Department announced.

Shannon Ray Singleton, 18, and Gary Wayne Stouard, 40, both of Wichita Falls, pled guilty today in U.S. District Court in Dallas to burning down a house in early March which Ruby Fleeks, an African-American woman, planned to live in with her two children.

"No American should live in fear of having their home attacked because of their race," said Assistant Attorney General Deval. L. Patrick. "We will not tolerate acts of racial hatred toward members of our society and we will continue to vigorously prosecute these crimes."

According to a two count information filed today, Stouard solicited Singleton on March 5 to set fire to a house at 2118 Bluff Street, directly across the street from Stouard's own home. Fleeks and her family were to move the next day, and had many of their belongings in the house already. Stouard offered to pay Singleton $50 and to provide him with the necessary supplies to carry out the act.

That night, Singleton obtained gasoline from Stouard's home and used it to set fire to the house, breaking a window to pour the gasoline before lighting it. After committing the act, Singleton sought refuge in Stouard's home to avoid detection by the police.

The Fleeks family was not able to move into the home.

"We treat this attack so seriously because it was aimed not simply at one African-American family, but at an entire community. It is a graphic reminder of how far we still have to go in race relations in this country," said Paul E. Coggins, U.S. Attorney in Dallas.

Count one of the information charged the two with conspiring to intimidate and injure the Fleeks family because of their race. Count two charged the two with committing a felony with the use of fire.

Sentencing will take place on October 21, 1996. Under the law, each faces up to 15 years in prison and a $500,000 fine.

96-371

***

Justice Department Sues Waukegan, Illinois for Discriminating Against Hispanic Families

WASHINGTON, D.C.—The Justice Department today sued a city in Illinois that enacted and enforced a housing code for the purpose of limiting the number of Hispanic family members who could live in the same home or apartment, in violation of the federal Fair Housing Act.

Under the city ordinance, Waukegan sought to restrict the number of persons related by blood or marriage who could live together in the same home. It permitted only a husband and wife, their children, and no more than two additional relatives to live in a home or apartment, regardless of its size.

The complaint, filed today in U.S. District Court in Chicago, asserted that city officials, who were aware that Hispanics often reside in extended families, engaged in discriminatory conduct by enacting the family-restrictive rule to limit the number of Hispanics in Waukegan. It stated that city officials repeatedly expressed their animosity toward the new Hispanic residents moving into the city and said they intended to prevent the Hispanics from "taking over" Waukegan.

> "No action taken for a discriminatory purpose has any place in our nation," said Assistant Attorney General for Civil Rights Deval L. Patrick. "If overcrowding is the problem, then place a limit on the number of people living together, not on the type of people."

Today's complaint also alleged that officials, including Donald Weakly, Director of Governmental Services, and Noah Murphy, Building Commissioner, specifically targeted Hispanics when enforcing the ordinance. On numerous occasions, officials ordered Hispanic families to vacate their homes, even though their homes were of sufficient size to accommodate the families. In fact, based on the records the city provided to the Justice Department, the only families forced to vacate their homes were Hispanic.

In June 1994, after experiencing a significant increase in its Hispanic population, Waukegan revised its housing code to include the new restrictive language. Before the provision was enacted, the city was even advised that it may violate the Constitution because of the way it restricts who can live together. Shortly thereafter, and after receiving numerous complaints from Waukegan residents, the Justice Department began investigating the city's housing policies.

For the past eight months, the Justice Department and the city have been engaged in negotiations to resolve the matter. Last week, Waukegan decided to end the negotiations.

"Hispanic families deserve a place to call home just like everyone else," said James B. Burns, U.S. Attorney in Chicago. "The Supreme Court has already said that similar restrictions on the types of family members who can live together violate the Constitution."

Today's complaint seeks a court order preventing the city from enforcing the ordinance and from discriminating on the basis of national origin, and requiring the city to pay damages to the victims of the discriminatory policies and civil penalties to the U.S. Treasury.

96-383

***

Montgomery Realty Company to Pay $30,000 for Allegedly Steering Blacks and Whites to Different Areas Because of Their Race

Case Stems from Justice Department Nationwide Testing Program

WASHINGTON, D.C.—A Montgomery, Alabama real estate company that was sued by the Justice Department for allegedly refusing to refer African-Americans to properties in predominantly white parts of town will pay $30,000 in damages, the Justice Department announced.

The case, brought last January, stems from the Justice Department's highly successful nationwide fair housing testing program. Under the program, trained pairs of African-Americans and whites posing as prospective tenants inquire about the availability of rental units. By comparing the experiences of the testers, investigators discover whether minorities were treated less favorably than whites.

The agreement, filed today in U.S. District Court in Montgomery, resolves Justice Department allegations that rental agents at Hamilton Realty Company based in Montgomery, steered African-Americans toward properties located in predominantly minority areas of the city and whites toward predominantly white areas. "Steering" occurs when a rental agent discloses different properties to applicants with the intent to concentrate persons in different areas according to race.

"Housing discrimination is usually subtle but it inflicts deep wounds on its victims and serves to segregate our society," said Assistant Attorney General for Civil Rights, Deval L. Patrick. "All Americans should have the ability to live in the neighborhood of their choice regardless of the color of their skin."

Under the agreement, the company, which owns and manages approximately 200 rental properties in the Montgomery area, will create a $30,000 fund to compensate any identified victims of the alleged discriminatory practice. Any money not paid to identified victims will be paid to the government as a civil penalty.

The suit alleged that Hamilton Realty rental agents did not tell African-Americans about properties located in predominantly white areas of Montgomery, while whites were told. It also claimed that agents would steer African-Americans toward properties located in predominantly minority areas of Montgomery and whites toward predominantly white areas.

"This lawsuit and the Consent Order entered today signal our continuing commitment to the principle that equal rights in housing for all people is a basic right of citizenship," said Redding Pitt, U.S. Attorney in Montgomery.

The Justice Department's testing program has produced 33 federal cases in nine states—Ohio, Michigan, California, South Dakota, Indiana, Missouri, Florida and Virginia—resulting in more than $3 million dollars in settlements. At any given time, the Justice Department is conducting testing in about a dozen cities.

Individuals who believe they may have been the victims of housing discrimination at any of the properties owned or managed by Hamilton Realty Company should call the Housing Section of the Civil Rights Division of the Justice Department at 202-307-3804, or the Central Alabama Fair Housing Center at (334) 263-4663.

96-532

BRAIN'S USE OF SHORTCUTS CAN BE A ROUTE TO BIAS

K. C. COLE

Study Questions

1. Define "cognitive weakpoints," "default assumptions," "availability-mediated influence," "believer perseverance," and "behavior confirmation biases."
2. How can each cognitive weakpoint lead to discrimination?

Affirmative action stirs up powerful emotions in both supporters and opponents. But while both sides battle for the hearts of voters, psychologists say the real issues have more to do with the mechanisms of the mind.

Human brains are finely tuned, decision-making machines designed to make quick judgments on a wide variety of confusing events. How far away is that car in the distance? Is that form in the shadows a garbage can or a man with a gun? Is that round red thing a cherry or a marble?

In general, the brain uses past experience to jump to the "most likely" conclusion. Yet these same assumptions can lead people grossly astray.

"This acceptance by the brain of the most probable answer," writes British perceptual psychologist Richard Gregory, makes it "difficult, perhaps somewhat impossible, to see very unusual objects."

When "unusual objects" are women and minorities, it may be impossible to see them as qualified for a variety of jobs, psychologists say.

"Even if you have absolutely no prejudice, you are influenced by your expectations," said Diane Halpern, professor of psychology at Cal State San Bernardino. "A small woman of color doesn't look like a corporate executive. If you look at heads of corporations, they are tall, slender, white males. They are not fat. They are not in a wheelchair. They are not too old. Anything that doesn't conform to the expectation is a misfit."

"Similarity is a strong predictor of attraction," said David Kravitz, psychologist at Florida International University. "So there is a natural human tendency to prefer and hire people like you."

A growing number of behavioral studies point to patterns of perception that influence how people view everything from the moon to minority job candidates. These patterns, experts say, confirm that perception is an active process in which people color the world with their expectations. They do not so much believe what they see as see what they believe.

The ideal of a society free of prejudice may not be possible, experts say, simply because of the makeup of the human mind. Stereotypes are not only inevitable, but essential for survival. If people couldn't make lightning-fast decisions on limited information, they would not be able to discriminate between friend or foe, shadow or object, far or near. To a very real extent, people have to judge every book by its cover. And once a judgment is made, virtually no amount of contrary evidence can turn it around.

People aren't normally aware of the amount of guesswork that goes on in the brain because these perceptual tricks hit upon the right answer the vast majority of the time. Not only do perceptual processes work to ensure survival, they allow people to make music, play baseball, create art. In fact, one of the great puzzles of cognitive science is how a mind capable of dreaming up the music of Mozart and the equations of quantum mechanics can make so many egregious mistakes.

Social psychologists are finding that the occasional errors that the mind makes reveal the hidden rules it uses to make decisions. For example, the brain uses apparent size to judge distance: People don't mistake a car in the distance for a toy because the brain knows through past experience that distant objects appear smaller; therefore the brain compensates, automatically making it larger.

But when the information is ambiguous, the brain often leaps to the wrong conclusion. For example, the moon appears to be much larger when it floats just above the horizon than when it shines overhead. The moon doesn't change size, but the brain's estimation of its distance does—in turn automatically changing its apparent size.

By studying how the mind can fool us, psychologists explore the nature of cognitive weak points. They have found that to a large extent, people see what they expect to see, and reject any information that would challenge their already established point of view. "It's the one thing that everyone agrees on," said psychologist Rachel Hare-Mustin, formerly of Harvard. "Unconscious prevailing ideologies are like sand at the picnic. They get into everything."

Errors about everyday objects tend to provide immediate feedback, which makes people unlikely to repeat them. Even a slight mistake in estimating the size of a step can lead to a serious fall.

But errors about other people can more easily slip by unnoticed. "If you're wrong about that car coming at you, it's going to run you down," said psychologist Jennifer Crocker of the State University of New York at Buffalo. "But if you're wrong about whether someone is stupid, you don't hire that person and you never find out how brilliant they are."

The subversive nature of unconscious thought is revealed by this riddle:

A father and son are en route to a baseball game when their car stalls on the railroad tracks. The father can't restart the car. An oncoming train hits the car. The father dies. An ambulance rushes the boy to a nearby hospital. In the emergency room, the surgeon takes one look and says: "I can't operate on this child; he's my son."

As cognition researcher Douglas Hofstadter pointed out, even intelligent, broad-minded people go out of their way to invent bizarre scenarios—sometimes involving extraterrestrials—to solve the riddle. What prevents most people from seeing that the surgeon is the boy's mother is the reliance of the brain on the "default assumption" that a surgeon is a man.

"A default assumption," Hofstadter explained, "is what holds true in what you might say is the 'simplest' or 'most likely' case. But the critical thing is that they are made automatically, not as a result of consideration and elimination."

Default assumptions are one of the strategies the brain uses to judge the most likely interpretation of an ambiguous situation. In effect, the brain calculates what psychologists call a "base rate"—the normal frequency of a certain event in a normal population.

Base rates have enormous survival value. A mail carrier who assumes that most pit bulls are dangerous is more likely to escape injury than a more open-minded colleague.

Other peculiarities of social perception have been uncovered in a wide variety of controlled experiments, mostly with college students. For example, subjects judge attractive colleagues as smarter, kinder and happier than their unattractive (but otherwise similar) counterparts.

They judge people perceived to be powerful as taller than less powerful people, even when they are actually the same height. They judge people living in poverty as less intelligent than people in affluent neighborhoods.

In one experiment, college students watched a short film of a girl taking a math test and getting a numerical grade. When the girl was portrayed in a suburban neighborhood, viewers remembered her score as higher than when she was shown in a ghetto—even though both the girl and the score were the same in both cases.

The brain also grabs for the most readily available image at hand. This automatic response—which psychologists refer to by the tongue-tangling term "availability-mediated influence"—can be easily manipulated.

In one frequently cited series of experiments, three groups of people were introduced to one of two bogus prison guards—one sweet natured and humane, the other sadistic and brutish. All three groups were later asked to make inferences about "prison guards in general."

The first group was told that whatever guard they met was typical of all prison guards. The second group was told nothing. The third group was told that the guard they met was not at all typical; in fact, they were specifically warned that any inferences they made from this one case was likely to be wrong.

Nonetheless, all three groups described "prison guards in general" as either kind or brutish, depending on which guard they met.

The experiment, described in the classic book, "Human Inference" by Lee Ross of Stanford and Richard Nisbett of the University of Michigan, presents what the authors describe as "a humbling picture of human . . . frailty." When presented with a single vivid "available" example, the mind tends to bury all other evidence under the carpet of the unconscious.

This reliance on one vivid example sheds light on one of the most painful contradictions of the affirmative action debate. Many white males, studies show, are angry because they are convinced that less qualified women and minorities are taking their jobs.

Yet minorities and women still feel excluded—and apparently for good reason. The recently published report of the Glass Ceiling Commission, established by legislation introduced in 1990 by then-Senate minority leader Bob Dole, concluded that 95% of top positions are still occupied by white men, even though they constitute only 43% of the work force.

"So much of the public discourse on this is debate by anecdote," said William Bielby, chairman of the sociology department at UC Santa Barbara. "We hear from so many students that they have a white friend from high school who couldn't get into UCSB, but a black kid got in with no problem. And we know how many black kids are on campus. If all those anecdotes were true, then 15% of our students, rather than 3%, would be black."

In the same way, Bielby said, it's easier to hang onto stereotypes in settings where only one or two women, for example, are in management positions. When only one woman occupies the executive suite, she becomes a target for all expectations about women in general. "But when the proportion of women is 40% or 50%," Bielby said, "[their colleagues] can see the extent to which the women differ among themselves and the men differ among themselves."

Psychologist Faye Crosby of Smith College conducted an experiment with a group of Yale undergraduate men that vividly showed how inequality becomes imperceptible on a case-by-case basis. Patterns of discrimination that are easy to see in a broad context become invisible when seen in individual instances.

Crosby and her colleagues created bogus job descriptions of various men and women at a hypothetical company. The students were instructed to look for unfairness in the salaries. Unknown to them, the women's salaries were rigged to be 80% of the salaries of comparable men.

When the students compared one man with one woman at a time, they did not see any unfairness. But when they saw all the salaries of all the men and all the women at the same time, they could easily spot the pattern.

Crosby stresses that this inability to see unfairness on a case-by-case basis has nothing to do with sexism or bad attitudes. It has to do with how the mind works. "We're not saying people are stupid. It's just [a normal cognitive process] like optical illusions."

However one's perceptions are planted, they soon become almost impossible to root out.

In a process psychologists call "belief perseverance," people do almost anything to cling to cherished notions. "If we were constantly changing the way we view the world, things would be too confusing," Crocker said. So people tend to discount evidence that contradicts their "schema," or theory about the world. "If you believe lawyers are slimy and you meet some who aren't, you don't revise your schema; you say; oh, that's an exception."

People also routinely change their memories, Halpern said, to fit their beliefs. If you think that successful people have to be aggressive, and you work with a successful person who is not aggressive "you remember that person as more aggressive," Halpern said. "What we remember depends very much on our biases and beliefs."

These self-fulfilling prophecies, known to psychologists as "behavioral confirmation biases," were dramatically illustrated by a series of experiments in which similar black and white job applicants were questioned by a white interviewer while researchers watched behind a one-way mirror. When the job applicants were black, interviewers sat farther back in their chairs, avoided eye contact, stumbled over their speech and posed fewer questions.

The Lessons of Illusions

Psychologists use illusions to catch the brain in the act of jumping to conclusions. Most of the time, these perceptual shortcuts work quite well, so we don't notice them. But in unusual situations—such as considering women and minority applicants for jobs traditionally held by white males—the same tricks can lead to egregious mistakes. Many psychologists believe that the unconscious mechanisms people employ to make judgments about other people are very similar to those behind visual illusions.

Note: The moon on the right has been made smaller to simulate the illusion.

True Moon

- **THE ILLUSION:** The moon appears larger when it's low on the horizon than when it's high overhead, even though the moon doesn't change size.
- **HOW IT WORKS:** When the moon sits low in the sky, the horizon serves as a reference point, making the moon seem unnaturally bigger. (If you view the moon upside down and the horizon becomes the sky—thereby changing the apparent distance—the illusion disappears.)
- **WHAT IT SHOWS:** That the brain can jump to the wrong conclusions when information is ambiguous. Also, that knowing something is an illusion does not make the illusion go away.

Shape and Form

- **THE ILLUSION:** A white triangle appears to float in front of three black circles, even though no triangle exists.
- **HOW IT WORKS:** The brain constructs the triangle as the most likely solution to the figure of three pie-shaped wedges. People who don't immediately see the triangle usually find it after someone points it out to them.
- **WHAT IT SHOWS:** That people can see something that doesn't exist, especially if they go looking for it. Also, that it's much easier to see something familiar.

Paris, Paris

- **THE ILLUSION:** A sign appears to read "Paris in the spring," but it actually has an extra "the."
- **HOW IT WORKS:** Since people do not expect to see a double "the," most do not perceive it.
- **WHAT IT SHOWS:** That expectation influences what people see.

Source: The Exploratorium, San Francisco. Researched by K. C. Cole / *Los Angeles Times*

The next part of the test was designed to look at the behavior of the job applicants. This time, the researchers became the interviewers. For consistency, all the applicants were white. With half of the applicants, the researchers intentionally mimicked the behaviors that the interviewers in the first part of the experiment used on blacks (sitting back, stumbling over words and so on); with the other half, they behaved as the interviewers had with whites—that is, they sat forward in the chairs, maintained eye contact, spoke clearly and asked more questions.

Other researchers watching from behind one-way mirrors evaluated how the applicants seemed to perform during the interview. The result was that the white applicants, when treated as the black applicants had been, were rated less confident, less articulate and less qualified for the job.

What makes these behaviors hard to correct is that they're completely unconscious; the brain jumps to conclusions in less than 100 milliseconds, "the time it takes to recognize your mother," Hofstadter noted.

In study after study, "the most important finding is that [biases] operate unconsciously, even in people who don't want them to," said Anthony G. Greenwald, psychologist at the University of Washington. One of the greatest misconceptions that people have, he said, "is that wanting to be fair is enough to enable you to be fair—not recognizing the unconscious forces that influence your judgments."

In the end, he says, the best approach to affirmative action may have nothing to do with putting people's hearts in the right place. Instead, it should come from understanding what goes on in the brain.

"If you understand that your car tends to drive to the left because your wheels are out of line, you can correct it," he said. Affirmative action, says Greenwald, is a way to compensate not only for past discrimination, but also for future discrimination "by persons who have no intent to discriminate."

TALKING PAST ONE ANOTHER

RICHARD T. SCHAEFER

Study Questions
1. What are the two competing definitions of racism?
2. Do you think that differences in the meaning assigned to racism affect people's opinion on whether racism is a problem?

When it comes to talking about race, I contend that on college campuses as in the larger society Whites, Blacks, Asians, and Hispanics hold different views. It is not a variation in accent or vocabulary that is important, but how the dominant Whites and subordinated African Americans and other minority groups have come to view race.

Robert Blauner (1989; 1992) writes that Blacks and Whites basically talk past each other. Blauner reached these conclusions through his in-depth interviews with Blacks and Whites stretching back to 1968. While not intended as a random sample, Blauner's observations help to explain why national surveys continue to show such sharp differences between Whites and Blacks on questions about a broad range of issues from race to employment to welfare policies. By extension, his observations offer insight in the presence of racial prejudice and incidents on a college campus.

Blauner found that Black and White Americans differ on their interpretations of social change from the 1960s through the 1990s because their racial languages define central terms differently, especially "racism." Racism once meant a belief in the superiority of Whites based on the inherent inferiority of Blacks. But in the 1960s, academics and civil rights leaders broadened the meaning of racism. Blacks have tended to embrace the enlarged definition, while Whites have resisted it. Whites object when Blacks form their own groups because Whites equate color consciousness with racism. This is especially evident when we see (on predominantly White college campuses) White students puzzled and annoyed by Black fraternities, Black/Latino cultural houses, and Miss Black Homecoming Queen contests.

Racism was first widened to include "institutional racism," incorporating the social structures that lead to racial segregation. Clearly, in society and on college campuses, the term "racism" refers to an atmosphere that comforts people of one race while making people of other races uncomfortable and unwanted. Blacks may use the term to mean "racism as result," expressing the view that any underrepresentation of minorities shows that racism is at work. Again, few Whites accept this interpretation. This should not be surprising because accepting the view that racism is widespread challenges the legitimacy of whatever success White individuals have enjoyed (Bobo and Kluegel 1993).

Typical of this difference in Whites' and Blacks' attitudes was the aftermath of the 1992 acquittal of four White Los Angeles police officers charged in the beating of Rodney King. Large majorities of Whites and overwhelming majorities of African Americans told pollsters that the verdict was wrong and justice had not been served. Yet when asked if the verdict "shows that blacks cannot get justice in this country," the responses differed—78 percent of Blacks said yes, compared to only 25 percent of Whites (Duke 1992). Even broadly directed questions elicit vast differences in outlook. A 1994 national survey found that 60 percent of Whites "think blacks and other minorities have the same opportunities as whites in the U.S." Yet only 50 percent of Hispanics and 27 percent of Blacks held the same opinion (Fulwood 1994). These contrasting perspectives are what William A. Gamson and his colleagues have termed competing "issue cultures." People frame social issues in different ways, calling upon contrasting metaphors, phrases, and other symbols (Gamson and Lasch 1983; Gamson and Modigliani 1987; see also, Bobo and Kluegel 1993).

These expanded definitions of racism do not make sense to White college students, and Whites in general, who tend to view racism as a personal issue. By and large the content of college curricula does little to unravel these differences. Whites find it difficult to differentiate between the charge that a social structure or institution is racist and the accusation that they, as participants in that structure, are personally racist.

Judith Lichtenberg (1992, p. 3), a professor of philosophy, summarizes this dichotomy:

> In general, white people today use the word "racism" to refer to the explicit conscious belief in racial superiority (typically white over black, but also sometimes black over white). For the most part, black people mean something different by racism; they mean a set of practices and institutions that result in the oppression of black people. Racism, in this view, is not a matter of what's in people's heads but of what happens in the world.

The expanded meaning of racism makes sense to many African Americans, Hispanics, Asian Americans, and Native Americans, "who live such experiences in their bones" (Blauner 1992). But these same expanded definitions of racism do not make sense to Whites, who find it difficult to differentiate between charges of a racist social structure and individual racists.

Whites' resistance to the view of racism as pervasive can be attributed to the dominant ideology in the United States that opportunity is plentiful, effort is economically rewarded and, hence, economic failure is largely deserved (Huber and Form 1973). Furthermore, Whites' own typical experience of relative economic success prevents their recognition of the continuing barriers to opportunity confronted by African Americans and other minorities (Kluegel and Smith 1986; Taylor and Pettigrew 1992).

African Americans talk and think of racism as an ongoing, pervasive condition of life, while Whites tend to talk and think of racism as individual actions, the bigoted exception. These differing perceptions help explain the frequent White response, "I am not racist," and Blacks' view that Whites are, at the very least, naive about the conditions in the nation they dominate.

The view emerging in post-1980 surveys indicates that Whites do not define racism as a serious problem. They object to measures seeking to reduce inequality on grounds they perceive as allegedly free of racial antipathy. Richard Lowry (1991) refers to this limited view of racial inequality and the mistaken perception that racial intolerance was a thing of the past as "yuppie racism."

Let's Spread the "Fun" Around: The Issue of Sports Team Names and Mascots

Ward Churchill

Study Questions

1. Before you read this article, did you have an opinion on the meaning of the "Tomahawk Chop"? What was that opinion?
2. Did your opinion change upon reading Ward's essay? Explain.
3. If your opinion changed to one against the "Chop", what elements of Ward's argument contributed to that change?
4. If your opinion remained in support or changed to one in support of the "Chop," why was Ward's essay unconvincing?

If people are genuinely interested in honoring Indians, try getting your government to live up to the more than 400 treaties it signed with our nations. Try respecting our religious freedom which has been repeatedly denied in federal courts. Try stopping the ongoing theft of Indian water and other natural resources. Try reversing your colonial process that relegates us to the most impoverished, polluted, and desperate conditions in this country. . . . Try understanding that the mascot issue is only the tip of a very huge problem of continuing racism against American Indians. Then maybe your ["honors"] will mean something. Until then, it's just so much superficial, hypocritical puffery. People should remember that an honor isn't born when it parts the honorer's lips, it is born when it is accepted in the honoree's ear.

Glenn T. Morris
Colorado AIM

During the past couple of seasons, there has been an increasing wave of controversy regarding the names of professional sports teams like the Atlanta "Braves," Cleveland "Indians," Washington "Redskins," and Kansas City "Chiefs." The issue extends to the names of college teams like Florida State University "Seminoles," University of Illinois "Fighting Illini," and so on, right on down to high school outfits like the Lamar (Colorado) "Savages." Also involved have been team adoption of "mascots," replete with feathers, buckskins, beads, spears, and "warpaint" (some fans have opted to adorn themselves in the same fashion), and nifty little "pep" gestures like the "Indian Chant" and "Tomahawk Chop."

A substantial number of American Indians have protested that use of native names, images, and symbols as sports team mascots and the like is, by definition, a virulently racist practice. Given the historical relationship between Indians and non-Indians during what has been called the "Conquest of America," American Indian Movement leader (and American Indian Anti-Defamation Council founder) Russell Means has compared the practice to contemporary Germans naming their soccer teams the "Jews," "Hebrews," and "Yids," while adorning their uniforms with grotesque caricatures of Jewish faces taken from the nazis' antisemitic propaganda of the 1930s. Numerous demonstrations have occurred in conjunction with games—most notably during the November 15, 1992, match-up between the Chiefs and Redskins in Kansas City—by angry Indians and their supporters.

In response, a number of players—especially African-Americans and other minority athletes—have been trotted out by professional team owners like Ted Turner, as well as university and public school officials, to announce that they mean not to insult, but instead to "honor," native people. They have been joined by the television networks and most major newspapers, all of which have editorialized that Indian discomfort with the situation is "no big deal," insisting that the whole thing is just "good, clean fun." The country needs more such fun, they've argued, and "a few disgruntled Native Americans" have no right to undermine the nation's enjoyment of its leisure time by complaining. This is especially the case, some have contended, "in hard times like these." It has even been contended that Indian outrage at being systematically degraded—rather than the degradation itself—creates "a serious barrier to the sort of intergroup communication so necessary in a multicultural society such as ours."

Okay, let's communicate. We may be frankly dubious that those advancing such positions really believe in their own rhetoric, but, just for the sake of argument, let's accept the premise that they are sincere. If what they are saying is true in any way at all, then isn't it time we spread such "inoffensiveness" and "good cheer" around among *all* groups so that *everybody* can participate *equally* in fostering the round of national laughs they call for? Sure it is—the country can't have too *much* fun or "intergroup involvement"—so the more, the merrier. Simple consistency demands that anyone who thinks the Tomahawk Chop is a swell pastime must be just as hearty in their endorsement of the following ideas, which—by the "logic" used to defend the defamation of American Indians—should help us all *really* start yukking it up.

First, as a counterpart to the Redskins, we need an NFL team called "Niggers" to "honor" Afroamerica. Halftime festivities for fans might include a simulated stewing of the opposing coach in a large pot while players and cheerleaders dance around it, garbed in leopard skins and wearing fake bones in their noses. This concept obviously goes along with the kind of gaiety attending the Chop, but also with the actions of the Kansas City Chiefs, whose team members—prominently including black team members—lately appeared on a poster looking "fierce" and "savage" by way of wearing Indian regalia. Just a bit of harmless "morale boosting," says the Chiefs' front office. You bet.

So that the newly-formed "Niggers" sports club won't end up too out of sync while expressing the "spirit" and "identity" of Afroamericans in the above fashion, a baseball franchise—let's call this one the "Sambos"—should be formed. How about a basketball team called the "Spearchuckers"? A hockey team called the "Jungle Bunnies"? Maybe the "essence" of these teams could be depicted by images of tiny black faces adorned with huge pairs of lips. The players could appear on TV every week or so gnawing on chicken legs and spitting watermelon seeds at one another. Catchy, eh? Well, there's "nothing to be upset about," according to those who love wearing "war bonnets" to the Super Bowl or having "Chief Illiniwik" dance around the sports arenas of Urbana, Illinois.

And why stop there? There are plenty of other groups to include. "Hispanics"? They can be "represented" by the Galveston "Greasers" and San Diego "Spics," at least until the Wisconsin "Wetbacks" and Baltimore "Beaners" get off the ground. Asian Americans? How about the "Slopes," "Dinks," "Gooks," and "Zipperheads"? Owners of the latter teams might get their logo ideas from editorial page cartoons printed in the nation's newspapers during World War II: slant-eyes, buck teeth, big glasses, but nothing racially insulting or derogatory, according to the editors and artists involved at the time. Indeed, this Second World War-vintage stuff can be seen as just another barrel of laughs, at least by what current editors say are their "local standards" concerning American Indians.

Let's see. Who's been left out? Teams like the Kansas City "Kikes," Hanover "Honkies," San Leandro "Shylocks," Daytona "Dagos," and Pittsburgh "Polacks" will fill a certain social void among white folk. Have a religious belief? Let's all go for the gusto and gear up the Milwaukee "Mackerel Snappers" and Hollywood "Holy Rollers." The Fighting Irish of Notre Dame can be rechristened the "Drunken Irish" or "Papist Pigs." Issues of gender and sexual preference can be addressed through creation of teams like the St. Louis "Sluts," Boston "Bimbos," Detroit "Dykes," and the Fresno "Faggots." How about the Gainesville "Gimps" and Richmond "Retards," so the physically and mentally impaired won't be excluded from our fun and games?

Now, don't go getting "overly sensitive" out there. *None* of this is demeaning or insulting, at least not when it's being done to Indians. Just ask the folks who are doing it, or their apologists like Andy Rooney in the national media. They'll tell you—as in fact they *have* been telling you—that there's been no harm done, regardless of what their victims think, feel, or say. The situation is exactly the same as when those with precisely the same mentality used to insist that Step'n'Fetchit was okay, or Rochester on the *Jack Benny Show,* or Amos and Andy, Charlie Chan, the Frito Bandito, or any of the other cutesey symbols making up the lexicon of American racism. Have we communicated yet?

Let's get just a little bit real here. The notion of "fun" embodied in rituals like the Tomahawk Chop must be understood for what it is. There's not a single non-Indian example deployed above which can be considered socially acceptable in even the most marginal sense. The reasons are obvious enough. So why is it different where American Indians are concerned? One can only conclude that, in contrast to the other groups at issue, Indians are (falsely) perceived as being too few, and therefore too weak, to defend themselves effectively against racist and otherwise offensive behavior. The sensibilities of those who take pleasure in things like the Chop are thus akin to those of schoolyard bullies and those twisted individuals who like to torture cats. At another level, their perspectives have much in common with those manifested more literally—and therefore more honestly—by groups like the nazis, aryan nations, and Ku Klux Klan. Those who suggest this is "okay" should be treated accordingly by anyone who opposes nazism and comparable belief systems.

Fortunately, there are a few glimmers of hope that this may become the case. A few teams and their fans have gotten the message and have responded appropriately. One illustration is Stanford University, which opted to drop the name "Indians" with regard to its sports teams (and, contrary to the myth perpetuated by those who enjoy insulting Native Americans, Stanford has experienced *no* resulting drop-off in attendance at its games). Meanwhile, the local newspaper in Portland, Oregon, recently decided its long-standing editorial policy prohibiting use of racial epithets should include derogatory sports team names. The Redskins, for instance, are now simply referred to as being "the Washington team," and will continue to be described in this way until the franchise adopts an inoffensive moniker (newspaper sales in Portland have suffered no decline as a result).

Such examples are to be applauded and encouraged. They stand as figurative beacons in the night, proving beyond all doubt that it is quite possible to indulge in the pleasure of athletics without accepting blatant racism into the bargain. The extent to which they do not represent the norm of American attitudes and behavior is exactly the extent to which America remains afflicted with an ugly reality which is far different from the noble and enlightened "moral leadership" it professes to show the world. Clearly, the United States has a very long way to go before it measures up to such an image of itself.

ANOTHER JAPANESE VERSION: AN AMERICAN ACTOR IN JAPANESE HANDS[1]

JAMES F. HOPGOOD

Study Questions

1. Describe the process by which Hopgood refines his understanding of the word "obsession" as it applies to Japanese "Deaners" and Japanese culture in general.
2. List the various substitutes for the word "obsession" that Hopgood considers.

Practically from the beginning of my research with the "Deaners" in 1989 (Hopgood 1991, 1992a)[2], I was aware of some Japanese interest in the late American actor, James Dean, along with other American "icons." As the research continued, the "Japanese connection" appeared again and again and to the point that I decided to explore its meaning hoping to arrive at an understanding of the interest in Dean in the Japanese context. In some cases, the interest in Dean was certainly more than casual and even appeared to be at the level of an "obsession." It turns out that exploring the "meaning" of James Dean for the Japanese and in Japanese culture is more enigmatic than I anticipated.

Several possibilities for this interest occur to me at this point and these are not necessarily exclusive of one another: (1) the Japanese are like us and become "obsessed" with things and the "obsession" with things is an extension and/or expression of a universal existential self. Unfortunately, there is a problem: While that may be true at a general, abstract level, why certain "things" from one culture become "obsessed" goes unanswered and when certain things from one culture become "obsessed" by people of a different culture, what is to be made of that? (*cf.* Brannen 1992: 218); (2) the Japanese, unlike Americans, are more likely to incorporate non-Japanese cultural elements into existing cultural patterns and practices and the Japanese fascination with American pop culture of the 1950s and '60s and associated artifacts present another example of the "Japanese form of cultural imperialism" (Brannen 1992). However, in 1956 Japanese film critics are reported to have given *East of Eden* 26 awards (Riese 1991: 274) indicating that Japanese interests in Dean and his films, at least, are not recent; and, finally, (3) the quest for meaning and fulfillment of "self" is directed towards the achievement of the Japanese value of "purity" (*jun and junjō*) (Lebra 1976, 1992) and the "obsession" with Dean for some is an expression of that quest.

How is Japanese interest in James Dean expressed? I will examine a few of the manifestations of this interest in the late American actor, before going on to an attempt to decipher Japanese interest in Dean.

Mass Media Cases

It may come as a surprise to Americans to see "Dean" brand cigarettes on sale in Japan. The video *The Japanese Version* (Alvarez and Kolker 1991) exhibits many examples of American culture that appear in Japan. Among them are two examples of James Dean. One shows a life-sized figure of Dean in the emblematic *Rebel Without a Cause* red jacket selling photos. The other example, in a Tokyo subway, uses Dean's image to sell electronics.

While traveling in Japan during July and August, 1994, I found Dean in several different locations and settings. In Kyoto along a narrow, shop lined cobblestoned street leading to a major temple and shrine complex at Kiyomizu, I encountered him in several of the shops. His image was available on mirrors, posters, *noren* (a certain type of curtain), window shades, wall hangings, postcards, and assorted other items. It may strike an American as somewhat "odd" to find images of Dean available in a setting closing associated with religious temples and shrines. In the Tokyo Tower, he was on exhibit in the Wax Museum and for sale in several shops. As in Kyoto, he could be purchased in a variety of forms. On one of the mirrors, was written: "One Tear for Summer Past, A Smile for Winter to be James Dean." In a flower shop located in Tokyo's World Trade Center, he appeared on a poster announcing an international AIDS conference.

Special publications covering his life and career are published in Japan in Japanese and bilingual, Japanese-English, editions. Copies of Dean's movies are available on video and recordings of the soundtracks from those movies are issued in Japan on compact disk. The list goes on and on. . . .

In *James Dean Story* (Hikaru 1992), a Japanese NHK Television program, Dean's life is explored seeking to uncover the reasons for his fame. This program is aimed at high school and college-age young people and is part of a TV series called *Biography* focusing on famous personalities.[3] A great deal of attention is given to the death of Dean's mother and the emotional scars left on him at age of nine. Also explored are later difficulties he encountered and his perseverance in seeking to become an actor. Also emphasized is Dean's acting talent. Dean's enthusiasm in racing motorcycles and sports cars is presented as an escape from disappointments.

Other Cases

On a lonely stretch of rural highway in southern California is a most remarkable site at the "town" of Cholame. Located between Salinas and Bakersfield, Cholame has a population of twenty-five, a cafe, and a small building that was once a U.S. Post Office. Cholame is within sight of where James Dean died as the result of an automobile accident on 30 September 1955. In front of the old post office building is a large monument dedicated to James Dean. It was erected by Japanese businessman Seita Ohnishi in 1977 at a cost of $50,000 (Riese 1991). Mr. Ohnishi is currently having a larger, more massive monument built in France at an estimated cost of $200,000. This larger monument is reported to be 14 feet high, 40 feet long, and to weigh 130 tons. When finished it will be shipped by sea to California.

Mr. Ohnishi is known as a major collector of Dean memorabilia. For example, he purchased the entire collection of negatives of the late photographer Sanford Roth from his widow. Roth was one of several well known photographers of the day who photographed Dean extensively. Roth was following in a Ford station wagon behind Dean in his Porsche Spyder when the fatal accident occurred. Subsequently, Ohnishi has published several books in Japan on Dean illustrated largely with Roth's photographs.

Ohnishi is reported (Riese 1991: 369) to have said of Dean:

> There are some things, like the hatred that accompanies war, that are best forgotten. There are others, like the love inspired by this young actor, that should be preserved for all time.

In the materials and data I have collected since 1989 there are numerous letters from Japanese fans written to the James Dean Foundation, members of the Dean and Winslow families, David Loehr of the James Dean Gallery, and to the "We Remember Dean International" Fan Club. There are, as well, dozens and dozens of cases of Japanese making pilgrimages to Fairmount and other sites associated with Dean. During 1995, for example, the Fairmount Historical Museum reported 95 visitors from Japan. That was the largest number for any country (Germany was second with 72).

Perhaps the most "interesting" case of a pilgrimage occurred on August 24, 1993. That evening at 10:25 p.m. I received a phone call from David Loehr from Fairmount. He sounded nearly hysterical. David is normally very "laid-back" and at first I thought someone close to him must have died.

A group of Japanese had arrived in Chicago earlier that day and then chartered a bus to Fairmount. The group consisted of a Mr. and Mrs. Masao Hiyashi, a daughter, and eleven friends. Mr. Hiyashi's 21 year old son, Kentaro, had died in an accident on a movie set in Japan two years earlier. The son was a very devoted fan of James Dean. The reason for their pilgrimage was the son always wanted to travel to Fairmount and the other places associated with Dean. They spent over four hours in Fairmount visiting the James Dean Gallery, the Fairmount Historical Museum, Dean's grave, the Winslow farm, and other Dean sites. They carried framed photos of the son and of Dean and numerous personal items belonging to the son. The photo of the son was carried and held up at each place visited so he could "see." At Dean's grave they spent an hour. While the group stood around the grave, the son's photo was placed at the grave and the mother took out personal items belonging to her son and placed them around the grave. Some of the personal affects were on the son when he died. The father lit two cigarettes (need I say who the cigarettes were for?) then set them up on pebbles to burn. Incense was also lit and the son's last pack of cigarettes placed on Dean's grave marker. There was lots of touching of the grave stone by members of the group and lots of photo taking. Members of the group took "souvenirs" consisting of pieces of grass, gravel, and other items from around the grave site, and placed them in plastic bags for the trip home. According to Loehr, their bilingual guide said that now the members of the group felt that the two spirits of Kentaro and Dean were "together" or "the same" (*isshō*). From Fairmount the group was traveling on to New York City to visit the places, haunts, and sites there associated with Dean. Perhaps their pilgrimage to Fairmount and New York was a paying-back of a "debt" (*on*) felt owed to Dean on behalf of the dead actor. I can not say at this juncture. Perhaps the explanation for this event lies elsewhere in Japanese culture or involves several dimensions, trajectories, or levels in Japanese culture. Later I learned that Mr. and Mrs. Hayashi donated $10,000 in memory of their son for the new "James Dean Memorial Park" in Fairmount.

But what do these cases tell us? What of Mr. Ohnishi? He is known for spending large sums of money to feed his "obsession." He could be, after all, just a Japanese "oddity," whatever that would be. But, is he and other

Japanese, like those described here, "obsessed" with Dean? I have discovered a problem in using that term in the Japanese case. The application of the term and concept of "obsession" in the Japanese case is highly problematic.

In August, 1993, I interviewed a Japanese colleague on this issue of "obsession."[4] Not an anthropologist, but an information systems specialist, he was raised and educated in Japan until age 18. He continues to maintain contacts with and to visit family and friends in Japan, although he now lives in St. Louis.

Our discussion on this issue was made difficult because of my use of the term "obsession." Although speaking in English he had no problem understanding what I meant, it became clear that he was uncomfortable with the application of the term "obsession" to the Japanese in the examples I used. He repeated many times that the Japanese are not "obsessed." I tried contrasting what I meant by comparing having a "hobby," with being "obsessed" with something. It turns out in that case "hobby," as in "working at a hobby" or "having a hobby," is not applicable. Using that contrast, it turns out that "obsession" in English is best. We could agree on using "obsession" as an objective, Western, term but agreeing on its applicability in the Japanese cultural context continued to be troublesome. Within the context of Japanese culture the sort of "obsession" as an attribute of *behavior* attached to James Dean or any other character, thing, or event becomes difficult to "place," position, or interpret, if conceived of as "obsession."

I can not be sure if this is only a "linguistic problem," that is, the experience of "obsession" exists for the Japanese, but it is identified and denoted by other terms, and without the negative connotations found in Western culture. When my Japanese colleague suggested "total immersion into an experience" as a trait of the Japanese I thought that could be it. But, does "immersion" in Japanese (*netchū*[5]) also carry the connotation of long term and excess of "obsession?" Apparently not, *netchū* applies to a temporary fascination and lacks the intensity of the English term "obsession."

Eventually Kasai suggested the term *yamitsuki,* "infatuation," as a possible near equivalent. This term apparently lacks the negative connotation, or stigma, of "obsession" in the Euro-American setting. There is also *yamitsuku,* meaning "be taken ill; be addicted to, become absorbed in, give oneself up [to]." Perhaps as a final thought, Kasai wondered if the relative lack of interest in Japan with psychological pathologies had anything to do with the general lack of a negative or pathological connotation with "obsession" leading to our confusion over the whole issue.

Still, there are other possibilities. Mathews (1996) explores the interesting term *ikigai.* Ikigai is defined as "reason for living, what one lives for" and possibly denotes the "obsession" demonstrated by Ohnishi and others. Takie Sugiyama Lebra (Personal communication 28 February 1995) suggests *akogareru* (to long, to yearn) or *muchō* (absorbed, engrossed, carried away). In the case of *muchō,* Lebra suggested a translation as "being crazy about." Certainly these terms contain some of the distinguishing attributes of our "obsession."

Perhaps another way to examine this problem is through the notion of "consumed" as in "totally consumed" by something. In Japanese this occurs as "exhaust," "exert", "endeavor," and other synonyms. The terms "possess" and "possession" also occur in Japanese. Perhaps the Japanese may conceptualize or experience the *"inward"* problem of something coming *into* them as in *"possessed,"* but not the *"outward"* quality of *becoming* obsessed. Nevertheless, I can not place these on the same scale of things as viewed by Western scientists or lay-persons; *i.e.,* that in Japanese "obsession" or "consumed" fit into the same Western dichotomous way of thinking.

To return to the Japanese TV program *James Dean Story:* is there any help to be found there in attempting to understand the appeal of Dean to the Japanese? Two important Japanese themes appear in this film. One is the pathos (*aikan*) of the tragic hero. The significant concern given to Dean's mother's death, the emotional scar that resulted, his failed love relationship with the actress Pier Angeli indicate this theme. (The notion of young, short-lived, romantic love links up well with the Japanese sense of aesthetics.) The second theme is *gaman,* perseverance or suffering, in the face of many difficulties as Dean struggled to make it as an actor.

A Few Closing Thoughts

Despite my difficulties in interpreting a Japanese attraction or "obsession" with Dean, there are a few points of linkage in Japanese culture worth exploring further. The themes of pathos and *gaman* noted in the Japanese TV program on Dean point to classic Japanese "mythic figures" or heros, like Yoshida Shōin (1830–1859) (de Bary 1988: 75 ff.). It seems that Shōin was a young samurai who defied Japanese seclusion laws and attempted to stow away on one of Commodore Perry's ships. He wanted to visit the West to see and learn for himself. He was caught and imprisoned. Later he was martyred for revolutionary activities, but he became a model for a new, modernizing Japan.

Could it be James Dean and other Western personalities are being transformed into a new type of *hitogami?* In traditional Japanese Shintō a *hitogami* is a mortal person who after death is worshiped as *kami,* a god or spirit. Is this, then, just an expression of "Japanese cultural imperialism" noted earlier and the "recontextualization" of which Brannen speaks in her piece on Tokyo Disneyland (1992: 219)? Perhaps it is, *on one level,* but on another, deeper level it may be an expression of the self's desire to "absorb" some of what makes a *kami* and thereby achieve that value of "purity" of which Takie Sugiyama Lebra speaks (1992: 117). The Japanese sense of aesthetics, as well, could be a clue by way of a connection with traditional notions of beauty that are attached to short-lived things, whether cherry blossoms or young warriors dying in battle (Lebra 1976: 166), *or* a beautiful young actor dying tragically on a lonely California highway.

References

Alvarez, Lewis and Andrew Kolker, producers and directors. 1991. *The Japanese Version.* Videocassette. New York: The Center for New American Media.

de Bary, William Theodre. 1988. *East Asian Civilizations: A Dialogue in Five Stages.* Cambridge: Harvard University Press.

Brannen, Mary Yoko. 1992. "Bwana Mickey": Constructing Cultural Consumption at Tokyo Disneyland. In *Re-Made in Japan,* edited by Joseph J. Tobin. New Haven: Yale University Press.

Goris, Richard C. and Yukimi Okubo. 1993. *Collins Shubun English-Japanese Dictionary.* Glasgow: HarperCollins Publishers.

Halpern, Jack, editor. 1993. *NTC's New Japanese-English Character Dictionary.* Lincolnwood, IL: National Textbook Company.

Hopgood, James F. 1991. "Saints and Stars: Exploration of Two Types of Charismatic Movements." Paper presented at the 90th Annual Meeting of the American Anthropological Association in Chicago.

—— 1992a. "What Would Durkheim Say About James Dean?" In *Sociology: A Global Perspective,* by Joan Ferrante. Belmont, CA: Wadsworth Publishing Co.

—— 1992b. "'Back Home in Indiana': Semiotics of Pilgrimage to Honor an American Icon." Paper presented at the 91st Annual Meeting of the American Anthropological Association in San Francisco.

—— 1994. "'Obsession' and 'Excess' in a Contemporary American Iconic Movement." Paper presented at the 93rd Annual Meeting of the American Anthropological Association in Atlanta.

—— 1995. "What Would Durkheim Say About James Dean?" In *Sociology: A Global Perspective,* Second Edition, by Joan Ferrante. Belmont, CA: Wadsworth Publishing Co.

——1997. "'Back Home in Indiana': Semiotics of Pilgrimage and Belief in Honor of an American Icon." In *Explorations in Anthropology and Theology,* Frank A. Salamone and Walter R. Adams, eds. Lanham and London: University Press of America.

Hikaru, Nishida, producer. 1992. "James Dean Story." TV program, NHK Television, Japan.

Mathews, Gordon. 1996. "The Pursuit of a Life Worth Living in Japan and the United States." *Ethnology,* 35 (1): 51–62.

Lebra, Takie Sugiyama. 1976. *Japanese Patterns of Behavior.* Honolulu: University of Hawaii Press.

———— 1992. "Self in Japanese Culture." In *Japanese Sense of Self,* edited by Nancy R. Rosenberger. Cambridge: Cambridge University Press.

———— 1995. Personal Communication. E-mail: February 28.

Riese, Randall. 1991. *The Unabridged James Dean: His Life and Legacy from A to Z.* Chicago: Contemporary Books.

Vance, Timothy J. 1993. *Kodansha's Romanized Japanese-English Dictionary.* Tokyo: Kodansha International.

Notes

[1] An earlier version of this paper was presented for an organized session, "Back to the Body (I): Text(ure), Tact(ile), (E)motion—The Sensor/Censure of Experience," at the 71st Annual Meeting of the Central States Anthropological Society in Kansas City, Missouri, March 17–20, 1994. The reference to "Japanese Version" is to a video film by Alvarez and Kolker (1991). In this video Alvarez and Kolker explore how examples of American culture, using Mickey Mouse, TV Westerns, pop culture of the 1950s, weddings, and so on, have been adopted and utilized by the Japanese.

[2] The reader may wish to consult Hopgood (1992b, 1993, 1995, and 1997) for more details on the larger project.

[3] My thanks to David and Yumiko Potter for their assistance in translating and interpreting critical portions of the *James Dean Story.*

[4] I want to thank my colleague Susumu Kasai for consenting to this interview and for his patience with my incessant questions about "obsession." The interview took place on 8 August 1993, in Wuhan, Hubei, P.R.C.

[5] I have consulted the following dictionaries regarding the meanings of Japanese terms: Jack Halpern, editor, *NTC's New Japanese-English Character Dictionary* (1993), Timothy J. Vance, *Kodansha's Romanized Japanese-English Dictionary* (1993), and Richard C. Goris and Yukimi Okubo, *Collins Shubun English-Japanese Dictionary* (1993).

Toward a New Vision: Race, Class, and Gender as Categories of Analysis and Connection

Patricia Hill Collins

Study Questions

1. Explain how race, class, and gender operate as interlocking categories that cultivate profound differences in our personal biographies.
2. Define the institutional, symbolic, and individual dimensions of oppression. Define the "oppressor within".
3. Give examples from Patricia Hill Collins' life which suggest she has come to recognize her own oppressor within. Describe the basic elements of the "new vision" Collins offers.

> The true focus of revolutionary change is never merely the oppressive situations which we seek to escape, but that piece of the oppressor which is planted deep within each of us.
>
> Audre Lorde
> *Sister Outsider*, 123

Audre Lorde's statement raises a troublesome issue for scholars and activists working for social change. While many of us have little difficulty assessing our own victimization within some major system of oppression, whether it be by race, social class, religion, sexual orientation, ethnicity, age or gender, we typically fail to see how our thoughts and actions uphold someone else's subordination. Thus, white feminists routinely point with confidence to their oppression as women but resist seeing how much their white skin privileges them. African-Americans who possess eloquent analyses of racism often persist in viewing poor White women as symbols of white power. The radical left fares little better. "If only people of color and women could see their true class interests," they argue, "class solidarity would eliminate racism and sexism." In essence, each group identifies the type of oppression with which it feels most comfortable as being fundamental and classifies all other types as being of lesser importance.

Oppression is full of such contradictions. Errors in political judgment that we make concerning how we teach our courses, what we tell our children, and which organizations are worthy of our time, talents and financial support flow smoothly from errors in theoretical analysis about the nature of oppression and activism. Once we realize that there are few pure victims or oppressors, and that each one of us derives varying amounts of penalty and privilege from the multiple systems of oppression that frame our lives, then we will be in a position to see the need for new ways of thought and action.

To get at that "piece of the oppressor which is planted deep within each of us," we need at least two things. First, we need new visions of what oppression is, new categories of analysis that are inclusive of race, class, and gender as distinctive yet interlocking structures of oppression. Adhering to a stance of comparing and ranking oppressions—the proverbial, "I'm more oppressed than you"—locks us all into a dangerous dance of competing for attention, resources, and theoretical supremacy. Instead, I suggest that we examine our different experiences within the more fundamental relationship of domination and subordination. To focus on the particular arrangements that race or class or gender take in our time and place without seeing these structures as sometimes parallel and sometimes interlocking dimensions of the more fundamental relationship of domination and subordination may temporarily ease our consciences. But while such thinking may lead to short term social reforms, it is simply inadequate for the task of bringing about long term social transformation.

While race, class and gender as categories of analysis are essential in helping us understand the structural bases of domination and subordination, new ways of thinking that are not accompanied by new ways of acting offer incomplete prospects for change. To get at that "piece of the oppressor which is planted deep within each of us," we also need to change our daily behavior. Currently, we are all enmeshed in a complex web of problematic relationships that grant our mirror images full human subjectivity while stereotyping and objectifying those most different than ourselves. We often assume that the people we work with, teach, send our children to school with, and sit next to in conferences such as this, will act and feel in prescribed ways because they belong to given race, social class or gender categories. These judgments by category must be replaced with fully human relationships that transcend the legitimate differences created by race, class and gender as categories of analysis. We require new categories of connection, new visions of what our relationships with one another can be.

Our task is immense. We must first recognize race, class and gender as interlocking categories of analysis that together cultivate profound differences in our personal biographies. But then we must transcend those very differences by reconceptualizing race, class and gender in order to create new categories of connection.

My presentation today addresses this need for new patterns of thought and action. I focus on two basic questions. First, how can we reconceptualize race, class and gender as categories of analysis? Second, how can we transcend the barriers created by our experiences with race, class and gender oppression in order to build the types of coalitions essential for social exchange? To address these questions I contend that we must acquire both new theories of how race, class and gender have shaped the experiences not just of women of color, but of all groups. Moreover, we must see the connections between these categories of analysis and the personal issues in our everyday lives, particularly our scholarship, our teaching and our relationships with our colleagues and students. As Audre Lorde points out, change starts with self, and relationships that we have with those around us must always be the primary site for social change.

How Can We Reconceptualize Race, Class and Gender as Categories of *Analysis?*

To me, we must shift our discourse away from additive analyses of oppression (Spelman 1982; Collins 1989). Such approaches are typically based on two key premises. First, they depend on either/or, dichotomous thinking. Persons, things and ideas are conceptualized in terms of their opposites. For example, Black/White, man/woman, thought/feeling, and fact/opinion are defined in oppositional terms. Thought and feeling are not seen as two different and interconnected ways of approaching truth that can coexist in scholarship and teaching. Instead, feeling is defined as antithetical to reason, as its opposite. In spite of the fact that we all have "both/and" identities (I am both a college professor and a mother—I don't stop being a mother when I drop my child off at school, or forget everything I learned while scrubbing the toilet), we persist in trying to classify each other in either/or categories. I live each day as an African-American woman—a race/gender specific experience. And I am not alone. Everyone in this room has a race/gender/class specific identity. Either/or, dichotomous thinking is especially troublesome when applied to theories of oppression because every individual must be classified as being either oppressed or not oppressed. The both/and position of simultaneously being oppressed and oppressor becomes conceptually impossible.

A second premise of additive analyses of oppression is that these dichotomous differences must be ranked. One side of the dichotomy is typically labeled dominant and the other subordinate. Thus, Whites rule Blacks, men are deemed superior to women, and reason is seen as being preferable to emotion. Applying this premise to discussions of oppression leads to the assumption that oppression can be quantified, and that some groups are oppressed more than others. I am frequently asked, "Which has been most oppressive to you, your status as a Black person or your status as a woman?" What I am really being asked to do is divide myself into little boxes and rank my various statuses. If I experience oppression as a both/and phenomenon, why should I analyze it any differently?

Additive analyses of oppression rest squarely on the twin pillars of either/or thinking and the necessity to quantify and rank all relationships in order to know where one stands. Such approaches typically see African-American women as being more oppressed than everyone else because the majority of Black women experience the negative effects of race, class and gender oppression simultaneously. In essence, if you add together separate oppressions, you are left with a grand oppression greater than the sum of its parts.

I am not denying that specific groups experience oppression more harshly than others—lynching is certainly objectively worse than being held up as a sex object. But we must be careful not to confuse this issue of the saliency of one type of oppression in people's lives with a theoretical stance positing the interlocking nature of oppression. Race, class and gender may all structure a situation but may not be equally visible and/or important in people's self-definitions. In certain contexts, such as the antebellum American South and contemporary South America, racial oppression is more visibly salient, while in other contexts, such as Haiti, El Salvador and Nicaragua, social class oppression may be more apparent. For middle class White women, gender may assume experiential primacy unavailable to poor Hispanic women struggling with the ongoing issues of low paid jobs and the frustrations of the welfare bureaucracy. This recognition that one category may have salience over another for a given time and place does not minimize the theoretical importance of assuming that race, class and gender as categories of analysis structure all relationships.

In order to move toward new visions of what oppression is, I think that we need to ask new questions. How are relationships of domination and subordination structured and maintained in the American political economy? How do race, class and gender function as parallel and interlocking systems that shape this basic relationship of domination and subordination? Questions such as these promise to move us away from futile theoretical struggles concerned with ranking oppressions and towards analyses that assume race, class and gender are all present in any given setting, even if one appears more visible and salient than the others. Our task becomes redefined as one of reconceptualizing oppression by uncovering the connections among race, class and gender as categories of analysis.

Institutional Dimension of Oppression

Sandra Harding's contention that gender oppression is structured along three main dimensions—the institutional, the symbolic, and the individual—offers a useful model for a more comprehensive analysis encompassing race, class and gender oppression (Harding 1989). Systemic relationships of domination and subordination structured through social institutions such as schools, businesses, hospitals, the work place, and government agencies represent the institutional dimension of oppression. Racism, sexism and elitism all have concrete institutional locations. Even though the workings of the institutional dimension of oppression are often obscured with ideologies claiming equality of opportunity, in actuality, race, class and gender place Asian-American women, Native American men, White men, African-American women, and other groups in distinct institutional niches with varying degrees of penalty and privilege.

Even though I realize that many in the current administration would not share this assumption, let us assume that the institutions of American society discriminate, whether by design or by accident. While many of us are familiar with how race, gender and class operate separately to structure inequality, I want to focus on how these three systems interlock in structuring the institutional dimension of oppression. To get at the interlocking nature of race, class and gender, I want you to think about the antebellum plantation as a guiding metaphor for a variety of American social institutions. Even though slavery is typically analyzed as a racist institution, and occasionally as a class institution, I suggest that slavery was a race, class, gender specific institution. Removing any one piece from our analysis diminishes our understanding of the true nature of relations of domination and subordination under slavery.

Slavery was a profoundly patriarchal institution. It rested on the dual tenets of White male authority and White male property, a joining of the political and the economic within the institution of the family. Heterosexism was assumed and all Whites were expected to marry. Control over affluent White women's sexuality remained key to slavery's survival because property was to be passed on to the legitimate heirs of the slave owner. Ensuring affluent White women's virginity and chastity was deeply intertwined with maintenance of property relations.

Under slavery, we see varying levels of institutional protection given to affluent White women, working class and poor White women, and enslaved African women. Poor White women enjoyed few of the protections held out to their upper class sisters. Moreover, the devalued status of Black women was key in keeping all White women in their assigned places. Controlling Black women's fertility was also key to the continuation of slavery, for children born to slave mothers themselves were slaves.

African-American women shared the devalued status of chattel with their husbands, fathers and sons. Racism stripped Blacks as a group of legal rights, education, and control over their own persons. African-Americans could be whipped, branded, sold, or killed, not because they were poor, or because they were women, but because they were Black. Racism ensured that Blacks would continue to serve Whites and suffer economic exploitation at the hands of all Whites.

So we have a very interesting chain of command on the plantation—the affluent White master as the reigning patriarch, his White wife helpmate to serve him, help him manage his property and bring up his heirs, his faithful servants whose production and reproduction were tied to the requirements of the capitalist political economy, and largely propertyless, working class White men and women watching from afar. In essence, the foundations for the contemporary roles of elite White women, poor Black women, working class White men, and a series of other groups can be seen in stark relief in this fundamental American social institution. While Blacks experienced the most harsh treatment under slavery, and thus made slavery clearly visible as a racist institution, race, class and gender interlocked in structuring slavery's systemic organization of domination and subordination.

Even today, the plantation remains a compelling metaphor for institutional oppression. Certainly the actual conditions of oppression are not as severe now as they were then. To argue, as some do, that things have not changed all that much denigrates the achievements of those who struggled for social change before us. But the basic relationships among Black men, Black women, elite White women, elite White men, working class White men and working class White women as groups remain essentially intact.

A brief analysis of key American social institutions most controlled by elite White men should convince us of the interlocking nature of race, class and gender in structuring the institutional dimension of oppression. For example, if you are from an American college or university, is your campus a modern plantation? Who controls your university's political economy? Are elite White men over represented among the upper administrators and trustees controlling your university's finances and policies? Are elite White men being joined by growing numbers of elite White women helpmates?

What kinds of people are in your classrooms grooming the next generation who will occupy these and other decision-making positions? Who are the support staff that produce the mass mailings, order the supplies, fix the leaky pipes? Do African-Americans, Hispanics or other people of color form the majority of the invisible workers who feed you, wash your dishes, and clean up your offices and libraries after everyone else has gone home?

If your college is anything like mine, you know the answers to these questions. You may be affiliated with an institution that has Hispanic women as vice-presidents for finance, or substantial numbers of Black men among the faculty. If so, you are fortunate. Much more typical are colleges where a modified version of the plantation as a metaphor for the institutional dimension of oppression survives.

The Symbolic Dimension of Oppression

Widespread, societally-sanctioned ideologies used to justify relations of domination and subordination comprise the symbolic dimension of oppression. Central to this process is the use of stereotypical or controlling images of diverse race, class and gender groups. In order to assess the power of this dimension of oppression, I want you to make a list, either on paper or in your head, of "masculine" and "feminine" characteristics. If your list is anything like that compiled by most people, it reflects some variation of the following:

Masculine	Feminine
aggressive	passive
leader	follower
rational	emotional
strong	weak
intellectual	physical

Not only does this list reflect either/or dichotomous thinking and the need to rank both sides of the dichotomy, but ask yourself exactly which men and women you had in mind when compiling these characteristics. This list applies almost exclusively to middle class White men and women. The allegedly "masculine" qualities that you probably listed are only acceptable when exhibited by elite White men, or when used by Black and Hispanic men against each other or against women of color. Aggressive Black and Hispanic men are seen as dangerous, not powerful, and are often penalized when they exhibit any of the allegedly "masculine" characteristics. Working class and poor White men fare slightly better and are also denied the allegedly "masculine" symbols of leadership, intellectual competence, and human rationality. Women of color and working class and poor White women are also not represented on this list, for they have never had the luxury of being "ladies." What appear to be universal categories representing all men and women instead are unmasked as being applicable to only a small group.

It is important to see how the symbolic images applied to different race, class and gender groups interact in maintaining systems of domination and subordination. If I were to ask you to repeat the same assignment, only this time, by making separate lists for Black men, Black women, Hispanic women and Hispanic men, I suspect that your gender symbolism would be quite different. In comparing all of the lists, you might begin to see the interdependence of symbols applied to all groups. For example, the elevated images of White womanhood need devalued images of Black womanhood in order to maintain credibility.

While the above exercise reveals the interlocking nature of race, class and gender in structuring the symbolic dimension of oppression, part of its importance lies in demonstrating how race, class and gender pervade a wide range of what appears to be universal language. Attending to diversity in our scholarship, in our teaching, and in our daily lives provides a new angle of vision on interpretations of reality thought to be natural, normal and "true." Moreover, viewing images of masculinity and femininity as universal gender symbolism, rather than as symbolic images that are race, class and gender specific, renders the experiences of people of color and of non-privileged White women and men invisible. One way to dehumanize an individual or a group is to deny the reality of their experiences. So when we refuse to deal with race or class because they do not appear to be directly relevant to gender, we are actually becoming part of some one else's problem.

Assuming that everyone is affected differently by the same interlocking set of symbolic images allows us to move forward toward new analyses. Women of color and White women have different relationships to White male authority and this difference explains the distinct gender symbolism applied to both groups. Black women encounter controlling images such as the mammy, the matriarch, the mule and the whore, that encourage others to reject us as fully human people. Ironically, the negative nature of these images simultaneously encourages us to reject them. In contrast, White women are offered seductive images, those that promise to reward them for supporting the status quo. And yet seductive images can be equally controlling. Consider, for example, the views of Nancy White, a 73-year old Black woman, concerning images of rejection and seduction:

> My mother used to say that the black woman is the white man's mule and the white woman is his dog. Now, she said that to say this: we do the heavy work and get beat whether we do it well or not. But the white

woman is closer to the master and he pats them on the head and lets them sleep in the house, but he ain't gon' treat neither one like he was dealing with a person. (Gwaltney, 148)

Both sets of images stimulate particular political stances. By broadening the analysis beyond the confines of race, we can see the varying levels of rejection and seduction available to each of us due to our race, class and gender identity. Each of us lives with an allotted portion of institutional privilege and penalty, and with varying levels of rejection and seduction inherent in the symbolic images applied to us. This is the context in which we make our choices. Taken together, the institutional and symbolic dimensions of oppression create a structural backdrop against which all of us live our lives.

The Individual Dimension of Oppression

Whether we benefit or not, we all live within institutions that reproduce race, class and gender oppression. Even if we never have any contact with members of other race, class and gender groups, we all encounter images of these groups and are exposed to the symbolic meanings attached to those images. On this dimension of oppression, our individual biographies vary tremendously. As a result of our institutional and symbolic statuses, all of our choices become political acts.

Each of us must come to terms with the multiple ways in which race, class and gender as categories of analysis frame our individual biographies. I have lived my entire life as an African-American woman from a working class family and this basic fact has had a profound impact on my personal biography. Imagine how different your life might be if you had been born Black, or White, or poor, or of a different race/class/gender group than the one with which you are most familiar. The institutional treatment you would have received and the symbolic meanings attached to your very existence might differ dramatically from what you now consider to be natural, normal and part of everyday life. You might be the same, but your personal biography might have been quite different.

I believe that each of us carries around the cumulative effect of our lives within multiple structures of oppression. If you want to see how much you have been affected by this whole thing, I ask you one simple question—who are your close friends? Who are the people with whom you can share your hopes, dreams, vulnerabilities, fears and victories? Do they look like you? If they are all the same, circumstance may be the cause. For the first seven years of my life I saw only low income Black people. My friends from those years reflected the composition of my community. But now that I am an adult, can the defense of circumstance explain the patterns of people that I trust as my friends and colleagues? When given other alternatives, if my friends and colleagues reflect the homogeneity of one race, class and gender group, then these categories of analysis have indeed become barriers to connection.

I am not suggesting that people are doomed to follow the paths laid out for them by race, class and gender as categories of analysis. While these three structures certainly frame my opportunity structure, I as an individual always have the choice of accepting things as they are, or trying to change them. As Nikki Giovanni points out, "we've got to live in the real world. If we don't like the world we're living in, change it. And if we can't change it, we change ourselves. We can do something" (Tate 1983, 68). While a piece of the oppressor may be planted deep within each of us, we each have the choice of accepting that piece or challenging it as part of the "true focus of revolutionary change."

How Can We Transcend the Barriers Created by Our Experiences with Race, Class and Gender Oppression in Order to Build the Types of Coalitions Essential for Social Change?

Reconceptualizing oppression and seeing the barriers created by race, class and gender as interlocking categories of analysis is a vital first step. But we must transcend these barriers by moving toward race, class and gender as categories of connection, by building relationships and coalitions that will bring about social change. What are some of the issues involved in doing this?

Differences in Power and Privilege

First, we must recognize that our differing experiences with oppression create problems in the relationships among us. Each of us lives within a system that vests us with varying levels of power and privilege. These differences in power, whether structured along axes of race, class, gender, age or sexual orientation, frame our relationships. African-American writer June Jordan describes her discomfort on a Caribbean vacation with Olive, the Black woman who cleaned her room:

> . . . even though both "Olive" and "I" live inside a conflict neither one of us created, and even though both of us therefore hurt inside that conflict, I may be one of the monsters she needs to eliminate from her universe and, in a sense, she may be one of the monsters in mine. (1985, 47)

Differences in power constrain our ability to connect with one another even when we think we are engaged in dialogue across differences. Let me give you an example. One year, the students in my course "Sociology of the Black Community" got into a heated discussion about the reasons for the upsurge of racial incidents on college campuses. Black students complained vehemently about the apathy and resistance they felt most White students expressed about examining their own racism. Mark, a White male student, found their comments particularly unsettling. After claiming that all the Black people he had ever known had expressed no such beliefs to him, he questioned how representative the view points of his fellow students actually were. When pushed further, Mark revealed that he had participated in conversations over the years with the Black domestic worker employed by his family. Since she had never expressed such strong feelings about White racism, Mark was genuinely shocked by class discussions. Ask yourselves whether that domestic worker was in a position to speak freely. Would it have been wise for her to do so in a situation where the power between the two parties was so unequal?

In extreme cases, members of privileged groups can erase the very presence of the less privileged. When I first moved to Cincinnati, my family and I went on a picnic at a local park. Picnicking next to us was a family of White Appalachians. When I went to push my daughter on the swings, several of the children came over. They had missing, yellowed and broken teeth, they wore old clothing and their poverty was evident. I was shocked. Growing up in a large eastern city, I had never seen such awful poverty among Whites. The segregated neighborhoods in which I grew up made White poverty all but invisible. More importantly, the privileges attached to my newly acquired social class position allowed me to ignore and minimize the poverty among Whites that I did encounter. My reactions to those children made me realize how confining phrases such as "well, at least they're not Black," had become for me. In learning to grant human subjectivity to the Black victims of poverty, I had simultaneously learned to demean White victims of poverty. By applying categories of race to the objective conditions confronting me, I was quantifying and ranking oppressions and missing the very real suffering which, in fact, is the real issue.

One common pattern of relationships across differences in power is one that I label "voyeurism." From the perspective of the privileged, the lives of people of color, of the poor, and of women are interesting for their entertainment value. The privileged become voyeurs, passive onlookers who do not relate to the less powerful, but who are interested in seeing how the "different" live. Over the years, I have heard numerous African-

American students complain about professors who never call on them except when a so-called Black issue is being discussed. The students' interest in discussing race or qualifications for doing so appear unimportant to the professor's efforts to use Black students' experiences as stories to make the material come alive for the White student audience. Asking Black students to perform on cue and provide a Black experience for their White classmates can be seen as voyeurism at its worst.

Members of subordinate groups do not willingly participate in such exchanges but often do so because members of dominant groups control the institutional and symbolic apparatuses of oppression. Racial/ethnic groups, women, and the poor have never had the luxury of being voyeurs of the lives of the privileged. Our ability to survive in hostile settings has hinged on our ability to learn intricate details about the behavior and world view of the powerful and adjust our behavior accordingly. I need only point to the difference in perception of those men and women in abusive relationships. Where men can view their girlfriends and wives as sex objects, helpmates and a collection of stereotypes categories of voyeurism—women must be attuned to every nuance of their partners' behavior. Are women "naturally" better in relating to people with more power than themselves, or have circumstances mandated that men and women develop different skills? Another pattern in relationships among people of unequal power concerns a different form of exploitation. In scholarly enterprises, relationships among students and teachers, among researchers and their subjects, and even among us as colleagues in teaching and scholarship can contain elements of academic colonialism. Years ago, a Black co-worker of mine in the Roxbury section of Boston described the academic colonialism he saw among the teachers and scholars in that African-American community:

> The people with notebooks from Harvard come around here and study us. They don't get to know us because they really don't want to and we don't want to let them. They see what they want to see, go back and write their books and get famous off of our problems.

Under academic colonialism, more powerful groups see their subordinates as people that they perceive as subordinate to them, not as entertainment as was the case in voyeurism, but as a resource to be benignly exploited for their own purposes.

The longstanding effort to "colorize" feminist theory by inserting the experiences of women of color, represents at best, genuine efforts to reduce bias in women's studies. But at its worst, colorization also contains elements of both voyeurism and academic colonialism. As a result of new technologies and perceived profitability, we can now watch black and white movie classics in color. While the tinted images we are offered may be more palatable to the modern viewer, we are still watching the same old movie that was offered to us before. Movie colorization adds little of substance—its contributions remain cosmetic. Similarly, women of color allegedly can teach White feminists nothing about feminism, but must confine ourselves to "colorizing" preexisting feminist theory. Rather than seeing women of color as fully human individuals, we are treated as the additive sum of our categories.

In the academy, patterns of relationships among those of unequal power such as voyeurism and academic colonialism foster reformist postures toward social change. While reformists may aim to make the movie more fun to watch by colorizing their scholarship and teaching via increased lip service to diversity, reformists typically insist on retaining their power to determine what is seen and by whom. In contrast, transformation involves rethinking these differences in power and privilege via dialogues among individuals from diverse groups.

Coming from a tradition where most relationships across difference are squarely rooted in relations of domination and subordination, we have much less experience relating to people as different but equal. The classroom is potentially one powerful and safe space where dialogues among individuals of unequal power relationships can occur. The relationship between Mark, the student in my class, and the domestic worker is typical of a whole series of relationships that people have when they relate across differences in power and privilege. The relationship among Mark and his classmates represents the power of the classroom to minimize those differences so that people of different levels of power can use race, class and gender as categories of analysis in order to generate meaningful dialogues. In this case, the classroom equalized racial difference so that Black students who normally felt silenced spoke out. White students like Mark, generally unaware of how they had been privileged by their whiteness, lost that privilege in the classroom and thus became open to genuine dialogue.

Reconceptualizing course syllabi represents a comparable process of determining which groups are privileged by our current research and pedagogical techniques and which groups are penalized. Reforming these existing techniques can be a critical first step in moving toward a transformed curriculum reflecting race, class and gender as interlocking categories of analysis. But while reform may be effective as a short term strategy, it is unlikely to bring about fundamental transformation in the long term. To me, social transformations, whether of college curricula or of the communities in which we live and work, require moving outside our areas of specialization and groups of interest in order to build coalitions across differences.

Coalitions Around Common Causes

A second issue in building relationships and coalitions essential for social change concerns knowing the real reasons for coalition. Just what brings people together? One powerful catalyst fostering group solidarity is the presence of a common enemy. African-American, Hispanic, Asian-American, and women's studies all share the common intellectual heritage of challenging what passes for certified knowledge in the academy. But politically expedient relationships and coalitions like these are fragile because, as June Jordan points out:

> It occurs to me that much organizational grief could be avoided if people understood that partnership in misery does not necessarily provide for partnership for change: When we get the monsters off our backs all of us may want to run in very different directions. (1985, 47)

Sharing a common cause assists individuals and groups in maintaining relationships that transcend their differences. Building effective coalitions involves struggling to hear one another and developing empathy for each other's points of view. The coalitions that I have been involved in that lasted and that worked have been those where commitment to a specific issue mandated collaboration as the best strategy for addressing the issue at hand.

Several years ago, masters degree in hand, I chose to teach in an inner city, parochial school in danger of closing. The money was awful, the conditions were poor, but the need was great. In my job, I had to work with a range of individuals who, on the surface, had very little in common. We had White nuns, Black middle class graduate students, Blacks from the "community," some of whom had been incarcerated and/or were affiliated with a range of federal anti-poverty programs. Parents formed another part of this community, Harvard faculty another, and a few well-meaning White liberals from Colorado were sprinkled in for good measure.

As you might imagine, tension was high. Initially, our differences seemed insurmountable. But as time passed, we found a common bond that we each brought to the school. In spite of profound differences in our personal biographies, differences that in other settings would have hampered our ability to relate to one another, we found that we were all deeply committed to the education of Black children. By learning to value each other's commitment and by recognizing that we each had different skills that were essential to actualizing that commitment, we built an effective coalition around a common cause. Our school was successful, and the children we taught benefitted from the diversity we offered them.

I think that the process of curriculum transformation will require a process comparable to that of political organizing around common causes. None of us alone has a comprehensive vision of how race, class and gender operate as categories of analysis or how they might be used as categories of connection. Our personal biographies offer us partial views. Few of us can manage to study race, class and gender simultaneously. Instead, we each know more about some dimensions of this larger story and less about others. While we each may be committed to an inclusive, transformed curriculum, the task of building one is necessarily a collective effort. Just as the members of the school had special skills to offer to the task of building the school, we have areas of specialization and expertise, whether scholarly, theoretical, pedagogical or within areas of race, class or gender. We do not all have to do the same thing in the same way. Instead, we must support each other's efforts, realizing that they are all part of the larger enterprise of bringing about social change.

Building Empathy

A third issue involved in building the types of relationships and coalitions essential for social change concerns the issue of individual accountability. Race, class and gender oppression form the structural backdrop against which we frame our relationship—these are the forces that encourage us to substitute voyeurism and academic colonialism for fully human relationships. But while we may not have created this situation, we are each responsible for making individual, personal choices concerning which elements of race, class and gender oppression we will accept and which we will work to change.

One essential component of this accountability involves developing empathy for the experiences of individuals and groups different than ourselves. Empathy begins with taking an interest in the facts of other people lives, both as individuals and as groups. If you care about me, you should want to know not only the details of my personal biography but a sense of how race, class and gender as categories of analysis created the institutional and symbolic backdrop for my personal biography. How can you hope to assess my character without knowing the details of the circumstances I face?

Moreover, by taking a theoretical stance that we have all been affected by race, class and gender as categories of analysis that have structured our treatment, we open up possibilities for using those same constructs as categories of connection in building empathy. For example, I have a good White woman friend with whom I share common interests and beliefs. But we know that our racial differences have provided us with different experiences. So we talk about them. We do not assume that because I am Black, race has only affected me and not her or that because I am a Black woman, race neutralizes the effect of gender in my life while accenting it in hers. We take those same categories of analysis that have created cleavages in our lives, in this case, categories of race and gender, and use them as categories of connection in building empathy for each other's experiences.

Finding common causes and building empathy is difficult, no matter which side of privilege we inhabit. Building empathy from the dominant side of privilege is difficult, simply because individuals from privileged backgrounds are not encouraged to do so. For example, in order for those of you who are White to develop empathy for the experiences of people of color, you must grapple with how your white skin has privileged you. This is difficult to do, because it not only entails the intellectual process of seeing how whiteness is elevated in institutions and symbols, but it also involves the often painful process of seeing how your whiteness has shaped your personal biography. Intellectual stances against the institutional and symbolic dimensions of racism are generally easier to maintain than sustained self-reflection about how racism has shaped all of our individual biographies. Were and are your fathers, uncles, and grandfathers really more capable than mine, or can their accomplishments be explained in part by the racism members of my family experienced? Did your mothers stand silently by and watch all this happen? More importantly, how have they passed on the benefits of their whiteness to you?

These are difficult questions, and I have tremendous respect for my colleagues and students who are trying to answer them. Since there is no compelling reason to examine the source and meaning of one's own privilege, I know that those who do so have freely chosen this stance. They are making conscious efforts to root out the piece of the oppressor planted within them. To me, they are entitled to the support of people of color in their efforts. Men who declare themselves feminists, members of the middle class who ally themselves with anti-poverty struggles, heterosexuals who support gays and lesbians, are all trying to grow, and their efforts place them far ahead of the majority who never think of engaging in such important struggles.

Building empathy from the subordinate side of privilege is also difficult, but for different reasons. Members of subordinate groups are understandably reluctant to abandon a basic mistrust of members of powerful groups because this basic mistrust has traditionally been central to their survival. As a Black woman, it would be foolish for me to assume that White women, or Black men, or White men or any other group with a history of exploiting African-American women have my best interests at heart. These groups enjoy varying amounts of privilege over me and therefore I must carefully watch them and be prepared for a relation of domination and subordination.

Like the privileged, members of subordinate groups must also work toward replacing judgments by category with new ways of thinking and acting. Refusing to do so stifles prospects for effective coalition and social change. Let me use another example from my own experiences. When I was an undergraduate, I had little time or patience for the theorizing of the privileged. My initial years at a private, elite institution were difficult, not because the coursework was challenging (it was, but that wasn't what distracted me) or because I had to work while my classmates lived on family allowances (I was used to work). The adjustment was difficult because I was surrounded by so many people who took their privilege for granted. Most of them felt entitled to their wealth. That astounded me.

I remember one incident of watching a White woman down the hall in my dormitory try to pick out which sweater to wear. The sweaters were piled up on her bed in all the colors of the rainbow, sweater after sweater. She asked my advice in a way that let me know that choosing a sweater was one of the most important decisions she had to make on a daily basis. Standing knee-deep in her sweaters, I realized how different our lives were. She did not have to worry about maintaining a solid academic average so that she could receive financial aid. Because she was in the majority, she was not treated as a representative of her race. She did not have to consider how her classroom comments or basic existence on campus contributed to the treatment her group would receive. Her allowance protected her from having to work, so she was free to spend her time studying, partying, or in her case, worrying about which sweater to wear. The degree of inequality in our lives and her unquestioned sense of entitlement concerning that inequality offended me. For a while, I categorized all affluent White women as being superficial, arrogant, overly concerned with material possessions, and part of my problem. But had I continued to classify people in this way, I would have missed out on making some very good friends whose discomfort with their inherited or acquired social class privileges pushed them to examine their position.

Since I opened with the words of Audre Lorde, it seems appropriate to close with another of her ideas. As we go forth to the remaining activities of this workshop, and beyond this workshop, we might do well to consider Lorde's perspective:

> Each of us is called upon to take a stand. So in these days ahead, as we examine ourselves and each other, our works, our fears, our differences, our sisterhood and survivals, I urge you to tackle what is most difficult for us all, self-scrutiny of our complacencies, the idea that since each of us believes she is on the side of right, she need not examine her position. (1985)

I urge you to examine your position.

References

Butler, Johnnella. 1989. "Difficult Dialogues." *The Women's Review of Books* 6, no. 5.

Collins, Patricia Hill. 1989. "The Social Construction of Black Feminist Thought." *Signs.* Summer 1989.

Harding, Sandra. 1986. *The Science Question in Feminism.* Ithaca, New York: Cornell University Press.

Gwalatney, John Langston. 1980. *Drylongso: A Self-Portrait of Black America.* New York: Vintage.

Lorde, Audre. 1984. *Sister Outsider.* Trumansberg, New York: The Crossing Press.

————. 1985 "Sisterhood and Survival." Keynote address, conference on the Black Woman Writer and the Diaspora, Michigan State University.

Jordan, June. 1985. *On Call: Political Essays.* Boston: South End Press.

Spelman, Elizabeth. 1982. "Theories of Race and Gender: The Erasure of Black Women." *Quest* 5:32–36.

Tate, Claudia, ed. 1983. *Black Women Writers at Work.* New York: Continuum.

WHITE-BLINDNESS

BRUCE N. SIMON

Study Questions
1. What are the two versions of color-bindness that Simon describes? What questions are associated with each version of color-blindness?
2. Which version does Simon recommend as the best approach for thinking about race? Why?

It's amazing how controversial such traditional legal doctrines as "innocent until proven guilty," "jury of one's peers," and "reasonable doubt" become when a black defendant stands accused of the murder of a white woman and man before a majority black jury, and is found not guilty. How easily presumption of innocence gets cast as racial loyalty. How quickly the people who decided that the state had not proved its case beyond a reasonable doubt are dismissed as unreasonable and perhaps incapable of reason. How smoothly the same fury that used to fuel lynch mobs claims the high moral ground by chastising the jury's failure of color-blindness.

I am referring to the O.J. Simpson spectacle—and particularly of white responses to it—but I am trying to raise larger questions about how we in the U.S. understand issues of race and racism, whiteness and color-blindness, democracy and justice. Were Johnnie Cochran's "playing the race card" and the jury's "choosing racial loyalty" over deliberation and evidence really the only times race impacted the Simpson case? Must our only response to the Simpson verdict and the Rodney King beating verdict be lamentations and jeremiads over the flagging commitment to color-blindness in the post-Civil Rights era? Or is it instead that the many race-saturated public spectacles of the '90s call on us to question what is typically meant by color-blindness and rethink the problem it is supposed to solve?[1] It's striking that so many observers and commentators could deploy a rhetoric of color-blindness while at the same time repeating coded racialized narratives—and not only have the contradiction go unnoticed but have the latter legitimized by the former. In response, I think it's high time we distinguished between different versions of color-blindness and clarified what color-blindness for white people entails.[2]

To this end, let's consider the most controversial aspect of the Simpson case to many liberal and conservative commentators. Not the fact that he "got off." Not even the "racial divide" that opinion pollsters so suddenly discovered (after decades of ignoring or downplaying more telling evidence). No, what really irritated these commentators was the charge that their conviction of Simpson's guilt was not neutral or objective—that their whiteness interfered with their judgment, particularly in evaluating the plausibility and relevance of police racism and incompetence. I'm going to personalize this issue and imagine myself in a thought experiment as a potential juror faced with a similar charge. Adhering to one version of color-blindness would lead me to ask the following questions in response: (1) What does my being white have to do with considering the evidence and making a decision? (2) What does my racial identity, an accident of birth, have to do with issues of evaluation or judgment? (3) Hasn't the concept of race itself been shown to be incoherent, self-contradictory, fallacious, arbitrary, without basis in scientific fact or religious doctrine? So (4) what influence can an illusion have on me or my habits of thought? Given the currency of this version of color-blindness, I suspect that most people would say that the answers are simple: being white shouldn't affect how I consider the evidence; my white racial identity has nothing to do with how I evaluate or judge; yes, race has been shown to have no basis in science; and since race doesn't exist, it should have no influence on my thought. In other words, to proponents of this version of color-blindness, it would be racist for someone to insist that my being white could influence, much less interfere with, my judgment. Case closed.

But I don't think the answers to the above questions are at all simple—in fact, I think they are the wrong questions in the first place. Which is to say that I have my doubts about this version of color-blindness. I certainly understand and feel its appeal—particularly given the horrible history that race-thinking has been such a constitutive part of in modernity, from the slave trade and slavery to genocide to ethnic cleansing. And I certainly agree that the concept of race is without scientific basis. But I want to question the assumption that if we stop noticing race, if we stop talking about race, if we stop thinking of ourselves as belonging to any race, then the system of racial oppression that those who have identified themselves as white have established will simply go away.[3] I want to question the assumption that to stop doing any of these things is at all simple or easy—or even desirable in all circumstances. I want to question the assumption that the best way to fight racism is to attack the notion of race by showing it to be a cognitive error.[4] For race is not only a concept, it is also a lived experience.[5]

Attention to race as social fact or lived experience does not conflict with the insight into the social construction of race, for we should not associate the idea of social construction with the notions of illusion or fallacy or cognitive error, but instead with such concepts as ideology and narrative.[6] Under this view, that is, I can fully agree that I am not "essentially" white, but at the same time I can't ignore, downplay, or dismiss the privilege being positioned as white tends to bestow, and not only in this country. Nor can I simply assume that how I've been positioned in and by U.S. race discourses and formations has nothing to do with how I experience or reflect upon the world. What this notion of race as social construction implies, then, is that some aspects of the version of color-blindness I've elaborated and criticized might be preserved as an end, but the model as currently understood has serious limitations as a means to justice in a multiracial democracy.

So let me pose an alternative set of questions that will bring out why I think my being white has a lot to do with how I might act as a juror: How does my self-perception and identification as "white" (both by myself and by others) affect my perceptions, experiences, thoughts, and judgments, not to mention my life chances? What does thinking of myself as "white" enable me to recognize or cause me to gloss over or elide? What relation does my "whiteness" have to other aspects of my identity—class, gender, sexuality, religion, political affiliations, order and area of birth, and on and on to even less obvious ones like the enjoyment I get out of watching The Tick, Daria, The Simpsons, Dr. Katz, The Critic, and Beavis and Butt-head?

Here's why I think these questions are better than the four questions I asked while ventriloquizing the first version of color-blindness. For one thing, the earlier set of questions takes for granted as natural and eternal the existence of "the white race." I would counter that this concept is of relatively recent origin, and that thinking of whiteness or race as a simple biological fact is a mistake.[7] So when I say that it matters that I'm white in how I view the Simpson case, I don't mean inability to understand people of "other races" ("it's a white thing, I can't understand"). Rather, I mean that being treated as white throughout my entire life (along with a range of other socially significant conditions—male, middle class, short, Jewish, from upstate NY [no, not just north of New York City—the real thing!], and so on) has contributed toward shaping my habits of mind and emotions, including what I tend to take for granted and my gut reactions, my attitudes toward the police, crime, authority, and the law, where I've lived, whom I hang with and am close to, and so on. What I'm saying is that "being white" is a learned phenomenon, and until I started thinking about what kinds of lessons I was learning (usually after a friend took the time to call me out on something), I didn't even recognize that I was being taught, much less question its value or consider the possibility of change.

For another thing, the first four questions above assume that color-blindness is always in and of itself a good thing.[8] But think about that word. When you are color-blind, you only see in black and white, right?

Isn't that counter-productive? Doesn't it actually reduce the question of race—the experience of living in a thoroughly racialized society—to a binary, instead of opening it up for interrogation? I can go on with this line of argument (the problems you run into when you reduce the complex history of racial discourse, racial projects, racial formations, and racial oppression to the realms of color, vision, and perception, particularly if you are committed to an anti-racist agenda that amounts to more than diversity management), but let's for the moment treat this kind of "I treat people as individuals" position charitably. I submit that if you are truly committed to color-blindness, then your task shouldn't be to go around lecturing to all those (usually people of color) who are still caught in the grips of race-consciousness, but instead to make the case to whites of the necessity of color-blindness, that is, the recognition and rejection of white racial privilege. Otherwise, a stated commitment to color-blindness will only function as an alibi for white blindness to history and to power. When "white-blindness" means that the most powerful institutions and actors stop furthering racial oppression by privileging whiteness, then, and only then, can a society legitimately call itself "color-blind." But by then using the limiting metaphor of vision and blindness to imagine racial justice will be unnecessary.

Historicizing the social construction of whiteness is an important part of recognizing the ways it operates today, so for those to whom these ideas are relatively new, I would like to recommend a few works that were crucial in advancing the analysis of "whiteness" and "the white race" and are indispensable still today:

- W.E.B. Du Bois, *The Souls of Black Folk* (especially the opening first few pages and the last chapter, but it runs throughout this 1903 book);
- W.E.B. Du Bois, "The Souls of White Folk," in his mid-'20s essay collection, *Darkwater;*
- W.E.B. Du Bois, *Black Reconstruction* (a thick tome from the early '30s that challenges the then-popular racist interpretations of the Reconstruction era [1865–1877], but still a classic, and the source of the "wages of whiteness" thesis);
- W.E.B. Du Bois, *Dusk of Dawn* (this 1940 autobiography/history of the pre-World War II era is still not often cited in discussions of Du Bois's career, but it is an absolutely crucial text for many reasons, including an imagined discussion with a white friend in the middle of the book);
- Ralph Ellison, *Shadow and Act* (largely ignored by whites in the academy in the 1950s, this is now the bible of the "race and American literature and culture" movement; see also "What America

Would Be Like Without Blacks" in *Going to the Territory* for an update of his ideas, and of course read his novel *Invisible Man* if you haven't already);

- Malcolm X with Alex Haley, *The Autobiography of Malcolm X* (don't believe the hype that puts him as the black demon to Martin Luther King's black angel; read this for yourself—he's one of the best at exposing white supremacy, not only as it worked in the past, but how it is working in the present as well);
- Audre Lorde, *Sister Outsider* (a major collection of short and accessible essays that problematize the whiteness of the '70s women's movement and put racism squarely on the table in a challenging and constructive manner);
- James Baldwin, "On Being White . . . and Other Lies," in *Essence* (from 1984; good, short, accessible);
- bell hooks, "Representing Whiteness in the Black Imagination" (in the collection *Cultural Studies,* ed. Lawrence Grossberg, et al., and elsewhere);
- Toni Morrison, *Playing in the Dark* (recent but very influential book on the literary construction of blackness and whiteness, and of course don't forget to read all her novels and the less well-known essay collections she's edited—on the Anita Hill/Clarence Thomas and O.J. Simpson spectacles);
- Cheryl Harris, "Whiteness as Property," in *Critical Race Theory,* ed. Kimberlé Krenshaw, et al.;
- Patricia Williams, "The Ethnic Scarring of American Whiteness," in *The House That Race Built: Black Americans, U.S. Terrain,* ed. Wahneema Lubiano;
- Kimberlé Crenshaw, "Color Blindness, History, and the Law," in *The House That Race Built: Black Americans, U.S. Terrain,* ed. Wahneema Lubiano.

The reason I cite these classics along with the more recent African Americanist work on whiteness is that any exploration of whiteness today is practically worthless if it doesn't engage, question, and respond to them. People of color have had to figure out white people and survive under white supremacy for centuries. These works represent the tip of the iceberg of black thinking on whiteness; I won't even try to survey the full range of thinking on whiteness by people of color. Nor is this the place to go into my response to the important work of a journal like *Race Traitor* (http://www.postfun.com/racetraitor/) or David Roediger's *Towards the Abolition of Whiteness* or Ian Haney López's *White by Law.* But I can at least recommend these and other recent works on the history and politics of whiteness: Richard Dyer, "White," *Screen* 29.1 (Winter 1988); Paul Kivel, *Uprooting Racism; Off White: Readings on Race, Power, and Society,* ed. Michelle Fine et al.; *Race Traitor,* eds. Noel Ignatiev and John Harvey; Mab Segrest, *Memoir of a Race Traitor;* Vron Ware, *Beyond the Pale;* Ruth Frankenberg, *White Women, Race Matters;* Reginald Horsman, *Race and Manifest Destiny: The Origins of American Racial Anglo-Saxonism;* Alexander Saxton, *The Rise and Fall of the White Republic;* David Roediger, *The Wages of Whiteness;* Eric Lott, *Love and Theft;* Theodore Allen, *The Invention of the White Race;* Karen Sacks, "How Did Jews Become White Folks?" in *Race,* eds. Steven Gregory and Roger Sanjek; Noel Ignatiev, *How the Irish Became White,* and David Roediger, "White Workers, New Democrats, and Affirmative Action," Neil Gotanda, "Tales of Two Judges: Joyce Karlin in *People v. Soon Ja Du;* Lance Ito in *People v. O.J. Simpson,"* and Howard Winant, "Racial Dualism at Century's End," all in *The House That Race Built: Black Americans, U.S. Terrain,* ed. Wahneema Lubiano.

In closing, let's not forget that classic American literature has produced some profound analyses of the ideology of whiteness, most notably Herman Melville's *Moby-Dick* and "Benito Cereno"; Harriet Beecher Stowe's *Uncle Tom's Cabin;* Mark Twain's *Adventures of Huckleberry Finn* and "Pudd'nhead Wilson"; William Faulkner's *Absalom, Absalom, Light in August,* and *Go Down, Moses;* and Flannery O'Connor's "The Artificial Nigger" and "The Displaced Person."

Notes

[1] This, at least, is what such collections as *Race-ing Justice, En-gendering Power,* ed. Toni Morrison (NY: Pantheon, 1992); *Reading Rodney King/Reading Urban Uprising,* ed. Robert Gooding-Williams (NY: Routledge, 1993); and *Birth of a Nation'hood,* ed. Toni Morrison (NY: Pantheon, 1997) suggest.

[2] Given the relativist and pluralist rhetoric that contemporary white supremacists are now deploying, it is especially important to be clear when discussing color-blindness and race consciousness with respect to white people. On the new racism, see Pierre-Andre Taguieff, "From Race to Culture: The New Right's View of European Identity," trans. Deborah Cook, *Telos* 98–99 (Winter 1993–Fall 1994) 99–125; Etienne Balibar, "Is There a Neo-Racism?" trans. Chris Turner, in Etienne Balibar and Immanuel Wallerstein, *Race, Nation, Class: Ambiguous Identities* (NY: Verso, 1991) 17–28; Etienne Balibar, "Racism as Universalism," *Masses, Classes, Ideas: Studies on Politics and Philosophy before and after Marx* (NY: Routledge, 1994) 191–204; Slavoj Žižek, *Tarrying with the Negative: Kant, Hegel, and the Critique of Ideology* (Durham: Duke UP, 1993) 226; Judith Butler, "Endangered/Endangering: Schematic Racism and White Paranoia," in *Reading Rodney King/Reading Urban Uprising,* ed. Robert Gooding-Williams (NY: Routledge, 1993) 1–12; Avery Gordon and Christopher Newfield, "White Philosophy," *Critical Inquiry* 20 (Summer 1994) 737–757 (reprinted in *Identities,* ed. Kwame Anthony Appiah and Henry Louis Gates, Jr.

[Chicago: U of Chicago P, 1995] 380–400); Kimberlé Crenshaw, "Color-Blind Dreams and Racial Nightmares: Refiguring Racism in the Post-Civil Rights Era," in *Birth of a Nation'-hood,* ed. Toni Morrison (NY: Pantheon, 1997) 97–168.

[3] For an introduction to the idea of racial oppression, see Theodore Allen, *The Invention of the White Race—Volume One: Racial Oppression and Social Control* (NY: Verso, 1994) 1–51. Attending to racial oppression entails strict scrutiny toward biologically-inflected notions of culture, as well, for "culture" is often invoked today to advance claims that in the past would have been made in terms of race. In other words, anti-racism means more than making culture-based instead of nature-based claims (cf. note 2).

[4] For further questionings of this assumption, see Avery Gordon and Christopher Newfield, "White Philosophy," *Critical Inquiry* 20 (Summer 1994) 737–757 (reprinted in *Identities,* ed. Kwame Anthony Appiah and Henry Louis Gates, Jr. [Chicago: U of Chicago P, 1995] 380–400); and Gary Peller, "Race-Consciousness," in *Critical Race Theory,* ed. Kimberlé Crenshaw, et al. (NY: New P, 1995) 127–158.

[5] This apparently simple idea has far-reaching consequences; see Lucius Outlaw, "Toward a Critical Theory of 'Race,'" in *Anatomy of Racism,* ed. David Theo Goldberg (Minneapolis: U of Minnesota P, 1990) 58–82; Michael Omi and Howard Winant, *Racial Formation in the United States: From the 1960s to the 1990s,* 2nd ed. (NY: Routledge, 1994); Evelyn Brooks Higginbotham, "African-American Women's History and the Metalanguage of Race," in *"We Specialize in the Wholly Impossible": A Reader in Black Women's History,* ed. Darlene Clark Hine et al. (Brooklyn: Carlson, 1995) 3–24; Kenneth Mostern, "Three Theories of the Race of W.E.B. Du Bois," *Cultural Critique* 34 (Fall 1996) 27–63.

[6] For introductions to ideology, see James Kavanagh, "Ideology," in *Critical Terms for Literary Study,* eds. Frank Lentricchia and Thomas McLaughlin (Chicago: U of Chicago P, 1990) 306–320; and *Mapping Ideology,* ed. Slavoj Žižek (NY: Verso, 1994). For examples of reading race as ideology and as narrative, see Wahneema Lubiano, "Black Ladies, Welfare Queens, and State Minstrels: Ideological War by Narrative Means," in *Race-ing Justice, En-gendering Power,* ed. Toni Morrison (NY: Pantheon, 1992) 323–363; Wahneema Lubiano, "Like Being Mugged by a Metaphor: Multiculturalism and State Narratives," in *Mapping Multiculturalism,* eds. Avery Gordon and Christopher Newfield (Minneapolis: U of Minnesota P, 1996) 64–75.

[7] I discuss why this is so, at length, in my "race" page on the internet (http://www.princeton.edu/~bnsimon/race.html). For a small sample of the best scholarship challenging the notion that science has had, or should have, a monopoly on defining "race," see Reginald Horsman, *Race and Manifest Destiny: The Origins of American Racial Anglo-Saxonism* (Cambridge: Harvard UP, 1981); Audrey Smedley, *Race in North America: Origin and Evolution of a Worldview* (Boulder: Westview P, 1993); Theodore Allen, *The Invention of the White Race—Volume One: Racial Oppression and Social Control* (NY: Verso, 1994); Michael Omi and Howard Winant, *Racial Formation in the United States: From the 1960s to the 1990s,* 2nd ed. (NY: Routledge, 1994); Ian Haney López, *White by Law: The Legal Construction of Race* (NY: NYU P, 1996).

[8] For arguments challenging this assumption, see Neil Gotanda, "A Critique of 'Our Constitution Is Color-Blind,'" in *Critical Race Theory,* ed. Kimberlé Crenshaw, et al. (NY: New P, 1995) 257–275; and Kimberlé Crenshaw, "Color Blindness, History, and the Law," in *The House That Race Built: Black Americans, U.S. Terrain,* ed. Wahneema Lubiano (NY: Pantheon, 1997) 280–288.

The author thanks Wendy Chun, Joan Ferrante, and Wahneema Lubiano for their invaluable aid in translating this essay from web to print.

Appendix A

Race—The U.S. Bureau of the Census (1996)

The concept of race as used [in 1990] by the Census Bureau reflects self-identification; it does not denote any clear-cut scientific definition of biological stock. The data for race represent self-classification by people according to the race with which they most closely identify. Furthermore, it is recognized that the categories of the race item include both racial and national origin or socio-cultural groups.

During direct interviews conducted by enumerators, if a person could not provide a single response to the race question, he or she was asked to select, based on self-identification, the group which best described his or her racial identity. If a person could not provide a single race response, the race of the mother was used. If a single race response could not be provided for the person's mother, the first race reported by the person was used. In all cases where occupied housing units, households, or families are classified by race, the race of the householder was used.

The racial classification used by the Census Bureau generally adheres to the guidelines in Federal Statistical Directive No. 15, issued by the Office of Management and Budget, which provides standards on ethnic and racial categories for statistical reporting to be used by all Federal agencies. The racial categories used in the 1990 census data products are provided below.

White—Includes persons who indicated their race as "White" or reported entries such as Canadian, German, Italian, Lebanese, Near Easterner, Arab, or Polish.

Black—Includes persons who indicated their race as "Black or Negro" or reported entries such as African American, Afro-American, Black Puerto Rican, Jamaican, Nigerian, West Indian, or Haitian.

American Indian, Eskimo, or Aleut—Includes persons who classified themselves as such in one of the specific race categories identified below.

American Indian—Includes persons who indicated their race as "American Indian," entered the name of an Indian tribe, or re-

503

ported such entries as Canadian Indian, French-American Indian, or Spanish-American Indian.

American Indian Tribe—Persons who identified themselves as American Indian were asked to report their enrolled or principal tribe. Therefore, tribal data in tabulations reflect the written tribal entries reported on the questionnaires. Some of the entries (for example, Iroquois, Sioux, Colorado River, and Flathead) represent nations or reservations.

The information on tribe is based on self-identification and therefore does not reflect any designation of Federally- or State-recognized tribe. Information on American Indian tribes is presented in summary tape files and special data products. The information is derived from the American Indian Detailed Tribal Classification List for the 1990 census. The classification list represents all tribes, bands, and clans that had a specified number of American Indians reported on the census questionnaire.

Eskimo—Includes persons who indicated their race as "Eskimo" or reported entries such as Arctic Slope, Inupiat, and Yupik.

Aleut—Includes persons who indicated their race as "Aleut" or reported entries such as Alutiiq, Egegik, and Pribilovian.

Asian or Pacific Islander—Includes persons who reported in one of the Asian or Pacific Islander groups listed on the questionnaire or who provided write-in responses such as Thai, Nepali, or Tongan. A more detailed listing of the groups comprising the Asian or Pacific Islander population is presented in Table 1 on p. 507. In some data products, information is presented separately for the Asian population and the Pacific Islander population.

Asian—Includes "Chinese," "Filipino," "Japanese," "Asian Indian," "Korean," "Vietnamese," and "Other Asian." In some tables, "Other Asian" may not be shown separately, but is included in the total Asian population.

Chinese—Includes persons who indicated their race as "Chinese" or who identified themselves as Cantonese, Tibetan, or Chinese American. In standard census reports, persons who reported as "Taiwanese" or "Formosan" are included here with Chinese. In special reports on the Asian or Pacific Islander population, information on persons who identified themselves as Taiwanese are shown separately.

Filipino—Includes persons who indicated their race as "Filipino" or reported entries such as Philipino, Philipine, or Filipino American.

Japanese—Includes persons who indicated their race as "Japanese" and persons who identified themselves as Nipponese or Japanese American.

Asian Indian—Includes persons who indicated their race as "Asian Indian" and persons who identified themselves as Bengalese, Bharat, Dravidian, East Indian, or Goanese.

Korean—Includes persons who indicated their race as "Korean" and persons who identified themselves as Korean American.

Vietnamese—Includes persons who indicated their race as "Vietnamese" and persons who identified themselves as Vietnamese American.

Cambodian—Includes persons who provided a write-in response such as Cambodian or Cambodia.

Hmong—Includes persons who provided a write-in response such as Hmong, Laohmong, or Mong.

Laotian—Includes persons who provided a write-in response such as Laotian, Laos, or Lao.

Thai—Includes persons who provided a write-in response such as Thai, Thailand, or Siamese.

Other Asian—Includes persons who provided a write-in response of Bangladeshi, Burmese, Indonesian, Pakistani, Sri Lankan, Amerasian, or Eurasian. See Table 1 for other groups comprising "Other Asian."

Pacific Islander—Includes persons who indicated their race as "Pacific Islander" by classifying themselves into one of the following groups or identifying themselves as one of the Pacific Islander cultural groups of Polynesian, Micronesian, or Melanesian.

Hawaiian—Includes persons who indicated their race as "Hawaiian" as well as persons who identified themselves as Part Hawaiian or Native Hawaiian.

Samoan—Includes persons who indicated their race as "Samoan" or persons who identified themselves as American Samoan or Western Samoan.

Guamanian—Includes persons who indicated their race as "Guamanian" or persons who identified themselves as Chamorro or Guam.

Other Pacific Islander—Includes persons who provided a write-in response of a Pacific Islander group such as Tahitian, Northern Mariana Islander, Palauan, Fijian, or a cultural group such as Polynesian, Micronesian, or Melanesian. See Table 1 for other groups comprising "Other Pacific Islander."

Other Race—Includes all other persons not included in the "White," "Black," "American Indian, Eskimo, or Aleut," and the "Asian or Pacific Islander" race categories described above. Persons reporting in the "Other race" category and providing write-in entries such as multiracial, multiethnic, mixed, interracial, Wesort, or a Spanish/Hispanic origin group (such as Mexican, Cuban, or Puerto Rican) are included here.

Written entries to three categories on the race item—"Indian (Amer.)," "Other Asian or Pacific Islander (API)," and "Other race"—were reviewed, edited, and coded by subject matter specialists. (For more information on the coding operation, see the section below that discusses "Comparability.")

The written entries under "Indian (Amer.)" and "Other Asian or Pacific Islander (API)" were reviewed and coded during 100-percent processing of the 1990 census questionnaires. A substantial portion of the entries for the "Other race" category also were reviewed, edited, and coded during the 100-percent processing. The remaining entries under "Other race" underwent review and coding during sample processing. Most of the written entries reviewed and coded during sample processing were those indicating Hispanic origin such as Mexican, Cuban, or Puerto Rican.

If the race entry for a member of a household was missing on the questionnaire, race was assigned based upon the reported entries of race by other household members using specific rules of precedence of household relationship. For example, if race was missing for the daughter of the householder, then the race of her mother (as female householder or female spouse) would be assigned. If there was no female householder or spouse in the household, the daughter would be assigned her father's (male householder) race. If race was not reported for anyone in the household, the race of a householder in a previously processed household was assigned.

Limitation of the Data. In the 1980 census, a relatively high proportion (20 percent) of American Indians did not report any tribal entry in the race item. Evaluation of the pre-census tests indicated that changes made for the 1990 race item should improve the reporting of tribes in the rural areas (especially on reservations) for the 1990 census. The results for urban areas were inconclusive. Also, the precensus tests indicated that there may be overreporting of the Cherokee tribe. An evaluation of 1980 census data showed overreporting of Cherokee in urban areas or areas where the number of American Indians was sparse.

In the 1990 census, respondents sometimes did not fill in a circle or filled the "Other race" circle and wrote in a response, such as Arab, Polish, or African American in the shared write-in box for "Other race" and "Other API" responses. During the automated coding process, these responses were edited and assigned to the appropriate racial designation. Also, some Hispanic origin persons did not fill in a circle, but provided entries such as Mexican or Puerto Rican. These persons were classified in the "Other race" category during the coding and editing process. There may be some minor

Table I   Asian or Pacific Islander Groups Reported in the 1990 Census

ASIAN	PACIFIC ISLANDER
Chinese	Hawaiian
Filipino	Samoan
Japanese	Guamanian
Asian Indian	Other Pacific Islander (1)
Korean	Carolinian
Vietnamese	Fijian
Cambodian	Kosraean
Hmong	Melanesian (3)
Laotian	Micronesian (3)
Thai	Northern Mariana Islander
Other Asian[1]	Palauan
Bangladeshi	Papua New Guinean
Bhutanese	Ponapean (Pohnpeian)
Borneo	Polynesian[3]
Burmese	Solomon Islander
Celebesian	Tahitian
Ceram	Tarawa Islander
Indochinese	Tokelauan
Indonesian	Tongan
Iwo-Jiman	Trukese (Chuukese)
Javanese	Yapese
Malayan	Pacific Islander, not specified
Maldivian	
Nepali	
Okinawan	
Pakistani	
Sikkim	
Singaporean	
Sri Lankan	
Sumatran	
Asian, not specified[2]	

[1] In some data products, specific groups listed under "Other Asian" or "Other Pacific Islander" are shown separately. Groups not shown are tabulated as "All other Asian" or "All other Pacific Islander," respectively.

[2] Includes entries such as Asian American, Asian, Asiatic, Amerasian, and Eurasian.

[3] Polynesian, Micronesian, and Melanesian are Pacific Islander cultural groups.

differences between sample data and 100-percent data because sample processing included additional edits not included in the 100-percent processing.

Comparability. Differences between the 1990 census and earlier censuses affect the comparability of data for certain racial groups and American Indian tribes. The 1990 census was the first census to undertake, on a 100-percent basis, an automated review, edit, and coding operation for written responses to the race item. The automated coding system used in the 1990 census greatly reduced the potential for error associated with a clerical review. Specialists with a thorough knowledge of the race subject matter reviewed, edited, coded, and resolved inconsistent or incomplete responses. In the 1980 census, there was only a limited clerical review of the race responses on the 100-percent forms with a full clerical review conducted only on the sample questionnaires.

Another major difference between the 1990 and preceding censuses is the handling of the write-in responses for the Asian or Pacific Islander populations. In addition to the nine Asian or Pacific Islander categories shown on the questionnaire under the spanner "Asian or Pacific Islander (API)," the 1990 census race item provided a new residual category, "Other API," for Asian or Pacific Islander persons who did not report in one of the listed Asian or Pacific Islander groups. During the coding operation, write-in responses for "Other API" were reviewed, coded, and assigned to the appropriate classification. For example, in 1990, a write-in entry of Laotian, Thai, or Javanese is classified as "Other Asian," while a write-in entry of Tongan or Fijian is classified as "Other Pacific Islander." In the 1990 census, these persons were able to identify as "Other API" in both the 100-percent and sample operations.

In the 1980 census, the nine Asian or Pacific Islander groups were also listed separately. However, persons not belonging to these nine groups wrote in their specific racial group under the "Other" race category. Persons with a written entry such as Laotian, Thai, or Tongan, were tabulated and published as "Other race" in the 100-percent processing operation in 1980, but were reclassified as "Other Asian and Pacific Islander" in 1980 sample tabulations. In 1980 special reports on the Asian or Pacific Islander populations, data were shown separately for "Other Asian" and "Other Pacific Islander."

The 1970 questionnaire did not have separate race categories for Asian Indian, Vietnamese, Samoan, and Guamanian. These persons indicated their race in the "Other" category and later, through the editing process, were assigned to a specific group. For example, in 1970, Asian Indians were reclassified as "White," while Vietnamese, Guamanians, and Samoans were included in the "Other" category.

Another difference between 1990 and preceding censuses is the approach taken when persons of Spanish/Hispanic origin did not report in a specific race category but reported as "Other race" or "Other." These persons commonly provided a write-in entry such as Mexican, Venezuelan, or Latino. In the 1990 and 1980 censuses, these entries remained in the "Other race" or "Other" category, respectively. In the 1970 census, most of these persons were included in the "White" category.

Source: U.S. Bureau of the Census (1996).

APPENDIX B

Federal and Program Uses of the Data Derived from Race and Ethnicity Questions—The U.S. Bureau of the Census (1990)

Race and Ethnic Origin

U.S. CODE CITATION	USES OF THE DATA/PROGRAM/AGENCY
Subject: Race (Q4)	
5 U.S.C.	
7201	Establishment and evaluation of guidelines for Federal affirmative action plans under the Federal Equal Opportunity Recruitment Program (Equal Employment Opportunity Commission)
7 U.S.C.	
612c	Determine qualification for various programs such as the Food Stamp Program under the Food and Agriculture Act of 1977 (Department of Agriculture)
12 U.S.C.	
2809	Compilation of data on home mortgage lending patterns of depository institutions by race, geographic area, housing conditions, and income (Federal Financial Institutions Examination Council)
2901–2905	Determination of whether financial institutions are meeting credit needs of race/Hispanic origin groups in low- and moderate-income neighborhoods under the Community Reinvestment Act of 1977 (Federal Reserve Banks)
13 U.S.C.	
141	Review of State redistricting plans (Department of Justice)
15 U.S.C.	
631	Assistance to minority businesses in low-income areas under the Minority Business Development Program (Minority Business Development Agency—Department of Commerce)
1691 *et seq.*	Monitor compliance of nondiscrimination requirements of creditors under the Equal Credit Opportunity Act (Civil Rights Division—Department of Justice)
20 U.S.C.	
631	Planning school construction sites in school districts with increased enrollment due to Federal activities (Department of Education)
25 U.S.C.	
13	Assessment of program needs for housing improvement under the Housing Improvement Program (Bureau of Indian Affairs—Department of the Interior and Indian Health Service—Department of Health and Human Services)
450, 450h	Funds allocation and planning and evaluation of tribal or Alaska Native village programs (Department of Health and Human Services and Bureau of Indian Affairs—Department of the Interior)
458	Planning needs of schools serving American Indian and Alaska Native children on or adjacent to reservations or Alaska Native villages under the Indian Education Assistance Act (Bureau of Indian Affairs—Department of the Interior)

1601 (P.L. 94-037) Assessment of needs under the Indian Health Care Improvement Act (Indian Health Service—Department of Health and Human Services)

28 U.S.C.
1861–1871 Determination that jurors are randomly selected representing a cross-section of the community under the Jury Act (Department of Justice)

30 Federal
Register 12319
32 Federal
Register 14303 Monitor and enforce nondiscrimination by government contractors (Department of Labor—responsible for administering Executive Order 11246, as amended, and Department of Justice—authority to enforce E.O.)

31 U.S.C.
6708–6713 Revenue sharing funds allocation to tribal councils (Department of the Treasury) and enforcement of nondiscrimination of funds allocation (Department of Justice) under the State and Local Fiscal Assistance Act of 1972, as amended

42 U.S.C.
242k Collection of vital, social, and health statistics (National Center for Health Statistics—Department of Health and Human Services)

628 Funds allocation to American Indian tribal organizations for child welfare services under the Adoption Assistance and Child Welfare Act of 1980 (Department of Health and Human Services)

1310 Research conducted on welfare dependency and income and employment characteristics to reduce dependency rates in Social Security Act programs (Social Security Administration—Department of Health and Human Services)

1786 Grants to American Indian tribes for supplemental food programs under the Child Nutrition Amendments of 1978 (Department of Agriculture)

1973aa–1a Enforcement of bilingual election requirements of Voting Rights Act and Amendments of 1982 (Department of Justice)

1975c(4) Commission on Civil Rights acts as clearinghouse for information on discrimination in housing, education, and employment under the Civil Rights Act of 1957, as amended

2000c–2 Technical assistance for school desegregation plans (Department of Education) and enforcement of desegregation plans (Department of Justice)

2000d Monitor compliance with nondiscrimination requirements for variety of Federally-assisted programs under the Civil Rights Act of 1964, as amended (various Federal agencies)

2000e Evaluation of affirmative action programs and discrimination in employment in the private sector (Equal Employment Opportunity Commission) and enforcement of nondiscrimination in employment by State and local governments (Department of Justice) under the Civil Rights Act of 1964, as amended

2000f Research on voting and voter registration (Commission on Civil Rights)

2001–2004 Planning new or renovation of existing sanitation facilities serving American Indian and Alaska Native houses, communities, and lands under the Indian Sanitation Facilities Act (Department of Health and Human Services)

2808	Grants to American Indian tribes and tribal organizations under the Community Services Block Grant Act (Department of Health and Human Services)
2992	Evaluation of program goals under the Native American Programs Act of 1974 as amended (Department of Health and Human Services)

42 U.S.C.—Con.

3035a	Conduct demonstration projects addressing needs of low-income, minority, American Indian, older, and limited English-speaking persons under the Older Americans Act of 1965, as amended (Health Care Financing Administration—Department of Health and Human Services)
3057	Social and nutritional services for older American Indians under the Older Americans Act of 1965, as amended (Administration on Aging—Department of Health and Human Services)
3601 *et seq.*	Monitoring and enforcement of antidiscrimination provisions of Fair Housing Act of 1968, as amended (Department of Housing and Urban Development and Department of Justice)
3766c	Monitoring and enforcement of provisions of Omnibus Crime Control and Safe Streets Act of 1968, as amended, against discrimination by law enforcement agencies receiving Federal funds (Department of Justice)
8623–8629	Grants to American Indian tribes for home energy assistance to low-income households under the Low-Income Home Energy Assistance Act of 1981, as amended (Department of Health and Human Services)
9835	Grants to American Indian tribal organizations for preschool programs for low-income and handicapped children under the Head Start Program (Department of Health and Human Services)
P.L. 81-507	Collection of data on the need and availability for scientific and technical personnel (National Science Foundation)
P.L. 96-516	Provide data to Congress, Federal policymakers, and other data users on the status of women and minorities in science and engineering (National Science Foundation)

Public Health Act

Sec. 306	Collection of data on illness and disability (National Center for Health Statistics—Department of Health and Human Services)
Sec. 401	Research on the prevalence, causes, and prevention of cancer under the National Cancer Act (National Cancer Institute—Department of Health and Human Services)
Sec. 455e(2)	Research on the mental health problems of minorities (National Institute of Mental Health—Department of Health and Human Services)

Subject: Spanish/Hispanic Origin (Q7)

5 U.S.C.

7201	Establishment and evaluation of guidelines for Federal affirmative action plans under the Federal Equal Opportunity Recruitment Program (Equal Employment Opportunity Commission)

12 U.S.C.

2809	Compilation of data on home mortgage lending patterns of depository institutions by race, geographic area, housing conditions, and income (Federal Financial Institutions Examination Council)

12 U.S.C.—Con.

2901–2905   Determination of whether financial institutions are meeting credit needs of race/Hispanic origin groups in low- and moderate-income neighborhoods under the Community Reinvestment Act of 1977 (Federal Reserve Banks)

13 U.S.C.

141   Review of State redistricting plans (Department of Justice)

15 U.S.C.

631   Assistance to minority businesses in low-income areas under the Minority Business Development Program (Minority Business Development Agency—Department of Commerce)

1516a   Publication of social, health, and economic statistics of Spanish origin persons (Department of Agriculture, Department of Commerce, Department of Health and Human Services, and Department of Labor)

1691 *et seq.*   Monitor compliance of nondiscrimination requirements of creditors under the Equal Credit Opportunity Act (Civil Rights Division—Department of Justice)

29 U.S.C.

8   Development of methods for improving collection and analysis of unemployment data for Spanish origin persons (Department of Labor in cooperation with Department of Commerce)

30 Federal
Register 12319
32 Federal
Register 14303   Monitor and enforce nondiscrimination by government contractors (Department of Labor—responsible for administering Executive Order 11246, as amended, and Department of Justice—authority to enforce E.O.)

31 U.S.C.

6708–6713   Revenue sharing funds allocation to tribal councils (Department of the Treasury) and enforcement of nondiscrimination of funds allocation (Department of Justice) under the State and Local Fiscal Assistance Act of 1972, as amended

42 U.S.C.

242k   Collection of vital, social, and health statistics (National Center for Health Statistics—Department of Health and Human Services)

1973aa–1a   Enforcement of bilingual election requirements of Voting Rights Act and Amendments of 1982 (Department of Justice)

1975c(4)   Commission on Civil Rights acts as clearinghouse for information on discrimination in housing, education, and employment under the Civil Rights Act of 1957, as amended

2000c–2   Technical assistance for school desegregation plans (Department of Education) and enforcement of desegregation plans (Department of Justice)

2000d   Monitor compliance with nondiscrimination requirements for variety of Federally-assisted programs under the Civil Rights Act of 1964, as amended (various Federal agencies)

2000e   Evaluation of affirmative action programs and discrimination in employment in the private sector (Equal Employment Opportunity Commission) and enforcement of nondiscrimination in employment by State and local governments (Department of Justice) under the Civil Rights Act of 1964, as amended

2000f	Research on voting and voter registration (Commission on Civil Rights)
3035a	Conduct demonstration projects addressing needs of low-income, minority, American Indian, older, and limited English-speaking persons under the Older Americans Act of 1965, as amended (Health Care Financing Administration—Department of Health and Human Services)
3601 *et seq.*	Monitoring and enforcement of antidiscrimination provisions of Fair Housing Act of 1968, as amended (Department of Housing and Urban Development and Department of Justice)
3766c	Monitoring and enforcement of provisions of Omnibus Crime Control and Safe Streets Act of 1968, as amended, against discrimination by law enforcement agencies receiving Federal funds (Department of Justice)
P.L. 81–507	Collection of data on the need and availability for scientific and technical personnel (National Science Foundation)
P.L. 96–516	Provide data to Congress, Federal policymakers, and other data users on the status of women and minorities in science and engineering (National Science Foundation)

Subject: Ancestry (Q13)

5 U.S.C.

7201	Establishment and evaluation of guidelines for Federal affirmative action plans under the Federal Equal Opportunity Recruitment Program (Equal Employment Opportunity Commission)

8 U.S.C.

1521–1523	Employment assessment of refugee population and compilation of secondary migration data on refugees under the Refugee Education Assistance Act of 1980, as amended (Office of Refugee Resettlement—Department of Health and Human Services)

15 U.S.C.

631	Assistance to minority businesses in low-income areas under the Minority Business Development Program (Minority Business Development Agency—Department of Commerce)
1691 *et seq.*	Monitor compliance of nondiscrimination requirements of creditors under the Equal Credit Opportunity Act (Civil Rights Division—Department of Justice)

30 Federal Register 12319 32 Federal Register 14303	Monitor and enforce nondiscrimination by government contractors (Department of Labor—responsible for administering Executive Order 11246, as amended, and Department of Justice—authority to enforce E.O.)

42 U.S.C.

242k	Collection of vital, social, and health statistics (National Center for Health Statistics—Department of Health and Human Services)
1310	Research conducted on welfare dependency and income and employment characteristics to reduce dependency rates in Social Security Act programs (Social Security Administration—Department of Health and Human Services)
1973aa–1a	Enforcement of bilingual election requirements of Voting Rights Act and Amendments of 1982 (Department of Justice)

1975c(4)	Commission on Civil Rights acts as clearinghouse for information on discrimination in housing, education, and employment under the Civil Rights Act of 1957, as amended
2000d	Monitor compliance with nondiscrimination requirements for variety of Federally-assisted programs under the Civil Rights Act of 1964, as amended (various Federal agencies)
2000e	Evaluation of affirmative action programs and discrimination in employment in the private sector (Equal Employment Opportunity Commission) and enforcement of nondiscrimination in employment by State and local governments (Department of Justice) under the Civil Rights Act of 1964, as amended
2000f	Research on voting and voter registration (Commission on Civil Rights)
3601 *et seq.*	Monitoring and enforcement of antidiscrimination provisions of Fair Housing Act of 1968, as amended (Department of Housing and Urban Development and Department of Justice)
3766c	Monitoring and enforcement of provisions of Omnibus Crime Control and Safe Streets Act of 1968, as amended, against discrimination by law enforcement agencies receiving Federal funds (Department of Justice)

Source: U.S. Bureau of the Census (1990).

REFERENCES

Introduction

Fish, Jefferson M. 1995. "Mixed Blood." *Psychology Today.* (November/December): 55–61+.

FRONTLINE. 1985. "A Class Divided" (transcript #309). Boston: WGBH Educational Foundation.

Gates, Henry Louis, Jr. 1995. "The Political Scene: Powell and the Black Elite." *The New Yorker* (September 25):64–80.

Gerth, Hans and C. Wright Mills. 1954. *Character and Social Structure: The Psychology of Social Institutions.* London: Routledge & Kegan Paul.

Kilker, Ernest Evans. 1993. "Black and White in America: The Culture and Politics of Racial Classification." *International Journal of Politics, Culture and Society* 7(2):229– 258.

Lee, Sharon M. 1993. "Racial Classifications in the U.S. Census: 1890–1990." *Ethnic and Racial Studies* 16(1):75–94.

Page, Clarence. 1996. *Showing My Color: Impolite Essays on Race and Identity.* New York: HarperCollins.

del Pinal, Jorge and Susan J. Lapham. 1993. "Impact of Ethnic Data Needs in the United States." Pp. 448–49 in *Challenges of Measuring an Ethnic World: Science, Politics and Reality,* edited by Statistics Canada and U.S. Bureau of the Census. Washington, DC: U.S. Government Printing Office.

Rohrl, Vivian J. 1995. "The Anthropology of Race: A Study of Looking at Race." *Race, Gender, and Class* 2(2):85–97.

———. 1996. 1990 *Census Lookup.* http://venus.census.gov/cdrom/lookup/.

———. 1994. *Current Population Survey Interview Manual.* Washington, DC: U.S. Government Printing Office.

U.S. Bureau of the Census. 1993. *1990 Census of Population and Housing Content Reinterview Survey: Accuracy of Data for Selected Population and Housing Characteristics as Measured by Reinterview.* Washington, DC: U.S. Government Printing Office.

Webster, Yehudi O. 1993. *The Racialization of America.* New York: St. Martin's Press.

Part I

Ashe, Arthur and Arnold Rampersad. 1993. Pp. 126–131 in *Days of Grace: A Memoir.* New York: Knopf.

Atkins, Elizabeth. 1991. "For Many Mixed-Race Americans, Life Isn't Simply Black or White." *The New York Times* (June 5):B8.

Brodeur, Paul. 1978. "The Mashpees." *The New Yorker* (November 6):62–150.

Cambridge International Dictionary of English. 1995. New York: Cambridge University Press.

Clifford, James. 1988. *The Predicament of Culture: Twentieth-Century Ethnography, Literature, and Art.* Cambridge: Harvard University Press.

Egan, Timothy. 1996. "Expelled in 1877, Indian Tribe is Now Wanted as a Resource." *The New York Times* (July 22):A1+.

Franklin, John Hope. 1990. Quoted in "That's History, Not Black History," by Mark Mcgurl. *The New York Times Book Review* (June 3):13.

Goffman, Erving. 1959. *The Presentation of Self in Everyday Life.* New York: Anchor.

———. 1963. *Stigma: Notes of the Management of Spoiled Identity.* Englewood Cliffs, NJ: Prentice-Hall.

Graham, Lawrence Otis. 1995. "Black Man with a Nose Job." Pp. 222–231 in *Member of the Club: Reflections on Life in a Racially Polarized World.* New York: HarperCollins.

Halter, Marilyn. 1993. "Identity Matters." Pp. 163–173 in *Between Race and Ethnicity: Cape Verdean American Immigrants, 1860–1965.* Champaign: University of Illinois Press.

Handler, Richard. 1986. "Authenticity." *Anthropology Today* 2(1):2–4.

Hongo, Garrett. 1994. "Asian-American Literature: Questions of Identity." *Amerasia Journal* 20(3):1–8.

———. 1995. "Introduction: Culture Wars in Asian America." Pp. 16–30 in *Under Western Eyes: Personal Essays from Asian America,* edited by G. Hongo. New York: Anchor.

Kothari, Geeta. 1995. "Where Are You From?" Pp. 153–173 in *Under Western Eyes: Personal Essays from Asian America,* edited by G. Hongo. New York: Anchor.

Kilker, Ernest Evans. 1993. "Black and White in America: The Culture and Politics of Racial Classification." *International Journal of Politics, Culture and Society* 7(2):229–258.

Kochiyama, Yuri. 1992. "Then Came the War." Pp. 10–18 in *Asian Americans,* edited by J. F. J. Lee. New York: New Press.

Kramer, Peter D. 1995. "A Rescue Without Cheers." *The New York Times Magazine* (July 16):15.

Montagu, Ashley. 1964. "The Concept of Race in the Human Species in the Light of Genetics." Pp. 12–28 in *The Concept of Race,* edited by Ashley Montagu. New York: Free Press.

Mura, David. 1996. *Where the Body Meets Memory: An Odyssey of Race, Sexuality, and Identity.* New York: Anchor.

Park, Robert. 1967. "Human Migration and the Marginal Man." Pp. 194–206 in *On Social Control and Collective Behavior: Selected Papers,* edited by Ralph H. Turner. Chicago: University of Chicago.

Riley, Patricia. 1992. "Adventures of an Indian Princess." Pp. 135–140 in *Earth Song, Sky Spirit,* edited by C. E. Trafzer. New York: Anchor.

Scales-Trent, Judy, 1995. "Choosing Up Sides." Pp. 61–65 in *Notes of a White Black Woman: Race, Color, Community.* University Park: The Pennsylvania State University Press.

Simmel, Georg. 1950. "The Stranger." Pp. 402–408 in *The Sociology of Georg Simmel,* translated, edited, and with an Introduction by K. H. Wolff. New York: Free Press.

Thomas, Robert McG., Jr. 1995. "Thyra Johnston, 91, Symbol of Racial Distinctions, Dies." *The New York Times* (November 29):B11.

Tovares, Joseph. 1995. "Mojado Like Me." http://www.hisp.com/mojado.html (May).

Uehara-Carter, Mitzi. 1996. "On Being Blackanese." http://www.webcom.com/~~intvoice/ mitzi.html .

Ugwu-Oju, Dympna. 1995. "Convent Convenience" and "The Undoing of Mama's Handiwork." Pp. 272–282 in *What Will My Mother Say: A Tribal African Girl Comes of Age in America.* Chicago: Bonus.

Van't Hul, Sarah. "How It Was for Me." Pp. 210–214 in *Testimony,* edited by N. Tarpley. Boston: Beacon.

Part 2

Angelou, Maya. 1987. "Intra-Racism." Interview on the *Oprah Winfrey Show.* (Journal Graphics transcript #W172):2.

Beech, Hannah. 1996. "Don't You Dare List Them As 'Other.'" *U.S. News and World Report.* http://www.usnews.com/usnews/issue/birace.htm.

Brown, Prince, Jr. Unpublished. "Biology and the Social Construction of the 'Race' Concept." Northern Kentucky University.

Finnegan, William. 1986. *Crossing the Line: A Year in the Land of Apartheid.* New York: Harper & Row.

Forbes, Jack D. 1990. "The Manipulation of Race, Caste and Identity: Classifying Afro Americans, Native Americans and Red-Black People." *The Journal of Ethnic Studies* 17(4):23–25.

Gimenez, Martha E. 1989. "Latino/'Hispanic'—Who Needs a Name?: The Case Against a Standardized Terminology." *International Journal of Health Services* 19(3):567–571.

Green, V. 1978. "The Black Extended Family in the United States: Some Research Suggestions." Pp. 378–387 in *The Extended Family in Black Societies,* edited by D. B. Shimkin, E. M. Shimkin, and D. A. Frate. The Netherlands: Mouton DeGruyter.

Haney López, Ian F. 1994. "The Social Construction of Race: Some Observations on Illusion, Fabrication, and Choice." *Harvard Civil Rights-Civil Liberties Law Review.* 29:39–53.

Hunt, William M. 1993. *U.S. General Accounting Office Data Collection: Measuring Race and Ethnicity is Complex and Controversial.* Testimony Before the

Subcommittee on Census, Statistics, and Postal Personnel. Washington, DC: U.S. Government Printing Office.

Knepper, Paul. 1995. "Historical Origins of the Prohibition of Multiracial Legal Identity in the States and the Nation." *State Constitutional Commentaries and Notes: A Quarterly Review* 5(2):14–20.

Lee, Sharon M. 1993. "Racial Classification in the U.S. Census: 1890–1990." *Ethnic and Racial Studies* 16(1):75–94.

Lock, Margaret. 1993. "The Concept of Race: An Ideological Construct." *Transcultural Psychiatric Research Review* 30:203–227.

Meier, August. 1949. "A Study of the Racial Ancestry of the Mississippi College Negro." *American Journal of Physical Anthropology* 7(1):227–240.

Montagu, Ashley, ed. 1964. *The Concept of Race.* Toronto: Free Press.

Morganthau, Tom. 1995. "What Color is Black?" *Newsweek* (February 13): 63–65.

National Center for Health Statistics. 1993. "Advanced Report of Final Natality Statistics." *Monthly Vital Statistics Report* 41(9).

Piper, Adrian. 1992. "Passing for White, Passing for Black." *Transition* 58:4–32.

Pollitzer, William S. 1972. "The Physical Anthropology and Genetics of Marginal People of the Southeastern United States." *American Anthropologist* 74(1–2):719–734.

Poston, Dudley L. Jr., Michael Xinxiang Mao, and Mei-Yu Yu. 1994. "The Global Distribution of the Overseas Chinese Around 1990." *Population and Development Review* 20(3):631–645.

Potter, David M. and Paul Knepper. 1996. "Comparing Official Definitions of Race in Japan and the United States." *Southeast Review of Asian Studies* 28(1):103–118.

Scales-Trent, Judy. 1995. "Choosing Up Sides." Pp. 61–65 in *Notes of a White Black Woman: Race, Color, Community.* University Park: The Pennsylvania State University.

Strickland, Daryl. 1996. "Interracial Generation: 'We Are Who We Are'." *The Seattle Times.* http://webster3.seattletimes.com/topstories/browse/html/race_050596.html .

Trillin, Calvin. 1986. "American Chronicles: Black or White." *The New Yorker* (April 14):62–78.

U.S. Bureau of the Census. 1989. *200 Years of U.S. Census Taking: Population and Housing Questions, 1790–1990.* Washington, DC: U.S. Government Printing Office.

———. 1994. *Current Population Survey Interviewing Manual.* Washington, DC: U.S. Government Printing Office.

———. 1996. "Race." In *Appendix B: Definition of Subject Characteristics.* http://www.census.gov/td/stf3/append_b.html .

Webster, Yehundi O. 1993. *The Racialization of America.* New York: St. Martin's Press.

Williams, David R., Risa Lavizzo-Mourey, and Rueben C. Warren. 1994. "The Concept of Race and Health Status in America." *Public Health Reports* 109(1):26–41.

Part 3

Bakalian, Anny. 1991. "From Being to Feeling Armenian: Assimilation and Identity Among Armenian Americans." Paper presented at the annual meeting of the American Sociological Association, Cincinnati, OH.

Benumof, Jonathan L. 1994. "In Reply." *Anesthesiology* 81(4):1082.

Breton, Raymond, Wsevolod W. Isajiw, Warren E. Kalbach, and Jeffrey G. Reitz. 1990. *Ethnic Identity and Equality: Varieties of Experience in a Canadian City.* Toronto: University of Toronto.

Brodeur, Paul. 1978. A Reporter at Large: "The Mashpees." *The New Yorker* (November 6):103.

Burns, Jim. 1993. "Fusion Cooking From the Pacific Rim." *American Visions* (October/November):36–38.

Cohen, David Steven. 1991. "Reflections on American Ethnicity." *New York History* 72(3):321–336.

Gimenez, Martha E. 1989. "Latino/'Hispanic'—Who Needs a Name?: The Case Against a Standardized Terminology." *International Journal of Health Services* 19(3):567–571.

Goble, Paul A. 1994. "Ethnicity as Explanation, Ethnicity as Excuse." *Special Warfare* 7(2):8–11.

Hirschman, Charles. 1993. "How to Measure Ethnicity: An Immodest Proposal." Pp. 547–560 in *Challenges of Measuring An Ethnic World: Science, Politics and Reality,* edited by Statistics Canada and U.S. Bureau of the Census. Washington, DC: U.S. Government Printing Office.

Infield, Henrik F. 1951. "The Concept of Jewish Culture and the State of Israel." *American Sociological Review* 16(4):506–13.

Kondo, Dorinne K. 1990. *Crafting Selves: Power, Gender, and Discourses of Identity in a Japanese Workplace.* Chicago: University of Chicago Press.

Leonard, Karen. 1993. "Historical Constructions of Ethnicity: Research on Punjabi Immigrants in California." *Journal of American Ethnic History* (Summer):3–26.

Mahmood, Cynthia K. and Sharon L. Armstrong. 1992. "Do Ethnic Groups Exist?: A Cognitive Perspective on the Concept of Cultures." *Ethnology* XXXI(1):1–14.

Nagel, Joane. 1995a. "Resource Competition Theories." *American Behavioral Scientist* 38(3):442–458, Thousand Oaks, CA: Sage.

———. 1995b. "American Indian Ethnic Renewal: Politics and the Resurgence of Identity." *American Sociological Review* 60(6):947–965.

———. 1994. "Constructing Ethnicity: Creating and Recreating Ethnic Identity and Culture." *Social Problems* 41(1):152–176.

Nathan, Andrew J. 1993. "Is Chinese Culture Distinctive?—A Review Article." *The Journal of Asian Studies* 52(4):923–936.

Ortega, Rafael and Marcelle M. Willock. 1994. "To the Editor: When Is Ethnicity Relevant in a Case Report?" *Anesthesiology* 81(4):1082.

del Pinal, Jorge and Susan L. Lapham. 1993. "Impact of Ethnic Data Needs in the United States." Pp. 447–471 in *Challenges of Measuring An Ethnic World: Science, Politics and Reality,* edited by Statistics Canada and U.S. Bureau of the Census. Washington, DC: U.S. Government Printing Office.

Rushdie, Salman. 1991. *Imaginary Homelands: Essays and Criticism 1981–1991.* New York: Viking Penguin.

Sprott, Julie E. 1994. "'Symbolic Ethnicity' and Alaska Natives of Mixed Ancestry Living in Anchorage: Enduring Group or Sign of Impending Assimilation?" *Human Organization* 53(4):314–315.

Stavans, Ilan. 1995. *The Hispanic Condition: Reflections on Culture and Identity in America.* New York: HarperCollins.

Toro, Luis Angel. 1995. "A People Distinct From Others: Race and Identity in Federal Indian Law and the Hispanic Classification in OMB Directive No. 15." *Texas Tech Law Review* 26(1219):1259–1263.

U.S. Bureau of the Census. 1996a. *1990 Census Lookup.* http://venus.census.gov/cdrom/lookup .

———. 1996b. "Ancestry." In Appendix B: Definition of Subject Characteristics. http://www.census.gov/td/stf3/append_b.html .

———. 1994. *Current Population Survey Interviewing Manual.* Washington, DC: U.S. Government Printing Office.

Verkuyten, Matkel. 1991. "Self-Definition and Ingroup Formation Among Ethnic Minorities in the Netherlands." *Social Psychology Quarterly* 54(3): 280–286.

Waters, Mary C. 1994. "Ethnic and Racial Identities of Second-Generation Black Immigrants in New York City." *International Migration Review* 28(4):795–820.

———. 1990. *Ethnic Options: Choosing Identities in America.* Berkeley: University of California Press.

White, Merry. 1988. *The Japanese Overseas: Can They Go Home Again?* New York: Free Press.

Winn, Peter. 1995. "A View From the South." Pp. 19–24 in *Americas: The Changing Face of Latin America and the Caribbean.* New York: Pantheon Books.

Part 4

Altbach, Philip G. and Gail P. Kelly, eds. 1978. *Education and Colonialism.* New York: Longman.

Banks, James A. 1993. "The Canon Debate, Knowledge Construction, and Multicultural Education." *Education Researcher* 22(5):4–14.

Bell, Derrick. n.d. *Race, Racism and American Law.* Boston: Little, Brown.

Blauner, Robert. 1972. "Colonized and Immigrant Minorities," in *Nation of Nations,* edited by Peter I. Rose. New York: Random House.

———. 1969. "Internal Colonialism and Ghetto Revolt." *Social Problems* 16 (4):393–408.

Brown, Prince, Jr. 1995. "Why 'Race' Makes No Sense: The Case of Africans and Native Americans." Pp. 377–381 in *Sociology: A Global Perspective,* 2nd ed. by Joan Ferrante. Belmont, CA: Wadsworth.

Carnoy, Martin. 1974. *Education as Cultural Imperialism.* New York: David McKay.

Constitution of the State of California: Annotated California Codes. 1996. "Article XIX, Chinese." St. Paul: West.

Freeman, Bonnie C. 1978. "Female Education in Patriarchal Power System." Pp. 208–209 in *Education and Colonialism,* edited by Philip G. Altbach and Gail P. Kelley. New York: Longman.

Gallagher, Charles A. 1995. "White Reconstruction in the University." *Socialist Review 94* 24(1+2):165–187.

Genovese, Eugene. 1974. *Roll, Jordon Roll: The World the Slaves Made.* New York: Pantheon.

Gould, Stephen Jay. 1983. *Hen's Teeth and Horse's Toes.* New York: Norton.

———. 1981a. *The Mismeasurement of Man.* New York: Norton.

———. 1981b. "The Politics of Census." *Natural History* 90(1):20–24.

Grillo, Trina and Stephanie M. Wildman. 1991. "Obscuring the Importance of Race: The Implication of Making Comparisons Between Racism and Sexism (Or Other-Isms)." *Duke Law Journal* 1991(2):401–403.

Harris, Cheryl I. 1993. "Whiteness as Property." *Harvard Law Review* 106(8):1746–50.

Hazel, Forest. 1985. "Black, White and Other." *Southern Exposure* 13(6):34–37.

Herrnstein, Richard and Charles Murray. 1994. *The Bell Curve: Intelligence and Class Structure in American Life.* New York: Free Press.

Jackson, John G. 1972. *Man, God, and Civilization.* Secaucus, NJ: Citadel Press.

Jacquard, Albert. 1981. "Science, Pseudo-science and Racism." *UNESCO Courier* 2(34): 23–28.

Jordan, Withrop D. 1974. *The White Man's Burden: Historical Origins of Racism in the United States.* New York: Oxford University Press.

Katz, William Loren. 1986. *Black Indians: A Hidden Heritage.* New York: Atheneum.

Kelly, Gail P. 1980. "The Schooling of Vietnamese Immigrants." In *Comparative Perspectives of Third World Women: The Implications of Race, Sex, and Class,* edited by Beverly Lindsey. New York: Prager.

Lyons, Charles H. 1978. "The Colonial Mentality: Assessments of the Intelligence of Blacks and of Women in Nineteenth-Century America." Pp. 181–206 in *Education and Colonialism,* edited by Phillip G. Altbach and Gail P. Kelly. New York: Longman.

Marger, Martin N. 1991. *Race and Ethnic Relations: American and Global Perspectives.* Belmont, CA: Wadsworth.

McElroy, John H. 1989. *Finding Freedom: America's Distinctive Cultural Formation.* Carbondale: Southern Illinois University Press.

Meneses, Eloise H. 1994.

Merton, Robert K. 1970. *Science, Technology and Society in Seventeenth Century England.* New York: Harper & Row.

———. 1976. *Sociological Ambivalence and Other Essays.* New York: Free Press.

Morrison, Toni. 1989. "Unspeakable Things Unspoken: The Afro-American Presence in American Literature." *Michigan Quarterly Review* 28(1):1–34.

Nash, Manning. 1962. "Race and the Ideology of Race." *Current Anthropology* 3(3): 285–293.

Park, Robert E. 1950. *Race and Culture.* New York: Free Press.

Pope-Hennesy, James. 1967. *Sins of the Fathers: A Study of the Atlantic Slave Traders 1441–1807.* New York: Knopf.

Pulliam, John D. 1991. *History of Education in America.* Columbus: Merrill.

Rogers, J. A., 1972. *Sex and Race.* Vol. 3. St. Petersburg, FL: Helga M. Rogers.

Rose, Arnold. 1951. *The Roots of Prejudice.* Paris: UNESCO Courier.

Rothenberg, Paula S. 1988. *Racism and Sexism.* New York: St. Martin's Press.

Scales-Trent, Judy. 1995. "On Being Like a Mule." Pp. 99–183 in *Notes of a White Black Woman: Race, Color, Community.* University Park: The Pennsylvania State University.

Schaefer, Richard T. 1995. *Race and Ethnicity in the United States.* New York: HarperCollins.

Thomas, William I. and Dorothy S. Thomas. 1928. *The Child in America.* New York: Knopf.

The U.S. Government Manual 1996/1997. 1996. "The Constitution of the United States. Washington, DC: U.S. Government Printing Office.

U.S. Reports. 1896. "Plessy v. Ferguson: Opinion of the U.S. Supreme Court." 163(537): 535–564.

Vidmar, Neil and Milton Rokeach. 1974. "Archie Bunker's Bigotry: A Study in Selective Perception and Exposure." *Journal of Communication* 24(1):36–47.

Zinn, Howard. 1995. *A People's History of the United States,* revised and updated. New York: HarperPerennial.

Part 5

Bateson, Mary Catherine. 1968. "Insight in a Bicultural Context." *Philippine Studies* 16: 605–621.

Barzun, Jacques. 1965. *Race: A Study in Superstition.* New York: TorchBook.

Behrangi, Samad. 1994. Quoted on p. 28 in "International Rural Education Teacher and Literary Critic: Samad Behrangi's Life and Thoughts." *Journal of Global Awareness* 2(1):27.

Berry, Michael. 1995. "Curse-Cultural Communication." *Word* 16(1):8.

Caldwell, Stephen H. and Rebecca Popenoe. 1995a. "Perceptions and Misperceptions of Skin Color. *Annals of Internal Medicine* 122(8):614–17.

————. 1995b. In Response to "Skin Color and Ethnicity." *Annals of Internal Medicine* 123(8):637.

Chideya, Farai. 1995. *Don't Believe the Hype: Fighting Cultural Misinformation About African-Americans.* New York: Plume.

Churchill, Ward. 1994. "Let's Spread the 'Fun' Around: The Issue of Sports Team Names and Mascots." Pp. 65–72 in *Indians Are Us?* Monroe, ME: Common-Courage.

Cole, K.C. 1995. "Brain's Use of Shortcuts Can Be a Route to Bias." *Los Angeles Times* (May 1):A8,A18–19.

Collins, Patricia Hill. 1993. "Toward a New Vision: Race, Class, and Gender as Categories of Analysis and Connection." *Race, Sex, and Class* 1(1):25–45.

Davis, F. James. 1978. *Minority-Dominant Relations: A Sociological Analysis.* Arlington Heights, IL: AHM.

Du Bois, W. E. B. 1899/1996 Reprint. *The Philadelphia Negro: A Social Study.* Philadelphia: The University of Pennsylvania Press.

Earnest, Les. 1989. "Can Computers Cope with Human Races?" *Communications of the ACM* 32(2):174–182.

Hopgood, James F. Unpublished. "Another *Japanese Version:* An American Actor in Japanese Hands." Northern Kentucky University.

Huth, Edward J. 1995. "Identifying Ethnicity in Medical Papers." *Annals of Internal Medicine* 122(8):619–621.

Jefferson, Thomas. 1815. "Virginia's Definition of a Mulatto." *The Jefferson Papers.* Washington, DC: Library of Congress.

Knepper, Paul. 1995. "Historical Origins of the Prohibition of Multiracial Legal Identity in the States and the Nation." *State Constitutional Commentaries and Notes: A Quarterly Review* 5(2):14–20.

Kuhn, Thomas. 1975. *The Structure of Scientific Revolutions.* Chicago: University of Chicago Press.

Lewis, David Levering. 1993. *W.E.B. Du Bois: Biography of a Race, 1868–1919.* New York: Holt.

Lorde, Audre. 1984. *Sister Outsider.* Trumansberg, NY: Crossing.

McBride, James. 1996. *The Color of Water: A Black Man's Tribute to His White Mother.* New York: Riverhead.

Mirza, M. N. and D. B. Dungworth. 1995. "The Potential Misuse of Genetic Analyses and the Social Construction of 'Race' and 'Ethnicity.'" *Oxford Journal of Archaeology* 14(3):345–354.

Reynoso, Cruz. 1992. "Ethnic Diversity: Its Historical and Constitutional Roots." *Villanova Law Review* 37(4):821–37.

Rohrl, Vivian J. 1995. "The Anthropology of Race: A Study of Ways of Looking at Race." *Race, Gender, and Class* 2(2):85–97.

Scales-Trent, Judy. 1995. *Notes of a White Black Woman: Race, Color, Community.* University Park: PA: The Pennsylvania State University.

Schaefer, Richard T. 1996. 1995 Presidential Address. "Education and Prejudice: Unraveling the Relationship." *The Sociological Quarterly* 37(1):1–16.

Simon, Bruce N. "White-Blindness." Unpublished. Princeton College.

U.S. Bureau of the Census. 1990. *Federal Legislative Uses of Decennial Census Data.* Washington, DC: U.S. Government Printing Office.

U.S. Department of Justice. 1996. "Selected Discrimination Cases Handled in 1996." Washington, DC: U.S. Government Printing Office.

U.S. Equal Employment Opportunity Commission. 1995. *Kinds of Cases Awaiting Action.* Washington, DC: U.S. Government Printing Office.

Williams, Gregory Howard. 1995. *Life on the Color Line: The True Story of a White Boy Who Discovered He Was Black.* New York: Dutton.

Wright, Lawrence. 1994. "One Drop of Blood." *The New Yorker* (July 25):53–55.

TEXT CREDITS

The numbers in parentheses after each entry are the page numbers on which the material appears.

Part I

From "Thyra Johnson, 91, Symbol of Racial Distinctions, Dies" by Robert McG. Thomas. *The New York Times,* November 29. Copyright © 1995 The New York Times Company. Reprinted by permission. (26–27)

From "Adventures of an Indian Princess" by Patricia Riley in *Earth Song, Sky Spirit,* edited by C. E. Trafzer. Copyright © 1992 Patricia Riley. Reprinted by permission of the author. (34–38)

From "Expelled in 1877, Indian Tribe is Wanted as a Resource" by Timothy Egan, *The New York Times,* July 22. Copyright © 1996 The New York Times Company. Reprinted by permission. (39–43)

From "Black Man With a Nose Job" in *Member of the Club* by Lawrence Otis Graham. Copyright © 1995 Lawrence Otis Graham. Reprinted by permission of HarperCollins Publishers, Inc. (44–50)

From "Culture Wars in Asian America" in *Under Western Eyes: Personal Essays from Asian America* by Garrett Hongo. Copyright © 1995 Garrett Hongo. Reprinted by permission of the author and the Liz Darhansoff Literary Agency, 122 Park Avenue, New York 10128. (51–55)

From "On Being Blackanese" by Mitzi Uehara-Carter. http://www.webcom/ ~intvoice/mitzi.html (July 22). Copyright © 1996 Mitzi Uehara-Carter. Reprinted by permission of *Interracial Voice* and the author. (56–58)

From "A Rescue Without Cheers" by Peter D. Kramer. *The New York Times,* July 16. Copyright © 1995 The New York Times Company. Reprinted by permission. (59–62)

From "The Burden of Race" by Arthur Ashe in *Days of Grace: A Memoir* by Arthur Ashe and Arnold Rampersad. Copyright © 1993 Jeanne Moutoussamy-Ashe and Arnold Rampersad. Reprinted by permission of Alfred A. Knopf, Inc. (62–66)

From *What Will My Mother Say: A Tribal African Girl Comes of Age in America* by Dympna Ugwu-Oju. Copyright © 1995 Dympna Ugwu-Oju. Reprinted by permission of Bonus Books, Inc., 160 East Illinois Street, Chicago. (67–73)

Part 2

Part 3

From "To the Editor: When Is Ethnicity Relevant in a Case Report?" by Rafael Ortega and Marcelle M. Willock. "In Reply:" by Jonathan Benumof. *Anesthesiology.* Copyright © 1994 American Society of Anesthesiologists, Inc. Reprinted by permission of Lippincott Raven Publishers. (191)

From "A View From the South" in *Americas: The Changing Face of Latin America and the Caribbean* by Peter Winn. Copyright © 1992 Peter Winn and WGBH Educational Foundation. Reprinted by permission of Pantheon Books, a division of Random House, Inc. (207–210)

From "A People Distinct from Others: Race and Identity in Federal Indian Law and the Hispanic Classification in OMB Directive No. 15" by Luis Angel Toro. *Texas Tech Law Review.* Copyright © 1995 by Texas Tech Law Review. Reprinted by permission. (211–215)

From "'Symbolic Ethnicity' and Alaska Natives of Mixed Ancestry Living in Anchorage: Enduring Group or Sign of Impending Assimilation?" by Julie E. Sprott. *Human Organization: Journal of the Society for Applied Anthropology.* Copyright © 1994 Society for Applied Anthropology. Reprinted by permission. (216–222)

From "Ethnicity as Explanation, Ethnicity as Excuse" by Paul A. Goble. *Special Warfare.* Reprinted by permission of J. F. Kennedy Special Warfare Center and School, Ft. Bragg, NC and the author. (223–230)

From *Ethnic Options: Choosing Identities in America* by Mary C. Waters. Copyright © 1990 The Regents of the University of California. Reprinted by permission. (235–238)

From "Reflections on American Ethnicity" by David Steven Cohen. *New York History.* Copyright © 1991 The New York State Historical Association. Reprinted by permission. (239–248)

From "Resource Competition Theories" by Joane Nagel. *American Behavioral Scientist,* edited by John H. Stanfield II. Copyright © 1995 Sage Publications, Inc. Reprinted by permission. (249–267)

Part 4

From "On Being Like a Mule" in *Notes of a White Black Woman: Race, Color, Community* by Judy Scales-Trent. Copyright © 1995 The Pennsylvania State University. Reproduced by permission of the publisher. (287–290)

From "Article XIX, Chinese." *West's Annotated California Codes: Constitution of the State of California.* Copyright © 1996 West Publishing Company. Reprinted by permission. (291–292)

Part 5

Photo Credits

Photos on page 14: Courtesy of Dr. Gregory H. Williams, author of *Life on the Color Line: The True Story of a White Boy Who Discovered He Was Black.*

Photos on page 15 (top): © National Muesum of the American Indian.

Photos on page 15 (bottom): Reproduced from the Collections of the Library of Congress.

Photos on page 16 (top left): Schomberg Center for Research in Black Culture, New York Public Library.

Photos on page 16 (top right): © Reuters/Allen Fredrickson/Archive Photos.

Photos on page 16 (bottom left): Strickler/Monkmeyer Press.

Photos on page 16 (bottom right): Grantpix/Monkmeyer Press.

Photos on page 17 (top left and right): Courtesy of Dagmar Schultz; Orlanda Frauenverlag.

Photos on page 17 (bottom left and right): © Leah Melnick/Impact Visuals.

Photo on page 18: Bobby Hussey 1996; Student, Northern Kentucky University.

INDEX